UNDERSTANDING HEALTH ECONOMICS

John Rapoport, Ph.D.
Mount Holyoke College

Robert L. Robertson, Ph.D.
Mount Holyoke College

Bruce Stuart, Ph.D.
Pennsylvania State University

AN ASPEN PUBLICATION®
Aspen Systems Corporation
Rockville, Maryland
London
1982

Library of Congress Cataloging in Publication Data

Rapoport, John, 1944-
Understanding health economics.

Includes bibliographies and index.
1. Medical economics.   2. Medical economics—
United States.   I. Robertson, Robert L.
II. Stuart, Bruce C.   III. Title.
RA410.R36   338.4'73621'0973   81-14987
ISBN: 0-89443-380-6   AACR2

Copyright © 1982 Aspen Systems Corporation

All rights reserved. This book, or parts thereof, may not be reproduced in any form or by any means, electronic or mechanical, including photocopy, recording, or any information storage and retrieval system now known or to be invented, without written permission from the publisher, except in the case of brief quotations embodied in critical articles or reviews. For information, address Aspen Systems Corporation, 1600 Research Boulevard, Rockville, Maryland 20850.

Library of Congress Catalog Card Number: 81-14987
ISBN: 0-89443-380-6

Printed in the United States of America

1 2 3 4 5

To our wives,
Nancy Rapoport
Janice Robertson
Lynne Stuart

Table of Contents

Foreword ix

Acknowledgments xiii

Chapter 1— Introduction 1

    What is Economics? 2
    Economics and Health Care 4
    Validation Services 8
    Conclusion 10

Chapter 2— The Market Model 13

    Remarks 14
    What is a Market? 15
    Demand 16
    Supply 20
    Market Equilibrium 21
    Prices and Allocation 23
    Equity and Efficiency 26
    Market Failure 27

Chapter 3— Empirical Tools and Measurement in
              Economics 35

    Economic Methodology? 36
    The Necessity of Measurement 36

Sampling and Tests of Significance 39
Simple Regression and Correlation 41
Multiple Regression 46
Multiple Regression: A Case Study.............. 47
Regression and Forecasting..................... 51
Trends in Aggregate Measures of Hospital Costs.... 52
Measurement and Index Numbers................ 58
What the Index Is 61
The 1978 Revision............................. 70
Future Revisions 73
Customary Price 76
Forecasting Hospital Expenditure Rates 83

Chapter 4— Demand for Health Services................... 95

Subpart B — National Health Planning Goals 96
Fundamentals of Demand Theory 98
Characteristics of Demand..................... 111
Empirical Studies of Demand................... 121
Doctor Office Visits........................... 123
Effects of Coinsurance: A Multivariate Analysis ... 130
Another Approach to Demand Estimation 138
Assumptions Related to Forecast Financial
    Statements 138

**Chapter 5— Theory of the Firm: Applications to Solo
    Practice 161**

Overview and Synopsis......................... 161
Economics of Solo Practice 164
A Not-So-Final Word 185

Chapter 6— Introduction to Hospital Economics 189

Structural Characteristics of the Industry 190
Hospital Production Functions................... 193
Hospital Production 193
Hospital Cost Functions........................ 200
Economies of Scale 201
Hospital Cost Functions........................ 204
Theories of Hospital Behavior 220
Economic Theories of Behavior in Nonprofit,
    Private Hospitals........................... 220

| | The Not-For-Profit Hospital as a Physicians' Cooperative | 241 |
| | Conclusion | 248 |

Chapter 7— Health Maintenance Organizations ... 257

	The HMO Concept.	257
	Choices and Results: A Selective Appraisal of HMO Performances	259
	Introduction and Summary.	260
	Optimal Scale in Medical Practice: A Survivor Analysis.	264
	Health Maintenance Organizations	271
	Foundations for Medical Care: An Empirical Investigation of the Delivery of Health Services to a Medicaid Population.	278

Chapter 8— Health Care Financing ... 291

	The Industry.	292
	Economic Models of Third Party Coverage	294
	Reimbursement Methodology.	299
	Reimbursement for Professional Services.	203
	Medicare and Medicaid Physician Payment Incentives	309
	Institutional Reimbursement	322
	Why Prospective Rate Setting?	326

Chapter 9— Industrial Organization. ... 349

	The Structure-Conduct-Performance Approach	350
	Regulation of For-Profit Hospitals.	352
	Regulating Competition in a Nonprofit Industry: The Problems of For-Profit Hospitals	353
	The Drug Industry.	370
	The Pharmaceutical Industry.	371
	Ethical Pharmaceutical Industry.	373
	Pharmaceutical Marketing	380
	Conclusion	385

Chapter 10— Technological Change ... 391

| | The Production Function and Technological Change. | 392 |

viii   UNDERSTANDING HEALTH ECONOMICS

        Effects of Technological Change on Costs.......... 393
        Changing Technology............................ 394
        Capital-Embodied Medical Costs................. 399
        Investment in Biomedical Research............... 401
        Research Costs.................................. 403
        Diffusion....................................... 411
        Case Study of Radioisotopes in U.S. Hospitals...... 413
        Government Policy and Technological Change..... 425
        Medical Advances and their Diffusion............ 425
        Certificate of Need.............................. 428
        Federal Regulations and Pharmaceutical
           Innovation 433
        Conclusion 438

Chapter 11— Economic Evaluation of Health Programs **447**

        Variables in Health Service Analysis.............. 448
        Analysis of Costs 451
        Economic Cost and Some Observations on its
           Measurement............................... 451
        The Uses of Cost Analysis 455
        Objectives 456
        Effects of Manpower Utilization on Cost and
           Productivity of a Neighborhood Health Center ... 462
        Analysis of Benefits............................. 467
        Application of Cost-Benefit Analysis to the
           Health Services 468
        Syphilis Control Programs...................... 475
        Cost-Benefit Analysis........................... 479
        The Economics of the Private Sector 481
        Cost-Benefit Analysis of a PKU Screening Program. 485
        Cost-Effectiveness Analysis..................... 495
        Mobile Health Services: A Study in Cost-
           Effectiveness............................... 497
        Conclusion 510

Glossary.. **519**

Index... **531**

Foreword

This book grew out of the authors' involvement in teaching a course in health economics for administrators and planners at the University of Massachusetts at Amherst. The course was taught on a self-study and self-paced basis. Students were given study materials and exercises to be completed by the end of the term and mailed to the instructors for grading and credit. All those participating were professionals currently working in health care organizations. The course was developed as part of a program of continuing education for health planners and administrators funded under contract No. HRA 232-78-0136 from the U.S. Bureau of Health Manpower to the Division of Public Health of the University of Massachusetts.

Although the study materials have been expanded and considerably reworked for this book, the intended audience is similar to that for the course. We anticipate that the typical reader of this book will be, or will be training to become, a professional in health administration or planning. We assume the reader has no prior work in economics, and we believe the subject as presented here is accessible to anyone with a sincere desire to study and master it.

Just the same, some general exposure to the health industry is assumed, and we do not try to survey the field before getting into economic concepts and tools. In most chapters, the cases or problems used as examples reflect the expected target readership in administration and planning; in other places they are of more general interest. The book assumes no knowledge of mathematics beyond the ability to read simple formulas and graphs. Some tools of economic statistics are developed in Chapter 3, but this is done in a nontechnical way, the object being to equip the reader to understand work that has used the techniques, rather than to impart a working knowledge of them.

The book has three basic objectives:

1. to introduce the reader to the economic concepts that underlie the production, distribution, and financing of health services
2. to develop an appreciation for the strengths and weaknesses of economic methodology in designing health programs and evaluating health policy
3. to expose the reader to important published research findings that affect future health policy development and the management of health care organizations

To study any new field adequately, readers need a specialized vocabulary both to understand and to use the analytic techniques of that discipline. Economics is no exception. New terms with specialized meanings are introduced and defined when needed, and are repeated at the end of the book in a comprehensive glossary. Words in the glossary are identified in italics the first time they are used in the text (except for excerpted selections, which are reprinted unchanged from their original styling).

The reader will be able to replicate certain, but not all, of the economic methods in the reprinted selections. Some of the techniques can be applied after the reading, others require outside assistance, still others are presented to provide general understanding of the tools used by professional health economists.

The specific coverage of the book and examples used are suggested by the following summary of chapter contents:

1. **Introduction.** This chapter surveys economics as a discipline and its relevance to decision making in the health field.
2. **The Market Model.** This chapter outlines the theory of economic behavior in competitive markets. Major topics include determination of equilibrium price under perfect competition, factors underlying supply and demand behavior, the concepts of equity and efficiency, and the nature and implications of market power and market imperfections. It presents some reasons why economists favor certain types of governmental regulations while tending to oppose other restrictions on the operations of free markets.
3. **Empirical Tools and Measurement in Economics.** Measurement techniques and statistical tools used in economic analysis are explained to help administrators and planners better understand the research results in later chapters. Topics include price index construction and use, sampling and tests of significance, multiple regression, and forecasting hospital costs.
4. **Demand for Health Services.** The theoretical foundations and practical applications of demand analysis are covered here. Topics include enabling factors and constraints on demand, the concept of

elasticity, and the techniques available to measure and forecast demand. Among the applications suggested are studies of factors influencing demand for medical care, including insurance and consumer cost sharing.

5. **Theory of the Firm: Application to Solo Practice.** This chapter develops the economic theory of the firm, the unit of production. Elements of decision making on production volume, input choice, and pricing are explored, using as an example the physician in solo practice.
6. **Introduction to Hospital Economics.** This chapter develops the analysis of the firm through an examination of various aspects of hospital economics. It covers the economics of production functions, cost functions, and hospital objectives.
7. **Health Maintenance Organizations.** In this chapter a relatively new form of organization for health care delivery, the health maintenance organization (HMO), is analyzed from an economic perspective. Physician productivity and utilization are considered and the possible effects of HMOs on health care costs are discussed.
8. **Health Care Financing.** Reimbursement and third party cost controls are the principal topics in this chapter. The mechanics of provider payment are analyzed critically from the perspective of the conflicting objectives of hospitals, physicians, insurance carriers, and regulatory agencies.
9. **Industrial Organization.** This chapter treats the competitive interaction of firms in an industry. The concepts of market structure, conduct, and performance are developed. Examples of analysis include the effects of competition between for-profit and nonprofit hospitals and various economic viewpoints on the pharmaceutical industry.
10. **Technological Change.** Economic approaches to analysis of the production, diffusion, and assessment of new technology in the health sector are covered in this chapter.
11. **Economic Evaluation of Health Programs.** This chapter is the capstone of the book. Techniques of economic evaluation are covered in depth, including cost analysis, cost-benefit analysis, and cost-effectiveness analysis. Their usefulness and limitations in practice are illustrated by studies of health center costs, PKU screening program benefits and costs, and the cost-effectiveness of mobile health services.

The reader will note that the book contains more excerpted material than do most texts. This reflects the authors' desire to make the coverage as professionally useful as possible. Administrators or planners need not be their own health economists. They can develop original studies using staff or consultant help. In researching a specific problem, however, the economics literature often can be relevant, and it is our hope that the reader will become better able to use it.

Thus, many selections are chosen because they are typical of the kind of article to be found in economics journals. Other selections are included because they represent important empirical findings, and a few simply because we thought their authors made the point as well as, or better than, we could. Some classic selections might appear somewhat dated with respect to data or other information. They are reprinted, usually without comment, due to their intrinsic merits.

One final point: Sources and reprint permissions for the many excerpts are grouped at the ends of the chapters in which the excerpts appear. Their footnotes, in their original style and numbering, and their lists of suggested readings also are assembled at the conclusions of the chapters. Tables and Figures, however, all are renumbered sequentially within each chapter because of duplications in some of the originals.

John Rapoport
Robert L. Robertson
Bruce Stuart
December 1981

Acknowledgments

We acknowledge with thanks the assistance of several persons in preparing this manuscript. Roger Kropf, Associate Director of the Health Administration Program at the University of Massachusetts-Amherst, was very helpful in the early stages of the preparation of the study materials from which this book evolved. Many parts of the text reflect his suggestions. We also would like to thank the planners and administrators who used the materials in a continuing education course at the University of Massachusetts-Amherst during 1979 and 1980. Their comments and questions led to substantial improvements in both the form and coverage of the book.

Others who deserve credit for the existence of this text include Seth Goldsmith, the principal investigator under U.S. Bureau of Health Manpower contract No. HRA 232-78-0136, which funded the continuing education course, and Ginny Carmody, Sandra Hart, and Helen Canney, who prepared the several drafts with efficiency and effectiveness. Herbert Klarman made useful suggestions about several sections of the manuscript. These individuals have our thanks, but of course bear no responsibility for errors in content or interpretation.

The three of us participated equally in all aspects of the preparation of this book. Our names as authors are listed alphabetically.

Chapter 1

Introduction

Everyone knows the importance of good health, and most people believe that health services can contribute to it. On the other hand, no one in the United States needs to be told that the nation's system of providing and using health services is plagued by serious problems. Some see the principal problems as inequities in access and use of care by low income persons. Others regard the main difficulties as shortages and in some cases surpluses of personnel to provide care. Still others believe that the system's primary deficiency is rapidly rising costs. These perspectives have at least one thing in common: economic elements are very much involved in both the problem and its potential solutions.

To focus on economics, as does this book, is not to ignore other ways of analyzing the health field. Clearly, many different disciplines and approaches can be useful. For example, sociologists might examine such concepts as stratification of the society into groups by education, race, and so forth, and the implications of those classes for decisions to use or not to use medical care. Psychologists would be concerned with, among other things, the determinants of consumer tastes and the reactions of patients, as well as providers, to the delivery of services. Among the concerns of political scientists would be the process of decision making leading to public (governmental) support for health programs. Part of the "tool kit" of geographers would be detailed measurements of distance and the effect of physical obstacles on the location of hospitals and other health care providers. And so it goes.

Economists are aware of these contributions; they are likely to take class, tastes, location, and the like as given and proceed into a more focused study of the relevance of prices, incomes, and related variables to health care. The details of this approach become clear in what follows.

WHAT IS ECONOMICS?

Over the years many definitions of "economics" have been offered. Today, all economists stress the fact of *scarcity* of *productive resources* and draw from it the concept of *opportunity cost,* which states that the real cost of producing something is whatever must be given up in order to do so. In a fully employed economy, for example, people might give up some hospital construction to build more hotels; in that case, the true cost of those hotels would be the potential hospital care that is sacrificed in the process. Choices in the use of scarce resources must be made. They boil down to four fundamental questions concerning production and distribution in any society: What? How? For Whom? and When?

The first choice concerns what to produce. Shall more services be delivered in hospitals or more provided outside them? More medical care or more hotels or more weapons? And so forth, for thousands of decisions. The second set of choices determines how those products are produced: more labor inputs (of what kinds?) or more machinery? Doctors or auxiliary workers or computerized axial tomography (CAT) scanners? It is necessary to choose, also, who receives those products. This third question (for whom?) involves decisions on the distribution of *income,* on ability to pay, and on other ways of determining entitlement to economic output. Should current family income determine the use of medical care, for instance? The final choices concern when the elements are to be produced: more now or more later?

Because scarcity is a fact of life, these four types of economic choices are relevant to any decision that involves resource use. Who makes the choices? Except in the hypothetical case of a pure economic dictatorship, they are made by individuals, business firms, and a variety of other economic units including government. Economics then is concerned with the analysis of choices at all levels ranging from the individual consumer or worker to national policy decisions.

In a real sense each economic choice is unique. It will depend on the decision maker's objectives and the conditions that prevail at the time the choice is made. To analyze all the variables involved in each and every case would be a hopeless task beyond the capacity of the most sophisticated computer. For this reason economists have developed analytic techniques that simplify reality and thereby concentrate attention on the basic elements of choice. Of these techniques, *marginal analysis* is the most important.

The term marginal analysis simply means looking at the effect of a small change. For example, consider a personal economic choice: Should I spend my income on food or clothing? Put that way, the question is not very meaningful. Obviously, I need both and undoubtedly will buy some of each. The issue is what combination will be chosen. That question can be approached through marginal analysis in the following way:

Assume some arbitrary division of income between food and clothing. Then consider spending a small amount, say $10, more on food instead of on clothing. This might mean one more restaurant meal and one less shirt. Do I gain more satisfaction from the additional meal than I lose from not having the new shirt? If so, I should reallocate my income toward food and away from clothing. If, on the other hand, the shirt gives me more satisfaction than the meal, I should not make the change and indeed should reallocate income in the opposite direction—that is, buy less food and more clothing. If the satisfaction gained from $10 more spent on food is just the same as the satisfaction lost from $10 less for clothing, the division of income is optimal.

An economist would say here that the *marginal utilities* are equal and the total *utility*, i.e., satisfaction, is at a maximum. This is just one example of marginal analysis, but the point has general applicability: optimal allocation can be identified by the equality of marginal measures.

In the process of analyzing choices, economists often distinguish between *positive* and *normative* economics. The former is an analysis of what happens or is expected to happen, and why. A major goal of positive economics is to achieve an understanding of economic behavior that will make it possible to predict such behavior. Facts help answer questions of positive economics. Controversies in this area can be resolved by a better theory, more data, or more sophisticated statistical techniques. Normative economics, on the other hand, deals with what ought to happen. Facts will not resolve differences among people on normative issues because the source of disagreement is not lack of understanding but differences in fundamental values. Economists have no special competence to decide purely normative social questions.

Unfortunately, the distinction between positive and normative analysis frequently is unclear in actual economic writing. Consider the controversy over physician fee inflation. Positive economic analysis might explain why physician fees have risen; it can be used to predict on the basis of certain assumptions what their rate of increase will be in the future; and, finally, it can project the likely effects of a policy designed to lower their rate of increase. However, to condemn the rate of increase as "bad" and assert that a policy designed to limit fees is socially desirable is in the realm of normative economics. The distinction is obvious here, but the reader familiar with the literature will know from experience that the positive and normative aspects of the controversy seldom are clearly labeled as such.

In using economic analysis (including that presented in this book) the reader thus should be particularly alert to instances where the analyst is engaging in positive and normative economics.

As in every other field of science, economics has evolved to the point where it encompasses a variety of subspecialties. Health economics is one of the more recent subspecialties of *microeconomics*. The term refers to study of the behavior of individual economic units as opposed to national economic aggregates, the subject of *macroeconomics*. Several older fields of microeconomics have contributed important concepts and techniques to the analytical tool kit of the health economist. For example, the behavior of individuals as users of health care services is studied using demand analysis, the basic concept of consumption economics. Production economics and the theory of the firm provide a starting point for analysis of the economic behavior of hospitals. The study of physicians' behavior as well as some aspects of the evaluation of health services utilization draws on concepts of labor economics. Industrial organization economics helps the understanding of competition among health care providers. In other words, the analytical methodology of health economics is a natural outgrowth of other established fields of microeconomics.

This development has not gone unchallenged, however. Some have suggested that the extension of economic analysis to health issues is inappropriate and invalid. They argue that health care is a unique service, not a product like shoes or bananas, and that it raises fundamental moral questions that cannot and should not be treated by traditional economic analysis. This argument is analyzed in the next section.

ECONOMICS AND HEALTH CARE

There are two common objections to economic analysis of the health care sector. One is basically ethical, the other technical. It sometimes is argued that because health is such an important goal it should be beyond economic considerations; that society should, literally, spare no expense in buying health services. Critics object on ethical grounds to the idea that in some sense society puts a price on the value of human life and health. The other objection concerns the definition of economic output and the uniqueness of the health services *industry*. "Health" is extremely difficult to measure, yet it is the fundamental reason for health care delivery. Economic analysis generally is applied to clearly defined and easily measured outputs. Since health is so hard to measure, economics becomes inapplicable, according to this view. Similarly, critics point out that standard economic theory deals with well-informed consumers buying products from profit-making firms. This certainly is not descriptive of most transactions in the health care sector.

Unfortunately, resource scarcity does not permit health care to be set aside as something apart from economics. On both societal and personal levels, resources have opportunity costs and choices must be made. Those who object to economic analysis of health issues on ethical grounds misunderstand the role of positive economics. Where there is scarcity there are opportunity costs. Economics involves finding the alternatives and calculating these costs, not making the actual choices. The ultimate decisions are made according to the ethical standards of the individual or society; economics simply points out the consequences. The basic questions of what, how, for whom, and when must be answered for health care just as for other things people want.

Social and Individual Considerations

The percentage of the *gross national product* (GNP—the total value of the economy's output) in the United States devoted to health care is around 9 percent. It could be greater, but that would mean there would be less of other things; it could be less than that, in which case people could have more of other things. Either way a choice is unavoidable. In this case it is a social choice influenced to a great extent by government policy, the political process, and the values they reflect.

Individuals, too, must decide how important health and health care are relative to other uses of income, time, and energy. All sorts of individual actions suggest that health is not an overriding goal. People smoke, drink too much, and go hang gliding. They are not forced to do these things, although in some cases they may be less than fully aware of the likely health consequences. To the extent that these decisions are made on the basis of correct and complete information, they would seem to be clear evidence that for the individuals involved, other things, such as social acceptance or excitement, are more important than health. In a free society, who is to say that such decisions are unacceptable?

Economic decisions also are quite relevant to the "how" question in the health care sector. The ultimate goal desired is not health services but health. If resources are being used wastefully, they are not producing the maximum possible health benefit. There may be disagreement about whether 9 percent is the right amount of GNP to be used for health services, but there is agreement that whatever resources are used should be employed in such a way as to produce the maximum possible benefits in health. The decision to eliminate waste or unemployment is easy—there is no direct opportunity cost. If resources are unused anyway, then by putting them into use society is not giving up anything. But, of course, the choice about which particular use to put them to does raise the issue of opportunity cost.

There may be questions about the production of health services short of outright waste. Diagnosis or treatment of disease can be accomplished by alternative methods, requiring different combinations of resources. Should the decisions about which methods to use be made without any attention to opportunity costs of resources? From the point of view of many physicians, the answer probably is "yes." Their training, professional standards, and work environment all suggest that the medical welfare of the patient should be pursued to the exclusion of all other considerations. On the other hand, from the point of view of the patient who is paying the bill, the insurance company executive, or the health planner, opportunity cost is a crucial concern.

Many current controversies about medical technology are of this type. The issues are perhaps most sharply defined in the case of noninvasive diagnostic technologies such as the CT scanner or automated blood analysis where the test itself poses no danger to the patient. Even if most of the time the test confirms the diagnosis based on physical examination, sometimes it turns up unsuspected disease. In both cases there is clear medical benefit, so it would contribute to the quality of care if it were done routinely. However, the equipment and the tests are costly and there are alternative uses for the resources either in or outside of the health sector. The policy maker or planner must weigh these alternatives against the medical benefit.

Equity or Distribution

Questions of equity or distribution come up frequently in economic analysis of health services. The issue of "who" is to receive a certain benefit is related closely to the decision about "what" and "how." The view that medical care should not be subject to economic calculation frequently surfaces in cases where a specific identified person is in obvious need of care. A highly publicized story of a child accident victim is a good case in point. Such a story evokes sympathy and often substantial donations. How can a wealthy society deny lifesaving care to the unfortunate child? In the publicized cases it seldom does. Where the victims are unidentified, "statistical" people, however, the result may well be different. Putting a full-scale trauma center in every community hospital would save the lives of a certain number of accident victims. But it is not known in advance who they are, so it becomes much harder to mobilize public support for such a program and easier for elected officials or executives to emphasize the high cost and relatively low benefits from such an expenditure.

Having accepted the fact that a goal such as "the best possible medical care for all" is unrealistic because of resource scarcity, society still has the problem of what the distribution should be. Perhaps it should have the best possible care for a few and a minimal level for everyone else. Maybe it should be the best possible for a few, moderate for most people, and minimal for the rest. The possibilities are endless, of course, and it must be kept in mind that individual preferences with regard to health care differ—some people would rather consume other things. Both what the distribution is and how the decision is made are of economic importance. In particular, to what extent does society want it made through government action and to what extent through the market mechanism?

Choices about "when" are perhaps best illustrated by the alternatives of preventive and acute medical care. An individual may choose to go to the dentist every six months for routine checkups or to go only when a toothache erupts. Public programs may focus on screening programs to detect disease, health education, or care of people with advanced disease. The attempt to find a balance between immediate and future health benefits involves opportunity costs as well as personal and social values. Once again, economic analysis can point out the alternatives and help identify the costs; it cannot determine the ultimate solution alone.

The Boundaries of 'Health'

Every field of study has its boundaries, and health economics is no exception. However, "health" is such a ubiquitous concept that it is not immediately clear where these boundaries are located. Consider the following: "Health care can be defined as those activities that are undertaken with the objective of restoring, preserving or enhancing the physical and mental well-being of people."[1] The range of services and goods covered by this definition is properly broad.

For some purposes, environmental health services, such as clean water, and other factors such as adequate housing might be included. For other purposes, the desired focus is medical care, the narrower set of services provided directly to patients such as contacts with physicians and dentists, hospitalization, and prescription drug use. In the latter case, observers and analysts of health care take other elements such as environmental services as constant (or *ceteris paribus,* as an economist would say). Such assumptions form the basis for implicit economic choices that might be justifiable for most regions of a wealthy country such as the United States, but would be dangerously misleading or artificial in developing countries where the greatest contribution to better health might be made through better water supply and similar environmental improvements.

While an economic examination of the production of health naturally involves health services, it need not exclude the relationships between other variables and health status. There is the obvious question (whose answer lies beyond economics) of the importance of genetic factors. The impact of personal habits and life styles also can be considered. Ample evidence now exists to support the statement that health can be affected significantly by smoking and alcoholic intake, diet, and other aspects of personal behavior. Economic studies can help to quantify the cost of such intakes and also the value of economic loss from their resulting health problems.

On the other side of the coin, health and medical services can provide things of value other than better health per se. Of particular interest to economists are the contributions that health care makes to the national economy in terms of greater output and higher personal incomes. Victor Fuchs, a leading health economist, considers several additional outputs of the health care industry in the following excerpt:

VALIDATION SERVICES[a]

One type of output that is not directly related to improvements in health can be traced to the fact that only a physician can provide judgments concerning a person's health status that will be widely accepted by third parties. This type of output is designated "validation services." . . . One familiar example is the life insurance examination. This examination may have some favorable impact on the health of the examinee, but it need not do so and is not undertaken primarily for that purpose. The insurance company simply wants to know about the health status of the person concerned. In obtaining and providing that information, the physician is producing something of value, but it is not health.

Other examples include a physician's testifying in court, providing information in a workmen's compensation case, or executing a death certificate.

The validation role of physicians is probably much broader than in these sharply defined cases. Consider the following situation: a person feels ill; he has various aches, pains and other symptoms. He complains and looks for sympathy from family, friends, neighbors and co-workers. He may seek to be relieved from certain responsibilities or to be excused from certain tasks. Doubts may arise in the minds of persons around him. Questions may be asked. Is he really ill? Is he doing all that he can to get well? A visit, or a series of visits, to one or more doctors is indicated. The patient may not have the slightest hope that these visits will help his health, and, indeed, he may be correct. Nevertheless, the service rendered by the physician cannot be said to result in no output. The visit to the doctor is a socially or culturally necessary act. The examination, the diagnosis and the prognosis are desired by the patient to provide confirmation to those who have doubts about him. Only the professional judgment of a physician can still the doubts and answer the questions.

The validation service type of output should not be confused with another type of problem that arises in measuring the output of health services; namely, that advance knowledge about the effect of health services on health is sometimes difficult to obtain. This problem is similar to the "dry hole" situation in drilling for oil. That is not to say that the work done in drilling dry holes results in no output. Rather, when the drilling operation is viewed in its entirety, some successes will be noted as well as some failures. All those who participate in the drilling operation are considered to be sources of the output. Similarly, if a surgeon operates on ten people and only six are helped, one should not say that no output occurred in the other four cases, if one could not determine in advance which cases could be helped and which could not. The output consisted of improving the health of six people, but this output was the result of a production process which encompassed the ten operations.

Other Consumer Services

The outstanding example of other consumer services produced by the health industry is the so-called "hotel" services of hospitals. Those hospital activities that directly affect health are difficult to separate from those that are equivalent to hotel services, but the latter clearly are not insignificant. One way of getting some insight into this question would be to study the occupational distribution of health industry employment. A very significant fraction consists of cooks, chambermaids, porters and others who are probably producing "other consumer services."[11]

In mental hospitals and other hospitals providing long-term care a major proportion of all costs are probably associated with producing consumer services other than health. The fact that these other consumer services would have to be provided somehow, either publicly or privately, if the patients were not in the hospital, is often neglected in discussions of how total hospital costs are inflated by the presence of people who are not really ill. Possibly some of these consumer services are actually produced more inexpensively in a hospital than on the outside. This point comes to the fore in New York City, now grappling with the problem of housing and feeding patients who have been discharged from mental hospitals, not because they are cured, but because the new drugs mean they no longer need to be confined to an institution.

Some of the services rendered by nurses outside hospitals also bear little relation to health, but nevertheless they may have considerable value to consumers. This type of service is likely to grow in importance with the increase in the number of elderly people with income who are seeking companionship and help with their daily chores.

The failure of mortality indexes to decline with increased expenditures for health services in recent years has led some people to conclude that mortality no longer measures health levels properly. But if most of these increased expenditures have gone for health services that largely produce "other consumer services" rather than health, a great deal of the mystery is removed.

CONCLUSION

From an economic standpoint, the health services industry is as complex as they come. Outputs are difficult to define and measure, consumer information is lacking, markets are noncompetitive. While none of these characteristics is unique, their widespread applicability and importance to buyers and sellers of health services alike make them notable. Although a few economists have chosen to stress the similarities rather than the differences, the authors would follow the majority viewpoint on the issue and say: "Yes, the health services industry is different from others."[2]

If the provision and use of health care are distinctive, as industries go, does that restrict the validity of economics in studying health problems? Of course, it means that some unusual problems are studied and that certain economic models must be modified to be useful. On the whole, though, the literature in the field, and the contents of the remainder of this book, show a practical-minded reader that economics can yield valuable lessons for the distinctive field of health care. So, the true test is in the reading to come.

NOTES

1. Victor R. Fuchs, "Health Care and the United States Economic System: An Essay in Abnormal Physiology," *Milbank Memorial Fund Quarterly*, 50 (April 1972), p. 211.
2. Selections illustrating the majority view include Victor R. Fuchs, "The Contribution of Health Services to the American Economy," *Milbank Memorial Fund Quarterly*, 44, part 2 (October 1966), pp. 67–70; and Herbert E. Klarman, *The Economics of Health* (New York: Columbia University Press, 1965), pp. 10–19. For the contrary (minority) case see, for example, Kong K. Ro, "Economics of Health Care: Is Medical Care Different?" in Program in Community Health Planning/Administration, *Economics in the Health Care System* (Cincinnati: University of Cincinnati, 1976), pp. 8–25.

SUGGESTED READINGS

Culyer, A.J., et al. *An Annotated Bibliography of Health Economics: English Language Sources.* London: Martin Robertson, 1977.

Fuchs, Victor R. "Health Care and the United States Economic System: An Essay in Abnormal Physiology." *Milbank Memorial Fund Quarterly* 50:211–237, reprinted in John B. McKinlay, editor, *Economic Aspects of Health Care.* New York: PRODIST, 1973, pp. 95–121.

———, *Who Shall Live?* New York: Basic Books, 1974.

Hogendorn, Jan S. *Modern Economics: An Introduction.* Cambridge, Mass.: Winthrop Publications, Inc., 1975, esp. Ch. 1.

Klarman, Herbert E. *The Economics of Health.* New York: Columbia University Press, 1965, esp. Ch. 1.

LaLonde, Marc. *A New Perspective on the Health of Canadians: A Working Document.* Ottawa: Government of Canada, 1974.

Lipsey, Richard G., and Steiner, Peter O. *Economics*, 5th ed. New York: Harper & Row Publishers, Inc., 1978, esp. Chs. 1, 2.

Mushkin, S. J. "Towards a Definition of Health Economics," *Public Health Reports*, September 1958.

Ro, Kong K. "Economics of Health Care: Is Medical Care Different?" in Program in Community Health Planning/Administration, *Economics in the Health Care System.* Cincinnati: University of Cincinnati, 1976, pp. 8–25.

Sorkin, Alan L. *Health Economics.* Lexington, Mass.: Lexington Books, D.C. Heath and Company, 1975, esp. pp. 1–8.

NOTE FROM FUCHS EXCERPT

11. Reed, Louis S., and Rice, Dorothy P., National Health Expenditures: Object of Expenditures and Source of Funds, 1962, *Social Security Bulletin*, 27, 11-21, August, 1964.

SOURCE AND PERMISSION

a. Reprinted from "The Contribution of Health Services to the American Economy" by Victor R. Fuchs, *Milbank Memorial Fund Quarterly*, 44, part 2 (October 1966), pp. 83–86, by permission of the *Milbank Memorial Fund Quarterly*, © 1966.

Chapter 2

The Market Model

This chapter presents the basic elements of the economic model of price determination in perfectly competitive markets. For many, perhaps most, readers it will be review. Price determination through the interaction of supply and demand is so central to modern economic analysis that it is covered in virtually every introductory economics course. Even those who have not had courses in economics undoubtedly will be familiar with the basic concepts and outline of the model. After all, the day-to-day professional activities of planners and health administrators require understanding of the behavior of those who produce and consume health services. However, a reminder is in order that *supply* and *demand* are technical terms to economists, and the reader should make sure that their precise technical meanings are well understood.

The model presented here is abstract, very general, and quite simple. To those who are involved professionally in health services it will seem unrealistic. It is. The intent is not to describe fully the real world but rather to focus on selected elements of reality that may provide some insights. Because it is so general, it necessarily is unrealistic, but this is a first step in the study of a complex reality. To take an analogy from physics, even though a frictionless surface or a perfect vacuum does not exist, analysis of the laws of matter under such unrealistic conditions is necessary as a first step to understanding behavior of matter under conditions that do exist. So it is in economics. The simple model presented here is modified, qualified, and complicated as the book progresses in order to increase its realism and usefulness.

A *competitive market* is defined by economists as one in which there are many reasonably well-informed buyers and sellers. Competition or the lack thereof is an important topic in many discussions of health policy. In some areas policies have been introduced to prevent competition or modify its effects. One argument in favor of certificate-of-need legislation, for example, is that competition among hospitals leads to overinvestment in expensive capital equipment. In other areas the problem may be not enough competition. Later in this chapter, a case where high drug prices resulted from lack of competition in the pharmaceutical industry is cited. Some now suggest that market competition may be a more effective regulatory tool than specific government actions. The following remarks by Michael Pertschuk, when chairman of the Federal Trade Commission, indicate elements of this view:

REMARKS[a]

As everyone must know, it's not easy to get a handle on the economics of health care, much less focus on the specific issue of competition. While there are examples of more flexibility in the field of physician training and practice—doctors' unions, prepaid group practices, community health cooperatives, free clinics, and so on—we have to admit that the practice of medicine remains one of the last strongholds of private entrepreneurship. Despite the large infusion of Federal, State, and local tax money into medical care, the physician population still operates with rather remarkable independence.

But physicians ought not to be singled out either for special honor or opprobrium. The entire health community—the *health industry,* if you will—has become the object of careful scrutiny by the public guardians of the country's trust and treasure. We all need the health industry so very much; it's not an overstatement to say that our lives depend on a strong, vigorous, responsive health industry. But not at any price. *Not at any price.*

That is our issue today and tomorrow. Accessible and affordable quality health care is something every American has come to expect. How many times in the past several years have consumers spoken of the "right" to quality health care, as if it were the same as the right to education or to police and fire protection? Yet, those other essential public services are supported out of a general tax base and are administered by officials subject to the rule of the ballot box.

No such controls are the rule in the health sector. Quite the contrary. The money is generated in a variety of ways: third-party payments, Government subsidies, reinsurance guarantees, private fund-raising, complex tax incentives, and old-fashioned cash fees for service.

The providers of care are generally not public officials. They are answerable primarily to their colleagues—and there is great suspicion that such accountability is more apparent than real. We know we need them—but we also know that, thus far, we have failed to control the escalating costs of the health care they provide.

We may conclude, one day in the future, that self-regulation—however inadequate—is better than stronger Government regulation. There is serious doubt that the Civil Aeronautics Board has been a boon to passengers. And after nearly 10 years of piled-on law and regulation, the Medicare and Medicaid programs have benefited the providers of health care as much—and in some cases more—than they have benefited patients.

Study of this chapter and those following will not provide definitive answers to the questions Pertschuk raises, nor will it settle the debate of whether more or less competition is the appropriate policy in any given instance. Nonetheless, an understanding of the market model presented here is essential for informed participation in that debate.

WHAT IS A MARKET?

Health care involves millions of economic transactions between buyers and sellers of goods or services. Consumers buy physical examinations, hospital care, and aspirin, among other things. Physicians provide a wide variety of services ranging from prescribing a cold remedy to performing open heart surgery. Hospitals act as sellers of such things as patient care, laboratory tests, or x-rays, and as buyers of a myriad of items as diverse as tissue paper and CT scanners. The analytical concept economists use to study all such transactions is the *market*. A market is buyers and sellers interacting to trade a particular good or service. Markets exist not only for goods and services sold to final consumers but all along the chain of production. For example, a consumer purchase of a bottle of aspirin represents a transaction in a final goods market. An x-ray machine sold by its manufacturer to a hospital is an example of an intermediate good transaction. The market for nursing services is an example of a market for a primary factor of production—labor. The term *factor of production*, or simply *factor*, refers to an input in the production process.

A market need not be in a particular geographical location although some are, e.g., the New York Stock Exchange. The spatial dimension is important if a market is to be defined properly, however. The proper geographical definition depends on where potential buyers and sellers are located. Many markets in the health care sector are local, since buyers and sellers are in the same city. This is true of most hospital services. On the other hand, for some specialized hospital services, the market may be regional or even national. Markets for many pharmaceutical products are worldwide since the product can be transported easily and international marketing and distribution arrangements exist.

The rest of this chapter lays out the fundamental groundwork for analysis of markets. The determinants of price and output in competitive markets are the focus of the next three sections, followed by interrelationships among different markets. The last section deals with the important issue of market imperfections and market failures. The concepts and terms presented here provide a basic foundation for later chapters.

DEMAND

Potential buyers of a good or service constitute the demand side of the market. The market demand at a given time is the total amount of the good that buyers are willing and have sufficient funds to purchase, for example the demand for aspirin. What determines the amount of aspirin consumers want to buy? One very important determinant is the price of aspirin. If the price is lower, other things remaining unchanged, the quantity demanded will be greater. This relationship is diagramed in Figure 2-1 in the form of a *demand curve*. The vertical axis plots the price of aspirin, the horizontal axis the number of units demanded. The unit of measure depends, of course, on the specific market being considered. If the focus is on sales in a small town, it might be the number of 100-tablet bottles, whereas the national market might be analyzed in terms of thousands of cases of 100-tablet bottles. In Figure 2-1, when the price is $3, the quantity demanded is 80. A drop in price to $2 leads to an increase in quantity demanded to 100. Thus, the demand curve shows for any price of aspirin how much buyers will demand, assuming other things such as income or tastes do not change.

Why does quantity demanded increase with a fall in price or, in geometric terms, why do demand curves slope down? One reason is that at lower prices the good becomes more attractive relative to other goods, and each individual who consumed some of it at higher prices will now consume more of it, substituting it for other goods in the consumption budget. Another reason is that some individuals who did not buy the good at all at the higher price may do so at the lower price. Thus, market demand increases when price falls, both because there is more demand by buyers

Figure 2-1 The Demand Curve

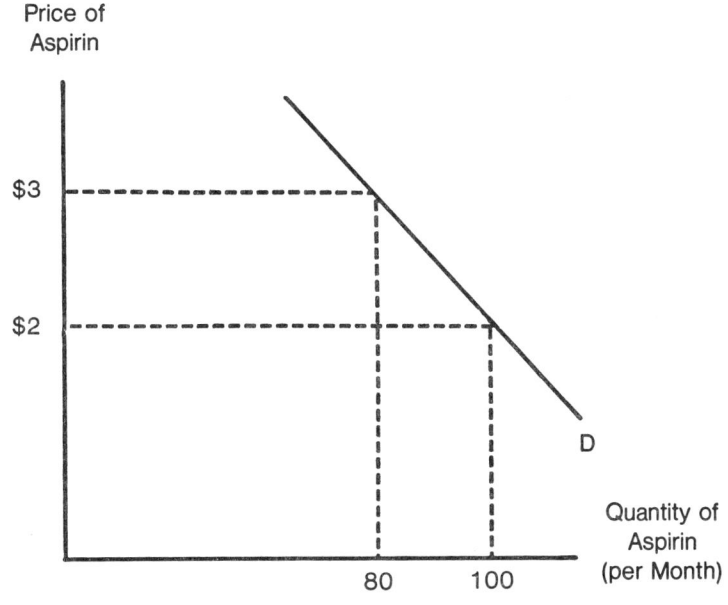

already in the market and because more buyers enter the market. The so-called *law of downward sloping demand* is almost universal; a fall in price, other things unchanged, almost always leads to a rise in quantity demanded.

How great will the increase in quantity be for a given price drop, however? Here there is considerable variation among products. The technical name for the responsiveness of quantity demanded to price change is the price *elasticity of demand*. (A detailed analysis of elasticity is given in Chapter 4.) If a small price change results in a large quantity change, demand is said to be highly *elastic*. If a small price change results in little quantity change, demand is *inelastic*. Elasticity is an important key in predicting the effect of policy proposals. For example, health insurance proposals differ with respect to the amount of *coinsurance* and *deductible* and, hence, the out-of-pocket price to the consumer for medical care. In such cases the difference between the proposals' effects on utilization of medical services depends on demand elasticity. Administrators often need to estimate demand elasticity in the course of their decision making. If the fee for outpatient clinic visits is raised, how much will the number of patients requesting appointments decrease? It might not change at all if patients have no convenient alternatives, but if other clinics are available and do not change their fees, some patients will go there instead. Should a health maintenance organization (HMO) raise its monthly premium? If it does, some members will change their coverage to another plan if such an alternative is available.

As these examples suggest, the most important determinant of demand elasticity is the availability of substitutes. A product with many close substitutes will have a very elastic demand curve. For instance, it might be expected that the demand curve for aspirin would be elastic since there are other nonprescription pain medicines that perform essentially the same functions. The demand for insulin or kidney dialysis would be quite inelastic, however, because of the lack of alternatives.

The slope of the demand curve is related to elasticity, but what determines the level or position of the curve? In Figure 2-2, why might there be demand curve D_1 instead of curve D_2 or D_3? Factors that shift a demand curve are elements other than the good's price. The most important are prices of other products, incomes of consumers, and tastes. If the price of a substitute falls, the good in question becomes relatively less attractive and its demand curve shifts leftward. For example, in Figure 2-2 a drop in the price of other pain medicines might cause the aspirin demand curve

Figure 2-2 Shifts in a Demand Curve

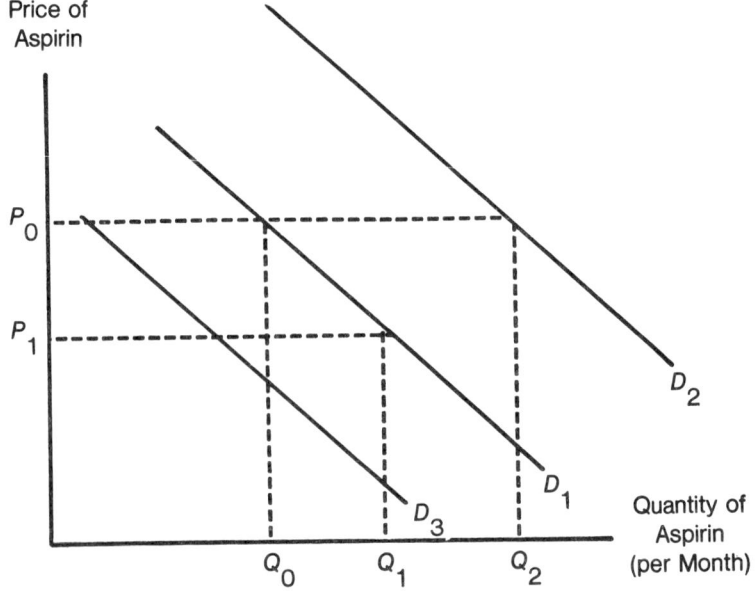

to shift from D_1 to D_3. A rise in income generally increases the demand for a good. (There are exceptions to this but they are not important in the health sector.) Thus, a rise in consumers' income might shift the demand from D_1 to D_2.

The term "tastes" often is used as a catchall for other factors influencing demand. Economists tend to leave the study of the underlying determinants of consumer tastes to psychologists and simply accept the fact that there are many possible noneconomic factors that can shift the demand curve. For example, consumer reaction to reports that taking aspirin can reduce the risk of heart disease might shift the demand curve rightward.

It is important to distinguish between moves along a given demand curve and shifts of the demand curve itself. Both cause a change in the quantity demanded but they are quite different analytically. In Figure 2-2, assume that if price initially is at P_0 and that D_1 prevails, then quantity demanded is Q_0. If a drop in price to P_1 leads to an increase in quantity to Q_1, this is a move along curve D_1. Alternatively, suppose that an increase in income results in an increase in quantity to Q_2. This is a shift of the demand curve itself. In other words, any time something other than a change in price of the good in question leads to a change in the amount of that good that consumers are able and willing to buy, a shift in demand has occurred. A rise in income causes a shift (rightward) of the demand curve for cosmetic surgery. An increase in strep throat infections causes a shift (rightward) of the demand curve for penicillin. A drop in the price of wheelchairs leads to a shift (leftward) of the demand curve for crutches and a move along the demand curve for wheelchairs. All of these, of course, depend on the *ceteris paribus* assumption.

The analysis thus far has assumed that the market is for a final good. What if the market is for an *intermediate good* or primary factor of production? Suppose, for example, that the demand for nurses is the issue. Most buyers are not final consumers but rather employers of nurses—hospitals, nursing homes, HMOs, and the like. How does this affect the analysis? For the most part, the above results still are valid, with some minor differences in interpretation. The demand for nurses is a *derived demand,* so called because it is derived from the demand for the final good, i.e., hospital services. The demand curve slopes down because at lower wages it will be advantageous for the employer to use more nursing labor, perhaps substituting it for other inputs. The level of the demand curve depends on the productivity of the input, which in turn is affected by the technological and organizational structure of the employing organization. For example, the demand curve for nursing labor will be shifted down by a technological innovation that permits some nursing tasks to be taken over by less skilled personnel, or shifted out (up) by an organizational change that enables nurses to take over some functions formerly performed by physicians.

Demand for many goods and services in the health sector is, of course, more complex than the simple example of aspirin used here. For hospital and physician services, the facts that payment comes from a third party rather than the consumer and that the purchase decision is influenced by the doctor introduce complications that are dealt with in Chapter 4.

SUPPLY

The other side of the market, sellers' behavior, is the subject of the theory of supply. The market supply in a given time period is the amount sellers want to sell. One important determinant of market supply is the prevailing price of the good. To suppliers, price represents an incentive for production; the higher the price, the greater the incentive to produce and sell the item. Thus, an upward sloping *supply curve,* such as the aspirin supply curve S_1 shown in Figure 2-3, is a common phenomenon. If the price is $2, sellers will produce 60 units per month; if the price rises to $3, this would provide enough incentive for an extra 20 units of production, or a total of 80 units.

More detailed consideration of the supply incentive suggests the key role that production costs play in supply decisions. A firm seeking a profit must weigh the price it receives from selling an additional unit of the good against the cost of inputs needed to produce it. As long as the former is greater than the latter, it will be profitable to produce the additional unit. The curve S_1 in Figure 2-3, then, is based on the cost of providing an additional unit of output at each level. The reason that the quantity supplied at a price of $3 is 80 units is that it would cost more than $3 to produce the 81st unit and, thus, companies would not carry production this far. This is, of course, an application of marginal analysis. The manufacturer weighs the cost of a small addition to output (marginal cost) against the revenue from the sale of the small addition (marginal revenue) and produces up to the point at which the two are equal.

Thinking of the *supply function* in terms of cost of production provides insight into the factors determining its level. Anything that tends to lower the cost of production will shift the supply curve rightward. For example, a drop in the cost of aspirin bottles or a technical change that permits aspirin to be produced more cheaply will shift the supply curve from S_1 to S_2 in Figure 2-3. A government regulation that requires aspirin manufacturers to install expensive pollution control equipment will raise production costs and shift the supply curve leftward from S_1 to S_3.

Figure 2-3 Shifts in a Supply Curve

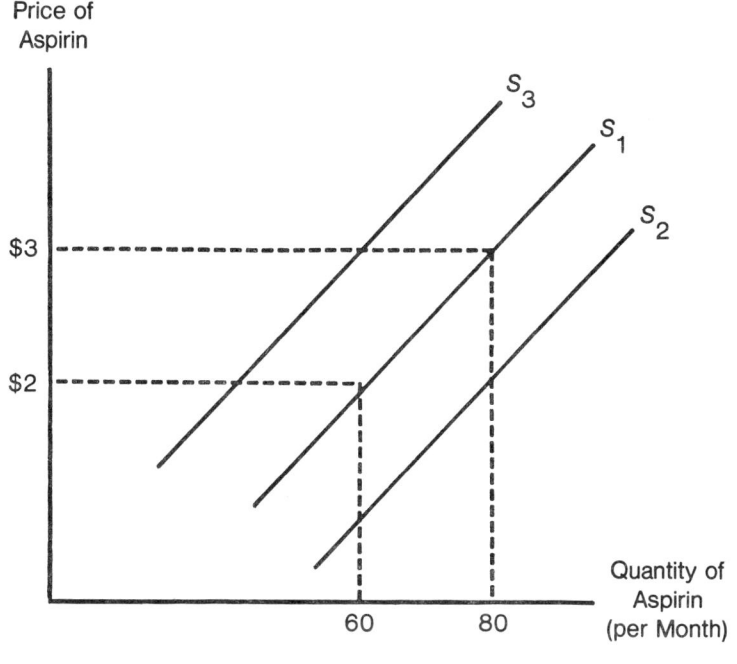

Does basic supply theory hold when suppliers are individual professionals or nonprofit firms, both of which are important suppliers of health care services? It does in most cases, as Chapters 5, 6, and 7 explore in detail. Nonprofit hospitals may be motivated by altruism and the desire to serve the community rather than to maximize profits but even so must consider the relationship between costs and revenues in making supply decisions. Physicians and other professionals are not motivated solely by the desire to earn income, but it is an important factor. The high income of physicians and the large number of persons who want to go to medical school are not unrelated, in the opinion of most economists.

MARKET EQUILIBRIUM

Supply and demand interact to determine the *equilibrium price* in a market. An equilibrium price is one that, if attained, will be maintained. That is, the equilibrium price is one from which there is no inherent tendency to change unless the underlying determinants of supply and demand are altered. In most markets it is the price that will tend to be realized.

Graphically, the equilibrium price is the figure determined by the intersection of the supply and demand curves. Figure 2-4 simply puts together the two sides of the now familiar aspirin market. The equilibrium in this market occurs at a price of $3 and a quantity of 80 units. At this price, and only at this price, is the quantity that buyers want to buy equal to the amount that sellers want to sell. If the actual market price is $3, the desires and expectations of both buyers and sellers are realized; neither has any incentive to take action that would change the price.

However, if the actual price is $2, buyers demand 100 units. Sellers are willing to supply only 60 units. There thus is an *excess demand* of 40 units—everyone who wants aspirin cannot obtain all they want. There is an incentive for buyers to bid the price up. As price rises, the quantity demanded falls off and quantity supplied increases until at a price of $3 they are equal and equilibrium is attained. A similar story can be told for prices above $3. If the original price is $5, it tends to fall because there is an *excess supply* at that level; sellers tend to cut price in order to unload their output.

What are called excess demand and excess supply above correspond in some sense to the terms *shortage* and *surplus* that are common in discussions

Figure 2-4 Equilibrium Price and Quantity

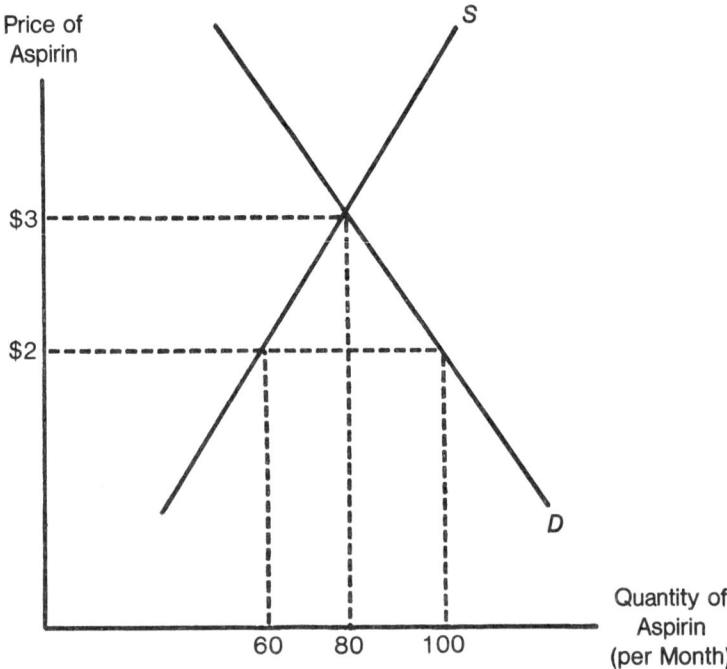

of the health care sector. The adjustment of price in the example eliminates the shortage or surplus without any policy other than independent action in the market by buyers and sellers. Price, in other words, plays the role of rationing the limited supply among those who want it. It does this by providing incentives for both suppliers and demanders to change their behavior until the quantities supplied and demanded are mutually consistent. In the absence of price adjustment there would have to be some way to determine who is permitted to buy the 60 units available at a price of $2. The rationing mechanism could be as complex as a government allocation scheme or as simple as a first-come-first-served rule. In some cases such mechanisms are more desirable than price as a rationing device, but they seldom work as automatically or as cheaply.

Changes in market equilibrium reflect changes in underlying economic conditions. This is accomplished through shifts in the supply and demand curves. In Figure 2-5, suppose the market for aspirin is initially in equilibrium at price P_0 and quantity Q_0, and demand rises to D_1 (perhaps because of research findings showing that the drug prevents heart disease). Initially, there may be an excess demand or a shortage of Q_0-Q_2, but as the price rises suppliers will expand output and a new equilibrium will be realized at price P_1 and quantity Q_1. Similarly, a shift down in demand or a shift up or down in the supply curve will lead to a new price-quantity equilibrium.

Two things must be noted about the analysis of supply and demand shifts. First, only the initial effect of the change is examined. In this example, the research findings probably will cause changes in demand for other drugs, methods of treatment of other diseases, future research plans, and so forth. All of these things could react back on the aspirin market. This analysis ignores them because of the *ceteris paribus* assumption. To take such effects into account requires a much more complicated economic model. The focus here is only on the demand shift and its initial effect on the equilibrium price of aspirin. Second, the model says nothing about the speed or time pattern of price change. Does the price rise from P_0 to P_1 the day after the research findings become known? Does it go up in several steps over the next few months? The model casts no light on these questions. All it says is that the new equilibrium price is P_1. It does not identify when that equilibrium price actually will be realized.

PRICES AND ALLOCATION

To explore more fully the economic role of price, it is necessary to expand the focus from a single market to consider price in the context of a series of interrelated markets. Price serves as a signal of the need for a

Figure 2-5 Changes in Market Equilibrium

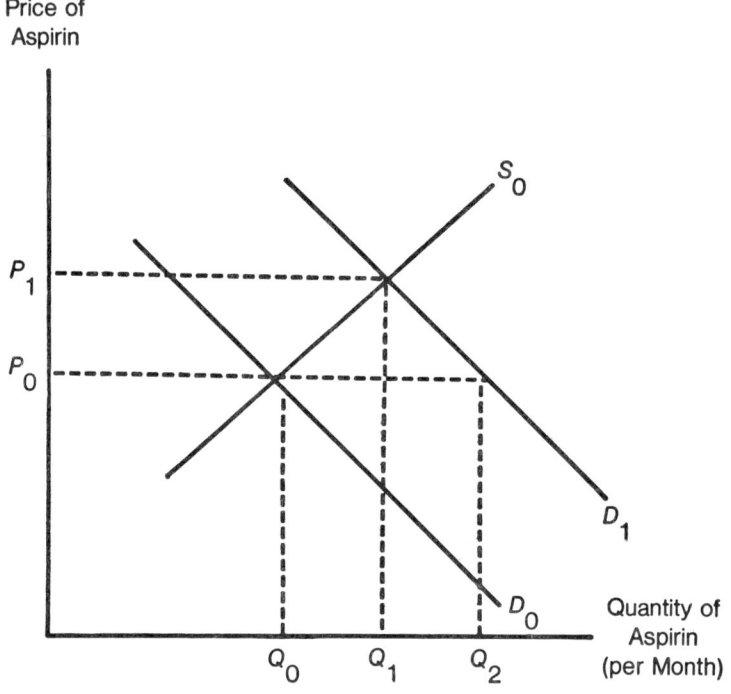

resource transfer, and a change in conditions in one market will set off a series of price moves in other markets in order to achieve the appropriate reallocations. (This, of course, is a relaxing of the *ceteris paribus* assumption.) To consider in brief outline a very simple example, suppose that because of a well-publicized research finding that "an apple a day keeps the doctor away," consumer demand for apples rises sharply, i.e., the apple demand curve shifts outward. This causes an increase in the price of apples and a higher equilibrium quantity supplied and demanded. The higher production quantity requires more inputs, shifting out the derived demand curve for apple pickers and raising their wages. The higher wage for pickers will induce some laborers to seek work in the orchards rather than in other jobs. Prices in other final goods markets also will change as demand for substitute goods changes. When all the effects have been realized, there will be a new allocation of inputs and a new set of goods produced by the economy. Price changes will have provided both a signal that a transfer of resources is needed and an incentive for individual actions by firms and workers to accomplish the transfer.

The facts that resource scarcity is reflected in prices and that the price system links markets together provide a basis for the argument that equilibrium prices in competitive markets are socially desirable prices and that equilibrium quantities are the socially correct quantities of goods to produce. Why is this so? In what sense is the equilibrium quantity determined by the market better than any other quantity?

The demand curve indicates the value placed on each unit of the good by some consumer. In Figure 2-6, P_0 is the value purchasers put on the last unit of the good, i.e., the Q_0th unit—the amount they are willing to pay. The height of the supply curve at Q_0 indicates the opportunity cost of the resources used to make the Q_0th unit of the good; that is, the value those resources would have in their next best alternative use. Their value in their next best use is, of course, determined by what consumers of the alternative product are willing to pay for the output of those resources.

Consider now output Q_1. Will it benefit society to expand production from Q_1-1 to Q_1? The amount someone is willing to pay for the additional unit is P_1. The opportunity cost of the resources needed to make it is only

Figure 2-6 Values for the Last Unit of a Good

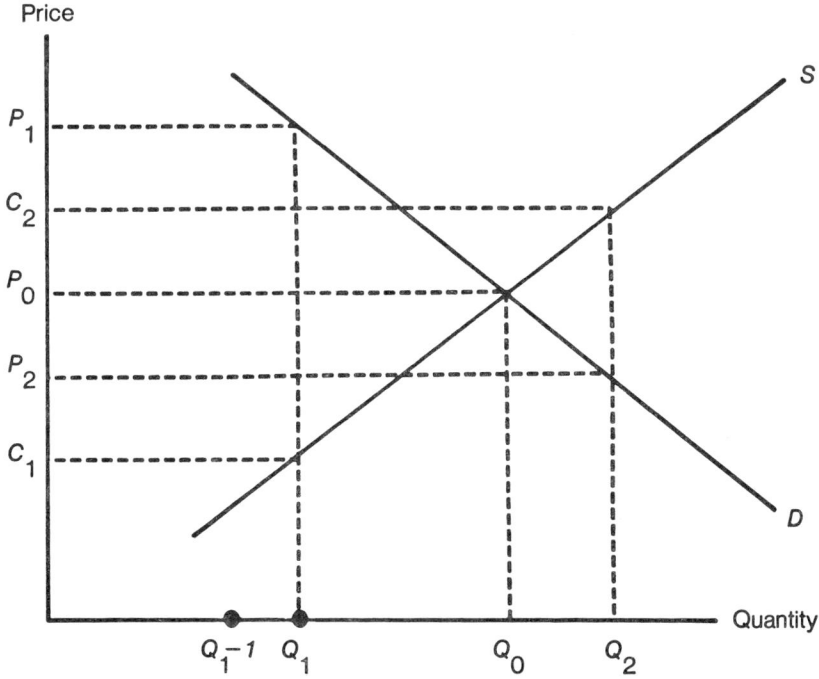

C_1. The difference P_1-C_1 represents the excess of the value of the resource in this use over what the value would be in the best alternative use. Thus it would pay society to give up some of whatever the alternative product is and transfer the resources to producing this good. It can be seen from the graph that this argument will hold at any output below Q_0. Conversely, at any output greater than Q_0, say Q_2, it would be better to cut back output since the resources saved by doing so would be more highly valued in an alternative use (i.e., C_2 is greater than P_2). Thus, at any output other than Q_0, consumers' welfare could be increased by a move toward Q_0; therefore, Q_0 is the optimal output. As Q_0 is the equilibrium output to which the perfectly competitive market will tend, its workings do yield a socially correct outcome.

EQUITY AND EFFICIENCY

Two broad analytical concepts that concern analysts studying the health sector are *equity* and *economic efficiency*. Efficiency means using available resources in a way that will yield the maximum possible benefits. Equity refers to the fairness with which those benefits are distributed. In the health sector, examples of issues mainly related to efficiency, or rather inefficiency, include the use of inpatient care when less expensive outpatient care would be equally beneficial and use of unnecessary laboratory tests. Problems related mainly to equity include inadequate access to health services for low income persons and maldistribution of physicians among urban and rural areas. Naturally, issues and policies never are "pure" equity or "pure" efficiency matters. In most cases, both types of concern are present, but the concepts are useful analytical tools.

Efficiency can be broken into two subcategories: *technical efficiency* and *allocative efficiency*. Technical efficiency means getting the largest possible output out of a given combination of inputs. Technical inefficiency corresponds closely to waste or mismanagement. Allocative efficiency means using inputs and producing outputs in the proper combinations to satisfy society's wants. The argument in the preceding section about the desirability of the output resulting from supply-demand equilibrium in competitive markets is, in fact, an allocative efficiency argument.

Equity often is discussed in terms of *income distribution*. Since income represents generalized purchasing power and thus command over goods and services, fairness of the distribution of goods and services among people relates to fairness of the underlying income distribution. Insofar as most income represents payment for factor services—wages, interest, rent, or profit—an income distribution is determined from the operation of a system of linked competitive markets, because factor prices also are determined by supply-demand equilibrium.

The basic determinants of factor prices and incomes in a market system, therefore, are the elements that influence the supply and the demand for factors. The most important are: (1) the availability of the factor and willingness of its owner to supply it, (2) the productivity of the factor, i.e., the extent to which it contributes to the output of the final good for which it is used, and (3) the demand for and the price of the final good.

To take a specific example, what determines the wages of hospital nurses in a competitive market? First, the number of nurses available in the local labor market. Second, the productivity of nurses in providing the final good—hospital care. (This depends, among other things, on the extent of nurses' training and experience and the technological and organizational structure of the hospital.) Third, the price of hospital services working through the derived demand for nurses.

Most people are not likely to view the income distribution results of the competitive market system as favorably as they view its efficiency. While there is a certain justice in rewarding individuals in proportion to their contribution to output, and good reason to do so in order to provide incentives for economically productive behavior, an income distribution based only on market forces probably is unacceptable in terms of broader social and political considerations. Furthermore, incomes received from property, and especially inherited property, are less likely to be applauded than labor earnings. In the United States and most other countries, government policies are designed to redistribute income. One way to do this is through a system of taxes combined with *transfers,* such as welfare or Social Security payments.

Many government programs in the health field have income redistributive aspects, a prime example being Medicaid. The view that health care is a "right" certainly implies that if the existing income distribution does not permit everyone to realize this right, then redistribution is in order. In effect, this is saying that health care is too important to be left to the market. However, rejecting the markets' income distribution and attempting to correct it by government action may have implications for technical and allocative efficiency. Achieving equity may have costs in terms of decreased efficiency; this trade-off is the source of much discussion and controversy in health economics.

MARKET FAILURE

In moving away from the restrictive assumptions of perfect competition to a more realistic view of the economy, a number of instances arise where the market fails to achieve efficiency. Four such situations are the subject of this section: market power, externalities, public goods, and imperfect information.

Market Power

Market power is a situation in which one or a small number of market participants acting jointly can affect the price. A limiting case is pure *monopoly* where only one seller exists and can control the price at which the good is sold. The major result of sellers' market power is to restrict the supply of the good and raise its price. That is, the monopoly equilibrium price is higher and the output smaller than would be the case if the same market were not monopolized. In a monopoly equilibrium, allocative inefficiency is reflected in the fact that the price charged to consumers is greater than the cost of production. Resources are valued more highly in this use by consumers than in alternative uses and society thus would benefit if output of the monopolized good were expanded. It is not in the monopolist's interest to expand output, however, because the resulting price fall would hurt its profit.

The wedge that monopoly drives between price paid by consumers and cost of resources can be quite large. The effect of monopoly has been observed in the drug industry where some market power is based on patents.

> From 1956 through the mid 1960s, the Pfizer Company and its four licensees sold the antibiotic tetracycline to druggists at a wholesale price of $30.60 per bottle of 100 capsules. Total sales at wholesale to drugstores exceeded a billion dollars during this period. Production costs ranged between $1.60 and $3.80 per bottle, and when doubts about the validity of Pfizer's patent began to mount, several unlicensed firms began producing and selling tetracycline at approximately $2.50 per bottle wholesale. Many similar cases of price-cost margins on the order of 900 per cent for patented drug products have been identified.[1]

A patent is a legal monopoly, and society receives benefits of increased innovation as a result of the patent system. But this example suggests how great the effect of market power can be. Another area in which market power arises is in the licensing of physicians and other health professionals. Of course, the number of physicians in a geographic market is typically large, so the monopoly model does not apply directly. To the extent that professional associations acting through influence on government licensing boards determine entry into the profession, however, the full results of market competition will not be achieved. For example, it has been argued that organized medicine, through control of medical education, has acted to restrict the supply of doctors and thereby raise physicians' incomes.[2]

Market power also can occur on the buyers' side where one or a few big purchasers acting jointly can control the price. The outcome of market power on the buyers' side, as could be expected, is a price below the figure that would prevail in a competitive market. In the health sector, buyers' market power is important since government and large insurance companies are the "buyers" of many services and for this reason can influence price. Market power on the buyers' side is, like monopoly, a source of inefficiency. Some economists note that the presence of buyers' market power can offset monopoly power in the same market and that this situation of countervailing power can be more desirable than a simple monopoly market.

Externalities

Another situation in which markets fail to achieve efficient outcomes is when there are side effects (economists use the term *externalities*) of either consumption or production. It is assumed implicitly in the discussion of markets that the supply curve reflects all the costs of producing the good and that the demand curve reflects all the benefits of consuming it. That is, the sellers, because they must pay them, take into account all costs of resource use in deciding how much to produce at each price; and the buyers, because they will enjoy them, take into account all the benefits of consumption in deciding how much to demand at each price. Through the self-interest of each party, all relevant information enters into the decision.

Often this is not the case. A good example of a negative side effect or externality of production is environmental pollution. A company polluting the air or water is using a valuable resource, one with alternative uses. By using water as a waste-carrying mechanism, the manufacturer is making it unfit for an alternative use, say drinking or swimming. But the company does not have to consider this in its economic calculation because it does not have to "buy" the water away from its next best alternative use. The private cost the concern must take into account is less than the true *social cost*, the opportunity cost of all resources used.

The implications of this are shown in Figure 2-7. The supply curve is labeled *private cost* to emphasize that the suppliers take into account only the costs they must bear. The *social cost* curve represents the private cost plus the external costs, i.e., those borne by others. The diagram suggests the type of misallocation that externalities can cause. The output realized

Figure 2-7 Social and Private Cost Curves

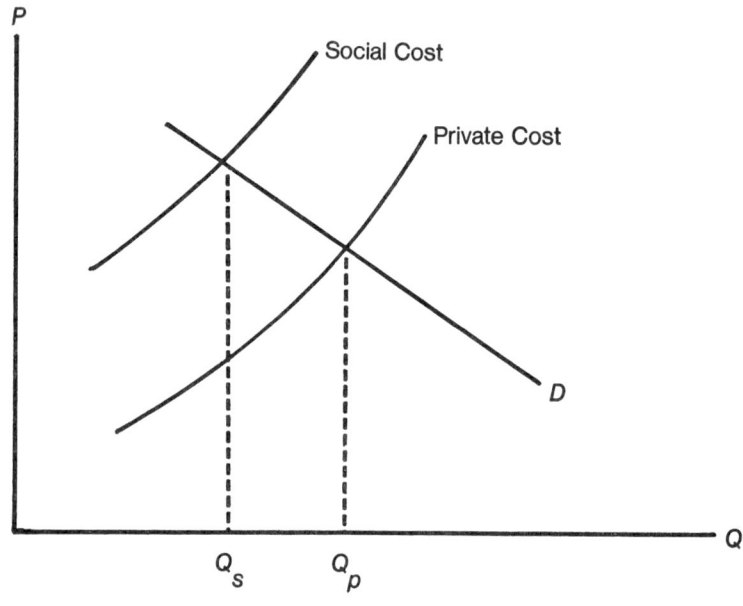

in an unregulated market would be Q_p. The socially optimal output, however, would be Q_s, at which all costs are balanced against the value the consumer places on the good. Thus, in the case of external costs, the tendency is for the market to produce too much of the good (Q_p instead of Q_s).

An example of a good with a consumption externality is a vaccination against a contagious disease. The benefit the person realizes from getting such a vaccination is that the individual will not contract the disease. However, by getting the shot, the person also confers a benefit on others: the reduced probability that they will catch the disease from the first individual. The situation can be analyzed in terms of Figure 2-8. The demand curve is labeled *private benefit* to emphasize that demanders base their decision on the benefits they will receive from their own vaccination. The *social benefit* curve is the private benefit plus the external benefits. The market will reach equilibrium at Q_p while socially the most efficient outcome is Q_s, a higher output level. The external benefit has led the market to produce too little of the good—in this case, too few vaccinations.

Externalities may justify some type of government intervention in the market on efficiency grounds. Types of such action include attempts to modify economic incentives for private firms (e.g., imposing an effluent

Figure 2-8 Social and Private Benefit Curves

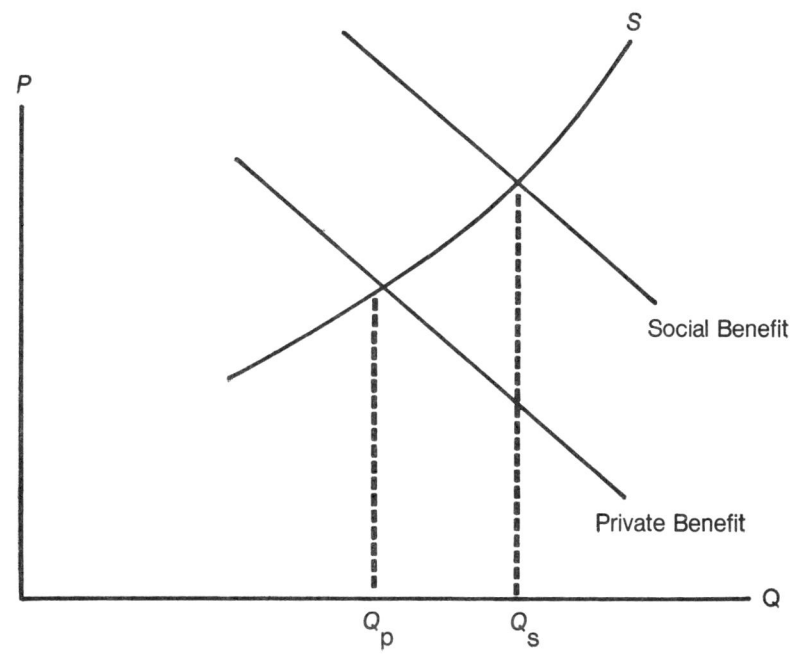

fee or tax on pollutants emitted), direct regulation (e.g., requiring the use of specific pollution control technology), and government provision of the good itself (e.g., an immunization program where the government provides vaccinations at no charge). Not all externalities call for federal or state intervention. Government programs require resources and may themselves be inefficient. Thus, the expense of such intervention must be balanced against the cost of the inefficiency generated by the externality before a policy is carried out.

Public Goods

Another case of market failure in which government must act is the *public good* situation where the market cannot or will not provide the good at all. Incentives for private entities to do so are lacking because the good cannot be sold in the usual way. There are two major characteristics that produce public good status. First there is nonexcludability in consumption. That is, a person who refuses to pay for a good cannot be prevented from consuming it or benefiting from it. Second, everyone must consume the same amount. A standard example of a public good is national defense. The hawk who favors high military spending and the dove who favors none at all each receives the same amount of protection from foreign attack, despite great differences in their preferences and willingness to pay for it.

An example of a public good in the health field is mosquito control. Everyone in the area involved must benefit to the same extent. The service must be financed through taxes. A private company could not simply offer it to individuals on the market at a price while excluding those who refuse to pay. A problem arises: How much mosquito control is the "right" amount? That is a question policy makers do not have to decide in the case of goods sold in competitive markets. As has been noted, the independent actions of many suppliers and demanders lead to an efficient solution there. For mosquito control, however, the decision must be made by government. Some of the economic tools of analysis that can help officials make such decisions are discussed in Chapter 11.

Imperfect Information

Finally, lack of perfect information may be a cause of market failure. The model of perfect competition assumes that all buyers and sellers are equally and fully informed about relevant economic conditions. All buyers must be aware of the availability, prices, and quality of goods from alternative sources. Sellers must have access on equal terms to information about the prices, characteristics, and availability of inputs as well as to technological information about the production process. Where there are restrictions on the free flow of information, market failures can result.

In the health field, an example of information availability is the question of whether health professionals should be permitted to advertise. Some economists believe that restrictions on advertising prevent consumers from obtaining information needed to make decisions and that as a result prices are higher than if advertising were permitted. Empirical research reported in 1980 provides some support for this hypothesis in the case of eye examinations and sales of eyeglasses. Prices are lower in markets where advertising by optometrists and opticians is permitted than in markets where it is prohibited or restricted by law.[3]

NOTES

1. F.M. Scherer, *Industrial Market Structure and Economic Performance* (New York: Rand McNally Co., 1970), p. 390.
2. Elton Rayack, "The Physicians' Service Industry," in Walter Adams, ed., *The Structure of American Industry,* 5th ed. (New York: Macmillan Publishing Company, Inc., 1977).

3. Federal Trade Commission, Bureau of Economics, 1980. *Staff Report on Effects of Restrictions on Advertising and Commercial Practice in the Professions: The Case of Optometry;* and James W. Begun and Roger D. Feldman, 1980. *A Social and Economic Analysis of Professional Regulation in Optometry,* U.S. Department of Health and Human Services, National Center for Health Services Research, Research Digest Series (DHHS Publication No. PHS 80-3285).

SUGGESTED READINGS

Mansfield, Edwin. *Microeconomics,* 3rd ed. New York: W. W. Norton & Co., Inc. 1979.

Newhouse, Joseph P. *The Economics of Medical Care.* Reading, Mass.: Addison-Wesley Publishing Co., 1978.

SOURCE

a. Reprinted from *Competition in the Health Care Sector: Past, Present and Future.* Warren Greenberg, ed., Federal Trade Commission, March 1978, pp. 11–13.

Chapter 3

Empirical Tools and Measurement in Economics

This chapter introduces some of the techniques used to apply economic theory to real world problems. Full understanding of the methodology used in economic research today requires several years of graduate training in mathematics and statistics. Obviously in the next few pages the authors cannot hope to impart this level of sophistication. However, an attempt is made to indicate the kind of problems that arise in empirical work and to illustrate the use of some of the major empirical tools of health economics research.

The first section of this chapter reviews conceptual issues involved with economic methodology. The following section discusses statistical sampling and significance testing. The next four sections present the basic elements of simple and multiple regression analysis, including the use of regression for forecasting hospital costs. Two selections deal with problems using index numbers—a study of the trend in prices of physicians' services and another look at forecasting hospital costs.

The elementary nature of this chapter must be reemphasized: it does not intend to impart the skills needed for performing empirical research. Econometric research is an art as well as a science and requires both practice and formal training. Those interested in more sophisticated applications are urged to take course work in mathematical economics and statistics. However, careful study of this chapter is important to an understanding of those that follow. Multiple regression and the other statistical tools presented here are used extensively by the writers whose works are excerpted in later chapters.

For readers who wish to delve further into the technical aspects of econometrics (or for those who have done such work and want a review) we would suggest a good starting point is *Statistics and Econometrics: A Problem-Solving Text* by Barry and Stephen Chiswick.[1] Other readings in econometric methodology and applications are listed at the end of the chapter.

ECONOMIC METHODOLOGY

All empirical economic studies involve four basic elements: (1) the assembly of facts, (2) the formulation of a hypothesis, (3) the construction of models to test the hypothesis, and (4) the interpretation of test results. In the following excerpt from a widely used introductory textbook, Lloyd Reynolds gives a good summary of the conceptual issues.

THE NECESSITY OF MEASUREMENT[a]

Economics has an advantage in that much of it deals with *quantities*. It is concerned with prices, hourly wage rates, numbers of people employed, amounts of goods produced and exchanged, quantity of money and credit in existence, government receipts and expenditures. These things are measurable in principle, though actual measurements fall short of perfection.

Precise measurement, then, is important for serious study of economics. If one man maintains that national output is higher this year than last, while another maintains firmly that it is lower, they cannot get any farther. Agreement on facts is an essential starting point. So we set out to measure total national output, production of specific goods and services, exports and imports, the money incomes of households, price levels and wage levels, and dozens of other things. One cannot approach economics without such measurements any more than natural scientists can operate without measures of mass or temperature.

Preparation and criticism of these measures is the task of *economic statistics*.

Measurement of what is happening is only the beginning. Our ultimate hope is to *explain* why things happen as they do. If we can explain past events, we have some chance of being able to *predict* future events. Science aims at prediction: and practical men are especially intrigued by the possibilities of prediction in economics, since profits and votes may hang on the outcome.

Horseback predictions can sometimes be obtained directly from economic statistics. For example, if you look at statistics of personal income in the United States over the last 30 years, you will find that on the average about 94% of personal income after taxes has been spent on consumption while 6% has been saved. Except for the war years 1942–45, when goods were hard to get and savings were abnormally large, the savings ratio has not varied far from the 6% average. Thus if you have to make a quick estimate of what personal savings will be next year, your safest course will be to take 6% of expected personal income.

Such rules of thumb are all right as far as they go. Their limitation is that they give no explanation of why the figures behave as they do. It is as though an engineer looked at a machine and observed that a particular wheel always went around so many times a minute but knew nothing about the principles governing the machine's operation. No engineer or physicist would be content to stop at this point. He wants to know *why* the machine behaves as it does. Until he knows this, he cannot be sure that another machine will behave in the same way, nor can he design a machine that would behave differently. Similarly, the economist wants to understand why the American people behave as they do about saving, food buying, working, and other things. He wants to discover the mechanisms behind the statistics.

How can he acquire this understanding? First, he can ask people why they made certain decisions. There are obvious drawbacks to this method. You can quiz only a small percentage of the population, and you can never be completely sure that you have a representative group. People do not always know why they did what they did, and if they do they may not be willing to tell. Interview questions have to be direct and simple, but the circumstances surrounding a decision are often complex. People can give more reliable answers about recent events than about events in the more distant past. Despite these difficulties, "survey research" has increased greatly in recent years and has added much to our economic understanding.

The standard method of physical science is the controlled experiment, but economists cannot use this method. We cannot shut people up in an isolated camp to observe their reactions. In any case, people's reactions under such artificial conditions would be different from their reactions in everyday life.

So what are we to do? Deprived of the possibility of actual experiments, the economist resorts to *intellectual experiments*. The process of intellectual experiment begins with *observations of behavior*. The important thing is observation of large numbers of families, or business concerns, or what not, rather than of isolated individuals. It isn't very interesting to know that when Mr. Jones got a $1,000 raise last year, he put $200 of this into extra saving. Mr. Jones may turn out to be an unusual specimen. But if we find out that all families in the United States received $20 billion more income last year and that $3 billion of this went into savings, this is significant. If we can break the total population down into groups, say by income level, and observe the different behavior in these groups, this is even more interesting.

The next stage is to sit down quietly in an armchair and try to reason out why people might have behaved as they did. One can think of many things that might influence family decisions about saving, including the family's present income, its expected future income, its accumulated wealth, fixed commitments for mortgages and time payments, and plans for children's education or other large future expenditures. From what we know of our own reactions, and from what we observe in statistical measurements, we try to estimate the probable strength of these various influences. This is the stage of *hypothesis building* or *theorizing*. At the end, we come out with a set of propositions that may be capable of explaining the facts. We can call this a *theory of household savings*.

Finally, we must go back to the facts and test our hypotheses against observed behavior. Our theory says, for example, that people will react in a specified way to a certain increase in their current income. Well, do they or don't they? The measures of what actually happens are the payoff. If they agree closely with our hypothesis, we can have some confidence that we are on the right track. If not, we must ask what went wrong and start over again. This step is termed *verification, hypothesis testing,* or *statistical inference*. Statistical inference is the economist's substitute for the laboratory he can never have.

It may be necessary to work back and forth several times between hypotheses and verification. We develop certain hypotheses in the first instance. We look at the facts. The facts don't quite fit. So we go back and change our hypotheses, perhaps making them more complicated to take account of things we have overlooked at first. Then we apply another test of statistics against our hypotheses. If we are lucky, the fit will be better, but the hypotheses may need still further revision; and so on and on. In the end, if we are clever as well as lucky, we may come out with a set of hypotheses that agree closely with observed behavior.

Before concluding that economics is an exact science, let's look a little farther. Economic hypotheses are always tested by reference to the past. They have to be, since we have no figures for the future. Yet it is the future in which we are really interested. Are we safe in saying that a formula which fits the facts pretty well for the years 1950–75 will work just as well in 1980? It will *if people continue to behave in the future as they have in the past.* This is an important qualification. Hypotheses about consumer purchases and savings are reasonably reliable, because consumers' tastes and habits seem to change rather slowly. But suppose, instead, that we were trying to predict how much companies will spend on new plants and machinery. This is a quite variable and unstable figure. Our hypotheses about it are less complete than for consumer behavior, and predictions are likely to be farther from the mark.

Even at best, economic predictions have an "iffy" character. No economist in his right mind would say flatly, "Butter sales next year *will* be 1,700 million pounds." Rather, he will say, "*If* the price of butter is [$1.70 per pound], *if* consumer income is $600 billion (and so on through several other ifs), *then* butter sales will be 1,700 million pounds." Even this statement is not sufficiently cautious. Statistical inference yields probabilities rather than certainties. So we must say something like, "If butter prices, consumer incomes, and other relevant factors are as stated, then the chances are 95 out of 100 that butter sales will be between 1,675 and 1,725 million pounds."

Note also that economic predictions relate to a *group* of consumers, companies, workers, or what not; and the larger the group, the more reliable the prediction. It is sometimes argued that economics can't possibly be a precise subject, because it deals with human beings and human beings are unpredictable. If this means that we cannot predict the economic behavior of the Brown family very reliably, the argument is correct. But the economist is not interested in the Brown family. He tries rather to say what 5 million or 50 million families will do under specified conditions, which is a much more feasible undertaking.

SAMPLING AND TESTS OF SIGNIFICANCE

Although economic prediction and analysis deal with the behavior of large groups of people, data often can be obtained on only a portion of the group at interest. This is called statistical sampling. The observed data represent a *sample* from a larger *population;* an important task of statistical analysis is to determine what can be learned from a sample about a population. For instance, one empirical health economics study investigated the hypothesis that hospital utilization differed between persons using a prepaid group practice and those covered by a "free choice" health insurance plan.[2] The study reviewed the medical records for a nine-month period of a group of about 2,700 schoolteachers, some of whom were covered by each kind of plan. A small portion of the results dealing with males shows the following:

Males Age	Surgical Admissions (per 1,000 persons)	
	Prepaid Group Practice	Free Choice Plan
35–49	15.9	60.8
50–64	42.9	77.7

The results seem to suggest that the prepaid group practice coverage is associated with lower surgical admissions (at least for men aged 35–64). But how sure can economists be of that? After all, these data are based on the experience of relatively few persons for a relatively short time. Perhaps these result from chance, the random fluctuation that characterizes most human behavior. On the other hand, perhaps they indicate that there really are important differences in utilization associated with variations in the type of health insurance coverage. Which is more likely correct?

This is a standard and very common statistical problem. Given some evidence from a sample, economists want to know how strong it is in support of a particular hypothesis about the population.[3]

What is called for here is a *test of significance*. This is a statistical computation that helps in making a judgment about the strength of sample evidence on the hypothesis. Note that it is impossible to be 100 percent sure, short of obtaining data on the whole population. However, common sense suggests that in this problem, the larger the number of people in the sample and the greater the observed differences, the stronger the evidence. The *hypothesis test* used in this case answers the question: "If in fact there were no real difference in surgical admission rates in the population between the two groups, how likely is it that (by chance) observers will note a difference in the sample as large as was seen?"

In the study above, the computation (a *t-test*) showed that the probability of a chance observation as great as the difference seen for males aged 35–49 is less than 5 percent. In other words, that difference is *statistically significant* at the 5 percent level. The difference for ages 50–64 is not statistically significant at the 5 percent level. A statistically significant result, then, is one that is unlikely to have occurred by chance; therefore, it is one that supports the hypothesis being tested. The level of the test—the level of significance—chosen by the researcher depends on how strong the evidence needs to be in order to deem it statistically significant. Conventional choices are 5 percent or 1 percent, but there is room for differ-

Empirical Tools and Measurement in Economics 41

ences among analysts, based in part on their assessments of the relative costs of making errors in decisions—that is, accepting a hypothesis that really is false or rejecting a true one from the sample results.

SIMPLE REGRESSION AND CORRELATION

Often it is necessary to explore the relationship between two variables. As has been seen, many economic models involve such functional relationships. The idea that one variable depends on another is key to the analysis of many types of administrative problems, as well. Consider, for example, the data in Table 3-1 for 12 short-term general hospitals in Portland, Oregon.

For obvious reasons, a hospital's payroll expense might be expected to be related to the number of employees. Mathematically if Y is the payroll expense and X the number of personnel, the economist suggests or hypothesizes that Y is a function of X, that is

$$Y = f(X)$$

where Y is referred to as the dependent variable and X the independent variable. This functional relationship is hypothesized to hold for all hospitals, yet the data come from only a sample. Again, the analyst is in a situation of wanting to use the sample data to draw conclusions about the entire population. Where the hypothesis in question involves a relationship

Table 3-1 Payroll Expense and Number of Personnel in Portland Hospitals

Hospital	Payroll Expense ($mil) (Y)	Personnel (X)
A	9.6	1,095
B	.4	87
C	9.8	1,195
D	10.6	1,530
E	5.0	900
F	.6	87
G	2.5	366
H	4.8	540
I	1.7	240
J	7.4	1,191
K	7.5	920
L	1.8	307

Source: Reprinted from *The 1973 AHA Guide to the Health Care Field* by permission of the American Hospital Association, ©1973.

between two variables, *correlation* and *regression* are appropriate statistical tools.

The data from the table are plotted in Figure 3-1. It appears that payroll expense is related to personnel and the relationship is positive, i.e., higher payroll expense is related to more personnel. The relationship is not "tight," however. If it were, all the points would be on a line. The scatter of points suggests an upward sloping line but with points off-line in a random fashion. This is indeed the notion that underlies the simple regression model: Y is related to X but is also influenced by error. Formally,

$$Y = f(X) + (\text{error}) = a + bX + (\text{error})$$

Figure 3-1 Relationship between Payroll Expense and Number of Employees

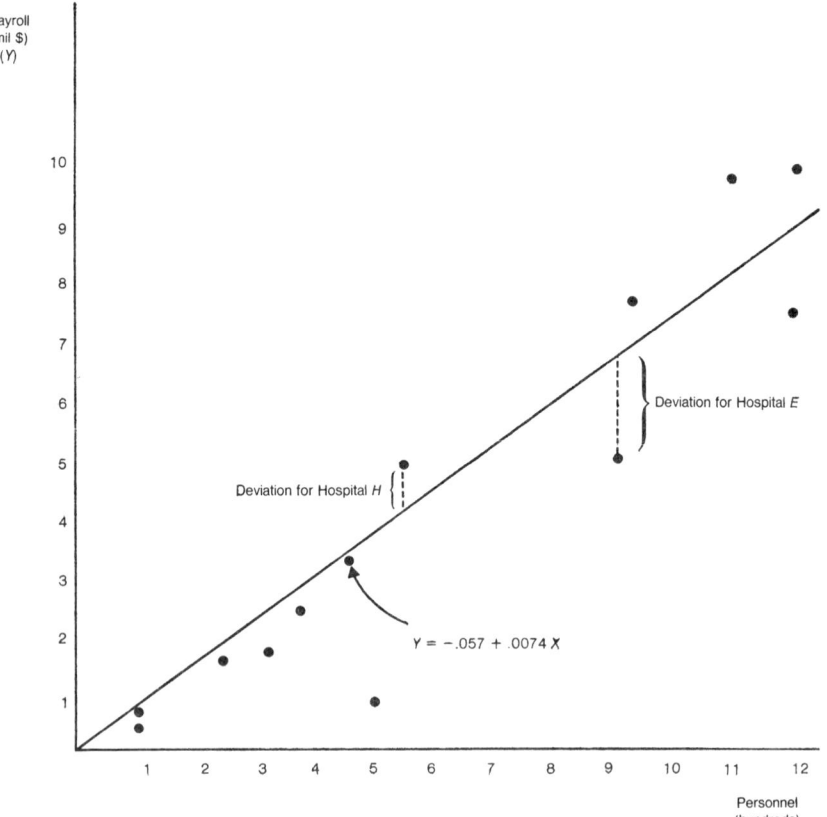

where a and b are constant terms that define the true linear relationship between X and Y (a is the intercept on the Y axis and b is the slope of the line). The source of the error is twofold. First, there may be important factors other than X that are systematically related to Y. Since these determinants of Y are not included explicitly in the equation, they appear as error. Second, the randomness that characterizes all human behavior means that the sample observation will not correspond exactly to the population relationship, which also appears as error.

Linear regression is a technique for "fitting" a line to a scatter of points such as that in Figure 3-1. That is, the regression computation determines values for a and b in such a way that the line best summarizes the relationship contained in the observed points. The problem is to determine a line that misses all the points by as little as possible. The amount by which any line misses a point is called the deviation. For example, in Figure 3-1 the deviation for hospital E is the vertical distance between the regression line for an observed X-value of 900 employees and the observed Y-value of $5.0 million in payroll expense for that hospital. Also shown is the deviation for hospital H: the vertical distance between the line for an X-value of 540 and the observed Y-value of $4.8 million.

The size of the deviation depends, of course, on where the line is drawn. The line that best fits the observed points is the one that makes the sum of squared deviations as small as possible. Why minimize the sum of squared deviations rather than simply the sum of deviations? Because some deviations will be positive and some negative, it would be possible to get a small sum by having large positive numbers offset by large negative ones. This clearly would defeat the purpose of the exercise, which is to choose a line that goes as close as possible to the points. Using the sum of squared deviations, which must be positive, avoids this problem.

The line that best fits the points in Figure 3-1 according to the *least squares* criterion[4] is:

$$Y = -.057 + .0074\,X$$

where $-.057$ is the estimated value of a and $+.0074$ the estimated value for b. These *regression coefficients* are computed from a sample so they are not the same as the "true" coefficients, a and b, but they are the best guess as to the values of a and b (which cannot be observed directly).

How good a guess is this? Two factors are relevant here:

1. The larger the sample, the better the regression coefficients are as estimators of the true values. This follows because the larger sample gives more information on which to base the estimate.

2. The estimates will be better if the points fall fairly close to a line than if they are widely scattered.

In Figure 3-2, it is possible that given the data points in Panel A and Panel B, regression estimates of the coefficients will be exactly the same, generating the lines shown. However, the economist would have much more confidence that the estimates in A represented the true situation. Indeed, in B, it might well be wondered if a relationship between X and Y exists at all. The analyst may have been unlucky and chosen a sample that indicates a linear relationship when in fact none really exists.

This suggests one major use of regression analysis—testing whether a relationship between two variables exists. The statistic commonly used for this purpose is the *correlation coefficient, r*. The correlation coefficient is computed from the sample observations and can take on values between -1 and $+1$. The sign of r indicates the direction of the relationship, i.e., the direction of the slope of the regression line. A positive correlation coefficient means a positively sloped line, that is, as X increases, Y does also. A negative correlation coefficient suggests that as X increases, Y falls.

Often the square of the correlation coefficient, r^2, is used, since it can take on only positive values. The size of r^2 relates to the extent to which the points vary around the line. In a situation like Panel A, where the points lie very close to the line, r^2 will have a value near 1. In Panel B, where the points are widely scattered, r^2 will have a lower value. Thus a high r^2 computed from sample observations is strong evidence of a relationship in the population, and the lower r^2, the weaker the evidence becomes.

Regression results also can be used for prediction. Suppose, for example, that the analyst desired to predict the payroll expense of a hospital (not included in the sample) with 1,000 employees. A logical approach would be to substitute 1,000 as the value of X in the regression equation and use the computed value of Y as the predicted payroll expense, i.e.,

$$\text{predicted } Y = -.057 + .0074X = -.057 + .0074(1{,}000) = 7.34$$

or $7.34 million. The accuracy of the prediction will depend on how good the estimates of a and b are and, in addition, on how close the new X value is to the sample X values. That is, 1,000 is in the general range of the X values in the sample (from 87 to 1,530), so it is fairly safe to make the prediction. If the hospital has 2,500 employees, the ground would be much shakier since 2,500 is far beyond the range of X-values on which the regression estimates are based.

Empirical Tools and Measurement in Economics   45

Figure 3-2 Scatter Diagrams for Different r^2 Values

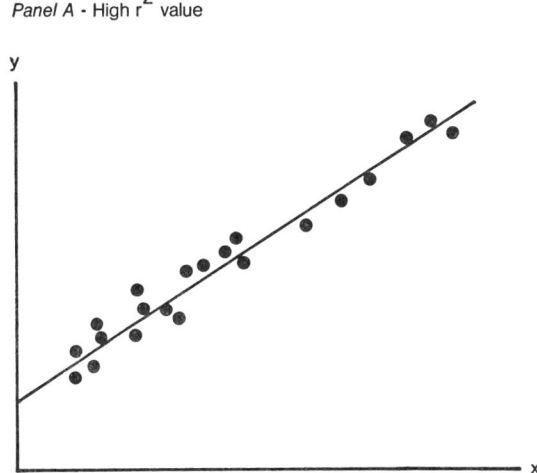

Panel A - High r^2 value

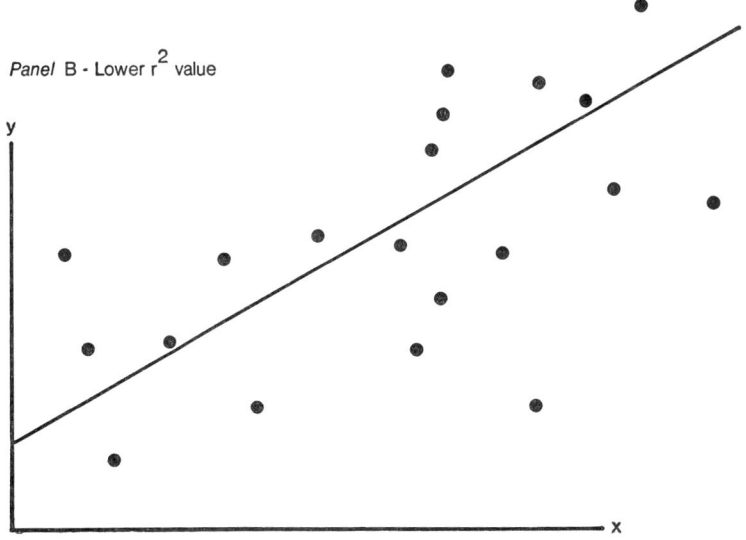

Panel B - Lower r^2 value

MULTIPLE REGRESSION

Multiple regression is an extension of simple regression and is probably the most commonly used statistical technique in economic research. It permits economists to represent the type of relationship where several independent variables acting at the same time affect the dependent variable. Although the two-dimensional graphical representation breaks down, the algebraic generalization is straightforward. The model now is

$$Y = a + b_1X_1 + b_2X_2 + b_3X_3 + \ldots b_nX_n + (\text{error})$$

where $X_1, X_2, \ldots X_n$ are n different independent variables and Y is the dependent variable. To continue with the example of hospital payroll expense, it can be hypothesized that payroll expense is related to both the number of employees and the number of beds in the hospital. The regression line then would be

$$Y = -.23 + .0031X_1 + .011X_2$$

The key to interpreting correctly multiple regression results is to remember that a regression coefficient shows the effect of the independent variable on the dependent variable when the other independent variables are held constant. In the example, there might be interest in the effect of bed size on payroll costs when personnel are held constant. It might be hypothesized that hospitals with more beds tend to have more specialized facilities and, thus, more specialized and highly paid workers. It may well be impossible to find several hospitals with the same number of workers but different numbers of beds to observe in order to test the hypothesis directly. Multiple regression allows this to be done statistically. The coefficient of X_2 (.011 in the equation above) shows the effect of a 1-unit change in bed size on payroll expense when personnel are held constant. That is, if bed size increases by 1 bed and the number of employees is unchanged, payroll expense is predicted to go up by $.011 million, or $11,000. The coefficient of X_1 (.0031) indicates that a 1-unit change in personnel, beds remaining constant, will lead to a change in payroll expense of $.0031 million, or $3,100.

Several statistics usually are presented along with regression estimates and are useful in interpreting the results. The most important are the standard error and *t-statistic* for each estimated coefficient and R^2 the squared multiple correlation coefficient for the equation as a whole.

Estimates are presented in a manner such as Table 3-2, which summarizes the results for the multiple regression in the example.

Table 3-2 Regression Results

	Dependent Variable: Payroll Expense		
Independent Variable	Estimated Coefficient	Standard Error	t-Statistic
Constant	−.23	.136	1.7
Personnel	.0031	.00086	3.6
Beds	.011	.002	5.5
R^2	.98		
D.F.*	9		

* D.F. = degrees of freedom.

The standard error and t-statistic relate to how good the statistical "fit" is with respect to the independent variable involved. (The t-statistic is simply the coefficient divided by its standard error.) Therefore, they give information about how strong the sample evidence is that there is in fact a population relationship between that independent variable and the dependent variable when other variables are held constant. The higher the t-statistic, the stronger the evidence that a relationship exists. A low t-statistic suggests that the independent variable may have no effect when other independent variables are taken into account, i.e., held constant. Roughly speaking, a t-statistic above 2 is evidence of statistical significance. (The exact value depends on sample size as well as the level of significance being used.)

The R^2 statistic is analogous to the squared correlation coefficient in simple regression. It indicates the goodness of fit of the equation as a whole. The most useful interpretation of R^2 is that it tells the percentage of variation in the dependent variable that is "explained" by all the independent variables together. Thus a high R^2 (closer to 1) is strong evidence that the equation captures the important factors influencing the dependent variable. The D.F. in the table refers to the degrees of freedom. This is a statistical measure related to the number of observations. The higher the degrees of freedom, the larger the sample size and, thus, the more confidence in the results.

MULTIPLE REGRESSION: A CASE STUDY

Regression analysis is used to investigate broad economic and policy issues but also is valuable in dealing with specific administrative and regulatory questions. The following example from the latter context provides additional insight as to the usefulness and interpretation of regression analysis. First, the issues involved are described. How regression analysis might be applied is then demonstrated. It must be reiterated that this chapter is not intended to equip the reader to perform such analysis but only to appreciate its applicability. The example, by the way, is based on an actual situation but the name of the institution has been changed.

Shackleton Community Hospital is a rural, 40-bed institution in New England. A state regulatory agency questioned the amount of money Shackleton was spending on respiratory therapy (RT), noting that its expenditure on this service was considerably greater than most hospitals its size and, indeed, was even more than some larger institutions. The agency felt that the expenditure was increasing the cost of care at Shackleton unnecessarily. The administrator, called upon to explain, offered the following points:

1. The hospital had on its medical staff an internist whose specialty was pulmonary disease. This doctor was well known in the region and her patients came from a wider geographical area than most of the hospital's patients. Thus, the hospital had more admissions for pulmonary disease than other hospitals its size.
2. The medical staff believed that the use of respiratory therapy was associated with shorter hospital stays. Therefore, while Shackleton's respiratory therapy expenditure was greater than that at similar hospitals, its average length of stay was less and the cost was not unnecessary or wasteful.

How might regression analysis be used to explore the issues raised here? Consider the regulator's initial assertion. It suggests that, first, there is a relationship between respiratory therapy expenditure and hospital size and, second, that Shackleton's RT expenditure is above what would be predicted by that relationship for a hospital its size. The simple regression framework applicable here is suggested in Figure 3-3. Each dot in the scatter diagram represents a hospital in the regulator's jurisdiction. The line is the least squares regression line fitted to these points. The dot representing Shackleton lies considerably above the line, i.e., it has a large positive deviation (also sometimes called the residual). The actual expenditure of $200,000 is $60,000 more than what the regression predicts for the "typical" 40-bed hospital.

The administrator's argument, in effect, is that simple regression is not appropriate here and that multiple regression is needed. The executive suggests that respiratory therapy expenditure (RT) depends not only on hospital size (S) but also on the number of pulmonary disease admissions

Figure 3-3 Regression of Respiratory Therapy Expenditure (*RT*) on Hospital Size (*S*)

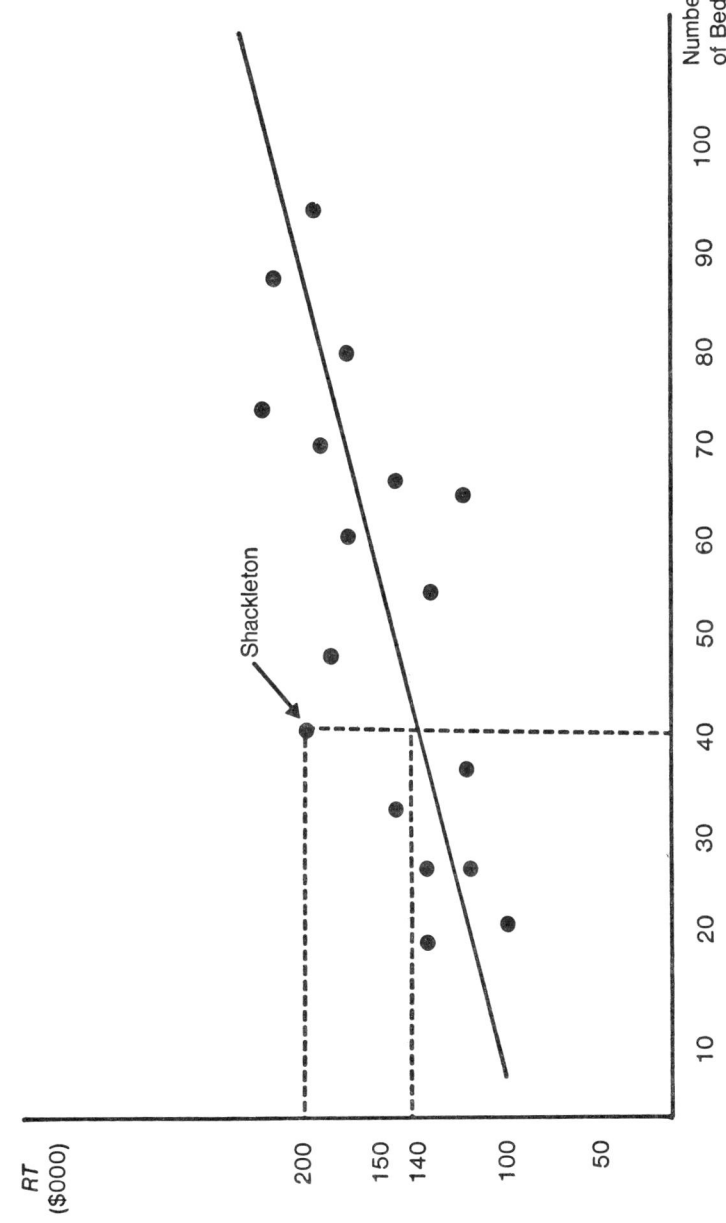

(P) and the average length of stay (L). The implied multiple regression equation then is

$$RT = a + b_1 S + b_2 P + b_3 L$$

According to the administrator's argument, if this regression is computed, b_1 and b_2 are found to be positive numbers since RT goes up with increases in S and P, and b_3 is negative since shorter L is associated with higher RT.

Suppose the regulator obtains information on all four variables for all the hospitals in that jurisdiction and computes the multiple regression equation. How can the results be analyzed? What aspects of the regression estimates are of interest? First, the regulator might check to see whether the algebraic signs of b_1, b_2, and b_3 are in fact as indicated above. Second, the t-statistics are examined to evaluate the strength of the statistical evidence. If, for example, b_3 has a very low t-statistic, it indicates that L really has no effect on RT when S and P are held constant. Third, the R^2 value is analyzed to see the extent to which the three independent variables together explain the variation in RT.

Finally, the regulator might look at the residual for Shackleton using the multiple regression rather than the original simple regression—that is, by plugging in the actual values for Shackleton's size, pulmonary admissions, and length of stay and computing the predicted value for RT from the regression equation. The difference between the actually observed value of $200,000 and this computed value is the residual. If it is small (or negative) it could be concluded that the administrator has correctly identified the reasons for the discrepancy between Shackleton's respiratory therapy expenditure and that of other hospitals its size. If the residual still is a large positive number, the administrator's explanation will be less convincing.

One point that should be emphasized is that statistical association does not imply the direction or even the existence of a causal relationship. It is easy in using regression analysis to think that changes in independent variables in some sense cause changes in the dependent variable. This is not necessarily correct. In the example above, the administrator's argument is that increased RT causes decreased length of stay, not vice versa. There might be two-way causation between RT and P: more RT is needed because there are more pulmonary patients, but it also is possible that pulmonary patients are attracted to hospitals that have large RT services. Advanced statistical techniques can take care of such problems to some extent, but the question of causation and statistical association remains an important philosophical and research issue. This is one reason why this example is oversimplified and should be considered only suggestive of the way statistical analysis actually is applied to such a problem.

REGRESSION AND FORECASTING

Another useful application of regression is for forecasting. This section presents a regression model used by Paul Feldstein for forecasting hospital costs. Before turning to that model, several additional regression concepts are introduced briefly. In the previous section the data on hospital personnel, beds, and payroll were drawn from several hospitals for the same year. This is called a *cross section* observation of different units at the same time. Another type of sample is a *time series*—observation of the same unit at different times. For example, Feldstein uses annual data on the United States for 16 years as the basis for his regression estimates. Time series regression estimates are useful for forecasting, since the equation relates the values of the independent variables in a given year to that of the dependent variable in that year. Thus, if some assumptions are made about the value of independent variables in a future year, the regression equation lets the value of the dependent variable for that year be predicted. In the Feldstein article, hospital costs are predicted on the basis of an assumption about the general level of inflation likely to be obtained in the economy in the future.

Another technique Feldstein uses is the *dummy variable*. Often an independent variable is not continuously variable but instead is a "yes or no" kind of phenomenon. For example, in some years of Feldstein's sample the Medicare program was in effect, and in other years it was not. In such cases the econometrician defines a variable that takes on the value of "0" or "1". For example, the variable MED below is defined to equal 0 in the years before Medicare and to equal 1 for the years when Medicare was in effect. (Actually, Feldstein goes beyond the usual procedure by assigning it the value .5 for the transitional year of 1966.) Thus the dummy variable is a way to quantify artificially a characteristic of the units observed that is not measurable in the usual way.

A third characteristic of Feldstein's analysis is his use of the natural logarithms of the variables. This is a common procedure where a constant growth rate or certain other nonlinear functions are involved. The effect is to linearize the relationships so the standard regression estimation techniques can be used. It does not change the interpretation of regression results as used in this book. Finally, Feldstein presents the regression coefficients in a slightly different format from that used earlier, but includes the same basic information about the equation.[5]

TRENDS IN AGGREGATE MEASURES OF HOSPITAL COSTS[b]

It is well recognized that measuring hospital output is no easy task. But in order to discuss trends in cost, one must focus on the cost of some unit. The units most commonly chosen for cost comparisons are patient day and admission (case). Neither one is in any sense a homogeneous unit; changes in the nature of the average patient day or the average case may have important effects on costs. Still, they are useful measures for some purposes, and as simple measures of the quantity of output, they are essentially all we have. For other purposes, the size of the population receiving care may be a more useful output measure. Major payors for hospital care are probably more interested ultimately in total costs or costs per capita than costs per patient day or per admission, since their total payouts depend on the total hospital expenses for the covered population.

The principal sources of national data on changes in hospital costs are the U.S. Bureau of Labor Statistics and the American Hospital Association. The BLS compiles an index of hospital room charges, based on movements in the price of the most common type of accommodation, currently a semi-private room, as a component of the Consumer Price Index (CPI). This index (a pure number without units attached) provides one indication of changes in the cost of a day of hospital care. It has been criticized as a highly imperfect measure of changes in hospital costs, however, in part because it is not a comprehensive index of charges, and in part because charges are not perfectly correlated with costs and a large portion of hospital payments are made on a cost basis.

The AHA collects and publishes data annually on utilization, finances and personnel of hospitals, based on a survey to which response rates generally exceed ninety percent. It also conducts a monthly Panel Survey in which it collects similar data from a sample (currently being expanded) of about one-fourth of all community hospitals. The AHA data permits calculations of average expenses per patient day and per admission, and the total expenses data can be divided by population figures to derive average expenses per capita.

Table 3-3 presents annual data on several measures of hospital costs. The first column under each measure gives its average level in each year; the second column gives its percentage increase over the previous year's level. EPPD is expenses per patient day; EPAPD is expenses per adjusted patient day; and EPC is expenses

Table 3-3 Common Measures of Hospital Costs

Year	C.P.I. An Avg.	C.P.I. % ↑	C.P.I. Services An Avg.	C.P.I. Services % ↑	C.P.I. Sp. Room Charge An Avg.	C.P.I. Sp. Room Charge % ↑	E.P.P.D. An Avg.	E.P.P.D. % ↑	E.P.A.P.D. An Avg.	E.P.A.P.D. % ↑	E.P.C. An Avg.	E.P.C. % ↑
1960	88.7	—	83.8	—	57.3	—	32.23	—			31.21	—
1961	89.6	1.0	85.2	1.7	61.1	6.6	34.98	8.5			34.15	9.4
1962	90.6	1.1	86.2	1.2	65.3	5.9	36.83	5.3			36.82	7.8
1963	91.7	1.2	88.5	2.7	68.6	5.1	38.91	5.6	35.11	—	39.96	8.5
1964	92.9	1.3	90.2	1.9	71.9	4.8	41.58	6.9	37.58	7.0	44.15	10.0
1965	94.5	1.7	92.2	2.2	75.9	5.6	44.48	7.0	40.56	7.9	47.26	7.0
1966	97.2	2.9	95.8	3.9	83.5	10.0	48.15	8.3	43.66	7.6	52.54	11.2
1967	100.0	2.9	100.0	4.4	100.0	19.8	54.08	12.3	49.46	13.3	61.18	16.4
1968	104.2	4.2	105.2	5.2	113.6	13.6	61.38	13.5	55.80	12.8	71.02	16.1
1969	109.8	5.4	112.5	6.4	128.8	13.4	70.03	14.1	64.26	15.2	82.49	16.2
1970	116.3	5.9	121.6	7.9	145.4	12.9	81.01	15.7	73.73	14.7	95.97	16.3
1971	121.3	4.3	128.4	5.6	163.1	12.2	92.31	12.9	83.43	12.1	108.63	13.2
1972	125.3	3.3	133.3	3.8	173.9	6.6	105.21	14.0	94.61	13.4	122.70	13.0
1973	133.1	6.2	139.1	4.4	182.1	4.7	114.69	9.0	101.78	7.6	135.80	10.7
1974	147.7	11.0	152.0	9.3	201.5	10.7	128.05	11.6	113.21	11.2	153.66	13.2
1975	161.1	9.1	166.6	9.6	236.1	17.2	151.42	18.3	133.08	17.6	183.50	19.4
1976	170.1	5.9	179.5	8.3	265.1	13.9	167.06	15.4	147.12	14.7	197.57	17.2

EPPD = Expenses per Patient Day
EPAPD = Expenses per Adjusted Patient Day
EPC = Expenses per Capita

per capita. For comparison purposes, data on the CPI and CPI for services are also presented.

Table 3-3 provides some indication of the way in which hospital costs have increased in the last 16 years. It points up, for example, that expenses per patient day have quintupled since 1960 and tripled since 1967, while expenses per capita have increased even faster. Part of this increase can be attributed to the general rise in prices in the economy. The CPI is generally interpreted as an index of the overall cost of living, and it has nearly doubled since 1960. It is sometimes argued that labor productivity increases more slowly in service industries (like hospitals) than other industries, and that, therefore, the costs of services should be expected to increase faster than the general price level. Table 3-3 indicates that the service component of the CPI has risen somewhat faster than the overall CPI, though the difference is relatively minor.

Clearly, hospital costs have—by any measure—increased much faster than the general price level in the last decade-and-a-half. But a closer examination of Table 3-3 reveals that while all the measures of hospital costs have moved very similarly over time, the relationship of the rate of increase of hospital costs to the rate of increase in the CPI has varied. Even during the pre-Medicare 1960s, hospital costs tended to increase annually at rates which were several percentage points faster than the CPI. But with the advent of Medicare in mid-1966, costs began to increase at a considerably faster rate. The CPI increased faster after 1965 than it had previously, but the differences between the rates of increase in the CPI and the measures of hospital costs also increased in the post-Medicare period. A definite narrowing of the gap between the rate of increase of the general price level and that of hospital costs occurs in 1973 and 1974 (also 1972 if you look at room charges). This correlates with the period of the Economic Stabilization Program. ESP placed special controls on hospitals from August, 1971, until April, 1974, somewhat longer than price controls remained on the rest of the economy. Evidence for the post-controls period is quite limited, but what evidence there is suggests a return to rates of hospital cost increase far in excess of increases in the CPI.

Figure 3-4 presents much of the information from Table 3-3 in graphic form. It is intended to depict movements in hospital costs since 1960 relative to the CPI. In order to focus on trends relative to the CPI, we have deflated (divided) EPPD, EPAPD and the

Figure 3-4 Trends in Hospital Costs

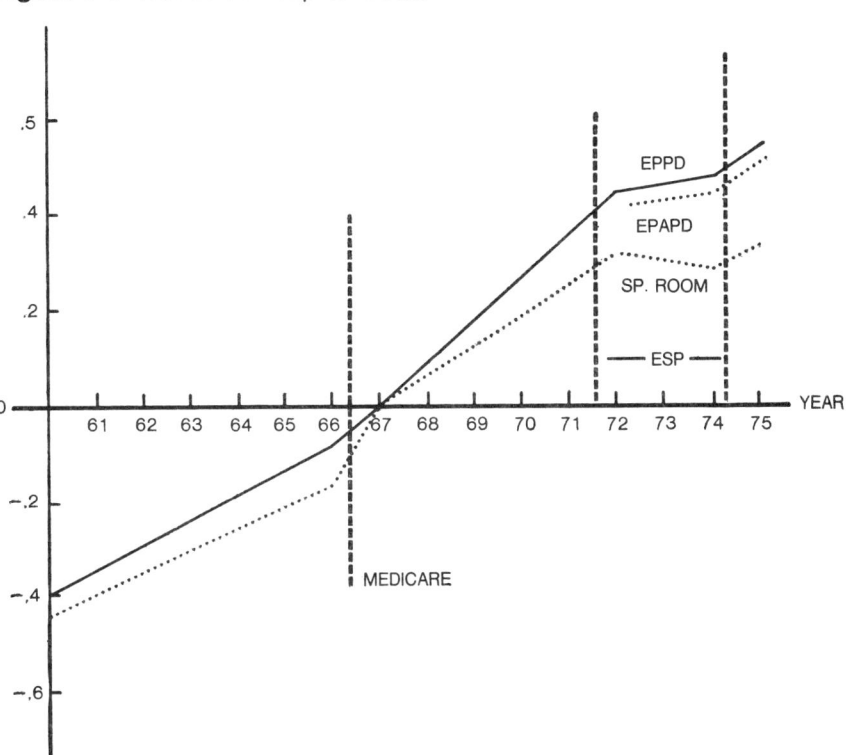

Source: Table 3-3.

room charge index by the CPI in each year, converted the former two to index numbers with 1967 = 100 (the room charge index was already in this form), and plotted the natural logarithms of these indices against time. The conversion to logs is carried out because it allows a constant growth rate to show up as a linear trend. The points are connected by line segments to indicate periods over which rates of increase relative to the CPI are roughly constant.

Two points already made in relation to Table 3-3 stand out clearly in Figure 3-4. One is that these three measures of hospital costs have moved very similarly over time. The trends in EPPD and EPAPD are virtually indistinguishable prior to 1972. The second point is that the post-1960 period can apparently be divided into several subperiods with regard to hospital costs. Furthermore, the divisions between the segments appear to coincide closely with the introduction of Medicare and the beginning and end of ESP.

We can carry this analysis of the trend in hospital costs a bit further by calculating some relatively simple multiple linear regressions. In Table 3-4 we present results of several ordinary least squares regressions. The dependent variable for regressions (1) and (3) is the percentage increase in EPPD; for regressions (2) and (4), the percentage increase in EPC; for regression (5), the percentage increase in EPPD minus the percentage increase in the CPI; and, in regression (6), the percentage increase in EPC minus the percentage increase in the CPI. In addition to a constant term, the independent variables include the percentage increase in the CPI, a dummy variable for the effects of Medicare (taking the value "0" for 1961–65, ".5" for 1966, and "1" thereafter), and a dummy variable for the effects of ESP (taking the value "1" in 1973–74, "0" otherwise). Data is taken directly from Table 3-3. Regressions (1) and (2) use data from 1961 through 1975, and all four independent variables. Regressions (3) and (4) use only the years 1967 through 1975. Since Medicare was in effect in all these later years, the constant picks up its effect also. Regressions (5) and (6) use data from 1961 through 1975, and are, in effect, regressions (1) and (2) with the coefficient on CPI constrained to equal one. All R^2's are quite high, and all calculated t-statistics are very large.

One interpretation of the results of regression (1) is the following: there is an unexplained rate of increase in EPPD, which would have occurred even if the CPI had remained constant and the Medicare program and ESP had never existed, equal to about

Table 3-4 Regression Results

	CONSTANT	CPI	MED	ESP	
(1) EPPD	5.4760	.78509	4.9911	6.9188	$R^2 = .94$ d.f. = 11
	(10.171)	(4.3249)	(5.2750)	(6.2435)	S.E.E. = 1.1
(2) EPC	7.7015	.68214	4.6216	6.2395	$R^2 = .88$ d.f. = 11
	(11.268)	(2.9602)	(3.8479)	(4.4354)	S.E.E. = 1.4
(3) EPPD	10.632	.77993		−7.0395	$R^2 = .95$ d.f. = 6
	(16.979)	(6.8824)		(10.197)	S.E.E. = .70
(4) EPC	12.285	.70106		−6.3638	$R^2 = .76$ d.f. = 6
	(8.2766)	(2.9252)		(4.3588)	S.E.E. = 1.5
(5) REPPD	5.2099		4.1829	−7.6928	$R^2 = .88$ d.f. = 12
	(10.475)		(6.2805)	(8.4570)	S.E.E. = 1.1
(6) REPC	7.3079		3.4263	7.3842	$R^2 = .79$ d.f. = 12
	(11.348)		(3.9731)	(6.2694)	S.E.E. = 1.5

The entries in the table are regression coefficients; beneath each coefficient is its calculated t-statistic.

EPPD = Expenses per Patient Day
EPC = Expenses per Capita
REPPD = Real Expenses per Patient Day
REPC = Real Expenses per Capita

1977 FORECASTS BASED ON THESE RESULTS, ASSUMING FIVE TO SIX PERCENT INCREASE IN CPI:

(1) %↑ EPPD = 10.5 + .8 (%↑ CPI) = 14.5 − 15.3
(5) %↑ EPPD = 9.4 + + % CPI = 14.4 − 15.4
(2) %↑ EPC = 12.3 + .7 (%↑ CPI) = 14.8 − 16.5
(6) %↑ EPC = 10.7 + %↑ CPI = 15.7 − 16.7

(*Editor's Note:* There is an apparent typographical error in the table above: In Equations 1, 2, and 6 there should be minus signs before the coefficients of ESP.)

5.5 percent per year. In addition, EPPD increased by 80 percent of all increases in the CPI. Medicare added about 5 percent to the annual increases in EPPD, and ESP subtracted about 6.9 percent from them. This explanation yields the prediction that future annual percentage increases in EPPD (assuming no major changes in government policy) will equal about 10.5 + .8 times the percent increase in the CPI. A similar explanation of the results of regression (2) can be made, leading to the prediction that future increases in EPC will equal 12.3 + .7 times the percent increase in the CPI. It is interesting that the use of only post-Medicare data to estimate these relationships in regressions (3) and (4) leads to almost identical predictions. Even when the assumption is made in regressions coefficients on the other independent variables change very little. If this assumption—that an increase in the CPI leads to a matching percentage increase in EPPD and in EPC—is made, the predictions become: percent increase in EPPD = 9.4 + percent increase in CPI, and percent increase in EPC = 10.7 + percent increase in CPI.

We then have our first and simplest method for forecasting hospital costs. Testing it out on our preliminary 1976 data in Table 3-3, we get predictions of 15.2 and 15.3 for the percent increase in EPPD, and 16.4 and 16.6 for the percent increase in EPC. These predictions compare rather favorably with our actual estimated values of 15.4 and 17.2. For 1977, since most forecasters are predicting five to six percent increases in the general price level (see *Business Week,* December 27, 1976, p. 52), this method leads to predictions of about 14.4 to 15.4 percent increases in EPPD, and 15.7 to 16.7 percent increases in EPC.

MEASUREMENT AND INDEX NUMBERS

The data in the above selection, and those used most frequently by policy makers, are not simply monetary measures of cost but rather are indexes. Theoretical models of price determination usually are constructed as if they were dealing with the price of a single economic good. But administrative or policy issues seldom involve only one good. A hospital administrator may be concerned with the cost of purchasing laboratory supplies, which can include several hundred different items whose prices are influenced by the same factors. A policy analyst might be concerned with the effect on the wages of nurses of a proposed regulation that will affect not one specific pay rate but many, since different scales apply to different types of nursing service, levels of nurses' education, type of institution, shift, and the like. A federal bureaucrat may be interested in the cost of physician services in relation to the expense of other consumer purchases, but there are many different kinds of physicians' services, all with their own prices. In each of these cases a critical issue is the measurement of change in a group of related variables over time. This may appear to be a rather simple problem at first blush, given the economist's propensity to measure performance in monetary terms (prices, costs, value of output, and so forth). However, it can become complicated quickly as demonstrated in the following example.

Consider a 100-bed hospital that fills 80 percent of its beds in one year and 82 percent in the following year. In this case output has risen from 29,200 days (.80 × 365 × 100 beds) to 29,930 days (.82 × 365 × 100) for an increase of 2.5 percent. Is the 2.5 percent figure correct? To be sure, it would be necessary to consider the possibility that changes have occurred in hours of nursing service, numbers of diagnostic tests, surgeries, drugs, and all the other services the hospital produces in the process of filling beds. The aggregate output may have risen by 2.5 percent or it actually may have fallen if fewer services are provided per patient day. To make matters more difficult, the services are not commensurable in quantitative terms. Adding together Darvon tablets, nursing hours, and phenylketonuria (PKU) tests obviously makes no sense. Only if all the services are measured by a common denominator can total output be analyzed. But which denominator? Even if a monetary unit is chosen, it can make a considerable difference whether the measure is actual cost or patient charges and whether the price (or cost) is for the beginning or the end of the period.

Similar problems in aggregation (or disaggregation, as the case may be) arise in attempting to measure economic performance in terms of changes in price, productivity, cost, income, and quality of care. The fact is that economic trends usually involve the interaction of many variables, and isolating the effect of one from the rest can be difficult. Multiple regression analysis and other multivariate techniques are useful tools, but frequently the administrator or planner will need quick and more readily obtainable indicators of change. Economic indexes are designed to fill this need. The remainder of this chapter explains what indexes are and how they are computed, using the Consumer Price Index (CPI) as an example. This is followed by examples of how index numbers can be used to study the trend in prices of physician services and to forecast hospital costs.

An *index number* is simply an expression of the percentage change in a particular numerical value (price, output, or such) over what it was in a base period, holding other variables constant. Say it is desired to measure the change in price of a collection of health services over time. Each transaction or expenditure during the period involves a price (p) times a quantity purchased (q). If the pq's are summed (Σ) for the base period and then for the current period, an expression of the percentage change in expenditures over time can be developed. But how is the effect of price changes segregated from quantity changes? There are two common approaches, one using the *Laspeyres* index and the other a *Paasche* index.

According to the Laspeyres index,

$$I = \frac{\Sigma(p_1 \, q_o)}{\Sigma(p_o \, q_o)} \cdot 100,$$

the aggregate price change from period 0 to period 1 for a collection of commodities (the q's) is determined by *weighting* each individual price change by the amount consumed during the base year (q_o). Another way to look at this is the following: The denominator is what a particular collection of goods actually costs in period 0. The numerator is what the same collection of goods will cost in period 1. Thus the procedure holds quantity constant by looking at the ratio of the values of the same market basket at two different price sets. Suppose a simple price index is needed for hospital care that measures the aggregate change in the private room rate, laboratory fees, and prescription drug charges from 1975 to 1981. The appropriate procedure using the Laspeyres index is to determine how much of each service was consumed during 1975 (the q_o's) and to use these quantities to weight the service prices in the numerator (1981 prices) and denominator (1975 prices) of the index.

A Paasche index is constructed similarly except that the quantities are derived from 1981 consumption patterns (q_1 instead of q_o)

$$I = \frac{\Sigma(p_1 \, q_1)}{\Sigma(p_o \, q_1)} \cdot 100$$

There is some controversy over which index formulation is superior. From a practical standpoint, the Laspeyres index is far easier to calculate on a periodic basis. The reason is that once the base quantities (weights) are determined, it is only necessary to collect price information thereafter. Where Paasche indexes are used, it is necessary to collect information on both current quantities and current prices. However, there is a drawback to the Laspeyres approach. Because the index uses historical patterns of consumption, it does not reflect shifts in consumption that themselves are related to price changes. For this reason it tends to overstate the true impact of price increases where substitute goods are available to the consumer. If the aggregate price of hospital care has doubled from 1975 to 1981 according to the Laspeyres index, does this mean that individuals (or insurance companies) have suffered the entire increase? Not if some individuals shifted to lower cost alternatives such as outpatient diagnostic tests or nursing home care. By the same token, a Paasche approach to measure the change in hospital prices will tend to understate the true impact of the increase because of the implicit assumption that individuals always have been using the (now) lower priced substitutes.

Despite these drawbacks, indexes based on the Laspeyres and Paasche approaches are widely used in government and industry. The familiar CPI and its components are but one example. Other broad-based price indexes include the Producers Price Index and the GNP *Deflator*.[6] The Federal Reserve Board routinely calculates an Index of Industrial Production. There are indexes for wage rates, productivity, and many other indicators of economic performance. In the health sector, specialized indexes measure changes in health status, quality of patient care, and costs per patient day in hospitals. The applications vary, but the basic mechanics of index number construction are quite similar. The next selection prepared by the U.S. Department of Labor in 1974 shows how the CPI is constructed. It should be noted that the CPI went through a major revision in 1978. The character of this latest revision is examined in another extract later in this chapter.

WHAT THE INDEX IS[c]

The Consumer Price Index (CPI) is a statistical measure of changes in prices of goods and services bought by urban wage earners and clerical workers,[1] including families and single persons. The index is often called the "cost-of-living index," but its official name is *Consumer Price Index for Urban Wage Earners and Clerical Workers*. It measures changes in prices, which are the most important cause of changes in the cost of living, but it does not indicate how much families actually spend to defray their living expenses. Prior to January 1964, the complete name for the index was: Index of Change in Prices of Goods and Services Purchased by City Wage-Earner and Clerical-Worker Families to Maintain Their Level of Living.

The index covers prices of everything people buy for living—food, clothing, automobiles, homes, housefurnishings, household supplies, fuel, drugs, and recreational goods; fees to doctors, lawyers, beauty shops; rent, repair costs, transportation fares, public utility rates, etc. It deals with prices actually charged to consumers, including sales and excise taxes. It also includes real estate taxes on owned homes, but it does not include income or personal property taxes.

Since January 1964, the index has applied to single workers living alone, as well as to families of two persons or more. The average size of families represented in the index is about 3.7 persons, and the average family income in 1960–61 was about $6,250 after taxes. The average income after taxes of single persons represented in the index was about $3,560.

The Meaning of the Index Measurement

The index measures price changes from a designated reference period. Beginning January 1971, the base reference period for the CPI is the annual average for 1967—as 100.0. (Index numbers are also available regularly on $1939 = 100$, $1947–49 = 100$, and $1957–59 = 100$ bases, and they can be converted to any desired base period.) An index of 110 means there was a 10-percent increase in prices since the base period; similarly, an index of 90 means a 10-percent decrease.

Movements of the index from one date to another are usually expressed as percent changes rather than changes in index points because index points are affected by the base period, while percent changes are not. Table 3-5 illustrates the difference between percent change and index points change.

The Bureau calculates a monthly index representing all urban places in the United States—The U.S. City Average Index—and a separate index for each of 23 Standard Metropolitan Statistical Areas.[2] The individual city indexes measure how much prices have changed in a particular city, from time to time; but they do not show whether prices or living costs are higher or lower in one city than in another. For example, consider the prices of a single item in two cities in 2 years:

	Price		Index, Year II
	Year I	Year II	(Year I = 100)
City A	$0.30	$0.60	200
City B	.40	.70	175

The price is higher in City B in each of the 2 years, but the relative increase in price in City B is less and therefore the index is lower.

Table 3-5 Percent and Index Point Changes

Period	Index		
	Base A	Base B	Base C
I	112.5	168.8	225.0
II	121.5	182.3	243.0
Index points change	9.0	13.5	18.0
Percent change	$\frac{9.0}{112.5} \times 100 = 8.0$	$\frac{13.5}{168.8} \times 100 = 8.0$	$\frac{18.0}{225.0} \times 100 = 8.0$

Uses of the Index

The Consumer Price Index is used widely by the general public to guide family budgeting and to understand what is happening to family finances. It is used extensively in labor-management contracts to adjust wages. Automatic adjustments based on changes in the index are incorporated in some wage contracts and in a variety of other types of contracts, such as long-term leases. In addition, the CPI is used as a measure of changes in the purchasing power of the dollar for such diverse purposes as adjusting royalties, pensions, welfare payments, and occasionally alimony payments. It also is used widely as a reflection of inflationary or deflationary trends in the economy.

Brief History of the Index

The Bureau of Labor Statistics has been calculating the Consumer Price Index for nearly five decades. The weighting factors, the list of items included in the market basket, and the cities in which price data were collected for calculating the index have been updated several times during that period. Initially, they were based on a survey of expenditures by wage earners and clerical workers in 1917–19. Because people's buying habits changed substantially by the mid-1930's, a new study was made covering expenditures in the years 1934–36 which provided the basis for a comprehensively revised index introduced in 1940 with retroactive calculations back to 1935.

During World War II, when many commodities were scarce and goods were rationed, the index weights were adjusted to reflect these shortages. Again in 1950, the Bureau made interim adjustments, based on surveys of consumer expenditures in seven cities between 1947 and 1949, to reflect the most important effects of immediate postwar changes in buying patterns. This adjustment was followed by the first comprehensive postwar revision of the index, which was completed in January 1953. At that time, not only were the weighting factors, list of items, and sources of price data updated, but many improvements in pricing and calculation methods also were introduced.

The most recent comprehensive revision of the index was completed in January 1964. To determine the current pattern of expenditures for goods and services by wage earners and clerical workers, the Bureau made a Consumer Expenditure Survey (CES) covering the period 1960–61.[3] The sample of cities in the survey included 72 urban areas which were chosen to represent all urban places in the United States, including Alaska and Hawaii.[4] Only 56 of the 72 areas comprise the list of cities in which price quotations are obtained for the index. In this most recent survey, as in those conducted earlier, the BLS obtained a detailed record of the kind, qualities, and amounts of all goods and services bought by each consumer unit (family or single person living alone) and of the annual amount spent for each item. A total of 4,912 urban wage-earner and clerical-worker families and 585 single workers provided such records.

The Market Basket

It is not feasible or necessary to obtain current price quotations on everything that consumers buy in order to calculate a valid index of changes in consumer prices. About 400 items have been selected objectively to compose the "market basket" for current pricing, beginning with the January 1964 indexes. Not all items are priced in every city. In order to make possible estimates of sampling error, two subsamples of items have been set up. These are priced in different cities and in different outlet samples. The list includes the most important goods and services and a sample of the less important ones.[5] In combination, these represent all items purchased. The content of this market basket in terms of items, quantities, and qualities is kept essentially unchanged in the index calculation between major revisions so that any movement of the index from one month to the next is due solely to changes in prices. A comparison of the total cost of the market basket from period to period yields the measure of average price change.

Price Data Collection

Prices are obtained by personal visit to a representative sample of about 18,000 retail stores and service establishments where wage and clerical workers buy goods and services, including among the establishments chain stores, independent grocery stores, department and specialty stores, restaurants, professional people, and repair and service shops. Rental rates are obtained from about 40,000 tenants. Reporters are located both in the city proper and in suburbs of each urban area. Cooperation of reporters is completely voluntary and generally excellent.

To insure that the index reflects only changes in prices and not changes due to quantity or quality differences, the Bureau has prepared detailed specifications to describe the items of the market basket. Specially trained Bureau representatives examine merchandise in the stores to determine whether the goods and services for which they record prices conform to the specifications. Where the precisely specified item is not sold at a particular retail establishment, the Bureau's representative obtains a detailed technical description of the item on which prices are quoted, in order to insure that prices will be quoted on the same quality and quantity from time to time.

Prices are collected in each urban location at intervals ranging from once every month to once every 3 months, with a few items surveyed semiannually or annually. Because food prices change frequently, and because foods are a significant part of total spending, food pricing is conducted every month in each urban location. Prices of most other goods and services are collected every month in the five largest urban areas and every 3 months in all other places. Pricing of foods is done on 3 consecutive days each month; rents and items for which prices are obtained by mail are reported as of the 15th of the month; pricing of other items extends over the entire calendar month. The Bureau uses many questionnaires to obtain data on streetcar and bus fares, public utility rates, newspaper prices, and prices of certain other items which do not require personal visit by Bureau agents. For a number of items, e.g., home purchase, college tuition, used cars, magazines, etc., data collected by other Government agencies or private organizations are used.

Index Calculation

A standard statistical formula[6] is used to calculate the Consumer Price Index from prices for the market basket items. Average price changes from the previous pricing period to the current month are expressed in percentage terms for each item, and the percent changes for the various goods and services are combined, using weighting factors based on the item's importance in family spending and that of other items which it represents. This composite importance is called the cost weight of the market basket item. There is a set of separate cost weights for each of the 56 urban locations included in the index. The following hypothetical example for pork illustrates the index procedure (see Table 3-6). Identical results could be obtained for pork by multiplying prices each period by the implied physical quantities included in the market basket, as illustrated in Table 3-7. The average change in pork prices is computed by comparing the sum of the cost weights in October with the comparable sum for September, as follows:

$$\frac{\text{October cost weight } \$33.85}{\text{September cost weight } \$33.00} \times 100 = 102.6$$

This means that pork prices in October were 102.6 percent of (or 2.6 percent higher than) pork prices in September.

Although the second method may appear simpler, in reality it is not. Deriving the implied quantity weights is an extra operation. Furthermore, the second formulation greatly complicates the handling of the numerous substitutions of reporters and items which occur constantly in repetitive index work. Consequently, the first method is the one actually used for the CPI. The second illustra-

Table 3-6 The Index Procedure

Sample item	September price	October price	Price relative Sept. = 100	September cost weight	October cost weight
Pork chops	$0.75	$0.77 1/4	103.00	$15.00	$15.45
Ham	.80	.82	102.50	8.00	8.20
Bacon	1.00	1.02	102.00	10.00	10.20
				$33.00	$33.85

tion, however, may assist the user to understand the meaning of the index mechanism.

After the cost weights for each of the items has been calculated, they are added to area totals for commodity groups and all items. The U.S. totals are obtained by combining area totals, with each area total weighted according to the proportion of the total wage-earner and clerical-worker population which it represents in the index based on 1960 Census figures. In this process, it is necessary to make estimates for cities in which price data are not collected in a given month. Finally, the U.S. totals for the current and previous months are compared to compute the average price change.

Seasonally Adjusted Indexes

In January 1966, the Bureau initiated publication of seasonally adjusted national indexes for selected groups and subgroups of the CPI for which there is a significant seasonal pattern of price change. Previously, the Bureau had made available seasonal factors, permitting users who wished to do so to calculate seasonally adjusted indexes.[7] Percent changes in the seasonally adjusted CPI have been published since February 1970. Seasonal factors and seasonally adjusted indexes used in these computations only are carried to two decimals. The factors used initially in computing the seasonally adjusted indexes were derived by the BLS Seasonal Factor Method using data for 1956–65.[8] These factors are updated at the end of each calendar year.

The seasonal adjustment does not affect the procedure for computing the original indexes. The unadjusted all items and group indexes are derived as described above. The seasonal calculations are a separate operation designed to make available data from

Table 3-7 The Market Basket

Sample Item	Implied quantity (pounds)	September price	September cost weight	October price	October cost weight
Pork chops	20	$0.75	$15.00	$0.77 1/4	$15.45
Ham	10	.80	8.00	.82	8.20
Bacon	10	1.00	10.00	1.02	10.20
			$33.00		$33.85

which normal seasonal fluctuations have been removed to facilitate analysis.

Limitations of the Index

The Consumer Price Index is not an exact measurement of price changes. It is subject to sampling errors which cause it to deviate somewhat from the results which would be obtained if actual records of all retail purchases by wage earners and clerical workers could be used to compile the index. These estimating or sampling errors are not mistakes in the index calculation. They are unavoidable. They could be reduced by using much larger samples, but the cost is prohibitive. Furthermore, the index is believed to be sufficiently accurate for most of the practical uses made of it.

Another kind of error occurs because people who give information do not always report accurately. The Bureau makes every effort to keep these errors to a minimum, and corrects them whenever they are discovered subsequently. Precautions are taken to guard against errors in pricing, which would affect the index most seriously. The field representatives who collect the price data and the commodity specialists and clerks who process them are well trained to watch for unusual deviations in prices which might be due to errors in reporting.

The Consumer Price Index represents the average movement of prices for wage earners and clerical workers as a broad group, but not necessarily the change in prices paid by any one family or small group of families. The index is not directly applicable to any other occupational group. Some families may find their outlays changing because of changes in factors other than prices, such as family composition. The index measures only the change in prices and none of the other factors which affect family living expenses.

In many instances, changes in quoted prices are accompanied by changes in the quality of consumer goods and services. Also, new products are introduced frequently which bear little resemblance to products previously on the market; hence, direct price comparisons cannot be made. The Bureau of Labor Statistics makes every effort to adjust quoted prices for changes in quality, and has developed special procedures for this purpose, including the use of technical specifications and highly trained personnel referred to previously. Nevertheless, some residual effects of quality changes on quoted prices undoubtedly do affect the movement

Explanation of the Index Formula

In the absence of major weight revisions or sample changes, the index formula is most simply expressed as:

$$I_{io} = \frac{\sum(q_o p_i)}{\sum(q_o p_o)} \times 100 = \frac{\sum(q_o p_o)\left(\frac{p_i}{p_o}\right)}{\sum(q_o p_o)} \times 100 \quad (1)$$

This is the customary, oversimplified way of writing a price index formula to show what the q's are held constant between major revisions. In actual practice, the basic data for weights are values, and the quantity and price elements of the "pq" values (p's and q's) are not separated.

With a weight revision, the formula becomes:

$$I_{i:o} = \frac{\sum(q_o p_{i\text{-}s})}{\sum(q_o p_o)} \times \frac{\sum(q_a p'_i)}{\sum(q_a p'_{i\text{-}s})} \times 100 \quad (2)$$

where

q is a derived composite of the annual quantities purchased in a weight base period for a bundle of goods and services to be represented by the specific item priced

p and p' are the average prices of the specific commodities or services selected for pricing (the superscript indicates that the average prices are not necessarily derived from identical samples of outlets and specifications over long periods)

$i\text{-}s$ is the month preceding a weight revision (most recently, December 1963)

i is the current month

a is the period of the most recent consumer expenditure survey (1960–61) from which the revised weights were derived

o is the reference base period of the index (1967).

The $(q_o p_o)$ or $(q_a p'_{i\text{-}s})$ base "weights" for a given priced item are the average expenditures in a weight base period represented by that item (including expenditures for the item itself and for other similar non-priced items).

In actual practice, this expenditure is projected forward for each pricing period by the price relative for the priced item:

$$(q_a p_i) = (q_a p_{i-1}) \left(\frac{p_i}{p_{i-1}}\right)$$

In practice, then, the index formula is as follows:

$$I_{i:o} = \frac{\Sigma(q_o p_{i-s})}{\Sigma(q_o p_o)} \times \frac{\Sigma(q_a p'_{i-1})}{\Sigma(q_a p'_{i-s})} \times \frac{\Sigma(q_a p'_{i-1})\left(\frac{p'_i}{p'_{i-1}}\right)}{\Sigma(q_a p'_{i-1})} \times 100 \quad (3)$$

Thus, although the cost weight changes with every change in price, the implicit quantity (q_o) or (q_a) remains fixed between major weight revisions.

The long-term price relative for each priced item $\left(\frac{p_i}{p_o}\right)$ in reality is:

$$R_{i:o} = \left(\frac{p_1}{p_o}\right) \cdot \left(\frac{p_2}{p'_1}\right) \cdot \left(\frac{p''_3}{p''_2}\right) \cdot \ldots \cdot \left(\frac{p''''_i \ldots}{p''''_{i-1} \ldots}\right)$$

That is, $R_{i:o}$ is the product of a number of short-term relatives. The susperscripts on the p's indicate that these average prices are not necessarily derived from identical samples of outlets and specifications over long periods. This chaining of monthly, or quarterly, price relatives based on comparable specifications in successive periods allows the requisite flexibility to make substitutions of items, specifications, and outlets.

THE 1978 REVISION[d]

[The 1978] revision, begun in 1970, constituted a large-scale effort to (1) update the weights assigned to the various spending categories, such as food, clothing, shelter, and medical care; (2) update the sample of items priced each month in the ongoing CPI; (3) update the sample of retail stores; and (4) modernize the conceptual basis and statistical methods employed in the CPI.

Many improvements and innovations have been introduced as a result of the revision, but only a few are visible in the final, published indexes. Index users can see that (1) a new index representing all urban consumers—80 percent of the population—has been issued in addition to the improved index for wage earners and clerical workers which represents roughly half of the urban population; (2) monthly or bimonthly indexes are published for 28 cities compared with 24 monthly or quarterly indexes formerly published; (3) regional indexes are available for urban areas of different population sizes; and (4) some more general index components cover a type of good or service instead of a very specific item.

In addition to visible changes resulting from innovations in the 1978 revision, less obvious improvements include these: (1) The updated fixed market basket reflects new patterns of consumption; (2) outlets surveyed are more representative of those which consumers actually frequent; (3) prices are collected in larger number of areas; (4) food price collections are spread throughout the month; and (5) monthly pricing has increased and bimonthly pricing has largely replaced quarterly pricing.

CPI for All Urban Consumers

An important addition to the 1978 revision is the new Consumer Price Index for all urban consumers. One major problem in any index revision is to determine just who should make up the index population. The previous index represented only wage earners and clerical workers and therefore was, strictly speaking, appropriate for only that group. A more comprehensive consumer price index was needed to reflect expenditures for the many population groups other than wage earners and clerical workers whose income payments are now being escalated and to measure inflation and guide monetary and fiscal policy for the Nation as a whole. Therefore, on May 24, 1974, the Commissioner of the Bureau of Labor Statistics, Julius Shiskin, announced the decision to develop two indexes—the traditional index for wage earners and clerical workers and a new index that would cover all urban consumers.

The comprehensive index covers all consumer households in a representative number of Standard Metropolitan Statistical Areas (SMSA's) and of small urban areas outside SMSA's. Some of these include rural areas, but other rural families, the military, and those in institutions are excluded from the index population. The result has been to increase the population coverage to about 80 percent of the total noninstitutional population compared with less than 45 percent in the past. Of the total, other rural families make up about 18 percent, and military personnel make up about 2 percent.

Expanded City Coverage

Monthly or bimonthly indexes are published for 28 cities compared with the previous 24. The previous sample of 56 Standard Metropolitan Statistical Areas was selected on the basis of the 1960 Census of Population using probability methods and was designed to represent wage earners and clerical workers from the entire urban portion of the country.

Improved Item Selection

The components of the CPI look different as a result of a new method of selecting the particular, detailed items to be priced each month. Under the previous system, a fixed basket of about 400 specific items was priced each month. Although most outlets in the survey carried the items as described, occasionally an outlet did not stock the item, and a replacement that fit the detailed description had to be chosen. This approach restricted the range that existed for each CPI component.

Under the 1978 revision, an improved process called "disaggregation" was designed for selecting the detailed items to be priced. In the previous process, BLS pricing agents were given detailed descriptions of items to be priced. Now, agents have more general descriptions to choose from. For example, the market basket item which was previously "Vitamin D, Grade A Homogenized milk in half-gallon containers" is now "Whole fresh milk." Through the disaggregation process, the pricing agent selects the specific kind of fresh whole milk that will be priced continuously in each outlet. By this process, each kind of whole milk is assigned a probability, or weight, based on the quantity of it the store sells. If Vitamin D, Homogenized milk in half-gallon containers makes up 70 percent of the sales of fresh whole milk, and the same milk in quart containers accounts for 10 percent of all whole milk sales, then the half-gallon container will have a 7 times greater chance of being chosen than the quart container. After probabilities are assigned, one kind of milk is chosen by an objective selection process based on the theory of random sampling. The particular kind of milk that is selected by disaggregation will continue to be priced each month in that outlet.

In the total market basket, all high-volume items are represented in proportion to their share of total expenditures. The range of items typically purchased now is more representative than it was under previous selection processes.

FUTURE REVISIONS

Improvements in the CPI will not stop with the most recent revision. Maintaining a tradition of research and analysis, the BLS will continue to update and review the CPI. Between major revisions, the BLS will conduct an ongoing Consumer Expenditure Survey and Point-of-Purchase Survey program. At the same time, analysts will study further such conceptual issues as population coverage, the treatment of housing, and quality change.

The Continuing Consumer Expenditure Survey

In the past, data on consumer income and expenditures have been collected every 10 to 15 years as a major component of large-scale programs to update and revise the CPI. Because detailed surveys of consumer expenditures are extremely complex, such surveys have historically been difficult, time consuming, and expensive. Although more than $20 million was spent on the 1972–73 Consumer Expenditure Survey, the 1978 revised CPI contains base year weights which were 5 years old at its first release. This lag results from the length and cost associated with such a massive survey. A smaller, continuing Consumer Expenditure Survey has therefore been adopted to reduce this lag, to eliminate periodic start-up costs, to increase the overall timeliness and efficiency of future CPI revision programs, and, for broader use, to report current data on consumer buying patterns.

Past expenditure surveys have not responded to the ongoing demand—from the public and private sectors—for current information on consumer spending and income. Current data on consumer expenditure patterns are important to policymakers both within and outside the government. For this reason, both the Administration and the Congress have endorsed the continuing Consumer Expenditure Survey program to collect data on an ongoing basis in 102 primary sampling units (geographic sampling areas). Eighty-five of these areas have been selected for ongoing price data collection. This design enables the BLS to revise the CPI and to establish a regular publication program of reporting on changes in consumer expenditures. As in 1972–73, the project will consist of both quarterly interview and diary survey panels. For each respondent, quarterly interviews will be conducted for 5 calendar quarters, with approximately 6,000 households interviewed each quarter. For the diary survey, two 1-week diaries will be obtained from about 4,800 households each year. After a 12- to 18-month start-up period, expenditure data will be published regularly 6 to 9 months after the reference period.

A Continuing Point-of-Purchase Survey

One of the important achievements of the 1978 CPI revision program has been the implementation of modern scientific sampling procedures to develop survey data for the selection of the CPI outlet sample. To insure that current and future CPI's properly reflect the market place on a continuing basis, a point-of-purchase survey will be conducted in one-fifth of the 85 Primary Sampling Units in the index outlet sample each year. From these surveys, a new outlet sample for each pricing area covered could be selected. Thus, over a 5-year period, the entire CPI outlet sample could be revised completely. The point-of-purchase approach to updating the CPI outlet sample represents a marked advance in CPI design and methodology.

Costs

Costs provided a major reason for changing the previous approach to CPI revision. The 1950–52 revision took 3 years and cost $4 million; the 1960–64 revision took 5 years and cost $6.5 million; the 1978 revision took 8 years and cost about $50 million. Most of these expenditures were made before 1975. The cost in 1975 dollars would be almost $56 million.

Endless delays and ever-rising costs—including those for gearing up for a decennial effort—suggest that a better process must be used to update the CPI. Over the past decade, statistical agencies the world over have shifted to smaller decennial or quinquennial programs supplemented by annual, quarterly, and monthly sample surveys.

As indexes go, the CPI generally is well regarded. However, there are shortcomings of which health administrators and planners should be aware. In the first place, the CPI for medical care charts price movements for a rather small sample of health services. As of the latest revision in 1978, the index prices four categories: professional services (12 items), hospital services (10 items), health insurance (4 items), and drugs and prescriptions (20 items). Thus, the index is of limited use in analyzing specialized service offerings. Because the price surveys are conducted in selected urban areas, the index also cannot be used to draw inferences concerning price differentials between urban and rural areas or among states.

A second drawback is the rather narrow definition of price used by the Bureau of Labor Statistics. The BLS defines institutional and professional prices as the "usual and customary fees" for given procedures or services. This represents but one of at least a dozen possible definitions of the term found in the economics and insurance literature:

1. Customary fee: sometimes referred to as the "usual and customary fee," this is the standard fee for a particular service charged by a given provider to most patients.
2. Average fee: the actual mean charge for a given service to all patients.
3. Sliding fee: a price that depends on the characteristics of the patient, usually rising with the individual's income.
4. Price received: actual revenue from billed charges net of bad debts or discounts.
5. Prevailing fee: the market price of some defined percentile of charges by providers in a given geographic area or specialty.
6. Controlled fee: a price established by government (other similar terms are "fixed fee," "negotiated rate," or "assigned fee").
7. Black market price: prices charged above controlled fees.
8. Shadow price: an accounting assignment of prices in cases where charges are not assessed to patients or insurers.
9. Out-of-pocket price: the patient's own price net of insurance payments.
10. Constant dollar price: current prices deflated to account for the effect of inflation.
11. Cost per service: price received by institutional providers under cost-based insurance contracts.
12. Cost per case: combined price for all services relating to treatment for a given illness.

It should be obvious from this list that the direction and magnitude of price changes can vary significantly over time, depending upon which definition is considered appropriate to the task at hand. In the next selection, Victor Fuchs and Marcia Kramer examine the historical trend in physician service prices between 1948 and 1968 using three alternative definitions. Their results demonstrate in graphic fashion how the familiar CPI may be inappropriate for measuring the change in physician prices over time.

CUSTOMARY PRICE[e]

The Bureau of Labor Statistics collects information every month from physicians concerning their "usual and customary fee," and this information forms the basis for the physicians' fee component that goes into the medical care portion of the Consumer Price Index. The customary fee index is a weighted average of standard fees charged for an office visit by "family physicians" (formerly "general practitioners"), for an appendectomy, and for other specified categories of visits. This index may behave very differently from an index that measures the average price actually received by physicians, or from one that measures the net price paid by patients.

Average Price Received

The average price received may deviate from the customary or nominal price for two principal reasons. First, physicians do not charge all their patients the customary fee [26]; they may charge poor patients significantly lower fees and may treat some without any charge. Secondly, physicians do not collect 100 per cent of the fees they do charge.

One of the uses of the price index is to obtain a series of the real quantity of services by deflating the expenditures series. For such purposes the appropriate price series is one that measures the average price received by physicians, not the customary price. To the extent that physicians charge less than their customary fee and to the extent that they fail to collect all the fees they do charge, deflation of expenditures by the customary fee would result in a biased estimate of quantity.

Our approach to both these problems is based upon the assumption that a physician is more likely to charge his customary fee and more likely to collect his charges when the service is covered by insurance. The extent of insurance coverage has two dimensions: the number of people carrying protection, and the average level of protection per person insured. In both aspects of coverage dramatic increases were recorded during the postwar period. The number of persons with private insurance coverage for physician expenses grew from approximately 34 million in 1948 to 160 million in 1968, and average annual benefits per insured rose from $4.61 to $23.57. The contrast between the initial and terminal years becomes even greater when the Medicare and Medicaid populations are included among the insured and expenditures made under these programs are added to those covered by private insurance. All third-party payments together accounted for 11 per cent of expenditures in 1948 and 57 per cent twenty years later (Figure 3-5).

The ratio of average price to customary price in any year depends upon the proportions of insured and uninsured in the population (I and N), the utilization per insured relative to utilization per uninsured (U), the fraction of customary price paid by insured persons (K), and the fraction of customary price paid by uninsured persons (k). More exactly,

$$\frac{AP}{CP} = \frac{U \cdot I \cdot K + N \cdot k}{U \cdot I + N}.$$

If everyone were fully insured ($N=0, K=1$), average price would equal customary price. Average price approaches customary price with increases in the percentage insured of the population, in the utilization ratio, and in the average payment ratio of insured persons. It is assumed that K varies with the fraction of insured persons' utilization covered by insurance. Starting from a lower limit of k, it reaches an upper limit of 1.0 when all services purchased by insured persons are fully covered. k is assumed to remain constant over time at 0.67. . . .

According to our formula, the ratio of average price to customary price rose from 0.72 in 1948 to 0.89 in 1968. The average annual rate of change of average price from 1948–68 was 4.2 per cent, compared with 3.2 per cent for customary price. The disparity in the growth rates of the two price series was larger before 1956 than after that date. This conforms with the results of Klarman et al., based on estimates of physician collection ratios [28], and of Martin Feldstein [16].

Figure 3-5 Growth of Third-Party Payment for Physicians' Services, 1948–68

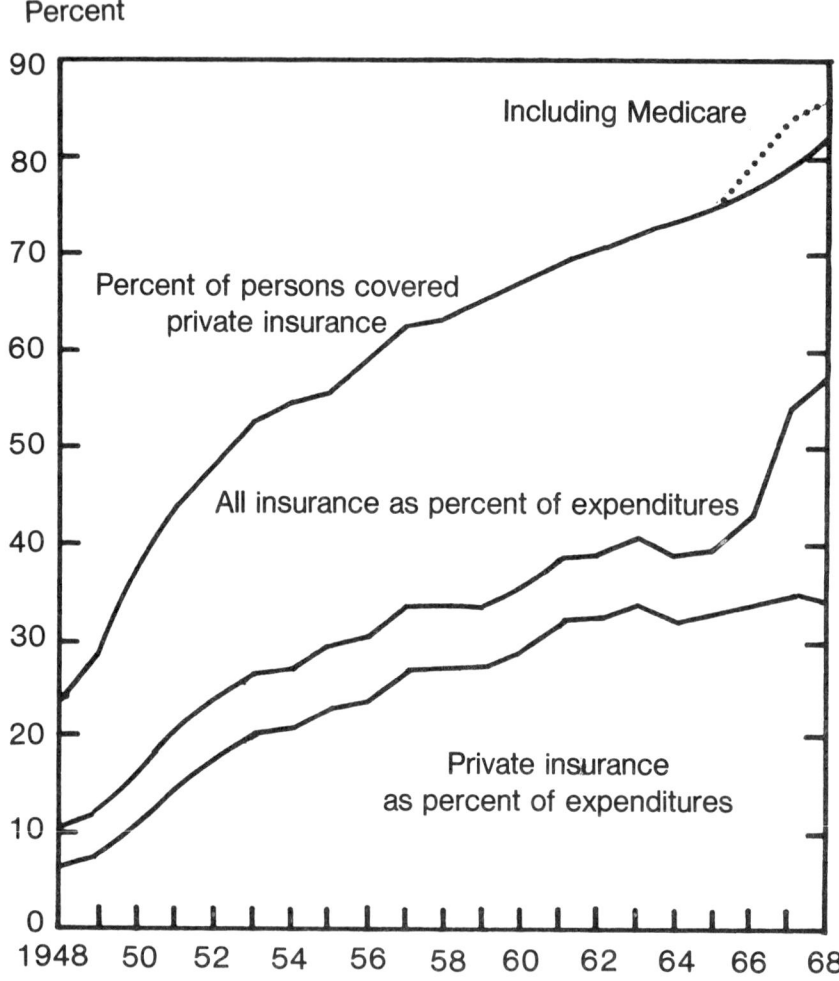

Net Price

While the growth of insurance coverage tends to raise the average price received by physicians relative to the customary price charged, it has the opposite effect on the net price paid by patients. To the patient, an increase in the share of the bill covered by insurance appears as a decrease in the price he pays. Following Martin Feldstein, we calculate net price as equal to average price multiplied by the fraction of expenditures the patient must pay directly:

$$NP = AP \cdot \left(\frac{\text{expenditures} - \text{third-party payments}}{\text{expenditures}}\right).$$

The three price series for physicians' services are presented in Tables 3-8 and 3-9 along with the Consumer Price Index for all goods and services. Table 3-9 shows that net price rose at the rate of 1.3 per cent per annum from 1948 to 1968. Its fastest growth was during 1956–66, and after 1966 it actually declined as a result of the large increase in third-party payments by government.

When net price rises more slowly than the price of other goods and services, physicians' services are relatively cheaper, and we might expect an increase in the quantity demanded. When net price rises faster than the Consumer Price Index, we might expect the reverse. The magnitude of the effect is determined by: (1) the differential change in price and (2) the elasticity of demand for physicians' services with respect to changes in price. Most observers believe this elasticity to be quite small. If so, differential price changes will not have much effect on demand. The main point to be noted, however, is that whatever the size of the effect, Table 3-9 shows that it would be in the direction of *lowering* demand in 1956–66 relative to 1948–56 or 1966–68.

Impact of Insurance on Growth of Expenditures

One of the factors commonly believed to be responsible for the sharp growth of expenditures for physicians' services is insurance (both private and public). According to this view, the growth of insurance coverage should be considered as an exogenous phenomenon rather than as a direct result of an increased demand for medical care. Given the additional coverage, patients found that the net price to them of medical care was lower, and they

Table 3-8 Price Indexes of Physicians' Services and All Goods and Services, 1948–68 (1956 = 100)

	Physicians' Services			All Goods and Services
Year	Customary Price	Average Price Received	Net Price Paid	Consumer Price Index
1948	79.3	71.0	91.1	88.5
1949	80.7	73.1	92.1	87.6
1950	82.5	76.6	92.4	88.5
1951	85.1	80.8	92.6	95.6
1952	88.8	85.6	93.6	97.7
1953	91.2	89.2	94.2	98.4
1954	93.8	92.3	96.5	98.8
1955	97.1	96.1	97.1	98.5
1956	100.0	100.0	100.0	100.0
1957	104.3	105.7	100.4	103.5
1958	107.9	109.4	103.7	106.3
1959	111.5	113.6	108.1	107.2
1960	114.3	117.4	108.9	108.9
1961	117.2	121.6	106.8	110.0
1962	120.7	125.5	109.9	111.3
1963	123.4	129.1	110.2	112.7
1964	126.5	132.2	117.0	114.1
1965	131.1	137.8	120.1	116.0
1966	138.6	147.6	122.2	119.4
1967	148.4	163.0	108.1	122.8
1968	156.7	173.7	106.6	128.0

responded by demanding more care. This increase in demand resulted in higher expenditures.

With respect to the period 1966–68, we find that this hypothesis fits well with the observed data. The rapid growth in expenditures coincided with a major increase in third-party payments, and, indeed, there appears to have been an absolute as well as a relative decrease in direct spending by patients after 1966 (see Tables 3-10 and 3-11).

On the other hand, this hypothesis is of no help in explaining the difference in growth rates before and after 1956. In fact, the relative growth of insurance was far more important in the first than in the second subperiod. We see that the differential between 1956–66 and 1948–56 in growth of direct expenditures by patients

Table 3-9 Rates of Change of Prices of Physicians' Services and All Goods and Services, 1948–68 (per cent per annum continuously compounded)

	1948–56	1956–66	1966–68	1948–68
Customary price	3.0	3.0	6.1	3.2
	(0.1)	(0.1)	(0.4)	(0.1)
Average price received	4.4	3.6	8.1	4.2
	(0.1)	(0.1)	(1.0)	(0.1)
Net price paid	1.1	1.9	−6.8	1.3
	(0.1)	(0.2)	(3.0)	(0.1)
Consumer Price Index	1.8	1.5	3.5	1.7
	(0.3)	(0.1)	(0.4)	(0.1)

Note: Standard errors of rates of change are shown in parentheses.
Source: Table 3-8.

was greater (4.3 per cent per annum) than the differential for all expenditures (2.5 per cent per annum). Thus, this approach yields the same conclusion as the comparison of net price with the Consumer Price Index, namely, that differential changes in insurance cannot explain the upsurge of utilization after 1956.

The Fuchs and Kramer study is significant for reasons that go beyond the issue of historical trends in physician prices. The findings demonstrate how sensitive measurement instruments are to underlying assumptions and definitions. Those who interpret trends should be attuned to the fact that data can be manipulated to support alternative, and sometimes opposing, conclusions. This is not to suggest that manipulation is always purposeful. It can be quite unintentional. For example, when an expenditure series is deflated by a price index, the residual usually is attributed to a pure quantitative or qualitative change in utilization. However, if the analyst begins with a measure of quantity (or quality) and deflates accordingly, the results may be very different because some of the increase may stem from the interaction of changes in quantity (or quality) and price on consumer expenditures.[7]

Perhaps the most serious shortcoming of the CPI relates to the measurement of hospital prices. Prior to 1972, the market basket of hospital services consisted of just three elements—the semiprivate room rate, the operating room rate, and an upper gastrointestinal (GI) x-ray diagnostic series. The BLS recognized that this short list was not reflective of actual utilization patterns, particularly given the dramatic increase in use of ancillary services in recent years. As a consequence, a major revision in 1972

Table 3-10 Relative Importance of Insurance for Physicians' Services, 1948–68

Year	Per Cent of Population with Private Insurance	Per Cent of Expenditures Paid by		
		Private Insurance	Public Programs	Patients Directly
1948	23.6	6.1	4.4	89.5
1949	28.1	7.4	4.8	87.8
1950	36.4	10.7	5.2	84.1
1951	43.3	14.4	5.7	79.9
1952	47.7	17.7	6.0	76.3
1953	52.5	20.0	6.3	73.7
1954	54.6	20.6	6.4	73.0
1955	55.5	22.8	6.7	70.5
1956	59.5	23.5	6.7	69.8
1957	62.7	26.7	7.0	66.3
1958	63.1	26.8	7.1	66.1
1959	65.6	26.9	6.8	66.3
1960	67.1	28.9	6.4	64.7
1961	69.3	31.9	6.9	61.2
1962	70.5	32.1	6.9	61.0
1963	72.2	33.5	6.9	59.6
1964	73.1	32.0	6.3	61.7
1965	74.9	32.9	6.3	60.8
1966	76.5	33.7	8.6	57.7
1967	78.8	34.4	19.3	46.3
1968	80.8	33.6	23.6	42.8

Note: Per cent of population covered by Medicare and/or private insurance in 1966–68: 1966, 79.1; 1967, 84.0; 1968, 85.9.

---

added a group of ancillary services, including physical therapy, oxygen, intravenous solution, electrocardiogram (EKG), antibiotics, tranquilizers, and laboratory tests. Nonetheless, the combined hospital index remains controversial. The reason is that most hospital services are not reimbursed on a usual and customary charge basis.

The Economic Stabilization Program (ESP) of 1971–74 brought the issue to a head. During Phase I of the ESP controls, hospital payments received under cost-based reimbursement contracts were not considered as "prices" and hence were not subject to the nationwide freeze on wages and prices. In regulations issued in December 1971, this loophole was closed but it took the Price Commission another nine months to clarify the units of output for which prices were to be controlled. In the end, control of hospital prices necessitated separate limitations on wage and salary expenses, costs

Table 3-11 Rates of Change of Third-Party and Direct Expenditures for Physicians' Services, 1948–68 (per cent per annum continuously compounded)

Per Capita Expenditures	1948–56	1956–66	1966–68	1948–68
Third parties	17.7 (1.4)	9.4 (0.2)	24.2 (6.0)	12.5 (0.5)
Patients directly	0.7 (0.5)	5.0 (0.5)	−5.9 (3.2)	3.2 (0.3)

Note: Standard errors of rates of change are shown in parentheses.

---

for goods and services purchased, new technology, and volume changes. Even so, the results were mixed. Viewed from the perspective of the average semiprivate room rate, the impact appears to have been marked indeed. In 1971 these prices rose by 12.2 percent; in 1973 the rate of increase was a mere 4.7 percent. But if cost per patient day is the measure of impact, the reduction is far less dramatic. In 1971 and 1973 these expenses increased by 12.9 percent and 9.0 percent, respectively. (See the Paul Feldstein selection earlier in this chapter, as well as the extract that follows.)

The ESP experience generated heated arguments about the long-term effectiveness of price control. The debate continued throughout the late 1970s as more states developed hospital rate-setting commissions and Congress considered a national hospital cost-containment program. Although apparently dead for the time being, the debate is sure to flare up again in the future. Then, as now, the disagreement between the health care industry and the regulatory and planning community will rest on the fundamental question of how best to measure changes in economic performance over time. In the final extract, Paul Feldstein attacks this issue in the context of forecasting future hospital expenditure rates. The selection is a continuation of the article earlier in this chapter, and concentrates on the problems of constructing hospital-specific indexes for labor and nonlabor expenses, an important point on which to conclude this chapter.

FORECASTING HOSPITAL EXPENDITURE RATES[f]

A . . . problem common to all price indices is the difficulty of separating changes in prices from changes in product quality. Quality improvements in inputs (e.g., increases in labor productivity) are akin to increases in the quantity of inputs or "intensity" of care, and if these are not adequately accounted for the price index will tend to overstate true price changes.

The availability of data often plays a role in decisions on index number construction, and makes compromises with theoretical purity necessary. Certainly this has been true in the case of hospital price indices. Data on the importance of various items in hospital budgets is quite limited, and researchers have had to do with what is available.

On the labor side in particular, the conceptual problems are somewhat greater than they are in indexing nonlabor prices. Although some noninputs which hospitals use are peculiar to the hospital industry, for such items as food, energy, and office supplies, hospitals account for only a small segment of the total market. It is probably true that for most nonlabor inputs that hospitals buy, the hospitals simply react to prices set in larger markets. The case of labor inputs is somewhat different. For a large proportion of workers—notably nurses and medical technicians of various kinds—hospitals are the most important employers. Nurses' salaries, in the short run particularly, are probably not very closely tied to the salaries of any other group in the economy. In addition, there is the often voiced hypothesis that hospital employees were traditionally paid less than workers doing equivalent jobs in other industries, and therefore rapid increases in hospital wages (in the 1960s at least) have been the result of a "catching-up" process.

So how are we to index hospital wages? The answer depends on the purpose for which the question is asked. If one's interest is in the *actual* trends in hospital wages and employment, then the simple procedure which is generally used may be as good as any. That procedure is to use the AHA Annual Survey data on number of full-time equivalent employees and payroll expenses to determine the average annual wage of hospital workers in each year. Changes in this average wage are interpreted as changes in the price of labor inputs. Changes in the quantity of labor used per patient day are measured as changes in the number of full-time equilavent employees per one hundred census, also calculated for AHA Annual Survey data.

Table 3-12 presents a breakdown of payroll expenses per patient day [PEPPD] into average wage and personnel per one hundred census [PP100C]. Note that in the 1966–75 period, payroll expenses per patient day increased 11.2 percent per year on the average. Wages increased at a rate of 8.3 percent per year and personnel per one hundred census at 2.9 percent. Some of the

Table 3-12 Payroll Expenses and Labor Inputs

	PEPPD		Wage		PP100C	
	An Avg.	% ↑	An Avg.	% ↑	An Avg.	% ↑
1960	20.08		3240		226	
1961	21.54	7.3	3349	3.4	235	3.8
1962	22.79	5.8	3507	4.7	237	0.9
1963	24.01	5.4	3638	3.7	241	1.7
1964	25.26	5.2	3864	6.2	242	0.4
1965	27.44	8.6	4072	5.3	246	1.7
1966	29.41	7.2	4097	0.6	261	6.1
1967	32.44	10.3	4475	9.2	265	1.5
1968	36.61	12.9	4918	9.9	272	2.6
1969	41.36	13.0	5380	9.4	280	2.9
1970	47.30	14.4	5827	8.3	292	4.3
1971	53.80	13.7	6530	12.1	301	3.1
1972	59.79	11.1	7062	8.1	310	3.0
1973	63.86	6.8	7383	4.5	315	1.6
1974	69.83	9.3	7802	5.7	326	3.5
1975	80.34	15.0	8649	10.9	339	4.0
1976	86.21	12.1	9202	9.0	343	3.0

increase in personnel must be attributed to the expansion of outpatient activity, but personnel per adjusted one hundred census still increased by about 2.5 percent per year during this period. Using this method of separating wage changes from changes in the quantity of labor, it appears first that labor expenses per patient day increased somewhat less rapidly than total expenses per patient day in the 1966–75 period (11.2 as compared to 12.7 percent per year), and second that most of the increase in labor expenses—about three-quarters of it—is accounted for by changes in wages. There are, of course, some problems with this simple method. One is that it takes no account of changes in the skill-mix of labor. If hospitals have over time been hiring more highly skilled (and therefore more expensive) workers on the average, then changes in the average wage will overstate changes in labor prices, while changes in the quantity of labor will be understated. Just the opposite is true if the mix of workers is shifting toward a lower skill level. This may not be a serious problem, since skill-mix appears to have changed very little over time. Martin Feldstein presents some evidence that the average skill level in hospitals was declining slightly during the 1960s. The AHA has recently calculated a skill mix index for the years 1969–74, taking the proportions of services performed by each of four categories of employees, weighting them by the average wage in each category, and summing them. This index increased by slightly more than three percent over the entire five-year period and there is no clear trend.

This method of measuring changes in prices and quantities of labor also ignores changes in labor productivity. If there is an upward trend in productivity among hospital workers (if a given number of workers can accomplish more now than it could in the past), then in a sense we will be overstating increases in labor prices and understating increases in the quantity of labor. Unfortunately, since productivity is normally defined in terms of units of output per unit of input, and since a wholly satisfactory measure of hospital output has not yet been developed, the whole notion of labor productivity in hospitals remains quite fuzzy.

We have been looking at how hospital wages have actually changed over time. If one is interested in determining an *appropriate* rate of wage increase for use in a reimbursement formula, then looking only at actual hospital wage changes is obviously unacceptable. For those classes of employees for whom large markets exist outside of hospitals, changes in the going market wage would seem to be an appropriate standard. Experts agree that by 1969 hospital personnel were being paid at least as well as workers in comparable jobs in other industries—the "catching-up" period is apparently over. The BLS publishes data on wages in a wide variety of jobs at a national level, and state governments often collect similar data at a more localized level. Information such as this may be of use in determining an appropriate rate of wage increase for those hospital employees who have close counterparts in other industries.

For those classes of workers for whom hospitals are the principal employers, the appropriate rate of wage increase is less clear. The minimum increase necessary to elicit the desired supply of personnel is one standard an economist might suggest. But it is not obvious how one might determine what this minimum necessary increase is. Furthermore, a wage increase sufficient to maintain the desired supply of nurses in the short run may not be sufficient to maintain the desired flow of individuals into training for nursing positions.

However, since the purpose of this paper is to forecast what costs will be rather than construct an index of what ought to be, we turn to the nonlabor portion of the increase in expenses per patient day. The nonlabor input side has drawn considerable attention in the past few years. Early attempts to separate changes in nonlabor input prices from changes in the quantity of inputs generally used the Wholesale Price Index (WPI) [now the Producer Price Index] as an index of price changes. The WPI is a comprehensive index of nonlabor input prices in the economy. The bundle of goods which the average hospital buys, however, is quite different from the bundle of goods that the average U.S. firm buys, and it is not obvious that the prices of these bundles should increase at the same rate. Primarily spurred by the growing interest in hospital rate-setting, researchers have begun to approach the problem of developing nonlabor price indices specific to the hospital industry.

One attempt was made by M. Feldstein, in the context of a study of geographic and intertemporal variations in the quality of hospital services. For weights in his index he used data from the 1963 U.S. input-output table, which contains information on the purchases of the hospital industry from other industries. Indices of the prices of the various components were derived from a number of sources. Several of the indices were unpublished deflators calculated by the U.S. Department of Commerce for manufacturing industries; others were components of the CPI or WPI. M. Feldstein notes that his index tracks very closely to the CPI during the period under study (1958–67), but he acknowledges that it would "be necessary to compare substantially longer time series . . . before deciding whether the consumer price could generally be used as a proxy for hospital nonlabor input price." M. Feldstein's procedure illustrates the method generally used in calculating hospital nonlabor price indices. That method is to find a source of data which breaks down hospital expenses by component (for use in determining weights) and to find indices (preferable existing ones) of the prices of the components. The assumption behind this procedure is that changes in the prices hospitals pay for nonlabor inputs are, or at least should be, closely tied to changes in the prices of similar goods in the broader economy. . . .

Rather than detailing the work of (others) . . ., we will present our own index of hospital nonlabor input prices. . . .

Table 3-13 gives our breakdown of nonlabor expenses by component, the weights that we used, and the indices used for each component. The weights are only estimates of the percentages of each component in total nonlabor expenses (we estimate that nonlabor expenses are about forty percent of total expense, so that if the weights in Table 3-13 are divided by 2.5, they give percentages of total expenses), derived mainly from data presented in the above-mentioned studies. We chose 1975 as our base year, because we felt that we could make our best estimates of the weights for that year. Each component price is scaled to equal one hundred in that year, so that in effect we have an index with (estimates of) 1975 quantities as weights. It is interesting to note that if these weights are even approximately correct, they indicate that three frequently cited sources of increased costs—food, fuel, and malpractice insurance—are still rather small portions of total expenses. According to these figures, for example, a full twenty percent rise in food prices would, in itself, increase total costs per day by only about eight-tenths of one percent. A twenty percent rise in fuel prices (disregarding feedback effects on other prices) would have only half that effect on total costs per day.

Most of the component indices used are components of the CPI or WPI. Probably the most troublesome categories to provide

Table 3-13 Estimated Weights and Indices Used

	Weights	Indices
Dietary	10.00	.5 (CPI Food at home) + .5 (WPI All Foods)
Laundry	2.50	.5 (CPI Laundry, flatwork) + .5 (CPI Sheets)
Fuel	5.00	WPI Fuel and related commodities
Maintenance and Repairs	3.75	CPI Maint. and rep.
Drugs	6.25	WPI Drugs and pharmaceuticals
Medical Supplies, X-ray Supplies, and Laboratory	27.50	WPI Industrial commodities
M.D. Fees	11.25	CPI, M.D. fees
Capital	15.00	.67 (Dept. of Commerce, Construction) + .33 (WPI Machinery and Equipment)
Insurance (Malp.)	4.25	AHA (see text)
Miscellaneous*	14.50	CPI All Items
TOTAL	60.00	
Estimated weight of nonlabor expenses in total expenses		40.0

*The miscellaneous category includes such items as office supplies, telephone, postage, accounting and legal fees, housekeeping, and blood, each of which individually is relatively minor.

indices for are malpractice insurance and capital expenses. Since malpractice premiums have been so volatile of late, and since capital expenses vary so much across hospitals, these categories are generally left out of indices designed for use in reimbursement formulas. In indexing malpractice premiums, we relied on data from AHA surveys for the years 1970–75, which showed an increase in premiums of over 800 percent during that period. Before 1970, malpractice premiums were far too small to have any appreciable effect on the index. We treat them before 1970 as changing at the rate of the all items CPI. The weight given to this component is also based on AHA survey data on the size of the average premium. We estimate that about two-thirds of capital costs were for fixed capital (buildings), and one-third was for movable equipment. The Department of Commerce composite index of construction costs is used as an index of fixed capital prices, and the WPI for machinery and equipment is used for movable equipment. Of course, if depreciation on existing capital is carried out on a historical cost basis, depreciation costs should not be affected by changes in the cost of new capital.

Indexing fuel prices is also somewhat of a problem area, since prices of different fuels have changed at widely different rates and prices vary considerably by region. We chose as a general index of fuel prices the WPI for fuels and related products, which more than doubled from 1972–75, while the CPI for fuel and utilities—another possible choice—increased only about forty percent.

Table 3-14 presents the values of our nonlabor price index for the years 1960–75 alongside the CPI and WPI values. Our index has been rescaled to equal 100.0 in 1967 for easier comparison. By way of comparison, we see that our index, like M. Feldstein's, appears to follow the CPI very closely, more closely than it does the WPI, until the years 1974–75. In those years our index showed much larger increases than the CPI. The total increase in our index since 1967 has been very nearly the same as that shown in the WPI, though the timing of increases has differed between the two indices.

It is perhaps worth stressing a point which may already be obvious. Our nonlabor price index at best provides a fairly good indication of how hospital input prices have increased on the average across the nation. There is actually a great deal of variation in the weights of various components in hospital budgets by region and by size and type of hospital. Prices and movements

Table 3-14 Three Price Indices

Year	Nonlabor Price Index	CPI	WPI
1960	90.6	88.7	94.9
1961	91.0	89.6	94.5
1962	91.5	90.6	94.8
1963	92.1	91.7	94.5
1964	92.9	92.9	94.7
1965	94.5	94.5	96.6
1966	97.3	97.2	99.8
1967	100.0	100.0	100.0
1968	103.2	104.2	102.5
1969	108.3	109.8	106.5
1970	114.0	116.3	110.4
1971	118.9	121.3	113.9
1972	125.3	125.3	119.1
1973	132.7	133.1	134.7
1974	152.3	147.7	160.1
1975	176.7	161.1	174.9

in prices also vary somewhat by region (regional differences in prices is one reason we would expect differences in the mix of inputs used). Thus it may not be justifiable to apply this index to any individual hospital or group of hospitals as a measure of the amount of nonlabor input price pressure on costs.

In spite of these difficulties, we have in Table 3-15 broken down the changes in nonlabor expenses per day into changes in our price index and residual changes, which are interpreted as changes in real inputs used per patient day. Nonlabor expenses per patient day are calculated by subtracting 115.4 percent of payroll expenses per patient day from total expenses per patient day, using AHA data. The extra 15.4 percent is our estimate of the importance of expenses on employee benefits and payments to interns and residents, which the AHA does not include in payroll expenses. Whether or not our breakdown is precisely accurate, several points seem apparent. One is that expenses on nonlabor inputs have been increasing considerably faster than expenses on labor inputs—about 15.8 percent per year from 1966–75 by our estimates, compared to 11.2 percent. Secondly, the increases in nonlabor expenses appear to be more heavily concentrated in real quantity increases than in input prices increases. We estimate that over the 1966–75 period nonlabor prices increased 6.6 percent per year on the average—less rapidly than wages—while nonlabor inputs per patient day increased about 9.2 percent per year. Only

Table 3-15 Nonlabor Prices and Inputs

Year	Nonlabor Expense Per Patient Day		Nonlabor Prices		Nonlabor Inputs Per Patient Day
	An Avg.	%	An Avg.	%	%
1960	9.06		90.6		
1961	10.12	11.7	91.0	.4	11.2
1962	10.53	4.1	91.5	.6	3.5
1963	11.20	6.4	92.1	.7	5.7
1964	12.43	11.0	92.9	.9	10.0
1965	12.81	3.1	94.5	1.7	1.4
1966	14.21	10.9	97.3	3.0	7.7
1967	16.64	17.1	100.0	2.8	14.0
1968	19.13	15.0	103.2	3.2	11.4
1969	22.30	16.6	108.3	4.9	11.1
1970	26.43	18.5	114.0	5.3	12.6
1971	30.22	14.3	118.9	4.3	9.7
1972	36.21	19.8	123.3	3.7	15.5
1973	41.08	13.4	132.7	7.6	5.4
1974	47.47	15.6	152.3	14.8	0.7
1975	58.71	23.7	176.7	16.0	6.6

in the last several years have increases in utilization of nonlabor inputs begun to slow down. We do not have the detailed data necessary to determine how the use of particular categories of nonlabor inputs has changed, but it seems likely that increases in use have been concentrated in medical supplies and capital, both fixed capital and movable equipment.

NOTES

1. Barry Chiswick and Stephen Chiswick, *Statistics and Econometrics: A Problem-Solving Text* (Baltimore: University Park Press, 1975).
2. R.L. Robertson, "Comparative Medical Care Use Under Prepaid Group Practice and Free Choice Plans: A Case Study," *Inquiry*, 11, no. 3 (September 1972): 70–76.
3. The computational and theoretical details of the appropriate procedure for dealing with this problem are too complex to be presented here. The following is intended to give only the general "flavor" of the approach.
4. The mathematical technique for determining the a and b values for the line that minimizes the sum of squared deviation is beyond the scope of this book. The estimation method described is sometimes called ordinary least squares (OLS). In cases where an equation is part of a simultaneous equation system or special problems are present, other techniques such as two-stage least squares (TSLS) are used.
5. The S.E.E. Feldstein gives in his tables is the standard error of estimate. Its use and interpretation are beyond the scope of the discussion here and unnecessary for the purposes of this book.

6. The term *deflator* is used to indicate a method of translating current money values into *constant dollars*—that is, removing the effects of inflation from the measure. The GNP deflator thus is a form of price index used to distinguish money increases in the GNP from real increases in production.
7. See Herbert Klarman et al., "Sources of Increase in Selected Medical Care Expenditures, 1929-1969." U.S. Department of Health, Education and Welfare, Social Security Administration, Office of Research and Statistics, Staff Paper No. 4, 1970.

SUGGESTED READINGS

Statistics and Econometrics

Beals, Ralph E. *Statistics for Economists: An Introduction.* New York: Rand McNally & Co., 1972.
Rao, Potluri, and Miller, Roger LeRoy. *Applied Econometrics.* Belmont, Calif.: Wadsworth Publishing Co., Inc., 1971.
Wonnacott, Thomas, and Wonnacott, Ronald. *Introductory Statistics for Business and Economics,* 2nd ed. New York: John Wiley & Sons, Inc., 1977.

Indexes: General

Neter, John; Wasserman, William; and Whitmore, G. A. *Applied Statistics.* Boston: Allyn & Bacon, Inc., 1978, Ch. 26.
Wonnacott and Wonnacott, *Introductory Statistics,* Chap. 23.

Indexes: Medical Care

Klarman, Herbert et al. "Sources of Increase in Selected Medical Care Expenditures, 1929-1969." U.S. Department of Health, Education and Welfare, Social Security Administration, Office of Research and Statistics, Staff Paper No. 4. Washington, D.C.: Government Printing Office, April 1970.
Scitovsky, Anne. "An Index of the Cost of Medical Care—A Proposed New Approach" in *The Economics of Health and Medical Care.* Ann Arbor: University of Michigan Press, 1964, pp. 128-142.
Scitovsky, Anne, and McCall, Nelta. *Changes in the Costs of Treatment of Selected Illnesses, 1959-1964-1971.* U.S. Department of Health, Education and Welfare, National Center for Health Services Research, NCHSR Research Digest Services, Publication No. (HRA) 77-3161. Washington, D.C.: Government Printing Office, 1976, pp. 4-17.

NOTES FOR CONSUMER PRICE INDEX EXCERPT

1. The definition of wage earners and clerical workers is based on the occupational classification used by the Bureau of the Census for the 1960 Census of Population and listed in the Alphabetical Index of Occupations and Industries. The group includes *craftsmen, foremen, and kindred workers,* such as carpenters, bookbinders, etc.; *op-*

eratives and kindred workers, such as apprentices in the building trades, deliverymen, furnacemen, smelters, and pourers, etc.; *clerical and kindred workers; service workers, except private household*, such as waitresses, practical nurses, etc.; *sales workers;* and *laborers, except farm and mine*. It excludes *professional, technical, and kindred workers*, such as *engineers and teachers; farmers and farm managers; managers, officials and proprietors, except farm; private household workers;* and *farm laborers and foremen*. A consumer unit included in the 1960-61 Survey of Consumer Expenditures was classified in the index group if more than half the combined income of all family members was obtained in a wage-earner and clerical-worker occupation and at least one family member was a full-time earner (i.e., worked 37 weeks or more during the survey year).

2. For New York and Chicago, the more extensive Standard Consolidated Areas are used.
3. The Surveys for Cincinnati and Anchorage covered expenditures in 1959, and those for Houston, Kansas City, Milwaukee, Minneapolis-St. Paul, and San Diego covered expenditures in 1963.
4. The selection of the city sample is described in "The Revised City Sample for the Consumer Price Index," Reprint No. 2352 from the October 1960 *Monthly Labor Review*.
5. The complete list is available on request.
6. See explanation of the Index Formula at end of excerpt.
7. See *Seasonal Factors, Consumer Price Index: Selected Series*, May 1963. (Bulletin 1366), U.S. Department of Labor, Bureau of Labor Statistics.
8. A detailed description of the BLS Seasonal Factor Method is available upon request.
9. Since there are two index populations (one of urban wage earners and clerical workers, and one of all urban households), items are selected to be representative of each of these populations. Selected items may vary from region to region and between index populations, but probability sampling procedures are used to maximize the overlap for efficiency in collection. Within selected items, in general, the goal is to use an objective probability process for the selection of goods "specified in detail," including proper representation of both big-volume and other goods.

NOTE FOR FUCHS AND KRAMER EXCERPT

5. This approach was proposed and applied by Martin S. Feldstein [16]. We have utilized additional data and relaxed some of his assumptions in deriving our average price series. An alternative approach employed by Klarman et al. [28] utilizes direct estimates of changes in collection ratios, but makes no adjustment for deviations between customary and actual charges.

REFERENCES FOR FUCHS AND KRAMER EXCERPT

16. Feldstein, Martin S. "The Rising Price of Physicians' Services," *The Review of Economics and Statistics*, 52 (May 1970): 121-133.
26. Kessel, Ruben A. "Price Discrimination in Medicine," *Journal of Law and Economics*, 1 (October 1958).

28. Klarman, Herbert et al. "Sources of Increase in Selected Medical Care Expenditures, 1929–69," U.S. Department of Health, Education and Welfare, Social Security Administration, Office of Research and Statistics, Staff Paper No. 4 (April 1970).

SOURCES AND PERMISSIONS

a. Reprinted from *Economics: A General Introduction*, 4th ed., by Lloyd Reynolds by permission of Richard D. Irwin, Inc., 1973, pp. 13–16. ᶜ 1973.

b. Reprinted from "Forecasts of Costs in the Hospital Sector" by Paul Feldstein, in *Proceedings: Health Care in the American Economy: Issues and Forecasts*, pp. 24–33, by permission of the Health Services Foundation, Chicago, ᶜ 1977.

c. Reprinted from "The Consumer Price Index: A Short Description," 1980, Washington, D.C.: U.S. Department of Labor, Bureau of Labor Statistics, 1974.

d. U.S. Department of Labor, Bureau of Labor Statistics, *The Consumer Price Index: Concepts and Content Over the Years*, Report 517 (Washington, D.C.: Government Printing Office, 1978).

e. Reprinted from "Determinants of Expenditures for Physicians' Services in the United States, 1948–68," by Victor Fuchs and Marcia Kramer, U.S. Department of Health, Education and Welfare, National Center for Health Services Research and Development, DHEW Publication No. (HSM 73-3013), 1972, pp. 7–10.

f. Reprinted from "Forecasts of Costs" by Paul Feldstein (supra), pp. 41–54.

Chapter 4

Demand for Health Services

Demand represents both one of the simplest and one of the most complex of economic concepts, but it is not difficult to grasp. As noted in Chapter 2, demand means simply the amount of a good or service that consumers are willing and able to buy at given prices. It can be a formidable concept to apply in practice because of the innumerable factors that influence and constrain individual purchasing decisions. Nonetheless, a working knowledge of demand is of singular importance to health administrators and planners alike. Every decision to expand or contract the supply of health services rests (or at least should rest) on knowledge of the demand characteristics for the population in question. If demand considerations are ignored, the result may be a glut of services that no one uses or a shortage that creates an undesired reduction in levels of health.

This chapter has three objectives:

1. to provide an understanding of the theoretical underpinnings of demand analysis;
2. to consider the properties of demand curves and their relationship to planning;
3. to examine the methods used in empirical studies of health services demand.

To the noneconomist, the initial sections may appear rather abstract and tenuous but they should be read carefully. When economists conduct demand studies, they are testing hypotheses that were developed initially in the form of theoretical models. Unless the theory is understood, the results may be seriously misinterpreted.

Health planning literature, in particular, includes numerous examples where demand tends to be confused with other theoretical concepts. Consider the following extract from the National Guidelines for Health Planning published in March 1978.

SUBPART B—NATIONAL HEALTH PLANNING GOALS[a]
(Reserved)

Subpart C—Standards Respecting the Appropriate Supply, Distribution, and Organization of Health Resources

§121.201—General Hospitals—Bed Supply

(a) *Standard.* There should be less than four non-Federal, short-stay hospital beds for each 1,000 persons in a health service area except under extraordinary circumstances. For purposes of this section, short-stay hospital beds include all non-Federal short-stay hospital beds (including general medical/surgical, children's, obstetric, psychiatric, and other short-stay specialized beds). Conditions which may justify adjustments to this ratio for a health service area include:

(1) *Age:* Individuals 65 years of age and older have a higher hospital utilization rate—up to four times that of the general population—than any other age group. Bed-population ratios for health service areas in which the percentage of elderly people is significantly higher (more than 12% of the population) than the national average may be planned at a higher ratio, based on analyses by the HSA [Health Systems Agency].

(2) *Seasonal population fluctuations:* Large seasonal variations in hospital utilization may justify higher ratios. Plans should reflect vacation and recreation patterns as well as the needs of migrant workers and other factors causing unusual seasonal variations.

(3) *Rural areas:* Hospital care should be accessible within a reasonable period of time. For example, in rural areas in which a majority of the residents would otherwise be more than 30 minutes travel time from a hospital, the HSA may determine, based on analyses, that a bed-population ratio of greater than 4.0 per 1,000 persons may be justified.

(4) *Urban areas:* Large numbers of beds in one part of a Standard Metropolitan Statistical Area (SMSA) may be compensated for by fewer beds in other parts of the SMSA. Health service areas which include a part of an SMSA may plan for bed-population ratios higher than 4.0 per 1,000 persons reflecting existing patterns if there is a joint plan among all HSAs serving the SMSA

which provides for less than 4.0 beds per 1,000 persons in the SMSA as a whole.

(5) *Areas with referral hospitals:* In the case of referral institutions which provide a substantial portion of specialty services to individuals not residing in the area, the HSA may exclude from its computation of bed-population ratio the beds utilized by referred patients who reside outside both the SMSA and the HSA in which the facility is located.

(b) *Discussion.* There is general agreement that the number of general hospital beds in the United States is significantly in excess of what is needed and that utilization of acute in-patient care resources is often higher than necessary. Excess bed capacity and use contribute to the high cost of hospital care with little or no health benefits. Empty beds are often filled by patients who could be cared for as well or better in less expensive ways, such as ambulatory care or home care.

The Institute of Medicine's Report on "Controlling the Supply of Hospital Beds" in 1976 recommended that the nation should achieve at least a 10% reduction in the bed-population ratio in the next five years and further significant reductions thereafter. The Institute statement noted: "This would mean a reduction from the current national average of approximately 4.4 non-Federal short-term general hospital beds per 1,000 population to a national average of approximately 4.0 in five years and well below that in the years to follow." Similarly a study reported by InterStudy of Minneapolis, Minn. the same year concluded that a 10% reduction in hospital bed supply would be a desirable and reasonable first step toward reducing excess hospital capacity.

As part of the process for determining this standard, the Department reviewed projections in State health facilities planning plans. Such plans have set targets for future hospital bed supply that, on an aggregate nationwide basis, project just under 4.0 beds per thousand. Many States set lower targets. Health Maintenance Organizations and similar groups have shown that high quality care can be provided with less than 3.0 beds per 1,000 population.

Thus, 4.0 beds per 1,000 population is a ceiling, not an ideal situation. HSAs are expected to identify the desirable local ratio, working closely with the State Health Planning and Development Agency and the Statewide Health Coordinating Council. It is anticipated that in subsequent plans HSAs will be required to indicate how they will reach a bed-population ratio of less than

3.7 per 1,000 population except under extraordinary circumstances. HSAs whose areas are now below the 4.0 per 1,000 level are urged to attempt to decrease bed-population ratios below 3.7 per 1,000 population. In areas where Federal medical facilities and Health Maintenance Organizations provide substantial services to local residents, lower ratios should be readily achievable. Population growth must be carefully analyzed; in many cases, this factor alone will bring the area below the target level if no unnecessary additional beds are built.

Under some conditions, a higher target ceiling may be justified by the HSA. Travel distance to the nearest hospital is one of the most important factors to be analyzed, especially in rural areas. A planning criteria of 30 minutes has been set, in line with the policies of many local and State health planning agencies around the country.

In reading this selection quickly, it would appear that demand plays no part in the process of setting standards for acute care bed supplies (the term "demand" is not even mentioned). If this were indeed true, the wisdom of national health planning policy might well be questioned. Demand considerations are implicit in the references to utilization differentials among health service areas. But this relationship can be confusing, since utilization and demand are two very different concepts. Utilization is realized demand; that is, the amount of service people are willing to purchase and actually do obtain at a given place and time. In other words, utilization patterns reflect underlying conditions of both demand and supply. Can demand be projected from utilization? Obviously not in cases where there is insufficient supply to meet desired (but unrealized) demand.

The confusion deepens when a distinction is made between necessary and unnecessary utilization. To the economist, demand is a value-free concept in the sense that no attempt is made to second-guess individual choices. The decision to buy a particular service may be viewed as good, bad, or indifferent depending on prevalent social values. But judgment must be distinguished from fact. Economics provide little insight into the normative issue of what constitutes necessary service. It can help in understanding the consequences of public decisions to promote or constrain demand.

FUNDAMENTALS OF DEMAND THEORY

The theory of demand presented in the next four sections may be summarized as follows. At the beginning is the supposition that people purchase only things they believe will provide satisfaction (or in economic jargon, *utility*). The satisfaction gained from consuming medical care is related to the value that individuals place on their own health status. When an individual suffers from illness or accident, there is the possibility that utility can be increased by purchasing one or more medical treatments. However, the objective need for such medical attention does not necessarily generate demand. The individual faces a number of important trade-offs. The value of improved health must be balanced against the loss of utility from other goods and services that no longer can be purchased if money is spent on medical care. The available income and structure of relative prices (for medical and nonmedical services alike) imposes a constraint. Individuals also may not know how much any given treatment will improve their health status and hence have difficulty making informed judgments.

All these factors must be considered in deriving demand curves for medical services. The analysis that follows is somewhat more sophisticated than that in basic economics textbooks. For the reader who is not familiar with introductory microeconomics, the eleventh edition of Samuelson's *Economics* contains a summary of utility and demand theory. Other useful sources are listed in the suggested reading list at the end of this chapter.

The Utility Function

Individuals gain satisfaction or utility from the possession and use of goods and services. The level of utility depends on many variables, including individual tastes and preferences, the quality of the good or service, and the time it takes to consume the item. Some commodities such as food, newspapers, and movies are enjoyed directly when purchased or shortly thereafter. These are known as *consumption* goods and may be differentiated from *investment* goods (housing, education, automobiles, and so forth) that provide a flow of service over time.[1]

Depending on the circumstances, medical care may be either a consumption good or an investment good. Preventive and rehabilitative services obviously have characteristics of investment; they are purchased on the assumption that treatment will yield future rewards in the form of improved health status. A physician office visit may be considered as an investment in the sense that the information gained may be used in future decisions regarding when and from whom to seek medical attention. Symptomatic treatment and the care of self-limiting illness are examples of consumption goods. They yield immediate utility to the patient but contribute few future benefits.

The belief that medical care will provide current and/or future utility is a necessary precondition for demand. But before an actual purchase is made, individuals must be convinced that the value of the care to them is at least equal to the value of the best alternative use of their incomes. (This example and the discussion following assume that individuals purchase all health services out-of-pocket. Insurance obviously will have an effect on demand. This effect is examined later in the chapter.)

Assume that a bricklayer has been saving for a new stereo system that costs $1,000. When the money finally is in hand, the individual develops a hernia that also happens to cost $1,000 to repair. Will the person have the operation? Not necessarily. If the pain from the hernia can be relieved by an inexpensive truss, the individual may decide to buy the stereo and forego (or at least delay) the operation. The decision will depend on the opportunity cost of the treatment,[2] in this case the utility gained from the purchase of the stereo system.

The choices people face when deciding whether to buy medical care seldom are this clearcut. But even when there is no single alternative, the individual still must decide whether the direct utility gained from medical care (improved health status) equals or exceeds the value of the utility potential contained in the income that must be spent to obtain the care. Experience notes that individuals differ widely in the relative values they place on health status and income. They also tend to place a lower value on additional units of a given commodity as their consumption of it increases relative to other commodities (the so-called law of *diminishing marginal utility*).

There is no direct way to measure individual utilities, but a simplified model should help to explain the underlying concepts. In Figure 4-1 the relative value an individual places on health status at a point in time is shown by means of an *indifference curve*. It is assumed here that the individual has less than perfect health and can use income (Y) to purchase various combinations of improved health (via medical care expenditures) and some composite collection of all other goods and services designated as $Y - M$ (income minus outlays for medical care). Health status is defined broadly here to include psychological as well as physical attributes perceived and desired by the patient. Thus, it includes such factors as better information about health and freedom from worry about disease as well as objectively measurable physical characteristics.

In Figure 4-1, improvements in health status (HS) are indicated as movements up the vertical axis (the actual units of measurement are arbitrary in this example), and income is measured in dollars on the horizontal axis. Each curve represents the combinations of HS and $Y - M$ that provide a constant level of utility for the individual in question. That is to say, the individual gains the same aggregate satisfaction from the combination (HS_1, $Y - M_1$) as from (HS_2, $Y - M_2$) or any other point on Curve 1. Because of this feature, the curve is known as an indifference curve. Conceptually, at

Figure 4-1 Indifference Analysis

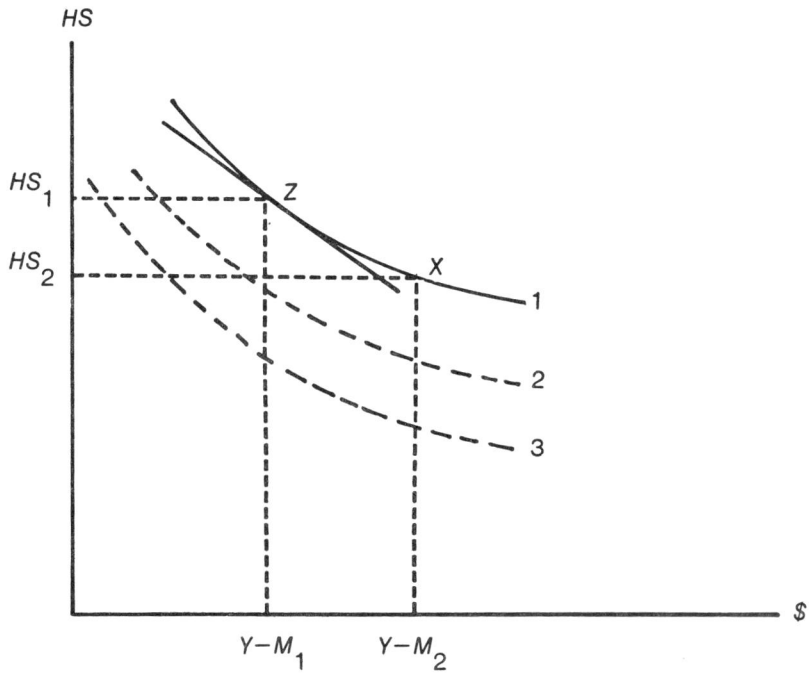

any point in time an individual has an infinite number of indifference curves, reflective of different levels of utility. While the individual is indifferent between any two points on a given curve, the person always will prefer a higher level of utility to a lower level (e.g., any point on 1 is preferred to any point on 2, and any point on 2 is preferred to any point on 3).

The collection of all possible indifference curves (sometimes referred to as an indifference map) comprises an individual's *utility function*. The law of diminishing marginal utility is reflected in the fact that each indifference curve is convex to the origin. This means that an individual must be given progressively more *HS* for every dollar of income that is given up (and vice versa) for that person to remain at the same level of utility. The rate at which the individual is willing to trade *Y* for *HS* is measured by the slope of the tangent to the curve at a given point (such as point *Z*) and is known as the *marginal rate of substitution* or simply as *MRS*. A high marginal rate of substitution of *Y* for *HS* means that health status is sufficiently important for the individual to give up relatively large amounts of income to purchase a cure. An example might be an emergency appendectomy. By the same logic, a low *MRS* of *Y* for *HS* means that a change in health status is not viewed as particularly important relative to uses of income other than for medical care.

The Production of Health Status

Up to this point, the analysis has made two tacit assumptions. The first is that individuals gain no direct satisfaction from the consumption of medical care per se, but rather demand it for its salutary effects on health status. This is not an unreasonable assumption for most types of health services, particularly if health status is defined broadly to incorporate peace of mind and mental health. A second and more critical assumption is that there is some direct and predictable relationship between the consumption of medical care and improvement in health status.

No medical regimen is 100 percent successful in every case. Even under the best of circumstances there is always the chance that the individual was misdiagnosed or that the treatment will be botched. All medical procedures are characterized by *risk* or *uncertainty*. The distinction between the two terms is important. Risk means that there is a known probability that the treatment will be successful. When an endodontist says there is an 80 percent chance that a root canal will save a tooth, the dentist is providing an estimated risk. What the expert means is that the procedure has been tried in enough similar cases that a probability of success can be calculated. In cases where there is insufficient information to calculate probabilities, the outcome is described as uncertain. Uncertainty is an inevitable concomitant of new or experimental medical procedures.

Both risk and uncertainty also arise from the fact that medical care is but one input in the production of health status. In a very real sense, individuals produce their own level of health. The production process incorporates such variable inputs as personal habits, occupation, living conditions, and medical treatments. It is subject to the constraints imposed by age, sex, genetic background, and a host of noncontrollable environmental and cultural parameters. A complete production function for health would incorporate all of these (and other) variables and parameters.

For purposes here, it is sufficient to concentrate on a partial *production function* for health in which all inputs except medical care are held constant (this is equivalent to defining the relationship between consumption of medical care and health for a cohort of individuals with similar personal and demographic characteristics). The analysis begins with a production function, $HS = f(D,M)$, where D is the diagnosis when less than optimal

Figure 4-2 Production Functions for Health Status

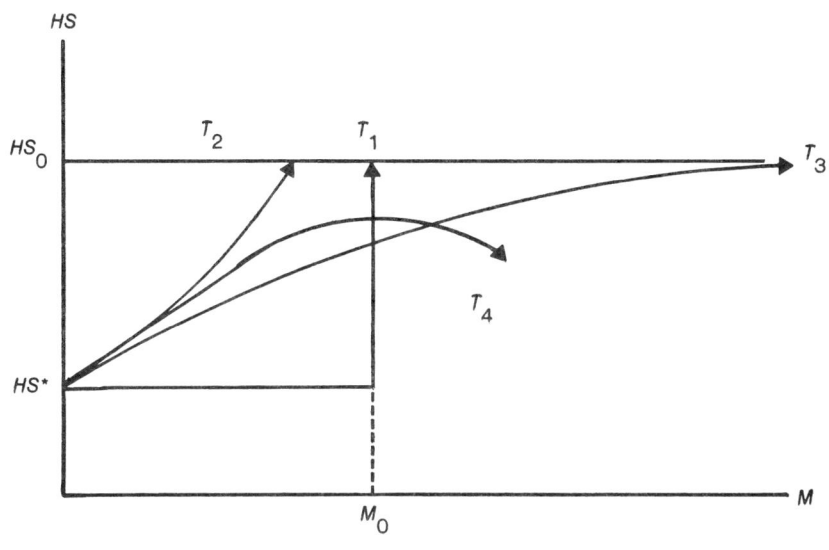

health status obtains, M the quantity of medical resources for a particular medical approach, and HS the expected health status associated with D and M.

The actual shape of the production function for a given diagnosis will depend on the medical technologies (T) involved. Figure 4-2 illustrates several possibilities. In this diagram HS is the health status before onset of some illness D, and HS^* is the health status after onset but before treatment. The first and simplest type of medical technology (T_1) is a discrete treatment process where M_0 medical care is necessary to produce any positive probability of recovery. Examples might include antibiotic treatments (ten days of penicillin may cure a strep throat but five days will have no effect) and most surgical procedures. A second type of technology (T_2) is a variable treatment process exhibiting increasing *marginal productivity* (e.g., where an additional unit of M produces a higher gain in HS than did the previous unit). The third type (T_3) is similar except that the treatment shows declining marginal productivity. There are numerous examples of both increasing and declining marginal productivity. Physical therapy usually produces few benefits in the early stages of treatment but improvement may become increasingly evident in later phases. The initial days of hospital care after surgery frequently show greater improvement than the days toward the end of the stay.

While in each of the first three cases there is a positive probability that the illness can be cured completely (return to HS_0) by consuming a given quantity of medical care, it is entirely possible that no amount of M will lead to a return to HS_0. Similarly, it is not inconceivable that using more than the medically optimal amount of care will result in an actual decline in HS (negative marginal productivity). These possible outcomes are shown as T_4 in Figure 4-2.

From the standpoint of demand analysis, it obviously is of critical importance whether the potential consumer (patient) is knowledgeable about the alternative treatment regimens (if alternatives exist) and the marginal productivity and probability of success associated with each. This issue has generated much confusion. On the one hand, there are those who argue that patients are at the mercy of physicians for all information regarding treatment and, more important, that physicians create the demand for their services by being selective in the way they share information with patients. On the other hand are those who assert that medical care essentially is no different from other goods of which the consumer is technologically ignorant. Uwe Reinhardt drives home this point (Table 4-1) by listing the technical properties of two stereo receivers offered by the same manufacturer at substantially different prices. Reinhardt goes on to say:[b]

Table 4-1 An Example of Complex Products

	MODEL A	MODEL B
Audio Section		
Continuous Power	25/35W (4Ω)	43.43W (4Ω)
	28/28W (8Ω)	35/35W (8Ω)
Power Amplifiers Section		
Frequency Response (at normal listening level)	15-40000Hz − 1dB	10-50000Hz + 1dB
Preamplifier Output	.8V (at rated input) 3V (max.)	.5V (at rated output) 2.5V (max.)
Power Amplifier Input	.8V (at rated output)	.5V (at rated output)
Voltage	1.6μV(20dB quieting)	1.4μV(20dB quieting)
Tuner Section		
FM Sensitivity	2.0μV (IHG)	1.8μV (IHF)
Capture Ratio	2.5dB	1.0dB
Image Frequency Rejection	Better than 85dB	Better than 90dB

and so on . . .

> Consider now a consumer without knowledge of electronics with an only moderately sensitive ear. It can be wondered how our consumer would necessarily be driven to select the right model from these and other models for his or her particular circumstances simply because true experts in the market have established reasonable prices for these models, given these experts' predilections and circumstances. Chances are that our consumer would rely on expert advice in making the selection; chances are that the consumer will take home a model that may not be the most appropriate for his or her particular circumstances, especially if the vendor is overstocked on a particular model or if profit margins differ among models. It could happen even to an economist!
> ... Even more apropos would be the case where a stereo system breaks down. Although the price of a new unit would limit the degree to which the service-intensity of repairs could be varied—a constraint usually absent in repairs on the human body—the market usually leaves room to vary that intensity for given technical malfunctions, especially for complicated gadgets.

The argument Reinhardt makes is that subtle forms of demand creation are an everyday feature of normal market operations. The reader undoubtedly can provide additional examples to prove the point. But is Reinhardt correct? Is there no fundamental difference between the demand for medical care and the demand for stereo equipment?

Demand creation by physicians might be expected to occur in situations where two conditions are met: (1) the service in question is one where consumers are unable to make a judgment about the need for and the results of the service; and (2) the method of payment is such that there is a possible divergence between the physician's economic self-interest and simultaneous role as agent for the patient. An example of such a situation is surgery under fee-for-service compensation. It has been suggested frequently that a certain proportion of operations financed in this way (hysterectomies and tonsillectomies in particular) are the result of demand creation.

Evidence on demand creation is far from conclusive. Some studies have shown that surgery rates are higher when surgeons are paid on a fee-for-service basis than when they are compensated in other ways. Correlations also have been noted between surgery rates and the number of surgeons in relation to population in the geographic area. Findings such as these are consistent with the demand creation hypothesis, but the statistical evidence is not strong and other studies have failed to find such an effect.[3] It should be emphasized in conclusion that demand creation covers only situations in which the physician induces the patient to purchase a treatment or service that the patient would not obtain if fully informed (e.g., the physician misrepresents the true probability and/or marginal productivity of the recommended treatment). The fact that physicians recommend treatment, and the treatment subsequently is carried out, does not constitute a priori evidence of demand creation.

Price and Income Constraints

From the patient's viewpoint the physician, as the individual's agent, should consider both the health consequences and economic effects of recommended treatments. There is some question whether the physician's fiduciary role extends to a consideration of ability to pay. Before the widespread adoption of health insurance, it was common practice for physicians to charge lower fees to less affluent patients. But even with insurance, the potential patient faces demand constraints in the form of the time cost of obtaining care, the out-of-pocket expense for the service in question (the amount after insurance benefits are deducted), and the prices of all other goods and services that compete for the individual's income.

Figure 4-3 Budget Lines

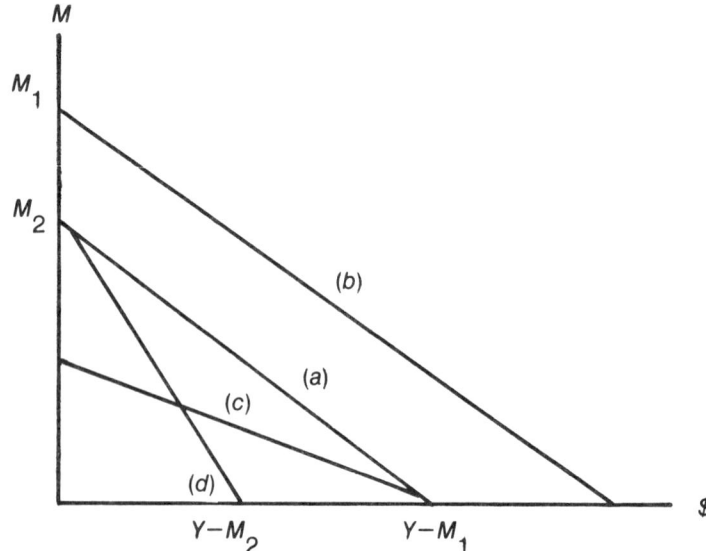

The effects of income and price constraints may be shown diagrammatically. In Figure 4-3, the *budget line* (*a*) represents all combinations of medical care (*M*) and all other goods and services ($Y-M$) that the individual can buy with a given income at given prices. That is to say, an individual can buy any combination on the line by spending the entire income on *M* and $Y-M$ (the composite good defined in connection with Figure 4-1), but by definition cannot purchase a combination to the right of the line. The distance of the budget line from the origin shows the level of income (and if income increases, the line shifts outward in a parallel fashion as shown by line *b*). The slope of the budget line, on the other hand, indicates the ratio of the price of *M* to the "price" of $Y-M$ (since $Y-M$ is a composite of all goods and services less medical care, its price is equivalent to the general price level or CPI less medical care). If the cost of medical care increases and the general price level stays the same, the individual's purchasing power is reduced. In Figure 4-3, a doubling of the price of medical care reduces the income/price line to (*c*). Similarly, if all other prices double and the cost of medical care remains unchanged, then the income/price line becomes (*d*).

Derivation of the Demand Curve

Figure 4-4 puts all this information together for the hypothetical individual. It can be used to derive the relationship between demand and price or income changes. Consider first each quadrant separately. Quadrant 1 is a particular version of Figure 4-2. For a disease that reduces health status from HS_0 to HS^*, the technology shown is the best perceived strategy available. Quadrant 2 is similar to Figure 4-1 (but backwards); each indifference curve represents a particular level of utility and the slope of the curve represents the marginal rate of substitution. As drawn, the curves are relatively steep and indicate that the consumer is willing to give up only a small amount of income to return from HS^* to HS_0.

Quadrant 4 shows the indifference curves in terms of medical care and income, rather than health status and income. That is, each curve in this quadrant shows all combinations of medical care and income-left-over ($Y-M$) among which the consumer is indifferent. The curves in quadrant 4 correspond exactly to the ones in quadrant 2. To illustrate this, consider point *X* on indifference curve A_3. According to quadrant 1, medical care in amount M' would achieve the health status (HS') associated with *X*. The 45° construction line in quadrant 3 simply permits plotting downward on the vertical axis the income left over, $(Y-M)'$, that corresponds to *X*. The point X' in quadrant 4 represents the same consumption decision and

Figure 4-4 The Demand Curve Derivation

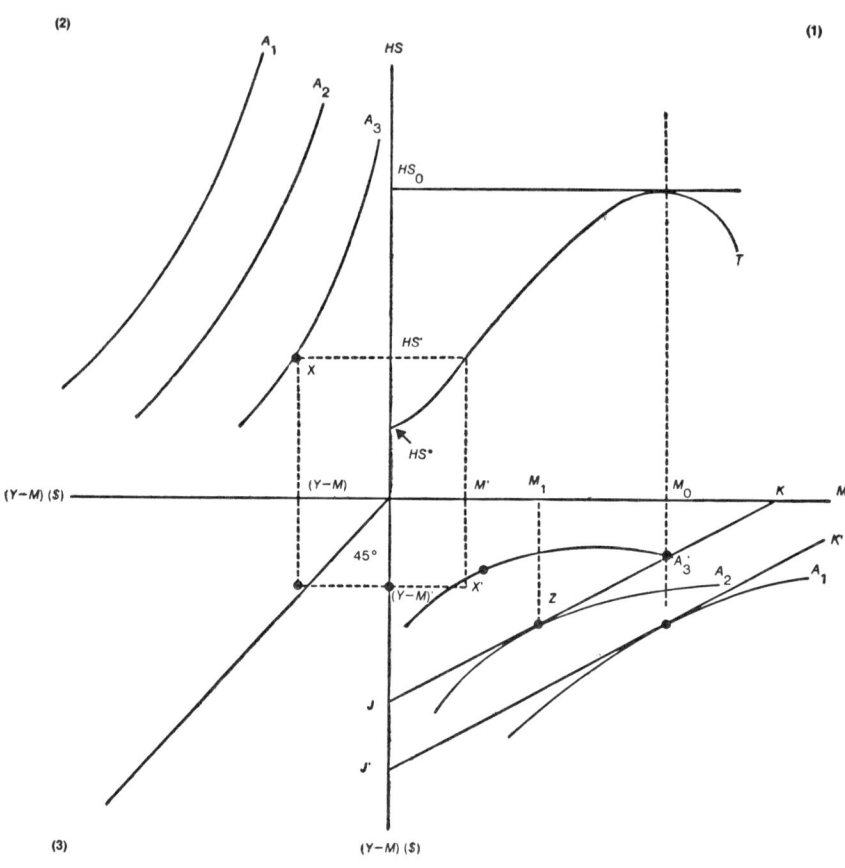

utility level as the point X in quadrant 2. A similar transposition performed for the other points on curve A_3 can generate curve A_3' in quadrant 4.

Finally, to derive the *demand function*, information must be introduced about the consumer's income and the prevailing prices. This is shown by the budget line JK that now is introduced in quadrant 4. Suppose prices and income yielded line JK. Since the individual cannot by definition purchase commodities beyond the budget line, the only choice is to maximize utility on the line. Maximum utility is obtained where the budget line is tangent to the highest possible indifference curve. In this example, tangency occurs at point Z, implying a demand for M_1 of medical care—clearly well below the quantity required to bring about complete restoration of health status.

The demand curve is derived from points of tangency such as point Z. Thus, a change in price or income and the resulting move in the budget line will lead to a new tangency point and a different quantity demanded. What would induce the individual in Figure 4-4 to demand the amount of medical care that would bring about full restoration of health status, i.e., M_0? One possibility is an increase in income that would shift the budget line to $J'K'$. Another change (not shown) that would produce this result would be a drop in the price of medical care.

How is the relationship between price and quantity demanded measured? Consider a demand function $Q = f(P)$ where Q is quantity of medical care demanded and P is the price. All other factors that influence demand were derived in the previous section and are summarized in the budget constraint and utility function (mapped out as indifference curves) shown in the first quadrant of Figure 4-5. Assume that the current out-of-pocket price for a unit of medical care is $10 and that the average "price" per unit of $Y-M$ also is $10. The price ratio is thus 1:1. The individual maximizes utility at point a by purchasing 4 units of medical care at a price of $10 each. This is shown in the second quadrant as point x. Assume now that the price of a unit of medical care drops to $5. If the general price level (less medical care) remains unchanged, this means that the individual can now purchase twice as much medical care per dollar of income and the budget line shifts upward to 1:2. The individual now maximizes utility at point b by pur-

Figure 4-5 Effect of Price Change on Demand

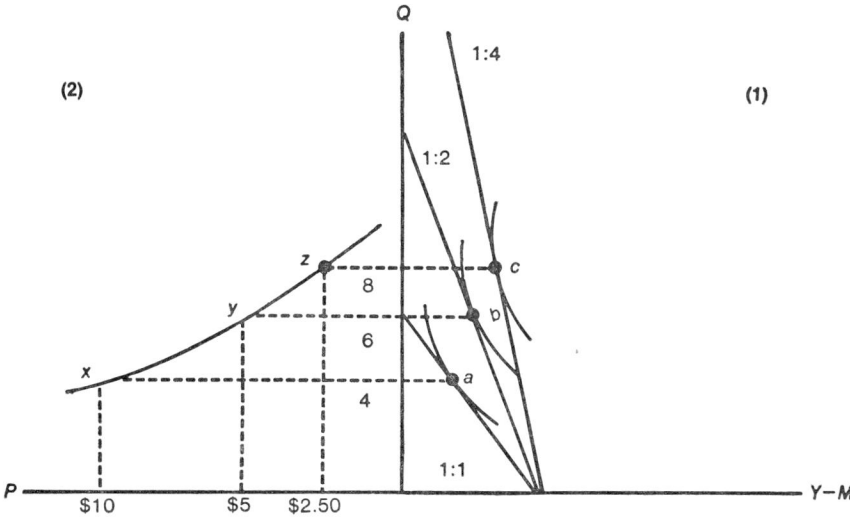

Figure 4-6 Aggregation of Individual Demands to Get Market Demand

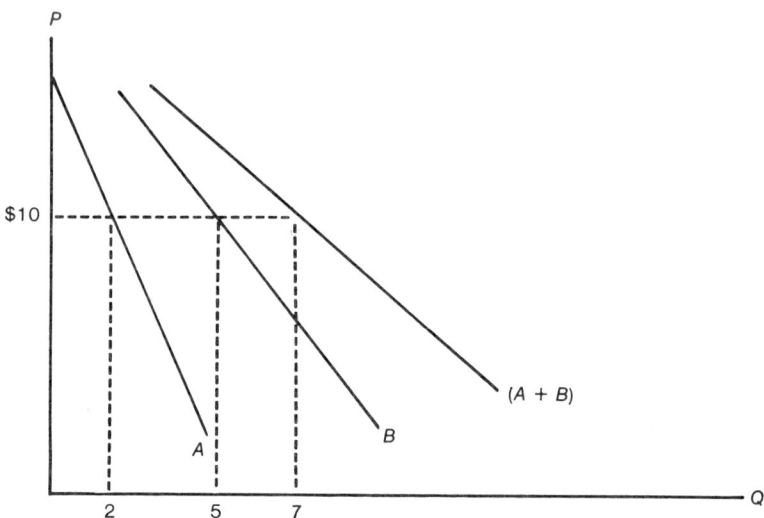

chasing 6 units of medical care at $5 each. This price/quantity relationship is shown at point y in the second quadrant. Similarly, if the price of medical care again drops in half to $2.50, the budget line shifts upward to 1:4 and the individual purchases 8 units of care at point z. Connecting the points described in the second quadrant produces the familiar demand curve where quantity demanded rises as price falls. It differs from the usual demand curve (Chapter 2) only in the sense that it is drawn from right to left and its vertical and horizontal axes are reversed.

Before consideration of the characteristics of this demand curve, one final note is in order. Up to this point the individual has been considered in isolation. However, if the market is to be examined for medical services, large numbers of individuals, each with unique demands, must be considered. While this may present a problem in empirical investigation, the aggregate or market demand is readily conceptualized. Since individual demand is measured in terms of the physical units of Q demanded by the individual at each price, the market demands may be derived simply by summing all individual demands. This process is shown in Figure 4-6, where A and B are individual demand curves and $(A + B)$ is the market demand curve. For example, at a price of $10 individual A will demand two units and individual B will demand five. Therefore, the market demand at $10 is seven units.

CHARACTERISTICS OF DEMAND

The demand curve for medical care exhibits a number of important properties. To understand these properties, it must be kept in mind that the quantity demanded, Q, is determined by the form of each of the three underlying elements: the utility function for health status $U = f(HS, Y - M)$, the perceived medical production function $HS = f(D,M)$, and the income/price constraints summarized in the budget line. If any of these elements change, there will be a corresponding change in demand. This raises interesting possibilities for the administrator and planner. While many of the elements underlying demand are not susceptible to deliberate change, others—including price, medical technology, and the organization of delivery—may be manipulated consciously as a matter of public or private policy. The elasticity concept introduced in Chapter 2 can be used to measure the response to a change in any of these variables.

Elasticity

As noted, medical care is not demanded for its own sake but rather is derived from the demand for health status. Thus, unless there is a negative change in HS (or some potential future drop in HS that can be avoided with preventive services), the individual will be completely unresponsive to any change in the price of medical care. The individual not only must experience a decline in HS but also must perceive that medical intervention, M, will do some good. Because the value of M is highly related to the diagnosis D, it follows that Q will be responsive to P only if the medical service in question will be helpful for the particular diagnosis. For example, if the aggregate price of physician services falls because surgeons reduce their fees for hemorrhoidectomies, this will not increase the demand for M if the individual is suffering from hepatitis. Similarly, if the hemorrhoidectomy is a discrete operation (Figure 4-2) and 10 "units" of medical treatment are necessary for there to be any improvement, a rational individual with D = operable hemorrhoids still will not be responsive to a change in price if the shift is insufficient to elicit a demand for the entire 10 units of treatment.

The responsiveness of quantity demanded to changes in the price of treatment is denoted as the *price elasticity of demand*, and is measured by dividing the percentage change in Q by the percentage change in P:

$$E = \frac{\frac{\Delta Q}{Q}}{\frac{\Delta P}{P}} = \frac{P(\Delta Q)}{Q(\Delta P)}$$

(The symbol Δ is used to represent "change in." That is, if Q_1 is the original quantity and Q_2 is the quantity after the change, then $\Delta Q = Q_2 - Q_1$.) The arc elasticity indicates the percentage changes between two points on the demand curve.[4] In this formulation it is customary to measure quantity and price at their average values (i.e., $Q = (Q_1 + Q_2)/2$ and $P = (P_1 + P_2)/2$), so

$$E = \frac{\frac{Q_2 - Q_1}{(Q_1 + Q_2)/2}}{\frac{P_2 - P_1}{(P_1 + P_2)/2}}$$

If the absolute value of E is greater than one, demand is said to be *elastic*, whereas if the absolute value is less than one, demand is *inelastic*. If the absolute value of E is equal to 1, the demand curve exhibits unitary elasticity. Consider the following example. The physicians in a community raise their fees for routine office visits from $12 to $15 and the observed demand drops from 7,000 to 6,000 visits per month. Is the demand elastic or inelastic? The information is shown in Figure 4-7. In this case the arc elasticity is less than one; hence, demand is inelastic:

$$E = \frac{\frac{12 + 15}{2} (1,000)}{\frac{6,000 + 7,000}{2} (3)} = 0.6923$$

It should be noted that because price and quantity always will change in opposite directions, E should have a negative sign to be technically correct. By convention, this sometimes is ignored and price elasticity of demand is considered to be positive. For many other elasticities, the sign is important, however.

The concept of price elasticity has several applications. First, since the product of price times quantity equals consumer expenditures (and provider revenues), the coefficient of elasticity can demonstrate what effect a change in price will have on expenditures (and revenues) for the commodity in question. If demand is elastic, a rise in price will result in a decrease in total expenditures; conversely, if demand is inelastic, a price rise will produce an increase in expenditures. In the previous example, the rise in physician fees resulted in expenditures of $90,000 ($15 × 6,000 visits) compared to $84,000 under the old price ($12 × 7,000 visits). If the aggregate demand for medical care is inelastic, then any increase in prices that exceeds the average increase for all prices (measured in terms of the

Figure 4-7 Elasticity and Inelasticity of Demand

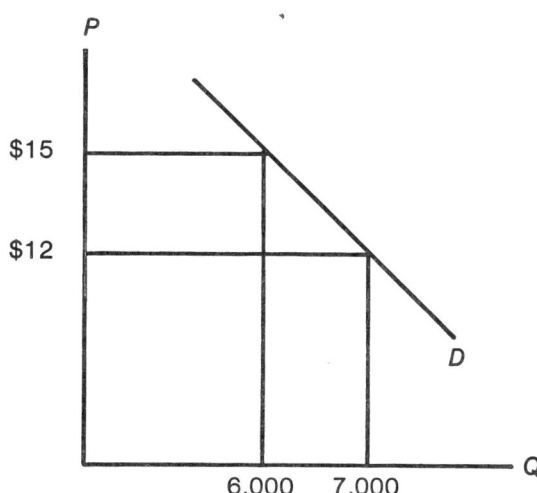

GNP deflator) will result in a higher proportion of the gross national product's going for medical care.

Another application of the elasticity concept relates to the individual's choice of medical treatment. Previous examples have assumed implicitly there is only one preferred technology for any given diagnosis. However, for many diagnoses there are a number of possible technologies. If the prices of the alternative technologies are the same, the individual will choose the treatment, T, that has the greatest expected effect on health status. But if the prices of the possible T's are different, the individual must incorporate price as a decision variable. The choice in this instance is determined by the *cross-elasticity of demand*. Take two possible treatment procedures, T_1 and T_2, that are at least partial substitutes for a given D. The cross-elasticity of T_1 for T_2 is defined as the percentage change in the quantity of T_2 demanded given a change in the price of T_1.

$$E = \frac{\frac{\Delta Q(T_2)}{Q(T_2)}}{\frac{\Delta P(T_1)}{P(T_1)}}$$

The closer T_1 and T_2 are to perfect substitutes, the higher will be the coefficient of cross-elasticity. For example, if T_1 and T_2 are treatments provided by two relatively competent doctors who happen to have offices in the same building, a high cross-elasticity of demand would be expected. But if these same two doctors were separated by 200 miles, the degree of cross-elasticity would be low indeed.

Generally speaking, if there is any positive cross-elasticity of demand, the goods T_1 and T_2 may be considered as substitutes: the higher the positive cross-elasticity of demand, the greater the range of substitutability. If there is a zero cross-elasticity of demand, the two goods are economically unrelated. If there is a negative cross-elasticity of demand, the goods are considered to be economic complements (that is to say, they are only or primarily useful in combination). An example of complementary goods is tires and cars. If the price of new cars increases, the demand for cars falls and the demand for new tires also will tend to drop. In other words, there is a negative cross-elasticity between the price of new cars and the demand for tires.

Demand under Insurance

Price changes for most goods and services can be triggered by various factors: rising production costs, a spurt in demand, or a change in the price of substitute services. One of the special characteristics of the demand for medical care is that it frequently is subsidized by health insurance. Because insurance reduces the out-of-pocket price for medical care at the point of purchase, the introduction or expansion of insurance coverage would be expected to increase demand. The fact that insured individuals demand more medical care than persons who must pay the full price out of pocket sometimes is referred to as *moral hazard*.[5] This has implications for both the insurance business and resource allocation.

Consider, for instance, the case of an insurance company that desires to sell medical coverage for a specific illness or collection of illnesses, D. What premiums should be charged? The company might look first at the past incidence of illness D among those it proposes to insure. Next, it might measure the actual medical expenditures for those who had suffered the illness(es). The product of the incidence times the outlay per case gives an actuarial estimate of the premium required. However, if the estimate of medical outlay is obtained from uninsured individuals, the premium may be set too low. Why? Because the uninsured individuals would have paid the market price for the care they received whereas insured individuals would pay little or nothing at the time of use. Newly insured persons, in other words, pay a lower out-of-pocket price and can be expected to increase their use of service accordingly. Clearly, since price is a factor in the quantity demanded, it must be explicitly incorporated into the rate-setting formula.

Figure 4-8 Demand Curves with Coinsurance

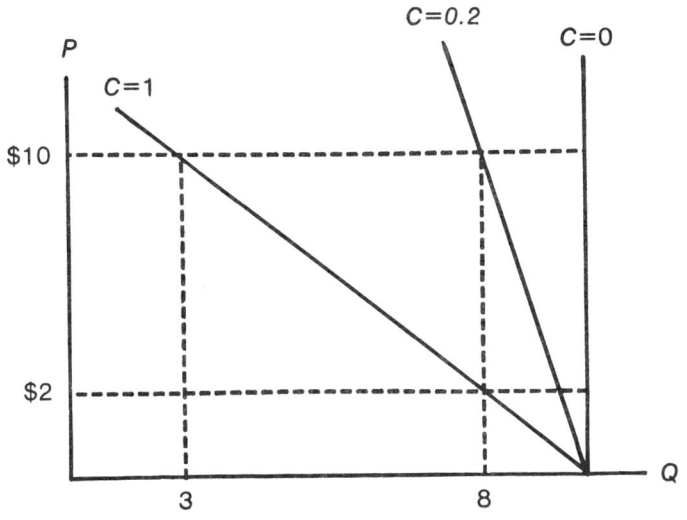

The allocative implications of this behavior can be viewed using the concepts of private and social cost. As seen in Chapter 2, when there are no market imperfections, the value put on the last unit purchased by the consumer (the marginal private benefit) is just equal to the marginal social cost of producing that unit. If insurance reduces the price as seen by the consumer to a level less than the marginal cost of production, more will be demanded than previously. Thus, the tendency is for "too much" medical care to be demanded under conditions of full insurance coverage.

One way that insurance companies combat this problem is through patient cost sharing. The typical policy requires that patients pay a portion of the cost of insured services in the form of deductibles, copayments, and/or coinsurance. Moreover, every insurance policy contains exclusions (services for which the patient must bear the entire expense) and most include maximum liability limits. In other words, the insured patient may face a bewildering array of prices that vary according to the amount and type of service.

To see how these forms of patient cost sharing affect demand, consider first the case of coinsurance. The coinsurance rate, C, determines the percentage of the total bill for which the patient is responsible. The percentage may vary between $C = 0$ (full coverage) and $C = 1$ (no coverage) as shown by the demand curves in Figure 4-8.

Take a typical comprehensive medical insurance policy that pays 80 percent of the cost of ambulatory care visits. A visit with a bill for $10 actually costs the patient only $2 (after the insurance is paid for). If the uninsured demand, $C = 1$, exhibits some degree of price elasticity, such an insurance policy must raise the demand for visits (in this case from 3 to 8). As the coinsurance rate falls, the elasticity of demand (measured against the true price of $10 per visit) declines. At a zero coinsurance rate, the patient is completely unresponsive to any change in billed price, and demand then is said to be perfectly inelastic. This is an important point to keep in mind. There frequently are statements that the demand for medical care is inelastic. Under full insurance coverage it is—by definition. This should not be taken to mean that uninsured or partially insured individuals are unresponsive to the price of care.

Deductibles and *copayments* represent other common forms of patient cost sharing. Both limit coverage to expenditures beyond a given dollar amount. The difference is that copayments are service-specific (e.g., $1 per prescription or $5 per physician visit) while deductibles count toward the purchase of any covered service. Suppose the policy contains a $100 deductible and no coinsurance. This means in effect that the patient is uninsured for the first $100 of expenditure for covered services and completely covered thereafter. Limits on maximum liability may be interpreted in an analogous fashion. Once the maximum is reached, the individual must pay the full freight.

The impact on demand of deductibles, copayments, and benefit maximums are somewhat difficult to model because of anticipation effects. An individual who expects to use $1,000 of medical treatments obviously will react differently to a $100 deductible than one who anticipates spending only $150. In the first instance, the insurance would cover 90 percent of the total, in the second just 33 percent. The effect of different anticipation rates is shown in Figure 4-9.

Assume that the individual has an insurance policy with a $100 deductible. The deductible can be met by various combinations of price and quantity (in the case shown by 10 visits at $10 per visit). If the individual anticipates that total expenditures during the policy period will be less than or equal to the deductible, the demand for the first $100 of service will be D_1. After this point is reached, demand will shift to D_2, assuming there is no coinsurance, or to D_3 if the coinsurance rate is 20 percent. However, if the insured individual anticipates expenditures greater than $100, the deterrent value of the deductible is lessened and the initial demand may be greater and more inelastic than D_1.

Anticipation effects also are a factor in the demand for medical care when the insurance carries benefit limitations. Most policies contain two types of limits: those applicable to a given service (e.g., 50 days of inpatient psychiatric treatment) and those applicable to total reimbursable expend-

Figure 4-9 The Effect of Anticipation Rates

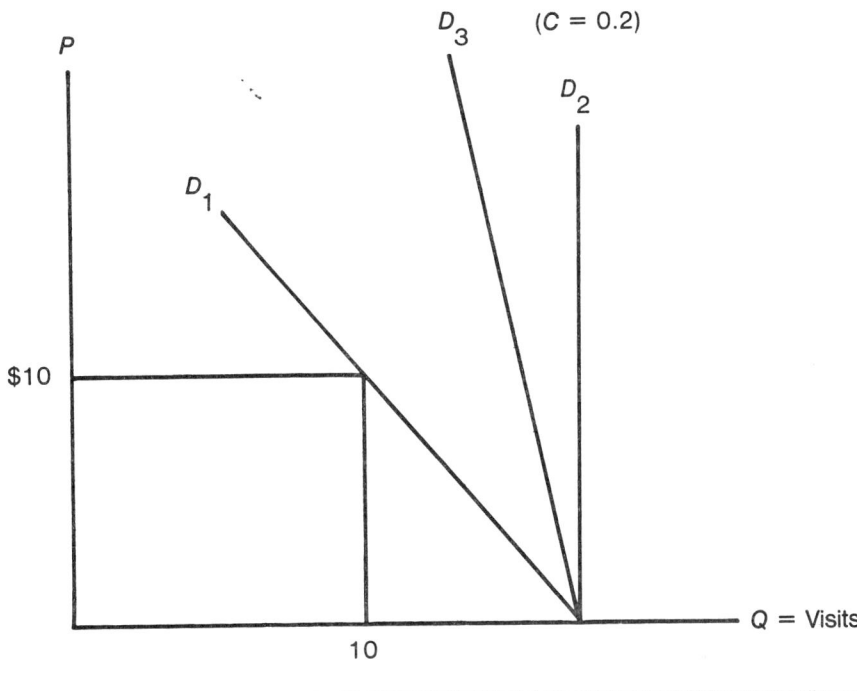

itures (e.g., a $10,000 maximum liability). The average policyholder will be affected by neither limit. But those who anticipate the possibility of exceeding a particular limit may cut back (i.e., demand becomes more elastic) as the limit is approached in order to conserve the remaining coverage.

Demand for Health Insurance: A Brief Digression

The preceding section dealt with the effects of health insurance on the demand for health care. A related question is: What determines the demand for health insurance? There is considerable literature on this topic, but the analysis is not fully developed here.[6] Rather, this section attempts merely to point out the major analytical concepts.

The demand for health insurance, as for any good, is related to price, income, and all the other variables typically included in demand functions. Demand for insurance, however, raises an additional issue: behavior toward risk. Insurance is a way of "buying out" of a risky situation. A simple example illustrates the point. Suppose a certain disease costs $1,000 to cure and on the average one in ten individuals will contract it. Any given person thus faces a 1/10 chance of incurring a $1,000 loss and a 9/10 chance of incurring no loss. The actuarial "expected loss" here is $100:

$$\text{Expected loss} = 1/10 \times \$1,000 + 9/10 \times \$0 = \$100$$

This expected loss represents two things. First, it is the maximum amount a risk-neutral person would be willing to pay for an insurance policy covering the cost of treatment for the disease. That is, such a person would be indifferent between the risky situation (with expected loss of $100) and the insurance policy (with certain loss of the $100 premium but no risk of financial loss from the disease). Second, the $100 is the premium an insurance company would have to charge to just break even, assuming there were no costs connected with writing and selling the policy, general administration, claims processing, profit, and any other aspect of running the insurance business. That is, for a large group, a premium of $100 per person would yield just enough revenue to cover claims.

Of course, since insurance companies do incur costs, the premium must be greater than $100. Furthermore, most people are willing to pay more than $100. That willingness in this case is evidence of *risk-averse* behavior. To buy out of the risky situation, the risk averter is willing to pay more than the actuarially fair price for the insurance. The disutility such a person suffers from a certain loss of, say, $150 may be equivalent to the disutility in a risky situation with an expected loss of $100. The fact that this type of attitude toward risk is relatively common accounts in part for the existence of the insurance industry.

Looking at the purchase of insurance in this framework suggests additional variables that must be incorporated in the demand analysis. One the degree of risk aversion among potential insurance purchasers. At an given price, a person who is strongly risk-averse is more likely to bu insurance than one whose attitude is closer to risk-neutral. Other factor; are the size of the potential loss and the probability of its occurrence. People tend to be more willing to pay for insurance against big losses than small ones because of the potentially disasterous economic consequences associated with major hazards. Willingness to pay for insurance also depends on the probability the loss will occur. If the loss is very probable, i.e., almost certain to occur, the actuarially fair premium will be so close to the size of the loss itself that most individuals will not be willing to buy the insurance. When the probability of loss is very small, they will be unwilling to pay very much for insurance. It is in the middle range of probabilities that demand will be highest.

These statements rest on two crucial assumptions. The first is that individuals are expert at calculating probabilities of loss. Mark Pauly argues that people tend to ignore major hazards with a low probability of occurrence (underinsure against catastrophic loss) while at the same time they overestimate the losses associated with highly probable events (overinsure against small losses.)[7] The second critical assumption is that individuals pay the full premium price for whatever insurance they maintain. In fact, private health insurance in the United States is heavily subsidized by the federal government and private business. Most large employers provide health insurance fringe benefits at little or no additional cost to their employees (except that aggregate wages are lower as a result). The Internal Revenue Service does not tax fringe benefits as ordinary income so, in effect, employees receive the policies tax free. Moreover, individual purchases of health insurance are tax deductible. The upshot of these factors is that the demand for health insurance of all types is greater than would be expected in an unsubsidized market.

Hypothetical Applications of Demand Analysis

As noted in earlier sections, elasticity measures may be used to examine the responsiveness of demand to changes in variables other than price. The principle is the same whether the variable is income, education, age, access, or any other influence on demand. In each case, elasticity is measured under ceteris paribus conditions; that is, holding constant all factors other than the variable in question. This requirement poses some thorny problems for empirical research that are dealt with in the following section. At this point it is appropriate to consider the circumstances under which an administrator or planner might apply demand analysis and elasticity measures.

Take the case of a hospital with a large, predominantly rural service area. The board of trustees is considering the establishment of satellite clinics to better meet the ambulatory service needs of the population. The question is whether there is sufficient demand to warrant the move. There really are two issues here.

First, if private physicians already are practicing in the potential satellite areas, there will be some competition for available patients. Do the proposed clinics have features (service offering, setting, price, and so forth) that might induce people to shift their primary source of care? Market surveys can be designed to provide initial answers. For example, the survey can ask residents to list first the services they receive from area physicians and then compare these with the services offerings proposed for the clinic.

Would the resident choose the clinic if the proposed services were in fact available? A more sophisticated approach is to list progressively more comprehensive service offerings on questionnaires given to selected subsamples of area residents. The results then can be formulated to estimate the elasticity of demand with respect to service availability. Similar techniques can generate estimates of elasticity for other relevant variables. In each case, the estimated responsiveness of (potential) demand can provide valuable information for the planning process.

The example can be taken a step further to the second issue. Presumably, the main reason for developing satellite clinics is to satisfy previously unmet demands rather than simply to pirate business away from other providers. Hospital administrators and institutional planners familiar with the work of Acton[8] know that a prime determinant of demand is the time it takes individuals to obtain services. As necessary travel time decreases, demand tends to increase. In the present case, the "time cost" elasticity of demand (that is, the percentage change in quantity demanded divided by the percentage changes in distance traveled) may be a crucial factor both in estimating potential use and in site selection. Once again, market surveys can be designed to provide the necessary information.

A second example of the use of demand analysis and elasticity measures involves the case of a financially strapped neighborhood health center operating in a section of the city undergoing significant demographic change. The center has experienced declining utilization for several years and the director is forced to seek grant support to keep the operation afloat. As part of the grant request, the director must provide a forecast of future utilization patterns. What information is necessary to make such a forecast?

This is a complex problem because there may be several interrelated reasons for the changing demand at the center. Obviously one possibility is that internal administrative factors are responsible—misscheduling, inappropriate hours of operation, or lack of bilingual staff. If these factors can be discounted, the director then must look to the underlying demand characteristics of the service area population. A review of medical records and encounter forms may indicate the type of change occurring in the service area. Census data also can help. But the director needs more than demographic information and must be able to relate these data to actual and projected utilization patterns.

Demand theory and existing empirical research suggest several hypotheses. For example, utilization tends to be positively related to age and income. If the average age of the service area population is becoming younger over time, this might explain part of the decline. In this case, the relevant measure is the age elasticity of demand (the percentage change in demand divided by the percentage change in average age). Likewise, if the population is becoming poorer (other things being equal), the appropriate measure is the *income-elasticity of demand* (the percentage change in demand divided by the percentage change in average income). If both types of change are occurring simultaneously, the director will need to use multiple regression analysis to determine the relative importance of each factor.

These two examples demonstrate the type of situation in which demand analysis can be used. Readers are encouraged to construct their own examples but they should be forewarned that the actual applications frequently raise serious conceptual and technical roadblocks. The excerpts in the next section illustrate what is meant.

EMPIRICAL STUDIES OF DEMAND

As can be seen from the supplementary reading list at the end of this chapter, there has been considerable empirical research into the economic determinants of demand in the last 15 years. Some of the studies are national in scope and are designed to provide insights into federal health policy issues, particularly the demand implications for national health insurance. Others are regional or local in nature. The results of these latter studies cannot be generalized but they demonstrate the type of demand estimation techniques that administrators and planners can apply in their own regions.

Virtually all of the retrospective demand studies (at least the respectable ones) use some form of multivariate technique, such as multiple regression analysis. It will be recalled from Chapter 3 that multiple regression analysis allows the significance of each variable in the equation to be estimated by holding all other variables constant. If the administrator wants to measure the responsiveness of demand to changes in price (or some other single variable), it obviously is essential that the results not be confounded by other changes in the system. For this reason, econometric demand models typically contain a number of noneconomic variables (such as age, sex, race, education, level of sickness, and the like) as controls.

It would be impossible here to provide a complete picture of the results of empirical demand studies or the techniques for doing such research. Instead, as illustrations of such work, excerpts are presented from two studies that focus on the same question: What is the relationship between coinsurance and demand for physician visits? Both studies use regression analysis. One uses data on a national sample of individuals who, of course, differ with respect to demand, insurance coverage, and other characteristics at a given point in time. This is an example of a *cross-sectional* approach. The second study uses data on one group of individuals at two different points in time, before and after a change in insurance coverage. This is an example of a *longitudinal* approach, or *time series*.

The first study, by Charles Phelps, is based on data from a 1971 national survey of health services utilization conducted by the Center for Health Administration Studies (CHAS) and the National Opinion Research Center (NORC) of the University of Chicago. A total of 11,822 individuals from all parts of the country were interviewed. The responses covered utilization and cost data (verified from hospitals, physicians, and insurance companies), plus a wealth of information on health characteristics, economic circumstances, and demographic variables. To calculate his elasticity measures, Phelps computes an implicit coinsurance rate that reflects the portion of expenditures for hospital care, surgical procedures, and physicians' office visits paid out-of-pocket.

In reviewing this selection, the reader should keep several factors in mind:

- The coefficients of elasticity do not reflect individual responses to actual changes in the variable in question (coinsurance rates, income, disability, education, etc.), but rather represent a composite of reactions by individuals in different circumstances. Would the results differ if, for example, the same individuals, over time, were faced with a change in health insurance coverage? (The selection following the Phelps study considers such a case.)

- The coinsurance variable calculated by Phelps is not coinsurance in the same sense as defined in the previous section but is an amalgam of coinsurance, deductibles, copayments, exclusions, and other forms of patient cost-sharing.

- The data were obtained from a sample survey. This is not the place for a detailed discussion of sampling bias and error, but the reader should recall from Chapter 3 that sample estimates may diverge from true population values.

- The demand functions estimated by Phelps explain a rather small proportion of the total variability in demand (the R^2's range from .115 to .256). Such low R^2's are typical of much econometric research.

Even though the t-ratios and F statistics may show statistical significance, there clearly are other factors and relationships affecting demand that are not captured by the estimating technique. The existence of these other factors means that the analyst never can be certain that the policy implications derived from the research will hold up in practice.

Following is the first excerpt from the Phelps study:

DOCTOR OFFICE VISITS[c]

Doctor office visits are less frequently covered by private insurance than are hospital services, but in 1970 there were still sufficient numbers of persons with insurance coverage to allow estimation of demand curves for MD office services. A major complication in these estimates was the presence of persons with special coverage for some services, but not for others. Major categories include persons receiving employment physicals; chest X-rays; services through school, industrial or armed forces clinics; and persons on welfare or Medicaid. For persons on Medicaid, the problem is that eligibility is uncertain, and demand does not follow usual patterns because of administrative "rationing." Inclusion of these persons in the sample obscures true relationships between coinsurance and utilization. Similarly, persons receiving care in special circumstances cannot have a coinsurance rate calculated accurately. For example, if the person has no insurance, but obtained a single physician visit as a pre-employment physical, the coinsurance (using the methods of calculation adopted for this paper) would be zero and demand would be one visit. To attribute the one visit to a zero coinsurance rate clearly does not represent the person's true situation. If the person has some mixed combination of free "unusual" visits and nonfree "normal" visits, it is even more difficult to infer what has really happened. Hence, all such persons are deleted from the sample before analysis.

The equations were estimated with 3,596 persons who had between one and 30 physician visits, under 100 disability days, incomes under $75,000, and did not receive Medicaid or have any "special conditions" physician visits. The results are shown in Table 4-2. The estimated effect of insurance on demand is large—demand for visits is over twice as high at full insurance as with no insurance. Health status variables accounted for a large amount of the explained variance; those with worse self-perceived health status and those with more frequent pain used noticeably more services. Disability days similarly increased demand for care. These variables show the importance of standardizing for health levels when estimating demand for care. Other control variables

Table 4-2 Physician Office Visit Demand Curve

	Visits		Expense	
Variable	Coefficient (t ratio)	Elasticity	Coefficient (t ratio)	Elasticity
Coinsurance	−0.0561 (9.25)	−1.38 at $\bar{C}$ −0.18 at C = 25%	−0.6426 (7.86)	−1.61 at $\bar{C}$ 0.19 at C = 25%
Income	−0.1079 E−04 (1.20)	−0.03	0.351 E−03 (2.91)	0.11
Appointment delay	−0.0771 (2.20)	−0.04	1.000 (2.12)	0.05
Travel time × wage	0.00175 (1.33)	0.02	0.0550 (3.11)	0.07
Wait time × wage	0.00107 (1.87)	0.03	−0.0021 (0.27)	—
Disability days	0.0699 (12.93)	0.12	0.4940 (6.78)	0.09
Good health	0.5748 (3.71)		2.533 (1.21)	
Fair health	1.9524 (8.67)		14.230 (4.69)	
Poor health	2.76 (6.16)		25.308 (4.20)	
Deceased	−0.1870 (0.14)		−12.623 (0.70)	
Pain very often	1.637 (4.78)		16.244 (3.52)	
Pain fairly often	1.499 (5.46)		8.691 (2.35)	
Pain occasionally	0.3807 (2.51)		7.571 (3.71)	
Welfare care (1 = yes)	−0.4733 (0.52)		−5.550 (0.46)	
Education	0.0477 (0.77)	0.05	3.847 (4.59)	0.38
Age	0.0167 (3.47)	0.13	0.3613 (5.59)	0.29
Sex (1 = female)	−0.0813 (0.58)		0.8376 (0.44)	
Race (1 = nonwhite)	−0.4307 (1.64)		1.0439 (0.29)	
Constant term	7.0194 (9.14)		44.305 (4.28)	
R^2 (Adjusted)	0.1946 (0.1904)		0.1070 (0.1022)	
F (d.f.) (significance)	45.485 (19, 3576) ($P < .00001$)		22,545 (19, 3576) ($P < .00001$)	
Std. error of Y:X	3.924 visits		$52.85	

were also important: age showed a positive association with use, and demand was about one-half visit lower for nonwhites than whites holding constant other factors. Family income had a slight negative effect (significant at the 0.22 level only) on demand, similar to the effect of income on hospital days. Demand was significantly lower for those persons facing higher waiting times to appointments, but travel and office waiting times showed a positive association with demand, contrary to the expectation that those variables would act as a price, reducing demand for care as they rose.

Expenditures for physician services is even more responsive to coinsurance than is use of physician services, which can only happen if better insurance leads persons to choose not only more services per person, but to use more expensive providers when they do use services. Expense is estimated to be three times higher at full coverage than with no coverage (compared with the doubling of demand between those two coverage levels). The third column of Table 4-2 shows equations predicting expense for physician visits at various coinsurance levels.

These equations were also estimated with various interactions between insurance coverage and income, health status, and at different coinsurance levels. The results were uniformly that the interactions were not significant in the demand equations, and these equations are not presented [10].

Phelps next summarizes the demand equation by showing the predicted value of demand at various coinsurance levels, assuming all other variables in the equation have a value equal to the sample average. These results are shown by his Table 4-3 and by his discussion of policy implications:

Table 4-3 Physician Office Visits and Expense: Fitted Values from Regression Equations

Coinsurance	Number of visits	Expense	Implied price per visit (Col. 2 ÷ Col. 1)
C = 0	9.07	$97.38	$10.74
C = 0.2	7.95	84.53	10.63
C = 0.5	6.27	65.25	10.41
C = 1.0	3.46	33.13	9.51
Level in 1970	4.00	39.23	9.81

Implications for Policy

Several questions can be posed about the effects of insurance on the health care system and upon the American people that can be tentatively answered from these analyses. First, what will happen to the distribution of services? Universal insurance could markedly improve the access of some persons to the health care system and the demand estimates show that lower coinsurance will increase demand extensively for medical services. Whether universal insurance would increase demand for any group of people depends as well on current levels of insurance and financing. For persons with relatively complete health insurance coverage, universal insurance would change little. For persons without private insurance, one must ask how universal insurance would change things relative to the effects of Medicaid and other free or reduced care public programs. As an example, consider demand for physician office visits by various income groups. Table 4-4 tabulates 1970 coverage for such care by income. There is a considerable discrepancy in private coverage across income groups (particularly for persons not in the labor force). This occurs because most private insurance held in 1970 was obtained through employer work groups, which provide insurance much cheaper than individual insurance contracts. But many of the people without private coverage have some governmental program covering their medical expenses. Persons over 65 had coverage under Medicare in 1970 and this category has since been broadened to include those individuals receiving Social Security disability payments. The 1970 CHAS-NORC Survey can give some indication of how many additional people are covered by Medicaid and similar programs by simply looking at the number of people who had doctor visits and received Medicaid. This understates the actual extent of Medicaid "coverage" in 1970, because some eligible persons will not have become sick, and hence will not have applied for or received any Medicaid payments. Yet as shown in Table 4-4, when persons receiving Medicaid or welfare medical payments are included, the apparent disparity in coverage is shifted. Including Medicare and Medicaid, the group with lowest coverage is that just above common Medicaid limits—the "near poor." Since the demand estimates were tested for interactions between income and coverage (none were found), the evidence suggests that the differences in demand between insured and uninsured

Table 4-4 Families with Doctor Office Coverage

Income (% of sample)	Group	Non-group	Private (subtotal)	Medicare	Medicaid	Public (subtotal)	Total
Under $3,000 (18.5%)	0.05	0.03	0.08	0.39	0.10	0.49	0.57
$3,000–4,999 (12.3%)	0.17	0.02	0.19	0.23	0.06	0.29	0.48
$5,000–6,999 (12.4%)	0.24	0.03	0.27	0.11	0.02	0.13	0.40
$7,000–9,999 (18.2%)	0.35	0.02	0.37	0.04	0.01	0.05	0.42
$10,000–14,999 (21.8%)	0.42	0.01	0.43	0.01	—	0.01	0.44
$15,000+ (16.9%)	0.41	0.03	0.44	0.03	—	0.03	0.47
All incomes (100%)	0.28	0.02	0.31	0.13	0.03	0.16	0.47

persons should hold for lower income persons as well as others. Thus, under universal insurance, the largest gains in physician use would come from the "near poor" group, chiefly under age 65.

A different question also arises. If the coverage of a large number of persons is shifted through universal insurance and demand therefore increases, could that demand be met by the delivery system? For hospital care, this does not appear to be much of a problem, since coverage is quite extensive for the entire population as Table 4-5 shows, either through Medicare and Medicaid or private insurance. Universal insurance, even without any coinsurance provisions, would therefore not be likely to increase demands beyond a point where the current delivery system could match the demands.

For physician office visits, the picture appears quite different. First, consider the composition of coverage of those with insurance for physician office visits. Analysis of verified insurance policies from this study shows that most private coverage for MD office visits is through major medical insurance rather than "basic" coverage. Most major medical plans, of course, contain some deductible provision which must be met before payment begins. For persons with minor illnesses, the deductible will typically not be met by expenses for one or two physician office visits and these persons are to some extent better described as having no insurance for such visits. For more serious illnesses, particu-

Table 4-5 Families with Health Coverage

Income (% of sample)	Group	Non-group	Private (subtotal)	Medicare	Medicaid	Public (subtotal)	Total
Under $3,000 (18.5%)	0.13	0.08	0.21	0.47	0.12	0.59	0.80
$3,000–4,999 (12.3%)	0.39	0.12	0.51	0.23	0.08	0.31	0.82
$5,000–6,999 (12.4%)	0.55	0.10	0.65	0.10	0.02	0.12	0.77
$7,000–9,999 (18.2%)	0.77	0.09	0.86	0.02	0.02	0.04	0.90
$10,000–14,999 (21.8%)	0.87	0.05	0.93	0.01	—	0.01	0.93
$15,000+ (16.9%)	0.81	0.12	0.93	0.02	—	0.02	0.95
All incomes (100%)	0.61	0.09	0.70	0.14	0.04	0.18	0.88

larly those involving hospitalization or repeated visits to the doctor, the patient can plan on the deductible being met, and would be likely to immediately act as if the insurance were paying for services.

Thus the question about the delivery system's ability to meet demands generated by universal insurance will largely depend upon the characteristics of the plan. If a deductible is present of a size similar to those in current major medical insurance plans (or under Medicare), demand will be increased some but not nearly to the extent that would occur under a plan with no deductible. If there are large overall shifts in demand (defined, again, as the number of people trying to see a doctor), it is likely that the current delivery system would not be able to absorb the increase. Nonprice rationing devices would automatically enter to reduce demand until it equaled observed utilization. For example, Canadian experience suggests that delays for appointments doubled when universal insurance was introduced in Canada. A similar experience resulted in Sweden when copayments for doctor visits were removed.

The demand estimates from the 1970 survey (see Table 4-2) show how increased waiting time between appointments and visits (appointment delay) reduces demand for care, holding constant other factors. Appointment time varied for the sample from zero days (about one-third of the sample) to over one month (coded 7 in the data). The estimates show that demand differences between those two levels of delay are over one-half of one visit (on average) per person per year, or greater than a 15 percent reduction from average demand in 1970 [13]. Thus, one way a medical system can equilibrate if there is a large demand increase is by delays in setting up appointments which ration available care.

The estimates presented in this chapter support the contention that increased insurance coverage could lead to increases in demand for medical services over a broad range of services. The estimated demand for physician office visits more than doubles under full coverage insurance relative to no insurance (see Table 4-3).

The increases in use that would actually occur depend heavily on the current distribution of insurance (public and private) in the country. Counting Medicare and Medicaid, it appears that the largest gains in coverage from a universal health insurance program would be for the low income group in terms of hospital insurance and for the near poor in terms of physician ambulatory care. Thus these groups would benefit most from introduction of universal insurance even if the universal plan made no special provisions for low income persons.

The Phelps article demonstrates how demand analysis can be used (with appropriate caution) to help formulate national policy. The next selection by Phelps, with Joseph Newhouse, analyzes a similar problem—the responsiveness of demand to coinsurance—but from a very different perspective. The data base in this case represents utilization information collected on a cohort of individuals enrolled in Group Health Plan (GHP) of Palo Alto, Calif., between 1966 and 1968. The study takes advantage of a "natural" experiment. Prior to 1967, the plan provided full ambulatory coverage with no patient cost sharing. But beginning in April of that year, GHP imposed a uniform 25 percent coinsurance on all services. The study uses data from GHP charge tags (billing forms) to analyze the difference in utilization rates among members for the years before and after the imposition of coinsurance. (The references to Scitovsky and Snyder in this excerpt refer to a preceding article in the *Social Security Bulletin* in which the same data were analyzed descriptively. That article is cited in the Suggested Readings at the end of this chapter.)

EFFECT OF COINSURANCE: A MULTIVARIATE ANALYSIS[d]

Methodology

This study considers the impact of coinsurance upon four variables only—physician visits, physician expense, ancillary services, and ancillary services expense. For each person in the study, the following data were also available: age, relation to the subscriber, sex, distance from the Palo Alto Medical Clinic, occupation group (at Stanford University), and family size.

Multiple regression methods were used to analyze these data. This technique permits the estimation of equations such as:

Physician visits = a_1 age of individual in years
+ a_2 distance from GHP clinic in miles
+ a_3 family size.

The a's in this equation are constants to be estimated from the data. They show the effect of changing one variable while holding the others constant. Thus, an individual who is 1 year older is hypothesized to make a_1 additional visits.

In this article the explanatory variables have not been entered in continuous form as in the above example. Rather, variables are broken into intervals or groups. Occupation is divided into faculty, other professional, and nonprofessional staff. Sex and subscriber variables are divided into five groups—male and female subscribers, male and female dependents, and children. Distance for dependents is divided into 5-mile segments, 0–5, 6–10, 11–15, 16–20, and greater than 20 miles; all subscribers are assumed to be in the 0–5 mile category. Age is divided into 0–4 years, 5–14, 15–18, 19–24, 25–44, 45–54, and 55 and over. When the individual being considered belonged to the category, the variable for that category took the value 1; otherwise it was zero. The advantage of this approach is that one does not have to assume, as in the above example, that each year or mile (or whatever) adds the same number of visits. The mean number of visits in each interval can be estimated by holding the other factors constant. (The family size variable is entered in continuous form.) For example, with other things equal, the mean number of visits among those aged 19–24 may be five, among those aged 25–44 it may be three, and among those aged 45–54 it may be four. No relationship among the age groups is assumed.

Initially, data for two years—1966 and 1968—were pooled, creating 5,134 effective observations. The explanatory variables listed above are virtually identical for each person in both years, except that age has increased by 2 years. These explanatory variables thus can only explain the level of visits by an individual, not any change between 1966 and 1968. In order to do that, a variable with the value 1 for all observations in the year 1968 and zero for all observations in 1966 was established. In 1968, of course, a coinsurance rate of 25 percent was in effect (that is, in 1968 patients paid 25 percent of the Clinic's normal fees but paid no money fees in 1966). The coefficient of this variable may be interpreted as the effect of a 25-percent coinsurance rate on the demand for medical care. Since virtually all other variables have been held constant, it is reasonable to expect that the only changes observed in demand were due to the introduction of coinsurance. By specifying the impact of coinsurance in such a way it is assumed that coinsurance led to an equal decline in visits or expense in each class. Evidence is presented below that this hypothesis cannot be rejected.

The technique of regression analysis leads to an estimate of the demand for physician visits and ancillary services and the changes in expenses for these services for a reference group. The reference group used for the following analyses was composed of persons in a family of four where the employed member was classified as nonprofessional staff and was a male subscriber aged 25–44. The estimated differences in levels of usage and expenses for groups of persons with different characteristics can also be calculated.

A word of caution is added here regarding these results. The decision to participate in the GHP could be made (or changed) by the family at any time. As a result, there may be some self-selection of persons in the plan in 1968 that would bias the results. About 300 of the original 2,870 members (10.6 percent) cancelled during the first year coinsurance was in effect; their overall use in 1966 was virtually identical to those who stayed in GHP. Therefore, it can be assumed that self-selection presents only a limited problem.

Demand for Physician Services

The basic finding of this article is the same as that of the Scitovsky-Snyder study: Coinsurance significantly reduces demand for medical care in this population, other things remaining the same. . . .

Table 4-6 Physician Visits and Expense and Change from Reference Group, by Selected Characteristics, 1966

Characteristic	Physician visits			Physician expense		
		Change from reference group			Change from reference group	
	Number	Number	Percent	Amount	Amount	Percent
Nonprofessional male subscriber, age 25–44, family of 4 (reference group)	¹²4.27			¹$66.81		
Not male subscriber, but—						
Female subscriber	5.14	³0.87	20.4	73.79	$6.98	10.4
Male dependent, adult	5.46	1.19	27.9	78.15	11.34	17.0
Female dependent, adult	6.80	¹2.53	59.3	108.83	¹41.02	61.4
Child	1.86	−2.41	−56.4	38.67	−28.14	−42.1
Not aged 25–44, but age—						
0–4	9.04	¹4.77	111.7	95.18	28.37	42.5
5–14	7.13	³2.86	67.0	83.13	16.32	24.4
15–18	7.25	³2.98	69.8	90.88	24.07	36.0
19–24	5.66	1.39	32.6	68.17	1.36	2.0
45–54	5.07	¹.80	18.7	80.58	¹13.77	20.6
55 and over	6.27	¹2.00	46.8	89.97	¹23.16	34.7
Not 0–5 miles, but—						
6–10	3.91	−.36	−8.4	56.29	³−10.52	−15.7
11–15	4.26	.01	−0.2	66.04	−0.77	−1.2
16–20	3.48	−.79	−18.5	57.34	−9.47	−14.2
21 and over	2.76	³−1.51	−35.4	48.09	³−18.72	−28.0
Employee in family not nonprofessional, but—						
Faculty	4.63	.36	−8.4	69.79	2.98	−4.5
Other professional	4.43	.16	−3.7	68.75	1.94	−2.9

¹ Significantly different from zero at 1 percent.
² Significantly different from zero at 5 percent.
³ Significantly different from zero at 10 percent.
⁴ Dependents only.

After the introduction of coinsurance all groups experienced declines of 1.37 in the average number of visits and $18.66 in average expense. The probability is .00005 that decreases this large would have been observed if coinsurance in fact had no effect.

The results of the analysis for predicting usage among groups are shown in Table 4-6 for physician visits and expense. Persons in the reference group averaged 4.27 visits in 1966. On the average, the number of visits in 1968 for each person in this group declined to 2.90 visits, or 32 percent; physician expense decreased from $66.81 in 1966 to $48.15 in 1968, or 28 percent.

Other demographic groups had somewhat different levels of usage. Table 4-6 also shows visits and expenses for groups of persons with different characteristics than the reference group. For example, if a person was a female dependent of a faculty member, aged 25–44, living 0–5 miles from the Clinic, and in a family of four, the mean difference from the reference group in the number of visits would be 2.53 (the difference for female dependents) plus 0.36 (the difference associated with faculty families), or a total difference of 2.89. The percentage change differs slightly across groups. The absolute decline is the same in each group, but each group had a different number of visits in 1966. The percentage reduction is slightly lower for faculty and other professional staff, higher for subscribers than for their dependents, and higher for dependents living further from the Clinic.

These results essentially corroborate the previous article's tables from the same data—that is, faculty members have higher utilization rates than other professional staff, who have higher rates than nonprofessional staff. Usage declines with distance from the source of care and follows a U-shaped pattern with respect to age. The U-shaped appearance is somewhat deceptive. Since all those under age 18 are considered children, the difference attributable to children should be added to those under age 18. Taking this into account produces a considerably less regular U shape. Even when all of these systematic patterns of demand for physician services are noted, the introduction of coinsurance is shown to have had a highly significant effect in reducing demand for physician services. Our analysis differs from that of the Scitovsky-Snyder study in that it holds all other variables constant while changing one variable—that is, it looks at the partial effect of each variable.

It has been suggested that the effects of coinsurance may be asymmetric. Behavior of persons when coinsurance goes from 0 to 0.25 may be different than behavior when coinsurance goes from 0.25 to 0. This result is not suggested by standard economic theory, but numerous institutional constraints may cause such a result. The question is clearly empirical and could be tested if a similar set of data could be found where a coinsurance provision had been removed, rather than instituted.

Expenditures for Physician Services

The physician expense column of Table 4-6 shows that spending for these services also decreased with the introduction of coinsurance but to a lesser degree than the number of physician visits (28 percent, compared with 32 percent for the reference group). A "visit" can imply a simple examination by a general practitioner or a complex specialized workup by a board-certified specialist. Thus, a simple-visit variable may be a somewhat ambiguous measure of the quantity of physician services demanded. Since expenses were not reduced by as large a percentage as visits with the introduction of coinsurance, one might infer that relatively inexpensive procedures had been reduced proportionately more than expensive procedures. The differences between "use" and "expense" do not, however, appear to be statistically significant at normal levels of hypothesis testing.[1]

Time Costs in the Demand for Services

In the demand equations, it is striking how much the usage by female dependents differs from that by the reference group. Female subscribers (who are in the labor force) used slightly more services than male subscribers (0.87 more visits per year, significant at 0.03 probability), but female *dependents* (many of whom, presumably, are not in the labor force) used, on the average, 2.53 more visits per year than male subscribers and 1.66 more visits per year than female *subscribers* (1.66 = 2.53 − 0.87). The null hypothesis of no difference between the utilization rates of female dependents and female subscribers can be rejected at a 0.001 level of probability. On the assumption that time cost is higher on the average for female subscribers than for female dependents, these data give striking evidence on how much time costs influence the demand for medical services. It has been suggested that the differences between the utilization rates of men and women may have been pregnancy-related. That hypothesis was tested in another regression by including a dummy variable for female dependents aged 45 and over (who should be past childbearing age). If the female dependents' dummy showed pregnancy effects, then the subgroup aged 45 and over should show lower use. The actual coefficient was -0.38 visits ($t = .78$), an insignificant difference. Another inference from this result is that the major differences between the use of physician services by men and women are probably not due to biological differences—a common justification—but to differences in the cost of time.

With this interpretation, a question can be raised concerning the relationship between sick-leave provisions and time costs for subscribers. Faculty and other professional subscribers hold jobs that require a certain amount of output rather than a certain amount of time, and, in fact, subscribers in these groups are generally not covered by sick-leave provisions. Thus, their visits would tend to come from time not devoted to market work, and time costs could be expected to be higher than they are for nonprofessional staff, where sick-leave provisions are more frequent. Moreover, sick-leave provisions only apply to employees paid hourly. Only 16 percent of the total number of employees work at an hourly rate (virtually all of whom are nonprofessional staff), and of these an undetermined number work less than half time and so would not be eligible for the health plan. Thus sick-leave provisions do not appear to be an important factor.

The average price per unit of service can be obtained by dividing annual expense by annual use. An overall average price per unit of $13.83 was obtained using the GHP data for both years ($69.14/5.00). With a 25-percent coinsurance rate, this means that in 1968 members paid an average of $3.46 more per visit than they did in 1966 when there was no coinsurance. From the GHP data an arc elasticity of demand for physician services—showing the percentage change in demand that results from a given change in monetary price—can be computed . . . . The arc elasticity of demand for a $3.46 increase in cost with a 25-percent coinsurance rate is -0.137;[2] a 10-percent increase in price would result in a 1.37-percent decline in visits.

This analysis is somewhat misleading regarding the sensitivity of medical care demand to total price, however. If a value of $10 were placed on time and transportation costs—so that the price of medical services jumped from $10 (with no monetary payment) to $13.46 (with the 25-percent coinsurance)—the arc elasticity would be: $(-1.37/\$3.46) \times (\$23.46/10.00) = -0.927$. Thus, a 10-percent increase in total price would result in a 9.3-percent reduction in the quantity of medical care purchased.

The elasticity figure is obviously quite dependent upon the value of other costs, including time costs. If a value of $5.00 were used for time costs, a 10-percent increase in total price would result in a 5.3-percent reduction in the use of services. If a value of $15.00 were used for time costs, a 10-percent increase in total price would result in a 13.2-percent reduction in the use of services. This line of reasoning suggests that very time-intensive services, such as hospitalization, would show quite small elasticities with respect to money price but possibly large elasticities with respect to total price.

Even though the elasticity coefficient is quite dependent on the value of other costs used in the equation, it does reveal why normal estimates of demand for medical services show price elasticities that are relatively low compared with other commodities—the base prices used are not really the total prices consumers consider when deciding how much of the service to purchase. Which price to use depends upon what one is trying to predict. If one wants to estimate the effects of a change in the monetary price on demand for medical care, the monetary price is sufficient. If one wishes to estimate demand for the services of a different medical care delivery system that will alter time or travel expenses, it may be necessary to consider the value of the consumer's time, travel distances, and the time required to obtain the services.

Both the Phelps and the Phelps and Newhouse studies establish the deterrent effect of patient cost sharing on the demand for physician office visits. In the previous Phelps study the elasticity of demand for visits nationwide was estimated at -0.18 at a 25 percent coinsurance rate; that is to say, a 10 percent increase in patient expense (above the 25 percent already paid) is estimated to reduce demand by 1.8 percent. This is strikingly similar to the -0.14 elasticity measure estimated from the Palo Alto data.

Nonetheless, care must be taken in extrapolating general conclusions from two such different studies. The cross-sectional analysis in the first study may be criticized because it does not actually measure the impact of a change in insurance coverage. The longitudinal analysis in the second measures such a change but there is always the possibility in before-and-after studies that the impact attributed to a shift in one variable may in fact be due to some exogenous change in the system. Phelps and Newhouse consider this possibility at the end of their presentation, as follows:

Possible Shortcomings of Study

Several factors could possibly limit the application of these findings. First, if some exogenous factor such as a local epidemic artificially increased demand in 1966, or some factor (such as a miracle) systematically reduced demand for the entire community in 1968, then the observed differences in these data could be attributed to factors other than or as well as the introduction of coinsurance. The GHP plan data in the Scitovsky-Snyder study, however, show essentially no change in visits to the Palo Alto Medical Clinic between the two years. Furthermore, the Kaiser Foundation Health Plan-Northern California reports a similar number of outpatient visits in the two years . . . .

In addition, it would be preferable, as mentioned earlier, to conduct an investigation of those who remained in the GHP in 1968 and those who chose some other source of insurance/medical care.[7] Unfortunately, no data are available on the demand of those persons in 1968 who left GHP, since they could presumably obtain their medical care from any provider in the community, rather than being restricted to the Palo Alto Clinic.

A final potential problem with this study is that, with the introduction of coinsurance in 1968, some persons enrolled in GHP may have continued their enrollment but purchased some of their medical care from other providers, presumably at full market prices. Doing this would be rational behavior if the total cost of some private services (including travel time) were lower than the costs of GHP. If such behavior occurred, then some of the observed reduction in care may actually be only a shift to other suppliers, rather than an actual decrease in the market quantities demanded. Such behavior would be more likely among those who lived far from the Clinic. As noted above, this could account for the greater reduction in demand for GHP services among those who live farther away. To the extent that this is true, the decrease in demand for an entire community would be less than estimated here for this particular prepayment group. As the preceding [Scitovsky-Snyder] article pointed out, however, an individual who intended to make much use of outside providers would probably have opted for alternative insurance coverage; thus, this factor does not appear to be significant.

Cautious interpretation of results is a byword of good empirical research. A useful rule of thumb is to be skeptical of studies that fail to consider the possible shortcomings and limitations of empirical findings. And if this warning is appropriate to historical demand analyses, it is doubly appropriate to forecasts of future demand. Forecasting is a tricky business in any field. The multiple influences and determinants of health service demand make accurate forecasting all the more difficult.

ANOTHER APPROACH TO DEMAND ESTIMATION

This section presents as a case study a typical noneconometric approach to demand forecasting based on a simple extrapolation of past trends. The setting is Yale-New Haven Hospital. In June 1979, the hospital received state authorization to float $59.5 million in tax-free revenue bonds to finance construction and renovation projects estimated to cost $65 million. (The difference is equal to an estimated $5.5 million in interest on invested bond receipts during construction.) Included in the bond prospectus is a forecast of hospital demand and utilization rates through 1985 prepared by a well-known hospital consulting firm. The reader is encouraged to contrast the analytic technique used by the consultants with the econometric methods of Phelps and Newhouse. Some additional issues are raised at the conclusion of this excerpt:

ASSUMPTIONS RELATED TO FORECAST FINANCIAL STATEMENTS[e]

Note 2—Assessment of Facilities Utilization

Our assessment of Hospital utilization, including inpatient, outpatient and ancillary service, is based upon various analyses of the demand for future Hospital services. The forecasts of utilization serve as a basis for the financial statement forecasts and are based upon the following factors:

- Patient origin data
- Projected population change in the Hospital's service area
- Admission use-rate trends
- Scope of medical programs and services offered
- Physician support for the proposed construction and renovation program

- Trends in Hospital admissions
- Changes in average length of stay by service
- Bed availability
- Effects of other area health care institutions' programs and facilities changes

Patient Service Area

The City of New Haven, Connecticut, is a major metropolitan area located in south central Connecticut. New Haven is the third largest city in Connecticut and is approximately 100 miles from other large metropolitan areas such as New York, New York, Boston, Massachusetts, and Providence, Rhode Island. The City has a stable economy supported primarily by small manufacturing companies and educational institutions. Yale University, as well as other colleges, is located in New Haven.

A forecast of bed need for the service area has been developed by the HSA [health systems agency] based upon an analysis of the following data:

- Service area demographic trends
- National health care trends and guidelines
- Population trends
- Admissions use-rates by town

The HSA, as a result of this analysis, has developed an area-wide health plan that outlines the demand for health care services within the service area. The HSA has reviewed the Hospital's proposed project and has determined that it is in conformity with the HSA's Annual Implementation Plan. The HSA's recommended bed complement for the Hospital is 889 beds, including newborn bassinets.

The Hospital's patient service area was defined as the result of a patient origin analysis of admissions based upon the period from October 1977 to September 1978. The service area was defined on a town-by-town admissions use-rate basis as follows:

- Primary Service Area—includes all cities and towns with an admissions use-rate per 1,000 population of 40 or more.

- Secondary Service Area—includes all cities and towns with an admissions use-rate per 1,000 population of 15 or more but less than 40.

- Tertiary Service Area—includes all cities and towns with an admissions use-rate per 1,000 population in excess of 8 but less than 15.

The service area of the Hospital, as defined, includes 30 cities and towns. Approximately 78.4% of the total 1978 Hospital inpatients resided in this area. The remaining inpatients resided in the following areas:

Other areas in Connecticut	18.5%
Other states	2.9
Other countries	0.2

Composition of Patient Service Area Admissions

	Use-Rate Per 1,000 Population	Percent of Admissions
	Notes A and B	
Primary service area:		
New Haven	70.4	30.49%
Branford	60.0	4.42
Guilford	53.8	2.80
West Haven	47.5	8.86
East Haven	45.8	3.71
Hamden	45.7	7.70
Madison	42.1	1.86
North Branford	40.6	1.61
Subtotal		61.45
Secondary service area:		
Woodbridge	39.7	1.18
North Haven	36.8	2.91
Clinton	32.6	1.22
Bethany	32.5	.49
Orange	28.2	1.45
Killingworth	24.0	.28
Westbrook	21.6	.35
Wallingford	17.2	2.06
Cheshire	16.9	1.24
Subtotal		11.18

Composition of Patient Service Area Admissions Cont.

	Use-Rate Per 1,000 Population	Percent of Admissions
	Notes A and B	
Tertiary service area:		
North Canaan	14.7	.16
Old Saybrook	14.2	.44
Essex	13.5	.23
Milford	13.0	2.25
Chester	12.6	.14
Old Lyme	11.9	.23
Ansonia	11.3	.76
Oxford	11.1	.21
Deep River	10.8	.14
Derby	10.3	.43
Durham	9.6	.17
Prospect	8.7	.20
Seymour	8.6	.40
Subtotal		5.76
Total		78.39%

Note A—The use-rate per 1,000 population in the service area is as follows: Primary—57.0; Secondary—25.8; Tertiary—11.8.

Note B—Population data include students residing in the service area whose primary address is outside the service area.

Source: Hospital records for the fiscal year ended September 30, 1978.

Population for the towns in the service area was determined from two sources. 1970 through 1978 populations are from *Estimated State Populations* per the Connecticut State Department of Health. Population projections for 1979 through 1985 were obtained from *Preliminary Population Projections—Connecticut Town by Age and Sex 1970–2000* prepared by the Division of Health Statistics, State Department of Health, with assistance from the Comprehensive Planning Division of the Office of Policy and Management.

The following table sets forth the historical, estimated, and projected population growth for the Hospital's service area.

	Population			
	Historical	Estimated	Projected	
	1970	1975	1980	1985
Primary service area:				
New Haven	137,707	132,300	131,800	132,000
Branford	20,444	21,300	22,500	23,000
Guilford	12,033	14,300	16,300	17,000
West Haven	52,851	54,000	54,900	56,900
East Haven	25,120	24,800	24,200	24,500
Hamden	49,357	50,000	51,300	52,500
Madison	9,768	12,100	13,300	14,200
North Branford	10,778	11,500	12,300	13,100
Subtotal	318,058	320,300	326,600	333,200
Secondary service area:				
Woodbridge	7,673	8,400	9,300	9,900
North Haven	22,194	23,000	24,000	24,200
Clinton	10,267	10,800	11,500	11,900
Bethany	3,857	4,300	4,600	4,900
Orange	13,524	15,000	15,800	16,200
Killingworth	2,435	2,900	3,400	3,700
Westbrook	3,820	4,700	5,000	5,200
Wallingford	35,714	35,000	37,400	38,600
Cheshire	19,051	21,100	21,800	22,800
Subtotal	118,535	125,200	132,800	137,400
Tertiary service area:				
North Canaan	3,045	3,100	3,100	3,000
Old Saybrook	8,468	9,100	9,400	9,600
Essex	4,911	5,000	5,200	5,300
Milford	50,858	51,200	51,100	51,900
Chester	2,982	3,200	3,400	3,600
Old Lyme	4,964	5,400	6,200	6,800
Ansonia	21,160	20,200	20,300	20,400
Oxford	4,480	5,200	6,100	6,700
Deep River	3,690	4,000	4,200	4,400
Derby	12,599	11,900	12,500	12,600
Durham	4,489	4,900	5,500	5,700
Prospect	6,543	6,700	6,900	6,800
Seymour	12,776	13,400	14,700	15,500
Subtotal	140,965	143,300	148,600	152,300
Total	577,558	588,800	608,000	622,900

The population projection indicates that there is a steady growth rate within the Hospital's patient service area during the forecast period. The rate of growth is an indication that the population is stable and that no major population shifts are expected.

Our analysis, based on Department of Health statistics, of the age distribution of the population within the patient service area as compared to the State of Connecticut indicates:

- The pediatric population, age 0 to 14, is expected to decrease between 1975 and 1985 at a lesser rate than the State of Connecticut.

- The adult population, age 15 to 64, is expected to increase between 1975 and 1985 at a lesser rate than the State of Connecticut.

- The aged population, age 65 and over, is expected to increase between 1975 and 1985 at a greater rate than the State of Connecticut.

- The total service area population is expected to increase at a rate slightly less than the Statewide growth rate during the period 1975 to 1985.

Comparative Age Distribution of Population

Age Category	Patient Service Area		
	1975	1985	Percent Change
0 to 14 (Pediatric)	145,500	124,900	(14.16)%
15 to 64 (Adult)	390,600	436,800	11.83
65 and over (Aged)	52,700	61,200	16.13
Total	588,800	622,900	5.79

Age Category	State of Connecticut		
	1975	1985	Percent Change
0 to 14 (Pediatric)	781,400	660,900	(15.42)%
15 to 64 (Adult)	1,975,600	2,298,800	16.36
65 and over (Aged)	274,800	315,700	14.88
Total	3,031,800	3,275,400	8.03

Comparative Percentage Age Distribution

	1975		Projected 1985	
Age Category	Service Area	State of Connecticut	Service Area	State of Connecticut
0 to 14 (Pediatric)	24.71%	25.78%	20.05%	20.18%
15 to 64 (Adult)	66.34	65.16	70.12	70.18
65 and over (Aged) ..	8.95	9.06	9.83	9.64
Total	100.00%	100.00%	100.00%	100.00%

Use-Rate Analysis

The following use-rate analysis is based on discharges from the Hospital per 1,000 population:

	Historical		Forecast	
	1975	1978	1979	1985
Primary service area	62.7	57.0	57.4	56.9
Secondary service area	28.5	25.8	25.4	25.0
Tertiary service area	11.9	11.8	11.5	11.4

This analysis indicates a stable to moderately declining use-rate through 1985. The decrease in the primary service area use-rate from 1975 to 1978 is the result of two factors:

- The decrease in the average length of stay
- The opening of a new facility at the Hospital of St. Raphael

Admissions for the first six months of fiscal year 1979 indicate that the use-rate is stabilizing. As a result, the use-rates in the three service areas are expected to remain relatively stable throughout the forecast period.

Area-wide Inpatient Utilization

[There are four] major acute care institutions within the Hospital's service area. The [following] table presents as of September 30, 1978 information relative to these hospitals:

	Yale-New Haven Hospital	Hospital of St. Raphael	Griffin Hospital	Milford Hospital
Location	New Haven	New Haven	Derby	Milford
Distance from Yale-New Haven Hospital (miles)	—	1	12	15
Service area	Primary	Primary	Tertiary	Tertiary
Bed complement —excluding newborn	826	482	245	148
Occupancy	82%	85%	82%	73%
Average daily room rate	$154	$156	$101	$120

All of these institutions are located within the planning jurisdiction of the HSA. Our discussions with hospital administrators and the HSA staff revealed that certain area hospitals are planning replacement and/or renovation programs that would change the bed complement of the service area during the forecast period. However, the HSA has indicated that no programs are planned to commence during the forecast period that would impact the operations of the Hospital. An outline of these plans is set forth below.

- The Hospital of St. Raphael recently expanded its capacity from 455 beds to 482 beds with the opening of a new facility. Currently the occupancy rate is high. The hospital has no plans to open additional nursing units or significantly change other services during the forecast period.

- Griffin Hospital is planning submission of a Certificate of Need application within the next year for an expansion of approximately 70 new beds in the general areas of psychiatric, medical and surgical and intensive care services.

- Milford Hospital at present is not anticipating any significant capital improvements.

Medical Specialties and Specialized Services

The Hospital has many missions. Its first is to provide patient care through:

- Primary services such as medicine, surgery, emergency, laboratory and radiological services;
- Secondary services such as intensive care, coronary care and ancillary services; and
- Tertiary services such as newborn intensive care, high risk maternity, CAT scanning and open heart surgery, to patients within the Hospital's service area as well as those who are referred to the Hospital from the surrounding area or from other areas throughout Connecticut and other states.

In addition, the Hospital seeks to provide the resources necessary to conduct or participate in educational programs needed to provide excellence in the training of health professionals as well as to participate in appropriate research in conjunction with the programs of Yale University, the Yale School of Medicine and the Yale School of Nursing.

Finally, the Hospital engages in a variety of outreach, support and cooperative programs with community agencies to attempt to ensure that the total needs of patients coming to the Hospital can be met in the most appropriate setting and in the most cost-effective manner.

With increased concentration of medical technology in centralized areas, the Hospital foresees its future growth in the area of tertiary care. To meet this objective, the Hospital has developed a medical staff of both full-time faculty members and community physicians that is qualified in many medical sub-specialty areas. The quality of its medical staff, as well as the commitment to providing tertiary care, has resulted in a number of formal cooperative programs with participating institutions throughout Connecticut. These programs are:

- Medical Education
  The Hospital is the primary teaching hospital of the Yale School of Medicine and provides a setting for clinical training of undergraduate medical students. Regarding graduate medical education, the Yale School of Medicine maintains affiliation agreements with a group of Connecticut hospitals for rotation of residents based in the Hospital's resident training programs.

Demand for Health Services 147

These hospitals include:

Griffin Hospital
Bridgeport Hospital
Norwalk Hospital
St. Vincent's Hospital
St. Mary's Hospital
West Haven Veterans Administration Hospital
Waterbury Hospital
Hartford Hospital
Hospital of St. Raphael
Newington Children's Hospital

- Cooperative Services
  The Hospital participates in a number of programs with other local or regional health institutions. These programs include:

  Alcohol Detoxification
  Alcoholism Services Organization of South Central Connecticut
  Community Disaster Response Plan
  EEG Interpretations
  EKG Interpretations
  Fetal Monitoring
  Laboratory Specimen Analysis
  Laundry Services
  Pharmacy Services
  Radiation Therapy
  Radiology-Physics
  Stroke Program
  Epilepsy Program

- Allied Health Education
  The Hospital is associated with many educational programs in the New Haven area. These include:

  Emergency Medical Technology
  Licensed Practical Nursing Programs
  Physician Assistant Program
  Registered Nursing Programs
  Radiology Technology

The impact of these services on the operations of the Hospital is that approximately 22% of its admissions are generated from an outer referral area which essentially surrounds its patient service area, as well as incorporates all of southern New England. These referrals can be attributed to both the cooperative programs detailed above and the existence of certain medical specialties and specialized services not available at other health care institutions in the region.

Medical Staff

The following table presents an analysis of the Hospital's medical staff as of September 30, 1978, and indicates the specialties, average age and percentage of admissions during the fiscal year ended September 30, 1978:

Specialty	Number of Staff	Number of Board Certified	Average Age	Percentage of Hospital's Discharges
Active staff:				
Anesthesiology	25	18	42	—
Clinical Laboratories	10	5	45	—
Dentistry	49	16	52	0.3%
Dermatology	19	17	48	0.6
Medicine	372	180	50	17.7
Neurology	18	11	42	1.4
Obstetrical/Gynecology	61	47	47	27.3
Ophthalmology	30	24	47	2.1
Pathology	11	9	44	—
Pediatrics	160	119	50	14.0
Psychiatry	97	60	49	1.3
Radiology:				
Diagnostic	36	35	46	0.1
Therapeutic	12	9	42	—
Surgery	134	114	50	35.2
Total	1,034	664		100.0%

Source: Hospital records for the period October 1, 1977, to September 30, 1978.

Approximately 71% of the Hospital's patient discharges for fiscal year 1978 were by physicians 49 years old or younger. The age distribution of physicians is as follows:

	Number of Admitting Physicians	Percentage of Hospital's Discharges
Age of Admitting Physician:		
30 to 39	314	39.52%
40 to 49	277	31.14
50 to 59	184	17.56
60 to 69	120	8.11
70 and over	68	0.76
Other (age not available)	71	2.91
Total	1,034	100.00%

Source: Hospital records for the period October 1, 1977, to September 30, 1978, exclusive of house staff discharges.

The Hospital continues to attract qualified physicians to practice in the community or to become affiliated with the Yale School of Medicine. During fiscal year 1978, the Hospital granted admitting privileges to 83 physicians whereas 48 physicians retired or relocated. The majority of these changes occurred on the full-time teaching staff. The specialties, average age and board certification of these physicians are as follows:

Specialty	Staff Additions			Staff Deletions		
	Number of Staff	Number of Board Certified	Average Age	Number of Staff	Number of Board Certified	Average Age
Dentistry	8		31	6		47
Dermatology	3	1	34	1	1	65
Medicine	28	19	34	18	5	49
Neurology	4		32	2		44
Obstetrics/Gyr.	6	1	32	4	2	52
Ophthalmology	9	4	34	2		59
Orthopedics	2		31			
Pediatrics	10	3	33	2	2	40
Psychiatry	1		39	6	6	42
Surgery	12	1	34	7	5	52
Total	83	29		48	21	

The Hospital has an extensive residency program as a result of its close affiliation with the Yale School of Medicine. No changes in the number of residency programs are expected to occur during the forecast period.

The Hospital's medical staff includes over 300 physicians who also hold faculty positions at the Yale School of Medicine. The incoming enrollment of the School of Medicine is limited to 102 positions per year and its students are selected from approximately 3,000 to 3,200 applicants.

Evaluation of Physician Support

Our evaluation of the future demand for Hospital services included a survey of all the staff physicians at the Hospital, including community as well as full-time faculty members. In conducting this evaluation, we performed the following procedures:

- Mailed confidential questionnaires (882) in November 1977 to all members of the Hospital's active medical staff. The questionnaire requested that the physicians respond to the following: future utilization of the Hospital's services; the impact of the construction and renovation on their practices; their affiliations with other hospitals; the impact of other hospitals' expansion programs on their practices; and group practice information.

- Conducted 24 confidential interviews in November 1977 with all chiefs of service and associate chiefs of service within the Hospital to obtain information with respect to their utilization of the Hospital's services and future support for the proposed program as well as their indications of their entire departments' future utilization of the facility.

- Conducted 13 confidential interviews in February 1979 with selected chiefs of service and associate chiefs of service to update data obtained during the interview process conducted in November 1977. The selection of the interviewees was based upon a review of the variance from the original forecasts obtained, as a result of comparing 1978 actual data with the physicians' original estimate of departmental utilization. Ten of the thirteen physicians had been previously interviewed. The other three physicians replaced chiefs of service who had been interviewed in November 1977.

Demand for Health Services 151

The responses to the physician questionnaires were tabulated and the results indicated that:

- Approximately 70% of the questionnaires mailed were returned.
- The number of questionnaires returned represented approximately 76% of discharges for the fiscal year ended September 30, 1977.
- There is substantial physician support for the construction and renovation program.
- The demand for Hospital utilization increases with the availability of a modern health care facility providing access to all technological and medical advancements.
- The Hospital will continue to be an outstanding tertiary care center and referrals from outside the service area will continue.

Inpatient Utilization

The forecast of inpatient utilization of the Hospital is based upon the following assumptions:

- Physician support for the Hospital and its programs as documented through the responses received from the confidential questionnaire mailed to 882 admitting physicians would continue.
- Population growth within the Hospital's service area is expected to be consistent with estimates published by the Division of Health Statistics, State Department of Health.
- Stabilization of inpatient use-rates within the Hospital's service area throughout the forecast period.
- The overall average length of stay would reflect a neutralization of two opposing trends: 1) the referral of more difficult

and more complicated cases from outside the primary service area; and 2) stricter utilization review procedures.

- Expansion and/or modernization programs of other area hospitals, either planned or under way, would have no adverse impact on the Hospital's inpatient utilization.
- The Hospital's close working relationship with the Yale School of Medicine would continue.

Upon review of the demographic analysis, the summary of the physicians' survey and the summary of the confidential interviews with the chiefs and associate chiefs of the various services, admissions, patient days and average length of stay were forecast through the year 1984.

The following schedule (page 153) summarizes the patient utilization actually achieved during the fiscal years 1973 through 1978, and the forecasts of these statistics for the fiscal years 1979 through 1984.

The decline in patient days from 1977 to 1978 is the result of two factors:

- The average length of stay decreased from 8.24 to 8.07.
- The opening of a new facility at the Hospital of St. Raphael.

Admissions are forecast to increase by only 1% as a result of the reduction in number of beds limiting inpatient utilization and the average length of stay is expected to decrease by approximately 3.0% for the fiscal years 1979 through 1984. The forecast reduction in average length of stay is based upon a department-by-department analysis of historical trends as well as discussions with chiefs of service. This decrease in average length of stay is forecast to continue during the forecast period.

The forecast admissions result from a slightly increasing population within the service area, the availability of beds as a result of a decreasing length of stay and the increase in referrals to the full-time faculty.

Emergency, Clinic and Private Referred Visits

The forecast of emergency room and outpatient visits is based on historical trends and projected population changes. The Hos-

Inpatient Statistics (Excluding Newborn)

	Average Beds Available for Use	Patient Days	Admissions	Average Length of Stay	Average Census	Occupancy Percent	Newborn Patient Days
Actual:							
1973	858	241,025	29,897	8.06	660	76.9%	20,896
1974	862	253,641	31,122	8.15	695	80.6	22,617
1975	819	254,993	31,264	8.16	699	85.3	23,259
1976	822	252,689	31,181	8.10	690	83.9	24,021
1977	818	252,109	30,557	8.25	691	84.5	25,361
1978	813	242,115	30,003	8.07	663	81.6	26,853
Forecast:							
1979	790	245,300	30,271	8.10	672	85.1	27,350
1980	790	245,200	30,401	8.07	670	84.8	28,000
1981	790	244,500	30,489	8.02	670	84.8	29,000
1982	765	241,000	30,304	7.95	660	86.3	29,900
1983	740	236,100	29,997	7.87	647	87.4	30,800
1984	740	236,900	30,238	7.83	647	87.4	31,300

pital's historical ambulatory visits for the years 1973 through 1978 and the forecast visits for 1979 through 1984 are as follows:

	Emergency Room	Clinic	Private Referred
Actual:			
1973	87,105	78,099	68,427
1974	87,924	81,403	73,631
1975	88,123	84,078	76,824
1976	91,809	84,973	89,490
1977	90,101	87,975	90,507
1978	90,099	87,140	89,172
Forecast:			
1979	90,100	87,500	86,800
1980	90,500	88,000	83,300
1981	90,800	88,300	83,600
1982	91,000	88,500	83,900
1983	91,300	88,800	84,200
1984	91,600	89,100	84,400

Emergency room visits are anticipated to increase 1.7% during the forecast period. Clinic visits are expected to increase 2.2% over the forecast period. These slight increases are primarily due to the projected increase of population in the Hospital's primary service area. Emergency room visits are also forecast to increase based upon the availability of a new and more accessible emergency room facility. Private referred visits are forecast to decline slightly in 1979 and 1980.

Ancillary volumes and related units of service were forecast based upon historical trends as adjusted by responses received from the physician survey and Hospital management's plans to reflect changes in patient mix, levels of service and new programs.

As suggested prior to this selection, the reader should contrast the approach used in the Yale-New Haven analysis with the economic approach presented earlier in the chapter. The following points are relevant to such a comparison:

1. A major issue is whether an adequate distinction is made here between demand and utilization. Is such a distinction important or relevant in this case?

2. The Yale-New Haven analysis is concerned with the total demand for the services of a hospital in a given area. The economic theory and empirical analysis presented earlier dealt with demand by an individual for medical care, and it was suggested that individual demands could simply be added up to get total market demand. Does the Yale-New Haven study bring in the determinants of individual demand? Does it assume that individual demand for hospital care is invariant among people, or over time, or that such variation is unimportant? Can total demand be understood without a model explaining the behavior of individuals?

3. Many of the variables suggested by the theory and found to be important in the econometric studies appear to be missing here. Income, insurance coverage, and the price of medical care relative to other prices are not included explicitly in the Yale-New Haven study. Are they not relevant here? Is there reason to believe that their effect is so small that they can be safely ignored?

4. The econometric studies and theory included much information about patients, their characteristics, and their decision making. The Yale-New Haven study devotes considerable attention to information about doctors. Is it making some implicit assumptions about "demand creation" by physicians? What are these assumptions and what is the basis for them?

The approaches taken in the Yale-New Haven study and in the earlier sections of the chapter obviously are quite different. This is not to suggest that one is "correct" and the other is "wrong." Health planning and administration are professions requiring many approaches and analytical skills from diverse disciplines. To the extent that readers are in a position where the quality and reliability of demand analyses must be evaluated, then clearly, they should become familiar with different methodologies. Economic theory and econometric analysis have important contributions to make in this area.

NOTES

1. Many, perhaps most, goods display characteristics of both consumption and investment. For example, food provides immediate gratification but good (or bad) nutrition has lasting effects on bodily development and general well-being. Education is an investment in the sense that it prepares individuals for future employment but it also can provide direct rewards in ego satisfaction.
2. In the economics literature, the term "opportunity cost" can mean either the cost or the gain associated with choices not made (opportunities forgone). It usually is employed to denote the value attached to the best alternative use of time or money.
3. Two examples of empirical studies in this area are: George Monsma, "Marginal Revenue and the Demand for Physicians' Services," in Herbert E. Klarman, ed., *Empirical Studies in Health Economics*. Baltimore: Johns Hopkins University Press, 1970. Charles E. Lewis, "Variations in the Incidence of Surgery," *New England Journal of Medicine*, 281 (October 16, 1969): 880–884.
4. The concept of point elasticity measures the elasticity at a single point on the curve. It is the limit of E as ΔQ and ΔP approach zero. That is, using calculus notation, the point elasticity is $\frac{dQ}{dP} \cdot \frac{P}{Q}$.
5. In insurance literature, moral hazard is defined as the "loss-producing propensity of the insured." There are two types of moral hazard. The first is where an individual substitutes insurance coverage for preventive behavior designed to reduce the risk (e.g., buying fire insurance rather than fireproofing a building). The second type is where individuals actively court the hazard in order to collect on the insurance (e.g., arson on an insured building). Both situations have ethical connotations, hence the term "moral" hazard. In the economics literature, on the other hand, the term is used to describe any price elasticity in the demand for insured services.
6. For a good summary treatment of this subject see Paul Feldstein, *Health Care Economics* (New York: John Wiley & Sons, Inc., 1979), Ch. 6.
7. For a discussion of the arguments see "Over-insurance: The Conceptual Issues" in Mark Pauly, ed., *National Health Insurance: What Now, What Later, What Never?* (Washington, D.C.: American Enterprise Institute, 1980), pp. 201–219.
8. J. Acton, "Nonmonetary Factors in the Demand for Medical Services: Some Empirical Evidence," *Journal of Political Economy* 83, no. 3 (June, 1975).

SUGGESTED READINGS

General Demand Analysis

Ferguson, C.E., and Gould, J.P. *Microeconomic Theory,* 4th ed. Homewood, Ill.: Richard D. Irwin, Inc., 1978, Chaps. 1–4.

Nicholson, Walter. *Microeconomic Theory: Basic Principles and Extensions*, 2nd ed. New York: The Dryden Press, 1978, Chaps. 3–6.

Overview of Health Services Demand

Arrow, Kenneth J. "Uncertainty and the Welfare Economics of Medical Care." *The American Economic Review* 53 (December 1963): 941–973.

Berki, Sylvester. *Hospital Economics.* Lexington, Mass.: Lexington Books, 1972, pp. 121-166.

Donabedian, Avedis. *Benefits in Medical Care Programs.* Cambridge, Mass.: Harvard University Press, 1976, pp. 41-47.

Feldstein, Paul. *Health Care Economics.* New York: John Wiley & Sons, Inc., 1979, pp. 74-133.

Hyman, Joseph. "Empirical Research on the Demand for Medical Care." *Inquiry* 8, no. 1 (March 1971): 61-71.

Kelley, Terence, and Schieber, George J. "Factors Affecting Medical Service Utilization: A Behavioral Approach." Washington, D.C.: The Urban Institute, 1972.

Klarman, Herbert E. *The Economics of Health.* New York: Columbia University Press, 1965, pp. 20-40.

─────────, ed. *Empirical Studies in Health Economics.* Baltimore: The Johns Hopkins University Press, 1970, pp. 73-170.

Mushkin, Selma, ed. *Consumer Incentives for Health Care.* New York: Prodist, 1974.

Newhouse, Joseph. *The Economics of Medical Care.* Reading, Mass.: Addison-Wesley Publishing Co., 1978, pp. 4-24.

Pauly, Mark. "The Economics of Moral Hazard: Comment." *The American Economic Review* 58, no. 3 (June 1968): 531-537.

─────────. *National Health Insurance: What Now, What Later, What Never?* Washington, D.C.: American Enterprise Institute, 1980, pp. 201-249.

Sorkin, Alan. *Health Economics.* Lexington, Mass.: Lexington Books, 1975, pp. 19-40.

Recent Empirical Studies of Health Services Demand

Acton, J. "Nonmonetary Factors in the Demand for Medical Services: Some Empirical Evidence." *The Journal of Political Economy* 83, no. 3 (June 1975): 595-614.

Chiswick, B. "The Demand for Nursing Home Services: An Analysis of the Substitution Between Institutional and Non-institutional Care." *The Journal of Human Resources* 11, no. 3 (Summer 1976): 295-316.

Cullis, J., and West, P. "Demand for Health Services and the Theory of Time Allocation." *Applied Economics* 8, no. 2 (June 1976): 81.

Freiberg, Lewis, and Scutchfield, F. Douglass. "Insurance and the Demand for Hospital Care: An Examination of Moral Hazard." *Inquiry* 13, no. 1 (March 1976): 54-60.

Fuchs, Victor. "The Supply of Surgeons and the Demand for Operations." *The Journal of Human Resources* 13 (Supplement, 1978): 35-56.

Holtmann, A.G., and Olsen, E. "The Demand for Dental Care: A Study in Consumption and Household Production." *The Journal of Human Resources* 11, no. 4 (Fall 1976): 546-560.

Inman, Robert. "The Family Provision of Children's Health, an Economic Analysis," in Richard Rosett, ed. *The Role of Health Insurance in the Health Services Sector.* New York: National Bureau of Economic Research, 1976, pp. 215-254.

Keeler, Emmett. "An Empirical Study of the Differences Between Family and Individual Deductibles in Health Insurance." *Inquiry* 14, no. 3 (September 1977): 269-277.

Lairson, David, and Swint, Michael. "A Multivariate Analysis of the Likelihood and Volume of Preventive Visit Demand in a Prepaid Group Practice." *Medical Care* 16, no. 9 (September 1978): 730-739.

Newhouse, Joseph. "On Having Your Cake and Eating it Too: An Analysis of Estimated Effects of Insurance on Demand for Medical Care." Paper R-1149-NC. Santa Monica, Calif.: The Rand Corp., April 1974.

Newhouse, Joseph, and Phelps, Charles E. "Price and Income Elasticities for Medical Care Services," in Mark Perlman, ed., *The Economics of Health and Medical Care*. London: Macmillan Publishing Co., 1974.

Newhouse, Joseph, and Schwartz, William. "Policy Options and the Impact of National Health Insurance." *New England Journal of Medicine* 290 (June 13, 1974): 1345–1359.

Phelps, Charles. "The Demand for Health Insurance: A Theoretical and Empirical Investigation." July 1973.

Phelps, Charles, and Newhouse, Joseph. "New Estimates of Price and Income Elasticity of Medical Care Services," in Richard Rosett, ed., *The Role of Health Insurance in the Health Services Sector*. New York: National Bureau of Economic Research, 1976, pp. 261–313.

Russell, L. "The Demand for Short-Term Hospital Admissions Under Medicare." *American Economist* 19, no. 2 (Fall 1975): 9–17.

Samuelson, Paul. *Economics*, 11th ed. New York: McGraw-Hill Book Company, 1980.

Schuman, Larry; Wolfe, Harvey; and Sepulveda, Jose. "Estimating the Demand for Emergency Transportation." *Medical Care* 15, no. 9 (September 1977): 738–49.

Scitovsky, Anne, and McCall, Nelda. "Coinsurance and the Demand for Physician Services: Four Years Later." *Social Security Bulletin* 40, no. 5 (May 1977): 19–26.

Scitovsky, Anne, and Snyder, Nelda M. "Effect of Coinsurance on Use of Physician Services." *Social Security Bulletin* 35, no. 6 (June 1972): 3–19.

Yett, Donald. "A Microeconometric Model of the Health Care System in the United States." *Annals of Economic and Social Measurement* 4, no. 3 (Summer 1975): 407–33.

NOTES FOR PHELPS EXCERPT

10. In the expenditure equation one interaction was significant at the 0.1 probability level—this interaction showed that the response to insurance (the demand elasticity) became smaller for sicker persons, suggesting that in terms of physician office visit expense, better insurance coverage will change demands of relatively sick persons less than slightly sick persons.

13. The coefficient on appointment delay in the demand equation was -0.077 ($t = 2.20$). Hence the difference in demand between zero days delay and seven days delay is $7 \times (-0.077) = -0.57$ visits per year. The average for the sample in this equation was four visits per year, so demand (holding constant other factors) would be $0.57/4.0 = 14$ percent lower with the longest waiting times than with no waiting time.

NOTES FOR PHELPS AND NEWHOUSE EXCERPT

1. The mean decrease in visits was estimated to be 24.07 percent of the demand in 1966 (calculated as the decline in average visits for the entire population), with a standard error around that estimate of 2.98 percent. The mean decrease in expense was estimated to be 23.78 percent, with a standard error around that estimate of 4.25 percent. To rigorously test the hypothesis of no difference between these means would require knowing the covariance between them. Computing this figure does not seem worth the computational costs.

2. The estimated own-price elasticity of demand for physician services of -0.14 is almost identical to an elasticity estimate of total medical expenditures from an entirely different data source. Using insurance premium data, that elasticity was computed to be -0.13 as the coinsurance rate changed from 20 percent to 25 percent. See Charles E. Phelps and Joseph P. Newhouse, *Coinsurance and the Demand for Medical Services*, Rand Report No. R-974.

7. The decision of GHP members to participate in the plan and to use its services should be analyzed in the context of a simultaneous equation model. On the basis of their use of services in 1966, persons dropping GHP appeared to be little different from those keeping plan membership, so the simultaneous equation bias is probably small.

SOURCES AND PERMISSIONS

a. Reprinted from *Papers on the National Health Guidelines: National Guidelines for Health Planning*, U.S. Department of Health, Education, and Welfare, Public Health Service, DHEW Publication No. (HRA) 78-643. Washington, D.C.: Government Printing Office, 1978, pp. 4-6.

b. Reprinted from "Competition Among Physicians" by Uwe Reinhardt, in Warren Greenburg, ed., *Competition in the Health Sector*, Washington, D.C.: Federal Trade Commission, 1978, pp. 164-165.

c. Reprinted from "Effects of Insurance on Demand for Medical Care" by Charles Phelps, in Ronald Anderson, Joanna Kravits, and Odin Anderson, eds. *Equity in Health Services: Empirical Analysis in Social Policy*, pp. 119-123, 125-130, by permission of Ballinger Publishing Co., © 1975.

d. Reprinted from "Effect of Coinsurance: A Multivariate Analysis," by Charles Phelps and Joseph Newhouse, *Social Security Bulletin* 35:6 (June 1972), pp. 20-23, 26.

e. Reprinted from *Preliminary Official Statement: Revenue Bonds, Yale-New Haven Hospital Issue, Series B-1979*, State of Connecticut, Health and Educational Facilities Authority, June 13, 1979, pp. 70-83.

Chapter 5

Theory of the Firm: Applications to Solo Practice

In economics, a *firm* is the decision-making unit concerned with production. This definition encompasses entities ranging from a single proprietor operating a corner drugstore to General Motors and other giant corporations. Despite the obvious differences between these two examples of a firm (and everything in between), at a certain level of abstraction they are quite similar. All have to operate in an environment characterized by certain technological, economic, and institutional constraints and to make decisions about how much output to produce, what inputs to use in the production process and how to use them, and how much to invest in the business for future production capability. This chapter and the following two show how basic concepts in the theory of the firm can be applied to the production of health services.

OVERVIEW AND SYNOPSIS

The firms providing health services are a diverse group in a number of respects:

1. The group includes both profit-oriented and nonprofit firms. Companies making drugs or medical equipment are examples of profit-oriented manufacturing corporations. Most hospitals are nonprofit organizations, but a significant minority are organized on a for-profit basis. Many firms in the health sector are independent professionals or groups of professionals whose net income is, in effect, the profit from the firm's operation.

2. The size of firm varies widely, ranging from one or a few workers in the case of a physician in solo practice to thousands of employees in large hospitals and manufacturing companies.
3. The nature of the competition in the markets in which firms operate differs. A primary care physician in a large city has many different competitors while a community hospital in a small town has none.

Despite this diversity, three central concepts are applicable to all firms and provide a useful structure for economic analysis. These three—the objectives of the firm, the constraints under which the firm operates, and the choices it must make—are detailed in Figure 5-1.

The classical economic assumption is that the firm's objective is to maximize profits. Where the firm is a one-person operation whose income is identical with profits, the assumption is perhaps most convincing, although even here other motives, such as altruism, may be present. When the firm is a complex organization, such as a corporation or a nonprofit hospital, the simple profit maximization assumption becomes less satisfactory. Many theorists have turned to an approach that attempts to determine the organization's objective through analysis of the interactions among members of the entity, each of whom may have different goals. Thus, the objectives of a corporation may result from a resolution of different motives of stock-

Figure 5-1 Structure for Economic Analysis of Firms

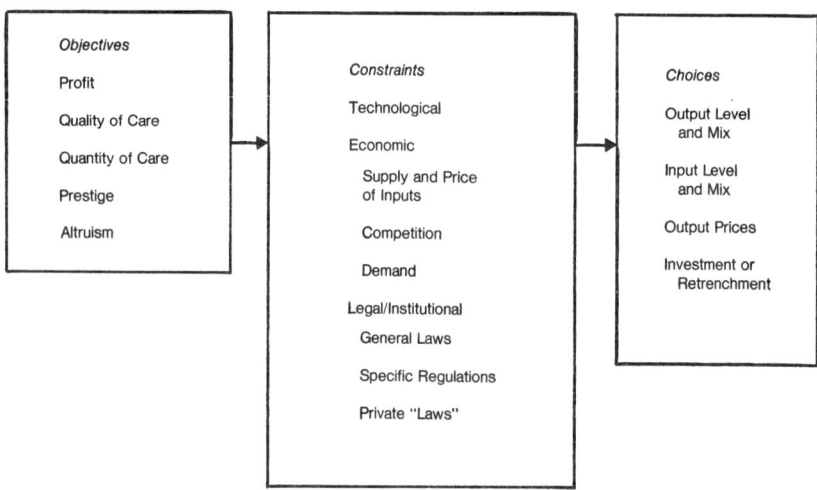

holders and management; a hospital's objectives may be determined by the relationship among trustees, administrators, and medical staff.

The technological constraint faced by a firm is the production function. This function describes the terms on which inputs can be transformed into outputs. A production function thus is an engineering relationship that indicates the maximum output that can be achieved from a given set of inputs. The difficulty of defining output and the fact that health services firms tend to produce several outputs simultaneously introduce obvious complications in applying this concept. The supply and price of inputs represent an economic constraint in the firm's production decision. Combined with the production function, input prices describe the *cost function*, a relationship between output level and production cost.

Another economic constraint is, of course, the demand for the firm's output. This depends on the underlying consumer demand for the output of all the firms in the market as well as on the proportion of total sales that any one company gets—that is to say, its market share. The latter is related to the number of competitors and the nature of their interaction in the market. Finally, firms have to operate within the applicable legal and institutional environment, including general laws and standards that affect all organizations (minimum wage laws, local zoning codes, occupational health and safety standards), specific government regulations relevant to the health sector (licensure, certificate of need, state regulations), and private "laws" promulgated by the providers themselves (standards set by the Joint Commission on Accreditation of Hospitals and medical specialty boards). Indeed, a major reason for better understanding of health service firms' behavior is to be able to predict their reactions to changes in these legal and institutional strictures.

Given its objectives and constraints, a firm makes several decisions or choices of particular interest to economists. First, it must decide on a short-run output level and output mix. What occupancy rate does a hospital seek? How does it allocate beds among medical, surgical, pediatric, or other uses? How many hours per week does a physician work? What determines the mix between inpatient and outpatient care in a health maintenance organization (HMO)? These are examples of the kinds of questions an economic analysis of output decisions might help answer.

In a longer run view, output choice is tied closely to investment decisions. Future capacity for production depends on investment today. Under what conditions will a hospital expand (or reduce) its number of beds? What determines the amount of research done by drug companies? These are examples of investment decisions that determine output in the long run. Finally, analysis of production should explain something about the mix of inputs firms use. Why has the use of paramedical personnel spread faster in some delivery organizations than others? What determines the staff/patient ratio in nursing homes? These are examples of input choices.

The reader is likely to be familiar with most if not all the organizations discussed in this and following chapters and may find the models oversimplified or unrealistic. The authors' purpose is not to provide the kind of detailed description and specific understanding that administrators must have of their own organizations. Nor is an attempt made to analyze the gamut of economic decisions faced by health care providers in the context of each sector of the industry. Rather, the approach is selective and sequential. A few important characteristics common to most firms are selected to show how health care organizations are likely to react to changes in demand, technology, and government regulation. The discussion of specific sectors of the health care industry emphasizes economic issues and analytic concerns that seem particularly germane.

The rest of this chapter focuses on solo practitioners. The basic microeconomic model of price and output determination for profit-making firms is developed first. The ramifications of this model then are discussed with respect to five topics of current interest: physician incomes, charity care, nonprice rationing, productivity and labor substitution, and the quality of professional medical services.

ECONOMICS OF SOLO PRACTICE

A substantial proportion of outputs in the health sector consists of ambulatory services produced in office-based or clinic-based practices by physicians, dentists, optometrists, and other independent health care professionals. These practices range from sole proprietorships offering a single service to large multispecialty groups. Some clearly are oriented to profit making, others are established as nonprofit private corporations, and still others are operated by government. Some provide health care on a *fee-for-service* basis, others operate their own insurance programs through capitation payment schemes. In short, there is no single (or simple) economic model that can hope to capture the diversity of objectives, production techniques, or financial arrangements for such a diverse group of organizations.

To highlight the usefulness of economics to an understanding of ambulatory care delivery, this analysis begins with a relatively simple form of organization typified by the physician in solo practice. Of the 433,600 physicians (M.D.s and D.O.s) active in the United States in 1979,[1] over half were solo practitioners. The percentage has declined gradually over the last three decades, but solo practices still represent the most prevalent form of ambulatory care delivery. Such practices are by definition "owned" by a single physician who makes all the decisions regarding what to offer patients, how much to make available, and how to produce it.

However, these decisions are tempered significantly by forces beyond the doctor's immediate control. The question of what to produce is constrained by the physician's education and training as well as by state licensure statutes. Licensing requirements also influence the method of production in that they specify the degree to which medical decisions and treatment protocols can be delegated to nonphysicians. Time is a most important constraint on how many services can be produced. The typical solo practitioner works 51 hours per week,[2] which leaves relatively little room for expanded production requiring commitment of the physician's own time.

The characteristics of demand represent another constraint. Even though physicians retain the legal right to refuse to accept patients, once they do take them on, the doctors have a fiduciary responsibility to treat such individuals according to accepted standards of medical practice. If the type of illnesses and accidents prevalent in the physician's service area change, then the production process must change accordingly.

The importance of these constraints should not overshadow the fact that physicians still retain discretionary power over a variety of economic variables. Consider the case of a solo practitioner who finds that demand has increased to the point where the practice clearly cannot accommodate all the patients who wish to be served. Possible responses might include:

1. raising the level of fees
2. increasing waiting time in the office and/or lengthening the appointment calendar
3. expanding the practice by hiring additional help, or
4. reducing the average amount of time spent with each patient.

Which option or combination of options would the physician choose?

This type of situation provides a useful context for exploring the economics of solo practice. The following sections examine the effects of each option in turn, using a device known as *comparative statics*. This is a new term, but the principle behind it was introduced in the aspirin example in Chapter 2. In technical terms it means the study of the relationship between two static equilibrium points, one before and the other after a particular change is introduced into the system, holding all other outside influences constant. In this case it means finding the equilibrium price and output levels for the solo practice prior to the increase in demand, then analyzing how these equilibrium levels will change for each of the possible responses to that rise in demand. The assumptions, behavioral models, and other information necessary to perform the analysis are presented as the discussion progresses.

Prices and Profits

The decision to raise price in the face of increasing demand is just the type of response that would be expected of a profit-making enterprise. To see why, the example is fleshed out with the hypothetical cost and revenue figures shown in Table 5-1. The left-hand column of the table shows the level of output measured in number of patient visits (units of the product) per week that the physician practice can produce. For the sake of simplicity it is assumed that the physician has no control over patient case mix and that the mix of visit types is the same at all levels of output. (These assumptions allow the practice to be treated as if it were producing a single homogeneous output. While there are economic models for multiproduct firms, they are considerably more complex.) It also is assumed that the physician either cannot or will not provide more than 120 visits per week; this number thus determines the maximum output of the firm.

The next column in the table measures total cost at each level of output. Even when no visits are produced, the practice still has positive costs of $500 per week. This reflects the fact that any firm has fixed costs, such as rent, interest, and depreciation on equipment that must be paid regardless of whether or not it is selling any services.

The third and fourth columns contain two additional measures of cost. The *average cost* (AC) measure is simply the total of fixed costs and variable costs (such as wages, medical and office supplies, and other expenses that increase as more visits are produced) divided by the level of output. For most firms, including the hypothetical office practice cited here, average costs will fall rapidly as output increases because fixed expenses are spread over a larger number of service units. At some point, however, average variable costs will tend to rise, generating a U-shaped average cost curve. The final expense measure, *marginal cost* (MC), is the additional expense of producing one more unit of output. (This is why the data elements in the MC column fall between the relevant output levels measured in visits per week.) The marginal cost curve, too, is U-shaped.

The information thus far provides some notion of what the physician must pay out to provide various levels of service, but gives no idea which level will generate the greatest profit. For this, information is needed on

Table 5-1 Physician Costs and Revenues at Different Levels of Output

Output Visits/Week	Costs in Period 1 and 2				Period 1 Revenue				Period 2 Revenue			
	Total Costs	Average Costs (AC) Per Visit	Marginal Costs (MC) Per Visit		Total Revenue	Average Revenue (AR) Per Visit	Marginal Revenue (MR) Per Visit		Total Revenue	Average Revenue (AR) Per Visit	Marginal Revenue (MR) Per Visit	
0	$ 500.00	0			0	0			0	0		
10	750.00	$75.00	$25.00		$ 600.00	$60.00	$60.00		$ 750.00	$75.00	$75.00	
20	950.00	47.50	20.00		1,000.00	50.00	40.00		1,250.00	62.50	50.00	
30	1,100.00	36.67	15.00		1,320.00	44.00	32.00		1,650.00	55.00	40.00	
40	1,220.00	30.50	12.00		1,600.00	40.00	28.00		2,000.00	50.00	35.00	
50	1,330.00	26.60	11.00		1,850.00	37.00	25.00		2,312.50	46.25	31.25	
60	1,440.00	24.00	11.00		2,100.00	35.00	25.00		2,625.00	43.75	31.25	
70	1,530.00	21.86	9.00		2,310.00	33.00	21.00		2,887.50	41.25	26.25	
80	1,610.00	20.13	8.00		2,480.00	31.00	17.00		3,100.00	38.75	21.25	
90	1,710.00	19.00	10.00		2,610.00	29.00	13.00		3,262.50	36.25	16.25	
100	1,860.00	18.60	15.00		2,700.00	27.00	9.00		3,375.00	33.75	11.25	
110	2,060.00	18.73	20.00		2,750.00	25.00	5.00		3,437.50	31.25	6.25	
120	2,310.00	19.25	25.00		2,760.00	23.00	1.00		3,450.00	28.75	1.25	

demand and revenue. The two are linked closely because what patients are willing and able to pay for services (demand) becomes revenue to the physician once those services are in fact provided. There are two sets of revenue figures in Table 5-1 representing the original demand conditions (Period 1) and the new, higher levels of demand (Period 2). The first set is used to determine the starting equilibrium point in the exercise on physician response to increased demand.

The three measures of Period 1 revenue are analogous to the cost measures discussed previously. Total revenues are the physician's gross weekly receipts. As would be expected, they increase as more visits are sold. However, the rate of increase declines with each additional 10 visits produced. The reason is that the physician faces a downward sloping demand curve. As the average price drops, existing "customers" are willing to make more visits and new patients who perhaps could not afford high fees are brought into the market. Although nothing is labeled as prices in Table 5-1, the *average revenue* (AR) figures produce this information. For example, given a weekly output of 10 visits, average revenue will equal $60 as long as the price is set at $60 per visit and patients are willing to pay this amount. Likewise, at 20 visits per week average revenue will be $50 if the price is $50 per visit. In other words, the average revenue schedule and the demand curve are identical.

The per visit revenue (price) must fall as output increases because of the downward sloping demand curve. In producing increasingly higher levels of output, the physician both loses some revenue from patients who would otherwise have paid higher prices and gains revenue from the additional demand associated with lower prices. The net effect is summarized under the heading of *marginal revenue* per visit (MR). The concept of marginal revenue is analogous to that of marginal cost, namely, the net addition to total revenues obtained from the sale of one more visit.

All the information necessary to determine which output level will maximize the physician's profit in Period 1 now is available. The rule for profit maximization is straightforward: keep producing as long as marginal revenues are greater than (or at least are not exceeded by) marginal costs or, in the notation used by economists, produce up to the level where MC = MR. In this example, this point is obtained at an output level of approximately 90 visits per week, a price (average revenue) of $29 per visit, and an average cost of $19 per visit. This is because, for the move from 80 to 90 visits, the marginal revenue ($13) exceeds the marginal cost ($10), while for the move from 90 to 100 visits the marginal revenue ($9) is less than the marginal cost ($15). The total profit of $900 per week [($29–$19) × 90] is the most the practitioner can earn, given the demand specified by the average revenue schedule and the production methods underlying the average cost schedule.

Before examining the implications of this solution, it is useful to recap the exercise using graphic analysis. Figure 5-2 represents Period 1 demand and cost conditions where average cost (AC), marginal cost (MC), demand and average revenue ($AR_1 = D_1$), and marginal revenue (MR_1) are plotted as curves by connecting the data points obtained from Table 5-1. The maximum profit output is the point where the MC and MR_1 curves intersect (the only output level where MC = MR), price is set at the highest level the market will bear at that output (the point on the demand/average revenue curve AR_1 above the intersection of the MR_1 and MC curves), and profit is represented as the difference between total revenue (AR_1 × Output) and total costs (AC × Output) shown as the shaded rectangle. The resulting profit-maximizing output of 90 visits per week and price of $29 are, of course, the same as determined previously from the table.

By acting as a profit maximizer, the physician ensures that the market will be in equilibrium. The $29 per visit average charge is the only price that will clear the market. There is neither excess demand nor excess supply at that point. However, if any of the underlying conditions change, then this equilibrium point also must change.

Consider now what might happen if demand increases and production costs remain constant at Period 1 levels. Such a situation is indicated in the final three columns of Table 5-1 that hypothesize an across-the-board 25 percent increase in the amount patients are prepared to pay for the physician's services or, to look at it another way, an increase in the volume of services that will be demanded at any price. Such a shift in demand might arise because of an improvement in the physician's reputation. It might occur because more patients have insurance for ambulatory care services. Whatever the reason, the physician must now reevaluate the price/output relationship.

If average fees were to be maintained at the Period 1 level of $29 per visit, patients would demand roughly 120 visits rather than the 90 visits actually produced in the first period. Producing the additional 30 visits would cost $600 per week (the marginal expense of moving from 90 to 100 visits is $15 for each such visit, from 100 to 110 it is $20, and from 110 to 120 it is $25, for a total of $600). The additional revenue generated for 30 visits at $29 is $870. Since the added revenue is greater than MC by $270 per week, it might be assumed that the physician has an unambiguous signal to increase production to 120 visits. However, this decision would be incorrect if the physician truly desired to maximize profit. The reason is that the doctor could earn more than an extra $270 if prices were raised and the level of output were constrained. For instance, if the output of 90 visits per week were maintained, the new Period 2 demand would allow the physician to increase the average fee to $36.25, thus generating an additional $652.50 per week ($36.25 − $29.00 × 90 over and above the

Figure 5-2 Graphic Analysis of Cost-Revenue Relationship

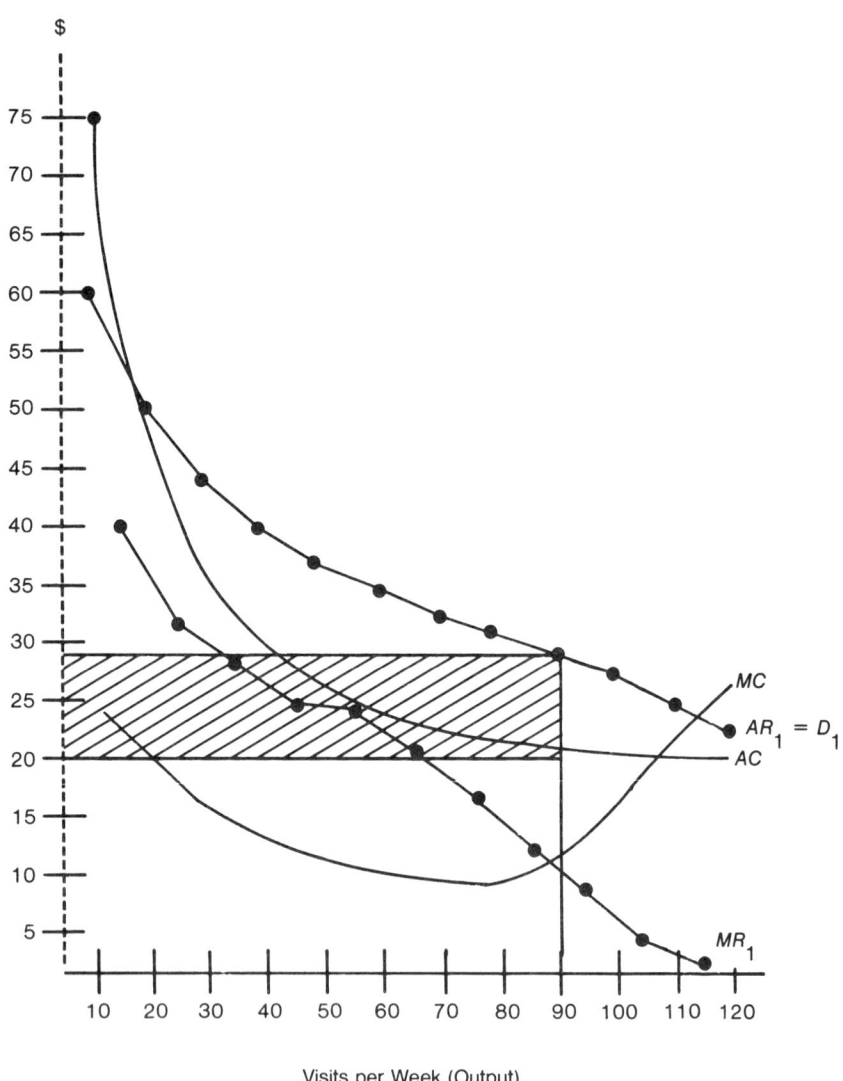

original Period 1 profits). This clearly is a preferable decision for the doctor, but it should be kept in mind that the rule of equating marginal costs with marginal revenues is still the one to follow. It just so happens that in this case MR_2 = MC between 85 and 95 visits; virtually all of the increase in demand thus would go to higher prices rather than to expanded output.

This price response can be graphed (Figure 5-3). The cost curves are identical to those in Figure 5-2 since it is assumed that there is no change in the production process or in the level of factor prices from Period 1 to Period 2. The only difference is in the average and marginal revenue curves that reflect the outward shift in demand. Here it is graphically evident why the profit-maximizing physician would not produce 120 visits per week. For every visit beyond the intersection of MC = MR, the additional cost of production exceeds the extra revenue generated. Likewise, for any level of output below the intersection (MC<MR) the physician could earn additional revenue by producing more visits. Just as in Period 1, there is a single price/output combination that will maximize profits and ensure a market equilibrium. The fact that an equilibrium price can be obtained in both periods satisfies the requirement for a comparative statics solution to the problem of rising demand.

Prices and Target Incomes

Some health economists argue that physicians are motivated more by certain predetermined income goals than by profit per se.[3] Known as the *target income hypothesis*, this theory suggests that as annual income rises, a worker (professional or otherwise) reaches a point where the potential for further income will be traded off for more leisure time. Once the target is obtained, higher rates of pay will lead to less rather than more work's being performed. The theory has considerable intuitive appeal but it does not explain how the individual chooses the target in the first place.

Assume the physician has a target income that, for the sake of argument, is set at $65,430, the median net earnings level for all physicians in 1977.[4] How will the solo practitioner meet this target with the change in demand hypothesized in the previous section? Since maximum earnings in Period 1 are approximately $46,800 a year for a 52-week work year ($900 per week times 52 weeks), it can be assumed that the practitioner will act as a profit maximizer. However, in Period 2 the maximum annual earnings are nearly $81,000, which exceeds the target by a considerable margin if the physician works 52 weeks. To reach the target precisely, the physician must balance three variables: the average price per visit, the average cost per visit, and the number of visits produced.

Figure 5-3 Maximizing Profit by Raising Prices

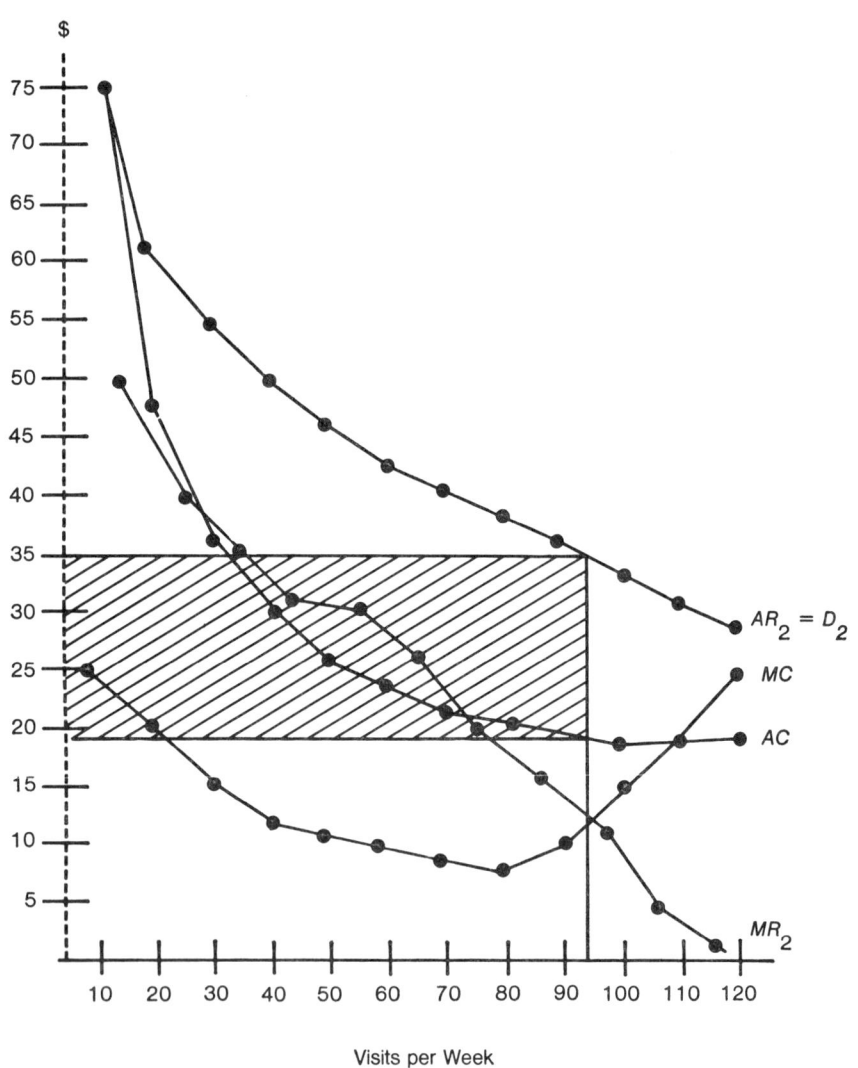

Visits per Week

One possibility would be to retain the previous profit-maximizing price of $36.25 and simply cut back the average workweek from 90 to 80 visits. The result ($2,900 in weekly revenue − $1,610 in weekly costs × 52 weeks = $67,080) would be very close to the income target. Alternatively, the physician might decide to cut the workyear by a little less than six weeks to obtain the same result. It can be demonstrated, however, that neither solution is optimal. The reason is that, given a volume of 80 visits per week for 52 weeks (or 90 visits per week for 46.2 weeks), the physician could charge an average price of $38.75 for Period 2. By failing to charge what the market will bear, the practice will lose revenue equal to $10,400 and create an excess demand of 520 visits for the year.

Even though the physician may not know the characteristics of the demand curve with precision, the existence of excess demand will become evident as the appointment calendar fills up and grows longer. The previous section showed that rising demand gives the physician a clear signal to raise prices. The same response would be expected if the physician's behavior conforms to the target income hypothesis. In this case the market clearing price will be higher still because of the output constraint introduced by the income target. If the demand curve were known, the practitioner could develop a set of simultaneous equations to determine just how much higher this price would have to be. From a practical standpoint, a trial-and-error approach to fee adjustment also could be used to reach an equilibrium price and desired income level.

Prices and Charity

The target income and profit maximization hypotheses have one point in common: both assume that the physician is ethically prepared to use the price mechanism to ration supply among all potential patients. However, in so doing some people will be denied care because they cannot afford it. This problem is not unique to the medical sector; it occurs whenever the price of a good or service is above zero. In most markets, producers and buyers accept this as a fact of economic life. What distinguishes the market for medical care is that some producers are willing to subsidize less affluent consumers at the expense of those with higher incomes. The process is known as *price discrimination* and at one time was practiced widely by physicians in this country. There is no hard evidence on how much subsidized or charity care physicians provide these days. It is known from the pioneering work on Fuchs and Kramer (Chapter 3) that price discrimination has tended to decline as coverage under private insurance and government health programs has expanded. But even if it no longer is practiced on a wide scale, it is probable that there are few physicians alive who have not provided some form of price discrimination, including giving charity care, at one time or another.

Various scenarios might be developed to show the effect of price discrimination on physician decisions regarding price and output levels. The simplest case is where the physician opts to provide a certain number of visits free of charge. Take, for example, the recent case of a community organization in western Massachusetts. The organization was concerned that the working poor and others ineligible for Medicaid but below the poverty line were unable to purchase adequate physician services. As a consequence it negotiated an agreement with a number of area doctors to set aside a given amount of time each month for free care. Assume that the solo practitioner was one of them and that this physician generously agreed to provide ten visits per week in charity care. What impact would this decision have on total output and prices charged to noncharity patients?

The answer can be found by referring back to Table 5-1. In Period 1, the physician had been producing and selling 90 visits per week. The commitment to provide charity care means that total production must rise to 100 visits to accommodate the new demand or that services to paying customers must be cut back to 80 visits per week or some combination in between. If the physician increases production by 10 visits, gross revenues will remain unchanged but costs will rise by $150 (marginal costs are $15 per visit between 90 and 100 visits). Net profit therefore will drop from $900 to $750 per week. If, on the other hand, the physician were to cut production to paying customers by 10 visits, total costs would remain the same and revenue would decline by $130 (marginal revenues are $13 per visit between 80 and 90 visits), assuming the doctor charged the market-clearing price of $31 (up from the original equilibrium price of $29). In this case net profit would equal $770, which obviously is preferable to $750. (It should be noted that any output other than 90 total visits will result in net revenues below $770 per week.) This, then, is what would be expected of the price-discriminating physician: total output will be the same as for the nondiscriminating practitioner, profits will be lower, and prices to paying customers will rise.

Time Costs and Queuing

Price discrimination is one, but not the only, method a physician might use to influence the allocation of services among different client populations. Another way is through queuing. In economic theory the *queue* (or waiting line) is an indicator that the market price is too low. If more people want to buy a service than suppliers are willing to make available at the going price, then customers must wait in line to get it. But they will not wait forever because time spent in the queue has a positive opportunity cost in terms of time lost from work or from leisure activities. An equilibrium of sorts will be established eventually when the marginal utility of the service to the last person in line (that is, the additional satisfaction to that person from purchasing and using the service) just equals the sum of the money price and time cost required to obtain it. At this point the queue will cease to grow.

To most economists, queues are viewed as an inefficient way to allocate services precisely because of the time costs involved. (These costs sometimes are referred to as *dead weight losses*, because an economic resource—the patient's time—is used with no corresponding increase in productive output.) But to the physician, queues can perform several useful functions. The typical physician employs two types of queues: the appointment calendar and the office wait. In a sense they are substitutes, because precise scheduling can reduce average waiting time. Nonetheless, each has its own unique economic characteristics. Consider first office waiting time.

No physician knows exactly how much time each patient visit will take. The appointments secretary may do a good job in scheduling but there always is the possibility that some patients will fail to show up or will take fewer minutes than estimated. Unless there is some built-in overbooking, the physician may find the day filled with unremunerative gaps. The queue would appear to be an obvious solution. However, if patients are to line up for service, there has to be adequate waiting room space to handle the load; this imposes a cost on the practice that must be balanced against the potential for increased revenue. Moreover, to induce patients to wait, the physician by definition must establish fees somewhat below the market prices that would obtain at zero waiting levels. In economic terms, the optimal queue is obtained when the revenue from a tight schedule just offsets the sum of additional waiting room costs and lost revenue from charging lower prices.

Going back to the original example, it can be assumed that this point would be reached at prices below $29 and $36.25 for Periods 1 and 2, respectively. How much lower would depend on patients' time values. If the practice served a patient population with relatively high time values, then the optimal queue would be shorter and the money price higher than if the patient population had low time values. Lacking direct information on these values, the practitioner is left with little choice but to experiment with different prices until the correct queue length is determined.

This example has tacitly assumed that the physician is a profit maximizer and, indeed, queuing is perfectly consistent with such a behavioral hypothesis. It should be noted, however, that the queuing solution introduces an equity implication not found in the traditional profit-maximizing solution. As long as the patient population exhibits mixed time values, the queue will create conditions that are relatively favorable to persons who may be unable to pay high money prices but are willing to bear high time costs. On the other side of the coin, the queue will tend to impose an additional burden on patients unwilling to wait in line.

This feature of queuing can be exploited for its own ends by physicians who refuse to practice overt price discrimination. Given a rise in demand, such a physician simply would allow the queue (excess demand) to develop beyond the profit-maximizing level, thereby rationing services on the basis of time rather than price. (The same result, incidentally, would be expected under government-imposed price controls.)

The potential reallocation engendered by queuing may involve medical as well as economic factors. No physician, hospital, or other health care provider follows a strict "first-come-first-served" rule in deciding who shall receive services. Rather, medical ethics require that the truly ill be given preference over the less ill; that patients who can benefit most from medical treatment be served before those for whom medical care is less helpful. It is a simple matter to rearrange the structure of a queue so that sicker patients are seen first. This is standard policy in most physicians' practices and no doubt is supported by a majority of patients. Nonetheless, from a business standpoint, the physician must realize that patients who are bumped back in line may just leave and seek services elsewhere. This applies to appointment schedules and waiting lines alike.

As noted, the appointment calendar is itself a type of queue. On the positive side, it allows the physician to minimize waiting room costs and to meet ethical obligations by scheduling emergency or high need patients first. Equally important, the calendar provides a buffer against minor fluctuations in demand. Day-to-day and even week-to-week changes in patient demand can be handled easily by contracting or expanding the appointment timetable.

On the negative side, there are costs associated with appointment queues just as there are with office waiting time queues. The most obvious is the salary of the appointments secretary or receptionist who performs the scheduling function. Beyond this are the opportunity costs imposed on patients, which may affect demand and hence the price a physician can charge for delayed services. From the patient's standpoint a future appointment does not use up currently available time; it does postpone the symptomatic relief or cure that the physician visit might entail. The strength of the perceived need thus is a prime determinant of whether a patient will accept a future appointment from one doctor or seek services elsewhere. At any given time patients will differ in the appointment delays they are willing to accept but, as the calendar lengthens, progressively more patients can be expected to refuse placement on the queue. As with other economic decisions confronting physicians, the optimal solution (in this case, the average delay in scheduling patients) will require a careful balancing of marginal costs and benefits.

Productivity and Labor Substitution

Rationing mechanisms based on queues or on changes in money prices are useful primarily as short-run responses to changes in demand. In the longer run, a substantial increase in demand raises the question of whether or not a firm should expand. This decision involves more than demand and revenue considerations. It requires a thorough evaluation of the production process to find the most efficient way to produce each level of output. It may turn out that more production can be obtained only by raising the unit cost of production (that is, the average cost curve slopes upward as output expands). Alternatively, it may be possible to increase productivity by using a different mix of inputs, thereby holding production costs in check.

These possibilities can be demonstrated in the context of the original example. It will be recalled that in Period 1 a profit-maximizing physician would produce 90 visits per week, given the production costs summarized in Table 5-1. A crucial, though unstated, assumption was that the production costs listed in the table represented the lowest possible expenditures consistent with each level and quality of output. If, for some reason, this assumption proves incorrect, then both the Period 1 and Period 2 equilibrium solutions will be different. In other words, before making any decision to expand, the physician first should test to see that the practice is technically and economically efficient. (The question of quality is considered in the next section.)

The test for technical efficiency really is an engineering question: Is maximum output obtained for every possible combination of inputs that might be used in the production process? Or, what amounts to the same thing, is the use of resource inputs minimized for every level of output? This test would be a simple matter if there were one and only one way to produce each output. (Economists refer to such a production process as having fixed input proportions.) In many instances, however, there are several and sometimes numerous ways that inputs can be mixed and matched to produce a given output. Such is the case with the typical physician practice according to the work of a number of health economists.[5] They argue that the production function for office visits exhibits variable input proportions in the use of labor. This means that, within limits, one type of labor (nurses, for example) can be substituted for another (physicians) without changing the characteristics of the output.

One way to tell whether there are variable input proportions in the production process is to conduct a time-and-motion study. This would entail a listing of all of the labor functions performed in the office, including clerical and managerial work as well as purely medical affairs. Next, the type of individual who performs each function in whole or in part would be determined, as well as how much time it should take, assuming each individual performed up to full potential. This information would then be summarized to show the maximum number of visits the practice could produce for various combinations of labor inputs. A simplified version of the results might look like Table 5-2, which measures physician hours on the vertical axis and allied health personnel (AHP) hours (combining nursing, clerical, and perhaps even physician extender inputs) on the horizontal axis. Arrayed in this fashion each visit total in the table is technically efficient. If, for example, the physician works 51 hours per week and uses 80 hours of allied health personnel time, the table indicates that the practice could produce a maximum of 90 visits per week. Alternatively, if the physician uses an additional 2 hours of hired help, it would be possible to produce one more visit per week. And so on.

There are two characteristics of the analysis worthy of note. First, it is evident from the circled numbers (indicating a weekly output of 90 visits) that there are several different ways to produce the same output. This is just what would be expected, since the two types of labor are at least partial substitutes. At the extreme, a physician with no office help would have to perform the functions of billing, scheduling, history taking, and other tasks typically carried out by allied health personnel. Under these circumstances the number of actual visits the physician could produce for a given number of hours practiced clearly would be less than if some help were hired. In other words, some of the physician's own time could be substituted for that of office help, or vice versa.

The second feature of note is that the two types of labor are not perfect substitutes. This goes without saying, of course, but the degree of substitutability must be known before an economically efficient combination of inputs can be determined. In economic terminology, the degree of substitutability is designated as the *marginal technical rate of substitution* or MTRS. (The MTRS is analogous to the MRS—marginal rate of substitution—introduced in the demand analysis in Chapter 4.) Because the two types of labor are not perfect substitutes, the MTRS varies with different combinations of inputs. This can be seen graphically in Figure 5-4 where an *isoquant* or "same quantity" curve has been drawn by connecting the input combinations associated with 90 visits (there is a separate isoquant

Table 5-2 Variable Input Proportions in the Production of Physician Office Visits

Physician Hours \ Allied Health Personnel Hours	66	68	70	72	74	76	78	80	82	84	86	88	90	92	94	96	98	100	102	104	106	108	110	112	114	116	118	120
58					85	87	(90)	93	95	97	97	99	99	101														
57					85	86	(90)	93	94	95	97	98	99	101														
56					84	86	88	92	93	95	96	97	98	100														
55					84	85	86	91	92	94	95	97	98	99	101													
54					83	84	86	(90)	92	94	95	96	97	99	100	101												
53						83	85	88	91	91	93	94	96	97	98	99	100	102										
52							84	86	91	92	94	95	96	97	98	99	100											
51							83	85	(90)	91	92	94	95	96	97	98	99	100	101									
50						81	83	85	88	91	91	92	93	94	95	96	97	98	99	100	101	102						
49						80	82	84	87	(90)	91	92	94	94	95	96	96	98	99	100								
48					79	81	83	86	88	91	92	93	94	95	96	96	97	98	99	100								
47				75	77	79	82	84	87	(90)	88	89	91	92	93	94	95	96	97	98	99	100	101					
46		71	74	76	78	79	82	84	87	(90)	91	92	93	94	95	96	97	98	99	100	101	102	102					
45	67	72	74	76	77	78	79	82	84	86	88	89	91	92	93	94	95	96	97	98	99	100	100	101				
44	61	65	70	73	74	76	77	78	80	83	86	88	89	91	92	93	94	95	96	97	98	99	100	101	101			
43		66	70	73	74	76	77	79	80	82	84	86	88	89	91	92	93	94	95	96	97	98	99	100	100	101	101	
42			67	71	73	75	76	78	79	80	82	83	85	87	88	(90)	91	92	93	93	93	93	94					
41				68	72	74	75	76	78	79	81	82	84	85	86	88	89	(90)	91	91	91	91	92					
40		64	66	68	72	74	75	76	77	79	80	81	82	83	84	86	87	88	88	89	89	(90)	89					
39			58	61	63	65	67	69	71	73	75	77	79	81	82	84	85	86	87	88	88	89						

Figure 5-4 Rates of Physician/Personnel Substitution

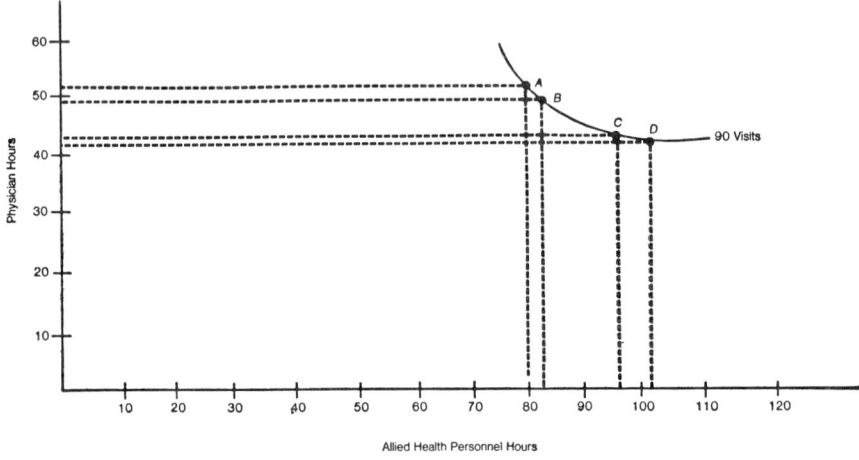

curve for each level of output). Between points *A* and *B* on the isoquant, two hours of physician time can be substituted for two hours of AHP time without changing the level of output; hence the MTRS is 2:2 or 1. But between points *C* and *D* it takes 6 hours of AHP time to replace a single hour of physician time (MTRS = 1.6 or 0.167). Thus, the MTRS decreases as one moves down the isoquant.

Alternatively, it could be said that the *marginal productivity* of a given input declines as the use of that input increases, holding all other inputs constant. To see that this is indeed true, consider a constant level of physician input of 45 hours in Table 5-2 and trace the effect on output as more and more hours of AHP time are employed. At relatively low levels of AHP use, the incremental or marginal additions to output are large. The marginal product declines as progressively more AHP hours are employed until it reaches zero at 101 visits per week. At this point the isoquant for 101 visits becomes parallel to the horizontal axis. The same phenomenon of declining marginal productivity applies to physician inputs. For any given level of AHP time, increasing additions of physician hours will yield progressively smaller additions to output. This explains why, in economic analysis, isoquant curves are always convex to the origin.

It might be suspected that a physician practice should avoid input combinations where the marginal productivity of one input is very low. This generally is correct because the cost of inputs (hourly wages, for example) will not decline just because the input becomes less productive. In other words, while every point on the isoquant (by definition) is technically efficient, not all combinations of inputs will be economically efficient.

To find the point of economic efficiency where each output is produced at lowest total cost, information on input prices is needed. Assume that the market wage (including fringe benefits) for AHP time averages $11 per hour. The physician input also has a "price" that is equal to what the doctor would have to pay to hire a replacement (or, alternatively, what the physician could earn by working for someone else). Say that the going rate for physicians is $22 per hour net of costs. With this information the total cost of production (including the value of the physician's time) can be determined at every point on the isoquant by simply adding up the hours for each type of labor and multiplying by its respective wage rate.

A particularly useful technique in this regard is shown in Figure 5-5. The parallel lines designated as $1,320, $1,958, $2,002, and $2,915 are *isocost* lines; that is, every point on a line corresponds to an identical cost in the amount shown. The slope of the line is determined by the ratio of the prices of one input for the other (in this case $11 divided by $22, giving a slope of −0.5). Consider the isocost line marked $1,320. It touches the vertical axis at 60 physician hours because 60 hours times a wage rate of $22 per hour equals $1,320. Likewise, the line touches the horizontal axis at 120 hours, because 120 hours of AHP time at $11 per hour also amounts to $1,320. Every point in between represents a combination of physician

Figure 5-5 Determining the Point of Economic Efficiency

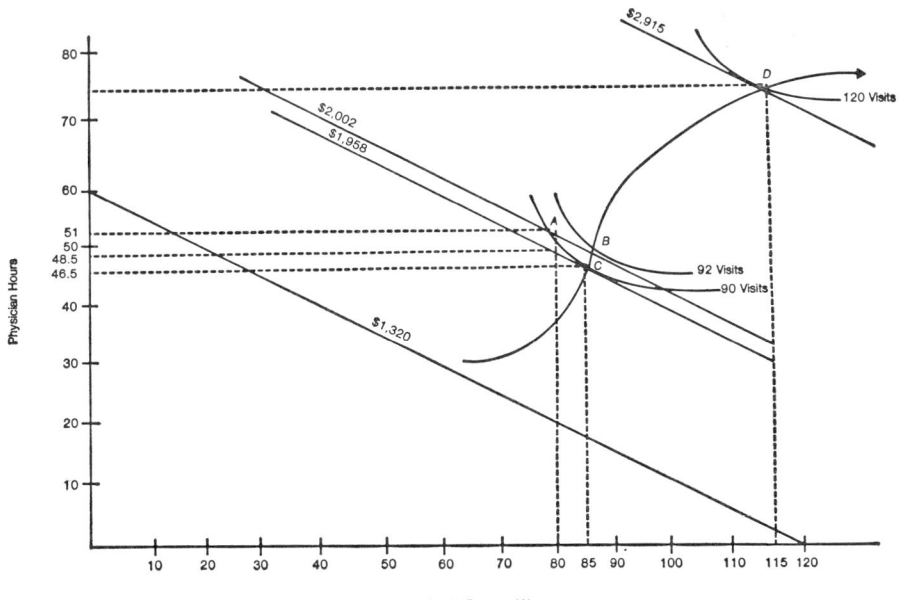

hours and AHP hours costing $1,320. The other parallel isocost lines can be interpreted in a similar manner, each for a given dollar outlay.

The quest for an economically efficient solution is now nearly complete. Assume that in Period 1 the practitioner began by working 51 hours per week and using 80 hours of AHP time (point A in Figure 5-5, derived from Table 5-2). As long as output equals 90 visits, this represents a technically efficient production process. But is it economically efficient? The answer is no, because, for a total cost of $2,002 (the value of the isocost line passing through point A), the physician could have produced 92 visits by shifting the input proportions to B (48.5 hours of physician time and 85 hours of AHP time). Alternatively, if 90 visits were considered optimal, then the most economical way to produce this output is as point C (46.5 and 85 hours of physician and AHP time, respectively) where the cost is $1,958. Only at points of tangency between an isocost line and an insoquant curve can the practice be said to be economically efficient. The line (not shown) connecting all such points in Figure 5-5 is known as an *expansion path*.

The expansion path has obvious implications for any decision to increase capacity. It will be recalled from the original example that in Period 2, patient demand was 120 visits per week at a price of $29 per visit. Starting again at point A in Figure 5-5, it can be seen that 120 visits could be produced if AHP hours were increased to 115 per week with an increase in physician hours to 75 (point D). Total cost would rise to $2,915 but the unit (average) cost actually would fall from $22 to $10.54 per visit. In this instance the practitioner could meet the increase in demand by simultaneously increasing the size and efficiency of the practice.

The theoretical expectation is that physicians always will wish to operate in an economically efficient fashion. Whether the objective is profit maximization, attainment of a target income, or optimal delivery of charity care, failure to be efficient will thwart the realization of that objective. However, the empirical literature suggests that physicians are far less productive than this model would predict. A consistent theme in this literature (well summarized in the book, *Physician Productivity and the Demand for Health Manpower*, by Uwe Reinhardt)[6] is that physician office practices underutilize auxiliary health personnel. Reinhardt's own estimates suggest that productivity could be increased by 30 to 50 percent if practitioners expanded their support staff to an average of four aides per physician.[7] Does this mean that physicians are ignorant of this productive potential? Here, as elsewhere, simple answers usually are wrong or misleading.

The fact is that physician productivity varies widely according to specialty, geographic region, and organizational characteristics of the practice. General practitioners rely more heavily on aides than do internists or obstetrics-gynecology (OBG) specialists;[8] physicians in the Southeast employ more than their counterparts in New England;[9] and group practices are heavy users of auxiliaries compared to solo practices.[10] In part, these differences reflect underlying technological constraints in the practice of medicine that limit the range of permissible labor substitution. In part, too, they reflect differences in state law and community standards of care that present legal or quasi-legal barriers to change. At the level of the individual office practice, differences arise because some physicians are more skilled in management than others and are better able to cope with the supervisory responsibilities of task delegation. Last but not least is the fact that individual physicians hold widely divergent views on the quality of care produced by allied health personnel.

Efficiency and Quality

There is a limit to how much new output can be created through efficiency improvements. To economists, that limit is determined at the point where no further cost reductions are possible without diminishing the value or quality of the output to consumers. In normal markets, buyer awareness of the characteristics that give a good or service value will be sufficient to guard against such diminution. But what about a visit to a physician's office? What are its qualitative characteristics, and how do they relate to the notions of productivity and efficiency in the production process?

One school of thought holds that the most relevant aspect of quality is the outcome of medical treatment.[11] If the outcome is good, quality is high; if the outcome is poor, quality is low. Proponents of this view do not deny that outcomes are related to the quantity of inputs used during treatment but they recognize that quantity alone cannot account for the myriad intangible factors that can lead to a cure in one instance while not in another. The main strength of this approach is that it properly emphasizes the end product in the production of health. However, as noted in Chapter 4, the production of health involves the life style of people and environmental inputs as well as medical care. It frequently is not at all clear how these inputs will interact in a given case. A physician with poor outcomes may be incompetent or simply unlucky.

A second approach to the quality issue focuses on tasks or processes in delivering medical treatments. As long as the tasks are performed properly, the provision of care can be said to meet a certain standard of quality regardless of outcome. This concept of quality was implicit in the discussion of physician productivity and labor substitution in the previous section. If a certain task can be performed competently by more than one type of labor, the choice of who carries it out is a matter for efficiency experts, not quality controllers. At first blush, it might appear that the task approach finesses the whole question of quality. It does—but only in the very limited context where some predetermined level of quality can be agreed upon. The task approach is of little help when the appropriate level of quality is itself at issue.

A third approach goes farther back in the production process to consider the attributes of those who perform the tasks. In its crudest form, this "structural" approach would rank labor inputs according to the individuals' education and training: the highest quality of care is provided by physician specialists by virtue of their superior training; specialists are better than general practitioners; GPs are better than nurse practitioners (NPs), who in turn are better than registered nurses (RNs) without such training; and so on down the line in the medical hierarchy. Aside from being elitist, this view of quality misses an essential point. Medical specialists may well perform certain defined tasks with more skill than someone with less experience but that does not mean they can perform all tasks better. The key to reaching an efficient solution without sacrificing quality is to identify which tasks can be performed equally well (and perhaps better) by the least costly form of labor available.

A slightly more subtle variant of the structural approach holds that while labor substitution can be accomplished without sacrificing quality, it takes those low in the hierarchy longer to perform a given task than it does for those at the top. There is a grain of truth here but it cannot be stretched very far. For example, there is a widely held belief that nurse practitioners can perform numerous routine therapeutic and diagnostic tasks as well as the average doctor, but take more time to do so. Indeed, economic evidence in the form of time-and-motion studies tends to back this up.[12] The problem here is in the assumption that the output is necessarily the same in both cases.

In manufacturing industries, outputs are the culmination of precisely delineated collections of labor tasks and capital inputs. In service industries, a task can be an input and an output simultaneously. The time a doctor spends with the patient is an input to the visit but it also serves as a convenient measure of output. On the same basis, if a nurse practitioner takes 30 minutes to perform a medical examination whereas the doctor takes only 20 minutes, it may mean the doctor is more productive, or the NP is providing more service, or some combination of the two. Such ambiguity obviously makes it difficult to distinguish productivity gains from quality losses and vice versa.

Consider now the case of a physician who responds to increasing demand pressure by reducing the average time spent per patient visit. Of all the responses considered thus far, this is the easiest to implement. Assume again that the solo practitioner works 51 hours per week in Period 1 and produces 90 visits. Of the 51 hours, some must be spent on nonmedical activities such as travel, signing insurance forms, and supervising the office staff. If 30 hours are spent in direct patient care, the average time per patient visit would be 20 minutes. By lowering the average to 15 minutes, the physician could meet the Period 2 demand for 120 visits without raising prices or working longer hours. The question is: Does the reduction in time reflect improved productivity or a reduction in quality?

From what has been said up to this point, the reader might well conclude that there is no answer. But economists are an ingenious lot and have developed a way out. It is based upon the notion that quality, like beauty, is in the eye of the beholder; that a good or service has no intrinsic quality other than that perceived by consumers. An important corollary is that people are willing to pay for quality in proportion to its perceived value. An economist's solution should now be apparent. If patients feel that a 25 percent reduction in visit time represents a decline in quality, then they will expect to pay less and demand will drop. On the other hand, if demand is unaffected, it can be inferred that quality has been maintained and that the reduced visit time represents improved productivity. Whether this conclusion satisfies those who are not economists by training must be decided by the reader.

A NOT-SO-FINAL WORD

This extended examination of the economics of solo practice has served two purposes. It has provided a theoretical and conceptual view of production economics not dissimilar to that found in most introductory microeconomics texts. It also has attempted to show how these economic concepts can be used to better understand the workings of small medical enterprises.

But lest the reader conclude that we have overplayed our hand, let us be the first to admit that physicians do not think exactly like economists (nor does anyone else, for that matter). The "solutions" reached here are stylized responses to simplified problems. In the real world, personal ideology and conditioned reflex surely are more important to decision making than economic rules. Yet, to twist the words of John Maynard Keynes, "Even practical physicians who believe themselves to be quite exempt from any intellectual influence are usually the slaves of some defunct economist."

NOTES

1. U.S. Department of Health and Human Services, Public Health Service, *Health, United States, 1980*, DHHS Publication No. (PHS) 81-1232. (Washington, D.C.: Government Printing Office, 1980), p. 79.
2. American Medical Association, Center for Health Services Research and Development, *Profile of Medical Practice, 1977* (Chicago: 1977), p. 136.
3. For a view of this hypothesis in depth, see "The Target Income Hypothesis and Related Issues in Health Manpower Policy," U.S. Department of Health, Education, and Welfare, Public Health Service, DHEW Publication No. (HRA) 80-27. (Washington, D.C.: Government Printing Office, 1980).
4. Arthur Owens, "Doctors' Earnings: Inflation Edges Ahead," *Medical Economics*, September 18, 1978, p. 241.
5. A useful review is presented in Uwe Reinhardt, *Physician Productivity and the Demand for Health Manpower* (Cambridge, Mass.: Ballinger Publishing Co., 1975), Chaps. 4 and 7.
6. *Ibid.*
7. *Ibid.*, p. 247.
8. *Ibid.*, p. 172.
9. *Ibid.*, p. 56.
10. *Ibid.*, p. 94.
11. A survey of the relation of outcomes to quality of care can be found in "Quality of Medical Care Assessment Using Outcome Measures," U.S. Department of Health, Education, and Welfare, National Center for Health Services Research, DHEW Publication No. (HRA) 77-3176 (Washington, D.C.: Government Printing Office, 1977).
12. Kenneth Smith, Marianne Miller, and Fredrich Golladay, "An Analysis of the Optimal Use of Inputs in the Production of Medical Services," *The Journal of Human Resources* 7 (Spring 1972): 208-225.

SUGGESTED READINGS

Blumberg, Mark. *Trends and Projections of Physicians in the United States, 1967-2002*. Berkeley, Calif.: The Carnegie Commission on Higher Education, 1971.

Kessel, Reuben A. "Price Discrimination in Medicine." *Journal of Law and Economics* 1 (October 1958): 20-53.

Long, Elliot. *The Geographic Distribution of Physicians in the United States: An Evaluation of Policy-Related Research*. Minneapolis: Interstudy, 1975.

Rayack, Elton. "The Physicians' Service Industry," in Walter Adams, ed., *The Structure of American Industry*, 5th ed. New York: Macmillan Publishing Company, 1977, pp. 419-456.

Ruffin, Roy, and Leigh, Duane. "Charity, Competition, and Pricing of Doctors' Services." *The Journal of Human Resources* 7, (Spring 1972): 212-222.

Somers, H., and Somers, A. *Doctors, Patients, and Health Insurance*. Washington, D.C.: The Brookings Institution, 1961.

U.S. Department of Health, Education, and Welfare, Health Care Financing Administration. "Price Setting in the Market for Physicians' Services," by David Juba. DHEW Publication No. (HDFA) 03012 9-79. Washington, D.C.: Government Printing Office, 1979.

U.S. Department of Health, Education, and Welfare, Public Health Service. "The Target Income Hypothesis and Related Issues in Health Manpower Policy." DHEW Publication No. (HRA) 80-27. Washington, D.C.: Government Printing Office, 1980.

U.S. Department of Health, Education, and Welfare, Public Health Service. "Analysis of Physician Price and Output Decisions," by Frank Sloan and Bruce Steinwald. National Council on Health Services Research (NCHSR) Digest Series, DHEW Publication No. (HRA) 77-3171. Washington, D.C.: Government Printing Office, 1977.

U.S. Department of Health, Education, and Welfare, Public Health Service. "Physician Requirements Forecasting: Need Based Versus Demand Based Methodologies." GMENAC Staff Papers, No. 3. DHEW Publication No. (HRA) 78-12. Washington, D.C.: Government Printing Office, 1978.

U.S. Department of Health, Education, and Welfare, Social Security Administration. "Study of Physicians' Income in the Pre-Medicare Period—1965," by Zachary Dyckman. DHEW Publication No. (SSA) 76-11932. Washington, D.C.: Government Printing Office, 1976.

U.S. Department of Health, Education, and Welfare, Social Security Administration. "Studies of Incomes of Physicians and Dentists," by Lorin Reed. Social Security Publication No. 69-19(3-69). Washington, D.C.: Government Printing Office, 1969.

Chapter 6

Introduction to Hospital Economics

It takes an intellectual leap of some magnitude to go directly from solo practices to hospitals. The economic characteristics of the two types of firms could scarcely be more divergent. The objectives and internal decision-making processes are different. Hospitals' legal and institutional constraints are more complex. And the production process in most office-based practices is simplicity itself compared to the sophisticated collection of procedures in the average hospital. If not at opposite ends of the economic spectrum, the two are sufficiently far removed that it might be asked whether the same techniques of economic analysis can be applied in both cases. The answer is a qualified "yes." The basic economic concepts underlying production, input costs, and price and output determination are equally applicable but the specification of hospitals' functional relationships is indeed more complicated.

Three functional relationships lie at the core of hospital economics and serve as the focus for this chapter:

1. The production function: How is the output of hospitals to be defined and measured? Given a measure of output, how can users be sure that inputs are combined in a technically efficient manner?

2. The cost function: Do hospitals operate so as to minimize the cost of production? Are there economies associated with hospital size? Can hospital cost functions in fact be determined empirically?

3. The objective function, perhaps the most important: Nearly 90 percent of all hospitals either are government-owned or operate as nonprofit corporations. For these facilities, any objective other than earning a surplus for the express purpose of enriching the owners is

theoretically possible. What are the alternative objectives? And how do they influence hospital price and output decisions?

The economics literature contains dozens of theoretical and empirical articles devoted to finding answers to such questions. Selected excerpts from that literature are reproduced in the following sections. Coverage of the field is expanded to include issues related to third party reimbursement (Chapter 8), competition among proprietary and nonprofit facilities (Chapter 9), and diffusion of technological innovation among hospitals (Chapter 10). With the exception of this last topic, the discussion is geared to short-term, acute care voluntary hospitals. A brief overview of the structural changes in the industry in recent years will suffice to show why the authors concentrate attention on these facilities.

STRUCTURAL CHARACTERISTICS OF THE INDUSTRY

Hospitals come in all shapes and sizes. The major categories (Table 6-1) are federal hospitals; acute care and specialized facilities operated by state and local governments; nonfederal long-term care institutions (primarily state facilities for psychiatric treatment but also those for tuberculosis and other such specialized facilities); voluntary, short-term general hospitals; and investor-owned or proprietary institutions.

It is clear from this table that over the last 30 years the industry has undergone simultaneous growth and decline. The long-term care sector has been in a period of retrenchment since 1950 because of changing patterns of institutionalization for the chronically ill and concurrent development of the nursing home industry. Capacity in the acute care sector, on the other hand, has expanded in all categories, with the greatest growth in the bed stock in voluntary institutions. Roughly 70 percent of all acute care beds now are found in these not-for-profit facilities.

The present interest in hospital economics can be related directly to the growth in the voluntary hospital sector. Some aspects of the growth may be seen in Table 6-2. The principal source of concern is what has happened within hospitals rather than the number of institutions per se. The number of voluntary hospitals actually reached a peak of 3,461 in 1967 and has declined steadily since then. Nonetheless, total bed capacity has risen rapidly (Columns 2 and 3) as a result of consolidation and growth among the existing institutions. More significant is the phenomenal increase in resources consumed per bed. As can be seen from Column 4, it is not attributable to changes in occupancy rates; rather, it results from increased

Table 6-1 The U.S. Hospital Industry: Number, Type, and Bed Capacity from 1950 to 1979*

Year	Total Hospitals	Total Beds (000)	Federal Hospitals	Federal Beds (000)	State & Local Short-Term General Hospitals	State & Local Short-Term General Beds (000)	Nonfederal Long-Term Care Hospitals	Nonfederal Long-Term Care Beds (000)	Voluntary Short-Term General Hospitals	Voluntary Short-Term General Beds (000)	Investor-Owned Short-Term General Hospitals	Investor-Owned Short-Term General Beds (000)
1950	6,788	1,456	414	189	942	131	1,343	762	2,871	332	1,218	42
1960	6,876	1,658	435	177	1,260	156	1,034	841	3,291	446	856	37
1965	7,123	1,704	443	174	1,453	179	944	788	3,426	515	857	47
1970	7,123	1,616	408	161	1,704	204	856	607	3,386	592	769	53
1975	7,156	1,466	382	132	1,840	215	795	387	3,364	659	775	73
1979	6,988	1,372	361	117	1,846	214	704	266	3,350	690	727	83

*Figures are for AHA-registered hospitals. A small number of nonregistered hospitals are excluded.
Source: Reprinted from *Hospital Statistics*, 1980 ed., by permission of the American Hospital Association, © 1980.

Table 6-2 Characteristics of Short-Term Voluntary General Hospitals, 1950 to 1979*

Year	(1) Hospitals	(2) Beds (000)	(3) Average Size (2) ÷ (1)	(4) Occupancy %	(5) Payroll Expenses per Bed	(6) Nonpayroll Expenses per Bed
1950	2,871	332	116	74.4	$ 2,554	$ 2,033
1960	3,291	446	136	76.6	5,742	3,538
1965	3,426	515	150	77.8	7,938	4,961
1970	3,386	592	175	80.1	14,088	9,836
1975	3,364	659	196	77.4	22,703	19,733
1979	3,350	690	206	76.5	34,845	34,675
% change 1950–1979	17%	108%	78%	−3%	1,264%	1,606%

*Figures are for AHA-registered hospitals.
Source: Reprinted from *Hospital Statistics*, 1980 ed., by permission of the American Hospital Association, © 1980.

expenditures for payroll and nonlabor (including *capital*) inputs. Even granting the impact of inflation, it is clear that far more real resources are used to produce acute hospital services today than was the case in earlier years.

Voluntary hospitals represent a growth industry in two respects: the first is related to the bed stock, the second is service-specific. To paraphrase a cliché, a day of hospital care isn't what it used to be. For a given diagnosis, the typical patient today spends fewer days in the institution but consumes far more ancillary services and specialized care than in years past. Virtually all of these services require additional personnel (which helps explain the rapid increase in payroll costs over time as shown in Column 5), but they also mandate new plant and equipment. Moreover, there is a strong correlation between the growth in basic capacity and the acquisition of new service capital at the individual hospital level and for the industry as a whole.

This last observation requires explanation. It is not clear whether hospitals grow in order to add new services or whether the expansion in service lines follows as a consequence of larger size. The direction of causality raises some interesting academic questions but the economic impact is the same either way. Size and service offerings are natural complements. The addition of new services can extend the hospital's marketing area and hence can create a higher demand for basic capacity. The high patient volume and cash flow made possible by increased size can improve the hospital's ability to gain financial backing for investment in new service lines. From an industry standpoint this mutually reinforcing process works well as long as aggregate demand and technology keep pace.

Up to the present, demand has been sufficient for voluntary hospitals to maintain occupancy as well as to increase capacity for both basic and ancillary services. How much more expansion can be supported in this fashion is anybody's guess, but the prospects appear limited. More than 90 percent of the population now has third party coverage for hospital care. There is little room for growth on this front even if a national health insurance plan ever is adopted. Moreover, developments in hospital rate setting and reimbursement controls (Chapter 8) may presage more concentrated efforts to constrain future growth in demand. On the other side of the coin, there is every indication that voluntary hospitals will continue to face expanding technological boundaries, new production possibilities, and ever more sophisticated ways to use additional resources. The economic challenge here is the familiar one of how best to meet society's competing wants in a world of resource scarcity. How hospitals will fare in the process is of obvious concern to administrators, planners, and policymakers alike. An understanding of the production function is a good place to begin.

HOSPITAL PRODUCTION FUNCTIONS

As noted in Chapter 5, the production function is an engineering relationship that indicates how resources (inputs) can be combined to produce various levels of output in a technically efficient manner. In the following excerpt, Sylvester Berki considers several reasons why it is difficult to find a good operational definition of hospital production. He then summarizes two well-known empirical efforts to measure hospital production functions.

HOSPITAL PRODUCTION[a]

To begin with, the production function available to the producing unit, in our case the hospital, is constrained in the short run by the resources of the hospital. The technical relationships between input combinations and output levels represented by the production function are those between *specific* inputs and specific outputs. At any given time the hospital may not have available to it the inputs *specified* in the technically best production function.

When the literature, and especially the criticisms of the operations of urban hospitals, attributes "inefficient" hospital operations to antiquated buildings and facilities, to the inadequacy of current equipment, and the lack of medically useful equipment, the meaning for the purposes of production analysis is that the inputs required for the attainment of technically efficient production are not present.

The best an existing producing unit can do, given some fixed inputs, is to use the technically best production relation, given its inputs. At this level, the identification of the best attainable technical production relationships (always keeping in mind the constraints established by the existing fixed inputs) is an engineering function. That is to say, if we are concerned not with *planning* a production unit but with the *operation* of an existing one, the problem of achieving a technically best combination of inputs, given that some of the inputs are fixed and in place, is one for engineers.

This problem in hospitals is complicated when the outputs are defined in outcome terms. To suggest that there may exist different input and technical production configurations to produce clearly developed X-rays is to pose a relatively simple engineering problem. But if we consider that the product is a successfully treated episode of illness, the outcome is always probabilistic and hence the objective is to find that technically feasible input configuration which maximizes the probability of a successful outcome. This implies that while the assumption of "homogeneous" or "invariant" or "fungible" outputs associated with different production functions may conveniently be made and then quickly forgotten in the analysis of some product outputs, all of whose dimensions can be specified, considerations of the effect of different technical combinations of inputs on the differential probabilities of successful medical outcomes must always be kept in mind. But even if we assume away the difficult issues imposed by the world of uncertainty in which hospitals operate, there are additional reasons why the technically best input combinations may not be present.

The combinations in which inputs can be used, that is to say, the substitutability among inputs, is constrained not only by technical factors but by institutional, professional, and social factors as well. Particularly in hospitals, where the largest component of input costs is labor costs, the non-technical constraints on the use of labor inputs which limit the attainable technological combinations of them must be recognized.

If the "output" is the treatment of a patient with the diagnosis of recent myocardial infarction, the "inputs" of physicians, nurses, nurses' aides, dietary and laundry facilities, chest X-ray, blood chemistry, E.K.G., possibly monitoring, inhalation therapy, and "days in bed" are all used. Clearly the services of nurses and nurses' aides are to a significant extent technically substitutable for each other: the R.N. can make the bed herself, or himself. The services of physicians are also technically substitutable for those of nurses to a significant extent: they too can make the beds, administer pharmaceuticals, take the temperature. And to some, but more limited, extent, the services of nurses are technically substitutable for those of physicians: they can both take the pulse rate, administer I.V., run the E.K.G. But nurses' aides, and most nurses, cannot read and interpret the E.K.G. or the chest X-ray. Further, at least during the diagnostic process, some services are substitutable for others, but not all are substitutes for each other. If the exact quantities of each of the inputs required to produce a "successful" treatment were known, a rough production function would result. If the substitutabilities among the various inputs were also known we would have a very acceptable production function. However, the extent to which the various labor inputs of different professional standing, technical training, and organizational status are substitutable for each other is determined by a complex set of role definitions which severely limit the technically feasible range of substitutions.

This issue in production and productivity may be seen from two perspectives. In one, we can posit that there are institutional, professional, and social constraints which establish the boundaries within which the technologically best combination of inputs, or production function, can be attained and that the objective is to identify and then to implement that production function. In the other view, the objective is to identify the best technical production function without considering non-technological constraints on the use of labor (and other) inputs and then to attempt to change the existing institutional and professional constraints which prevent its operationalization. While both of these perspectives are somewhat simplistic, they partly account for the very different evaluations of productivity in hospitals one finds in the literature. . . .

The two basic approaches to the identification of the production function in the economic literature have been *statistical* and *engineering*. In the statistical approach we attempt to identify the production function indirectly by studying an appropriate sample of costs and outputs from which a cost function is estimated. Given the successful identification of the cost function, we can then derive from it the underlying production function. In the engineering approach the focus is on the detailed description of the production relationships in physical terms. The emphasis is on the use of engineering data to develop a technical production function directly, from which, given input prices, resource constraints, and desired outputs, we estimate the implied cost functions.

Production functions may be studied at differing levels of aggregation. The production function of a single department may be identified. This has been the approach of administration-oriented systems analysts using the analytic and research techniques of operations research. The production function for a single hospital may be identified and, further, the production function for aggregates of hospitals may be studied. "A production function for acute hospitals can be a useful tool for studying several practical problems: economies of scale, optimum input proportions, and the measurement of productive efficiency" (133, p. 90).

While much operations research work has been done on individual hospital departments, or even on smaller units, in terms of identifying nurse staffing patterns, radiology department scheduling, and related aspects of hospital operations, they have not considered the hospital as an organization of interdependent producing units and hence their results are of questionable value even for the limited purposes for which they were designed. There have been few attempts to study production functions in the hospital as a whole. We next consider two such attempts.

Estimated Hospital Production Functions

The major attempt to estimate production functions for hospitals was undertaken by M. Feldstein. Defining the hospital's output to be the sum of weighted case categories, with relative average costs as weights, he experiments with various configurations of three basic aggregate production functions. . . . The basic difference among the three functional forms relates to their different assumptions about the elasticity of input substitution. . . . After various forms of input specification, and the use of different estimating techniques appear to yield few satisfactory results, this effort is abandoned in favor of a more generalized model (133, p. 120).

The "more general model of production relations" is a recursive system of five equations in beds (B), medical staff (M), drugs and dressings (D), nursing (N), and housekeeping (H) as inputs. Of the five inputs only B and M are exogenously determined, or constrained, beds by existing physical facilities and medical staff by the staffing rules applicable in the British National Health Services (from where the data originate) and the existing supply conditions. Drugs and dressings inputs are determined by the two constrained inputs B and M, while the levels of the other two factors are not considered to influence output levels, but are to be determined by the intensity of hospital operations itself, the level of output. Thus of the five inputs, output is determined by only three, B, M, and D, while the other two N and H are output determined. While beds are measured in physical units, all other inputs are measured in money terms as expenditures. Output, as in the other models, is measured in terms of weighted case categories. Hence both the measures of inputs and of outputs are highly aggregative.

In the five equations model then, output is seen as determined by the three inputs of beds, medical staff, and drugs and dressings, of which only B and M are fixed. The results show slightly decreasing returns with increasing output scale. Output, however, could be increased by a reshuffling of inputs, with less nursing and housekeeping activities and increases in the medical staff (133, p. 123). Whether the tentative nature of the analysis justifies the policy conclusion that "A general expansion of the medical staff and a reallocation in favor of larger hospitals seems warranted" is debatable (133, p. 123).

The conclusion is also baffling in view of the fact that, given the nature of the model, the inputs to be minimized (nursing and housekeeping) are endogenously determined: their levels are a function of the size of hospital output. That they are endogenously determined implies that there exists some technical relationship between their use and some dimension of output, whether captured in the definition used or not. Hence a reduction in the output-determined inputs implies a change in some dimension of output. If that dimension is considered relevant, what the model predicts is that for some other input combination more of a *different* output could be produced. Only if the output dimension changed is considered undesirable or irrelevant is Feldstein's conclusion valid. Hence the meaning of his statement that "the possibility of increasing hospital output by decreasing the amenity standard becomes clear" (133, p. 123) implies that he considers "amenity standards" to be an irrelevant dimension of output. In that case his conclusion is valid. However, since his definition of output excludes any consideration of other quite relevant dimensions of output, such as the quality of care and discharge status, it is also obvious that output measured in patient days, weighted or not, could be substantially increased by stacking patients in wards, two to a bed.

What would be desirable is a less aggregative production function, a production function of treatment. This would entail the specification of medical and hotel type services by diagnostic category for a successful termination of the inpatient phase of an illness episode. In its absence one can only speculate on the substitutability of such aggregates as "beds" and "medical staff": more complex cases may require higher numbers of time-intensive procedures, such as complex blood chemistry or BMR surveillance, and fewer medical-staff intensive inputs, resulting in longer stays and lower medical staff inputs. Other types of case complexity may require the opposite combination. Feldstein's analysis, therefore, is an interesting and careful exercise in econometrics, with some misspecification of output, but its operational fruitfulness as he cautions, is yet to be demonstrated.[a]

An attempt to identify a much more disaggregated production function of the medical services in the hospital has been undertaken by Dowling (120). Considering the hospital to be a multiproduct firm composed of a series of departments, analogously to the model we propose in chapter 1 [of Berki's book, not included in this extract], the focus of the study is narrowed to the production of medical services for inpatient care. Output is measured by patient case load decomposed into fifty-five diagnostic categories, each equally weighted on the assumption that the hospital's objective is to maximize its total patient care. The inputs are specified in engineering terms and measured in the appropriate physical units as services flowing to patients in the different diagnostic categories. The model is a linear programing one in which it is assumed that the input coefficients by diagnostic categories are fixed. That is to say, the basic assumption, whose applicability is later tested, is that to each diagnostic category there corresponds a well-defined and invariant medical service mix in terms of nursing days, specified operations, prescriptions, laboratory tests, etc. The next step is to specify the functional relationships between the service producing departments and the patients by diagnostic categories to which the services are rendered, the hospital's technology matrix.

The technology matrix is initially specified by fourteen medical service departments and fifty-five diagnostic categories and the input-output coefficients are estimated by regression techniques.[b] The absence of available data for two departments (p. 178) limited the analysis to twelve types of services. Tests for the linearity of the coefficients revealed that in the case of three additional departments (inhalation therapy, ECG, and IPPB) the input coefficients did not meet the linearity assumptions, leaving the model with eight specified inputs.

In a linear programing approach, the problem is to estimate the input coefficients, specify the outputs, and, given the constraints on resources (input capacities), estimate the optimum feasible outputs in terms of the number of patients in the specified diagnostic categories that can be treated. That is, both the optimum volume and diagnostic mix are estimated as well as the trade-offs among the various diagnostic categories that can be accommodated.

Using an argument similar to Feldstein's (133, pp. 120–24), Dowling assumes that the so-called minor departments do not have rigid capacity limits and hence they do not act as constraints on output. He considers that of the eight departments for whose outputs the coefficients can be accurately estimated and accepted to be linear, only five enter the production process. Output, in diagnosis specific patient days, is therefore seen to be a linear function of five departmental service inputs: nursing days, laboratory, radiology, delivery rooms, and operating rooms (120, pp. 177–83). The capacities of the departments producing these services are estimated by considering both physical and institutional constraints, such as "normal" weekly periods during which operations are carried out. After trying various specifications of the linear programing model, Dowling concludes that the study hospital "operated at from 78.5 to 85.1 percent of optimum efficiency" (p. 228), that is, that it could have treated significantly more patients without exceeding its capacity.

Perhaps the most interesting finding of this study is that specification four of the model, which considers institutionally (or what Dowling calls "experienced") constrained capacities and where the minimum permissible solution values for outputs are constrained to the actual number of patients by diagnostic category treated during the study year (p. 206, ff.), the major binding constraint is the number of operating room hours (p. 211). That is to say, while in actual terms the hospital produced some 15 percent below its feasible optimum output, *had* it been on its production possibility surface, the constraint with the highest shadow price would have been operating room hours: for each unit increase in operating room hours 0.76 more patients in the surgical categories could have been treated. In general the findings on the other constraints (pediatric, medical-surgical, psychiatric, obstetric, and newborn patient days), while more disaggregated and hence more specific, are in accord with Feldstein's finding that the constraints are imposed by beds and staffing, while laboratory tests, drugs, X-rays and other ancillary services are nonbinding.

Dowling's formulation is both ingenious and potentially fruitful in demonstrating the approach to a detailed specification of the production processes within the hospital. But, as he recognizes, a number of problems remain. One major problem, to those who are interested in the quality dimension of medical care, is that that dimension is not captured. In further attempts with the linear programing approach, quality should be incorporated into the output. Further, there are some serious difficulties with the assumption that in the hospital's objective function all treatments to patients, regardless of their diagnostic class, are weighted equally. This is recognized by Dowling and discussed at length by Feldstein, who demonstrates that the use of different weighting schemes (equal weights, by duration or by average cost of stay) yield very different results in terms of what the binding constraints are (133, p. 180).

HOSPITAL COST FUNCTIONS

Closely related to the production function is the cost function, a relationship between cost and output level. Conceptually, the problem of defining costs is easy. Costs relevant for economic analysis are opportunity costs—the values of resources in their best alternative use. Unfortunately, the data on costs that generally are available are based on accounting records of money payments for inputs. These may not reflect true economic costs for a variety of reasons, including externalities and inadequacy or inaccuracy of data, so the matter of giving empirical content to the economic concept is quite difficult. The problem is complicated when dealing with a multiproduct firm, such as the typical community hospital. Some techniques of cost finding commonly used in empirical analysis are reviewed in Chapter 11. Here, studies that use available data to estimate hospital cost functions are considered.

A major reason for estimating hospital cost functions is to investigate the relationship between cost and hospital size, that is, *economies of scale* (or *scale economies*). The framework is presented well by Alan L. Sorkin.

ECONOMIES OF SCALE[b]

Conceptually, the question of the existence of returns to scale is straight-forward. In the production of hospital services, just as in the production of any good or service, certain resources, or factors of production, are utilized as inputs in order to obtain a given output. Returns to scale are concerned with the relationship that exists between the inputs and the output. Specifically, the question of returns to scale focuses on what happens to the level of output as the quantity of inputs increases. If the inputs are increased in equal proportional amounts, and output grows at a constant rate, then there are constant returns to scale (constant costs); if output grows at an increasing rate, there are increasing returns to scale (decreasing costs); and if output rises at a decreasing rate, there are decreasing returns to scale (increasing costs).

Economies of scale can result from the specialization of factors of production. For example, the division of labor may permit greater specialization resulting in increased productivity. It seems reasonable to expect that division and specialization of nursing services in hospitals would result in economies of scale. These economies may also result from the use of certain indivisible factors of production. To the extent that certain "lumpy" inputs were required in the production of hospital services, economies of scale would result from the use or combination of factors in more efficient proportions concomitant with higher levels of output. A number of facilities might be suggested that seem to be indivisible in this sense. It is probably impossible, for example, to construct one-half of a pathology laboratory.[9]

Diseconomies of scale, if they exist at all, are usually associated with the inefficiencies of very large-scale management. For example, if a hospital becomes sufficiently large, the burden of administration may become so great that average costs would rise.

Economics textbooks have generally depicted long-run average cost curves as being U-shaped (Figure 6-1). The reason for this is that at lower levels of output economies of scale are important, but at higher levels of output all of these economies are fully

Figure 6-1 Long-Run Average Cost Curve

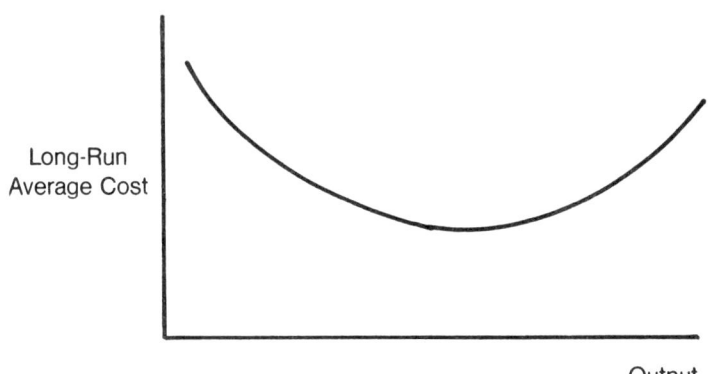

exploited and the diseconomies of exceedingly large scale may have a major influence on costs. The concept of an optimal size follows from the balancing of these forces. If average cost first falls and then rises as the level of output increases, the optimal size is that which coincides with a minimum average cost.

The existence of economies of scale in the production of hospital services is significant from a policy viewpoint. First, the prevalence of nonprofit enterprises in this industry implies that certain incentives for efficiency that are present in profit-making enterprises are missing or inoperative in the hospital industry. Moreover, forces external to the market influence the construction of new facilities and the expansion of existing facilities. Rational planning requires some indication of the relationship between hospital size and hospital costs.[10] Thus, planning agencies need to know whether or not there is an optimal size for different types of hospitals.

Two empirical methods have been utilized to determine the relationship between cost and output in a firm or group of firms. One approach has been to select a particular firm and study its costs and output over a period. This is known as the time-series method. The other approach, which is used in virtually all hospital cost studies, is to select a particular time period and observe the relationship between cost and output for a large number of firms. In either case, cost analysis is often complicated by variations in product quality and by inability to segregate costs by product for multiproduct firms. Both of these complications are particularly important in an analysis of hospital costs.

Variations in the quality of a particular hospital service undoubtedly exist among hospitals and they probably exist within a single hospital as well. For example, two different hospitals may have facilities for open-heart surgery, but there can be major differences in the quality of care and treatment. Usually higher quality is associated with higher costs of production and, conceptually, cost analysis requires standardization for quality variations.[a] Unfortunately, it is extremely difficult to quantify this particular dimension of quality and its influence on costs cannot be estimated directly.

A further complication for hospital cost analysis results because the output statistics do not reflect differences in the kinds of services provided in different hospitals. Hospitals are essentially multiproduct firms and total costs are not generally segregated for the different products produced. Thus, for example, two hospitals that produce the same range of services may have different average costs because they produce different proportions of these services or a different range of services associated with a dissimilar case mix.

Determination of the optimum allocation of hospital resources involves consideration of both the costs incurred by hospitals themselves and the costs associated with hospitalization that are borne by staff, patients, and visitors. Perhaps the most obvious external cost is travel cost, measured in terms of both dollar outlay and the psychological cost of time consumed.[11]

In any given community, average travel cost per patient day will depend upon a variety of factors such as the location of hospitals, the distribution and characteristics of the population, and the pattern of travel routes. In general, however, one can assume that if the sizes of hospitals were increased (with constant utilization rates), their geographic service areas would expand and, consequently, average travel cost (for both doctors and patients) would rise.[b] In Figure 6-2, line AA relates the average cost per patient day incurred by the hospital to the size of the institution, line BB represents average travel cost, and line CC indicates their sum. Note that the optimum size of a hospital is reduced (from OS_1 to OS_2) when travel cost is considered. While travel cost obviously affects the optimal size and location of hospitals, only the costs actually incurred by hospitals, and reflected in their accounts, have been considered by economists who have done empirical work relating hospital size to cost.

Figure 6-2 Effect of Travel Expenses on Hospital Costs

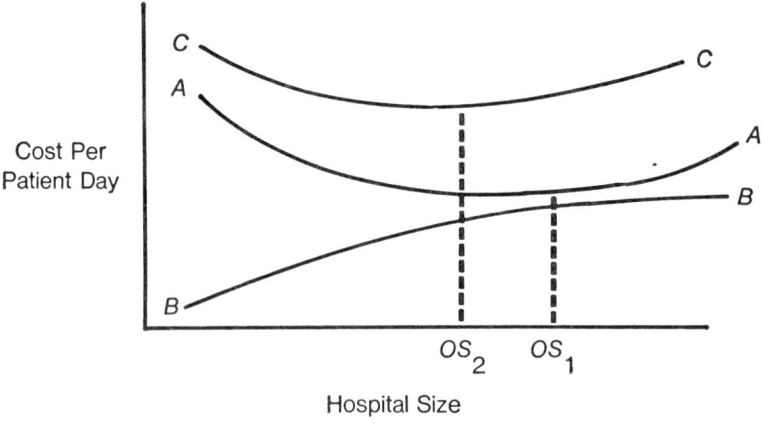

A - average cost of hospital services
B - travel cost to hospital
C - total cost

Many econometric attempts to estimate hospital cost functions have been carried out in recent years. The studies differ in methodology, data used, and results. While most investigators have found some economies of scale for hospitals, that conclusion is far from unanimous, and the specific results concerning the extent of economies and the optimal size vary widely. The findings of some of the major studies are summarized in Table 6-3.

A detailed review of these studies is not presented here (it is contained in Berki, pp. 87–119). Instead, there follows in some detail an example of how economists have attempted to estimate hospital cost functions. This selection by Judith and Lester Lave is more technical than most others in the book and is not essential for understanding later material. Thus, it can be omitted or merely skimmed. For the interested reader, however, it gives a good example of the problems and possibilities of empirical research in health economics.

HOSPITAL COST FUNCTIONS[c]

The estimation of cost functions has received wide attention in recent years (see John Johnston, Alan Walters). Curve fitting techniques have given way to careful investigations of firm (or industry) models. Economists have begun to explore the possi-

Table 6-3 Results of Studies on Economies of Scale*

Investigator	Existence of Economies of Scale	Minimum Long-Run Average Cost Point in Terms of Beds
Cohen[a]	Yes, strong	150–350 depending on output definition
Cohen[b]	Yes, strong	540–790 depending on quality measure
Ingbar and Taylor[c]	No	—
Lave and Lave[d]	Probably yes	—
Lave and Lave[e]	Probably no and if so, very weak	—
Francisco[f]	No	—
Klarman[g]	Yes	—
Carr and Feldstein[h]	Yes	190
Ro[i]	Yes	900
M.S. Feldstein[j]	Yes	300–900 depending on equation specification
Panel on Hospital Care[k]	No	—

Source: Reprinted from *Hospital Economics* by Sylvester Berki by permission of Lexington Books, D.C. Heath and Company, © 1972, p. 115.
*References cited here are listed in a separate section at the end of this chapter.

bilities that the cost function of a firm may shift over time (in a neutral or non-neutral fashion) and that a cross-section of firms may not all have the same cost function. More recently, investigators have attempted to account for errors of observation and the possibility of a simultaneous equations bias due to the level of cost affecting the rate of output (see Marc Nerlove).

All of these problems, with some added wrinkles, occur in estimating a cost function for a multi-product firm (see Ralph Pfouts). Even in the simplest terms, the multi-product firm requires a host of independent variables (one for each product) instead of a single one. Added to this difficulty is the likelihood that the quality of at least one product will change over time or that products will be differentiated across firms.

There are three problems that should be stressed. First, most econometricians would agree that an estimated cost function, rather than being a "true" specification of the transformed production function, is but an approximation over a relevant range. The nature of the approximation and the extent of the "relevant range" becomes more difficult to specify when there are many products. Hence, it seems even more advisable to regard the cost function of a multi-product firm as an approximation over a relevant range.

Second, regardless of whether one or many outputs is involved, estimated marginal costs tend to be sensitive to the specification of the function. This observation leads one to be cautious in estimating single product cost functions; it should lead one to be even more cautious in estimating multi-product cost functions. For such functions, it is essentially impossible to reflect the underlying cost structure in a single function (which is susceptible to estimation). The estimates from any multi-product cost function must be used with care.

The third difficulty arises when the measure of output is not a good one. For example, some firms (such as automobile manufacturers) produce a host of different advertised models and possible optional features. If each of the possible products were counted separately, it is inconceivable that a cost function could be estimated: There would be thousands of products. Either one must use a "composite output measure" or some measures of output mix.[1]

The hospital is a multi-product firm; it produces varying quantities of education, research, community services, outpatient care, and, its predominant activity, inpatient care. None of these activities is homogeneous across hospitals. In addition to the problems discussed above, the estimation of the hospital cost function is complicated by the difficulty of measuring the quality (appropriateness and competence) of each of the many services produced by the hospital.

The most commonly used measure of hospital output is unidimensional: the number of patient days produced.[2] The implicit assumption that all patient days are the same, both within and across hospitals, is obviously incorrect. In addition, the assumption is not a useful one in practice since the estimates of cost functions based on it have been characterized as nonsensical.[3] Several alternative measures have been suggested. However, much work remains to be done in defining and measuring the output of hospitals.[4]

In this paper we develop a method for estimating the hospital cost function which attempts to deal with the problems stemming from the multi-product nature of output. With data consisting of time-series on many firms, the multi-product nature of each firm can be accounted for in either of two procedures; both of them are based on the assumption that, while the output mix differs among hospitals, it is constant within a hospital (over a short time period). The first procedure involves two stages of analysis and allows the cost function to differ among hospitals. In the first stage, a relation between average cost, utilization, size, and time is estimated for each hospital. The second stage is a search for the causes of the variation in the estimated parameters among hospitals. The second procedure is based on the more limited assumption that all hospitals have the same cost function. Here, the data are pooled (to form a cross-section time-series) and a single cost function is estimated.

Although we are concerned directly with hospitals, we believe that our techniques are applicable to other multi-product and multi-service industries. In Section I we describe the estimation procedure in detail. In Section II the results are presented, and in Section III the conclusions are discussed.

I. The Estimation Procedure

The Two-Stage Procedure

The cost per patient day (total cost divided by total patient days) may be written as in equation (1),

$$AC_{it} = f_{it}(U_{it}, S_{it}, X_{it}) \qquad (1)$$

where U_{it} is utilization (output as a percent of capacity)[5] in period t, S_{it} is hospital size (the number of beds) in period t, and X_{it} is a vector which characterizes the product mix (both the diversity and quality of services provided) of hospital i in period t. As written, there is no presumption that the function remains constant over time in a given hospital or is the same across hospitals. So general a case is not considered. We do assume that the functional relations remain stable over short periods of time for each hospital but that neutral shifts in the function may occur.

As noted in the introduction, there is no satisfactory measure of hospital output. However, under special circumstances, the problem can be handled. We assume that the product mix of a hospital remains constant over a period of a few years.[6] If, as we assume, the hospital output vector is subject to proportional (or balanced) shifts, X remains unchanged over the period within a given hospital. If we were estimating a cost function for hospital

i from time-series data, X_{it} could be dropped from equation (1), as shown in equation (2).

$$AC_{it} = A(t)f_i(U_{it}, S_{it}, e_{it}) \qquad (2)$$

The $A(t)$ allows a neutral shift of the function over time. Insofar as output is not subject strictly to proportional expansion, an error e_{it} will be introduced. If there are additional variables (influencing the cost function) which are omitted, they would also contribute to an error term.

According to convention, short-run average (total) cost is a U-shaped function of output while the long-run average cost curve may display increasing, decreasing, or constant returns to scale. Most empirical studies of the short-run cost function have found an L-shaped relation (see Johnston and Walters). There are many reasons to expect an L-shaped curve for hospitals, the prime one being that hospitals tend to staff for a higher than average level of utilization so they can be ready on a stand-by basis. A functional form consistent with the L-shaped short-run average cost is the generalized Cobb-Douglas or linear in logarithms form. Another argument for this specification is that hospital costs have risen sharply in recent years. It seems likely that the variance of the error term in equation (2) is directly proportional to the size of AC. Thus, we specify the average cost curve for hospital i as in equation (3).[7]

$$\log AC_{it} = a_{i0} + a_{i1}t + a_{i2} \log U_{it} \qquad (3)$$
$$+ a_{i3} \log S_{it} + e_{it}$$

With a number of observations on each hospital over time, the parameters of equation (3) can be estimated for each hospital i. The coefficient of the time variable (t) indicates all changes in average cost which are geometrically related to time and are not accounted for by variation in utilization or size. Neutral technological change would contribute to a negative a_{i1}; increasing factor prices to a positive a_{i1}. In this model there is no way of separating cost reductions from cost increases and hence a_{i1} is a net inflation coefficient for each hospital. The coefficient of a_{i2} will indicate whether a hospital is operating on the declining portion of the short-run cost curve. Similarly, the coefficient of a_{i3} will indicate (if a hospital expanded) whether it captured economies of scale.

The output of this estimation procedure will be four estimated parameters for each hospital. The estimated relation for each hospital is a rather conventional time-series cost function. One might now ask: why do these parameters vary across hospitals? Is there any systematic way to explain differences in these parameters among hospitals? To answer these questions, a second-stage procedure is necessary.

Stage Two

Differences in hospital characteristics should lead to differences in the hospital cost function. Large hospitals tend to have more specialized facilities, the cost of which has been rising rapidly. They also tend to be located in urban areas where the price of labor inputs has been rising rapidly. However, large hospitals are generally run by trained managers who should be more efficient and better able to adapt to changing factor prices and technology. On balance, it is difficult to predict whether large hospitals should experience more or less inflation. Similarly, one can consider rural versus urban hospitals, or teaching versus nonteaching hospitals. Rural hospitals have lower absolute costs, but it is difficult to predict whether this gap is narrowing or widening over time. If, in fact, factor prices are rising more rapidly in the urban areas, one would predict that the gap is widening. Teaching programs tend to raise average costs. Hospitals with extensive teaching programs have the newest equipment. As medicine grows more expensive, these hospitals lead the way. We would expect that advanced teaching hospitals have had the highest rate of inflation, followed by teaching hospitals.

The management of a hospital tends to be permissive. Virtually all patients have their bills paid by insurance or government; even self-pay patients rarely worry about cost when hospitalization is required. The medical staff, which bears no responsibility for costs, generally makes all decisions about medical care. Possibly the only important check on cost is provided by a comparison of hospitals. If a hospital's costs rise more rapidly than those of comparable hospitals, some pressures will be exerted by Blue Cross, patients, and conscientious doctors. This behavioral observation provides the basis of a crude dynamic theory. Hospitals with relatively high initial cost will, *ceteris paribus,* tend to experience a slower rate of cost increase in the future.

This investigation of the variation of the a_{i1} can be formalized in a regression as shown in equation (4).

$$a_{i1} = b_0 + b_1 \log S_{i0} + b_2 P_i + b_3 M_i$$
$$+ b_4 AT_i + b_5 T_i + b_6 \log AC_{i0} \quad (4)$$
$$+ b_7 \log U_{i0} + e_{i1}$$

Here S_{i0} is the size of the ith hospital in the first period, P_i and M_i are dummy variables indicating the hospital's location (Pittsburgh, other urban, or rural); AT_i and T_i are dummy variables representing the hospital's teaching status (advanced teaching, teaching, or nonteaching), AC_{i0} and U_{i0} are, respectively, the hospital's average cost and utilization rate in the first period.

We also investigated the other parameters, a_{i2} and a_{i3}, using the explanatory variables of equation (4). We cannot, however, conjecture about the signs of the coefficients.

The Laves ran into certain data problems in trying to estimate their model. These are detailed in the next section, which also presents the estimation results. The reader interested in empirical research or in a detailed application of multiple regression analysis should read this section. Others may skim it or skip directly to the Laves' summary and conclusion at the end of the excerpt.

The Data: Some Difficulties

Data were obtained on 74 western Pennsylvania hospitals for the period 1961–67. In all, 14 semiannual observations were obtained on each hospital. Cost and utilization data were obtained from *Comparative Financial and Statistical Information,* a report by Blue Cross of Western Pennsylvania. Pennsylvania hospitals are required to submit semiannual reports to the Insurance Commissioner of Pennsylvania. These reports are checked and summarized by the audit staff of Blue Cross. Data on hospital size, number of facilities, geographical location, and teaching status were obtained from unpublished data series by Katherine Barker of Blue Cross of Western Pennsylvania. Her data on hospital size and number of facilities were based on information published in the annual August issue of *Hospitals, Journal of the American Hospital Association.*

After the analysis described in Section I was performed, we went on to extend the results and corroborate them with data from Blue Cross of Greater Philadelphia. When the Pittsburgh data were aggregated into annual observations, a consistent result was that all coefficients agreed with the semiannual analysis except that of utilization; it fell from $-.6$ to $-.3$. The latter value was nearly identical to the parameter estimates from the Philadelphia (annual) data. In all cases, the estimated parameter was extremely significant (more than ten times its standard error). The consistency between Pittsburgh and Philadelphia results implied that $-.3$ was the correct estimate. However the inconsistency between semiannual and annual results (for Pittsburgh data) was disconcerting since it implied that the underlying structure was not compatible with our model.

An inquiry into data collection revealed that the first semiannual observation (for each hospital) is an estimate, unaudited by Blue Cross. At the end of the year, Blue Cross subjects the annual estimate to an intense audit to determine costs for purposes of reimbursement. The second semiannual observation is then calculated as the difference between the audited annual figure and the estimated first half costs, i.e., it is a residual. Questions were raised about the accuracy of the first semiannual cost estimates.

We investigated the possibility of errors in the semiannual figures by inserting a dummy variable for first or second half of the year (F takes on a value of 0 if the observation is for the first half and a value of 1 if it is for the second half). The correlation between F and utilization is $-.5$, indicating that the occupancy rate is significantly higher in the first half than it is in the second. When F is inserted in the regression, all parameter estimates are nearly identical to those from the annual data.

The apparent explanation is that, since costs have been rising rapidly (more than 3 percent annually for these hospitals), hospitals tend to underestimate first half costs systematically (by about 2 percent and thus overestimate second half costs by 2 percent). When this underestimate is combined with the systematic difference in utilization, the estimate of marginal cost is biased downward. The artificially low average cost of the first half occurs when there is high utilization; the artificially high average cost of the second half occurs when there is low utilization. Thus, the cost increase due to higher utilization is systematically underestimated. The only parameter affected by adding F to the regressions is the coefficient of utilization; we present the results of the extended model in the sections which follow.

II. The Results

The Two-Stage Procedure

In the first stage of the two-stage procedure, we estimated equation (3), with F added for each of the 14 hospitals in our sample. With 14 observations, there were 9 degrees of freedom. The results were in accordance with our expectations and the coefficients of determination were almost always greater than .9.

The coefficients of the time dummy variable, a_{i1}, had a mean of 3.28 percent (indicating a mean rate of inflation of 3.28 percent) and a standard deviation of 1.04 percent. This coefficient was almost invariably significant and it ranged from .7 percent to 6.0 percent. A histogram showed the distribution of the coefficient to be unimodal with its median almost identical to the mean.

The coefficient of utilization a_{i2} had a mean of $-.605$ and a standard deviation of .591. Thus, on average, variable cost was 40 percent of total cost. The coefficient was generally significant with a range from -2.775 to .893. A histogram showed the distribution of this coefficient to be unimodal with its median approximately equal to its mean.

The coefficient of size, a_{i3}, had a mean of $-.333$ and a standard deviation of 2.418. The coefficient was almost never significant with a range from -13.4 to 8.5. Although the distribution of the coefficient was unimodal, the median was about $-.03$. Very little can be said about the slope of the long-run average cost curve from these results. The coefficient of period had both mean and standard deviations equal to .020; it ranged from $-.029$ to .100 with a single mode and median at .020.

Stage two, where we were attempting to explain the variation in a coefficient among hospitals, was frankly a search for significant coefficients. We were attempting to learn whether the variation in each of the coefficients could be explained by hospital characteristics, how much of the variance could be explained, and which variables had an affect. Many explanatory variables were tried.

Hospital Cost Increases

Five regressions, reported in Table 6-4, were used to explain the variance in the inflation coefficient across hospitals. The dependent variable, a_{i1}, is the rate of cost increase for hospital i, after accounting for cost changes due to variation in utilization

Table 6-4 Hospital Cost Increases[a,b]

$$a_{i1} = b_0 + b_1 \log AC_0 + b_2 \log S_0 + b_2 \log U_0 + b_4 AT + b_5 T + b_6 P + b_7 M + b_8 \log K_0 \quad \bar{R}^2$$

	b_0	$b_1 \log AC_0$	$b_2 \log S_0$	$b_2 \log U_0$	$b_4 AT$	$b_5 T$	$b_6 P$	$b_7 M$	$b_8 \log K_0$	$\bar{R}^2$
(1-1)	.240	−.047 (2.41)	.024 (4.67)	0.035 (−1.58)						.210
(1-2)	.272	−.052 (−2.46)		−.024 (−1.06)	.013 (3.68)	.009 (3.41)				.154
(1-3)	.178	−.036 (1.52)		−.007 (−.34)						.047
(1-4)	.294	−.058 (−2.59)	.016 (2.14)	−.036 (1.60)	.004 (.78)	.005 (1.40)	.004 (1.15)	−.005 (1.61)		.213
(1-5)	.659	−.060 (−2.72)	.021 (2.60)	−.058 (2.27)	.002 (.43)	.004 (1.24)	.001 (.20)	−.003 (−.25)		
							.002 (.54)	−.003 (−.94)	−.061 (−1.70)	.235

[a] Values of the *t*-statistic are shown in parentheses under the coefficients, in Tables 6-4, 6-5, and 6-6.
[b] There were 74 observations:

Variable	Mean	Variable	Mean	Variable	Mean
a_{i1}	.003	$\log U_0$	2.888	P	.324
$\log AC_0$	3.406	AT	.208	M	.338
$\log S_0$	2.249	T	.364	$\log K_0$	4.975

or size. These regressions explain nearly one-fourth of the variation in a_{i1}, correcting for the loss in degrees of freedom. In the first regression the inflation coefficient for each hospital is a function of its initial cost per patient day (AC_0), its initial size (S_0) and its initial utilization rate (U_0). The signs of the coefficients indicate that, *ceteris paribus,* hospitals with high initial average costs tended to have relatively smaller rates of cost increase; large hospitals tended to have relatively larger rates of cost increase; and hospitals with high initial utilization tended to have relatively smaller rates of cost increase. Both the coefficients of AC_0 and S_0 are significant; the coefficient of U_0 approaches significance.

The signs of the regression coefficients accord with our expectations. Large hospitals tend to have teaching programs, more specialized treatment facilities, and to be located in large cities. We speculate that the costs of teaching programs and specialized care have risen more rapidly than the cost of simple care. We also speculate that urban wage rates have risen relative to rural wage rates. All three of these factors would tend to account for the positive coefficient of S_0. These data do not permit investigation of our speculations; we intend to pursue them in future research.

The negative coefficient for U_0 is difficult to interpret. Since it is widely recognized that short-run marginal cost is a fraction of average cost, hospital administrators realize that one way of holding down cost is to keep the utilization rate high. Thus, the negative coefficient for U_0 might be taken to mean that hospitals with high utilization are, *ceteris paribus,* hospitals with a concern for holding down costs.

Regressions (1–2), (1–3), (1–4), and (1–5) contain variables indicating the nature of a hospital's teaching program and location. A hospital is classified as having an advanced teaching program (AT), a teaching program (T), or no teaching program. Three dummy variables can be used to describe these classifications. Note that one variable must be excluded to fit the regression. The excluded variable (those hospitals with no teaching program) has a coefficient of zero, relative to hospitals with teaching programs (actually, the coefficient of the excluded variable is part of the constant term). The location of a hospital is also defined in terms of three dummy variables. If a hospital is located in Pittsburgh or the surrounding counties, it is classified as P. If it is in one of the other western Pennsylvania counties which has at least 50 percent of its residents in cities, it is classified as M.

Otherwise, it is classified as rural and, relative to P and M hospitals, has a coefficient of zero.

In regression (1–2) the coefficients of AT and T indicate that hospitals with advanced teaching programs averaged a 1.3 percentage point (per year) higher rate of cost inflation than hospitals with no teaching programs; hospitals with regular teaching programs averaged a 0.9 percentage point (per year) higher inflation than hospitals with no teaching programs. In regression (1–4), when variables representing hospital location are included, the size of the teaching coefficients decreases (as would be expected). The coefficients, however, still indicate that the rate of cost inflation was higher in advanced teaching hospitals than in teaching hospitals, and higher in teaching hospitals than in nonteaching hospitals.

In regression (1–3) the coefficients of P and M indicate that hospitals in Pittsburgh had a .4 percentage point greater increase in cost than rural hospitals; Metropolitan hospitals had a .5 percentage point lower rate of cost increase than rural hospitals. Since neither M nor P is significant, there is no conclusive evidence for our conjecture that rural hospitals probably experienced a lower rate of cost inflation than urban hospitals.

In the final regression, the initial value of the size index number is added. If hospitals grew rapidly, their value of K_0 will be quite small; hospitals that did not grow will have a K_0 of unity. The negative coefficient for K_0 indicates that hospitals which grew most rapidly had the greatest rate of cost increase; hospitals which did not grow at all had the smallest rate of cost increase. However, this effect is not significant.

The Utilization Coefficient

The regressions analyzing the variation in a_{i2} the coefficients of the utilization index are reported in Table 6-5. (The coefficient of the utilization index carries the interpretation that a 1 percentage point increase in mean utilization implies an a_{i2} percentage point decrease in mean average cost.) In interpreting the results of the regressions it should be remembered that, since the utilization coefficient is negative, a small coefficient is one which is large in absolute value.

In the first regression the independent variable is K_0, the initial value of the size index. The negative sign indicates that hospitals

Table 6-5 Variation in Utilization Coefficient

a_{i2}	$= b_0$	$+ b_1 \log K_0$	$+ b_2 \log S_0$	$+ b_3 \log U_0$	$+ b_4 \log AC_0$	$+ b_5 AT$	$+ b_6 T$	$+ b_7 P$	$+ b_8 M$	$\bar{R}_2$
(2–1)	16.669	−3.472								.030
		(−1.80)								
(2–2)	15.162	−3.128						−.184	−.429	.096
		(−1.67)						(−1.14)	(−2.69)	
(2–3)	14.784	−3.041				.037	−.183	−.173	−.430	.098
		(−1.62)				(.18)	(−1.16)	(−.93)	(−2.70)	
(2–4)	−6.329			2.846	−.640	−.002	−.237	−.225	−.461	.115
				(2.18)	(−.48)	(−.01)	(−1.47)	(−1.12)	(−2.91)	
(2–5)	3.219	−1.596	.009	2.335	−.691	.005	−.225	−.195	−.446	.096
		(−.72)	(.02)	(1.48)	(−.51)	(.02)	(−1.12)	(−.94)	(−2.70)	

There were 74 observations: mean a_{i2} = .605, mean a_{i3} = −.333

Table 6-6 Variation in First-Half Coefficient

a_{i4}	$= a_0$	$+ a_1 \log K_0$	$+ a_2 \log S_0$	$+ a_3 \log U_0$	$+ a_4 \log AC_0$	$+ a_5 AT$	$+ a_6 T$	$+ a_7 P$	$+ a_8 M$	$\bar{R}^2$
(3–1)	.269			.041	−.116					.070
				(.87)	(−2.77)					
(3–2)	.228		.012	.058	−.108			−.004	−.017	.169
			(1.15)	(1.35)	(−2.49)			(−.59)	(−3.14)	
(3–3)	.270			.055	−.120	.012	−.005			.128
				(1.24)	(−2.84)	(1.68)	(.94)			
(3–4)	.244			.060	−.115	.007	−.006	−.006	−.017	.226
				(1.43)	(−2.64)	(1.37)	(−1.19)	(−.94)	(−3.24)	
(3–5)	.277	−.006	−.002	.060	−.115	.010	−.006	−.006	−.017	.203
		(−.08)	(−.12)	(1.17)	(−2.60)	(1.04)	(−.88)	(−.89)	(−3.10)	

There were 74 observations: mean a_{i4} = .020

which experienced the greatest increase in size had the largest a_{i2} (smallest a_{i2} in absolute value). That is, hospitals experiencing the greatest increase in size had the greatest increase in average cost when utilization increased. In other words, the hospitals which grew the most had the highest marginal cost.[9]

The second regression adds variables for the location of each hospital. The negative coefficients mean that urban hospitals have lower marginal cost than rural ones. Teaching status is added in regression (2–3). There is some indication that teaching hospitals have lower marginal cost than either advanced teaching or non-teaching hospitals.

The fourth regression substitutes initial utilization and average cost for K_0. The significance of location and teaching variables is enhanced and the coefficient of determination is increased. The positive, significant coefficient of initial utilization is interpreted to mean that hospitals with high utilization have high marginal cost, i.e., increases in utilization do not lower average cost much.

Regression (2–5) collects all of the variables in a single regression. Initial size is of no significance and K_0 loses its significance in the presence of other variables. The adjusted coefficient of determination falls when these additional variables are entered.

Variations in First-Half Coefficient

Our attempts to explain the variation in the first-half coefficient a_{i4} are presented in Table 6-6. This coefficient is an estimate of the extent to which first-half average cost was systematically underestimated by a hospital; the mean underestimate is 2 percent. Regression (3–1) indicates that large hospitals were more guilty of underestimation than small ones, that hospitals with high initial utilization and low initial average cost were also most guilty of underestimation. Regression (3–2) adds location variables. Not surprisingly, urban hospitals are less guilty of cost underestimation than rural hospitals. Teaching variables are substituted for location variables in regression (3–3) and the coefficients indicate that advanced teaching hospitals are more guilty of underestimation than are other hospitals. Regression (3–4) combines the variables of the last two regressions and has an adjusted coefficient of determination greater than .22; the coefficients are unchanged in the combined regression. In the final regression, K_0 and S_0 are added with no effect; the other coefficients are unchanged and the adjusted coefficient of determination falls due to the loss in degrees of freedom.

Our attempts to analyze the a_{i3} proved completely fruitless. No variable had a significant simple or partial correlation coefficient. Since few of the a_{i3} were significant, we can only conclude that the size coefficients appear to be random numbers.

III. Summary and Conclusion

In applying our method for estimating cost functions of multi-product firms to the hospital industry, much of our investigation consisted of a search for significant coefficients. This search was made necessary because there is little knowledge of the functional form of the cost relationship or of which explanatory variables to include. We were able to specify a number of signs, but there were many that eluded prediction. For these reasons, our conclusions should be viewed as tentative. It should be noted that at the time this analysis was first undertaken we had available only nine observations on each hospital. With one exception the results of the preliminary analysis were remarkably similar to results reported here using the extended data. To our surprise, the variables used in the pooled regressions continued to have similar signs and magnitudes; occasionally some of the significance tests changed.[12] Another significant change in specification came when the first-half dummy variable was added. With the exception of the utilization coefficient, adding this variable had almost no effect on the results. Further evidence is provided by comparing these results to those derived from replicating the procedure with annual observations for Pittsburgh and Philadelphia hospitals. Even the interaction variables continue to display similar coefficients.[13]

Our method of accounting for the multi-product nature of the hospital is computationally simple and plausible. Some elaborate methods have been tried and it is of some interest to compare results.

One question that has received much attention is the relationship between marginal and average cost. The commonly held belief is that an empty bed is about 75 percent as expensive as a full one, i.e., marginal cost is a small percentage of average cost. Our results suggest that the short-run average cost curve is L-shaped and that marginal cost is a large percentage of average cost; we estimate that marginal cost is between 40 and 65 percent of average cost. These results disagree with those of P. Feldstein who found that only 20 percent of cost is variable. There is no real contradiction here since his results are for one month periods while ours are for six month periods; one would expect that a higher percentage of cost is variable as the length of the period grows long. Our results are supported by the analyses of M. Feldstein and Ingbar and Taylor. In analyzing cost per patient week, Feldstein finds that marginal cost is approximately equal to average cost (although the focus of his book is an analysis of cost per patient). Ingbar and Taylor estimate a similar relation (not transformed into logarithms) and find that average cost is affected little by changes in utilization. Although it is a bit difficult to come up with a single figure for percentage variable, their results suggest that marginal cost is about 80 percent of average cost.

Second, our results indicate that if economies of scale exist in the hospital industry, they are not very strong. In most cases the sign of our K variable was negative which means that as a hospital grew it captured some economies of scale. The sign, however, rarely attained significance, which accords with the results of Ingbar and Taylor, Berry, and M. Feldstein.

Thirdly, our results suggest that the rate of cost increase has been accelerating (as would be indicated by conventional price indices): the cost per patient day increased 2.1 percent in 1961 and 6.5 percent in 1967 (the first year of Medicare). We would add that conventional price indices should *understate* the rate of cost increase since both size and utilization increased in western Pennsylvania hospitals over the period and their coefficients were negative.

We conclude that the proposed method of estimating hospital costs seems fruitful. However, one important problem not answered is that of determining the absolute level of cost for a hospital; we have concentrated on explaining changes in cost. The determination of the level of cost is an important problem, and the subject of future research.

One of the strong points of the Laves' article is its candid acknowledgment of certain inevitable difficulties in estimating hospital cost functions. Some of them, as they note, are related to statistical questions. Others pertain to the fundamental difficulty in defining the output of a hospital. This is not the place to extend that discussion. At a minimum, however, readers should be aware of a still continuing debate among specialists on the output question. One interesting development in this regard has been the classification of hospital cases into "diagnosis-related groups" (DRGs) for purposes of costing and third party reimbursement. This is discussed further in Chapter 8.

THEORIES OF HOSPITAL BEHAVIOR

Classical microeconomic theory makes no distinction among firms according to objective function. All firms are assumed to be profit maximizers. Economists know, of course, that this behavioral hypothesis is not realistic in every case—some firms are hungrier for profits than others—but at least it establishes a yardstick against which the actual performance of proprietary organizations can be measured. Unfortunately, there is no behavioral analog for nonproprietary organizations. The nonprofit status of voluntary hospitals has a specific meaning from a legal standpoint, but to economists this represents an exclusive rather than inclusive classification: If not profits, then what?

In the following selection, Karen Davis surveys the literature on hospital objectives, then evaluates the various hypotheses by comparing economic decisions by nonprofit hospitals with those of profit-making ones. Although the empirical portions of the study are outdated (the data are from the 1960s), the methodology still is pertinent today.

ECONOMIC THEORIES OF BEHAVIOR IN NONPROFIT, PRIVATE HOSPITALS[d]

Major changes in the financing of hospital care in the United States have been made in the last decade. With the implementation of Medicare in 1966, twenty million elderly persons became eligible for hospital care financed by the federal government [14]. Medicaid, involving state and federal financing of health care, paid $4.6 billion for the medical care of low-income individuals in 1969 [15]. In addition, private health insurance coverage for hospital benefits increased from $140 million in 1960 to $152 million in 1968 [13].

Recently, additional reforms in the financing of hospital care have been advocated. Proposals ranging from a national health insurance scheme to universal private health insurance have been presented. The success of various schemes in providing quality hospital care at reasonable cost to increasing segments of the population rests in large part on the response of hospital managers to economic incentives. Yet until recently little attention has been given to the motivation of those who control major decisions in nonprofit hospitals.

Perhaps because suppliers of hospital care are largely nonprofit organizations (in the legal sense that owners may not receive dividends), it has been assumed that those who control major decisions pursue goals other than profit maximization. Weisbrod, for example, dismisses profit maximization because "public opinion opposes profit" [17, p. 18].

Instead various divergent hypotheses have been advanced, including (1) recovery of costs; (2) output maximization; (3) output and quality maximization; (4) utility maximization; and (5) cash flow maximization. The following sections will review various hypotheses of decision-making suggested in the literature and derive their implications for price determination. Then preliminary evidence bearing on the validity of the various hypotheses will be examined.

Recovery of Costs

The most prevalent view of prices is that the price of each service is set equal to the average cost of providing the service. This view of hospital pricing is based upon the assumption that nonprofit organizations are interested only in serving the public and have no desire to make any profits. Ingbar and Taylor, for example, depict the nonprofit hospital as an organization aiming primarily to recover its costs:

> The typical short-term hospital is not interested in making a profit as such. Being a voluntary and charitable institution, it is content to cover its costs and sets its charges accordingly [6, p. 74].

Guidelines set forth by the American Hospital Association for pricing hospital services emphasize the recovery of cost theme. In addition to covering costs, it is recommended that charges be set high enough "to cover the funds necessary for plant expansion due to improvement of services required to keep pace with technological and scientific advances" [1].

Assuming that hospitals set the price of a hospital service at a percentage markup over its cost, the important question becomes what determines the amount of markup. If the markup is solely determined on the basis of "need" for investment, how is the "needed" investment determined? Do competitive pressures play a role in determining the markup?

The internal rate structure could give some evidence on this question. If competitive pressures are unimportant, prices on all services could be marked up uniformly. The latter is, in fact, the policy recommended by the American Hospital Association:

> The rate charged for each individual service should reflect properly the operating expenses of the service rendered plus an equitable share of the other financial needs for which the patient is responsible [1].

In practice, however, hospitals have typically set room charges lower relative to costs than charges for ancillary services such as x-rays and laboratory tests [10, p. 923].

Part of the diversity of markups may be attributed to competitive pressures or differences in demand elasticities. On the basis of an interview study of hospital administrators, Kaitz reported:

> Each of the six hospital administrators stated that the cost of providing a service is the initial base upon which prices are set. . . . The prices established from these standards are subsequently modified for competitive factors. . . . Each of the administrators stated that the price for routine services (room and board) was set as close to its formula-computed cost as possible because of the competition between hospitals for patients [7, pp. 38–39].

Empirical testing of the simple version of cost-pricing (prices set equal to average operating costs) is fairly straightforward. All that needs to be ascertained is whether nonprofit hospitals in fact make profits. The more sophisticated version in which prices are set at a percentage markup over cost with the markup determined by the "need" for investment is somewhat more difficult to ascertain.

Output Maximization

A different objective of nonprofit hospitals has been proposed by Long:

> Short-term general hospitals are typically organized as independent units under the control of self-perpetuating boards of directors. Profit maximization is clearly not the force directing their behavior. Insofar as I have been able to determine it, the guiding principle is a desire

to maximize the number of patients seen subject to several constraints. There is a financial limit specified by the sponsoring agency [2; 9, pp. 211–26].

Klarman has also noted this objective:

> It has been postulated that a voluntary hospital aims to maximize the welfare of society by serving as many patients as possible, subject to certain constraints. One is that the size of its deficit cannot exceed specified limits [8, p. 121].

A modified version of this motivation has been suggested by Reder. He asserts:

> ... hospitals ... tend to be run as though their objective was to maximize the weighted number of patients treated (per time period), the "weights" being the professional prestige of doctors attending them [12, p. 480].

If the demand for hospital services is sensitive to price, hospitals can increase the number of patients served by reducing price. If the hospital faces a breakeven constraint and produces only one service, price of the service would be set equal to average cost at expected output just as in the average cost model. Hospitals, however, are multi-service firms so that prices of services which have little effect on the number of patients treated (such as some ancillary services) could be raised to positive profit levels. The profits on ancillary services could then be used to subsidize losses on room services (since reduction in room rates could be expected to increase number of patients served).

Implications of this model of pricing are, therefore, as follows:

1. Hospitals will break even overall;
2. Hospitals will make losses on those services for which the number of patients desiring admission is sensitive to the price charged;
3. Hospitals will make profits on those services whose prices have little effect on the number of patients desiring admission; and
4. An increase in the supply of funds to the hospital (such as

increased donations or reimbursement in excess of costs as provided by Medicare) will lead to a reduction in prices charged (assuming no shift in the cost curve).

Evidence on the first implication is presented below. The practice of charging relatively lower prices for room services and higher prices for ancillary services is consistent with the second and third implications. Experience with the Medicare program sheds some light on the validity of the fourth contention. Under Medicare, hospitals were reimbursed at cost plus a 2 percent additional allowance for the care of aged persons [16]. According to this hypothesis, prices charged non-Medicare patients could be expected to decline. Instead, prices climbed precipitously, and overall rates of return increased [4].

A longer-run version of the output maximization hypothesis, however, would consider the need for funds to increase capacity. If the capacity constraint is binding, setting prices above the breakeven point may not reduce the number of patients served in the short run and it would provide some funds for expansion so that more patients could be served in the long run. Hospitals might make profits on all services in order to acquire funds for expansion. Under this version, hospitals with high occupancy rates could be expected to set prices in excess of average costs.

A quantity-maximizing hospital will differ from a profit-maximizing hospital primarily in the quantity of output provided. In the short-run, for any given bed size, a quantity-maximizing hospital can be expected to serve a greater number of patients, and in the long run a quantity-maximizing hospital can be expected to increase output at a faster rate than will a profit-maximizing hospital. For any given level of output, however, both the profit-maximizing hospital and the quantity-maximizing hospital will hire factor inputs in such a way as to minimize the cost of providing that level of output.

Quality and Quantity Maximization

A variant of the output maximization hypothesis is output and quality maximization subject to a breakeven constraint.[1] Proponents of this hypothesis of hospital behavior have, in general, begged the question of defining quality. Newhouse suggests criteria indicative of quality such as personnel per patient or availability of various facilities, but ends by letting quality be represented by a vector of undefined characteristics [11]. Feldstein calls quality a "catch-all term to denote the general level of amenities provided to patients as well as additional expenditure on professional staff" [5, pp. 158–62]. Both of these interpretations tend to emphasize the quantity of inputs used in producing any given level of output.

A more output-oriented definition of quality might be in terms of the probability of successful treatment. Higher quality care would be defined as that which results in a higher probability of successful treatment than does low quality care. A hospital which does not have highly skilled personnel or specialized equipment such as cobalt therapy units and open-heart surgical facilities could still provide high quality care (in the sense of high probability of successful treatment) for a wide range of case types, but would be unable to provide high quality care for some case types. The difficulty of defining quality in an output-oriented sense has led to the use of input criteria.

A quantity-quality maximizing hospital is likely to provide a lower quantity of care than a quantity maximizing hospital. It will also use more inputs in providing any given level of care than either a quantity-maximizing hospital or a profit-maximizing hospital.[2] This occurs because the quantity produced by the quantity-quality maximizing hospital will embody a higher level of quality which is likely to require more factor inputs than the same quantity (but lower quality) provided by the profit-maximizing hospital, or the quantity-maximizing hospital. If the "production" of higher quality requires primarily capital input, use of labor in producing a given level of output may not differ substantially between a quantity-quality maximizing hospital and either a quantity-maximizing hospital or a profit-maximizing hospital.

Utility Maximization

The utility maximization hypothesis includes the quantity and quantity-quality maximization hypotheses as special cases. The principal interpretations given to this hypothesis, in fact, are quite similar to those of the quantity-quality hypothesis. According to Reder, hospital administrators maximize their own utility which is a function of the size of the hospital, extensiveness of modern equipment, and professional prestige of doctors on the staff, i.e., $U_1 = U_1(K,D)$ where K is hospital capital and D is a weighted sum of doctors on the staff with the weights being professional prestige [12].

Reder also argues that the hospital's ability to attract and retain doctors on its staff is a function of the range of capital equipment of the hospital:

> Because doctors can admit patients into only one or two hospitals they have an incentive to become affiliated with hospitals which are as fully equipped as possible, so that they may treat hospitalized patients for as wide a range of ailments as their competence (as they judge it) permits. . . . Hospitals that wish to attract men of outstanding qualifications to their staffs are therefore impelled to expand the inventory of their equipment and the range of services they are able to offer. This serves to reinforce the usual prestige motives for expansion and improvement inherent in any organization [12].

Since the number of doctors on the staff can be expressed as a function of the hospital's specialized capital equipment, i.e., $D = D(K)$, the utility function may be rewritten as $U_2 = U_2(K)$.

It is possible that administrators also derive utility from providing services as well as simply having the facilities and equipment available so that $U_3 = U_3(X, K)$ where X is output of hospital services. This is identical to the quantity-quality maximization case in which quality is defined simply as availability of capital equipment.

The special form of the utility function $U_4 = U_4(X)$ also reduces to the quantity maximization hypothesis.

Cash Flow Maximization

According to this hypothesis, the hospital maximizes the difference between revenue and out-of-pocket expenses, i.e., operating expenses other than depreciation expenses [3]. Economic return to equity capital is not included as an expense, although interest expense on borrowed funds is. The basic rationale for this hypothesis is similar in some respects to that of the quantity-quality maximization hypothesis and the utility maximization hypothesis. An excess of funds over costs is desired so that additional facilities may be continuously added without the necessity of relying on gifts, government funds, or borrowed funds. It differs from the other hypotheses in that it predicts that the hospital will make a profit (in the sense that revenues exceed expenditures).

Upper constraints on prices may be posed by various social or political factors, such as public outcry at excessive charges, repercussions from powerful organizations such as Blue Cross or Congressional committees from prices that are "too far out of line," or aggressive price competition from other hospitals. The importance of the first cause is lessened by the limited information available to the public. Complaints of excessive charges from powerful agencies may be countered with difficult-to-refute arguments regarding the superior quality of care rendered. Since patients have little information about variations in hospital charges among hospitals, and little choice regarding selection of hospital, the third type of constraint mentioned above may not be significant.

Cash-flow maximizing hospitals will minimize the short-run cost of producing any level of output. That is, all non-capital factors will be hired up to the point where the marginal revenue product of the factor is equal to its cost.[3] The quantity of capital services, however, depends not upon a minimum cost criteria, but upon the availability of funds in the past (including philanthropy, government grants and retained earnings).

Profit Maximization

Before turning to the empirical evidence on hospital behavior, it should be pointed out that even a profit-maximizing hospital has some incentive to acquire specialized facilities since such facilities can be expected to increase demand and revenue. Acquisition of dental surgical equipment will bring in dental surgery patients who might otherwise have been treated in a dental office. Acquisition of specialized facilities may also have an indirect effect on demand by increasing the number of doctors affiliated with the hospital. This stems primarily from the institutional restriction which requires patients to be hospitalized where their doctors are affiliated. The relevant market facing the hospital, therefore, depends upon the number of doctors affiliated with the hospital, the size of their clientele, and the extent to which doctors are affiliated with more than one hospital. Increasing the number of doctors affiliated with the hospital is likely to shift the demand curve for any given period to the right.

The main way in which a hospital can attract more doctors is by increasing the specialized equipment which it has available. Since doctors may be affiliated with only one or two hospitals, they prefer to be affiliated with fully equipped hospitals which can treat a wide variety of hospitalization cases. A profit-maximizing hospital, therefore, can be expected to acquire specialized facilities to the point where marginal revenue from additional facilities is equal to the marginal cost of more facilities.[4]

Empirical Evidence

The following sections will examine the available empirical evidence in an attempt to determine which hypotheses of nonprofit hospital behavior are corroborated by the data and which hypotheses are inconsistent with observed hospital behavior. Several approaches will be pursued.

First, since a number of hypotheses are based on the assumption that nonprofit hospitals break even—either as a direct goal or as a constraint in the pursuit of other goals—evidence on the profits of nonprofit hospitals and on the behavior of price-cost margins will be presented. If, in fact, nonprofit hospitals attempt to break even, then profits of nonprofit hospitals should be zero on average and price-cost ratios should be constant.

Another approach is to compare behavior of nonprofit hospitals with that of for-profit hospitals. It is commonly assumed that for-profit hospitals are more concerned with the pursuit of profit than nonprofit hospitals. If such is the case, marked differences between the two forms of organizational control should be apparent. By identifying particular areas in which nonprofit hospitals diverge from for-profit hospitals, some information on the type of objectives pursued by nonprofit hospitals may be obtained. For example, if nonprofit hospitals grow at a faster rate than for-profit hospitals, then it is possible that nonprofit hospitals place a growth maximization goal above a profit maximization goal. If non-profit hospitals acquire specialized facilities at a more rapid rate than for-profit hospitals, then perhaps utility derived from specialized facilities or quality enhanced by specialized facilities may be more important to nonprofit hospitals than to for-profit hospitals.

Several aspects of the provision of hospital services will be compared between the two types of hospitals: (1) quantity of services provided in the short run and in the long run; (2) growth in capacity for caring for patients; (3) use of factor inputs; (4) rate of acquisition of specialized facilities.

Net Incomes of Nonprofit Hospitals

Since the principal empirical implication of the cash flow maximization hypothesis and the cost-plus pricing hypothesis which differs from the quantity, quantity-quality, and utility maximization hypotheses is that nonprofit hospitals, in fact, make profits, this section will examine nonprofit hospital profit rates over time and across geographical areas.

As indicated in Table 6-7, nonprofit revenues have exceeded nonprofit hospital expenses for every year from 1961 to 1969 with the exception of 1962. Furthermore, net incomes (revenue less expenses) have risen markedly over the period from $91 million in 1961 to $400 million in 1969. Translated into rates of returns, nonprofit hospitals have experienced a rise in net income as a percent of plant assets from 1.39 in 1961 to 3.19 in 1969. The return on sales (total revenue) followed a similar pattern, increasing from 1.94 in 1961 to 3.19 percent in 1969. Net income per patient day has climbed from $.71 in 1961 to $2.34 in 1969.

The profitability of nonprofit hospitals is not uniform across geographical areas. On a state basis, average nonprofit hospital net income ranged in 1969 from 0.0 percent of plant assets in Rhode Island to 9.62 percent of plant assets in Mississippi. In no state did average nonprofit hospital incomes fall below zero, and all but one state had positive profits.

The determinants of variation in net income rates of return across states have been investigated in an earlier study [4]. Net incomes were found to be most influenced by governmental financing of Medicare patients, the monopoly position of hospitals, occupancy rate of hospitals, the extent to which government hospitals serve charity patients, and the extensiveness of Blue Cross reimbursement plans. Hospitals in states with a higher percentage of Medicare patients have higher net income ratios. The net income ratio is higher in states with sparsely located hospitals, indicating that monopoly power may influence returns. Hospitals in states with high occupancy rates have higher hospital net incomes, a fact which is consistent with the "need" for investment theory of pricing as well as with cash flow and profit maximization theories.

Table 6-7 Revenue, Expenses, and Net Income for Nongovernmental Nonprofit Hospitals, 1961–69

Year	Total revenue (in millions)	Expenses (in millions)	Net Income (in millions)	Plant assets (in millions)	Net income ratio		Annual rate of change		
					Total revenue	Plant assets	Total revenue	Expenses	Plant assets
1961	$ 4,675	$ 4,584	$ 91	$ 6,541	1.94	1.39	9.86	10.74	5.90
1962	4,996	4,999	–3	7,010	–.06	–.04	6.87	9.04	7.17
1963	5,622	5,491	132	7,592	2.34	1.74	12.54	9.84	8.29
1964	6,154	6,039	115	8,217	1.87	1.40	9.46	9.99	8.23
1965	6,870	6,643	227	9,078	3.31	2.50	11.63	10.00	10.49
1966	7,674	7,435	239	9,752	3.11	2.45	11.70	11.93	7.42
1967	9,146	8,806	339	10,457	3.71	3.24	19.18	18.44	7.23
1968	[a]10,653	10,317	337	11,490	3.16	2.93	16.48	17.15	9.87
1969	12,537	12,137	400	12,523	3.19	3.19	17.68	17.64	9.00
Annual average:									
1961–65	5,664	5,551	112	7,688	1.88	1.40	10.07	9.92	8.02
1967–68	9,899	9,562	338	10,973	3.44	3.09	17.83	17.80	8.55
1967–69	10,779	10,420	359	11,490	3.35	3.12	17.78	17.74	8.70

[a] Estimated from 1968 revenue data on nongovernmental community hospitals based on the assumption that nongovernmental nonprofit revenue is 93.15 percent of nongovernmental community hospital revenue, as in 1969.

Source: Guide Issue, *Hospitals* (annual issues).

Contrary to popular belief, therefore, nonprofit hospitals do make substantial profits, and these profits have been increasing over time. Demand-and-supply factors have been found to be important in determining the profits obtained by nonprofit hospitals in various areas.

These findings are inconsistent with both short-run and long-run theories of hospital behavior based upon quantity, quantity-quality, and utility maximization subject to a breakeven constraint. Since equity capital comes largely from government grants, philanthropic gifts, and retained earnings, and since nonprofit hospitals may not make payments to owners, a hospital desiring to maximize the short-run quantity of services would set prices low enough to earn a zero cash flow (defined as net income plus depreciation). Hospitals following this pattern of behavior should evidence negative net incomes, rather than positive as observed.

Hospitals desiring to maximize quantity, quantity-quality, or utility over the long run, however, may initially desire to accumulate surpluses which could be used in acquiring facilities which will allow an expansion of output and an upgrading of quality. Hospitals reaching a long-run equilibrium in desired capital would then be expected to earn zero net incomes. Since net incomes have risen rather than declined over the last decade, there is no evidence of an adjustment toward a long-run maximization of quantity, quantity-quality, or utility position. Instead non-profit hospitals have accumulated larger and larger surpluses over time at the same time that per-capita incomes, insurance coverage, and government financing of hospital care have increased. This trend in net incomes is consistent with the view that hospitals attempt to maximize cash flow in order to expand continuously capital facilities. The maximum attainable return has increased with rising income, insurance coverage, and government funds.

Quantity of Services Provided by Nonprofit and For-Profit Hospitals

If nonprofit hospitals tend to maximize the quantity of hospital services provided, while for-profit hospitals tend to maximize profits, nonprofit hospitals should serve more patients than for-profit hospitals. Most descriptions of the quantity maximization hypothesis have emphasized the number of patients as the unit of quantity, but number of patient days may also be the maximum [5, pp. 158–62; 11].

As shown in Table 6-8, nonprofit hospitals do serve more patients and render more days of hospital care than for-profit hospitals which would seem to support the quantity maximization hypothesis. Upon closer examination, however, three findings alter this conclusion: (1) over time for-profit hospitals have increased quantity of care provided at a faster rate than nonprofit hospitals; (2) for hospitals of a given bed size, for-profit hospitals serve more patients than nonprofit hospitals; and (3) for-profit hospitals have expanded capacity for serving patients at a faster rate than nonprofit hospitals. If for-profit hospitals are more inclined to discriminate on the basis of price, output will be higher. A profit maximizing, perfect price discriminating monopolist will provide an output indicated by the intersection of the demand and marginal cost curve. A quantity maximizing, non-price discriminating, breakeven hospital will provide an output indicated by the intersection of the demand and average cost curve so that for a rising average cost curve the quantity maximizing hospital will still provide a greater output.

If nonprofit hospitals are long-run quantity maximizers, one would expect nonprofit hospitals to increase the number of patients provided hospital care at a faster rate than for-profit hospitals. The opposite, in fact, is true. For-profit hospitals increased admissions by 35 percent from 1961 to 1969 compared with 16

Table 6-8 Trends in Quantity of Care Provided, Nonprofit and For-Profit Short-Term Hospitals, 1961–1969

Year	Admissions per hospital		Patient days per hospital	
	Nonprofit	For-Profit	Nonprofit	For-Profit
1961	5,136	1,847	38,543	10,761
1962	5,240	1,947	39,598	11,459
1963	5,338	2,045	40,544	12,221
1964	5,472	2,125	41,843	13,006
1965	5,546	2,152	42,722	13,629
1966	5,600	2,177	44,352	14,137
1967	5,634	2,245	46,297	15,560
1968	5,731	2,389	48,206	16,612
1969	5,933	2,494	49,831	17,312
Percent increase (1961–1969)	16%	35%	29%	61%

Source: Guide Issue, *Hospitals* (annual issues).

percent for nonprofit hospitals. Patient days per hospital increased 61 percent in for-profit hospitals and only 29 percent in nonprofit hospitals over the same period. This evidence, then, is inconsistent with long-run quantity maximization for nonprofit hospitals and profit maximization for for-profit hospitals.

Examination of the occupancy rate and case-flow rate (admissions per bed) of nonprofit and for-profit hospitals reveals that the larger number of patients served by nonprofit hospitals is largely a consequence of their larger average size. As shown in Table 6-9, for a given bed capacity, for-profit hospitals see more patients than do nonprofit hospitals. Overall in 1969, for-profit hospitals handled 38.8 cases per bed while nonprofit hospitals handled only 35.1 cases per bed. The same relationship holds for each major bed size category. This evidence is inconsistent with a short-run quantity maximization hypothesis for nonprofit hospitals if for-profit hospitals maximize profits. If nonprofit hospitals maximize number of patients served in the short-run for any given bed size, nonprofit hospitals should serve more patients than for-profit hospitals. Again, the reverse is true.

Examination of the growth in hospital capacity also sheds some light on alternative hypotheses of behavior in nonprofit hospitals. If nonprofit hospitals maximize growth, or long-run quantity of services, while for-profit hospitals maximize profits, we would expect to observe a faster expansion of capacity in nonprofit hospitals than in for-profit hospitals. Table 6-10 indicates that in fact the reverse is true. Average bed size of for-profit hospitals has increased 40 percent from 1961 to 1969 while average bed size of

Table 6-9 Capacity Utilization of Nonprofit and For-Profit Short-Term Hospitals, by Bed Size, 1969

Bed size	Admissions per bed		Occupancy rate	
	Nonprofit	For-profit	Nonprofit	For-profit
All bed sizes	35.1	38.8	81.1	74.9
6–24 beds	34.9	43.0	55.2	61.7
25–49 beds	34.6	39.9	64.7	69.1
50–99	32.1	40.2	73.5	74.4
100–199	36.7	36.4	78.3	78.0
200–299	36.6	38.5	82.6	82.5
300 and over	33.9	37.2	84.6	79.2

Source: Guide Issue, *Hospitals* (August 1, 1970).

Table 6-10 Growth in Capacity, Nonprofit and For-Profit, Short-Term Hospitals, 1961–1969

Year	Average bed size		Plant assets per hospital (000s)	
	Nonprofit	For-profit	Nonprofit	For-profit
1961	139	45	1,979	255
1962	141	47	2,095	271
1963	143	49	2,237	307
1964	147	53	2,415	374
1965	150	55	2,650	354
1966	155	56	2,835	312
1967	159	57	3,021	395
1968	165	62	3,350	402
1969	169	63	3,653	510
Percent increase (1961–1969)	22%	40%	85%	100%

Source: Guide issue, Hospitals (annual issues).

nonprofit hospitals has increased only 22 percent. In terms of plant assets, for-profit hospitals have also expanded at a more rapid rate. Plant assets per hospital in for-profit hospitals doubled from 1961 to 1969 while nonprofit hospital plant assets per hospital increased by 85 percent.

Use of Factor Inputs

Most interpretations of the quality maximization hypothesis have interpreted quality in the sense of quantity of inputs devoted to hospital care, particularly capital facilities, rather than quality in the sense of output (better health, more rapid recovery, less impairment of life or productivity).

Table 6-11 presents some evidence on the quantity of inputs per day of hospital care provided by nonprofit and for-profit hospitals. Nonprofit hospitals employ more capital (measured by plant assets) per day of care rendered than do for-profit hospitals. In addition, nonprofit hospitals have been increasing the plant asset to daily census ratio at a faster rate from 1961 to 1969 than have for-profit hospitals. Plant assets per average daily census in nonprofit hospitals increased from 18.7 in 1961 to 26.8 in 1969, an increase of 43 percent. Over the same period, plant assets per average daily census in for-profit hospitals increased from 8.6 to 10.8, a 26 percent increase.

Table 6-11 Labor and Capital Inputs Per Day of Hospital Care, Non-Profit and For-Profit, Short-Term Hospital, 1961–1969

Year	Plants assets per daily census		Personnel per daily census	
	Nonprofit	For-profit	Nonprofit	For-profit
1961	18.7	8.6	2.40	2.05
1962	19.3	8.6	2.41	2.08
1963	20.1	9.2	2.44	2.14
1964	21.1	10.5	2.47	2.12
1965	22.6	9.5	2.52	2.18
1966	23.3	8.1	2.64	2.34
1967	23.8	9.3	2.68	2.33
1968	25.4	8.8	2.76	2.37
1969	26.8	10.8	2.84	2.44
Percent increase (1961–1969)	43%	26%	18%	16%
Bed size, 1969				
6–24 beds	15.9	6.2	2.2	2.5
25–49	17.8	8.3	2.3	2.4
50–99	21.2	10.7	2.4	2.5
100–199	24.6	10.9	2.6	2.4
200–299	26.5	9.7	2.8	2.4
300 and over	28.4	20.8	3.0	2.4

Source: Guide Issue, *Hospitals* (annual issues).

Differences in quantities of labor devoted to the production of hospital care between nonprofit and for-profit hospitals are not quite so marked. Full-time equivalent personnel per average daily census in nonprofit hospitals increased 18 percent from 2.40 in 1961 to 2.84 in 1969, while the ratio for for-profit hospitals changed from 2.05 in 1961 to 2.44 in 1969, a 16 percent increase.

These measures of factor inputs, of course, are quite aggregated and may conceal important differences in the types of labor and capital used by the types of hospitals. For example, for-profit hospitals may have more employees engaged in direct patient care per day of hospital care than do nonprofit hospitals. Table 6-11 indicates that small for-profit hospitals have more employees per day of care than nonprofit hospitals have. As bed size exceeds one hundred beds, nonprofit hospitals tend to employ more personnel per patient day. This could occur, for example, if large nonprofit hospitals tended to hire more highly specialized personnel engaged in the provision of ancillary services.

In summary, nonprofit hospitals use substantially more capital input per day of hospital care provided than do for-profit hospitals, and slightly more labor input per day of care. These findings are consistent with the cash flow maximization hypothesis (which emphasizes the desire to acquire additional capital while hiring that combination of labor which minimizes the cost of providing any level of output) and with a narrower version of utility and quality maximization where utility or quality comes primarily from capital inputs, not labor inputs.

Specialized Facilities

Since many of the theories of hospital behavior which have been proposed emphasize the desire of the hospital to acquire specialized facilities either because it increases the quality of care rendered or because it increases the utility of hospital decision-makers, it is interesting to investigate this factor in more detail.

One measure of the extent of specialized facilities relative to more basic types of capital such as beds is the ratio of plant assets to beds. If nonprofit hospitals tend to have more specialized facilities per bed than do for-profit hospitals, the ratio of plant assets to beds in nonprofit hospitals should exceed that of for-profit hospitals. Table 6-12 presents these ratios for the period from 1961 to 1969 as well as the ratios for various bed size classes in 1969. As shown, nonprofit hospitals have almost three times as high a ratio of plant assets to beds as do for-profit hospitals. In addition, nonprofit hospitals increased this ratio at a slightly faster rate over the period (an increase of 51 percent for nonprofit hospitals versus an increase of 42 percent for for-profit hospitals). Broken down on the basis of bed-size category, the ratio is still twice as high for nonprofit hospitals as for for-profit hospitals. It may be concluded, therefore, that nonprofit hospitals have exhibited a tendency to use more capital per bed than do for-profit hospitals.

A more direct comparison of specialized facilities between the two types of hospitals is shown in Tables 6-13 and 6-14. Table 6-13 shows the proportion of all nonprofit hospitals and the proportion of all for-profit hospitals possessing eight specialized facilities: blood bank, pharmacy, physical therapy department, pathology laboratory, premature nursery, postoperative recovery room, radioactive isotope therapy, and intensive care units. Table 6-14 presents the same information for all nonprofit hospitals with

Table 6-12 Plant Assets Per Bed, Nonprofit and For-Profit, Short-Term Hospitals, 1961–1969

	Plant assets per bed	
Year	Nonprofit	For-Profit
1961	14.3	5.7
1962	14.9	5.8
1963	15.6	6.3
1964	16.5	7.1
1965	17.6	6.4
1966	18.3	5.5
1967	19.0	6.9
1968	20.3	6.4
1969	21.6	8.1
Percent increase (1961–1969)	51%	42%
Bed size, 1969		
6–24 beds	8.8	3.8
25–49	11.5	5.7
50–99	15.6	8.0
100–199	19.3	8.5
200–299	21.9	8.0
300 and over	24.0	16.5

Source: Guide Issue, *Hospitals* (annual issues).

100 or more beds and for all for-profit hospitals with 100 or more beds.

For each type of facility, a greater proportion of nonprofit hospitals acquires the facility than for-profit hospitals. This is particularly true when no adjustment is made for bed size, but holds up even when only hospitals with one hundred or more beds are compared. For-profit hospitals lag behind nonprofit hospitals especially for such facilities as radioactive isotope and premature nursery. In 1969, 44 percent of for-profit hospitals with one hundred or more beds had radioactive isotope therapy while 68 percent of nonprofit hospitals with one hundred or more beds had such facilities. Premature nursery facilities are interesting in that both nonprofit and for-profit hospitals have moved out of this area since 1964, although for-profit hospitals seem to have moved out most rapidly. In 1964, 43 percent of all for-profit hospitals had a premature nursery versus 62 percent of all nonprofit hospitals. By 1969, only 25 percent of for-profit hospitals had such a facility while 53 percent of nonprofit hospitals continued to have this facility. This decline may be following the decline

Table 6-13 Proportion of Nonprofit and For-Profit, Short-Term Hospitals with Various Specialized Facilities, 1961–69

Year	Blood bank Non-profit	Blood bank For-profit	Pharmacy Non-profit	Pharmacy For-profit	Physical therapy Non-profit	Physical therapy For-profit	Pathology lab. Non-profit	Pathology lab. For-profit	Premature nursery Non-profit	Premature nursery For-profit	Postoperative recovery room Non-profit	Postoperative recovery room For-profit	Radioactive isotope Non-profit	Radioactive isotope For-profit	Intensive care Non-profit	Intensive care For-profit
1961	62.5%	31.8%	59.4%	31.9%	51.0%	29.8%	62.3%	27.1%	60.7%	41.2%	64.7%	34.2%	31.6%	9.0%	14.3%	8.0%
1962	62.7	30.8	60.0	33.0	52.9	31.3	62.7	27.5	61.9	42.3	67.2	38.8	32.4	8.4	17.7	9.1
1963	63.0	34.8	61.4	37.3	54.8	33.9	63.5	30.1	62.5	42.7	69.5	46.5	33.8	9.6	21.7	10.6
1964	64.8	36.3	64.9	41.9	57.4	37.0	65.8	33.0	63.7	42.8	72.2	51.4	36.1	12.0	25.8	13.0
1965	67.3	39.9	66.7	43.2	60.2	37.4	67.1	35.5	63.7	42.3	74.9	55.0	38.4	12.0	32.5	15.1
1966	*	*	69.9	49.1	61.4	36.4	71.3	42.0	60.5	36.4	76.7	61.6	37.5	11.0	*	*
1967	*	*	72.9	48.2	63.6	40.7	72.3	42.7	59.7	35.8	77.4	60.4	*	*	*	*
1968	*	*	79.0	55.1	*	*	*	*	56.8	29.1	79.1	62.0	*	*	50.9	27.1
1969	71.3	47.4	*	*	68.8	43.0	*	*	52.5	24.8	79.7	63.8	42.4	17.5	53.9	29.6

*Indicates data unavailable.
Source: Guide Issue, *Hospitals* (annual issues).

Table 6-14 Proportion of Nonprofit and For-Profit, Short-Term Hospitals of 100 Beds or More with Various Specialized Facilities, 1961–69

Year	Blood Bank		Pharmacy		Physical therapy		Pathology lab.		Premature nursery		Postoperative recovery room		Radioactive isotope		Intensive care	
	Non-profit	For-profit	Non-profit	For-profit	Non-profit	For-profit	Non-profit	For-profit	Non-profit	For-profit	Non-profit	For-profit	Non-profit	For-profit	Non-profit	For-profit
1961	82.0%	72.4%	91.0%	71.1%	78.5%	38.2%	94.7%	82.9%	79.4%	59.2%	93.2%	80.3%	59.9%	35.5%	24.2%	13.2%
1962	82.1	72.8	92.0	77.8	80.0	49.4	94.9	80.3	80.1	59.3	94.7	85.2	60.9	40.7	30.6	12.4
1963	82.4	69.3	92.8	81.8	81.7	53.4	94.9	79.6	80.2	56.8	95.5	92.1	62.5	39.8	38.2	18.2
1964	83.7	73.5	94.1	85.7	83.2	57.1	95.6	78.6	80.2	54.1	96.4	91.8	65.0	39.8	44.4	26.5
1965	84.6	72.8	94.8	86.4	85.4	60.2	95.8	83.5	80.5	56.3	97.3	90.3	67.3	39.8	53.5	33.0
1966	*	*	96.1	91.5	86.3	65.1	96.2	84.9	78.6	50.0	97.6	94.3	65.9	34.0	*	*
1967	*	*	97.1	91.2	86.9	72.6	96.3	88.5	76.9	46.9	98.0	96.5	*	*	*	*
1968	*	*	98.1	91.7	*	*	*	*	73.7	44.6	98.2	96.7	*	*	77.2	63.6
1969	86.4	79.1	*	*	89.4	72.9	*	*	69.8	41.1	98.0	96.9	68.2	44.2	80.2	71.3

*Indicates data unavailable.
Source: Guide Issue, *Hospitals* (annual issues).

in number of births in the nation. With fewer births, the profitability (or "need" depending upon one's point of view) of premature nurseries may have declined. It is possible that for-profit hospitals may lease facilities to a greater extent than nonprofit hospitals. If so, possession of facilities may overstate the difference between services provided.

In general the evidence on specialized facilities supports the quality-quantity maximization, utility maximization, and cash flow maximization hypotheses. Nonprofit hospitals do appear to acquire specialized facilities to a greater extent than do for-profit hospitals.

Summary

Although several theories of behavior in nonprofit hospitals have been presented in the last few years, as yet these theories have not been subjected to any rigorous empirical testing. This paper has attempted to make a first step in this direction by presenting some preliminary evidence on the likely validity of five alternative hypotheses: (1) recovery of costs; (2) output maximization; (3) output and quality maximization; (4) utility maximization; and (5) cash flow maximization.

The basic assumption that nonprofit hospitals break even—which is a direct goal in the recovery of cost model and a constraint in the output maximization, quality-quantity maximization hypothesis, and the utility maximization hypothesis—is not substantiated by the available evidence. Nonprofit hospitals, in fact, make rather sizable profits and these profits have been growing over time.

Comparison of nonprofit and for-profit hospitals provides some interesting insights into the principal points of divergence in behavior between the two types of organizational control. Among the most important findings are the following:

1. Although nonprofit hospitals serve more patients per hospital than do for-profit hospitals, this is largely a consequence of their larger average size.
2. For-profit hospitals in the same bed-size category as nonprofit hospitals serve more patients (and render more patient days of care) per bed than do nonprofit hospitals.
3. For-profit hospitals have increased output in the last decade at a faster rate than have nonprofit hospitals.
4. For-profit hospitals have expanded capacity for treating pa-

tients at a more rapid rate in the last decade than have nonprofit hospitals.
5. Nonprofit hospitals employ more capital per day of care rendered than do for-profit hospitals.
6. Small for-profit hospitals have more employees per day of care than do nonprofit hospitals. As bed size exceeds one hundred beds, nonprofit hospitals tend to employ more personnel per patient day.
7. Nonprofit hospitals have almost three times as high a ratio of plant assets to beds as do for-profit hospitals.
8. A greater proportion of nonprofit hospitals than for-profit hospitals possesses such specialized facilities as blood bank, pharmacy, physical therapy department, pathology laboratory, premature nursery, postoperative recovery room, radioactive isotope therapy, and intensive care units.

Although the evidence in this paper is quite tentative and does not represent a rigorous statistical test of alternative hypotheses, it does suggest that some simple models of nonprofit hospital behavior should be discarded and more dynamic models developed. Future empirical testing should be oriented toward differentiating between hypotheses with a view to finding a reasonable model of hospital behavior upon which public policy decisions can be based.

The theories reviewed in this article assume implictly that the hospital decision maker is the administrator, who may act to balance the interests of various constituencies such as trustees, medical staff, patients, and the general community.

The approach taken by Mark Pauly and Michael Redisch, in contrast, emphasizes the role of the medical staff. In the following excerpt they present the hospital as an organization run by physicians whose goal is to maximize their own incomes. This is, to say the least, a controversial assumption. It has not been investigated directly, and Pauly and Redisch include no empirical test in their article. Nevertheless, the work represents a provocative application of economic analysis based on profit maximization to a nonprofit firm.

THE NOT-FOR-PROFIT HOSPITAL AS A PHYSICIANS' COOPERATIVE[e]

In this paper we propose an alternative model in which the physician emerges as a traditional income maximizing economic agent who is "discovered" in a decision-making role within this not-for-profit enterprise. Our model is similar to the model of the firm customarily used by economists, in that it is based on the assumption of net income maximization. Only a somewhat unusual definition of net income is needed to enable us to apply in our short-run analysis many of the conclusions of the orthodox model of the firm. In the longer run, however, our model, while still based on net-income maximization, yields different predictions about the institution's response to changes in demand and supply parameters.

Specifically, we assume that the group of attending physicians on the hospital's staff enjoys *de facto* control of the hospital at any point in time. Given this assumption, we develop a model in which the hospital operates in such a way as to maximize the net income per member of the physician staff.

I. The Model

We simplify the problem initially by assuming that patients pay the full market price for care, and that the decision-making group in the hospital is able to impose its collective will on individual members. . . .

The product produced in the hospital is hospitalization services. We shall assume that this output can be represented by a single variable Q.[3] To produce this output, physical capital (K), nonphysician labor (L), and physician or medical staff labor (M) are used. The production process can be summarized by the production function

$$Q = F(K, L, M) \qquad (1)$$

In European countries in which physicians who treat patients in the hospital are employed by and paid by the hospital, this three-input production function is the obvious one.[4] But in the United States, the hospital patient is subject to two separate billings. The hospital charges him only for the use of capital and nonphysician labor. The physician presents a separate bill for the use of his "personal" physician's services. This dual billing system has led to a conceptually false dichotomy in much of the health economics literature. The physician and hospital are often viewed as independent economic entities selling services in functionally segmented health markets. This view appears to provide the rationale for the hospital-administrator-oriented, output-maximization theories of hospital behavior. . . .

We propose an alternative view. It seems obvious that the patient's demand is primarily for the service produced by the physician and hospital acting in combination, not for the separate components, even though there probably is a separate demand for some attributes, such as amenities, or additional patient days for recuperating, that the hospital alone produces.

The critical assumption of our model is that the physician staff members enjoy *de facto* control of hospital operations and see to it that hospitalization services are produced in such a way as to maximize their net incomes. The appearance of physician control is not hard to establish. The staff physicians have direct control over the number and types of patients admitted and over the types of services they receive; they control output. The staff physicians can determine, within rather broad limits, what use of the hospital will be made in treating a patient; they control many of the production decisions. They have indirect control over many other aspects of the hospital's operation, such as capital investment and the level of nursing care, in the sense that no administrator can afford to incur the displeasure of the medical staff, interfere with medical staff prerogatives, or make decisions which will deter large numbers of physicians from remaining on the hospital's staff or using that hospital for their patients. The trustees, who have nominal control over the hospital's operation, usually look to the medical staff when making decisions on operations or capital investment.

We first assume that the physicians on the staff of a hospital at any point in time act in such a way as to maximize the sum of the money incomes of all staff members. Such an assumption implies a process of group decision making resulting in a kind of perfect cooperation not likely to be observed in practice. It also ignores nonmonetary components of a physician's income, such as leisure time and prestige, which are likely to be of some importance. Nevertheless, this model is useful as a bench mark from which to consider the effects of alternative assumptions.

We postulate an economic short-run period as one in which the number of physicians on the hospital staff, M, remains constant. Each physician is presumed to supply a constant, homogeneous amount of medical input.

The patient's demand is primarily for the service produced by the physician and hospital acting in combination, not for the separate components. This can be formalized by postulating a demand function for "hospitalization services" faced by the physician staff that takes the form

$$Q = Q(P_T), \frac{\partial Q}{\partial P_T} < 0 \qquad (2)$$

where P_T is the combined price paid by the patient for the physician and hospital components.[5, 6] [For those unfamiliar with calculus, the notation here simply means that as P_T rises, Q declines; that is, the demand curve slopes down.]

We also assume that the hospital component of P_T is set so as to allow the hospital to just break even, with no gain or loss.[7] That is, we assume that the hospital price P_h is set to produce the equality:

$$P_h Q = wL + cK \qquad (3)$$

where P_h is the unit price the hospital charges for use of non-physician labor and capital, w is the wage rate for nonphysician labor, and c is the user cost of capital.[8]

The hospital is to be run so as to maximize the net incomes of the physicians on the staff at any point in time. If the number of physicians in the short-run analysis is taken as given at $\overline{M}$, the problem is to maximize $P_T Q - P_h Q$ (which is equal to $P_T Q - wL - cK$) subject to the production function (1), with the level of M set at $\overline{M}$, and the demand curve (2). This problem is obviously identical to that facing an orthodox profit-making firm with one input held constant. The marginal conditions for optimal employment of labor and capital are the same, namely, that marginal factor costs equal their respective marginal revenue or value products.[9]

It may be useful at this stage to contrast the model of the nonprofit hospital just developed with the orthodox model of the profit-maximizing firm. In the latter case, all labor inputs and capital services financed by debt are paid their competitive costs. Nondebt capital then obtains the residual income, which is usually assumed to consist of payment of the opportunity cost of that capital (normal profits) and economic profit. The only difference between this model and the physician-profit maximization model of the hospital is that in the latter it is the physician input, rather than the nondebt capital input, which obtains economic profits, the residual income. If a profit-maximizing firm submitted two bills for its services—one just covering the cost of labor and debt-financed capital, produced in a "nonprofit" firm, and the other from a separate legal institution covering the services of equity capital, the analogy would be complete. . . .

Pauly and Redisch then explore the implications of the model under different assumptions about hospital staffing policy, physician cooperation, and insurance coverage. The following gives their views on the origin of nonprofit enterprise and their major conclusions:

VI. Toward a Theory of the Not-For-Profit Enterprise

To this point we have taken the not-for-profit nature of the typical American hospital as given. In this section we offer an explanation of why this organizational form has arisen.

There are two ways in which the hospital might operate if it were on a profit-maximizing basis. It might combine the services of nonphysician labor and physical capital, and sell them to or through the physician, who combines them with his own input to produce the output of hospitalization services. Alternatively, the hospital might perform the job of combination itself, hiring the physician input and selling the final output. In either case the direct control over the use of non-physician labor and capital would not be held by the physician. In the first case, he would have to use the market for control, which is not always as efficient in the sense of minimizing all costs, including transactions costs, as direct control. In the second case, he himself would be under the direction of the supplier of equity capital. It is surely possible that there are some products which are not produced efficiently when a representative of the owners of equity capital directs their production, or when the market is used to organize the production process instead of the use of direct controls within a single organization. The most efficient method might be for the supplier of an important component of the labor input to direct the production process.

This would tend to happen when human capital is important in the production of some output and when the flow of services of that human capital cannot well be directed from outside, but is controlled by the person in whom the capital is embodied. As Armen Alchian and Harold Demsetz have noted, the wage system tends to break down when marginal products cannot be monitored closely. This may be a reasonable conjecture in the case of the production of hospital services. Many of the decisions the physician has to make are decisions which cannot be supervised directly, and which have contingent outcomes. There probably need to be some incentives for the physician. Financial interest in the outcome of his actions is one such incentive, and that incentive is at its greatest when the physician bears the full residual income, when the consequences of his actions are not spread over suppliers of physical capital.[15]

The production process requires some physical capital. In a labor-managed firm in which most of the assets of labor are embodied in nontransferable human capital, not all of the physical capital can be borrowed, since collateral cannot be provided. Another necessary condition therefore for the emergence of the not-for-profit form would seem to be the willingness of individuals to contribute for its equity capital. In principle, contributions could either be voluntary or provided through government. Where voluntary contributions are sufficient, government contributions would not be expected to emerge. On the other hand, voluntary contributions may arise in precisely those cases in which the government fails to act. They may also arise in cases in which the government through tax deductibility subsidizes private contributions. The source of contributions, whether unsubsidized voluntary, subsidized voluntary, or governmental, is not critical to the argument, except to the extent that one form (for example, government) implies more external control over physicians' actions than another.

These contributions could be motivated by a desire on the part of contributors to make output available to themselves or to those whom they would like to see consume it. That is, the motivation could either be based on the potential receipt of private benefits or of external benefits. Contributions are a logical way for potential purchasers of the outputs of labor-managed firms to make possible production of the output, which they or those about whom they are concerned will use. If there are barriers to entry by profit-seeking firms (as there are in higher education and, to some extent, in the hospital industry as well), potential consumers may be willing to contribute if that is the only way that output, which yields them consumers' surplus, can be made available. It is not surprising that private not-for-profit firms which sell output—hospitals, universities, symphony orchestras—tend to provide output which is used *not* by the poor, but partly by the contributors themselves.[16]

VII. Conclusion

The main thrust of the model we have suggested here, and the one which differentiates it from models of the not-for-profit hospital that have been suggested by others, is the use of the maximization of physicians' income as the characteristic function. The potential absence of perfect cooperation distinguishes it from similar models of producers' cooperatives. In a methodological sense, our model seems to be more attractive than those which simply assume that the not-for-profit organization maximizes a variable such as "quantity of output," because it explains what the organization does in terms of the economic motivation of those who control it.

More importantly, it appears to provide an appealing explanation of some peculiar characteristics of not-for-profit hospitals. The supposed quality consciousness of such hospitals, for example, is easily explained; "quality" is a synonym for application of nonphysician labor and capital in physician-income-enhancing ways, and noncooperative behavior could easily lead to "too high" quality. "Duplication of facilities" probably owes its existence to closed staffing and lack of perfect cooperation. Other aspects of hospital behavior could also be explained by considering their effect on physicians' income; the pattern of investment, for example, might be best explained by changes in the ability of capital to enhance physicians' incomes. The inelastic supply response of hospitals to Medicare and Medicaid is also consistent with our model.

Even the average size of hospitals, which seems, by most accounts, to be below the optimal or cost-minimizing level, can easily be explained. In the first place, empirically observed cost curves may be misleading, if we add the physician input. But more importantly, in a period of rising prices our model shows that hospitals will tend to be small, and for two reasons. First, smallness tends to permit maximization of net income per physician. Second, smallness is necessary to permit coordination of the medical staff.

A narrower range of possible observations is consistent with our model than with the general utility-maximization model. Appropriate choice of the variables to enter the utility function can make almost any observed behavior consistent with utility maximization. In particular, the definition of quality is not clear. Our model specifies the variable in the objective function. In principle it will also predict quantitative as well as qualitative responses, in the sense that physician income can be measured while utility cannot. Unfortunately, at present hospital-specific data on physicians' incomes or prices do not exist which would permit us to provide a conclusive test of the model. Nevertheless, we hope that more data can be made available to test this model.

CONCLUSION

At the beginning of this chapter, the authors indicated that our aim was to introduce the topic of hospital economics. After perusing the foregoing selections the reader, with some justification, may question whether this approach actually was "introductory" at all. In defense, it should be noted that the heavy emphasis on theoretical concepts and methodological issues (and some rather sophisticated ones, at that) was done with a definite purpose in mind. The nonprofit hospital (as well as the nonprofit firm in other sectors of the economy) remains one of the least understood economic organisms. Because there is no generally accepted model of nonprofit behavior, it is extremely difficult to predict how voluntary hospitals will react to changes in their economic environment. It is important that the reader grasp the implications of this fact before moving on to issues of direct policy relevance. In this sense, our treatment of hospital economics has indeed been "introductory."

SUGGESTED READINGS

Berry, Ralph E. "Product Heterogeneity and Hospital Cost Analysis." *Inquiry* 7 (March 1970): 67–75.

——————. "Cost and Efficiency in the Production of Hospital Services," *Milbank Memorial Fund Quarterly* 52 (Summer 1974): 291–313.

Clarkson, Kenneth W. "Some Implications of Property Rights in Hospital Management." *Journal of Law and Economics* (October 1972): 363–384.

Feldstein, Martin, and Schuttinga, James. "Hospital Costs in Massachusetts: A Methodological Study." *Inquiry* 13 (March 1977): 22–31.

Jacobs, Philip. "A Survey of Economic Models of Hospitals." *Inquiry* 11 (June 1974): 83–97.

Lee, M. S. "A 'Conspicuous Production' Theory of Hospital Behavior." *Southern Economic Journal* (July 1971): 48–58.

Newhouse, J. P. "Toward a Theory of Non-profit Institution: An Economic Model of a Hospital." *The American Economic Review* (March 1970): 64–70.

Pauly, M. V. "Hospital Capital Investment: The Roles of Demand, Profits and Physician." *The Journal of Human Resources* 9 (Winter 1974): 7–20.

NOTES FOR BERKI EXCERPT

a. This reminds one of the aptness of Leontieff's dictum: ". . . in all too many instances sophisticated statistical analysis is performed on a set of data whose exact meaning and validity are unknown to the author or rather so well known to him that at the very end he warns the reader not to take the material conclusions of the entire 'exercise' seriously" (238, p. 3).

b. The initial fourteen services specified are: nursing and intensive care unit, measured in patient days, blood units, ECG examinations, IPPB treatments, laboratory tests performed, intravenous fluids administered, prescriptions, X-rays, deliveries, and oxygen, anesthesia, operating room and recovery room services measured in hours (120, p. 154).

REFERENCES FOR BERKI EXCERPT

120. Dowling, William. *A Linear Programming Approach to the Analysis of Hospital Production.* Ph.D. dissertation, University of Michigan, 1970.

133. Feldstein, M.S. *Economic Analysis for Health Service Efficiency.* Chicago: Markham Publishing Co., 1968.

238. Leontief, Wassily. "Theoretical Assumptions and Nonobserved Facts." *The American Economic Review* 61, no. 1 (March 1971): 1–7.

NOTES FOR SORKIN EXCERPT

a. This is the case especially with respect to cardiac surgery. One factor determining the level of quality is whether or not enough operations are done to maintain a high level of skill among the members of the team.

b. As pointed out by W. John Carr and Paul J. Feldstein, in addition to travel cost, account should be taken of possible increases in morbidity and mortality arising directly from the time it takes to get to hospitals.

REFERENCES FOR SORKIN EXCERPT

9. Berry, Ralph E. Jr., "Returns to Scale in the Production of Hospital Services." *Health Services Research,* Vol. 2, no. 2, Summer 1967, p. 125.

10. Ibid.

11. Carr, W. John, and Feldstein, Paul J., "The Relationship of Cost to Hospital Size." *Inquiry,* Vol. 4, no. 2, June 1967, p. 49.

REFERENCES CITED IN TABLE 6-3 (BERKI)

a. H. A. Cohen, "Variations in Cost Among Hospitals of Different Sizes," *Southern Economic Journal,* January 1967, 355.

b. _____ , "Costs and Efficiency: A Study of Short Term General Hospitals." Ph.D. dissertation, Cornell University, 1967.

b. _____, "Hospital Cost Curves with Emphasis on Measuring Patient Care Output," in H. E. Klarman, ed., *Empirical Studies in Health Economics*. (Baltimore: The Johns Hopkins University Press, 1970), pp. 279–293.

c. M. L. Ingbar and L. D. Taylor, *Hospital Costs in Massachusetts*. (Cambridge, Mass.: Harvard University Press, 1968).

d. J. R. Lave and L. B. Lave, "Hospital Cost Functions: Estimating Cost Functions for Multiproduct Firms." Xeroxed. Pittsburgh: Carnegie Mellon University, Graduate School of Industrial Administration, December 1968.

e. _____, "Hospital Cost Functions," *The American Economic Review* 60, no. 3 (June 1970): 379–395.

f. E. W. Francisco, "Analysis of Cost Variations Among Short Term General Hospitals," in H.E. Klarman, ed., *Empirical Studies in Health Economics*, pp. 321–332.

g. H.E. Klarman, *The Economics of Health*. (New York: Columbia University Press, 1965).

h. W. J. Carr, and P. Feldstein, "The Relationship of Cost to Hospital Size," *Inquiry*, June 1967, pp. 45–65.

i. K-K. Ro, "Determinants of Hospital Costs," in *Yale Economic Essays*, 1968, pp. 185–257.

j. M. S. Feldstein, *Economic Analysis for Health Service Efficiency*. Chicago: Markham Publishing Co., 1968.

k. U.S., National Advisory Commission on Health Manpower, *Report of the National Advisory Commission on Health Manpower*, 1967.

NOTES FOR LAVE AND LAVE EXCERPT

1. The multi-product nature of output can be taken into account either by deriving a composite output measure which is a weighted sum of the various outputs or by including measures of the proportions of each output as explanatory variables. The former procedure simplifies estimation but depends on deriving a set of meaningful weights (for an example, see Franklin Fisher, et al.). In the latter procedure the estimated coefficient of each proportion is interpreted as being the relative marginal cost of producing that one type of product. Estimation is more difficult since the cost function must have a simple specification.

2. A more relevant measure is the number of cases treated. M. Feldstein has used this measure in studying British hospitals. The question of whether patients or patient-days is the better measure cannot be settled a priori. The better measure is the one which is more homogeneous across hospitals, given the cost function specified. It was our judgment that the patient-day was more homogeneous, although there is little data with which to justify our belief.

3. For a review of hospital cost literature, see J. Lave, and J. Mann and D. Yett.

4. One alternative to the patient-day involves counting the specific tasks performed by the hospital staff, e.g., lab tests, meals served, number of operations. But these tasks are inputs to the "restoration of health and alleviation of pain," not measures of the output itself, see M. Ingbar and L. Taylor. Another alternative, involving the construction of a composite measure of output, has been undertaken by D. Saathoff and R. Kurtz and H. Cohen. The authors are currently investigating other approaches to composite output measures. Several attempts have been made to improve the patient-day as a measure.

Introduction to Hospital Economics 251

M. Feldstein, W. Carr and P. Feldstein and R. Berry have stratified by available facilities or corrected for case mix.

5. This measure is often called the hospital occupancy rate and is measured as the ratio of total patient-days to available patient-days (bed days).
6. This hypothesized constancy of the product mix over a short period of time is being investigated by the authors. Some preliminary results suggest the hypothesis is a reasonable one; see Lave and Lave working paper. Any variation in case mix would probably be associated with a change in size; for our data the correlation between the log of hospital size and number of specialized facilities is .76. Thus, we can expect that the size variable would tend to pick up some of the variation in case mix.
7. To determine the correct functional form, we tried a quadratic specification. No evidence could be found that the square of the utilization variable was relevant; the coefficient of size squared indicated that average cost declined slightly as size increased (there was no evidence that cost began to increase at the larger sizes). Thus, an L-shaped cost curve seemed to best describe the data.

There is no simultaneous equations problem in estimating hospital cost functions. The hospitals we study are nonprofit and accept all paying patients as long as there is space, i.e., hospitals do not choose their rate of output, but rather are constrained to accept all cases offered. In addition, it seems likely that the cost of the hospital has little effect on the demand for its services. Most patients have their expenses covered by insurance of some other "third party." In addition, one would presume the demand for hospital services is inelastic with respect to price.

Some evidence on these questions comes from looking at the correlation of the occupancy rate with cost. If patients chose among hospitals on the basis of price, one would expect to observe a negative correlation between occupancy rate and average cost; the correlation is positive and is .26. Secondly, one would expect that high cost hospitals would grow less rapidly than would low cost ones; the correlation between average cost and an index number of size (indicating the rate of growth of each hospital) is .37. Thus, what evidence there is supports the hypotheses.

9. To be precise, hospitals which grew the most had total costs rise most (as a percentage increase) when utilization increased. One must be careful in making the statement ... in the text since a small sign might indicate something other than a large marginal cost. For example, if two hospitals had the same (dollar value of) marginal cost, the one with lower average cost would have its total cost rise more rapidly as utilization increased.
12. The only important change in the results reported in Table 6-4 occurs in the coefficient of M. In the first estimation, M had a positive sign and was about one-third the magnitude of the coefficient of P; these results were much more in line with expectations than the negative M shown in Table 6-4. Our previous estimation converted a clerical error into a positive coefficient for $\log K_0$ in Table 6-5. As in our current Table 6-5, the coefficient of AT continued to be implausible in some regressions. In the former estimation, we were able to explain about 10 percent of the variation in a_{i3}; the range of estimated coefficients was considerably smaller, from -3.50 to 4.46. Apparently the shorter time-series generated spurious significance. In the pooled regression, any time a coefficient was significant, neither the sign nor magnitude changed as more observations were added. Previously, the coefficient of $\log K_{i0}$ tended to be positive and insignificant; now it is negative and insignificant. In the first estimation, the interaction variables were not so stable in sign; $t(\log S_{i0})$ generally had a negative (insignificant) coefficient; $t(\log S_{i0})$ sometimes had a negative coefficient.

13. Space limitations prevent us from presenting both Pittsburgh and Philadelphia annual results here; we do this in our forthcoming paper in *Inquiry*. ["Estimated Cost Functions for Pennsylvania Hospitals," *Inquiry* vii, no. 2, June 1970, pp. 3–14.]

REFERENCES FOR LAVE AND LAVE EXCERPT

R. Berry, "Returns to Scale in the Production of Hospital Services," *Health Service Research*, Summer 1967, 2, 123–39.

W. Carr and P. Feldstein, "The Relationship of Cost to Hospital Size," *Inquiry*, Mar. 1967, 4, 45–65.

H. Cohen, "Variations in Cost Among Hospitals of Different Sizes," *Southern Econ. J.*, Jan. 1967, 33, 355–66.

M. Feldstein, *Economic Analysis for Health Service Efficiency*, Amsterdam 1967.

P. Feldstein, *An Empirical Investigation of the Marginal Cost of Hospital Services*, Chicago 1961.

F. Fisher, Z. Griliches, and C. Kaysen, "The Costs of Automobile Model Changes since 1949," *J. Polit. Econ.*, Oct. 1962, 70, 433–51.

M. Ingbar and L. Taylor, *Hospital Costs in Massachusetts*, Cambridge, Mass. 1968.

J. Johnston, *Statistical Cost Analysis*, New York 1960.

J. Lave, "A Review of the Methods Used to Study Hospital Costs," *Inquiry*, May 1966, 3, 57–81.

―――― and L. Lave, "Estimated Cost Relations for Pennsylvania Hospitals," *Inquiry*, 1970 forthcoming.

―――― and ――――, "The Extent of Role Differentiation Among Hospitals," working paper, Carnegie-Mellon Univ., Apr. 1970.

J. Mann and D. Yett, "The Analysis of Hospital Costs: A Review Article," *J. Bus., Univ. Chicago*, Apr. 1968, 41, 191–202.

M. Nerlove, *Estimation and Identification of Cobb-Douglas Production Functions*, Chicago 1965.

R. Pfouts, "The Theory of Cost and Production in the Multi-Product Firm," *Econometrica*, Oct. 1961, 29, 650–68.

D. Saathoff and R. Kurtz, "Cost Per Day Comparisons Don't Do the Job," *Modern Hospital*, Oct. 1962, 99, 14–16.

A. Walters, "Production and Cost Functions: An Econometric Survey," *Econometrica*, Jan.-Apr. 1963, 31, 1–66.

A. Zellner, "An Efficient Method of Estimating Seemingly Unrelated Regressions and Tests for Aggregation Bias," *J. Amer. Statist. Ass.*, June 1962, 57, 348–68.

Blue Cross of Western Pennsylvania, *Comparative Financial and Statistical Information*, Pittsburgh 1966.

NOTES FOR DAVIS EXCERPT

1. For a discussion of this hypothesis, see Newhouse [11]. Feldstein also derives the implications of a model based upon a utility maximization model where utility is a function of number of cases treated, average duration of stay per case, and the quality of care [5].

2. Although Newhouse argues that a quantity-quality maximizer will hire factors to the point where the marginal revenue product of a factor equals its marginal factor cost in the same way that a profit maximizer will, this is only true if both the quantity-quality maximizer and the profit maximizer produce the same quality output. In fact for any given level of output, the quantity-quality maximizer is likely to provide a higher quality service which will presumably require more inputs [11].
3. This may be demonstrated as follows:

$$\max CF^* = pQ - wL + \lambda[Q - \overline{F(K,L)}]$$
$$\frac{\partial CF^*}{\partial Q} = MR + \lambda = 0 => -\lambda = MR$$
$$\frac{\partial CF^*}{\partial L} = -w - \lambda \frac{\partial F}{\partial L} = 0 \to w = MRP_L$$

4. In this case, the decision maker maximizes profits:

$$\max \pi^* = p(Q,K) \cdot Q - wL - rK + \lambda[Q - F(K,L)]$$
$$\frac{\partial \pi^*}{\partial Q} = MR + \lambda = 0 => -\lambda = MR$$
$$\frac{\partial \pi^*}{\partial L} = -w - \lambda \frac{\partial F}{\partial L} = 0 => w = MRP_L$$
$$\frac{\partial \pi^*}{\partial K} = \frac{\partial P}{\partial K} \cdot Q - r - \lambda \frac{\partial F}{\partial K} => r = MRP_N + \frac{\partial P}{\partial K} \cdot Q$$

that is, capital services are used to the point where the marginal factor cost is equal to the additional revenue which can be produced with another unit of capital, plus the additional revenue which stems from the fact that with more capital any given level of output can be sold at a higher price (K shifts the demand curve).

REFERENCES FOR DAVIS EXCERPT

[1] American Hospital Association, *Factors to Evaluate in the Establishment of Hospital Charges*, Chicago, American Hospital Association, 1966.

[2] William J. Baumol, *Business Behavior, Value and Growth*, New York, The Macmillan Company, 1959.

[3] Karen Davis, *A Theory of Economic Behavior in Nonprofit, Private Hospitals*, unpublished doctoral dissertation, Rice University, May 1969.

[4] ──────── , *Net Income of Hospitals, 1961–1969*, Washington, D.C., Social Security Administration, 1970.

[5] Martin S. Feldstein, *Economic Analysis for Health Service Efficiency*, Amsterdam, North Holland Publishing Company, 1967.

[6] Mary Lee Ingbar and Lester D. Taylor, *Hospital Costs in Massachusetts*, Cambridge, Mass., Harvard University Press, 1968.

[7] Edward M. Kaitz, *Pricing Policy and Cost Behavior in the Hospital Industry*, New York, Frederick A. Praeger, Inc., 1968.

[8] Herbert E. Klarman, *The Economics of Health*, New York, Columbia University Press, 1965.

[9] Millard F. Long, "Efficient Use of Hospitals," in *The Economics of Health and Medical Care*, Ann Arbor, University of Michigan Press, 1964, pp. 211–226.
[10] Walter J. McNerney and Study Staff, *Hospital and Medical Economics*, Chicago, Hospital Research and Educational Trust, 1962, p. 923.
[11] Joseph P. Newhouse, "Toward a Theory of Nonprofit Institutions: An Economic Model of a Hospital," *The American Economic Review* 60:64–74 (March 1970).
[12] Melvin W. Reder, "Some Problems in the Economics of Hospitals," *The American Economic Review* 55:472–81 (May 1965).
[13] Louis S. Reed, "Private Health Insurance, 1968: Enrollment, Coverage, and Financial Experience," *Social Security Bulletin* 32:19–35 (December 1969).
[14] U.S. Department of Health, Education, and Welfare, *First Annual Report of Medicare*, Washington, D.C., Government Printing Office, 1968.
[15] ──────── , *Medicaid: Selected Statistics*, Washington, D.C., Government Printing Office, 1970.
[16] ──────── , *Principles of Reimbursement for Provider Cost*, Washington, D.C., Government Printing Office, 1967.
[17] Burton A. Weisbrod, "Some Problems of Pricing and Resource Allocation in a Non-Profit Industry—the Hospitals," *Journal of Business* 38:18–28 (January 1965).

NOTES FOR PAULY AND REDISCH EXCERPT

1. See Paul Ginsburg, p. 42.
3. Derivatives of two quite different surrogates for hospital output have been used most often by economists doing empirical research. One is based on the number of inpatient days and outpatient visits at the hospital while the other is concerned with the number of cases treated in the hospital. The "case treated" corresponds most closely with the measure of output implied by our model.
4. This was the form used by M. Feldstein (1967) in his study of hospitals in the United Kingdom.
5. Some empirical justification of this assumption may be found in Donald Yett et al., where it was estimated that the elasticity of demand for *hospital* output with respect to *surgeons'* fees is 0.7.
6. If the market for output is perfectly competitive, $|\partial Q/\partial P_T|$ will be infinite; otherwise, the individual hospital demand curve for output will have a negative slope.
7. If the hospital received contributions, it may set a target loss equal to the contributions, but this will not alter our analysis. Moreover, after the fact the hospital may have a profit or loss, but this is assumed to result wholly from stochastic factors.
8. The interpretation of the user cost of capital c is worth comment. When capital is provided through borrowed funds, the interpretation is clear; c is equal to $(r+d)P_K$, where r is the interest rate at which the funds were borrowed, d is the depreciation rate, and P_K is the price of capital goods. When unrestricted donations are used to pay for the marginal unit of capital, the user cost is $(r'+d)P_K$, where r' is the opportunity cost of using contributed funds for hospital physical capital, i.e., the rate which could have been earned on those funds if they had been invested elsewhere (say, in government bonds). When donations are made with the restriction that they be used for physical capital investment, they will affect the marginal user cost of capital only if the

hospital receives so much in donations that it does not have to turn to any other source for funds for capital investment (unless, of course, the conditions for contribution of restricted funds specify a certain amount of the hospital's own funds as matching payments). If restricted donations fall short of the amount which, given the interest rate r, the hospital wishes to invest so that the hospital borrows, the relevant *marginal* user cost of capital must involve the interest and depreciation rates. Except for the case in which restricted donations are so large that the amount of capital that is brought with them exceeds the amount which would be indicated by the marginal conditions, donations, whether unrestricted or restricted, are really equivalent to lump sum subsidies. Only if the hospital's price and output policies affect contributions (and within wide margins, they do not seem to) should contributions be treated as other than lump sum grants. In a world of uncertainty, however, the total of donations past and present may affect a lender's willingness to lend, since they provide collateral. Even in this case, current donations are likely to be important only if they are large relative to total nonborrowed capital.

9. The model implies cost minimization in the sense that, given the physician input, quantities of labor and capital are chosen which, given their marginal supply prices, minimize costs. Cost minimization is also a characteristic of output-maximization models. However, normative conclusions that have been derived from empirical cost function studies regarding socially optimal scale of hospital facilities are considerably weakened when it is realized that there is no reason to suppose that, in comparisons across hospitals or over time, the physician input actually is constant, or even variable in a random way. The physician input has been left out of cost and production function studies of $U.S.$ hospitals. Unless the physician input is specified or is known to be a constant ratio to K and L, there is no way of knowing the true social costs of all the inputs associated with any scale of output, and hence no way of determining the cost-minimizing scale. Observed decreasing hospital costs, for instance, may only represent a systematic increase in physician input with size. Furthermore, when we allow imperfect cooperation of the physician staff in our model in a later section, we will find that minimization of even nonphysician costs in the technical sense by the hospital is a very unlikely conclusion.

15. To see this, think of each physician as a "firm." The socially most efficient institutional arrangement is the one which maximizes the net present value of this firm. The present value is a contingency, depending on the state of nature (for example, what's really wrong with his patients, whether an epidemic occurs, etc.) and the amount of effort that the physician makes. The amount of effort, in turn, depends upon the share of profits the physician receives. The appropriate share for the physician, even given the greater risk he bears, may be approximately equal to one.

16. This last point is an important consideration. It is sometimes alleged that these firms have attained a nonprofit status so that they may better provide services to the poor. However, the recent experience in this country is for the poor to receive health services from government operated hospitals, to receive education in government operated institutions, and not to partake at all of the output of symphony orchestras, theatre groups, or private universities.

REFERENCES FOR PAULY AND REDISCH EXCERPT

M. Feldstein, "Hospital Cost Inflation: A Study of Nonprofit Price Dynamics," *Amer. Econ. Rev.*, Dec. 1971, 61, 853–72.

P. Ginsburg, "Capital in Non-profit Hospitals," unpublished doctoral dissertation, Harvard Univ. 1970, p. 42.

SOURCES AND PERMISSIONS
a. Reprinted from *Hospital Economics* by Sylvester Berki by permission of Lexington Books, D.C. Health and Company, © 1972, pp. 51–52, 54–58, 115.
b. Reprinted from *Health Economics* by Alan L. Sorkin by permission of Lexington Books, D.C. Heath and Company, © 1975, pp. 80–83.
c. Reprinted from "Hospital Cost Functions" by Judith Lave and Lester Lave, *The American Economic Review,* 60, no. 3 (June 1970) by permission of the American Economic Association, © 1970, pp. 379–389, 393–395.
d. Reprinted from "Economic Theories of Behavior on Nonprofit, Private Hospitals" by Karen Davis, *Economic and Business Bulletin,* 24 (Winter 1972) by permission of the *Journal of Economics and Business,* © 1972, pp. 1–13.
e. Reprinted from "The Not-For-Profit Hospital as a Physicians' Cooperative" by Mark Pauly and Michael Redisch, *The Economic Review* 63, no. 1 (March 1973) by permission of the American Economic Association, © 1973, pp. 87–90, 97–99.

Chapter 7

Health Maintenance Organizations

The traditional office-based solo practice of medicine based on fee-for-service payment is slowly giving way to other forms of practice. Groups of various sorts have become important in the delivery of professional services. The type of organization that has attracted perhaps the most attention for its features on financing and delivering care is the health maintenance organization (HMO). This chapter describes HMOs and analyzes several aspects of their economic performance.

THE HMO CONCEPT

A caution is in order in studying HMOs: some of these organizations embody both unique financial mechanisms and distinctive modes of delivering care. For example, some HMOs are linked to specific group practices and hospitals while others—similarly financed—are not as closely tied to providers. The effects of the financial scheme should be distinguished from those of the delivery mode when such firms are described and analyzed, but that is not accomplished easily.

Health maintenance organizations and their forerunners have existed in the United States for many years. Only recently, however, has the HMO terminology come into widespread use. The principal characteristics of these organizations are:

1. There is a contract between the HMO and the consumers (or their representative) who are the "enrolled population."
2. A regular (usually monthly) premium to cover specified (and typically broad) services is paid for, or by, each enrollee to the HMO; few additional charges are levied because the payment mechanism is not basically fee-for-service.

3. The HMO contracts with professional providers to deliver the services due the enrollees; the basis for reimbursing those providers varies among HMOs (as explained later).

There are two basic types of HMOs that the public tends to confuse. One is the prepaid group practice (PGP), the other the medical care foundation, frequently referred to as an independent (or individual) practice association or IPA. There are several differences between the two. First, in the foundation there is a clear organizational separation between the HMO itself and the providers. Second, the PGPs are site-specific, whereas foundations contract with the entire range of solo practitioners, specialized groups, and multispecialty groups in a geographic region. Finally, and probably most important, the PGP physicians are likely to be reimbursed on a salary basis or (less frequently) at a flat rate related to the number of enrollees (that is, on a capitation basis), while foundations generally reimburse their associated professionals through fee-for-service.

This chapter presents a partial, rather than full, application of the theory of the firm to the case of HMOs. The aim is to provide a practical appraisal of these organizations based on a selective survey of HMO objectives, constraints, and performance indicators. Although this chapter is less theoretical than the previous two, the reader will find that many of the conceptual issues discussed in the context of solo practice and voluntary hospitals apply with equal force to health maintenance organizations.

The objectives of the prepaid group practice type of HMO are related to the customary nonprofit nature of those organizations. As in the case of voluntary hospitals, it is not certain what the motivations might be, though many theories exist. It might be speculated that the "recovery of costs" theory of behavior in Karen Davis' selection in the previous chapter fits many, if not most, PGPs. Medical care foundations pose a more complicated issue because of the separate identities of their key units: the foundation itself and its associated "firms" of physicians. While the latter have some sort of profit orientation—perhaps also with a concern for patient quantity and (less tangibly) for personal prestige—the foundation per se might have the same objectives as a PGP.

Constraints upon HMO operations are not substantially different from those applicable to hospitals and solo practices. In the technological category, the main feature is the multiplicity of production functions involved, since HMOs can incorporate independent professionals such as physicians, miscellaneous other personnel, pharmacies, laboratories, and even hospitals. An attempt to generalize the technological factors that apply to all forms of HMOs would be fruitless, given the heterogeneous characteristics of the organizations.

The most important economic constraint is the competition the HMO faces. Although it is rather rare for HMOs to compete directly against each other, there are metropolitan areas in the country where such competition exists (Minneapolis, New York City, and Rochester, N.Y., for example), and there are other areas where a PGP is matched against a foundation (as in parts of California). More important, HMOs represent a potential source of competition to conventional service providers. As far as demand is concerned, HMOs' notable characteristics are the group nature of enrollment, usually employment-based, and the influences on consumers of the third party payment incorporated into the HMO financial scheme.

The other important constraints are institutional-legal ones. The conventional regulatory system, including credentialing of professionals and institutions, applies, of course. In the past, PGPs faced sharp legal restraints on their activities in some states, but these have been abandoned. Foundations confront a special institutional environment in their relations with medical societies; to cover them would require a chapter all its own. The federal government now influences HMO development through subsidies for organizations that qualify; the extent of such subsidies can be expected to affect the future financial viability of these organizations.

CHOICES AND RESULTS: A SELECTIVE APPRAISAL OF HMO PERFORMANCES

The decision criteria that all firms use in choosing levels of output, inputs, and investments apply equally to HMOs, with the proviso that foundations must be examined in conjunction with their associated providers. Here, the focus is on the results of certain basic choices made by HMO administrators and practitioners, interacting with consumers. Of special concern are two different types of performance having economic implications:

1. The economic efficiency with which specific services or sets of services are delivered when enough time is allowed to vary the quantities of all resources used. This raises the issue of economies of scale in HMO operations along with other efficiency questions.
2. The impact on utilization of the full range of HMO services. This raises the issue of cost savings through substitutions among different services.

The concluding portion of the chapter deals with HMO effectiveness and, very briefly, quality of care issues.

Economic Efficiency

A debate has raged over the impact of group practice on the efficiency of providing specific medical services and/or sets of services, such as physician office visits. Foundations typically are composed of medical groups as well as solo practitioners, so the question concerns them, but the group practice role has been argued more sharply in regard to PGPs. One set of issues concerns physician productivity: do individual doctors produce more services in a given time by virtue of practicing in a group? A second and related set concerns economies of scale in the delivery of care: do groups achieve cost savings through bigness per se?

Before the mid 1960s, assertions that large groups enjoyed economies of scale were commonplace despite any hard evidence on the subject. Later in the decade a counterattack was begun by some economists who saw little in theory or practice to support those claims. However, these economists typically did not distinguish between PGPs and other organizational forms of delivery. For example, one frequently cited study of scale economies among internists covered relatively few groups, none of which was a prepaid group practice.[1]

The flavor of the skeptics' case probably is best tasted in the work of Joseph Newhouse. The following brief excerpt from his principal paper on the subject reports the results of a rough cost comparison of a few ambulatory service organizations, none an HMO, with 20 private practices; his empirical findings are omitted. They show (for his limited data) lower costs for the private physicians than for large organizations or clinics. In this article, Newhouse goes beyond his theory of groups and cost evidence to speculate on what public policy should be concerning group practice. Only his introduction and theoretical section are excerpted, but readers might wish to read more of the article to appraise the implications he draws, especially in the light of the data available then and from more recent studies.

INTRODUCTION AND SUMMARY[a]

This article presents a theoretical and empirical discussion of how costs of outpatient medical practice vary with the size of the group providing services. It focuses upon an element which seems to have been ignored by those advocating increased emphasis upon group practice, namely, the incentives facing the individual physician to keep the cost of his practice down and his work effort high. Cost and revenue-sharing schemes are more prevalent as group size increases; therefore, any individual physician is less likely to have to bear the financial consequences of his decision. Likewise, the reward he obtains from additional work effort falls. Thus, we would predict that total costs would rise as an individual physician's share of costs falls because of greater X-inefficiency [13, 5].[1] We would also predict that hours worked would fall as the individual physician's share of marginal revenue falls. The situation reaches an extreme in hospital outpatient clinics. Since the cost to the patient is often kept below the market price in these clinics with the deficit made up from philanthropy and from the state, the incentive to control costs is at a minimum. Likewise, the incentive for a physician to work additional hours or to see as many patients as possible in the hours he works is at a minimum, since his reward for the additional effort will, in the usual case, be purely psychic.

We report some findings on the costs of outpatient medical practice. They are based on data from a small number of physicians and outpatient clinics. The physician data became available when a group of physicians indicated that they might be interested in moving into a new office building. As part of ascertaining their preferences for certain features of the new office building, cost information upon their practices was gathered. One of the major questions of interest was the comparison of the overhead costs of the private physician with cost information from three outpatient clinics we had studied. The expected result was found: namely, that overhead costs of private physicians are very much below those of outpatient clinics. The second question of interest was how costs varied by size of practice. Many health policy experts, for example, Fein [8], have advocated group practice as a method for achieving economies. Bailey [3], however, has contended that the productivity of the physician does not change as the size of his practice increases. In our sample, as might be expected because of the regression fallacy, there are initial increasing returns to scale.[2] However, the minimum cost point is at 860 visits per month. More importantly, however, we included a variable which measured the presence or absence of cost-sharing arrangements. It was significant with the expected sign, and its size showed that the magnitude of potential economies of scale is offset by additional X-inefficiency.

Revenue-sharing will clearly decrease the marginal reward to physicians. Bailey [2], in fact, finds that as group size increases, the number of hours worked decreases. In our sample, dividing the practitioners who share revenue from those who do not, those who share revenue do work less, but it is a very small amount and not statistically significant. The sample, however, is quite small.

We conclude by considering the implications of our analysis for public policy. The findings should give pause to those who believe that large clinics and large groups can give more efficient care than physicians working alone or in small groups and hence that group practice should be subsidized. Besides being more costly, the clinics we have observed are much less pleasant settings in which to receive care. The cottage industry may not be so bad after all.

The Economic Theory of Groups

The economic theory of groups is well understood. (See, for example, Olson [21]). Olson shows that when the output of a group is a public good (that is, a good from which no one can be excluded), each individual will have an incentive to minimize his input into the group. As the discrepancy between the reward to the individual from additional effort and the cost to him of that effort widens, the incentive grows stronger to reduce his input into the group. Olson remarks that:

> ... when a partnership has many members, the individual partner observes that his own effort or contribution will not greatly affect the performance of the enterprise, and expects that he will get his prearranged share of the earnings whether or not he contributes as much as he could have done. The earnings of a partnership, in which each partner gets a prearranged percentage of the return, are a collective good to the partners, and when the number of partners increases, the incentive for each partner to work for the welfare of the enterprise lessens [21, pp. 54–55].

The tendency to work "for the welfare of the enterprise" is less, the larger the group, for at least two reasons. First, assuming an equal sharing arrangement, the reward to the individual from his actions is less, the greater the number of individuals sharing in that reward. Second, the forming and enforcing of informal agreements whereby each partner agrees to work a certain amount is clearly easier in a smaller group.

At one extreme is the solo practitioner. Since he keeps all his net revenue (after taxes), we would expect that the incentive to control costs and work long hours would be maximized. With group practice, the incentive for each physician to devote effort to maximize net revenue will clearly depend upon his share in that revenue. How are shares determined? Of 4,289 medical groups surveyed by the American Medical Association in 1965 (80.8 percent of the total number), 12 percent divided net income according to the dollar amount of fees charged accountable to each physician [1, p. 30]. An additional 34 percent divided net income into nonequal shares, where, in some cases, amount of fees generated was one of the factors determining the share. (Examples of other factors might be seniority and original capital investment in the group.) Thirty-seven percent of the groups divided net income equally. Thus, some groups attempt to take account of the individual's effort to generate additional revenue by making his share dependent upon gross revenues generated. Almost none, however, appears to recognize extra effort to control cost.

At the other extreme from the solo practitioner are large outpatient clinics. If overhead costs of private practitioners get too far out of line, their fees will reflect that, and they may find themselves with fewer patients. Although cross-elasticities of demand between physicians are likely to be low, it is doubtful that many physicians would survive very long with overhead costs of the magnitude we observed in clinics.[3] By contrast, clinics can pass their costs along to third parties such as the Medicaid program or to private philanthropy which may underwrite any deficit in the entire operation. Charges to patients are kept at rates below what they would pay on the market, so that high clinic costs do not drive patients elsewhere. The community at large bears the penalty through increased philanthropic donations, higher taxes, and larger insurance premiums. Thus we would expect the highest costs of all in such clinics because of the highest X-inefficiency. The X-inefficiency comes both from the lack of incentive to control costs and from the lack of market forces which could weed out inefficient producers.

Other economists have responded in support of the view that medical groups can offer economic advantages, including economies of scale. One such position is that of H.E. "Ted" Frech and Paul Ginsburg. They point out some methodological difficulties that plagued earlier researchers and offer a new approach. Although their "survivor model" has yet to be generally accepted, it provides a good way to view the efficiency issue. As the selection indicates, Frech and Ginsburg add a useful component for purposes here: a separation in their data of prepaid groups from fee-for-service practices. Their findings (omitted from the selection) in favor of the efficiency of prepaid groups should encourage the advocates of PGPs, although it is clear that additional research would be useful. The results of such work gradually are becoming available.[2]

OPTIMAL SCALE IN MEDICAL PRACTICE: A SURVIVOR ANALYSIS[b]

Introduction

The issue of optimal scale in medical practice has received a great deal of attention in the literature.[1] Researchers have used a variety of methods to determine the relative efficiency of solo versus group practices of various sizes. The empirical results have unfortunately not been consistent. They have run the gamut of weakly favoring solo practice[2] to asserting that groups of over 30 physicians are most efficient.[3] The purpose of this paper is to point out some of the measurement problems that have plagued these studies (and are likely to hinder similar studies in the future) and to estimate relative efficiency by a method which does not encounter these problems—survivor analysis.

The a priori case for economies of scale in medical practice is based upon technical indivisibilities. Larger practices can make use of the services of paramedical personnel to perform many of the simpler tasks in delivering medical care. Large units of capital can be used more effectively in large practices, allowing provision of more services on site.

A number of diseconomies of scale have also been pointed out. A key one is the inefficiency inherent in managing large firms. As Pauly points out,[4] if the organization is set up as a pure sharing partnership, each member has the incentive to minimize his labor input—the classic free-rider problem. In addition to the incentive problem, communication and coordination become more expensive as organizations grow. Besides heavier management costs, larger units cause patients to incur higher transportation costs to purchase services. And, if physicians dislike large practices, higher compensation will be needed to attract them to work in these settings.

Conventional Methods

Past empirical research on the issue has attempted to measure economies through comparison of physician income, costs, or output between different sizes of practice. Studies such as Boan's and Egan's compared income per physician among practices.[5] However, important inputs are measured incorrectly. This type of study assumes that physician-time input does not vary by size of group. If this is not the case, practices where physicians spend long hours will appear to be more efficient. In addition, the nonpecuniary aspects of physician compensation, such as preferences for large or small organizations and variability of hours worked, are neglected. Controlling for different abilities of physicians is extremely difficult and ignored in practice. It is quite likely that ability of physicians does vary systematically with the size of the organization, partly because group physicians are younger. Finally, smaller practices allow physicians to take a greater part of their compensation in kind for tax avoidance, causing measured income to understate real income.

The direction of bias resulting from these measurement problems is not determinate. For instance, if, as we suspect, physicians work longer hours in smaller practices, the studies would make those sizes appear to be relatively more efficient than they really are. On the other hand, the presence of more highly skilled physicians in large groups or physician distaste for working in large groups would result in the opposite error. Consequently, we cannot deduce the direction of error in Boan's result that group practice is more efficient than solo practice or Egan's conclusion that groups of over 30 physicians are optimal.

Comparisons of costs are subject to similar problems. Newhouse looked at nonphysican cost per office visit, while Yett looked at tax-deductible expenses per physician.[6] These studies avoid the problems of variation in physician-time input and compensation in kind, but cannot control for quality of service variation and physician preferences or substitution of physician time for other inputs. Further, it covers only a small part of total cost. Most cost comparisons also suffer from omission of patient time and transportation costs, which clearly vary with practice size.

Likewise, productivity studies are beset by measurement problems, which differ according to the productivity measure used. For instance, if office visits per physician are studied, physician-time input, quality of care, and patient time and transportation costs may vary with group size. Billings per physician are affected by physician-time input, ability of the physician, and physician preferences. Reinhardt has been successful in eliminating some of these sources of variation via the incorporation of additional independent variables into a regression analysis.[7] In general, however, data of this sort are difficult to come by and are often of poor quality. For instance, Bailey's data show a negative correlation of practice size with hours worked,[8] while the *Medical Economics* survey data used by Reinhardt show the opposite. Both the quality of physicians (input) and the quality of care (output) are exceedingly difficult to measure, as there is no agreement as to how to evaluate them. Kovner is able to avoid some of the measurement problems by studying different size physician offices within one large organization (Kaiser),[9] although the applicability of the results to other settings is somewhat limited and overhead costs common to all offices and patient travel time are left out of the analysis.

Further, all these conventional measures of economies of scale suffer a common problem. They all measure costs (or income or productivity) for the existing firms in each size class, while the relevant magnitude for both private and public decision making is cost to the marginal firm entering or leaving each size class. Transportation costs, preferences for certain sizes on the part of physicians and consumers, and other factors are likely to cause costs experienced by a marginal firm in a given size class to differ from the previous experience of firms already in that class. At equilibrium, it is likely that average costs incurred by existing practices will vary with size class while the costs to a marginal firm will be constant across size classes.[10] Consequently, rank order of average costs in a size class is an unreliable guide to that for costs to marginal firms.

The Survivor Model

Difficulties in measuring inputs and outputs need not present barriers to the estimation of efficient sizes for medical practice. As long as physicians maximize some utility function,[11] their actions will cause the most efficient sizes of medical practice to thrive and those least efficient to decline. By studying the changing patterns of market shares of the various sizes of medical practice one can determine relative efficiencies.[12]

The underlying model is quite simple. Physicians will alter their size of practice when another appears to be more profitable in terms of the physician's utility function. In pursuit of this goal, practice sizes that are most efficient in an economic sense will be chosen. Efficiency will take account of more than physician-time input and accounting costs and will include physician and patient preferences, costs of time and transportation, quality of care, and other considerations. By studying changes in practice size, the net impact of all variables including those that could not be measured in conventional studies can be perceived. Over time, the size distribution of medical practices will tend toward an optimum where all sizes are equally efficient *at the margin*. Until this optimum is reached, those sizes that are growing most rapidly can be identified as most efficient at the margin.

It should be pointed out that an assumption of slow adjustment is required here. If adjustment was instantaneous, studies of changes in market shares would only identify changes in equilibrium rather than the differential efficiencies at the margin resulting from slow adjustment toward a new equilibrium. Use of a short time period for study helps to insure that movement toward an equilibrium is more important than changes in the equilibrium.

While observed changes in market share are considered to reflect a part of the movement toward an equilibrium, declining-size groups will not ultimately vanish. Variation in tastes among consumers and physicians, in market sizes, and in transportation systems will cause practice sizes that are currently relatively inefficient at the margin to be present in the equilibrium size distribution.

Limitations of the Analysis

The most important difficulty with this type of analysis is that it considers only private costs and benefits. The most obvious source of divergence between private and social efficiency is monopoly. To the extent that larger group practices attain more monopoly power, their social economic efficiency will be overstated by the analysis. However, as Shepherd argues,[13] this is less of a problem in atomistic industries—like medical care. Further, it is not clear that larger groups have more monopoly power than smaller ones. Kessel has shown that substantial monopoly power by individual practitioners is possible due to sanctions of organized medicine applied to price cutters and restrictions against advertising.[14] When one considers that the high cost of information is an important cause of whatever monopolistic market structure exists in medicine,[15] it is likely that the information produced by large groups tends to make the industry more competitive. Since larger groups are in the best position to engage in price competition and tend to provide more information than small groups, it is indeed likely that the social optimum will contain more large firms than the observed private optimum.

A second source of divergence of private from social costs concerns the tax advantages of smaller groups and solo practice. In a smaller organization, it is easier for physicians to take part of their income in kind. Also opportunities to take payment for services in cash and not report the income for tax purposes are more common in small practices. Tax advantages cause the socially optimal distribution to have fewer small practices than the private one.

A third important source of divergence might be institutional barriers restricting certain sizes of groups, which may obscure the social efficiency of these size classes. While organized medicine has opposed prepaid medical practice, this constitutes only a small fraction of medical groups. Fee-for-service groups have not been opposed.[16] Also, while state laws generally prohibit the "corporate practice of medicine," courts have consistently held that corporations owned by physicians may provide medical care,[17] and most groups are legally organized as partnerships. Insofar as the barriers have had effects, they have depressed the private returns at the margin to larger groups and prepaid groups.

Definition of the industry must be more precise than under conventional methods. Fortunately, the data available for this study permit disaggregation into single-specialty, multispecialty, and general-practice groups. Results for these categories are consistent with those from the basic data set of all office-based medical practice—an industry far more homogeneous than many SIC-coded groups of firms.

Another limitation is that the analysis does not indicate the quantitative dimensions of the optimal size distribution of practices. Since declining sizes need not vanish in equilibrium, only the qualitative difference between equilibrium and the present distribution can be identified.

Empirical Analysis

Medical practices are classified according to the number of physicians, a dimension which serves as a proxy for other scale variables. The change in market share between 1965 and 1969 is computed for each size classification, and these relative growth rates are compared. Further, medical practices are disaggregated into single specialty, multispecialty, and general-practice categories and separately analyzed. Production, demand, and physician-supply functions may vary across the three practice types. An additional disaggregation by location (census region) is performed to see if the observed pattern of market-share changes is the mean of divergent regional patterns or reflects a consistent pattern throughout the United States. Finally, the correlation of group size with presence of a group manager and with method of physician compensation will be examined to explain the observed pattern of relative growth rates.

Data on the size distribution of medical practice for 1965 and 1969 have been obtained from two American Medical Association surveys of the entire population of group practices combined with survey data on all office-based practices.[18]

• • •

Summarizing the empirical evidence, survivor analysis indicates that groups are more efficient than solo practice at the margin. Among groups, both large and small groups appear to be more efficient than middle-sized (7–25 physicians) practices. This inverted U-shaped average cost curve may be due to indivisibilities in management services and the adverse incentives of sharing arrangements. Multispecialty and prepaid groups are relatively more efficient than single-specialty and fee-for-service groups, respectively, as evidenced by the higher growth rates of the former categories.

Conclusions

With regard to private costs and benefits, one can conclude that the optimal size distribution of medical practice will have more groups in the size ranges identified as most efficient at the margin and fewer physicians in solo practice. It is also likely that optimal practice arrangements include more prepaid groups and more multispecialty groups. The authors are not aware of any empirical results that point to a systematic difference in the socially efficient optimum from the observed private one. These results do not imply that there should be no solo practice. Some patients and physicians will have a preference for this mode, and some consumers will put a high value on transportation time. It is a limitation of the analysis that only the direction of change toward the optimal distribution is pointed out and not the magnitude of the change.

The analysis is based upon a presumption that firm size is changing toward the optimum. In the absence of evidence that the social optimum differs from the private, any policy prescriptions based upon the analysis should be limited to whether or not to expedite the process of adjustment. There has been an increase of 29 percent of physicians in groups and an 8 percent decline in solo practice over the 1965–69 period. There is no a priori reason to think that optimal private and social adjustment rates differ. Subsidizing adjustment would suffer from the usual problems with subsidies such as development of vested interests seeking their maintenance. In addition, an effective subsidy would make it extremely difficult to recognize when the optimal distribution is achieved.

A more promising form of intervention would involve removing some of the legal barriers to the optimal organization of the medical practice industry in order to insure that movement toward an optimal private structure is also one toward an optimal social structure. These measures would include removing bars against prepaid groups, corporate practice of medicine, and advertising. [Ed. note: Many of those bars have been removed since this article was written.]

Impact on Utilization

Another aspect of HMOs' performance concerns their impact on the pattern of use of the entire range of medical services in the system. Probably no argument in favor of HMOs—at least, their PGP variety—has been asserted more frequently and strongly than that they offer appreciable cost savings. The key to the case is reduced utilization of days in hospitals, especially because of lower admission rates. Many observers also have noted lower rates of use of certain surgical procedures. There have been occasional critics, such as the economist Herbert Klarman, who have attempted to explain the differences largely in terms of limited access of PGP patients to hospital beds. Still, much evidence has accumulated to support the cost savings argument, and little exists to refute it, so it is likely to be accepted by almost all neutral observers.[3]

Although the reduced use of hospitals is a fact, there are associated questions that remain to be answered. One is the relative importance of the various causal factors related to lower utilization under HMOs: financial incentives for physicians to economize on care ordered, breadth of services covered by prepayment, access to beds, and peer review and other organizational features. The first of the two selections below, by M.R. Chassin, carefully distinguishes among those factors and points to needed future research. In the second article, John Holahan provides strong evidence to bolster theoretical speculations that most of the gains are likely to accrue to PGPs rather than to foundations.[4] If so, much of the public discussion of HMO "savings" has been muddled by a failure to make that distinction. The policy implications are important. Why, for example, should the federal government subsidize all forms of HMOs if only PGPs offer economic advantages? Further research and debate on this question appear called for.

HEALTH MAINTENANCE ORGANIZATIONS[c]

One of the principal arguments used by advocates of HMOs in support of further diffusion of this form of medical care is that it is less expensive than traditional fee for service medicine. The major reason cited for this effect is the often reported low hospital utilization rates experienced by HMOs. Theoretically, there are many possible explanations for this observed phenomenon. What follows is an analytic framework synthesized from many sources.*

By definition, an HMO has underwritten the financial risks of caring for a population. The less expensively it can render this care, the greater the surplus it realizes. A clear financial incentive may also be directly transmitted to the physician in the form of salary bonuses or other remuneration. Another possible explanation is that HMOs provide, again almost by definition, comprehensive ambulatory care. It has been argued that this will lead to lower hospital utilization. The data presented in the previous section [not included here] strongly suggest that this is not the case. A third factor is peer review. Once a hospital admissions policy has been established by the administration of an HMO, perhaps on the basis of the financial incentive described above, it is frequently enforced by a committee of physicians who review individual admissions for their compatibility with the policy. A final factor is bed availability. Several HMOs operate their own hospitals and prohibit their physicians from hospitalizing the group's patients anywhere but in their own facility. The number of beds in the HMO's hospital can then be manipulated by the group's administration to achieve policy goals.

It is important from the perspective of cost containment to weigh the relative importance of each of these effects and to decide which are the most critical to the success of an HMO in reducing hospital utilization.

The HMO experience has been exhaustively reviewed by Donabedian[30] and Roemer and Shonick.[110] Only selected individual studies which have been published since 1973 will be examined at length here. Donabedian reviews the extensive literature documenting the fact that family subscribers of HMOs pay less for their medical care annually than do families who receive care from fee for service practitioners and who are covered by more traditional forms of insurance. This saving is principally attributable to decreased rates of hospitalization. These prepaid groups may provide more ambulatory care than traditional medicine, but the additional expense of this care is more than offset by the fewer hospital days experienced by the HMO patient population. This decrease in hospitalization occurs both in medical and surgical categories, although reported rates of surgery are generally far lower among HMO patients than among comparable control groups.

Roemer and Shonick offer data indicating that per capita expenditures for hospitalization were 11 to 18 percent lower for California's Kaiser Plans than for patients cared for by traditional medicine. Furthermore, it has been the Federal Employee Health Program's continuing experience that its members who elect HMO coverage consistently show lower hospitalization rates. These rates which are "especially striking for elective surgical admissions,"[110] have been estimated to represent a 20 to 25 percent reduction in hospital days for HMO patients.

Luft has recently reviewed the relationship between HMOs and health care costs.[84] His conclusions are similar to those stated above. He found that California's Kaiser Plans were associated with 10 to 40 percent lower total health care costs than suitable comparison groups with traditional forms of insurance coverage. His data also show that HMOs deliver slightly more ambulatory care but strikingly less hospital care to their members. He estimates that HMO members spend 25 to 40 percent fewer days in hospital than their fee for service counterparts. This reduction was spread about equally between surgical and non-surgical hospitalizations.

The available HMO utilization data are of course plagued by the problem of self-selection. All the studies on HMOs have been done retrospectively on population groups that have already chosen the coverage they prefer. It is not unreasonable to expect that populations selected in this way will differ in their health status. Until the current Rand Health Insurance Study, there was no study that used random sampling of a population group to assign HMO or traditional care. Roemer and Shonick present some evidence that a slightly higher risk population may elect HMO coverage. This is important because, if it is true, it means that the HMO reductions in hospitalization take on added significance in that their population is sicker than the average.

A more recent study by Gaus et al. confirms and extends some of these earlier findings.[47] These authors compared 1975 data from more than 8,000 Medicaid families divided among 10 HMOs and 10 control populations matched for age, family size, geographic area, and Medicaid program status. The control populations received their care through traditional fee for service medicine. As expected, there were striking differences in hospital utilization. The HMO patients experienced 340 total days of hospital care per 1,000 persons, including 208 days for surgical care. The control group showed 888 total hospital days and 318 for surgical care. Medical Care Foundations were included in this analysis and did not show significant differences from the control groups. In an attempt to evaluate the extent of selection bias, data were gathered on patients' prior health status, data which revealed no differences between the HMO groups and the fee for service groups.

Weighing the most important factors in the HMO achievement of lower hospitalization rates, Roemer and Shonick cite and concur with Klarman that control over bed availability is the most important factor in this process. It is true that the most often cited HMO, Kaiser-Permanente, maintains a bed/population ratio which is roughly 2/1000, or less than half the national average. New York's Health Insurance Plan (HIP), which provided some of the earliest data on the low rate of HMO hospital utilization,[27] does not own hospitals. But in the early years of the program, its physicians had a difficult time obtaining staff privileges in many New York City hospitals, thus creating a functional constriction of bed supply. Klarman cites data that later HIP reports have failed to show the same large differences in hospital utilization that were shown by the earlier studies.[79] One possible explanation for this is increased availability of admitting privileges to HIP doctors. These data have been used to emphasize the importance of limited access to hospital beds in the HMO's ability to decrease hospital utilization.

Many other HMOs that have demonstrated low hospital utilization, however, neither own their own hospitals nor have a problem obtaining admitting privileges in community hospitals.[103] Donabedian stresses different factors:

> The available data on hospital utilization are consistent with the notion that prepaid group practice through changing the nature of the incentives to the physicians and introducing professional controls lowers the hospital utilization rates for many surgical and nonsurgical conditions.[30]

● ● ●

A study from Marshfield, Wisconsin, apparently contradicts much of the above experience with HMOs.[14] The Marshfield Clinic has operated for many years as a fee for service group practice of salaried physicians. In 1971, approximately 15 percent of its patients were brought under a prepayment plan that was worked out among the Clinic, Wisconsin Blue Cross, and the local community hospital in which the Clinic hospitalizes all its patients. The remainder of the Clinic's patients continued to pay for their care on a fee for service basis. The majority of them carried standard Blue Cross and Blue Shield policies that did not reimburse for most ambulatory care. Both groups were then followed for two full years, and their use of outpatient and inpatient services was tabulated. The authors state that the physicians in the Clinic had no knowledge of the payment status of individual patients.

The prepaid patients made much greater use of outpatient physician visits than their fee for service counterparts. In the year prior to the change in financing, the group of people that eventually became the prepaid group had 1.84 visits per person per year, while the others averaged 1.34 visits. In the year following the change, the prepaid group increased to 3.69 visits per person, while the group that remained fee for service rose slightly to 1.49 visits. In the second year of the study the difference was maintained: the prepayment group registered 3.68 visits and the fee for service group averaged 1.73. All three of these differences are statistically significant. The fact that there was an initial difference in utilization rates suggests that there may have been some initial adverse self-selection in the prepaid group, a suggestion which was not substantiated by the hospitalization data. These changes in the utilization rates support the previously described relationship of ambulatory physician visits to changes in copayment: whenever the net price of these services decreases, utilization increases.

The hospitalization data, on the other hand, surprised the authors: consistent with other data on HMOs, they expected a decrease in hospital utilization rates for the prepaid group. In the year prior to the change in financing, the group that chose prepayment experienced 413.5 hospital days per 1000 population, while the rest of the Clinic's population showed 408.4. In the first year of the study, the prepayment group increased to 656.5 days per 1000 and the fee for service group increased slightly to 464.3 days. Again, this difference was maintained in the second year of the study with the prepayment group experiencing 635.4 days per 1000 and the rest 414.6 days. These latter two differences were statistically significant.

This observation of increased hospitalization in the prepaid group has been the source of some consternation among analysts. When examining the Marshfield Clinic for the requisite factors involved in achieving decreased hospitalization, however, the data conform to previous studies. None of the three major factors was operating in the Clinic. There was no restriction of bed supply for the prepaid group as opposed to the fee for service group; both maintained the same access to the community hospital through their Clinic doctors. There was no separate peer review established to monitor hospitalization of the prepaid group members. In fact, it is not apparent from the report of the study that any sort of peer review was operative at Marshfield. Finally, it is not clear who bore the financial risk for the hospital care of the prepayment group. The fact that the Clinic physicians did not even know the payment status of the patients strongly indicates that it was not the Clinic. If the Clinic did bear the financial risk, then this physician ignorance of payment status means that the Clinic failed to act on its financial incentive. If this is the case, one possible explanation may be that only 15 percent of the Clinic's population was covered under prepayment, and this proportion may have been too small to motivate the Clinic administration to modify the behavior of its physicians.

Therefore, the Marshfield experience represents a group of patients that received increased ambulatory coverage without any of the structural alterations in the organization of their care that have proven effective in decreasing hospitalization. Prepayment by itself is clearly insufficient. Under these circumstances, prior experience would lead one to predict an increased hospitalization rate for the group receiving increased ambulatory benefits.

In summary, HMOs probably do care for their patients less expensively than traditional fee for service medicine. This is achieved primarily by impressive reductions in hospitalization rates for both medical and surgical conditions; some HMOs have demonstrated particularly striking decreases in elective surgery. This decrease in hospitalization is not attributable to increased ambulatory coverage, but rather to a combination of structural factors that all appear to be effective. The effects of these factors—financial incentives not to hospitalize, strong peer review procedures to determine the appropriateness of decisions to hospitalize, and restriction of bed supply available to physicians—may be additive; the more of them that are present, the larger may be the reduction in hospital utilization.

Furthermore, the above factors can be efficacious even when they are applied outside the kind of organizational structure usually associated with an HMO. Densen and his co-workers reported in 1962 on data generated by members of a department store union served by two different forms of medical insurance.[28] The union itself administered a program of hospital insurance that covered all its members, and there were two programs of outpatient care available to the membership. One was HIP, and the other, administered directly by the union, paid solo practitioners on a fee for service basis for ambulatory care. Both union members and physicians were subjected to a continuous educational program designed to encourage conservative use of medical services. Thus, in addition to bearing the financial risk for hospitalization, the union initiated its own review procedures. The results showed that hospital utilization rates for these two groups were identical; after adjusting for age and sex, the HIP group had 53.5 hospital days per 100 population, while the union plan had 53.4. The two groups, although self-selected, were comparable on several population parameters and across broad disease classifications. In addition, both these rates of hospitalization were comparable with the lowest rates achieved by HIP in other reported settings at that time. This example represents the application of the techniques of financial incentive and review procedure by a consumer group with an impact on hospitalization equivalent to that of an effective HMO.

What are the policy implications of these findings? From the viewpoint of cost containment, it appears that the HMO concept, employing the three factors outlined above, can be effective in reducing the cost of medical care for the individuals it serves. Moreover, economists argue that the very presence of the HMO as a competitor induces the fee for service sector of the medical market to make changes in its operations that result in cost saving. Some see the recent formation of Medical Care Foundations by local medical societies as an example of this phenomenon. The magnitude of this effect cannot be reliably estimated, and it must depend to some extent on the ability of the HMO to secure a sizeable share of the medical market. This has not yet happened, partially because the expansion of HMOs is severely hampered by insufficient administrative expertise, by hostility from fee for service medicine, and by misunderstanding on the part of consumers. Some would add the hindrance of governmental regulations to this list.[37, 38] It is probably not reasonable to expect that even a large minority of the population will be covered by HMOs in the near future.

● ● ●

What can be said of the quality of care provided by HMOs? It has been demonstrated that HMOs under the proper circumstances reduce hospitalization. Does this mean that they are delivering better quality care? Worse? The answer is not clear.†

A very early study showed that HIP patients had lower rates of prematurity and perinatal mortality than a control population served by fee for service medicine.[116] The relationship of this finding to decreased hospitalization is obscure; it is more likely related to expanded ambulatory care. There is a paucity of data relating to whether low HMO hospitalization rates are associated with better, equal, or worse quality when compared to fee for service medicine. Densen and his colleagues, in a previously cited study, reported on the relative hospitalization rates for HIP and traditionally served patients, all of whom were members of a particular labor union.[27] The group of patients that transferred from HIP to the other plan had higher rates of surgery than did those who had been in the other plan continuously. One possible explanation of this finding is that HIP doctors and other doctors disagreed over the advisability of surgery for these patients, the HIP physicians electing to manage their illnesses without operation, but fee for service physicians electing to manage them with surgery. Even if this were the case, it is still impossible to tell from the data which group of physicians is delivering the better quality care.

Whether HMOs hospitalize too little, or fee for service medicine hospitalizes too much, is unknown. More likely it will be found that for certain conditions, one or the other is true. Preliminary data from the Seattle Prepaid Health Care Project indicate that certain surgical procedures may not be performed often enough by HMOs.[29] It may be that HMO medicine is simply lower quality medicine at a discount price. On the other hand, it may be that HMOs have succeeded in weeding out unnecessary hospitalizations and in maximizing efficiency of outpatient operations, thus delivering better or at least equal quality of care at a lower cost. The truth is entirely unknown at the present time.

FOUNDATIONS FOR MEDICAL CARE: AN EMPIRICAL INVESTIGATION OF THE DELIVERY OF HEALTH SERVICES TO A MEDICAID POPULATION[d]

The health care system in the United States is commonly criticized for encouraging excessive utilization, permitting inefficient modes of service delivery, and for absorbing an inordinate share of the nation's resources. In particular, it has been argued that fee-for-service solo practice medicine has resulted in too little concern with the efficient delivery of health care. Because the physician's income varies directly with the number of (and complexity of) services rendered, the physician has a strong incentive to provide people with more services than "necessary." Concern with alternative reimbursement arrangements has led in recent years to considerable interest in health maintenance organizations (HMOs).

The basic objective of health maintenance organizations is to offer comprehensive health services to voluntarily enrolled consumers through annual contracts on a fixed price (capitation) basis. The fixed price is expected to cover the cost of all needed services for some period such as a year. There are two basic organizational forms of HMOs: the prepaid group practice and the foundation for medical care. The prepaid group practice is usually associated with a large-scale, multi-specialty provider organization. Unlike traditional forms of medical practice, the prepaid group practice has strong incentives to provide consumers with a combination of health services produced in a technically and economically efficient manner. Considerable evidence has accumulated in recent years which supports the argument that prepaid group practices lead to fewer unnecessary hospital admissions, shorter hospital stays, substitution of ambulatory care for in-hospital care, and greater emphasis to preventive care.[1] They may also reduce costs of health care delivery because of the more efficient use that can be made of specialized facilities and manpower, the savings in procurement of drugs and appliances, the efficiency permitted in record keeping, billing, and other clerical tasks, etc. Other sources of efficiency that have been demonstrated include more *rational* use of prescription drugs,[2] substitution of psychiatric care for general physician services,[3] and substitution of extended care and home health services for hospital days.[4] Finally, a large multi-specialty group practice may offer considerable savings in patient time by providing a wide range of services in a single location.

The foundation for medical care form of an HMO, sometimes referred to as individual practice association, is characterized by a number of individual health care providers not formally integrated into a larger organization. Individual providers maintain separate practices and are paid for services by the foundation on a fee-for-service basis. Because the foundation itself is prepaid, it needs to control costs and attempts to do so through extensive use of local audit and peer review. If, after extensive peer review of physicians' claims, total billings are found to exceed the fixed budget, all physicians will receive pro rata reductions in payments. Individual solo practices are maintained intact under the foundation plan, so costs are unlikely to be reduced through more efficient provider organization (i.e., scale economies, greater economies, greater use of non-physician personnel). Rather, the economies are expected to be derived from less use of hospital services and control of unnecessary physician visits, ancillary services, and prescription drugs. Foundations seem especially well suited for delivery of care in rural areas. Because foundations retain the solo practice mode of delivery, they are likely to offer patients greater convenience, which is of particular importance to patients for whom transportation is difficult. Finally, while foundations are not likely to be as efficient in delivery of care as HMOs, they have been considerably more popular with physicians and appear to be growing at a much faster rate.

In this paper we present arguments and some empirical evidence that foundations for medical care may not be effective mechanisms for the long-term control of costs. The major problem with fixed budget, fee-for-service arrangements is that all physicians in the association have an incentive to overprovide because gains from overprovision will typically exceed the losses from the pro rata reductions. That is, those physicians responsible for excessive provision will reap some remuneration for those services, while pro rata reductions will apply to all physicians in proportion to their total billings. This places an extraordinary burden on the foundation's peer review mechanism to control unnecessary services and create equity in physician remuneration. Failure to do so is likely to create resentment toward the program on the part of those physicians who have not abused it. Physicians who believe they suffer inordinately from pro rata reductions are likely to refer services to other providers, most likely hospital inpatient and outpatient departments as well. Alternatively, they will be less likely to participate in the foundation, which reduces the availability of private physician care to those covered by prepayment contracts with the foundation.[5]

While a rather large literature on prepaid group practices has developed in the past decade, little empirical research on the impact of foundations has been undertaken.[6] This paper will represent the results of an empirical investigation of the effect of the San Joaquin Foundation for Medical Care on the provision of selected health services in the California Medicaid program during 1969 and 1970. During fiscal years 1969 and 1970, the San Joaquin Foundation was "at risk" under the Medi-Cal program for all physicians' services—visits, diagnostic services and surgery. The Foundation was not at risk for hospital charges—inpatient or outpatient—but was responsible for service of private physicians rendered in those settings. It was also not at risk for prescription drugs at that time. Data from the California Medicaid paid claims system permit us to estimate the net impact of the San Joaquin project on utilization rates for several services, including those for which the Foundation was at risk.

The net impact is important because the fiscal intermediary (Blue Shield) which reviewed claims in other counties also attempts to control unnecessary utilization. While it is not itself at risk, Blue Shield is legally required to systematically examine claims to determine that both providers and beneficiaries are eligible to participate in the program and that the service provided is a covered benefit and medically necessary or appropriate. It presumably had some need to be concerned with the state's assessment of its performance because of the presence of other insurance firms which could perform the intermediary function. The foundation model, if it is to replace insurance firms by providing a closer link between the insurance and provider functions, must show evidence that it can monitor the delivery of care in a more effective fashion than those available alternatives. Foundations could be viewed as desirable if their review process results in a higher quality of care. However, the effect of peer review on quality of care was beyond the scope of this study.

Careful investigation of the effects of foundation-type HMOs is warranted because of their potential to dominate or monopolize the delivery of health care in their market area.[7] Foundations, in fact, seem to be consciously designed to monopolize care in particular regions and appear to have occasionally been developed in response to the threat of entrance into the market of an HMO. Monopoly control of a market area could have severe adverse effects on capitation rates or the quality of care, or both.

The San Joaquin experience is also worth examination because its approach to utilization control, i.e., extensive peer review, served in part to foster interest in what have now become Professional Standard Review Organizations (PSROs). PSROs are presently being established throughout the country to review claims for services covered by Medicare and Medicaid. Unlike the San Joaquin Foundation, however, PSROs operate independently of a budget constraint. Nonetheless, some of the conclusions of this paper may be applicable to PSROs as well.

Examination of data from the California Medicaid program to assess the effectiveness of foundation-type HMOs has several advantages. First, the population used in this study—AFDC adults and children throughout the state—is quite homogeneous. Second, reimbursement arrangements facing physicians (in counties other than San Joaquin) and hospitals were uniform throughout the state. The Medicaid program had not entered into any other prepayment arrangements in the state during the years of this study. Third, the Medicaid program is administered by the California Department of Health, and its policies are uniform throughout the state. Thus, the influence of extraneous factors is lessened. Fourth, because we are examining behavior of Medicaid recipients, money prices and insurance coverage which are normally critical factors in affecting utilization are irrelevant.

Methodology

Model Specification

The basic approach of this paper is to estimate sets of regression equations for each of six services: 1) physician visits; 2) surgery; 3) laboratory, X-ray, and other diagnostic services; 4) hospital inpatient care; 5) hospital outpatient care; and 6) prescription drugs. The units of observation are age-sex groups in each county. The basic model used in the paper is fairly comparable for all services. We argue that utilization rates for health services in Medicaid depend on the availability of physicians, the specialty composition of physicians, the racial and ethnic composition of the population, the extent of local support for the Medicaid program as well as the age and sex composition of the population. Many of these variables can be hypothesized to operate in different directions for different services. A dummy variable for the San Joaquin County cells was employed to test whether utilization rates for various services would have been different in the absence of the prepayment project in that county.

• • •

Conclusions

This study was unable to find evidence that the San Joaquin Foundation had any utilization or cost reducing impact. The Foundation was prepaid by the state to deliver health services to all Medicaid eligibles in its jurisdiction. Unlike the traditional prepaid group practice, which not only faces the incentives of budgetary limits on expenditures but also attempts to reap significant economies through substitution of ambulatory care settings for hospital inpatient services and various types of allied health professionals for more highly trained physicians, the Foundation attempts to control costs through peer review.

While the results of this study cast doubt on claims that foundation-type HMOs relying on peer review can result in sizable fiscal savings, three important qualifications deserve mention. First, the study was limited to an analysis of one foundation over a two-year period in one state's Medicaid program. Second, peer review may be of significant value to society if it upgrades the quality of care in many localities.[23] Assessment of changes in the quality of care, however, was beyond the scope of this study. Third, the utilization and cost control experience of the San Joaquin Foundation was analyzed in comparison with the claims examination and review functions performed by California Blue Shield. The purpose of this study was not to assess the relative merits of the review *processes* used by the two systems. Casual observation seemed to indicate that both made efforts to review carefully for excessive utilization and inappropriate care during the two-year period. It is possible that research would find that peer review systems can yield significant fiscal savings when introduced in areas where fiscal intermediaries are less capable in performance of the utilization review function.

Prepayment is cited by many health experts as a critical weapon in the effort to induce physicians to constrain health care costs. The logic of the argument is persuasive. However, it seems that the prepayment incentives affect the decision making of the individual physician in prepaid group practices far more than they do under the foundation approach. It is probably too difficult to enforce significant controls on service provision through claims review. Peer review can at best curtail gross excesses in service delivery and, in the process, control the generation of excessive incomes. It may also increase the quality of care in some instances.

It seems unlikely, based on evidence presented in this paper, that the chances of a major general reduction in health care costs through peer review of physician services is very great. The issue is whether the value society places on control of excessive service delivery and of incomes of abuse-prone physicians (most likely a small proportion of all physicians)—as well as on whatever improvements in quality occur—exceeds the cost of claims review. That issue clearly needs further evaluation.

HMOs and the Effectiveness of Medical Outcomes

A final question concerning how well HMOs perform must be addressed. The evidence of lower utilization of certain surgical procedures under HMOs (at least, PGPs) is quite strong. Supporters of HMOs have argued that this indicates the avoidance of unnecessary surgery, while others have suggested that perhaps physicians in HMOs do not provide enough surgical treatment. Clearly, quality of care is indirectly at issue. Measurement to resolve the surgery use question has been very difficult.

As Chassin notes at the end of his survey (excerpted above), evidence from a Seattle project suggests that inappropriate procedures in fee-for-service practices explain only a part of the difference from the surgical volume at a PGP, so the relatively low level at the latter requires further study (and, perhaps, some defense).[5] In his review of existing studies, Luft finds questionable support for the argument that HMOs achieve lower surgery rates by avoiding "unnecessary" surgery. He notes that HMOs appear to do less surgery of all types, not just fewer of those procedures usually considered discretionary.[6]

To investigate the matter further would require a move from studies of efficiency into the realm of effectiveness or outcomes of care—clearly beyond the usual scope of economics. At this point, it is possible only to identify this interesting question and to say that the few comparative studies of effects conducted to date, far from indicating undesirable outcomes of PGPs (because of low surgical rates, bed shortages, or whatever), have produced some results in favor of that type of HMO along with other findings that are less clear.[7]

NOTES

1. Richard M. Bailey, "Economies of Scale in Medical Practice," in Herbert E. Klarman, ed., *Empirical Studies in Health Economics* (Baltimore: Johns Hopkins University Press, 1970), pp. 255–273.

2. One recent example of research findings—related more to productivity than to economies of scale and not isolating PGPs—is Noralou P. Roos, "Impact of the Organization of Practice on Quality of Care and Physician Productivity," *Medical Care* 18 (1980): 347–359.

3. In addition to the readings suggested below, a useful summary of evidence appears in Harold S. Luft, "How Do Health-Maintenance Organizations Achieve Their 'Savings'?" *New England Journal of Medicine* 298 (1978): 1336–1343.

4. This view is endorsed by Luft, who says, "There is no documented evidence that costs for enrollees in individual practice associations [foundations] are lower than those for people with conventional insurance." Ibid., p. 1337.

5. James P. Lo Gerfo, et al., "Rates of Surgical Care in Prepaid Group Practices and the Independent Setting," *Medical Care* 17 (1979):1–10. See also the exchange of letters to the editor between R. Handschin and L. Gerfo in *Medical Care* 17 (1979): 1149–1153.

6. Luft, especially pp. 1340–1342.

7. There are citations of research done at the Health Insurance Plan of Greater New York (HIP) and of literature surveys in the paper by Chassin, which is excerpted above, as well as in Luft. See also papers suggesting that slightly lower work loss resulting from sickness is associated with lower rates of certain surgical procedures for female school teachers: Robert L. Robertson, "Economic Effects of Personal Health Services: Work Loss in a Public School Teacher Population," *American Journal of Public Health* 61 (1971): 30–45; ─────── , "Comparative Medical Care Use Under Prepaid Group Practice and Free Choice Plans," *Inquiry* 9 (1972): 70–76.

SUGGESTED READINGS

Bailey, Richard. "Economies of Scale in Medical Practice," in Herbert E. Klarman, ed., *Empirical Studies in Health Economics*. Baltimore: John Hopkins University Press, 1970, 255–273.

Davis, Karen, and Schoen, Cathy. *Health and the War on Poverty*. Washington: The Brookings Institution, 1978.

Donabedian, Avedis. "An Evaluation of Prepaid Group Practice." *Inquiry* 6 (March 1969): 3–27.

Gaus, Clifton R., et al. "Contrasts in HMO and Fee-for-Service Performance." *Social Security Bulletin* 39 (May 1976): 3–14.

Gavett, J. William, and Smith, David B. "A Comparison of the Hospital Cost Experience of Three Competing HMOs." *Inquiry* 15 (December 1978): 327–335.

Hollister, Robert M., et al., eds. *Neighborhood Health Centers*. Lexington, Mass.: Lexington Books, D.C. Heath and Company, 1974.

Klarman, Herbert E. "Economic Research in Group Medicine," in First International Congress on Group Medicine, *New Horizons in Health Care: Proceedings*. Winnipeg, Canada: The Congress, 1970, 178–193.

Lo Gerfo, James P., et al. "Rates of Surgical Care in Prepaid Group Practices and the Independent Setting: What Are the Reasons for the Differences?" *Medical Care* 17 (January 1979): 1–10. (Also: Handschin, R., vs. Lo Gerfo, J. P. *Medical Care* 17 (November 1979): 1149–1153.)

Luft, Harold S. "How Do Health-Maintenance Organizations Achieve Their 'Savings'?" *New England Journal of Medicine* 298 (June 15, 1978): 1336–1343.

Morehead, Mildred A. "Evaluating the Quality of Medical Care in the Neighborhood Health Center Program of the Office of Economic Opportunity." *Medical Care* 8 (March–April 1970): 118–131.

Robertson, Robert L. "Comparative Medical Care Use Under Prepaid Group Practice and Free Choice Plans." *Inquiry* 9 (September 1972): 70–76.

──────. "Economic Effects of Personal Health Services: Work Loss in a Public School Teacher Population." *American Journal of Public Health* 61 (January 1971): 30–45.

Roemer, M. I., and Shonick, William. "HMO Performance: The Recent Evidence." *Milbank Memorial Fund Quarterly* 51 (Summer 1973): 271–317.

Roos, Noralou P. "Impact of the Organization of Practice on Quality of Care and Physician Productivity." *Medical Care* 18 (April 1980): 347–359.

Sorkin, Alan L. *Health Economics*. Lexington, Mass.: Lexington Books, D.C. Heath and Company, 1975, 145–155.

Sparer, Gerald, and Johnson, Joyce. "Evaluation of OEO Neighborhood Health Centers." *American Journal of Public Health* 61 (May 1971): 931–942.

NOTES FOR NEWHOUSE EXCERPT

1. X-inefficiency is the economist's name for that type of inefficiency which reduces the output produced from a given set of inputs below the maximum obtainable.
2. For an explanation of the regression fallacy, see p. 45 [in original article].

3. Cross-elasticity of demand is the percentage change in visits to one physician as the result of a 1 percent change in the fee of another physician. If this is low, it means patients are not likely to change physicians because of a change in fees.

REFERENCES FOR NEWHOUSE EXCERPT

1. American Medical Association. *Survey of Medical Groups*. Chicago: American Medical Association, 1968.
2. Richard M. Bailey. "A Comparison of Internists in Solo and Fee-for-Service Group Practice in the San Francisco Bay Area." *Bulletin of the New York Academy of Medicine* 44 (November 1968): 1293–1303.
3. —————. "Economies of Scale in Medical Practice." In *Empirical Studies in Health Economics*, Herbert Klarman, ed. Baltimore: Johns Hopkins Press, 1970.
5. William S. Comanor and Harvey Leibenstein. "Allocative Efficiency, X-Efficiency and the Measurement of Welfare Losses." *Economica* 36 (August 1969): 304–309.
8. Rashi Fein. *The Doctor Shortage*. Washington: The Brookings Institution, 1967.
13. Harvey Leibenstein. "Allocative Efficiency vs. 'X-Efficiency.' " *The American Economic Review* 56 (June 1966): 392–415.
21. Mancur Olson, Jr. *The Logic of Collective Action*. Cambridge, Mass.: Harvard University Press, 1965.

NOTES FOR FRECH AND GINSBURG EXCERPT

1. Empirical studies include J.A. Boan, *Group Practice* (Ottawa: Royal Commission on Health Services, 1966); Donald E. Yett, "An Evaluation of Alternative Methods of Estimating Physicians' Expenses Relative to Output," *Inquiry* 4 (March 1967): 3–27; Joel Kovner, "Production Function for Outpatient Medical Facilities" (Ph.D. thesis, University of California, Los Angeles, 1968); Douglas M. Egan, "Income and Productivity of Physicians in Fee-for-Service, Multi-specialty Group Practice" (unpublished paper, 1969); Richard M. Bailey, "Economies of Scale in Medical Practice," in *Empirical Studies in Health Economics*, ed. Herbert E. Klarman (Baltimore: Johns Hopkins University Press, 1970); Joseph P. Newhouse, "The Economics of Group Practice," *Journal of Human Resources* 8 (Winter 1973): 37–56; and Uwe E. Reinhardt, "A Production Function for Physician Services," *Review of Economics and Statistics* 54 (February 1972): 55–66. Note that the term "optimal scale" is used instead of "economies of scale." The latter concept is too narrow for this problem because it implies a constant product across group size. Since physicians and consumers may both have preferences for certain group sizes, and quality of care may vary with group size, product may not be constant. Market evaluations of these variations must be taken into account in judging that one size is more efficient than another.
2. Newhouse.
3. Egan.
4. Mark Pauly, "Efficiency, Incentives and Reimbursement for Health Care," *Inquiry* 7 (March 1970): 114–31.
5. See n. 1 above.
6. Ibid.
7. Ibid.

8. Ibid.
9. Ibid.
10. For a particular example, if large groups are serving a group of consumers who tend to prefer large practices and have low transportation costs, an additional large group would have to draw on consumers who have less affinity for large groups and whose transportation is more expensive. Thus, although the average costs of large groups may be lower than those of small groups, the costs to a marginal practice could be higher. This distinction between average costs and cost at the (entry) margin has not been made in previous studies.
11. The function need not be restricted to income but can include leisure, interesting cases, preferences for organizational forms and sizes, and other considerations.
12. George J. Stigler ("The Economies of Scale," *Journal of Law and Economics* 1 [October 1958]: 54–71) pioneered use of this analysis for the steel and automobile industries. See also T.R. Saving ("Estimation of Optimum Size of Plant by the Survivor Technique," *Quarterly Journal of Economics* 75 [November 1961]: 569–607) and L. Weiss ("The Survivor Technique and the Extent of Suboptimal Capacity," *Journal of Political Economy* 72, no. 3 [June 1964]: 246–61) for their applications and W.G. Shephard ("What Does the Survivor Analysis Show about Economies of Scale?" *Southern Economic Journal* 37 [July 1967]: 113–22) for a discussion of the technique.
13. Shepherd, p. 115.
14. Reuben A. Kessel, "Price Discrimination in Medicine," *Journal of Law and Economics* 1 (October 1958): 20–53.
15. H.E. Frech III and Paul B. Ginsburg, "Imposed Health Insurance in Monopolistic Markets: A Theoretical Analysis," unpublished paper (1972).
16. Kessel.
17. David B. Starkweather, "Regulation of Health Insurance: A Review," *Medical Care Review* 27 (April 1970): 335–71; ibid. (May 1970), pp. 474–93.
18. B.E. Balfe and M.E. McNamara, *Survey of Medical Groups in the U.S., 1965* (Chicago: American Medical Association, 1968); C. Todd and M.E. McNamara, *Survey of Medical Groups in the U.S., 1969* (Chicago: American Medical Association, 1971).

NOTES FOR CHASSIN EXCERPT

* For a sample of other authors' analyses, the reader is referred to Greenlick[32] and Hill.[67]
† For a more thorough review of the literature on HMOs and quality of care, the reader is referred to Donabedian,[30] Roemer and Shonick,[110] and Brook.[15]

REFERENCES FOR CHASSIN EXCERPT

14. Broida, J.H., Lerner, M., Lohrenze, F.N., et al.: Impact of membership in an enrolled, prepaid population on utilization of health services in a group practice. *N. Engl. J. Med.* 292:780, 1975.
15. Brook, R. H.: Critical issues in the assessment of quality of care and their relationship to HMOs. *J. Med. Educ.* (Part II) 48:114, 1973.
27. Densen, P. M., Jones, E. W., Balamuth, E., et al.: Prepaid medical care and hospital utilization in a dual choice situation. *Am. J. Public Health* 59:1710, 1960.

28. Densen, P.M., Shapiro, S., Jones, E.W., et al.: Prepaid medical care and hospital utilization. *Hospitals* 36:62, November 16, 1962.
29. Department of Health Services, School of Public Health and Community Medicine, University of Washington. *The Seattle Prepaid Health Care Project: Comparison of Health Services Delivery,* November, 1976.
30. Donabedian, A.: An evaluation of prepaid group practice. *Inquiry* 6:3, 1969.
37. Enthoven, A.C.: Consumer-choice health plan (first of two parts). *N. Engl. J. Med.* 298:650, 1978.
38. Enthoven, A.C.: Consumer-choice health plan (second of two parts). *N. Engl. J. Med.* 298:709, 1978.
47. Gaus, C.R., Cooper, B.S., and Hirschman, C.G.: Contrasts in HMO and fee-for-service performance. *Soc. Sec. Bull.* May, 1976, p. 3.
52. Greenlick, M.R.: The impact of prepaid group practice on American medical care: A critical evaluation. *Ann. Am. Acad. Pol. Sci.* 399:100, 1972.
67. Hill, D.B.: Identification of hospital cost determinants: A health planning perspective. *Inquiry* 13:61, 1976.
79. Klarman, H.E.: Approaches to moderating the increases in medical care costs. *Med. Care* 7:175, 1969.
84. Luft, H.W.: How do health maintenance organizations achieve their "savings"? *N. Engl. J. Med.* 298:1336, 1978.
103. Perrott, G.S.: Federal employees health benefits program III: Utilization of hospital services. *Am. J. Public Health* 56:57, 1966.
110. Roemer, M.I., and Shonick, W.: HMO performance: The recent evidence. *Milbank Mem. Fund Q.* 5:271, 1973.
116. Shapiro, S., Jacobinzer, H., Densen, P.M., et al.: Further observations on prematurity and perinatal mortality in a general population and in the population of a prepaid group practice medical care plan. *Am. J. Public Health* 50:1304, 1960.

REFERENCES FOR HOLAHAN EXCERPT

1. Donabedian, A.: "An Evaluation of Pre-Paid Group Practice," *Inquiry,* 6, March 1969; and Roemer, M. I., and Shonick, W.: "HMO Performance: The Recent Evidence," *Milbank Memorial Fund Quarterly,* Summer 1973.
2. McCaffree, K. M., and Newman, H. F.: "Prepayment of Drug Costs Under a Group Practice Prepayment Plan," *American Journal of Public Health,* 58 (July 1968).
3. Follette, W., and Cummings, D. A.: "Psychiatric Services and Medical Utilization in a Prepaid Health Plan Setting," *Medical Care,* 5, 1 (January-February 1967).
4. Hurtado, A. R.; Greenlich, M. R.; McCabe, M., and Seward, F. G.: "The Utilization and Costs of Home Care and Extended Care Facility Services in a Comparative Prepaid Group Practice Program," *Medical Care,* 10, 1 (January-February 1972).
5. If the system in the long run operates to eliminate all physicians who do not overprovide, then there will no longer be any gain to those who remain because they will all be overproviders and should all have some pro rata reductions. Unless the peer review mechanism was extremely effective, this would tend to increase the capitation rates charged by the plan, increase costs of public programs contracting with it, and reduce the competitiveness of the foundation in the private market.

6. One previous study has examined the impact of the San Joaquin Foundation on aggregate utilization rates. That study (Foline E. Gartside, "The Utilization and Costs of Services in the San Joaquin Prepayment Project," Univ. of California, Los Angeles, 1971) compared the utilization experience of Medicaid recipients in San Joaquin County with that of Ventura County in the first six months of the prepayment project, February 1968–July 1969. Ventura County was chosen because it has comparable population size, percentage of the labor force in agriculture, household income, and population ratios of hospital beds and physicians. The study found lower utilization rates (as measured by costs per eligible person) in San Joaquin for most services. An examination of only the AFDC population yielded similar conclusions. The study reported average monthly cost of $17.44 per eligible person in Ventura County vs. $14.80 in the San Joaquin County. The differences in physician services were $5.87 vs. $5.20 in the Ventura and the San Joaquin county groups. Unfortunately, the analysis was complicated by several factors. First, individuals eligible for both full and part-year were used in the comparison. Preliminary tabulations prepared early in the present study showed markedly higher utilization rates for most services for part-year eligibles. The Gartside study notes that Ventura County had higher turnover rates—a higher ratio of part-year to full-year eligibles. Second, the study combined *all four counties* in the San Joaquin project—San Joaquin, Amador, Calavaras, and Tuolumne. The latter three are low density, heavily rural counties and it may not have been appropriate to include them. Third, the study contained no statistical control for other factors such as the racial or ethnic composition of the population and did not adequately control for the age and sex composition of the population. Finally, no tests of statistical significance were reported.
7. Havighurst, Clark C.: "HMO's and the Market for Health Services," *Law and Contemporary Problems,* Vol. XXXV, No. 4, Autumn 1970.
23. Newport and Roemer compared perinatal mortality rates for poverty populations covered by the San Joaquin Foundation and a comparison county and found no significant differences. See John Newport and Milton I. Roemer: "Comparative Perinatal Mortality Under Medical Care Foundations and Other Delivery Models," *Inquiry,* 12, March 1975.

SOURCES

a. Reprinted from "The Economics of Group Practice" by Joseph Newhouse, *Journal of Human Resources* 8, 1 (Winter 1973), pp. 37–40, 54–55, by permission of The Board of Regents of The University of Wisconsin System, © 1973.
b. Reprinted from "Optimal Scale in Medical Practice: A Survivor Analysis" by H. E. Frech III and Paul B. Ginsburg, *Journal of Business* 47 (January 1974), pp. 23–28, 36, by permission of the University of Chicago Press, © 1974 by the University of Chicago. All rights reserved.
c. Reprinted from "The Containment of Hospital Cost: A Strategic Assessment" by M. R. Chassin, *Medical Care* 16 (October 1978), Supplement, pp. 14–20, 52–55, by permission of J. B. Lippincott Company, © 1978.
d. Reprinted from "Foundations for Medical Care: An Empirical Investigation of the Delivery of Health Services to a Medicaid Population" by John Holahan, *Inquiry* 14, no. 4 (December 1977), pp. 350–354, 360, 366–367, by permission of the Blue Cross Association, © 1977. All rights reserved.

Chapter 8

Health Care Financing

The traditional economic theory of the firm assumes that producers are either *price takers* or *price setters*. Where many firms provide similar products and compete among themselves to satisfy market demand, the usual assumption is that each company will face a given market price, hence the term price taker. Where there is just one or, at most, a few producers, each firm can raise or lower prices and still be assured some share of the market, hence the term price setter.

This simple classification is sufficient to analyze provider behavior in most markets where buyers pay sellers directly for the goods or services received. However, in the health services marketplace, transactions are complicated by the fact that payment frequently comes from some third party, be it an insurance company or a *fiscal agent* or *intermediary* for a government program such as Medicare or Medicaid. Standard economic predictions of market behavior break down in such cases if the third party is large enough to influence price and output decisions.

Health care administrators need not be reminded of the ubiquitous influence of third party payment on their managerial decisions. In 1978, more than 90 percent of the $76 billion spent on hospital services represented reimbursements from *third party payers*.[1] For physician office practices and nursing homes, the percentages were 66 and 54, respectively.[2] The growing importance of third party coverage has spawned an industry of consulting firms catering to providers' need to understand and cope with various payment mechanisms. At the same time, the major insurance *carriers,* together with federal and state authorities, are busy devising strategies to limit the ever-increasing cost of third party coverage, which, it is estimated, will reach the phenomenal level of $210 billion by 1985 even without the passage of national health insurance.[3]

What can economics contribute to an understanding of health care financing? Several things. The principal elements of every financing scheme are economic in character: the prices to be paid for each unit of output, the number of units of output to be covered, and the timing of payment. If they have information on the cost and method of production, economists are in a position to identify the underlying incentives that providers face, given a particular type and level of payment. Moreover, because different payers use different reimbursement mechanisms, economists can test hypotheses regarding which method is best suited to reaching a particular objective, such as provider participation, efficiency of production, or quality of care. Finally, this process can yield useful information on the implicit trade-offs facing policymakers in the design and implementation of major funding programs, such as a possible national health insurance program.

THE INDUSTRY

The term third party payer is a generic expression covering four entities: private insurance companies, independent health plans, government health programs, and claims payment agents. A *payer* may fit into a single category or span several. For example, Blue Cross plans are private insurance companies but they also play a role as claims payment agents for Medicare, which is a federal program. Medicaid is another government health program that covers 53 separate state and territorial jurisdictions. In some states, the Medicaid agency handles all payer functions, including eligibility and benefit determination, general administration, and claims review and payment. In other states, private fiscal agents process claims. And in still others, risk-sharing arrangements are made with independent health plans. The distinctive characteristics of third party payers are described briefly next.

The private health insurance industry in the United States is composed of three different types of firms: commercial stock companies, mutual companies, and nonprofit insurance plans. More than 300 commercial corporations sell health insurance. Most are life or casualty companies; except for a few, health insurance is a sideline both in terms of number of policies sold and premium income generated. Nevertheless, it is a significant sideline—producing some $23 billion in premium revenues in 1977.[4] The major nonprofit insurers (140 Blue Cross and Blue Shield plans and a growing number of Delta Dental plans) sell only health insurance. In 1977, their combined premium revenues totalled approximately $20 billion.[5] In terms of gross enrollment, the nonprofit plans covered 90 million persons in 1977, compared to 118 million for commercial carriers.[6]

There are important organizational differences among insurers. The stock companies (such as Aetna, Travelers, and Connecticut General) are private stockholder-owned corporations and operate in the national marketplace. The same is true for mutual companies (Mutual of Omaha, Metropolitan Life, Prudential, and the like), except that the policyholders also are the owners. Commercial firms are subject to state insurance laws and federal and state taxation but are exempt from federal antitrust laws in most cases. Blue Cross, Blue Shield, and Delta Dental, on the other hand, are organized under special state enabling laws that grant an exclusive franchise to a geographic territory (either an entire state or a part thereof) and to a particular line of insurance. (In all but a few states Blue Cross sells just hospital coverage, Blue Shield is limited to medical insurance, and, as the name suggests, Delta Dental sells only dental insurance.) Their nonprofit status gives them tax exemption but in return they are subject to more stringent state regulation than are commercial insurers.

The business end of the health insurance industry is conducted in much the same way regardless of ownership characteristics. None of the companies actually delivers health services; they all market and underwrite policies designed to spread the risk of economic loss associated with health services utilization. At one time the nonprofit carriers operated under a philosophy very different from the commercial companies. Differences still exist but they are far less noticeable today than even ten years ago.

The major nonprofit and commercial carriers together account for more than 90 percent of the private health insurance sold in the country. The rest is underwritten by several hundred small independent health plans organized by consumer cooperatives, unions, universities, businesses of various sorts, and medical groups. Health maintenance organizations fall within this category, as do the self-insurance plans promoted by several manufacturing companies. Some are insurance carriers in the traditional sense; others not only sell insurance but also provide the health services as well. They serve highly localized populations but are competitively important only in certain metropolitan areas such as New York, Washington, Minneapolis, Los Angeles, Seattle, and the San Francisco Bay area.

All the independent plans combined generated $4.5 billion in premium revenues in 1977.[7] Large in absolute dollar terms, this amount pales in comparison to the $43 billion earned by insurance companies (commercial and nonprofit) and the $58 billion budgeted for personal health care services by government in the same year.[8] This latter figure overstates somewhat the role of federal and state government as third party payers because a third of all such expenditures is for direct public medical services by the military, the Veterans Administration, state hospitals, public health activities, and other "socialized" health and medical programs. But when all is said and done, no other influence in the health insurance market matches that of government. The four largest government third party programs—

Medicare, Medicaid, the Federal Employees Health Benefits Plan (FEHBP), and the Civilian Health and Medical Program of the Uniformed Services (CHAMPUS)—account for more than 50 percent of the nation's hospital revenues and nearly a quarter of physician incomes.

The government both competes and cooperates with the private insurance industry. It competes in the sense that private carriers would sell more policies in the absence of government financing. It cooperates with the industry in providing contracts for the administration of the claims payment process. More than 80 percent of government third party payments is handled by private contractors known variously as intermediaries (for the hospital side of Medicare), carriers (for medical insurance under Medicare), and fiscal agents (the term used by state Medicaid programs). An ironic result is that because of intermediary contracts, Blue Cross plans actually disburse more funds on behalf of government beneficiaries than for Blue Cross subscribers.

ECONOMIC MODELS OF THIRD PARTY COVERAGE

Before turning to how third party payers reimburse providers, some economic theorizing is in order. Chapter 4 noted that one of the principal effects of health insurance is to change the demand for care. Because insurance reduces the out-of-pocket price to consumers, the demand curve shifts outward and becomes more inelastic with respect to market price. In other words, at any given level of market price, insured consumers will demand more than they would if uninsured and, if price should happen to rise, will be deterred less by the increase than if they were uninsured. In aggregate terms, the strength of these demand-side effects is a function of the depth of coverage (the percentage of the average medical bill paid by third parties) and the breadth of coverage (the percentage of the population with insurance).

But insurance and third party payment can have supply-side effects as well, a point often overlooked. Consider the model in Figure 8-1. The curves D_1, D_2, and D_3 represent, respectively, uninsured demand, demand under a health insurance policy with a percentage coinsurance feature, and fully insured demand. If supply is perfectly elastic, as shown by the horizontal line S, the impact of insurance will be to raise total consumption from Q_1 to Q_2 (with coinsurance) or Q_3 (with full coverage). However, if the supply curve is less than perfectly elastic, say S' instead of S, then prices as well as consumption patterns will be affected. Under full coverage, consumption still will rise to Q_3, but the market price paid by third parties will increase from P_1 to P_3. Prices will be somewhat lower with coinsurance

Figure 8-1 Alternative Demand and Supply Elasticities under Insurance

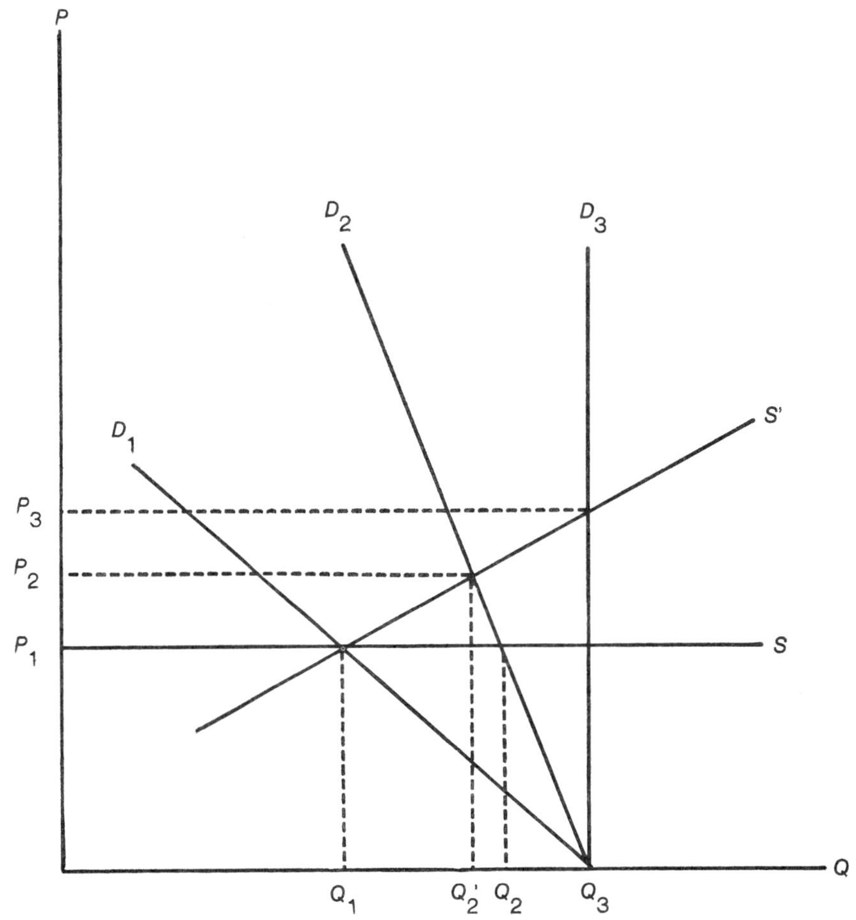

than with full coverage (P_2' instead of P_3), but so too will be the amount consumed (Q_2 rather than Q_3). The upshot is that supply elasticity is an important ingredient in any understanding of the impact of third party coverage.

Is the supply of health services price elastic? Surprisingly, perhaps, economists have spent far less effort in measuring health sector supply elasticities than demand elasticities. It is known that provider output is relatively more responsive to price in the long run than in the short run (as is the case in most industries). It also is known that supplier response is constrained by professional education requirements of state licensure, by facility planning requirements imposed under certification-of-need programs, and by other impediments to entry. The best guess, then, is that supply is relatively price inelastic for most segments of the health services industry, at least in the short-to-intermediate time range. If correct, this means that the impact of expanded insurance coverage should fall more heavily on price than on quantity consumed. And, indeed, recent expenditure patterns tend to bear this out.

It is necessary to emphasize, however, that the degree of supply elasticity cannot be inferred directly from expenditure trends. The reason is that changes in third party coverage can lead to provider responses different from those implied by a simple supply curve. Figure 8-1 assumes that providers will move out along a given supply curve if demand increases. In fact, it can be demonstrated readily that such a response is unrealistic when demand is inelastic at the intersection of the old supply curve and the new demand curve.

Consider, for example, how a physician might react to increased patient insurance coverage. In Figure 8-2 a hypothetical preinsurance demand measured in visits per week is shown as D_1 together with three possible output choices. For the sake of simplicity, assume that the physician is a profit maximizer and that profits are a fixed proportion of total sales revenue. This means that the preinsurance output level produced will be 100 visits rather than 50 or 150, because total revenues (hence, profits) are higher at a market price of $8 per visit than at either $12 or $4. The point of maximum total revenue occurs where demand elasticity is equal to 1.0; on a linear demand curve, this point is found midway between the line's horizontal and vertical intercepts.[9]

What is the impact of insurance? If its only effect were to shift the demand curve to the right without changing its slope (a shift from D_1 to D_2), then the supply curve S would prevail because revenues generated at the new market price of $10 ($S = 120$) would be greater than revenues at any other price. The key is the elasticity of demand. If insurance simultaneously increases demand and makes consumers less responsive to changes in market price (as has been argued it will), then the physician has a clear signal to produce less output at any given price than in the prior case. This is shown in Figure 8-3, which hypothesizes a new, more inelastic demand curve, D_2'. Once again, the physician will choose the output that generates the most revenue given the new demand situation: in this case, 100 visits at a price of $16, not the 130 visits at $11 that the supply curve S would have led the doctor to expect. Here, increased demand results in no output increase, only a rise in price.

Figure 8-2 Shift in Demand with Insurance

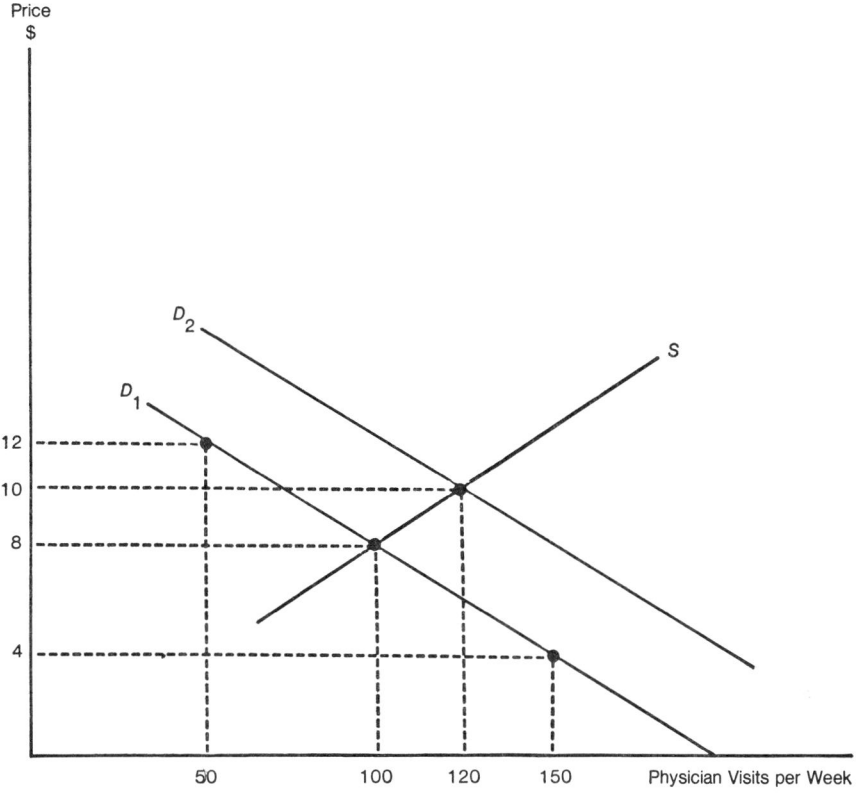

There is nothing particularly startling about these results. Indeed, this example is just an extension of monopoly pricing models found in most introductory microeconomics texts. What is significant is that insurance may increase the effective market power of providers, even nonprofit providers, and can produce very high price increases in the absence of buyers' market power.[10] It will have this effect as long as third parties act as willing pawns and pay rates sufficient to clear the market. As might be expected, most third parties refuse to play the role.

The theory of competition holds that if there is market power on the supply side, but many buyers, then buyers will lose in the sense of having to pay monopoly prices. If there is market power on the buyer side as well, then almost anything can happen. Price and output decisions no longer are

Figure 8-3 Change in Demand Elasticity with Insurance

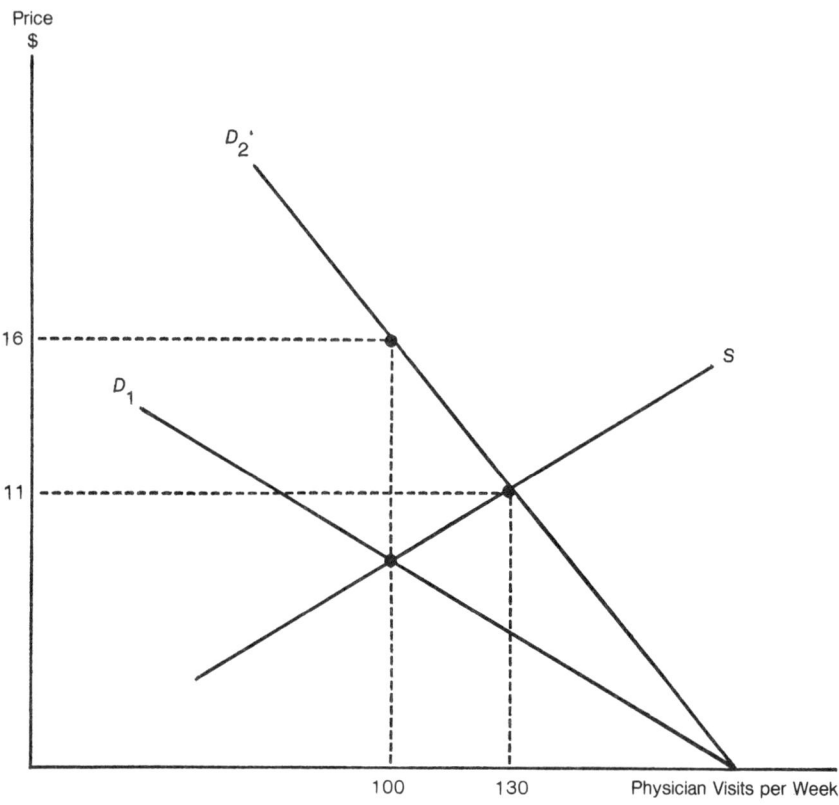

determinate in the market and other factors, such as relative bargaining strength, public opinion, and legal strictures, come into play. This situation (known in economics as *bilateral market power*) occurs in the present market for insured health services. Sellers gain market power by virtue of consumers' inattentiveness to market price, and buyers gain market power through the concentration of purchasing power in the hands of a few large third parties.

As noted in the previous section, the largest third party payers are government programs. There is little question that these programs have the potential to exercise market power. But what of the thousand or so private third parties? By most standards, the private health insurance industry is not heavily concentrated on the national level. The four-firm and eight-firm concentration ratios are low compared to other comparably sized industries.

Yet such measures are misleading. To be sure, there is competition in the market and, given the prevalence of bulk sales (group policies account for 85 percent of commercial insurers' business and an even larger segment of Blue Cross and Blue Shield business), it can be argued that sellers and buyers are relatively well informed. But the degree of competition varies widely from state to state, depending upon the market share held by Blue Cross and Blue Shield. In some states that share is virtually nil, whereas in others it approaches 80 percent.[11] Because these two systems have exclusive franchises, they do not compete with each other. And when market shares reach the 70 to 80 percent range, it may be asked whether these plans face serious competition from commercial insurers either.

It is known that the lack of competition in such markets confers power on the insurer, but market behavior cannot be predicted on the basis of this knowledge alone. The nonprofit status of these two plans, the market share held by government, and the existence of countervailing power on the provider side, all serve to complicate the analysis. The one thing that can be said with certainty is that reimbursement policies play a critical role.

REIMBURSEMENT METHODOLOGY

Reimbursement schemes can be bewilderingly complex but they all derive from the same simple formula:

$$R = \sum_{b}(P_b N_b)$$

where

R = the total reimbursement granted the provider over some specified period of time
b = 1, 2, 3 . . . n, the categories of reimbursable items or services (known as *rate bases*)
P_b = the dollar rate or payment amount per unit of b
N_b = the number of units of b delivered during the period

To see how this works, consider the case of a physician who sees 25 Blue Shield patients in a week. The amount the insurance company pays will depend on the three elements specified in the above formula. Since Blue

Shield plans typically reimburse on a fee-for-service basis, the rate bases will be defined in terms of medical procedures. For example,

$b = 1$ for routine office revisit
$b = 2$ for short initial visit
•
•
•
$b = 15$ for complete physical examination with history
•
•
•
$b = 75$ for appendectomy, no complications

and so on for every reimbursable service. The rates or fees for each service are determined in a variety of ways, depending on the policy of the particular plan. For the moment, assume that P_1 (routine office revisit) = $10, P_2 (short initial visit) = $15, and P_{15} (complete physical exam with history) = $75. Now, all that need be done is tabulate the number of procedures performed in each category to establish the reimbursement amount. If the physician performs 7 routine office revisits, 15 short initial visits, and 3 complete physical exams, the total payment from Blue Shield will be $520 for the week:

$$\$520 = (\$10 \times 7) + (\$15 \times 15) + (\$75 \times 3)$$

Fee-for-service (FFS) payment schemes similar to this are widely used by private insurance companies and public programs. In terms of the number of bills processed each year, FFS is by far the most important reimbursement method in the country today. However, measured in dollar volume, the most significant are the cost-based mechanisms used to reimburse health care facilities. Other approaches, such as capitation and prospective rating schemes, may be expected to gain predominance in the future.

The range of payment methodologies is depicted in Tables 8-1 and 8-2. The first table provides a list of alternative rate bases, the second a list of different methods of *rate determination*. Although there are some traditional combinations (e.g., piece rates for physician services and cost for routine daily hospital care), it is possible to construct a reimbursement scheme by taking any of the nine payment bases listed and combining it with any of the nine rate determination methods. Simple logic thus suggests that there are 81 different ways to pay health care providers.

Table 8-1 Alternative Rate Bases

Base	Explanation	Example
Service Supplied		
a. Piece	Individual item in service	Practitioners' services, drugs, ancillary services in institutions
b. Case	All services associated with a particular treatment regimen	Some physician and dental packages (e.g., maternity care and orthodontia)
c. Day, routine	All routine room, board, and nursing services provided per inpatient day	Common rate base for hospitals and nursing homes
d. Day, inclusive	All services (routine and ancillary) provided per inpatient day	Hospitals under a few state Medicaid plans
Number of Patients		
a. Treated	Same base regardless of differences in resources used in treatment	Rare: physician payment under old British poor laws
b. Treated successfully	Money-back guarantee	None current: physician payment in pre-revolutionary China
c. Eligible for treatment	Same base whether or not treatment is provided	Capitation plans, HMOs, panel practice in Britain
Time		
a. Spent on treatment	Actual time worked measured in minutes or hours	Base for wage payments and for setting some professional fees
b. Available to treat	Contractual commitment to work, usually specified as hours per week and weeks per year	Base for salary payments

Actually, there are many more than 81 counting hybrids, subtle variations, and payer-imposed rate restrictions and rate base limitations. It would be virtually impossible to catalog them all; and if the task ever were attempted, it soon would be out of date because new methods are being introduced constantly. All the authors can reasonably hope to do here is provide the following general economic understanding of professional and institutional reimbursement mechanisms.

Table 8-2 Alternative Methods of Rate Determination

Rate	Explanation	Example
Price (Charge, Fee)		
a. Individual provider	Prices set by practitioner or institution	Billed charge, customary charge (Medicare), usual charge (Blue Shield)
b. Market	Prices established by supply and demand in service area or set at some percentile of individual provider prices	Average price per services, prevailing charge (Medicare), customary charge (Blue Shield)
c. Scheduled	Prices fixed by government or payer or negotiated between payer and provider	Fee schedules commonly used by commercial insurers and Medicaid programs
d. Relative value	Fee schedule uses points rather than prices assigned to each procedure; a dollar conversion factor transforms a relative value scale into a fee schedule	Medicare physician payment in California and certain other states
Cost		
a. Individual provider, historical	Audited costs over a given period of time (usually a year) in the past	Basis for Blue Cross and Medicare hospital reimbursement
b. Individual provider, prospective	Historical costs projected forward according to some given formula	Common method for nursing homes and hospitals under some state Medicaid programs
c. Individual provider, budgeted	A form of prospective cost determination based on line item budget reviews	Governmental health facilities
d. Group related	Reimbursement tied to cost performance of institutions classed by geographic area, service offering, and/or other characteristics; may be historical or prospective	Nursing homes under some state Medicaid programs
e. Cost-plus	Typically historical cost with percentage add-on for community service or as a return on owners' equity for proprietary facilities	Hospitals (Blue Cross), Medicare (pre-1968), nursing homes under some state Medicaid programs

REIMBURSEMENT FOR PROFESSIONAL SERVICES

Basic Models

The typical independent practitioner receives reimbursement from private patients and from several third party payers. This is important to keep in mind because the incentives usually associated with one form of payment or another may differ depending on the combination of sources of revenue and the relative importance of each source of total income. In general terms, the practitioner's gross revenue is the sum of the revenue obtained from each payer (including self paying patients).

Gross revenue is not desired for its own sake but rather for the profit or net revenue it generates. This may seem self-evident but the point can be lost easily. For example, it frequently is asserted that fee-for-service reimbursement creates an incentive for the provider to deliver more and more services. True? Not if the cost of producing the service is above the fee received. In other words, it is essential to consider costs as well as gross receipts. Three types of outlays are relevant to most practices: (1) fixed costs, such as office rental and equipment; (2) labor costs; and (3) costs of medical and office supplies. Net revenue then can be calculated as gross revenue minus the sum of the three types of cost.

There is a fourth type of cost that also is relevant to small owner-operated businesses such as medical or dental practices: the opportunity cost the owner bears by being an entrepreneur rather than, say, an employee in a large firm in the same industry. One way to calculate this opportunity cost is to price the owner's time commitment to the business at the market wage for similar types of work. If the opportunity cost then is subtracted from net revenues, the remainder will equal the implicit profit earned by the practice.

The implicit profit, of course, can be either positive or negative—which is precisely why opportunity costs are essential to understanding provider behavior under alternative reimbursement schemes. Consider the example of fee-for-service once again. No one would seriously expect a physician to lose money delivering services, but what if the net revenue per service billed is below the doctor's opportunity cost (i.e., what if the implicit profit rate is negative)? Putting the question in these terms helps explain why physician participation in the Medicaid program is a problem in states with low pay rates.

Reimbursement Mechanics

There are several quite different types of reimbursement known collectively as fee-for-service. The simplest is the billed charge, whereby the practitioner sets the fee and bills the patient directly for all services. If third parties are involved at all, it is only through patient indemnification, not through any formal process of dictating acceptable rates. The revenue generated under billed charges is the product of three factors: the rate base (services), the rate charged per service, and the collection ratio. The fact that charges are billed directly means that the practitioner is at risk for all collections. The collection ratio (billed charges divided by total receipts) will reflect just how risky the business is. If there are any bad debts, the revenue will be less than the sum of billed charges. Moreover, bad debts can increase costs because of repeat billings and the services of collection agencies.

Both risk and collection costs tend to be lower under third party fee-for-service mechanisms. The oldest form of such reimbursement is payment on the basis of fixed fee schedules. Fee schedules are used by roughly half of the nation's Blue Shield plans, by some 26 state Medicaid programs, and by many commercial insurance companies.[12]

The simplest form of fixed fee schedule entails a single list of covered services and payment rates applicable to all participating practitioners. More complex systems differentiate fee schedules according to class of practitioner (medical specialists versus general practitioners), service site (office, clinic, outpatient department, etc.), and even geographic location. Payment is made either to the patient in the form of an indemnity or to the practitioner as direct reimbursement. Under indemnity plans, practitioners are free to set their own rates and bill patients for all services provided. Patients, in turn, are responsible for the entire billed amount, but many submit a copy of each bill to the third party for reimbursement at the scheduled rates. These rates never can exceed the actual billed charges, and typically are less. Because the obligation of the third party is fixed in dollar amount, patients face out-of-pocket prices that vary with the level of billed charges.

Different procedures apply under direct reimbursement or service benefit plans. Depending on the type of program, payment may be assigned or nonassigned. *Assignment* means that the practitioner agrees to accept the scheduled rates as payment in full. Medicaid, for example, requires assignment as a condition of participation for all medical providers. Other plans allow practitioners the option of accepting assignment on a patient-by-patient or service-by-service basis. In the case of nonassignment, each bill is reimbursed at the fee schedule rate (less any deductible or coinsurance), and practitioners then charge patients for the difference. This process, known as *balance billing,* is common in Canada.

Fixed fee schedules have always been popular from the payer's standpoint. Before 1960 they were the most common method of physician reimbursement. Fee schedules are relatively easy to administer; they require no extensive recordkeeping by individual practitioners; and, most important of all, they permit the payer some control over prices. This last feature explains why fee schedules generally are unpopular with practitioners. Even if they are determined through organized bargaining procedures involving the payer and practitioner representatives, they quickly become outdated during inflationary periods. Any systematic failure to adjust fee schedules in response to changes in private charges results in practitioner dissatisfaction, which in turn can lead to lower assignment rates (if allowed by the payer) or to outright nonparticipation by practitioners.

Pressures of this sort during the late 1950s and 1960s led many Blue Shield plans to adopt another form of reimbursement known as payment on the basis of *usual, customary, and reasonable* charges, or UCR for short. Following enactment of Medicare and Medicaid in 1965, UCR also was adopted as the principal means of practitioner payment under government programs. Unfortunately, Medicare regulations used different terminology, specifying payment of "customary and prevailing" charges. The two approaches are the same, however, as is apparent below.

The heart of the UCR approach is the practitioner's own schedule of private charges. The third party payer collects information on the level of billed charges for each service or procedure on behalf of every participating practitioner. Over time, profiles can be constructed showing the range of fees a given practitioner charged for a particular type of service. The median charge in such a profile is designated as the *usual fee* under UCR procedures and as the *customary charge* under Medicare procedures (hereafter the term "usual" is used in both contexts). Since the profile is updated constantly, the usual fee will follow the trend in actual billed charges.

The usual fees form the basis for another type of profile containing information on all practitioners who bill for a given service. These lists (one for each service category) rank practitioners' usual charges from lowest to highest and are known as *customary charge* (UCR) or *prevailing fee* (Medicare) profiles. (To avoid confusion over the two meanings of the term "customary" charges, the Medicare terminology is used here.) Every payer who uses the basic UCR methodology has established a given percentile of the prevailing fee profile for each service as the maximum amount it will pay any practitioner. Under Medicare the limit is set at the 75th percentile of usual charges. Blue Shield plans typically set the limit between the 80th and 95th percentile of usual charges. In other words, only practitioners with the highest fees in relation to their peers receive reimbursement at rates below the level of usual charges.

The remaining feature of UCR reimbursement is the meaning of a *reasonable fee*. Reasonable is defined in similar terms by all UCR payers (including Medicare) as the lowest of the actual charge (the billed amount), the practitioner's own usual fee, and the percentile limit on usual charges (the prevailing charge). To protect against the possibility that practitioners will impose higher fees on insured patients, the charge also must not exceed the amount billed for similar services to all other patients during the same time period.

UCR payment schemes are far more expensive to administer than are fixed fee approaches because of the data storage and computational facilities necessary to generate the thousands upon thousands of profiles required by the payer. Moreover, what is an advantage to the practitioners—the automatic adjustment of fees—is a disadvantage to the third party payer in that control over prices is lost. In fact, UCR schemes are widely criticized as being inflationary because practitioners have little to lose by submitting ever higher billed charges.[13] The billed charge may not be paid in full, but it will enter the system and serve to increase future usual and prevailing fee profiles. This fact has not been lost on third parties under pressure to constrain their costs.

Two ways to contain costs under UCR are to freeze usual charges and to reduce the percentile limits used to determine the prevailing fee. Both are used widely, particularly under public programs. Freezing usual charges is a popular approach with state Medicaid administrations. Such freezes typically specify a past date (to preclude any anticipatory price increases by practitioners) and may be maintained for months or even years. The longer the freeze is kept in force the greater is the difference between practitioners' current billed charges and what the state considers to be their usual fees. Reimbursement rates are fixed for each practitioner, but the relative differences in reimbursement levels among physicians that existed on the freeze date are retained. In other words, the freeze creates a fixed variable fee system.

Constraints on the prevailing fee have a very different impact. Blue Shield plans from time to time have taken this approach by lowering the percentile cutoff a few points. By definition such action affects only practitioners with the highest usual fees; however, for those few, reimbursement levels are reduced, not just frozen as in the previous case. It should be noted, however, that the level of reasonable charges still may rise in the face of a reduction in the percentile limit. The reason is that the dollar value of any percentile point on the prevailing fee profile increases each time the level of usual charges rises.

The Medicare program uses another type of control on the prevailing fee. Instead of percentile adjustments, the Health Care Financing Administration indexes the prevailing fee so that an annual dollar maximum is established for each service. These dollar limits then are increased each year by a percentage factor designed to cover increases in costs (not prices) of office-based practices. However, every year since the control was instituted the cost index has been lower than the annual increase in physician fees. The upshot is that the effective percentile limit on prevailing fees has declined each year. With each reduction, more and more physicians find that their usual charges are above the allowable indexed prevailing fee. As this trend continues, the Medicare "customary and prevailing" reimbursement system will devolve into a fixed fee schedule under which nearly every physician will be paid the same base amount for the same service. However, it will be a fixed fee system with all the cumbersome administrative aspects of UCR, and as such has little to recommend it.

There have been numerous attempts to develop fee-for-services programs that are as easy to administer as fixed fee systems but have the flexibility associated with UCR. The most notable are the *relative value schedules* (RVS) developed in California and elsewhere. The RVS begins with a list of reimbursable procedures and services as does any other fee-for-service approach. However, instead of rates' being assigned directly to service bases, each procedure is given a weight in *relative value units*. A relative value unit is an arbitrary number designed to facilitate uniform comparisons among services according to the average time it takes to perform a procedure or the level of professional skill required. The number 1.0 typically is assigned to a standard service such as a routine office revisit. All other services then are calculated as multiples of this one; e.g., an allergy shot might be a 0.5, whereas a complicated surgical procedure might rank at 80 or above.

The point of the RVS is that it establishes a single ranking system for all physician services. However, this does not mean that every doctor receives the same payment for the same service. To determine the amount of reimbursement due the physician, the RVS units must be multiplied by a dollar conversion factor. For example, if the conversion factor is $15 and the physician provides 20 services in a week with a cumulative RVS total of 35 units, then revenue will equal $525. Under some RVS systems, the physician picks the conversion rate, while in others the payer assigns different rates to identifiable groups of physicians by specialty, geographic location, or type of practice setting. The flexibility possible in rate determination makes the RVS approach an attractive alternative to either fixed fee or UCR systems.

As popular as fee-for-service is, it is not the only way physicians and other health practitioners are paid. Indeed, if the health-related work force is taken as a whole (including nurses, other allied health personnel, and clerical workers in hospitals), the most common methods are wages and salaries, whereby payment is tied to time worked rather than services delivered. Wage and salary methods are less risky than fee-for-service from the perspective of the practitioner because business expenses typically are picked up by the employer. They also engender different incentives for productivity and quality of output.

Like fee-for-service, time-based payment schemes can be simple or complex. They range from single rate systems (such as those used by some hospitals to contract for physician coverage of emergency rooms) to programs replete with scores of employee categories, pay scales, and promotion procedures. The rates may include elements of seniority, longevity, or productivity. They may even be tied to the profitability of the provider. For example, some physician group practices pay their members a basic salary plus a bonus. In such cases, the revenue received by one member of the group depends upon the salaries and rates of productivity for all members in the group. The dynamic implications are fascinating.

Of all the major forms of practitioner reimbursement, the most controversial surely is *capitation*, a method whereby the provider collects a set fee that entitles the patient to any quantity of covered services deemed necessary by the provider. Capitation payment has received considerable attention in the context of the HMO debate, but its roots lie in the British experience of paying general practitioners. This dual association has led to some confusion as to what the term really covers. To some, capitation payment means the monthly amount an individual pays to a health maintenance organization in order to be eligible for service. That overly simple usage is synonymous with the term insurance premium except that in this case the insurer also is the provider. It should be emphasized that just because the HMO receives capitation funds does not mean that the practitioners who work in the organization are paid on a capitation basis. In fact, if the HMO is of the group practice variety, the practitioners probably are salaried. On the other hand, if the HMO is a medical foundation plan or independent practice association (IPA) the normal reimbursement procedure is fee-for-service.

Whereas few health plans in this country pay physicians on a capitation basis, the approach is the cornerstone to ambulatory care reimbursement in Great Britain. Capitation is perhaps the simplest of all payment schemes. It is composed of two parts, a *panel* of individuals who agree beforehand to receive all outpatient physician services from the doctor in question, and a fixed capitation fee per panel member per month.

Capitation is a risky form of reimbursement for physicians because the revenue received is not tied directly to services delivered or to costs of practice. If the patients on the panel demand a high volume of services, the net revenue and implicit profit rates will be low. But if patient volume is low, then profits can be very lucrative. Proponents of capitation argue that this risk is healthy in that it forces physicians to be cost conscious and to be wary of providing unnecessary services. Detractors argue that the approach rewards underservice and unnecessary referrals to medical specialists or health facilities. There probably is some truth to both assertions. The British have managed to steer a middle path by modifying the basic capitation to account for differences in practice costs and patient characteristics. They reduce the risk further by permitting the physician to charge extra for certain services, notably evening and weekend calls.

Incentives and Implications

Several different approaches to practitioner reimbursement have been considered and a few advantages and disadvantages of each have been outlined. But which is best? Unfortunately, there is no simple answer because the question itself is complex: The best system for whom? The best under what circumstances? The best in terms of which objective? These issues—and some tentative answers—are presented well in the following selection written by four economists from the U.S. Health Care Financing Administration. While the focus is upon Medicare and Medicaid, the analysis can be applied readily to physician reimbursement schemes used by private insurance and other health plans. (The term CPR in the excerpt refers to the *customary, prevailing, and reasonable charge,* which is equivalent to the UCR terminology used earlier.)

MEDICARE AND MEDICAID PHYSICIAN PAYMENT INCENTIVES[a]

> The incentives in the Medicare and Medicaid physician payment systems and their effects on six interrelated aspects of health care costs and beneficiary access to care were analyzed. Research results and data presented indicate that Medicare and Medicaid physician payment incentives are inconsistent with current public policy goals of (1) containing inflation in fees and expenditures, (2) encouraging physician participation in public programs, (3) improving the geographic and specialty distributions of physicians, (4) encouraging primary care instead of surgery, and also outpatient rather than inpatient treatment.

> Three principal and interrelated concerns of health care policymakers are (1) controlling health care costs, (2) improving access to health care services, and (3) promoting high quality care. Although physician spending is only one-fifth of total health ex-

penditures, physician decisions significantly affect costs, access and quality because physicians direct over 70 percent of all health care spending.[1] This paper analyzes the incentives in Medicare and Medicaid physician payment policies and discusses their influence on health care costs and access for the programs' beneficiaries. While the relationship between physician reimbursement and quality of care is important, measurement problems and paucity of reliable data render it beyond the scope of this paper.

This analysis focuses on the effects of Medicare and Medicaid reimbursement practices on six interrelated dimensions of access and costs. The paper does not concentrate on theoretical models of physician behavior but rather it points out the direction of the economic incentives contained in current Medicare and Medicaid reimbursement policies. While the most direct effect on costs is inflation in physician fees and the most direct access impact is on physician participation in the Medicare and Medicaid programs, other factors are also important. These include incentives (both in terms of relative fees and benefits covered) for physicians to specialize rather than practice general medicine, to locate in physician-dense areas, to treat patients in hospitals rather than in outpatient settings, and to provide nonprimary care instead of primary care services. All of these have significant short-run, as well as long-run effects on Medicare, Medicaid, and total system costs.

We focused on Medicare and Medicaid physician reimbursement for three reasons. First, Medicare and Medicaid account for over one-fifth of physician spending. Second, detailed information on reimbursement methods, administrative practices, and rates encompassing the entire Nation for a large number of medical procedures is available for these programs. Third, since Medicare reimbursement is designed to pay the "going rate" in the private market, Medicare fees are believed to generally represent private sector payment patterns.

• • •

Physician Reimbursement and Inflation

Inflation is one of the most pressing problems in the health care sector. Over the past 11 years, physician fees have increased 20 percent faster than the overall cost of living. Per capita expenditures on physician services have increased 29 percent faster than per capita spending on all goods and services. About 70 percent of these increases were due to price increases, while the remainder resulted from increases in the quantity and changes in the mix of services provided per capita.

With respect to physician fee inflation, studies of CPR and fee schedule approaches suggest that CPR is more inflationary.[3] Under CPR, two factors create an environment in which physicians can influence reimbursement levels and rates of increase. These factors are (1) physician determination of CPR charges and (2) administrative practices used by carriers in calculating CPR screens. First, CPR implicitly encourages physicians to raise their fees because the higher the rate of increase in fees this year, the higher the CPR screens next year. Therefore, collectively, physicians can influence the level and rates of increase in Medicare and Medicaid CPR reimbursement rates. Second, several administrative practices may contribute to fee inflation.[4] These include using separate reimbursement rates for general practitioners and specialists, using local geographic areas for calculating separate CPR screens, and merging comparable private health insurance information with Medicare and Medicaid physician charge data. For example, the more localities and specialty designations, the greater is the potential for a small number of physicians to determine the levels and rates of increase in the fee screens.

In addition to fee inflation inherent in the reimbursement method, other characteristics of Medicare and Medicaid contribute to inflation in physician expenditures. These include (1) selective assignment provisions in Medicare; (2) "moral hazard" (i.e., induced use of medical services due to insurance); and (3) the lack of an effective mechanism to monitor and influence utilization patterns for physician services.

First, the selective Medicare assignment policy permits physicians to offset the fee restraints of the CPR screens since, on unassigned claims, physicians can charge beneficiaries more than the program pays. Second, since Medicaid has no cost-sharing and since about 70 percent of Medicare beneficiaries have their cost-sharing paid by supplementary private health insurance or Medicaid, the net cost of additional services is relatively small. Therefore, patients and physicians have few financial incentives to limit the utilization of services. Third, the lack of a utilization review system coordinated among all payers severely limits the ability to monitor patterns of care. This is especially important because under any fee-for-service system physicians can compensate for reimbursement rate limitations by increasing the quantity of services they provide or by redefining or upgrading the standard treatment patterns to include, for example, more diagnostic services or more frequent visits.

To counteract the inflationary pressures generated by price increases, the Congress mandated, through Section 224 of the 1972 Social Security Act amendments, the only enduring national effort to restrain price escalation for physician services under Medicare and Medicaid. Beginning with fiscal year 1976, a national economic index was applied to the Medicare and Medicaid programs to limit increases in prevailing charges to increases in the cost of maintaining an office practice and increases in general earnings in the labor force. This, in effect, limits increases in program recognized fees to a level based on general (not medical care) inflation and productivity increases.

While the economic index generally reduces the absolute increase in Medicare-allowed reimbursements by 1½ to 2 percentage points a year, it does not affect actual physician charges. Moreover, the economic index limit on fees may lead to an increase in the number of visits or a decrease in the quality of a visit. Furthermore, the economic index is locking into place all the existing prevailing charge imbalances between high and low fee regions and among physicians of different specialties. This occurs because as physicians' actual fees continue to increase at a faster rate than the economic index limit, over time an increasing number of claims will be paid at the Medicare prevailing charge. In effect, the prevailing charge screens are becoming fee schedules that represent historic geographic and specialty reimbursement differences.

At first glance, fee schedules would seem to have greater potential for containing inflation in fees than would the CPR system by removing physicians from exclusive control of the secular trend in fees. Additionally, by changing the relative prices of services, fee schedules could help reduce total expenditures for physician services by, for example, encouraging primary care instead of surgery. While there is some evidence that fee schedules can restrain the rate of increase in prices, they have not proven as effective in containing total expenditures on physician services.[5]

Physician Participation

Medicare and Medicaid physician reimbursement policies directly influence physician willingness to participate and thus affect beneficiaries' access to care. Medicare has greatly improved financial access to care for the aged. However, the selective Medicare assignment system has resulted in inadequate financial protection for beneficiaries on the 50 percent of claims that are unassigned. Beneficiary out-of-pocket costs for physician charges in excess of Medicare reasonable charges increased nationally from $81 million in 1969 to $699 million in 1977.

The bulk of criticism of public programs, however, has been lodged against Medicaid. According to "conventional wisdom," Medicaid fees are greatly depressed. They discourage office-based private practice physicians from accepting Medicaid patients, thereby forcing patients to seek care in higher cost hospital outpatient departments, emergency rooms, or in "Medicaid mills," which circumvent depressed fees through an increased volume of services per patient. This in turn leads to a separate system of care for the poor apart from mainstream medicine.

Comparison of Medicare, Medicaid, and private insurance reimbursement levels indicates the relative financial access to care among these groups. Table 8-3 shows 1975 national average fees for Medicare, Medicaid, and the "best" Blue Shield plan and the physicians' usual fee for each of seven specific medical procedures from a survey conducted by Sloan et al.[6] For the follow-up office visit, which is a fairly common procedure and thus may be a good indicator of routine access to care, Medicare and Blue Shield fees are very close (the "best" Blue Shield fees are 5 percent greater than Medicare fees). Similarly, for four of the other six procedures Medicare fees average at least 92 percent of the highest Blue Shield fees. Second, both Medicare and Blue Shield fees average about 75 to 80 percent of what physicians report they usually charge. Thus, as measured by third-party reimbursement levels, it would seem that Medicare patients are on about the same financial footing as are Blue Shield patients in seeking access to care.[7]

On the other hand, Medicaid fees average about 75 to 80 percent of Medicare and Blue Shield fees and about 60 percent of physicians' usual fees for the seven procedures. Reimbursement data from the Medicare and Medicaid programs confirm these results. From 1975 surveys of Medicare and Medicaid reimbursement rates, indices based upon a nationally representative basket of 29 specific medical services indicated that Medicaid reimbursement rates averaged 82 percent of Medicare fees for general practitioners and 77 percent for specialists. However, while Medicaid

Table 8-3 Mean Physician and Insurer Fees, 1975 (in Dollars)

	Physicians	Insurers		
	Usual Fee	Blue Shield "Best Fee"	Medicare Fees	Medicaid Fees
Follow-Up Hospital Visit on Day After Patient Is Admitted	$ 13.93	$ 10.73	$ 10.00	$ 7.63
Routine Follow-Up Office Visit	11.59	9.22	8.79	7.20
Inguinal Hernia Repair	303.97	244.82	233.21	170.57
Diagnostic Dilation and Curretage	149.06	113.97	104.43	76.72
Complete Blood Count	8.04	7.79	6.17	5.63
Suture of a Simple Laceration	22.26	19.04	16.55	13.68
Electrocardiogram	19.66	17.05	15.76	13.47

Source: Sloan et al., *A Study of Administrative Costs in Physician's Offices and Medicaid Participation,* Final Report, Health Care Financing Administration, June 1977.

---

reimbursement rates were virtually equal to Medicare reimbursement levels in 20 States, in 11 States they were less than 70 percent.[8]

With respect to physician participation in Medicare, survey data indicated that while 18 percent of physicians were always willing to accept Medicare assignment, 30 percent of physicians never accepted assignment.[9] Moreover, Paringer found that physicians' willingness to accept Medicare assignment was highly related to Medicare reimbursement levels—a 1 percent increase in reimbursement levels would result in a 0.5 to 1.5 percent increase in the assignment rate (controlling for other factors).[10]

With respect to Medicaid participation, data from Sloan et al. show that 32 percent of physicians do not treat Medicaid patients. In analyzing the impact of Medicaid reimbursement rates on physician willingness to treat Medicaid patients, Sloan et al. found that, holding other factors constant, a 10 percent increase in average Medicaid fees would increase physician participation by 7 percent. Hadley and Lee, as well as Held, Manheim, and Woolridge, found similar results.[11] Thus it appears that physician participation may be relatively sensitive to Medicare and Medicaid reimbursement levels. However, these studies also indicate that increases in Medicare or Medicaid reimbursements, accompanied by commensurate reimbursement increases by other payers, could lead to increased physician expenditures with no change in Medicare and Medicaid physician participation.

Geographic and Specialty Distribution

Much national concern exists over the geographic and specialty maldistribution of physicians. This maldistribution has limited access to primary care services and increased health care costs through the provision of more intensive and, consequently, higher priced services. The literature on physician location and specialty choice indicates that financial incentives play a major role in the physician decision process. Nevertheless, from a Federal policy perspective, Medicare and Medicaid reimbursement practices should support, or at least not contradict, government policies to attract physicians into shortage specialties and underserved areas.[12]

Medicare and Medicaid reimbursement policies may affect physician location choices because reimbursement rates vary among geographical areas. In 1975, Medicare carriers divided the country into over 290 different reimbursement areas varying in size from subcounty areas to entire States (there were only 6 State-wide reimbursement areas in 1975). State Medicaid programs have established about 185 different reimbursement areas, 34 of which are complete States. In 1975, Medicare general practitioner and specialist fees averaged 23 percent higher in metropolitan than nonmetropolitan counties, while there was no difference in average Medicaid fees. Adjusting for cost-of-living differences, the Medicare metropolitan/nonmetropolitan fee difference was reduced to 8 percent, while Medicaid fees were actually 12 percent higher in rural areas. However, the results for Medicaid can largely be attributed to the fact that 34 States paid physicians the same fee regardless of location within the State.[13]

Table 8-4 shows the relationship between physician density and average Medicare and Medicaid prevailing charges for specialists. A continuum exists from the least to the most physician-dense areas for Medicare specialist fees. Prevailing charges average 33 percent higher in counties with more than 175 physicians per 100,000 population than in counties with fewer than 75 physicians per 100,000 population. In contrast, there appears to be very little relationship between Medicaid fees and physician density. (The

Table 8-4 Mean and Range for Medicare and Medicaid Specialist Fee Indices by County Physician Population Ratio and County Per Capita Income, 1975

	Number of Counties	Medicare		Medicaid	
		Mean	Range	Mean	Range
All Counties	3,074	100	70–192	100	49–179
Physicians Per 100,000 Population (1973)					
< 24	314	85	71–126	108	61–145
25–74	1,747	85	70–126	101	49–154
75–124	704	82	70–132	99	49–179
125–174	182	102	71–154	103	49–142
175–224	70	113	75–154	102	49–150
225–299	25	110	77–154	94	49–134
300+	32	113	80–192	90	49–145
Per Capita Income (1970)					
< $2,499	628	83	70–103	101	61–142
$2,500–$2,999	877	83	70–113	102	49–145
$3,000–$3,499	874	87	70–117	100	49–145
$3,500–$3,999	479	99	70–154	98	49–154
$4,000–$4,499	153	100	75–154	101	49–145
$4,500+	63	121	75–192	100	49–179

Source: Medicare Carrier Survey, Intermediary Letter 74–19, June, 1974; Medicaid State Survey, SRS Action Transmittal 75–25, June, 1975.

correlation between physician density and Medicare specialist fees is .32 and −.07 for Medicaid fees.)[14]

The relationship between county per capita income and average Medicare and Medicaid fees is displayed in Table 8-4. The data show that average Medicare specialist prevailing charges are directly related to county per capita income. Medicare fees average 30 percent higher in the high-income counties compared with the low-income counties. Average Medicaid fees are virtually constant across all counties regardless of per capita income. (In fact, the correlation between per capita income and Medicare specialist fees is .40 and −.03 for Medicaid fees.)[14]

While higher practice costs in physician-dense and high-income areas could explain the inverse relationship between these factors and Medicare reimbursement levels, several studies question such a relationship.[15] Thus, to the extent that Medicare fees reflect private market patterns, existing physician fee patterns may provide financial incentives for physicians to locate in high-income, physician-dense metropolitan areas.

Some critics contend that, other things being equal, Medicare and Medicaid physician reimbursement policies have encouraged increased specialization. While three pieces of data give credence to this argument, it must be recognized that specialists may provide a different type of higher quality service. First, in fiscal year 1975, all but six carriers, encompassing 91 percent of Medicare physician payments, recognized specialty reimbursement differentials. Under Medicaid, specialist reimbursement differentials are less common, occurring in 25 states with 48 percent of physician payments.

Second, Schieber et al.[16] found statistically significant differences between general practitioner and specialist Medicare reimbursement rates for 27 of 39 procedures though differences generally were less than 10 percent. Of the 27 procedures with statistically significant differences, specialists' fees were higher than those of general practitioners in 19 cases, and the types of services with higher specialist than general practitioner fees were medical visits and surgery, which represent about three-quarters of Medicare physician reimbursements.

Third, based on a 5 percent sample of Medicare claims, Table 8-5 shows the average annual rate of growth in Medicare allowed charges for selected specialties between 1968–1972, 1972–1975,

Table 8-5 Average Annual Rates of Growth of Medicare Reasonable Charges by Specialty and by Place of Service, for Selected Years, 1968–1975 (Percent)

	1968 to 1972	1972 to 1975	1968 to 1975
Specialty			
All Physicians	5.4	7.3	6.2
All Specialists	5.8	7.8	6.7
General Practitioners	3.0	4.7	3.7
Internal Medicine	4.2	5.9	4.9
General Surgery	7.8	5.3	6.7
Place of Service			
All Places	5.4	7.3	6.2
Doctor's Office	4.1	2.4	3.4
Inpatient Hospital	7.1	12.2	9.3

Source: Unpublished preliminary data from Medicare 5 percent sample of beneficiary claims.

and 1968–1975. During each of these periods, the rates of growth of the two primary care specialties—general practice and internal medicine—were less than the rates of growth for all physicians and for specialists. Thus, the observed general practitioner/specialist reimbursement differentials and the slower rates of growth in allowed charges for primary care specialties indicate that the Medicare program does not provide economic incentives for physicians to choose primary care specialties.

Place of Treatment and Type of Service Rendered

A frequent criticism of the existing health care system is that it contains financial incentives for physicians to treat patients in the hospital when treatment on an outpatient basis might be equally suitable. Another criticism is that the current system encourages expensive, technologically oriented medical care rather than routine primary care services. While the following analysis of physician reimbursement rates provides some evidence that these allegations have merit, it must be remembered that the specific features of health insurance benefit packages also provide strong incentives with respect to place and type of service rendered.

Two pieces of evidence from the Medicare and Medicaid programs suggest that current physician reimbursement rates contain financial incentives for physicians to treat patients in the hospital as opposed to their offices. As shown in Table 8-6, national average reimbursement rates for initial visits for general practitioners and specialists indicate that both of these groups can receive Medicare and Medicaid reimbursements 14 to 20 percent greater if the initial visit is performed in the hospital instead of in the physician's office. For follow-up visits, physicians can receive reimbursement under Medicare averaging 13 to 21 percent more in the hospital than in the office and 3 to 7 percent more under Medicaid.

While hospitalized patients may be sicker and require more intensive physician care (e.g., on average, hospital visits are approximately 20 percent longer than office visits[17]), the physician himself bears none of the overhead expenses (e.g., rent, labor cost, equipment, drugs, etc.) associated with treating the patient in the office when treating a patient in the hospital, although he must bear time and transportation costs in going to the hospital. Since practice expenses compromise about 40 percent of a phy-

Table 8-6 Medicare and Medicaid National Average Medical Visit Fees, 1975 (in Dollars)

Procedure	Medicare General Practitioner	Medicare Specialist	Medicaid General Practitioner	Medicaid Specialist
Initial Office Visit	$29.00	$36.60	$23.00	$26.20
Follow-Up Office Visit	8.20	9.80	7.20	7.80
Initial Hospital Visit	34.70	42.40	26.30	30.50
Follow-Up Hospital Visit	9.90	11.10	7.70	8.00
	Ratios			
Initial Visit: Hospital/Office	1.20	1.16	1.14	1.16
Follow-Up Visit: Hospital/Office	1.21	1.13	1.07	1.03

Source: See Table 8-4; national average fees are county fees weighted by county population relative to U.S. population.

sician's gross revenues, the net value of the office visit reimbursement rate, after deducting office expenses, is even less compared with the hospital visit fee. For example, not considering physician time and transportation costs to the hospital, the after expense value of the Medicare specialist follow-up office visit fee is $5.90 (60 percent of $9.80) compared with $11.10 for the follow-up hospital visit—a difference of 88 percent. Even adjusting for the longer time to perform a follow-up hospital visit,[17] there is a 57 percent difference between the hospital visit fee and the net value of the office visit fee.

Second, Table 8-5 also contains data on the average annual rates of change in Medicare reimbursement rates from 1968–1975 by place of service. Over this period, Medicare reimbursement rates for services rendered in the hospital compared with the doctor's office increased more than two and one-half times as fast as services rendered in the doctor's office. While this result might be attributable to changes in the mix of services, the relative rates of increase are indicative of incentives favoring in-hospital treatment.

Some evidence suggests that Medicare and Medicaid reimbursement policies reward surgical procedures more generously than medical visit services. Table 8-7 contains hourly equivalent Medicare and Medicaid specialist remuneration rates for several medical visit and surgical procedures (i.e., adjusted for physician time to perform the procedure).[18] Using only operating room time data for five surgical procedures, Medicare fees translate into an

Table 8-7 Medicare and Medicaid Specialist Mean Fees Per Hour for Selected Procedures, 1975

Procedure	OR Time	Operating Room (OR) Time		Total Time*		
		Medicare Fee Per Hour	Medicaid Fee Per Hour	Total Time (Hrs)	Medicare Fee Per Hour	Medicaid Fee Per Hour
Surgical Procedures						
Hernia Repair	1.47	$193	$142	4.43	$64	$47
Appendectomy	1.33	225	165	5.62	53	39
Cholecystectomy	2.44	186	140	7.19	63	48
Radical Mastectomy	3.00	188	134	7.26	77	55
Colectomy	3.31	194	135	8.84	73	51
Average		$197	$143		$66	$48
Medical Visit Procedures						
Initial Office Visit	0.77	$48	$34	\multicolumn{3}{l}{Fees Per Hour Ratio: Surgical to Medical Visit Procedures}		
Follow-Up Office Visit	0.19	52	42			
					Medicare	Medicaid
Initial Hospital Visit	0.84	51	36	OR Time	3.94	3.86
Follow-Up Hospital Visit	0.22	50	36	Total Time	1.32	1.30
Average		$51	$37			

*Total time = operating room time plus time for medical visits.

Source: See Table 8-4 for fees; Medical visit times from U.E. Reinhardt, *Physician Productivity and the Demand for Health Manpower: An Economic Analysis* (Cambridge, Mass: Ballinger Publishing Co., 1975, p. 157. Operating room times are from E.F.X. Hughes, V.R. Fuchs, J.E. Jacoby, E.M. Lewitt, "Surgical Workloads in a Community Practice," *Surgery*, 71, 317 (March, 1972).

equivalent of $197 per hour for surgery compared with $50 per hour for medical visits. Similarly, under Medicaid, the five surgical procedures average $143 per hour compared with $37 per hour for medical visits. Assuming these procedures represent hourly fee patterns for all surgery and all medical visits, and assuming that physicians of a given specialty can substitute the performance of surgery and medical visits, these results suggest that surgical procedures are about four times more lucrative than medical visits for both Medicare and Medicaid. However, this comparison overstates the relative profitability of surgical procedures because the reimbursement rate for surgery generally includes not only the operation itself but also pre-and post-hospital office visits within a specified period of time. Adjusting to include both operating room time and time for pre- and post-operative hospital and office visits,[19] results in surgical procedure reimbursement are 32 percent higher under Medicare and 30 percent higher under Medicaid than for performing medical visits.

Preliminary results from a study of the resource costs of various medical and surgical procedures by Stason and Hsiao substantiate these findings. Even after adjusting for several factors, Stason and Hsiao found hourly surgical reimbursement exceeds by several times hourly reimbursement for medical visits.[20] Much more work needs to be done on this subject, including studying a larger number of procedures and developing better measures of the intensity and skill required to perform surgical and medical procedures. However, preliminary evidence suggests that the current Medicare and Medicaid reimbursement rates give physicians financial incentives to perform surgery as compared with medical visits where procedures can be substituted.[21] However, since Medicare and some Medicaid physician reimbursement methods are based on existing private market fee structures, they may only reflect fee patterns inherent in the overall health system.

Summary

The study used selected physician reimbursement data from Medicare and Medicaid program experience to analyze the nature and direction of the incentives contained in these programs and their effects on several important public policy issues. Implicit in the discussion was the basic economic assumption that prices affect physician behavior. However, given the limited nature of the data (e.g., Medicare and Medicaid) and the lack of behavioral relationships, the discussion has concentrated only on the empirically observed direction of the relationships.

The results from this analysis suggest several hypotheses. First, the CPR physician reimbursement method employed by Medicare, Medicaid, and many private insurers is inherently more inflationary than fee schedules. Second, Medicare beneficiaries appear to have about the same financial access to care as Blue Shield subscribers, but Medicaid patients are at a distinct disadvantage. Moreover, physician participation in public programs appears to be highly responsive to reimbursement levels. Third, Medicare and, to a lesser extent Medicaid, would appear to provide financial incentives for physicians to locate in high-income, physician-dense metropolitan areas and to choose specialty over primary care practice. Fourth, Medicare and Medicaid may also provide incentives for physicians to treat patients in hospital settings and to perform surgical, as opposed to medical visit, procedures.

Given that the customary, prevailing and reasonable charge system was designed to reflect the private market and that it operates essentially as a physician-determined reimbursement system, these results are not surprising. However, if national health insurance is to use the reimbursement system to promote cost containment and access to care as policy goals, then this analysis suggests that our predominantly laissez-faire reimbursement system will need to be modified.

INSTITUTIONAL REIMBURSEMENT

Hospitals, nursing homes, and other health care facilities provide an array of medical services only slightly more complicated than the reimbursement procedures under which they operate. As if the intricate payment schemes developed by Blue Cross, Medicare, and Medicaid were not enough, roughly a third of the states impose hospital rate setting or review and every state has some form of capital expenditure control over health facilities. To top it all off, third party payers have a habit of changing the rules as soon as the institutions begin to comprehend the game. The combination of complexity, diversity, and inconsistency makes it virtually impossible to present a complete picture of institutional payment methods used in the country today. The following pages concentrate on the basic charge and cost-related systems and convey a taste of how these systems can influence provider behavior.

Payment Mechanics

A few Blue Cross plans and most commercial insurance companies pay health facilities on the basis of billed charges. The mechanics are similar to those discussed under the same heading in the previous section—with two exceptions. First, no third party payer reimburses the entire range of services available in today's hospitals and nursing homes. Some services are not reimbursed because they exceed coverage limits, others may not be directly related to patient care, and still others are considered unnecessary by the payer. The upshot is that the facility typically will have to collect a part of the bill from the patient even though that individual may be "fully" insured.

The second exception relates specifically to Blue Cross plans that pay charges less a percentage "discount." These plans typically pay 95 to 98 percent of charges, with the reduction usually justified as a quantity discount. There is some argument as to whether this is a legitimate justification based on lower administrative costs or whether it is simply a manifestation of the market power exercised by Blue Cross. In either event, the Blue Cross service contracts specify that the institution is not to charge the patient for any percentage reduction in billed charges. If the charges are realistic to begin with, such procedures force the institutions to raise lost revenues from some other group of patients. This process, known as *cross-subsidization* (where one class of patients in effect subsidizes the cost of the care for some other class of patients), is a perennial issue in hospital reimbursement.

Reimbursement of billed charges works reasonably well when they are stable and bear some direct relationship to costs, but these conditions are difficult to maintain during inflationary periods. Charge payers have developed several techniques to handle such situations, including limitations on allowable rate increases and the imposition of maximum charge-to-cost ratios. The type of controls on rate increases differs from payer to payer but the effects are similar to the constraints on usual and prevailing fees considered in the last section. The few payers who impose maximum charge-to-cost ratios play a different tune. Their systems maintain the appearance of paying charges; in reality, they are cost-based reimbursement schemes.

Cost-related or cost-based reimbursement has been the predominant form of institutional payment since 1965 when the Medicare and Medicaid statutes specified that hospitals be paid on a "reasonable cost" basis. Just what is reasonable and what is a cost have been the subject of heated debate ever since. The issues hinge on two factors—cost finding or accounting and cost apportionment.

Most payers use similar standards for cost finding, such as the following:

- Costs are to be retroactively determined and verified by public audit.
- Costs for labor, consumables, and minor equipment are to be the incurred purchase prices for the items in question.
- Costs for building and major equipment are to be accounted for on an accrual basis over the useful lifetime of the assets.
- Costs are not to exceed what a prudent buyer would pay for the same good or service in an arms-length transaction.
- Allowable costs must be reasonably related to patient care in the institution.
- Costs associated with noncovered services, unnecessary care, and experimental medical procedures are considered disallowed costs.

Unfortunately, conformity in standards does not ensure harmony in the system. Disputes between hospitals and third party payers over cost-finding procedures have centered on two areas: the perennially tough accounting questions of overhead allocations and depreciation methodology, and the vague meaning of "patient-related" and "medically necessary." The reader can peruse the *Medicare and Medicaid Guide,* a publication updated biweekly and published by Commerce Clearing House, Inc., to see how these battles are progressing.

Disagreements over cost finding are the prelude to even more heated arguments over cost apportionment. If every hospital received its entire revenue from a single source, there would be no issue of cost apportionment. But because facilities serve patients insured by various payers, there must be some method of deciding what proportion of costs is to be reimbursed by each payer. The two basic methods of cost apportionment used today are the *average per diem* (APD) approach, and the *ratio of charges-to-charges applied to costs* (RCCAC) approach. An appreciation of the differences between these two methods is essential to any understanding of cost-based payment mechanics.

Both begin with a retrospective audit of the institution's costs over some specified period in time, usually a year. The audit simply determines what costs were incurred or accrued during the period; the payer then must make a separate determination of which costs are to be allowed and which disallowed. Once this has been accomplished, the payer determines its obligation according to the APD or RCCAC cost apportionment method. Under the average per diem method,

$$R_k^t = \frac{\sum_j PD_{jk}^{t-1}}{\sum_j \sum_k PD_{jk}^{t-1}} (TC^{t-1} - D_k^{t-1})(1 + r)$$

where

R_k^t = revenue from payer (k) obtained in the current year (t) for costs incurred in prior accounting year ($t-1$)

PD_{jk} = number of patient days utilized by subscriber or beneficiary (j) under contract with reimburser (k)

TC^{t-1} = total audited costs in period $t-1$

D_k^{t-1} = costs disallowed by k

r = percentage "plus" factor, if any

In this case, the apportionment of allowed costs is determined by the proportion of total patient days accounted for by the payer in question.

But there is one major hitch. No hospital can wait until its costs are audited to receive reimbursement. Therefore, this method requires some form of interim payment as services are being delivered. The two most common forms of interim payment are based on charges in the current year and per diem costs in the previous year. Whichever method is used, the hospital is subject to a cost settlement at the end of the accounting period, when the sum of the interim payments is compared with the payer's obligation, R_k^t. Cost settlement may result in additional payments due the hospital (the typical case) or repayment by the hospital to the third party for any excess of interim payments over the payer's obligation.

As with most forms of retrospective cost-based reimbursement, the average per diem methodology has been criticized for its supposed lack of incentives for hospital efficiency and cost consciousness. However, before turning to these issues, there is another problem with APD reimbursement, which for a time led to its virtual abandonment by the major third parties: cross-subsidization. An implicit assumption behind apportionment by APD is that the per-day costs for service are about equal for all classes of patients. Where this assumption is violated, the payer whose patients incur lower-than-average costs subsidizes the party whose patients incur above-average costs. Such an unstable situation cannot last long.

Before 1965, the majority of Blue Cross plans across the country used the APD methodology and urged that it be adopted under the Medicare program then in Congress. Two arguments were put forth. First, the method was cost based and thus (somehow) appropriate for nonprofit hospitals. Second, it could be administered easily even on behalf of hospitals with crude and outdated accounting systems. Neither point was challenged seriously; rather, Congress rejected APD because it meant that Medicare patients (and hence the government) would be subsidizing nonelderly Blue Cross patients. Why? The costs per patient stay were known to be significantly higher among aged patients—but, since these individuals stayed longer, the costs of auxiliary services were spread over more days and, as a result, the average per day costs were lower. Congress was willing to pay its share of hospital expenditure, but no more. The question remained: how could that be assured.

After much debate, the system known by its acronym as RCCAC was adopted. Instead of patient days, billed charges (C) would be used in cost apportionment:

$$R_k^t = \frac{\sum_i \sum_j (N_{ijk}^{t-1} C_{ijk}^{t-1})}{\sum_i \sum_j \sum_k (N_{kjk}^{t-1} C_{kjk}^{t-1})} (TC^{-1} - D_k^{t-1})(1 + r)$$

Here the cost base is the same as under the ADP method, but the proportion of that base picked up by a payer (k), such as Medicare, is determined by summing the charges to Medicare patients over the year and dividing by the sum of charges to all patients (including Medicare).

The logic behind the ratio of charges-to-charges approach is that any systematic cost differential in patient treatments will be reflected in the actual charges for services provided. This may be true, but only if the hospital has a consistent pricing policy across all departments. Cross-subsidization still will be a problem if the hospital uses different markups for different services (e.g., low for maternity and emergency care, high for pharmacy, laboratory, and radiology). Realizing this, payers have devised methods to combat it. Medicare and most Blue Cross plans now use a form of RCCAC known as the departmental method, whereby the ratio of charges-to-charges is applied to fully costed department revenue centers; that is to say, each department that bills patients is allocated its own direct costs plus a portion of the cost of all nonrevenue-producing departments (e.g., scheduling, maintenance, administration). In this way, interdepartmental differences in pricing do not affect the reimbursement received by the institution.

Incentives and Implications

As noted, retrospective cost-based reimbursement has been attacked by economists and others for its misdirected incentives. Cross-subsidization is only one problem, and one of the easier to solve, at that. Additional concerns include possible adverse effects on productivity, efficiency, and overall economy of operation. On the other side of the coin is the potential for overinvestment in service intensity, quality, and patient amenities. Such concerns have generated interest in alternative forms of institutional reimbursement, especially those that set rates prospectively. In the following excerpts, William Dowling examines the drawbacks of current cost-based payment schemes, then explores the economic implications of prospective rate setting.

WHY PROSPECTIVE RATE SETTING?[b]

Prospective rate setting evolved in response to the dramatic and persistent rise in hospital costs that began in the mid-1960s. It was then (and continues to be) widely believed that the cost inflation problem can be traced to an absence of cost containment incentives in the prevailing methods of paying hospitals—the payment of costs (determined retrospectively) and the payment of billed changes (set unilaterally by institutions themselves). Prospective rate setting was seen both as a means of exerting more external influence over hospital activities and plans, and as a means of building cost containment constraints and/or incentives into hospital payment. All prospective rate setting systems claim cost containment as a primary objective. State rate setting laws, for example, typically assign an agency or commission the job of assuring that hospital rates reflect "the costs of efficient production of services" or "the economy-wide inflation rate," or that they are, simply, "reasonable." The range of cost-influencing factors considered in judging the reasonableness of rates varies greatly, however. Some rate-setting systems focus on per unit costs, emphasizing efficiency or productivity; others look more broadly at aggregate hospital costs, emphasizing efficiency and utilization; others look even more broadly at aggregate system costs, emphasizing efficiency, utilization, and the supply of beds, facilities, and services. In general, rate setting agencies and programs also recognize the need to preserve the ability of hospitals to provide quality care and to remain financially viable.

In a number of states, hospitals acted through their associations to encourage the development of prospective rate setting systems, hoping that impartial rate setting authorities would come to agree with them that the cost inflation problem was largely attributable to factors beyond their control. These authorities might help explain this to the public and might even serve as advocates for hospitals with regard to certain of their financial problems. In addition, hospitals hoped that all third parties would be willing to pay rates set by independent rate setting agencies or programs, thereby ending the imposition by the different third parties of arbitrary cost or rate ceilings, different definitions of allowable costs, and different reimbursement practices. This, in turn, would help hospitals achieve the goal of "equal payment for equal services" and end the practice of shifting costs not reimbursed by third parties to self-pay patients. Both hospitals and third parties believed they would benefit from the financial predictability prospective rate setting makes possible.

● ● ●

Analytics of Prospective Rate Setting

Cost-Volume-Revenue

The financial incentives and implications of prospective rate setting can be analyzed by means of a conventional break-even

Figure 8-4 Cost-Revenue-Volume Relationship

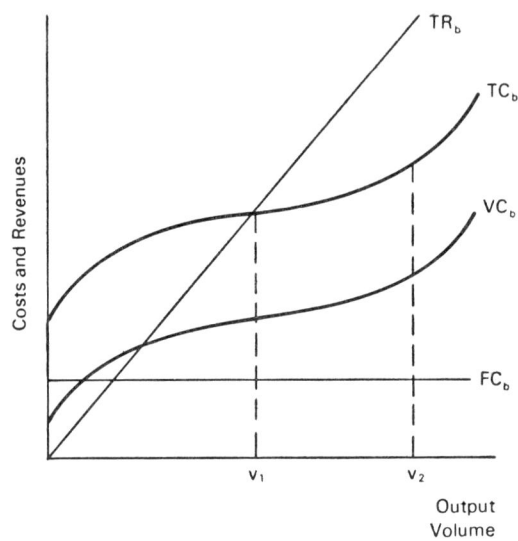

model. Figure 8-4 is a graphic presentation of the cost-revenue-volume relationships for a hypothetical hospital. Output volume is measured along the horizontal axis (in discharges, days, or services) and costs and revenues along the vertical axis. Suppose the hospital's budgeted fixed and variable costs at different possible volumes are shown by the curves FC_b and VC_b, giving budgeted total costs at different possible volumes of TC_b. Assuming that both self-pay patients and third parties pay fixed charges or rates per unit of service, budgeted total revenue would increase in direct proportion to volume as shown by the straight line TR_b. In actual practice, of course, costs and revenues are only budgeted for some relevant range of volume like $v_1 - v_2$.

Figure 8-5 is a simplified version of Figure 8-4, showing the hospital's TC_b and TR_b approximated by straight lines. In the absence of prospective rate setting or any other constraint on charges, the hospital would presumably set its charges so that TR_b would exceed TC_b by some desired operating margin, m_b, at its expected volume, v_b. If actual volume equals expected volume and the hospital's expectations about costs and revenues are right, the hospital would end the year with an actual operating margin of m_b. If actual costs begin running higher than expected as shown

Figure 8-5 Simplified Cost-Revenue-Volume Relationship

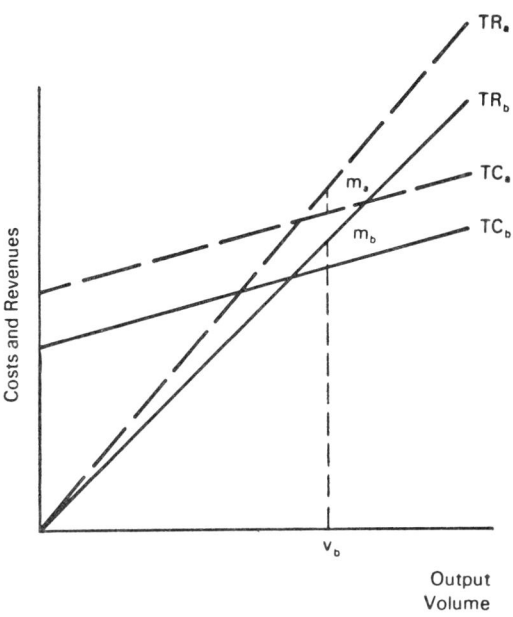

by TC_a, the hospital would presumably increase its charges during the year (again assuming no constraint on rate setting) to a level that would generate total revenue TR_a and operating margin m_a ($m_a = m_b$). This illustrates why it is felt that billed charges payment systems, in which hospitals are free to increase their charges at will, fail to provide cost containment incentives. Rather than finding ways to prevent costs from increasing more than expected, hospitals can just increase their charges to cover them. From Figure 8-5, it can also be seen that if actual volume turns out to be greater than expected volume, the hospital would end up with an operating margin greater than m_a or m_b whether TC_a and TR_a or TC_b and TR_b apply. This illustrates why it is felt that billed charges payment systems encourage increases in utilization. The greater the volume, the greater the operating margin.

Retrospective Reimbursement

Figure 8-6 illustrates the financial situation of a hypothetical hospital under retrospective cost reimbursement. Abstracting

Figure 8-6 Retrospective Cost Reimbursement

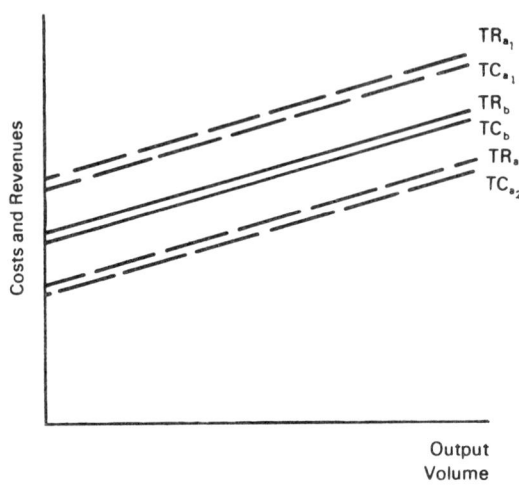

from the realities of nonallowable costs and nonrecognized financial requirements, and assuming for simplicity that all revenue comes in the form of cost reimbursement, this method of payment means that the hospital's revenues would always just equal its costs, whatever they happen to be (i.e., TR and TC would be the same). If actual costs begin running higher than expected as shown by TC_{a1}, the hospital's revenue would still cover its costs as shown by TR_{a1}, since payment is based on costs. On the other hand, if the hospital contained its costs to TC_{a2}, it would only receive revenue TR_{a2}. This illustrates why cost reimbursement is so often criticized as a scheme under which "whatever a hospital spends, it gets back." Clearly, cost reimbursement fails to provide cost containment incentives; hospitals are neither penalized for cost increases or rewarded for finding ways to prevent them.

Incentives Contrast

The financial incentives inherent in prospective rate setting contrast sharply with those of the conventional methods of reimbursement. Suppose a prospective rate setting system sets per case, per day, or per specific services rates for each participating hospital at a level just high enough to generate sufficient revenue to cover the hospital's approved budgeted costs and provide an

Figure 8-7 Prospective Payment

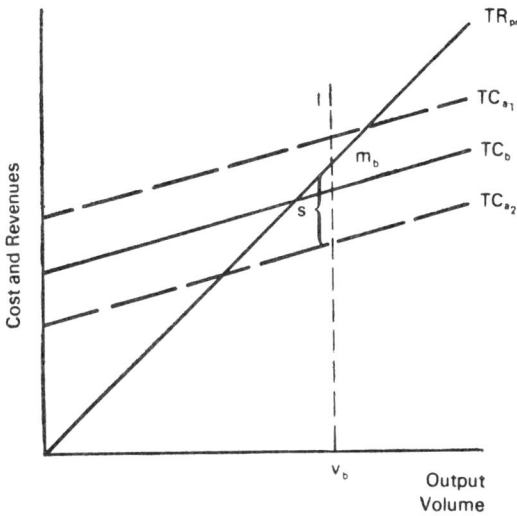

agreed upon operating margin at the expected output volume. Figure 8-7 illustrates this situation for a hypothetical hospital. TC_b represents the hospital's approved budgeted costs, TR_{pr} the revenue that the hospital's prospective rates will generate at different output volumes, m_b the agreed upon operating margin, and v_b the expected volume. Note that the hospital's rates are set in advance of the prospective year based on budgeted vs. actual costs, with the hospital's budget first reviewed for reasonableness. Once set, the hospital's rates are considered fixed for the year.

Suppose the hospital's actual costs for the year exceed its approved budgeted costs as shown by TC_{a1}. Under a prospective payment system, the hospital would suffer a loss equal to 1, since it would not be free to increase its rates. On the other hand, if the hospital is able to contain its costs to TC_{a2}, it would earn a surplus s, substantially greater than the agreed-to operating margin m_b. In contrast to both billed charges systems (where hospitals are free to set their own charges) and cost reimbursement systems, prospective payment systems provide a penalty for greater than expected cost increases. Higher costs mean financial losses. Thus, once a hospital's prospective rate is set, it faces a strong "negative incentive" to keep its costs below its rate. In contrast to cost reimbursement systems (where containing costs results in less revenue) prospective payment systems provide a "positive incentive" to keep costs down—the possibility of earning a surplus.

It should be noted, however, that it is not clear why a nonprofit hospital would prefer to contain its costs during the prospective year in order to earn a surplus to spend in future years. Why wouldn't it simply spend whatever it wishes each and every year (which a hospital theoretically could do under charges or cost reimbursement)? What is the advantage, in other words, of deferred spending? This is one of the key issues surrounding prospective rate setting. Some observers argue that prospective rate setting really offers no positive incentive to hospitals (at least, not to nonprofit hospitals which cannot distribute surpluses to their owners), since by cutting costs to earn a surplus, a hospital is just putting off expenditures it could make during the prospective year while risking lower rates in future years. It does appear that the negative incentive of the possibility of a loss must be present for prospective rate setting to work. However, some observers argue that the positive incentive inherent in prospective rate setting should be emphasized more. Prospective rates should be set so that efficient hospitals can make a surplus. Surpluses so acquired should place hospitals able to make them in an advantageous position with regard to some objectives they value. For example, planning agencies might place more emphasis on the cost of capital in considering competing expansion, modernization, or new service proposals. If several hospitals are seeking approval to add a particular new service, perhaps approval should be given to the one that could finance the project most cheaply as a result of its ability to accumulate enough surplus to obviate the need to borrow and incur debt service expenses.

Efficiency

Whether the planning process is formally structured along these lines, some proponents of prospective rate setting argue that over time efficient hospitals would find it easier than inefficient hospitals to keep their costs below their rates, and would, therefore, be more likely to expand (perhaps using accumulated surpluses). Inefficient hospitals would tend to suffer losses, forcing them to curtail their operations. Thus, there would be a gradual shift from less efficient to more efficient hospitals in the long run. This argument assumes that prospective payment systems can be designed to be sufficiently sensitive to reward efficient hospitals (which may not necessarily have the lowest costs) and penalize inefficient hospitals (which may not have the highest costs). It is not clear, however, that the prospective payment systems currently in operation are sophisticated enough to discriminate between efficient and inefficient hospitals. In large part, the problem is caused by an inability to measure output mix and quality accurately enough to know when a hospital's costs are unjustifiably out of line.

• • •

Basis of Payment

Prospective rate setting systems differ in terms of the basis of unit of payment for which rates are set. This feature is important because the payment unit determines the incentives posed by the system and hence how hospitals are likely to react to it. The alternative bases of payment that might be used are as follows:

1. Apportionment of total budget
2. Apportionment of departmental budgets
3. Capitation
4. Case
5. Day
6. Specific services

Total Budget

The apportionment of total budget method might work in the following way. Hospitals would submit budgets to a rate setting agency or program setting forth and justifying their expected prospective year costs and financial requirements. The agency would assess the reasonableness of each hospital's budget, perhaps by comparing its costs to the costs of similar hospitals, to cost standards, to expected inflation trends, or by a line by line budget review. Hospitals would be asked to defend or modify any parts of their budgets appearing out of line. Agreement on a final budget satisfactory to both parties might be automatic if a budget, as originally submitted or as modified, fell within acceptable parameters, or agreement might be reached through a formal hearings process, an informal negotiations process, or a combination of the two. Once a hospital's budget was agreed upon, each third party would be obligated to pay its share of budgeted costs, regardless (following the basic principle of prospective payment) of the costs actually incurred by the hospital during the prospective year. Apportionment of budgeted costs to different third parties could be based on each third party's share of the hospital's charges, admissions, or patient days, or could be determined by the departmental RCC method (applied to budgeted vs. actual costs). The hospital would be guaranteed its budgeted costs whatever the proportions paid by the different third parties. For example, if a budget of $6,000,000 were agreed upon for a hospital, the hospital would get this amount regardless of what its costs actually turned out to be. If a particular third party were responsible for half the hospital's patients; it would be obligated to pay $3,000,000 (which it might simply forward in monthly $250,000 installments). Quarterly checks could be made to determine each third party's exact share of the $2,000,000 due the hospital for the quarter.

Michigan Blue Cross and Washington's State Hospital Commission are currently experimenting with the apportionment of budget method of prospective payment. Military and Veterans Administration hospitals and hospitals in a number of Canadian provinces essentially operate on fixed budgets set in advance of each operating year. Obviously, this approach to prospective payment provides an incentive to control both the cost per unit and volume of services provided, since both contribute to the total cost of operating an institution. In actual practice, provision would undoubtedly be made to adjust the budgeted cost figure agreed to for a hospital, if its actual costs or volume diverge substantially from its budgeted costs because of major, uncontrollable, unpredictable occurrences. It merits repeating, however, that automatically adjusting what a hospital is paid based on how it actually operates during the prospective year removes the incentive to control operations.

Departmental Budgets

The apportionment of departmental budgets method of prospective payment is similar, except that cost figures are set for individual departments, and each third party's payment responsibility is determined by the proportion of each department's services going to its patients. The advantage of this approach is the "fine tuning" it makes possible in focusing financial incentives on specific areas of operation. In addition, it allows the elimination of departments over which the administrator has little or no control from prospective rate setting. Or, only the routine daily service and "hotel" cost centers might be included under the assumption that their costs are less influenced by changes in case mix, intensity of service, technology, etc., than the ancillary cost centers. The Connecticut Hospital Association has experimented with a modified version of the departmental budgets method in setting cost targets.

Capitation

The capitation method of prospective payment, as an approach to hospital vs. physician payment, would work best where hospitals are associated with or part of health plans or health maintenance organizations. Each hospital would agree to provide to the enrollees of the plan with which it is associated all needed hospital services in return for a fixed amount per person per year. Although it is conceivable that the capitation approach to payment could be used for hospitals not associated with health plans, this would require that groups of people in areas served by one or more hospitals identify themselves with specific hospitals that would accept responsibility for meeting their hospital needs. It is difficult to see how this would work in metropolitan areas. People do not identify directly with hospitals as they do with physicians, and so it would be difficult to determine which hospital was responsible for which people unless physicians were involved. Nevertheless, in a 1964 experiment conducted by Colorado Blue Cross in Yuma County, Colorado, the Plan made capitation payments to the two hospitals in the County which in turn agreed to provide all hospital services needed by Blue Cross subscribers. Yuma County is quite isolated, however, and each hospital's share of Blue Cross' business in the County was well known.

Per Case, Per Diem

Per case, per diem, or per specific services prospective rates are more familiar. The actual determination of per unit rates can be done by dividing approved budgeted costs by expected volume, or by asking hospitals to propose rate structures that will generate just enough revenue to cover approved budgeted costs at expected volumes, or by applying some sort of formula to project historical costs forward into prospective rates or to translate hospital and patient workload characteristics into prospective rates. The only operating per case rate prospective payment program is an experiment being conducted by Blue Cross of Northeastern Pennsylvania with two hospitals in Wilkes-Barre. However, Phase IV of the Economic Stabilization Program, which of course was never implemented because of the termination of the program, would have employed as its basic cost control mechanism a limit of 7.5 percent on annual increases in revenue per case. In the prospective rate setting programs sponsored by Blue Cross plans, choice of a payment unit generally follows the approach to reimbursement that the plan used before. Thus, plans that reimbursed costs tend to set per diem prospective rates, and plans that paid billed charges tend to set specific services rates.

Specific Services

A practical advantage of using specific services as the bases of payment is that services represent a common denominator applicable to all purchasers of hospital services—Blue Cross, commercial insurance, self-pay patients, Medicare, Medicaid, etc. Third parties reimbursing hospitals' all-inclusive per diem costs tend to prefer per diem prospective rates. However, it would be inappropriate to charge individual self-pay patients average per diem rates, since some would end up paying for much more service than they actually used and some for less. Therefore, either a dual rate structure would be required to satisfy third parties and individual self-pay patients, or all purchasers would have to agree on specific services as the basis of payment. State commissions, concerned about getting all purchasers to pay the same rates for the same services, seem to favor specific services rates, and several commissions have attempted to get Medicare and Medicaid to waive their cost reimbursement regulations and agree to pay the rates they set. Another advantage of specific service rates is that they permit the costs of similar services to be compared across hospitals. This might encourage patients and physicians to give costs more weight in choosing hospitals. It has also been suggested that third parties might use this information to make co-payment and deductible payments by patients dependent on the costliness of the hospitals they use.

A disadvantage of specific services rates is that hospitals charge for hundreds of services, and a detailed review of the "reasonableness" of each rate is impossible. In practice, prospective rate setting agencies and programs typically review budgeted costs, not rates. Once a hospital's budget is agreed upon, the hospital is asked to propose a rate structure that will generate just enough revenue to cover its approved budget at its expected volume (perhaps adhering to certain guidelines; for example, that rates be set such that each patient service department comes within specified parameters of breaking even). Presumably, the commission would check the hospital's financial reports at the end of the year to determine if the rates proposed by the hospital and approved by the commission did in fact generate only the allowed revenue. Despite this shortcut (i.e., elimination of reviews of hundreds of individual rates), some commissions are beginning to consider requesting that all hospitals under their jurisdiction use a considerably simplified, uniform rate structure.

Impact of Prospective Rate Setting on Hospital Operation

The impact a prospective rate setting system is likely to have on hospitals depends in large part on the basis of payment used, because the incentives posed by the different payment units differ. The areas of hospital operation that might be affected by prospective reimbursement can be identified a priori by considering the factors that determine costs in hospitals. The following is proposed as a complete although general list of these cost-influencing factors.

1. Cases treated
2. Case mix
3. Length of stay
4. Intensity of service
5. Scope of service
6. Amenity level
7. Quality level
8. Efficiency
9. Input prices
10. Investment in the improvement or maintenance of human and physical resources
11. Teaching programs

It is proposed that hospitals must act through these variables in attempting to keep their costs below their perspective rates. Further, given the payment unit used by a prospective rate setting system, the changes in these areas of operation that might be expected to occur can be predicted. It should be emphasized, however, that these predictions are based on the assumption that prospective payment is the only constraint or incentive to which hospitals must respond. Clearly, other goals and pressures affect hospitals; therefore, the predictions proposed may not hold in any particular situation.

Table 8-8 shows the changes in the areas of operation expected to occur under the different payment units. The payment units are ordered from the most aggregate to the most specific. It is important to note that hospital revenue under the first three payment units is not directly related to output, since once the amount to be paid is set for the prospective year, it does not vary with the actual quantity of services provided in that year. Under the other three payment units, which are in effect different measures of output, hospital revenue is directly related to output.

As Table 8-8 shows, the total budget, departmental budgets, or capitation bases of payment discourage increases in *cases treated* and *lengths of stay* because these methods of payment do not link the amounts hospitals are paid to the number of patients admitted or days of care provided. Hospitals might attempt to admit more selectively and to discharge patients sooner to alternative facilities or to their homes. Depending on the adequacy of payment for out-of-hospital services, hospitals might develop pre-admission testing, outpatient surgery, outpatient diagnostic and treatment services, and home care programs to prevent or shorten hospitalizations.

In addition to the incentive to reduce admissions and patient days, these bases of payment provide an incentive for hospitals to contain increases in per unit costs by changing the mix of patients treated and by changing the nature of the services provided them. Hospitals might admit fewer complex or serious case types, thereby shifting toward a less costly *case-mix*. Hospitals might discontinue (or delay adding) costly programs and services, thereby reducing the *scope of service* they offer. These actions tend to reinforce each other. Hospitals might also curtail the *amenity level, quality level,* and *intensity of service* they provide. An incentive exists for hospitals to improve *efficiency*, both by increasing input productivity and by shifting toward a less costly input mix. Assuming that hospitals have some buying power, an incentive exists to resist increases in *input prices*. An incentive also exists to reduce *investments in human and physical resources*. Cuts might be made in programs designed to improve employee

Table 8-8 Expected Changes in Hospital Performance under Alternative Payment Units

	Areas of Performance (Cost-Influencing Variables)										
Payment Unit	Cases Treated	Length of Stay[1]	Complexity of Case-Mix[2]	Intensity of Service[1]	Scope of Service	Amenity Level	Quality Level	Efficiency	Input Prices	Investment in Resources	Teaching Programs
Total hospital budget	↓	↓	↓	↓	↓	↓	↓	↑	↓	↓	↓
Departmental budgets	↓	↓	↓	↓	↓	↓	↓	↑	↓	↓	↓
Family or person (capitation)	↓	↓	↓	↓	↓	↓	↓	↑	↓	↓	↓
Case or stay	↑	↓	↓	↓	↓	↓	↓	↑	↓	↓	↓
Day	↑	↑	↓	↓	↓	↓	↓	↑	↓	↓	↓
Specific services	↑	↑[3]	↑	↑	↑	↓	↓	↑	↓	↓	↓

[1]It is assumed that intensity of service and length of stay are not substitutes (i.e., hospitals do not have to increase intensity in order to discharge patients sooner). Underlying this assumption is the belief that reductions in lengths of stay would come from the last few days of hospitalization, which are primarily convalescent.

[2]Admissions and case-mix are interrelated in that the case types that would be denied admission if admissions were reduced would be the least complex. Therefore, the case-mix of hospitalized patients that would result would include a higher proportion of more complex case types. At the same time, however, a hospital could attempt to select easier case types whenever possible.

[3]The direction of change in length of stay depends on the occupancy level. If a hospital is operating at high occupancy and has patients waiting for admission, payment on a per service basis should cause it to discharge patients sooner (reducing the average length of stay) in order to substitute patients requiring the more service-intensive first few days of hospitalization. Hospitals operating at low occupancy could both admit more patients and increase the length of stay to increase the quantity of services produced. The direction of change indicated is based on the observation that hospitals have extra or unfilled beds much of the time.

*Reprinted with minor modifications from Dowling, W.L. "Prospective Reimbursement of Hospitals." *Inquiry* 11:3 (Sept. 1974).

morale and productivity and in programs designed to prevent deterioration of equipment and physical plant (although such actions would tend to increase costs in the long run). Finally, an incentive exists to curtail *teaching programs,* both because of the direct expenditures involved, and because of the indirect impact of these programs on case-mix, intensity of service, and scope of service.

The overall effect of using any of these bases of payment in a prospective rate setting system should be to discourage increases in both the quantity and cost per unit of hospital services, so that increases in aggregate costs should be slowed.

In contrast, the overall effect on aggregate costs of using any of the output-related bases of payment—cases, days, or specific services—cannot be predicted, since they simultaneously motivate hospitals (1) to increase output (both to directly increase revenue and to spread fixed costs over more units of output to reduce the average cost per unit); and (2) to contain increases in the cost per unit of output, by containing the amenity level, quality level, intensity, and scope of service provided; by increasing efficiency; and by containing input prices, investments in resources, and teaching programs.

Specifically, payment of a fixed amount per case would motivate hospitals to admit more patients, but, if possible, to admit less complex case types, to shorten stays, and to reduce the intensity and scope of services provided. Payment of a fixed amount per day would motivate hospitals to increase the days of care provided, by increasing admissions and lengths of stay, and to shift from more costly to less costly days by admitting less complex case types and by reducing the intensity and scope of services provided. Payment of fixed amounts for specific services (e.g., nursing care, laboratory tests, surgical procedures, x-rays, etc.) would motivate hospitals to provide more services by increasing admissions and lengths of stay to increase the number of patients requiring services, and by increasing the intensity of service provided. In contrast to the other payment units, hospitals might attempt to admit the more complex case types, since they need the most services.

Figures 8-8 and 8-9 contrast the incentives inherent in the output-related and non-output-related bases of payment. Figure 8-8 illustrates the situation of a hypothetical hospital operating under prospective per case, per day, or per specific service rates. TC_b represents the hospital's approved budgeted costs, TR_{pr} the rev-

Health Care Financing   341

Figure 8-8 Prospective Per Case, Day or Specific Service Rates

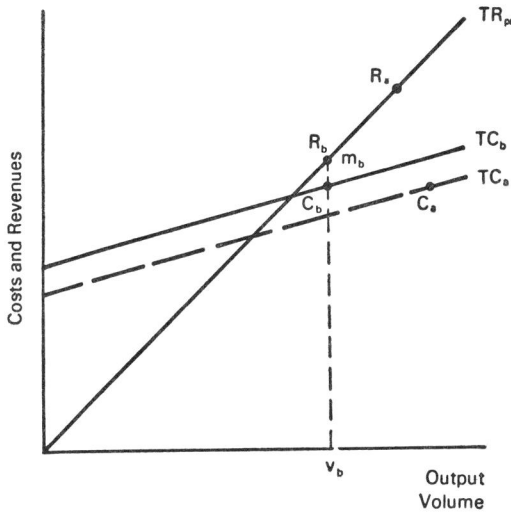

Figure 8-9 Prospective Total Budget Payment Program

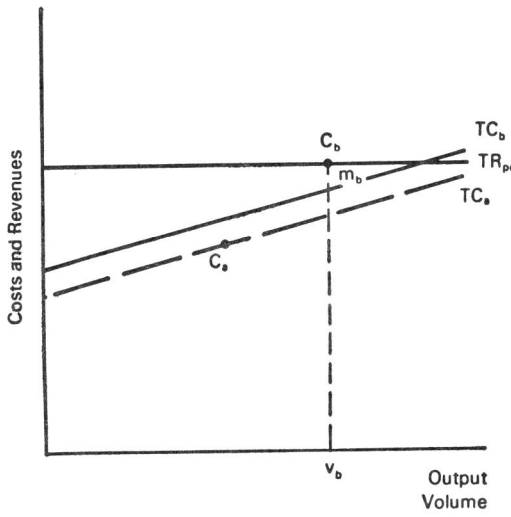

enue the hospital's prospective rates will generate at different volumes, m_b the agreed to operating margin, and v_b the expected volume. Since TR_{pr} depends directly on volume, an incentive exists to increase volume or at least to keep it from falling below v_b. In addition, an incentive exists to contain costs (as represented by TC_a), whatever the volume. Both actions act to increase the operating margin. Since increases in volume increase costs while cost containment efforts reduce them, it cannot be predicted whether actual total costs C_a will be above or below budgeted total costs C_b. It is quite possible, however, for actual revenue R_a (which is equivalent to patient and third party outlays) to exceed budgeted revenue R_b.

Figure 8-9 illustrates the situation of a hypothetical hospital operating under a prospective total budget payment program. TC_b represents the hospital's approved budgeted costs and TR_{pr} its guaranteed total revenue, set so as to provide an agreed upon operating margin m_b at the expected volume v_b. Since TR_{pr} does not depend on volume, an incentive exists to reduce volume or keep it from rising above v_b. A cost containment incentive TC_a also exists. Since both actions act to reduce costs, actual total costs C_a should be below budgeted total costs C_b. It is not possible for actual revenue to exceed budgeted revenue, since the approved budget figure is all the hospital will be paid.

All of the output related payment units then provide an incentive for hospitals to increase output, and this might be reinforced by long-run goals of growth and prestige. Of concern, of course, is whether inappropriate use would result. It should be emphasized that no payment unit is without potential negative impacts, and this is a dilemma that must be faced in designing prospective rate setting systems. It appears that controls over quality and utilization may assume more importance as cost containment incentives are introduced. Another approach would be to aim additional financial incentives directly at certain areas of operation; for example, by directly rewarding hospitals for reducing their average length of stay.

In summary, hospitals can attempt to contain costs in different ways. The actions hospitals are likely to take under prospective rate setting systems will depend on the basis of payment used. Selection of the payment unit, therefore, depends on how one wishes to change hospital performance. Hospitals could be left free to respond as best fits their situation, or additional controls could be applied to influence their responses. Hospital preferences for the different payment units would depend in part on their expectations about future use. If an increase in use is expected, the output related payment units would be preferred; if a decrease is expected, the budget or capitation payment units would be preferred. The magnitudes of the changes in operations predicted to occur under prospective rate setting depend on several factors:

1. The tightness of the prospective rates. Obviously, if hospitals must take extreme measures to maintain their financial viability, changes would be greater than if the rates were more "reasonable."
2. The firmness of the prospective rates. If rates are adjusted for actual volume or for changes in case-mix, input prices, etc., the impact of prospective rate setting would be moderated.
3. The size of potential rewards or penalties. This depends on the proportion of any difference between actual costs and prospective rates that hospitals are at risk for and on the proportion of their patients covered by prospective payment. Also, if hospitals are able to offset potential losses by increasing charges to self pay patients, the influence of prospective rate setting would be moderated.
4. The present state of hospital performance. Admissions or lengths of stay, for example, might decrease more under the appropriate payments units in hospitals where inappropriate use is occurring than in those where there is little overuse.
5. The disposition of physicians toward cooperating with hospital cost containment efforts. Admissions, case-mix, length of stay, etc., depend largely on decisions made by physicians; and therefore, changes in the medically related areas of operation require their support.

● ● ●

Dowling goes on to detail some of the administrative and technical problems associated with prospective rate setting. He concludes that:

Despite the problems, prospective rate setting appears to have considerable potential. . . . It should lead to better budgeting, planning, cost-finding, and cost control. It should make cash flow and revenue more predictable. It may provide a basis for straightening out differences in payment among different third parties.

Perhaps most important, it gives administrators and financial managers a clear mandate to attack the cost problems in their institutions.[14]

In 1976, when Dowling wrote, it indeed appeared that prospective rate setting was just over the horizon. Some 35 systems were then in operation and several more were in the planning stages. In 1981, we still are looking forward to the "potential" of prospective rating. The number of systems has increased over the last five years, but at a modest rate. New Jersey and Georgia, for example, were experimenting with a new system of hospital payment based on "diagnostic related groupings" (DRGs). On the other hand, a sunset decision in Colorado allowed that state's hospital rate-setting commission to go out of business.

For a time, emphasis and energy was focused on national solutions, particularly former President Carter's hospital cost control bill, which urged prospective revenue limitations as the next logical step after rate setting. The lopsided failure of hospital cost containment legislation suggests that the proposed solutions have overshot the problem, at least as perceived by important policymakers.

The present climate appears to favor consolidation and retrenchment rather than new political experiments in cost control and reimbursement design. Even among academic economists, caution seems to have replaced an earlier enthusiasm for new regulatory ventures. The recent theoretical work of Sloan and Steinwald, for example, suggests that economists such as Dowling may have been too sanguine in their predictions of hospital behavior under alternative reimbursement schemes.[15] The earlier discussion here of the implications arising from bilateral market power would support this view. But while such thoughts may provide solace to those who seek to maintain the status quo, it will not necessarily be maintained. Lack of knowledge can just as easily lead to impulsive and misguided policy. The fact that economists disagree on policy prescriptions is not news to readers of this book. It simply sweetens the challenge ahead.

NOTES

1. R. Gibson, "National Health Expenditures, 1978," *Health Care Financing Review* 1, no. 1 (Summer 1979): 26.
2. *Ibid.*
3. M. Freeland, G. Calat, and C. Schendler, "Projections of National Health Expenditures, 1980, 1985, and 1990," *Health Care Financing Review* 1, no. 3 (Winter 1980): 17.
4. M. Carroll and R. Arnett, "Private Health Insurance Plans in 1977: Coverage, Enrollment, and Financial Experience," *Health Care Financing Review* 1, no. 2 (Fall 1979): 20.

5. *Ibid.*
6. *Ibid.*, p. 18.
7. *Ibid.*, p. 20.
8. Gibson, p. 32.
9. For an explanation of the analysis and geometry leading to this conclusion see E. Mansfield, *Microeconomics: Theory and Applications* (New York: W. W. Norton & Co., Inc., 1970), pp. 85–88.
10. To see how insurance might induce a shift in the supply curve of a nonprofit hospital, consider the following scenario. Assume the hospital has a multiple objective function with elements relating to quantity, quality, and service intensity. Assume also that the facility has no preinsurance expansion plans and is content to break even on costs and revenues. The hospital's expenditures on inputs (costs) reflect the balancing of objectives necessary to maintain internal equilibrium within the facility. Production is carried out to the point where average cost (AC) equals average revenue (AR), thus assuring neither profit nor loss. With increased insurance coverage, the demand curve (which also is the average revenue curve) shifts outward and becomes more inelastic. How will this facility respond? If the only objective were to maximize quantity of output, the hospital simply would move along its AC curve to a new break-even point with AR. In that case AC would be the supply curve. But what of the other objectives? If quality and service intensity are important objectives, the hospital might maintain current output levels, raise patient charges, and earn a surplus (profit) to be used later to buy new equipment or renovate the facility. In this instance, the AC (supply) curve would shift upward because of the new expenditures, thereby resulting in a new break-even point consistent with the higher level of charges. This same result would occur if the facility decided to reward labor with higher wages or increase the degree of administrative slack (e.g., accept lower worker productivity). As long as there are multiple objectives, and some of them are cost inducing, the hospital will shift its supply curve in response to insurance coverage.
11. H. Frech and P. Ginsburg, "Competition Among Health Insurers," in W. Greenberg, ed. *Competition in the Health Care Sector: Past, Present, and Future* (Germantown, Md.: Aspen Systems Corporation, 1978), p. 169.
12. I. Burney, G. Schieber, M. Blaxall, and J. Gabel, "Medicare and Medicaid Physician Payment Incentives," *Health Care Financing Review* 1, no. 1 (Summer 1979), p. 63.
13. There is a catch here. As noted, no third party will pay billed charges that exceed the practitioner's current charge to noninsured patients. In other words, for higher billed charges to be reimbursed, the practitioner must raise fees to all patients. From the practitioner's standpoint this means that future revenue generated from higher charges to insured patients must be balanced against possible revenue losses resulting from reduced demand on behalf of noninsured patients.
14. W. Dowling, "Prospective Rate Setting: Concept and Practice," *Topics in Health Care Financing* 3, no. 2 (Winter 1976), p. 35.
15. F. Sloan and B. Steinwald, *Insurance Regulation and Hospital Costs* (Lexington, Mass.: Lexington Books, D.C. Heath and Company, 1980), p. 34.

SUGGESTED READINGS

Berry, Ralph. "Prospective Rate Reimbursement and Cost Containment: Formula Reimbursement in New York." *Inquiry* 13, no. 3 (September 1976): 288–301.

Dickerson, O. D. *Health Insurance,* 3rd ed. Homewood, Ill.: Richard D. Irwin, Inc., 1968.

Dowling, William, ed. "Prospective Rate Setting." *Topics in Health Care Financing* 3, no. 2 (Winter 1976).

Feder, Judith; Holahan, John; and Marmor, Theodore, eds. *National Health Insurance: Conflicting Goals and Policy Choices.* Washington, D.C.: The Urban Institute, 1980, pp. 73–128, 301–348.

Feldstein, Paul, and Goddeens, John. "Payment for Hospital Services: Objectives and Alternatives." *Health Care Management Review* 2 (Fall 1977).

Holahan, John; Spitz, Bruce; Pollak, William; and Feder, Judith. "Altering Medicaid Provider Reimbursement Methods." Washington, D.C.: The Urban Institute, 1977.

Krisay, John, and Wilson, Andrew. *The Patient as Consumer: Health Care Financing in the United States.* Lexington, Mass.: Lexington Books, D.C. Heath and Company, 1974.

Pauly, Mark. "Efficiency, Incentives, and Reimbursement for Health Care." *Inquiry* 7, no. 1 (March 1970): 114–131.

Ruchlin, Hirsch, and Rosen, Harry. "Short-Run Hospital Responses to Reimbursement Rate Changes." *Inquiry* 17, no. 1 (Spring 1980): 54–61.

Sloan, Frank, and Steinwald, Bruce. *Insurance, Regulation, and Hospital Costs.* Lexington, Mass.: Lexington Books, D.C. Heath and Company, 1980, pp. 11–40, 65–90.

Zubkoff, Michael; Raskin, Ira; and Hanft, Ruth, eds. *Hospital Cost Containment: Selected Notes for Future Policy.* New York: Prodist, 1978, pp. 324–400.

REFERENCES FOR BURNEY ET AL. EXCERPT

1. See M. A. Redisch, "Physician Involvement in Hospital Decision Making," in M. Zubkoff, I. Raskin and R. Hanft, *Hospital Cost Containment: Selected Notes for Future Policy* (New York: 1978); and J. R. Gabel and M. A. Redisch, "Alternative Physician Payment Methods: Incentives, Efficiency, and National Health Insurance," *Milbank Memorial Fund Quarterly/Health and Society,* 57, 1 (Winter 1979).

3. See F. Sloan and B. Steinwald, "The Role of Health Insurance in the Physician Services Market," *Inquiry,* 10, 4 (December 1975); United States Department of Health, Education, and Welfare, Social Security Administration, *A Report on the Results of the Study of Methods of Reimbursement of Physicians' Services Under Medicare* (SS Publication No. 92-73, (10–73), Washington, D.C., July, 1973); J. Holahan, "Physician Availability, Medical Care Reimbursement, and Delivery of Physician Services: Some Evidence From the Medicaid Program," *Journal of Human Resources,* X, 3 (Fall 1975); Z. Dyckman, *A Study of Physicians' Fees,* Council on Wage and Price Stability (Washington: 1978); J. Holahan, J. Hadley, W. Scanlon, R. Lee and J. Bluck, "Paying for Physician Services Under Medicare and Medicaid," *Milbank Memorial Fund Quarterly Health and Society,* 57, 2 (Spring, 1979).

4. As discussed below, this potential has been mitigated to a certain extent by the application of an Economic Index that limits the annual rate of increase in Medicare and Medicaid prevailing charges.

5. For example, these situations have been observed in certain provinces in Canada following the establishment of negotiated fee schedules for the National Health Insurance program. Although the composite Canadian physician fee index increased only 3.7 percent per year between 1969 and 1971, physicians' net incomes increased by 27.0 percent and per capita expenditures by 33.5 percent per year during that period. While

some of this increase is due to payment for services that previously were written off as bad debts, Lewin and Associates, *Government Controls on the Health Care Systems: The Canadian Experience,* HEW-OS-74-177 (Washington, D.C.: January, 1976) observed that there is a growing feeling that "many Canadian physicians have been increasingly manipulating the services they provide in light of the nature of the fee schedule in order to achieve their income goals."

6. F. Sloan, J. Cromwell and J. B. Mitchell, *A Study of Administrative Costs in Physicians' Offices and Medicaid Participation,* Final Report, Health Care Financing Administration, June 1977.
7. However, to the extent that the cost-sharing requirements in Blue Shield plans are less extensive than those in Medicare, the net value of the fee may be greater under Blue Shield since physicians' bad debt experience may be lower.
8. I. L. Burney, G. J. Schieber, M. O. Blaxall, and J. R. Gabel, "Geographic Variation in Physicians' Fees: Paying the Physician Under Medicare and Medicaid," *J. Am. Med. Assn.,* 240, 13 (September 22, 1978).
9. Further analysis of data collected by Sloan et al., op. cit.
10. L. Paringer, "The Medicare Assignment Rates of Physicians: Their Responses to Changes in Reimbursement Policy," Contract No. 600-76-0054, Health Care Financing Administration, March 1979.
11. Sloan et al., op. cit., pp. 205–244; J. Hadley and R. Lee, "An Econometric Analysis of Physician Participation in the Medicaid Program," Contract No. 600-76-0054, Health Care Financing Administration, April 1978; P. J. Held, L. M. Manheim, and J. Wooldridge, "Physician Acceptance of Medicaid Patients," Mathematica Policy Research Staff Paper SP-78B-02, August 30, 1978.
12. *Medicare and Medicaid Reimbursement Policies* (Washington, D.C.: Institute of Medicine and the National Academy of Sciences, March 1976), p. 229.
13. I. Burney and J. Gabel, "Reimbursement Patterns Under Medicare and Medicaid," Conference on Research Results from Physician Reimbursement Studies, Health Care Financing Administration, February 1978; I. Burney et al., op. cit.
14. Similar results were obtained for general practitioners. Medicaid results may be due to the use of State-wide areas for reimbursement purposes.
15. See C. Berry, R. Freiden, P. Held, and J. Wooldridge, "Abstract from Report on the Physician, Capacity Utilization Telephone Surveys," unpublished paper (Princeton: Mathematica, Inc., May 1976); M. S. Blumberg, "Physician Visits Per Week and Price Per Visit," unpublished paper, April 25, 1977; and J. R. Cantwell, "A Cross Sectional Econometric Analysis of Physician Location and Pricing," paper presented at the Midwestern Economic Association (April 1976).
16. G. J. Schieber, I. L. Burney, J. B. Golden, and W. J. Knaus, "Physician Fee Patterns Under Medicare: A Descriptive Analysis," *New Engl. J. Med.* 294, 1089 (May 13, 1976).
17. Medical visit times are from U. E. Reinhardt, *Physician Productivity and the Demand for Health Manpower: An Economic Analysis* (Cambridge, Massachusetts: Ballinger Publishing Company, 1975), p. 157.
18. Operating room times were obtained from E. F. X. Hughes, V. R. Fuchs, J. E. Jacoby and E. M. Lewitt, "Surgical Workloads in a Community Practice," *Surgery,* 71, 317 (Mar. 1972) for five surgical procedures common to both the Medicare and Medicaid fee surveys and Hughes et al. Hourly equivalent fees were calculated by converting the operating room times into hours (e.g., 89.4 minutes = 1.49 hours) and dividing

national average Medicare and Medicaid fees for the procedures by the hourly operating room time. The same methodology was used with medical visit times from Reinhardt, op. cit., to calculate hourly equivalent medical visit fees.

19. One pre-operative hospital visit, one post-operative hospital visit per day and one biweekly post hospital discharge visit up to the total period of care specified in the procedure coding manual of the California Medical Association, *1964 Relative Value Study* (San Francisco, California, 1964) was used. Medicare lengths of stay data come from U.S. Social Security Administration, Office of Research and Statistics, *Medicare Health Insurance for the Aged, 1970: Length of Stay by Diagnosis* (Washington, D.C., 1973).
20. W. B. Stason and W. C. Hsiao, "Toward Developing a Relative Value Scale for Medical and Surgical Services Based on Resource Costs," Contract No. 600-76-0058, Health Care Financing Administration, January 31, 1979.
21. See M. S. Blumberg, "Rational Provider Prices: An Incentive for Improved Health Delivery," in G. K. Chacko, ed., *Health Handbook, 1978* (Amsterdam, The Netherlands: 1978) for similar results.

SOURCES AND PERMISSIONS

a. Source: Reprinted from "Medicare and Medicaid Physician Payment Incentives" by Ira Burney et al., by permission of *Health Care Financing Review* 1, no. 1 (Summer 1979): 62–78.
b. Reprinted from "Prospective Rate Setting: Concept and Practice" by William Dowling, *Topics in Health Care Financing* 3, no. 2 (Winter 1976): 9–10, 11–15, 19–27, by permission of Aspen Systems, Inc., Copyright © 1976.

Chapter 9

Industrial Organization

Full understanding of a firm's behavior requires some attention to the competitive environment of the market in which it operates. As mentioned in Chapter 2, theoretical price competition implies many small firms producing identical products. In such an industry, firms individually have no market power, that is, they cannot control price and must simply sell at the price determined by supply and demand. A competitive industry serves the consumer well in that its prices will equal the cost of production and output will be at the socially optimal level. Theoretical monopoly, on the other hand, is the case where a firm has total market power. In the short run, before rivals might enter the industry, the monopolistic firm can set price at any level it desires since there are no firms selling highly substitutable products to which the consumer may turn to escape the high price. Monopoly results in allocative inefficiency because the profit-maximizing monopolist will restrict output and raise price in relation to the output and price that would be realized under perfect competition.

Real industries in the economy, including those in the health care sector, correspond exactly to neither the pure competition nor the pure monopoly model, but rather lie somewhere on the continuum between them. *Oligopoly* denotes an industry with a few large rivals that recognize their independence. It is in this kind of situation that many of the most interesting and important patterns of economic interaction are found. Industrial organization is the area of economics that attempts to understand the relationships concerning the structure of an industry, the nature of the competitive interaction among the firms in it, and the resulting economic performance.

In this chapter, the importance of these relationships is demonstrated in the context of the hospital and drug industries. However, before turning to these industries, it is useful to review an analytical framework that economists have developed to conduct industrial organization studies. The framework is the so-called structure-conduct-performance approach. Its central hypothesis is that the structure of an industry is a major determinant of firms' behavior, which in turn explains the industry's economic performance.

THE STRUCTURE-CONDUCT-PERFORMANCE APPROACH

The size distribution of firms in an industry is a key element of *market structure*. An industry dominated by a small number of relatively big firms is a likely candidate for market power problems. It should be emphasized that it is size of firm in relation to the market that is relevant, not simply absolute size. Thus, in determining market structure, the definition of a market in geographical and product terms is very important. For example, a 100-bed hospital is not big compared to most health facilities in the United States, but if it is the only one in an isolated community, it is a monopolist in that market for hospital services.

Another very important element of market structure is condition of entry. If it is easy to enter an industry, market power cannot persist in the long run. The existence of high profits will induce firms to enter the industry; this increased supply will lead to a price drop and eventually erode the position of market power. Many things can act as a barrier to entry, however. Often there is a legal barrier, such as where a monopoly position is based on patent ownership. Another entry barrier particularly common in the health sector is government licensing. Entry to the hospital industry, the nursing home industry, and almost any profession that provides health care services depends on obtaining a government license. There is the potential that this licensing requirement can serve as an entry barrier to protect the market power of firms or people already in the industry.

Whether the licensing authority acts this way in any particular case is, of course, a matter for empirical investigation. Whatever the specific situation, in the terminology of the model at the start of Chapter 5, the economic constraint of limited competition can be influenced by legal constraints, such as regulations. Other aspects of market structure involve the cost conditions of the industry, including the extent of scale economies; the degree of diversification of firms among different product lines; the extent to which products of one are differentiated in the minds of consumers from those of others; and the number and size distribution of buyers.

Conduct refers to the behavior of firms toward one another as well as toward suppliers, employees, and customers. A major aspect of conduct is pricing policy. Often in an oligopoly there is a strong incentive for firms to cooperate in pricing and to act jointly in setting the figure at a monopoly level. Price-fixing agreements are illegal under United States antitrust laws but behavior patterns short of explicit agreement can have similar effects and often skirt the border of illegality.

Price discrimination means charging different prices for the same good or service where the variations in price are not related to differences in the cost of production or distribution. For example, a drug firm may have one set of prices for hospital pharmacies and another for nonhospital buyers. An extreme case of price discrimination is charging a different price to each customer. This is possible where the thing being sold is a personal service, such as medical care. Price discrimination raises questions of equity as well as economic efficiency. Under most circumstances it is socially harmful and can result in an antitrust violation. But there may be exceptions. For instance, many would argue that the price-discriminating surgeon who performs operations free for poor persons while charging a high price for the same operation to those who can better afford it is deserving of praise rather than condemnation.

Another important aspect of conduct that often is quite controversial is advertising and promotion. Advertising tends to draw fire when it is seen to be manipulative, misleading, or excessive. This is particularly likely where the advertised product involves questions of health. Examples of this are the advertising and labeling of cigarettes and television advertising to children for presweetened cereals. On the other hand, for the market to work well buyers must have adequate information about products, prices, and sources of supply. Advertising is one way of disseminating such information. It has been alleged that professional or trade association bans on advertising have contributed to a lack of price competition and have served as an entry barrier to the industry, resulting in increased market power and decreased consumer welfare. Examples in the health care sector include advertising by physicians and of eyeglass and retail drug prices advertising. Other aspects of conduct important in some industries are product style change, types of sale, lease or franchise contract, repair and service policy, and legal tactics.

Evaluation of *performance* involves a judgment about the industry's overall economic effect on society. Dimensions of performance that are used frequently are efficiency, technological progressiveness, product safety and quality, and income distribution effects. One indicator of performance is profit. In perfect competition, price is at the level of cost so profit is very low. Monopolies on the other hand set price above cost with resultant high profits. This suggests that high profits in an industry may be symptomatic of market power and poor performance with respect to allocative efficiency. This conclusion must be qualified somewhat, since there may be other reasons for high profits, at least to some firms in an industry on a short-run basis. For example, high profits that represent a reward to research and development and the associated risk taking in search of innovation or profits that are present because of rapid demand growth do not indicate poor performance.

Evaluation of performance may require subjective judgments. What is the socially "best" performance with respect to technological innovation? There is no very good measure to guide such a judgment. The quality as well as the quantity of innovations are important in addition to the way they are used. Technological change has revolutionized the practice of medicine, but there are questions raised about the cost-effectiveness and necessity of use of some of the new technologies. (Some of those matters are discussed in the next chapter.) What should an industry's effect on the distribution of income be? It very much depends on what values people hold concerning desirable patterns of income distribution. In evaluation of performance, it is necessary to be particularly conscious of the fact that normative economics is involved.

Government policy plays a major role in influencing the structure, conduct, and performance of industry. The antitrust laws as well as regulation by the Federal Trade Commission and federal authorities in the areas of health and safety apply to all industries. Other federal regulation is specific to such industries as electric power, transportation, banking, and insurance. The health sector, of course, is regulated by governments at all levels from federal to local. Such regulation affects performance both through its effect on structure (such as entry barriers) and conduct (such as pricing and reimbursement policies). One goal of industrial organization analysis is to help policymakers predict the ultimate effects of such policies on the industry. It is illustrated below. Explaining the adoption of regulations also might be of interest, but lies outside the scope of this book.[1]

The rest of this chapter presents two examples of industry studies in the health sector. The first selection discusses arguments for government regulation of for-profit hospitals. The second examines some of the controversial issues involving the pharmaceutical industry.

REGULATION OF FOR-PROFIT HOSPITALS

Two segments of the hospital industry that are in competition with each other are nonprofit and for-profit facilities. The latter represent a relatively fast-growing part of the industry. The nature of the relationship between profit and nonprofit hospitals has been the subject of considerable controversy and some research. The following article by William D. White reviews the issues from the standpoint of regulatory policy that might affect forprofit hospitals. This selection is illustrative of some of the many uses of industrial organization analyses for understanding the behavior and performance of health care institutions.

REGULATING COMPETITION IN A NONPROFIT INDUSTRY: THE PROBLEM OF FORPROFIT HOSPITALS[a]

The American hospital industry is dominated by nonprofit institutions. Nonetheless, there exists a small number of forprofit hospitals.[1] These hospitals presumably maximize profits. The motives of nonprofit hospitals are not completely clear. Traditionally they have enjoyed a quasi-public utility status and, at least in theory, pursue socially desirable goals such as providing care to patients who cannot afford to pay for hospital services. The literature on the behavior of nonprofit hospitals suggests that size and status considerations and the welfare of staff physicians also may play an important role in determining the actions of these institutions.[2] However, even if nonprofit hospitals may not always try to maximize social welfare, they have played an important historical role in activities like providing subsidized care for the needy. In contrast, forprofit hospitals usually avoid providing any subsidized care unless they are forced into it by social and political constraints.[3]

To the extent that nonprofit hospitals seek objectives other than that of profit maximization, they may adopt pricing and investment policies that make them potentially vulnerable to competition from forprofit hospitals. Assuming that they do this for socially desirable reasons, this raises a basic public policy question. Should the government protect nonprofit hospitals from this kind of competition by regulating the pricing and investment behavior of forprofit hospitals?

For many years, the number of forprofit hospitals was declining in the United States and the question of regulating them did not seem like a particularly important issue. But during the last ten years, there has been a rapid growth in forprofit hospital chains, while public and private subsidies to nonprofit hospitals, which in the past have tended to give them a competitive advantage over forprofit hospitals, have been declining.[4] Meanwhile, the growth of certificate-of-need regulation, designed to limit new investments in hospital facilities, has forced policy-makers to make choices between permitting forprofit and nonprofit hospitals to expand. As a result, there has been a good deal of debate over the relative merits of the two types of hospitals and their ability to serve the needs of the communities involved.

Unfortunately, arguments in this debate have tended to be fragmented. Most empirical studies look at specific differences between forprofit and nonprofit hospitals in case mix, quality of care, and cost, rather than the impact of forprofit hospitals on the overall welfare of the consumer.[5] Critics of forprofit hospitals focus on quality and equity issues. They complain that these institutions engage in "unfair" competitive practices such as "cream skimming" (admitting patients on a selective basis that reflects their ability to pay and the ease with which they can be treated, rather than their need for medical care). They also argue that forprofit hospitals deliver less sophisticated care than nonprofit hospitals and may be tempted to lower the quality of services in order to increase their earnings. Supporters of forprofit hospitals emphasize the cost side of the picture and the advantages of free markets. They argue that forprofit hospitals are more efficient than nonprofit hospitals and suggest that increased competition in the industry could keep down the rising cost of hospital care.

Because of this piecemeal approach, it is often easy to lose sight of the underlying issues in the debate and focus on details like differences in case mix. The purpose of this paper is to try to clarify the debate by presenting the main theoretical arguments for regulation of competition by forprofit hospitals on a systematic basis using simple economic models. While a full empirical analysis is beyond the scope of this paper, we will briefly consider the relevance of these arguments to current conditions in the industry and employ this discussion to suggest a number of potentially useful areas for future research.

The discussion that follows is divided into three parts. The first section briefly describes the existing structure of the hospital industry and addresses the prospects for change in the industry. The second section develops models of the behavior of nonprofit hospitals and the possible impact of competition by forprofit hospitals. These models are then used to consider the main theoretical arguments for regulating forprofit hospitals. The section also discusses the relevance of these theoretical arguments under current industry conditions. The final section summarizes our conclusions and suggests areas for future research.

In the models considered in this paper, nonprofit hospitals encounter problems with competition from forprofit hospitals because, for charitable reasons, they voluntarily deviate from profit maximizing behavior. But many of the problems of nonprofit hospitals are analogous to problems encountered with competition in regulated industries where prices are set by the government. Examples include the problems of licensed carriers with unlicensed carriers in various areas of the transportation industry as well as those of the post office with private firms which also wish to carry mail. Economists have long been interested in the problems of setting prices in regulated industries, and the discussion that follows draws extensively on the marginal cost-pricing literature.[6] At the same time, this paper may provide some insights into the problem of dealing with competition in regulated industries.

Industry Characteristics

Expenditures on hospital services account for nearly half of all expenditures on health in the United States. They have attracted widespread attention not only because of their absolute magnitude, but also because of their rapid rate of increase in price, which is now around 15% a year.

On the supply side of the market for hospital services, individual institutions tend to be small and the industry is highly decentralized. Unlike many public utilities, there is little evidence of economies of scale in hospitals above fairly low-level output, and there is no real argument for regulating them because they are natural monopolies.

On the demand side of the market, equity considerations and insurance arrangements play an important role in determining the demand for hospital services. There is a strong social preference in this country for assuring that some sort of minimum level of hospital services is available to individuals who are seriously ill, regardless of their ability to pay. In the past, most of this type of care was provided directly by public or private nonprofit hospitals in the form of free or subsidized services. More recently, the government has begun to subsidize purchases of medical care directly through programs like Medicare and Medicaid. However, there are a number of gaps in these programs and there are still significant groups in the population who have little or no access to medical care.

Over time, the demand for hospital services can fluctuate a good deal for individuals and for the industry as a whole, and these fluctuations can be difficult to predict. For example, an individual may fall ill at any time, while a natural disaster or a major accident can sharply increase the total demand for hospital services with little or no warning. Since hospital services must be consumed as they are produced and speed is often critical in determining the value of these services to consumers, there is a strong incentive to maintain a high level of peak-load capacity in the industry to meet regular fluctuations in demand and unexpected emergencies. Difficulties in predicting demand also create an incentive for individuals to purchase insurance, and approximately 90% of Americans now have some form of hospitalization insurance.

Under existing insurance programs, patients' out-of-pocket expenditures on hospital services tend to be low and they bear only a small part of the total cost. Critics of this system, such as Martin Feldstein, argue that it is largely responsible for the rapid increase in hospital costs because it does not create any incentive for patients to try to hold down hospital expenditures.[7] At the same time, these critics emphasize that many Americans do not have adequate insurance against major medical expenditures and some have no coverage at all. They call for an overhaul of the existing insurance system not only to contain costs, but also for equity reasons. . . .

Arguments for Regulation

Forprofit hospitals may be able to expand their market share at the expense of nonprofit hospitals if they can offer patients the same service at a lower price or a higher quality service at the same price. Arguments for regulation focus on three main types of practices that may make this possible: 1) price discrimination; 2) average cost-pricing; 3) not using least-cost techniques because of externalities. There also is a fourth point: Forprofit hospitals may be able to increase their market share if there are lags in the availability of capital to nonprofit hospitals, which do not adjust quickly to increases in the demand for hospital services.

The approach in this section is to discuss the importance of these four problems and examine arguments for regulation for each case in turn. Unfortunately, there has not been much empirical research in most of these areas and so our discussion is necessarily rather theoretical. For simplicity, we assume in this discussion that nonprofit hospitals can be treated as a group.[8] We also assume that forprofit and nonprofit hospitals are equally efficient and that there is no difference in the quality of the services they produce unless specifically stated otherwise.

Price Discrimination

Price discrimination occurs when producers charge different prices to different consumers for the same services. In the health industry this term is also used to refer to cross-subsidization where hospitals charge above cost for some types of services in order to generate profits to subsidize purchases of other types of services sold at below cost. Data in Table 9-1 suggest that this practice is widespread. As we can see from the table, hospitals have tended to consistently charge more than cost for services such as laboratory tests, operating room services and radiology services, while delivery room services are priced below cost.[9]

Table 9-1 Ratio of Patient Revenue to Direct Costs of Selected Ancillary Services, 1962–68

Year	Revenue/direct-cost ratios						
	OR	DR	AN	R	L	PT	PH
1962	1.43	0.97	1.62	1.37	1.70	1.27	2.12
1966	1.37	0.81	1.50	1.28	1.63	1.28	2.02
1967	1.39	0.95	1.89	1.86	1.98	1.21	2.13
1968	1.37	0.99	1.81	1.60	1.74	1.30	2.01
Average annual:							
1962–66	1.40	0.89	1.55	1.34	1.66	1.26	2.05
1967–68	1.38	0.97	1.85	1.73	1.86	1.26	2.07

Key: OR = Operating Room, DR = Delivery Room, AN = Anesthesiology, R = Radiology, L = Laboratory, PT = Physical Therapy, PH = Pharmacy.

Source: Davis, K., "Hospital Costs and the Medicare Program," *Social Security Bulletin* (August 1973), p. 26.

There are two main arguments for price discrimination. The first is that price discrimination may increase equity, the second that it may perform a quasi-insurance function. In the equity case, nonprofit hospitals may charge wealthy patients a premium for hospital services and use the profits from these services to subsidize purchases of services by less affluent individuals. For example, private hospital rooms, used mainly by financially better-off patients, may be priced above cost, while beds in wards used primarily by poorer patients may be priced below cost. Alternatively, as Hellenger suggests, hospitals may charge a premium for services such as diagnostic tests that generally tend to be covered by insurance, even for needy patients through programs like Medicare; these profits are then used to subsidize services that usually are not covered, such as obstetrical services.[10]

Now consider the possible impact of competition by forprofit hospitals. If patients who can pay are unwilling to bear the costs of subsidizing poor patients voluntarily, forprofit hospitals may be able to bid these patients away from nonprofit hospitals. One way they can do this is by offering lower prices. But, since most hospital care is paid through insurance, the demand for hospital services tends to be price inelastic. Even so, consumers may still be sensitive to changes in the quality of services. So may the physicians who act as patients' agents. This may encourage forprofit hospitals to compete with nonprofit hospitals by offering higher quality service at the same price, rather than lower prices. Better food, nicer rooms, and better staffing arrangements and technical services are all possible examples of quality improvements that could attract patients or physicians to forprofit hospitals.[11]

If this kind of quality competition occurs, we may not observe any direct price competition. Nevertheless, if forprofit hospitals are successful in attracting patients who have been paying for services at above cost, the only patients who will be left in nonprofit hospitals in this model are those who are either subsidized or who pay for services at cost. Unless funds are available from sources other than those based on price discrimination, nonprofit institutions will face two choices: Either they can continue to treat patients who cannot pay and go bankrupt, or they can begin treating only those patients who can pay the full cost of service.

The basic equity argument for regulation in this case is that some patients lack the resources to pay for hospital care and will not receive it unless nonprofit hospitals are able to generate revenues from price discrimination. In many ways, this is similar to the argument often made for expanding regulation in industries where regulation is used as a tax along the lines described by Posner.[12] For example, this kind of argument has been used to justify regulating outside competition in order to allow the post office to do things such as subsidizing rural mail service at the expense of urban patrons. The same argument also has been used to justify protecting regulated airlines and railroads from outside competition where trunk lines are used to subsidize feeder routes.

Based on the experiences of these industries, there are two main ways to use regulation to deal with competition. One is to ban competition completely. This is the approach used by the post office for first class mail. It has the advantage of being easy to administer. But it may not be politically feasible in the hospital industry and could remove a valuable source of innovation. A second approach is to regulate the quality and price of services that are sold by forprofit hospitals. This would allow forprofit hospitals to continue to exist. But it has the disadvantage of being difficult to administer.

Under a system of price regulation, any time the price of hospital services is set above cost, there will be strong competitive pressures for forprofit hospitals to find some way to improve the quality of the services they provide so that they can either attract patients directly from nonprofit hospitals or attract them indirectly by attracting their physicians, thereby making additional profits. Conversely, any time the price of a service is set below cost, there will be strong competitive pressures for forprofit hospitals either to try to avoid offering the service or, if they are forced to offer it, to depreciate the quality of the service they provide so that patients will prefer to go to nonprofit hospitals.

The second argument for protecting price discrimination is that it enables nonprofit hospitals to perform a quasi-insurance function. Rafferty and Schweitzer suggest that nonprofit hospitals may price services so that patients with small expenditures on hospital services help subsidize patients with major illnesses.[13] This kind of price discrimination will tend to reduce the cost of major illness, while increasing the cost of minor illnesses. In effect, it amounts to a form of compulsory insurance, since everyone using these hospitals is forced to participate.

Again, pricing some services above cost and others below cost may lead to a welfare loss as a result of the underutilization or overutilization of services. The argument for price discrimination in this case is that gains from insurance effects exceed any efficiency losses that result from distorting prices. The argument for regulation is that forprofit hospitals will bid away all of the patients with less serious illnesses and nonprofit hospitals will no longer be able to perform this insurance function.

The validity of price discrimination and insurance arguments for regulating competition hinge on the availability of subsidies and insurance from other sources. A comprehensive system of national health insurance would presumably eliminate the need for regulation for equity and insurance reasons, since everyone would already have adequate insurance and be fully protected against financial hardship. In contrast, there seems to have been a strong argument for regulation during the early part of this century when direct subsidies to patients were rare and the insurance system was completely inadequate. The current situation is more difficult to evaluate. Government subsidies have increased sharply and health insurance is now widely available. But as we noted earlier, there are still gaps in the system. The key empirical question is whether nonprofit hospitals currently help fill these gaps and whether their contribution in this area is large enough to merit government intervention.

Average Cost-Pricing

Average cost-pricing occurs when producers set the price of a service equal to the average cost of producing this service. This is the standard method of pricing hospital services and it is built into most insurance reimbursement schemes. For example, the price for a hospital bed is usually set equal to the average cost of keeping a patient in a bed for a day in a hospital.

In a competitive equilibrium, average cost-pricing will have the same effect as marginal cost-pricing if consumers purchase identical services and there is no variation in costs over time. However, average cost-pricing amounts to an implicit form of price discrimination if the cost of producing a service varies either (1) within a given pricing category (i.e., consumers do not receive identical services for the same price), or (2) over time. We can illustrate the first type of implicit price discrimination by considering the case where there is a heterogeneous patient population in a hospital.

There is no nationally accepted scheme of classifying patients by the amount of care they need. But existing studies in this area suggest that there is a good deal of variation in the amount of care hospital patients require depending upon how sick they are. For example, staffing models developed for general nursing units by Georgette, Pardee and others suggest that seriously ill patients may require twice as much nursing care as average patients, while other studies suggest that seriously ill patients make up a significant minority of the patient population in hospitals.[14]

There are several different ways in which hospitals could charge for a day in a hospital bed under these conditions. One approach is to monitor services on an individual basis and charge each individual for the cost of the services that they actually receive, including regular nursing services. In this case, seriously ill patients may end up paying considerably more than patients who are less ill. The second alternative is to use average cost-pricing and charge all patients the average cost per bed of these services. In this case, less ill, low-cost patients will end up subsidizing seriously ill, high-cost patients. This type of implicit price discrimination may result in a welfare loss if it leads low-cost patients to underutilize services and high-cost patients to overutilize them. But average cost-pricing may also increase welfare by significantly reducing monitoring costs, since hospitals need only monitor the total cost of services and the number of patients instead of the cost of providing services to each patient. The net impact on welfare will depend on the magnitude of the two types of effects.

A third type of approach, which is usually not used in hospitals, is to screen patients in advance and charge them on the basis of expected treatment costs. Screening costs are likely to vary with the level of accuracy that is desired and the type of screening. For example, it may be relatively easy for a physician to make a general qualitative judgment about whether or not a case of appendicitis will involve expensive complications. But it may be quite difficult to make a more precise evaluation. It also may be more difficult to arrive at the same kind of judgment using only quantitative data. Since third-party payers may be reluctant to pay for services on the basis of qualitative judgments, this may explain why hospitals do not use screening to set prices directly.

But they may still use it indirectly. Suppose that nonprofit hospitals use average cost-pricing. Forprofit hospitals may be able to engage in "creaming" by using screening to identify low-cost patients and bidding these patients away from nonprofit hospitals while refusing to admit expensive patients. In this case, nonprofit hospitals will be left only with the high-cost patients in each category and this will tend to push up the average cost of treatment in these hospitals. If nonprofit institutions continue to adhere to an average cost-pricing rule, they will be forced to raise prices and the process will begin again. If this process continues indefinitely, nonprofit hospitals will gradually be pushed out of the market and end up with only the most expensive patients in each category.

The most expensive patients in any category also are likely to be the patients with the most complicated illnesses. They will tend to require more sophisticated care than low-cost patients. The relative cost of caring for patients with complicated illnesses in separate facilities compared to the cost of caring for them in facilities with other patients will depend largely on the number of patients involved. In smaller communities, where the absolute number of patients is small, separating care may substantially increase costs. The argument for using regulation to protect nonprofit hospitals from creaming when they use average cost-pricing is that caring for low-cost and high-cost patients in separate facilities is inefficient.

Empirically, two main questions are involved: First, is average cost-pricing in the public interest to begin with, or have nonprofit hospitals and third-party payers simply adopted this system of pricing for their own convenience? Second, assuming that average cost-pricing is desirable for at least some categories of services, is it inefficient to treat high-cost and low-cost patients in separate facilities?

There are not many data on monitoring costs in hospitals. However, monitoring-cost arguments have sometimes been used against marginal cost-pricing in public utilities, where outputs are less complex and easier to measure than in hospitals.[15] The demand for hospital services appears price inelastic and this suggests that efficiency losses from average cost-pricing are probably relatively small. But this may be mainly the result of insurance arrangements. Feldstein suggests that demand might be a good deal more sensitive to prices if there were more coinsurance.[16] In this case, efficiency considerations might be very important. Evidence on economies of scale is not clear, although there does seem to be some positive relationship between the quality of care and the overall size of hospitals.

The cost of patient services can vary with occupancy rates in hospitals as well as with the mix of patients. As we can see from Table 9-2, monthly occupancy rates may vary substantially over

Table 9-2 Monthly Occupancy Rates for Community Hospitals by Bed Size: 1977

Bed size	Average monthly occupancy rate for year (%)	Range in monthly occupancy rates during year (%)
Under 50	43.8	37.7–51.7
50–74	54.2	50.3–60.9
75–99	64.4	61.5–71.1
100–149	70.6	65.4–75.4
150–199	76.9	71.3–81.6
200–299	77.7	71.1–82.1
300–399	80.4	72.8–84.4
Over 400	80.9	74.0–84.5
Total	74.4	68.4–79.0

Source: National Hospital Panel Survey, American Hospital Association.

the year. Many hospitals also report significant variations in weekly occupancy rates.[17] Maintaining excess capacity to meet peak loads can be expensive. If hospitals use average cost-pricing, this will spread the costs of maintaining peak-load capacity over the entire patient population. This amounts to a de facto form of price discrimination to the extent that patients who use hospitals in off-peak periods end up subsidizing patients who use services during peak periods. Forprofit hospitals may be able to bid patients away during off-peak periods in this case by operating institutions with no excess capacity at normal levels of demand and by offering lower prices or providing a mix of services that is more attractive to patients or physicians than is the mix offered by nonprofit hospitals.

Assuming that nonprofit hospitals continue to maintain the same amount of excess capacity as they have in the past, this will lead to an increase in the ratio of peak-load capacity to normal capacity in these hospitals during off-peak periods. As a result, average costs will rise in nonprofit hospitals, since they will now have a higher proportion of empty beds during normal periods. If nonprofit hospitals continue to follow an average cost-pricing rule, the industry will tend toward an equilibrium in which nonprofit hospitals provide peak-load services and forprofit hospitals provide normal services.

This type of situation will not necessarily be socially undesirable if the costs of providing peak-load services are independent of the normal level of operation in hospitals (i.e., there are no economies of scale). The argument for regulating forprofit hospitals is that there are in fact significant economies of scale in providing peak-load services in hospitals that also provide off-peak services.

One alternative to regulation is to use peak-load pricing. There is ample literature on peak-load pricing for public utilities which suggests that marginal cost-pricing may be socially more efficient than average cost-pricing. Long and Feldstein specifically consider this kind of problem for hospitals, while Ro suggests that multipart pricing could help shift peak loads in the industry and enable hospitals to make more efficient use of plant and equipment.[18] For example, since demand usually falls during holidays, it might be possible to increase efficiency by offering lower prices during these periods.

However, these gains may be offset by increased monitoring costs. Multipart pricing may be especially expensive to administer if fluctuations in demand cannot be predicted in advance and prices depend on stochastic variables. Furthermore, Dreze argues that some element of price discrimination will be unavoidable if demand is stochastic.[19] This means that nonprofit hospitals may still be vulnerable to competition from forprofit hospitals even if they use marginal cost-pricing. Multipart pricing also raises equity issues. The idea of charging patients higher rates because they happen to become ill when a large number of other people are also ill is not very appealing, especially if demand is stochastic.

Unless there is a large stochastic element in demand, it is difficult to defend any pricing system that does not attempt to price services, at least in part, at marginal cost over time. However, if full peak-load pricing is not feasible for either equity or efficiency reasons, a second alternative may be for the government to use tax revenues to subsidize these services. Assuming that peak loads really are a problem this may be more efficient than using regulation to protect average cost-pricing.

Externalities and Quality Issues

Externalities occur when the actions of one individual in a market affect the welfare of others through nonmarket means. A standard example is the treatment of infectious diseases. If someone with an infectious disease goes to a hospital for treatment, that person will gain if treatment improves his or her own health status. At the same time, society as a whole may benefit if treatment limits the spread of disease to the rest of the population. These social benefits are an externality in the sense that while they are the result of a market transaction (an individual purchases medical services for his own benefit), they are not traded in the market. Precisely because they are not traded, the welfare impact of externalities may be difficult to measure because we cannot observe a price for them, although we may be able to make indirect inferences using cost-benefit analysis.

Hospital services may generate externalities in two ways: First, there may be externalities associated with the consumption of hospital services. For example, there are a number of studies in the public health literature that suggest there may be significant externalities from the treatment of infectious diseases along the lines we have just described. Second, there may be externalities from the process involved in producing hospital services in a nonprofit setting independent of any externalities from the consumption of these services per se.

In their discussions of nonprofit hospitals, Titmuss and others suggest that the act of giving for nonpecuniary motives may have a social value that is difficult to capture in market terms.[20] Underlying this view is the concept that society is ultimately a corporate venture based upon mutual cooperation and trust between individuals, rather than upon competition. Markets may increase efficiency, but they may also destroy the fabric of society by undermining socially symbolic acts that provide the means for individuals to reaffirm their participation in the social order.

Titmuss calls this kind of interaction "the gift relationship." He focuses on blood donations in his analysis of this type of relationship.[21] A direct nonmarket transfer of this sort is unusual in most other areas of the hospital. But his arguments suggest that there still may be important externalities involved in using and participating in maintaining voluntary institutions that do not occur when health care is provided in forprofit institutions. For example, there may be a much greater sense of community participation if care is produced in nonprofit hospitals than in forprofit hospitals.

We can begin our discussion of arguments for regulation by considering externalities from the consumption of hospital services. If there are externalities from subsidizing certain services, nonprofit hospitals may increase welfare by using price discrimination to finance the production of these services by charging prices above cost for services that do not involve externalities.

The argument for this type of behavior is that gains from externalities outweigh any efficiency losses from distorting prices. The argument for regulation contends that competition from forprofit hospitals makes it impossible for nonprofit hospitals to engage in this kind of activity. The main argument against regulation here is that it may be more efficient for the government to directly subsidize the production of services which result in externalities, as in fact is often done with programs like venereal disease clinics.

Turning to arguments for regulation where there are externalities from producing hospital services in a nonprofit setting, critics of nonprofit hospitals have often suggested that they are more expensive than forprofit hospitals. If this is true, nonprofit hospitals ultimately may not be able to compete with forprofits in the open market even though the social benefits of using nonprofit institutions outweigh the added costs. Therefore, it may be desirable either to regulate competition by forprofit hospitals or to subsidize nonprofits. The main empirical questions here are whether there really are important externalities from using nonprofit hospitals and the extent to which forprofit hospitals are less costly than nonprofit hospitals.

Even in the absence of externalities, critics of forprofit hospitals suggest that any apparent differences in efficiency between forprofit and nonprofit hospitals may be illusionary because of differences in the quality of services they provide. They note that forprofit hospitals have an incentive to reduce the quality of services if such action increases profits. They may be able to get away with this if quality changes are very difficult for consumers to detect because of the complexity of medical services and the high level of uncertainty about the outcomes of many of these services. In theory, consumers should be able to rely on their physicians to evaluate the quality of these services for them. However, if these physicians own stock in forprofit hospitals, this may bias their judgment. Even if they do not, hospital managers may be able to put pressure on them if physicians are employees or value their admitting privileges at forprofit hospitals. Therefore, another reason for regulating forprofit hospitals is to protect consumers against these types of abuses that can develop within the doctor-patient relationship.

Under a comprehensive system of national health insurance, it would presumably be possible to subsidize nonprofit hospitals if there really are significant externalities from the gift relationship. Nonetheless, abuses of the doctor-patient relationship do not seem very amenable to taxes or subsidies. If they are indeed a serious problem, regulation may be the only solution available. In this context, it is interesting to note that many of the issues discussed here about externalities and abuses of the agent relationship are also important in the education industry where, historically, there have been strong objections to forprofit institutions.

Adjustment Lags

Problems with adjustment lags can occur if forprofit hospitals adjust more rapidly than nonprofit hospitals to increases in the demand for hospital services. Traditionally, nonprofit hospitals have received large capital subsidies from public and private sources. These subsidies reduce capital costs and may give nonprofit hospitals a competitive advantage over forprofit hospitals. But they also may reduce flexibility, since it can be difficult to generate capital quickly from these sources. As a result, there may be significant lags before nonprofit hospitals respond to increases in demand, which Pauly estimates may be as long as four to eight years.[22]

Adjustment lags may create excess demand at existing price levels. Rafferty suggests that the usual response by nonprofit hospitals to this situation is to ration services by need, rather than by price, and to hold prices at existing levels.[23] Patients with more urgent problems are usually given preference over those with problems where treatment can be deferred. The result is that queues may form for services such as elective surgery.

This may create a large potential market for the services of forprofit hospitals. These hospitals may be able to enter the market for hospital services by providing care to patients who have been forced to wait in queues. If the response of forprofits to increases in demand is more rapid than the response of nonprofit hospitals, new capacity in the industry will take the form mainly of forprofit hospitals specializing in the treatment of paying patients with less urgent problems. Patients with serious illnesses that require more sophisticated care, as well as those who cannot pay, will end up concentrated in nonprofit hospitals.

There is little direct evidence on the investment behavior of forprofit hospitals. But Steinwald and Neuhauser found that forprofit hospitals tend to concentrate in areas where there has been rapid growth in population and income.[24] Both variables are closely associated with increases in the total demand for hospital services and this tends to support the hypothesis that forprofit hospitals can respond more quickly to changes in demand than can nonprofits. At the same time, studies by Schweitzer and Rafferty and others have found that forprofit hospitals on average admit patients who need a less capital-intensive mix of services than patients in nonprofit hospitals.[25] This supports the hypothesis that forprofit hospitals tend to treat patients with less complicated illnesses, although it is not clear from the data whether the needs of these patients are less urgent than those of patients treated in nonprofit hospitals.

From an efficiency standpoint, investments in forprofit hospitals as a result of lags in the response time of nonprofit hospitals are undesirable if this kind of investment pattern increases the long-run cost of medical care. If forprofit hospitals are oriented toward paying patients with uncomplicated illnesses, they may invest in more comfortable, but smaller and less sophisticated facilities than nonprofit hospitals. Once this capacity is in place, it may be difficult to alter. Even if forprofit hospitals eventually convert to nonprofit status, the original investment decisions made by these institutions could shape the organization of the industry in a given area for years to come, especially if certificate-of-need legislation limits total investments in the industry.[26]

On the other hand, if forprofit hospitals can adjust more quickly to changes in demand than nonprofit hospitals, restrictions on forprofit institutions may result in longer waiting times for care for less seriously ill patients. While longer waiting times may not endanger patients' lives, longer waits may still add significantly to the pain and suffering associated with illnesses, a welfare loss that should not be overlooked.

Because of certificate-of-need legislation, the issue of whether to regulate hospital investments is largely academic. The question is whether or nor regulators should limit new investments to nonprofit hospitals. The basic argument for this policy is that the short-run gains from permitting investments in forprofit facilities are less important than the long-run losses in efficiency that may result from this type of investment. An additional argument contends that a rapid increase in the number of forprofit hospitals may create a financial crisis for nonprofit hospitals if they have traditionally depended on price discrimination to finance things such as free care and peak-load capacity. This may result in a good deal of temporary disruption in the industry that may not be worth the trouble. If investment lags are really a problem for nonprofit hospitals, it may be much easier to try to improve capital markets for these institutions than to endeavor to make all the other sorts of adjustments that may be necessary if forprofit firms are allowed to enter the market. In practice, however, these types of problems seem to be largely a thing of the past. Nonprofit hospitals now have much better access to regular capital markets and enjoy far more flexibility than formerly.

Conclusions

The purpose of this paper has been to present arguments for regulation of competition by forprofit hospitals on a systematic basis and to briefly consider the implications of these arguments in light of industry conditions. The theoretical analysis suggests that it may be in the public interest to regulate competition by forprofit hospitals if nonprofit hospitals: 1) engage in price discrimination; 2) engage in average cost-pricing; 3) do not use least-cost methods of producing services for socially desirable reasons, or 4) if there are lags in the speed with which nonprofit hospitals adjust to increases in demand.

Based on this analysis, an extreme free market position (i.e., that regulation will never increase welfare) is clearly not justified a priori on theoretical grounds. However, it is also clear from our discussion that regulation of competition by forprofit hospitals will not necessarily always be socially desirable. Simply because forprofit hospitals are able to increase their market share at the expense of nonprofit hospitals is not sufficient evidence that regulation is needed. For example, success of forprofit hospitals may simply reflect lax management practices by nonprofit hospitals. The impact of regulation in any given case will depend on the way in which nonprofit hospitals actually behave, on other government policies, and on market conditions.

Given this discussion, how relevant are the arguments considered in this paper for public policy in light of conditions in the industry? No attempt has been made here to carry out a full empirical analysis. But the previous section suggests several general conclusions and points up a number of areas where further research is badly needed.

Specifically, it appears on one hand that in the past there have been strong arguments for regulation because of equity considerations and problems with inadequate insurance and capital markets. On the other hand, a comprehensive system of national health insurance would probably eliminate equity problems and provide a vehicle for dealing with efficiency problems involving average cost-pricing and peak loads. In this case, the only real arguments for regulation that would remain are those involving externalities and the possible impact of competition by forprofit hospitals on the relationships between communities and hospitals and between doctors and patients.

Under current conditions, the need for regulation seems problematic. Health insurance is now widely available and government programs have reduced equity problems. But large gaps still exist in the system and nonprofit hospitals may play an important role in filling these gaps. In addition, competition by forprofit hospitals may also create problems because of externalities and the current system of average cost-pricing. As a result, it may be possible that more regulation could increase welfare.

But these issues clearly need further study. A large number of important empirical questions remain unresolved. For example, how important is price discrimination in financing care for patients who cannot pay under the current system? How large are rationing costs in the industry? Are there really serious problems with peak loads? Is there any evidence of the importance of the gift relationship in determining the behavior of nonprofit hospitals? These questions are not easy to answer. But answering them would provide a much better basis for evaluating arguments for regulation of forprofit hospitals. And even in the absence of problems with forprofit hospitals, these questions raise issues that may be important to consider if we are interested in increasing the overall efficiency of the industry and providing a more equitable system of health care delivery.

THE DRUG INDUSTRY

Many inputs used by health services providers and consumed directly by purchasers of health services are products from firms entirely within the profit-oriented manufacturing sector of the economy. Perhaps the most important of these products in terms of effects on health and on the cost of care are drugs. The drug industry also is an important target of government regulation.

The pertinent questions about the economics of the drug industry require going well beyond the analysis of individual firms' behavior and, for reasons noted at the beginning of this chapter, to take an industrial organization approach to the industry. What is the relationship between market structure and competitive interaction? How does the industry's overall performance measure up?

The economic performance of the drug industry is a matter of considerable debate. Some economists see it as highly monopolistic and socially irresponsible and call for more government regulation to protect consumers' safety and pocketbooks. Others see it as a technologically innovative, highly competitive source of modern advances in medical care and believe that current government regulation is harmful to its economic and technological performance. The following outlines the major points of contention in this debate. The authors make no attempt to indicate our own conclusions on this controversial theme; that task is left to the reader.

The pharmaceutical industry includes ethical (prescription) drugs and proprietary (over-the-counter) products. The focus here, and the category probably of most interest to administrators and planners, is the former. Several hundred firms manfacture ethical drugs. Most of these are very small producers of generic drugs. Some small firms are "repackaging houses" that buy generic products and resell them under their own brand names. The large manufacturers and marketers of branded drugs are a group of 30 or so companies.

Economists look to the size distribution of firms as one indicator of an industry's competitiveness. A commonly used measure is the four-firm *concentration ratio,* that is, the percentage of total sales accounted for by the four largest firms. Roughly speaking, the higher the concentration ratio, the greater the divergence of the industry structure from perfect competition and the greater the likelihood that market power and lack of price competition exist. For drugs, the four-firm concentration ratio is around 25 percent and the eight-firm ratio about 40 percent. These are not high figures compared to other U.S. industries. However, critics argue that these figures do not accurately reflect the structure of the industry. Walter Measday writes:

THE PHARMACEUTICAL INDUSTRY[b]

Although some drug companies are much larger than others, there do not appear to be any industrywide dominant firms such as those one finds in automobiles, steel, or a number of other industries. Instead, the bulk of the market is shared among 20 to 30 leading firms, with a substantial fringe of competitors.

This is the view of the industry emphasized by the Pharmaceutical Manufacturers Association and not a few outside observers. To accept such a view uncritically, however, is to ignore the fact that the over-all drug market is fragmented into a number of separate, noncompeting therapeutic markets: Antibiotics are not substitutes for antidiabetic drugs, and tranquilizers are not substitutes for vitamins. Manufacturers do not compete on an industrywide basis, and, hence, concentration must be evaluated within the various therapeutic groups of drugs in which competition does occur.

When this is done, even on the basis of the fragmentary data available, it is clear that high levels of concentration within important therapeutic classes are a more meaningful element of structure than the relatively moderate level for the industry as a whole. Examples can be found from the overly broad therapeutic classes used by the Bureau of the Census. The four largest producers of central nervous system drugs (including a wide variety of products from aspirin and other analgesics through tranquilizers to anesthetics) accounted for 43 per cent of the market in 1972, whereas the eight largest had 63 per cent. In the anti-infective drug class (including antiparasitic products, antibiotics, antimalarials, and even simple antiseptics), the four largest firms held 45 per cent and the eight largest 67 per cent of the market. For preparations affecting neoplasms, the endocrine system, and metabolic diseases (lumping together drugs for the treatment of cancer, arthritis, and diabetes with the oral contraceptives, anti-obesity drugs, and others) the four and eight company concentration ratios were, respectively, 48 and 70 per cent. These are high, not low, concentration ratios, and they would be much higher still were the bureau census to compute them on the basis of realistic therapeutic divisions rather than agglomerating widely diverse products into broad categories.[8]

Another aspect of the pharmaceutical industry, concentration of bulk drug production, is an important consideration even when there may be an impressive number of suppliers of any given finished product on the market. The Tariff Commission identifies the manufacturers of roughly 650 bulk medicinal chemicals. In 1972, only six of these were produced by more than four manufacturers, while nearly 500 were available from a single domestic source.[9]

The nature of this type of concentration can be readily illustrated. Ascorbic acid (vitamin C) in dosage form is offered by more than 100 companies; the entire output of the vitamin itself, however, is produced by Merck, Pfizer, and Hoffmann-LaRoche.

Finished reserpine products are offered by at least 60 suppliers; S. B. Penick is the sole manufacturer of the active drug. Meprobamate (Miltown) tablets are available from nearly 50 suppliers; the actual drug is manufactured by Abbott and Millmaster Onyx. It is obvious, in such cases, that the bulk producers may have considerable power to control the effectiveness of competition by their selling policies.

In short, concentration ratios for the pharmaceutical industry as a whole convey a somewhat misleading impression of the industry, although they are useful in the broad sense of supplying information on the number and approximate size distribution of drug firms. From a standpoint of the influence of industry structure on competitive behavior, however, it is necessary to go beyond the industrywide ratios and examine concentration in therapeutically significant categories and in bulk drug production. On this basis, it appears that high concentration in these separate categories, rather than the moderate concentration of the entire industry, is the dominant structural characteristic.

Others argue that concentration ratios are misleading indicators of competition in this industry and that analysis should focus on dynamic factors, that is, changes over time in the market shares of firms. Jerome Schnee and Erol Caglarcan argue that from a dynamic viewpoint the industry is very competitive:

ETHICAL PHARMACEUTICAL INDUSTRY[c]

The ethical pharmaceutical market is a dynamic one. Competition results in rapid firm turnover; that is, shifts in market share rankings among the largest firms. Between 1962 and 1972, sixteen of the 21 largest pharmaceutical firms changed market positions. Nine firms improved their market rank, some by eight to ten positions. Twelve firms either failed to improve their market positions or dropped in rankings. The average absolute rank change was 4.1 positions (Table 9-3).[14] Only one industry, petroleum, has higher turnover than the drug industry. . . .

Analysis of seventeen therapeutic markets during the 1956-65 decade further illustrates the industry's dynamic market characteristics. The average market share position of the firms ranked first declined from 39.8 percent in 1956 to 14.5 percent in 1965. Similar declines occurred for the firms ranked second; their average market position dropped from 15 percent in 1956 to 7.1 percent in 1965.[16]

Table 9-3 Firm Turnover for the Leading 21 Firms in the Ethical Pharmaceutical Industry, 1962–72

Company	Market Share of Hospital and Drugstore Sales (percent of industry total)		Rank in Terms of Market Share		Change in Rank between 1962 and 1972
	1962	1972	1962	1972	
Lilly	7.2	7.9	1	1	0
Hoffmann-La Roche	4.0	7.5	10	2	+ 8
American Home Products	6.1	6.6	3	3	0
Merck	4.9	6.0	6	4	+ 2
Bristol-Myers	3.4	4.2	13	5	+ 8
Abbott	3.9	3.7	11	6	+ 5
Pfizer	3.8	3.6	12	7	+ 5
Ciba-Geigy	4.2	3.6	8	8	0
Upjohn	5.8	3.5	4	9	− 5
Squibb	4.1	3.4	9	10	− 1
Smith Kline	6.3	3.3	2	11	− 9
Johnson & Johnson	1.3	2.7	21	12	+ 9
Schering-Plough	2.4	2.7	15	13	+ 2
Parke-Davis[a]	4.6	2.7	7	14	− 7
Searle	2.2	2.5	17	15	+ 2
Lederle	5.3	2.3	5	16	− 11
Sandoz-Wander	1.6	2.0	19	17	+ 2
Robins	1.9	2.0	18	18	0
Sterling	2.4	1.9	16	19	− 3
Burroughs Wellcome	1.4	1.8	20	20	0
Warner-Lambert[a]	2.6	1.7	14	21	− 7
Average absolute change in rank between 1962 and 1972					4.1[b]

[a] Parke-Davis was merged with Warner-Lambert in late 1970; rank and market shares computed as if firms had not merged. Market share of the combined firm in 1972 was 4.4 percent, or fifth in rank.

[b] Computed with Parke-Davis and Warner-Lambert changes based on their ranks as if they had not merged.

Source: D. Cocks, "Production Innovation and the Dynamic Elements of Competition in the Ethical Pharmaceutical Industry," *Drug Development and Marketing*, ed. Robert B. Helms (Washington, D.C.: American Enterprise Institute for Public Policy Research), p. 241.

A further indication of the competitive market structure of the pharmaceutical industry is the entry and exit exhibited within therapeutic submarkets. Between 1963 and 1972 there were more than five successful new entrants in 15 of the 17 product classes analyzed in one study.[17] The average 1972 market share of new entrants exceeded 10 percent with individual market shares ranging as high as 33 and 43 percent. . . . Exit occurred in 16 of the 17 therapeutic classes.

Obviously, entry into a therapeutic market could be by entirely new firms from outside the drug industry or by pharmaceutical firms that did not previously market products in that particular market. In either case, the market positions of the existing firms are likely to be affected. New entrants are likely to create additional competition and lower prices. For example, on the basis of his study of the 1963-1972 period, Telser concluded that pharmaceutical prices tend to fall in response to entry of new firms.[18]

An aspect of drug industry performance of particular interest to those concerned with health care costs is pricing. Critics of the industry argue that prices are at monopoly levels. Demand is inelastic with respect to price, which makes it possible for prices to be raised considerably above costs. Some of the reasons for this inelastic demand and its implications are detailed by Measday as follows:

> The nature of demand for individual ethical drugs, however, is very nearly unique, at least where private buyers are concerned. With most consumer products, the consumer himself makes the buying decision. For ethical drugs, in the words of the late Senator Kefauver, "He who orders does not buy; he who buys does not order." The decision is made for the consumer by his physician when the latter writes out a prescription, generally by brand name. The pharmacist is usually obligated to fill the prescription exactly as it is written.[4] If, for example, the physician has specified Achromycin, the druggist must supply American Cyanamid's brand of tetracycline and not the identical product offered by Pfizer, Bristol, Squibb, or Upjohn. The average patient may not even know what he has purchased, apart from the fact that it is a bottle of small pink pills, or large white ones, or yellow capsules; in the majority of cases, neither the physician nor the pharmacist tells him clearly what has been prescribed.
>
> The customer's ignorance of the product is matched by his ignorance of prices. The most prevalent retail markup on ethical

drugs is 40 per cent of the retail price (that is, 66⅔ per cent above the cost to the druggist). In any major metropolitan area, however, a given prescription may be filled over a wide range of prices. Some druggists may accept much lower margins, offering substantial savings to customers. Others, especially in the case of less expensive prescriptions, may employ a minimum "professional fee," which results in a higher markup. A quantity of pills that costs the druggist $1.50 would be retailed at $2.50, but might be available in some outlets for $2.00, or in others for as much as $3.50, depending on the pricing policy of the retailer.

Comparatively few customers will shop around to have a prescription filled at the lowest price. Until recently, this would have been difficult in any case because only one state, Ohio, permitted prescription drug advertising. In 1972, for example, the Michigan Board of Pharmacy sought to revoke the licenses of pharmacists employed by a chain that advertised nothing more than a 10 per cent discount on prescriptions for senior citizens. Since 1972, however, a number of states (20 by the end of 1974) have enacted legislation either permitting advertising or requiring in-store posting of prescription drug prices.

Next, consider the physician, who is frequently described as the purchasing agent for his patient's drug requirements. In contrast to other purchasing agents, most physicians have little knowledge of price or price alternatives. This stems from what is probably a distortion of an ancient and excellent principle: The physician's prescription of a drug should be based solely on his judgment of the best therapy for his patient. Thus, in the flood of advertising and promotional literature with which the major drug companies inundate the medical practitioner, there is never any mention of price, nominally on the ground that such commercialism might be interpreted as an attempt to taint professional judgment. The physician who is concerned about drug prices must find them out in the same way as anyone else; and, with the best will in the world, he simply has no time to engage in economic research.

Finally, remember that the patient has visited his doctor in the first place because he is experiencing certain symptoms that worry him even if they do not incapacitate him; the doctor's prescription offers him the hope that these symptoms can be cured. The patient will have the prescription filled, unless he has absolutely no resources (either of his own or through public aid) to pay the cost. When this underlying reason for seeking medical advice is viewed in juxtaposition to the inability of either the physician or the patient to include price as a factor in the buying decision, we can see that the demand for prescription drugs, either in the aggregate or as individual products, approaches closer to complete inelasticity with respect to price than the demand for any other commodity that readily comes to mind.

In the institutional sector of the market (hospitals and governmental agencies), the demand for ethical drugs in the aggregate is probably as inelastic as it is in the private prescription sector. Total demand will depend on such factors as hospital patient loads or the number of people eligible to receive drugs through governmental channels, rather than on drug prices. Within the aggregate framework, however, the demands for many individual drugs and particularly for different brands of the same drug may exhibit considerable elasticity.

A majority of the nation's hospitals have adopted formularies from which staff physicians are expected to prescribe as a means of holding down hospital costs. The purpose of a formulary can be understood from the foreword to the one issued by the Baltimore City Health Department: "The principal criteria for admission of substances to this formulary are therapeutic efficacy, simplicity, and economy." Therapeutic efficacy is clear enough. Simplicity is achieved by limiting the number of drugs in the formulary. If, say, 40 or 50 drugs on the market are available to treat the same illness, the formulary committee will choose four or five for inclusion. In this connection, it may be noted that there are upwards of 7000 ethical drug products (single drugs and combinations of two or more active ingredients) offered to the medical profession by the industry. The director of one of the leading hospitals in the country has stated that a formulary containing only 400 of these products covers more than 99 per cent of patients' drug requirements.[5] Economy is achieved both through simplicity and through a common provision that the hospital pharmacy may fill any prescription on a generic basis—that is, if a staff physician prescribes Meticorten, the pharmacy may dispense equally reliable, but much less expensive, generic prednisone.

In the institutional market, as distinct from the private prescription market, therefore, price becomes an important influence in the choices made by purchasing authorities. The degree of this influence may vary considerably according to the ability and objectivity of the decision makers, and drug manufacturers woo these decision makers even more assiduously than they do individual practicing physicians. Some hospitals and agencies have done an excellent job; at the other extreme, the state of New Mexico, in the mid-1960s, used the *Physicians' Desk Reference* as its official "formulary."[6] This is a commercial advertising compendium, distributed free to physicians and utilized almost exclusively by the major drug companies. Despite such variations in standards, it is clear that price elasticity of demand can be a significant factor in the institutional market. It is becoming even more significant as both hospital costs and public expenditures for out-of-hospital prescription drugs for the needy and elderly continue to rise.

To summarize, two submarkets for ethical drugs can be distinguished. The private prescription market accounts for between two thirds and three fourths of total demand, and the institutional market for one quarter to one third. In the former, demand—whether considered in the aggregate for different drugs within the same therapeutic class, or for individual brands of the same drug—is extraordinarily inelastic. In the latter, because price is a factor in decisions involving choices among different drugs for the same therapeutic purpose and in choices among alternative brands of a given drug, an important element of price elasticity may be introduced into the demand functions for individual products and brands.

Another area of controversy is drug marketing. Ethical drugs are not advertised directly to consumers. They are advertised in medical journals, but most promotional efforts by the drug firms go into direct mail advertising and sales persons who call on doctors in person. The amount spent on marketing and promotion is large in absolute terms and as a ratio to sales when this ratio is compared to that for other industries. Critics of the industry believe that it is too large and represents a waste of resources. Others see the function as one of physician education and note its importance in informing practitioners about proper use of a complex product. Conclusions about drug marketing ultimately are value judgments. Is it "educational" or "brainwashing?" The following two excerpts outline the opposing positions. As Measday writes:

> "Educational effort" (as the industry prefers to call drug promotion) is directed almost entirely to the select group of about 250,000 practicing physicians who are in a position to decide what drugs and which brands will be purchased by the ultimate consumers. The effort begins when the physician is still a medical

student and continues throughout his active career. For the leading companies, drug promotion has been successful in developing brand and company loyalties within the profession, which can be far more effective in maintaining sales than the therapeutic value of the particular drugs promoted. Furthermore, it is a mode of competition requiring enormous resources beyond the reach of all but the major firms in the industry.

The funds devoted to drug promotion can only be guessed. In the course of the Kefauver investigation, 22 companies reported that advertising and promotional expenses for their drug operations alone amounted to $580 million in 1958; the subcommittee staff estimated that the industry total was $750 million.[18] Allowing for increases in salesmen's salaries and expenses, advertising rates and mailing costs, as well as the growth in manufacturers' shipments, a conservative estimate for 1974 would be well over $1 billion. The magnitude of this sum can be appreciated best in terms of the small audience courted by the drug companies—the expenditure averages at least $5000 per physician.[19]

● ● ●

This persuasion function may be considered either education or brainwashing, depending on how one views the industry. There is some evidence for the latter point of view. The detail man has neither enough of the doctor's time nor the qualifications to present a balanced scientific report on the product he is pushing. At best, he will give a one-sided, but reasonable, presentation of the benefits of the drug. At worst, his approach raises serious ethical questions.

● ● ●

From the standpoint of market performance, the issue of drug advertising and promotion has a significance that transcends its economic cost. Almost any drug good enough to be useful has some potential for toxicity. A number of distinguished pharmacologists are in agreement that drug company promotional efforts have led to overprescribing on a large scale, which has created an increasingly serious problem of illness, hospitalization, and deaths caused by the drugs themselves. It is in the area of product promotion that the basic conflict between the goal of the drug company as a profit-seeking organization and its function of meeting a vital human need is most evident.

Gilbert D. Harrell, a marketing expert, has a more positive view of the sales representative, as noted in this excerpt:

PHARMACEUTICAL MARKETING[d]

In general, when the product is complex, the more effective sales presentation relies on a strategy based on technical information rather than nontechnical persuasion. Pharmaceutical salespeople stimulate sales by communicating important information to physicians.

A pharmaceutical company's medical sales representatives are an important part of its information program. These individuals receive continuous in-house training in pharmacology and other medical aspects of drug use so that they may convey up-to-date information to physicians, hospital personnel, pharmacists, and other health professionals. The sales representative has the responsibility to promote to medical professionals in a manner which will encourage the appropriate use of pharmaceutical and other health care products and services. To accomplish this task, sales representatives must understand selected therapeutic treatment goals, the complexities of patient management, product distribution, and applicable federal and state regulations regarding labeling and distribution of pharmaceuticals. More importantly, they should have a thorough technical understanding of the advantages and limitations of each product or service before calling on a physician.

The advisory nature of the sales message and the exchange of technical information afford a two-way communication flow, by personal contact, which is more instructive than the one-way promotion characteristic of much retail marketing. The sales representative serves several functions for both the physician and the firm, among which are the following:

1. A source of information on drug products. The sales representative is able to convey to the physician information on new drugs and new information on old drugs.
2. A conduit to the expertise available to the physician through the professional staff of the pharmaceutical firm. The sales person communicates messages to the physician from the experts within the pharmaceutical company. In doing so he can answer questions of a limited scope or convey specific information requested by the physician.

3. A messenger of information from the physician to others in the firm. This affords the firm sensitivity towards its customers, provides on-the-spot information concerning possible adverse reactions with drugs, better forecasting and, therefore, product efficiency.
4. A problem solver in the drug distribution system. The sales person can help monitor inventory levels, sometimes make deliveries, and maintain surveillance of the appropriate distribution of pharmaceuticals.
5. A forum to discuss with the physician therapeutic alternatives and patient management problems. The sales person will discuss those of his products he believes have the potential to fill this need for the physician.

A final topic of controversy is the profits of drug firms. On the one hand, high profits in an industry are of concern since they represent a large excess of price over cost and, thus, possible inefficient allocation. There also are equity implications in that profits represent an income transfer from consumers of the product to the firms' owners. On the other hand, adequate profit opportunities are essential for an industry to be able to attract capital and to provide incentives for entrepreneurship and the risk taking associated with technological innovation.

As with the other areas examined, different economists have studied drug industry profitability and reached sharply differing conclusions. Measday argues that high drug profits are indicative of undue market power:

> Table 9-4 shows the average rates of return on stockholders' investment from 1958 to 1975 for 12 large companies, the drug industry as a whole, and all manufacturing. During the entire period, the annual rates of return for all manufacturing averaged 11.0 percent, compared to 18.1 percent for the drug industry and 19.7 percent for the 12 large companies.[30] Furthermore, as Table 9-4 suggests, there has been relatively less variation in drug industry profits than in all manufacturing. The industry's profits after taxes rose in every year from 1958 ($343 million) to 1975 ($1.6 billion), including those years in which net manufacturing income as a whole declined. Few, if any, other industries in the economy can match this record.
>
> A coterie of distinguished economists retained by the PMA explained to the Nelson subcommittee, in 1968, that the rate of return in this industry reflects a substantial risk factor. If this were so, during a reasonable period of time, losses would presumably

Table 9-4 Rates of Return on Average Stockholders' Investment,[a] Pharmaceutical Industry and All Manufacturing, 1958–1975 (in per cent)

Year	12 Large Companies		Drug Industry	All Manufacturing
	Average	Range		
1975	20.5	13.2–29.5	17.8	11.6
1974	21.3	14.8–29.9	18.8	14.9
1973	21.8	14.8–30.3	19.0	12.8
1972	20.6	14.1–28.4	18.6	10.6
1971	19.9	8.9–31.0	17.9	9.7
1970	19.6	14.5–29.2	17.6	9.3
1969	20.8	14.2–28.5	18.4	11.5
1968	18.8	9.0–26.1	18.3	12.1
1967	19.0	10.4–28.1	18.7	11.7
1966	21.1	14.4–29.8	20.3	13.4
1965	21.0	14.3–32.7	20.3	13.0
1964	18.9	13.6–33.0	18.2	11.6
1963	17.8	11.2–32.7	16.8	10.3
1962	17.1	6.3–33.0	16.8	9.8
1961	17.6	10.3–32.7	16.7	8.8
1960	18.4	10.3–31.6	16.8	9.2
1959	20.3	11.5–37.5	17.8	10.4
1958	20.3	13.3–35.4	17.7	8.6

[a] Net profit as a per cent of the average of net worth at the beginning and end of each year.

Source: FTC, *Rates of Return for Identical Companies in Selected Manufacturing Industries* (Washington, D.C.: U.S. Government Printing Office, annual); FTC "Quarterly Financial Reports" (Washington, D.C.: U.S. Government Printing Office); company annual reports.

---

offset extreme profits so that something approaching the average return in the economy would result. There is no evidence that this has occurred. In the most recent 5-year period, 1971–1975, the average rate of return in manufacturing was below 12 per cent. Abbott Laboratories and Richardson-Merrell were the poorest performers among the large companies; yet their returns during the period averaged 14 per cent or more, substantially above that for manufacturing generally. At the other extreme, Merck, Schering, and American Home Products each averaged 26 percent or better.

Thus, although variation in profits from company to company does exist, the "risk" appears to lie between earning a normal rate of return and some significant multiple of a normal rate. This would seem to support what has been said earlier concerning the barriers to effective price competition in the industry.

Schnee and Caglarcan, on the other hand, offer several other explanations for observed high profit rates:

Drug Industry Profitability

The drug industry is one of the more profitable sectors of the U.S. economy. In fact, in terms of figures found in company annual reports, the rate of return for this industry is higher than it is for most other industries (Table 9-5). Consequently, questions have been raised regarding the appropriateness of the relative level of drug industry profitability, since profitability rates sometimes have been used in determining the reasonableness of prices.

Therefore, it seems necessary to explain why the accounting rates of return for this industry are above the average for all industries. Explanations are of two distinct types. Some economists contend that accounting profits tend to overstate the real rate of return in the pharmaceutical industry.[32] They point out that because R & D expenditures are treated as a current expense rather than as an investment, rates of return in drug company financial reports are inflated. For example, on the basis of a comparative analysis of rates of return for drug and other firms, Curley concludes that "conventional accounting procedures necessarily result in biased measures of rates of return."[33] Moreover, this bias is not uniform among industries or even different firms within an industry.

According to Solomon, treatment of intangible assets and depreciation affect reported profit figures. These numbers also depend on the average life of assets, the ratio of working capital to total capital, the time pattern of cash flows, and the firm's growth rate.[34]

Accounting rates of return tend to be most severely overstated in those industries, such as pharmaceuticals, for which research and development constitutes a major proportion of investment outlays. Using a sample of six drug companies, Friedman estimated that capitalization of R & D expenditures would reduce the average rate of return by 4.4 percentage points, thus making the pharmaceutical industry's rate of return more comparable with the similarly adjusted rates of other industries.[35] Therefore, simple comparisons of the type made in Table 9-5 suffer from

Table 9-5 Rate of Return on Equity: After Taxes, 1964–1976

Year	All Manufacturing	Drugs and Medicines
1964	11.6	18.2
1965	13.0	20.3
1966	13.5	20.3
1967	11.7	18.7
1968	12.1	18.3
1969	11.5	18.3
1970	9.3	17.6
1971	9.7	17.9
1972	10.6	18.6
1973	13.1	19.2
1974	14.9	18.8
1975	11.5	17.5
1976	13.9	18.0

Source: Federal Trade Commission, *Quarterly Financial Reports,* various issues.

various distortions that result from infirmities in accounting conventions.

Researchers have used variables such as risk, growth in demand, and R & D intensity to explore the determinants of an industry's rate of return. In a 1967 study, Conrad and Plotkin found a significant relationship between risk and the rate of return on total capital for companies within 59 industries. The pharmaceuticals ranked fourth in rate of return and fourth in risk. The Conrad-Plotkin model explained a substantial portion of the rate of return differential for drug firms.[36]

Fisher and Hall used a different measure of risk.[37] They measured risk as dispersion of returns over time, as opposed to measuring dispersion across industries as Conrad and Plotkin had done. Nevertheless, both methodologies yielded premiums for risk. The intra-industry comparison showed a risk premium of 8 percent for pharmaceuticals. However, the figure was 1.7 percent when risk was measured as dispersion over time. Conrad and Plotkin pointed out that part of the reason for the discrepancy between the two numbers was that the Fisher-Hall calculations suffered from autocorrelation problems, which reduced the explanatory power of the model.

Similarly, Barges and Hickey identified growth in demand for the industry's products as a significant determinant of return on investment. High growth requires additional capital investment.

To attract such capital, higher-than-average returns must be offered; i.e., the "growth premium." In their study, Barges and Hickey attempted to measure the size of this growth premium. However, they were somewhat less successful than Conrad and Plotkin in explaining the drug industry rate of return surplus over the all manufacturing industry rate.[38]

In a 1974 study, Smith also concluded that the drug industry's higher rate of return reflected both a premium for risk and a premium for growth in pharmaceutical demand.[39]

... concern has been expressed over the drug industry's deteriorating rate of return on R & D investment. Clymer, for example, contends that huge increases in the costs and length of drug R & D and an accompanying decline in new product introductions have combined to sharply reduce the rate of return on R & D investment below 5 percent.[40] Schwartzman estimates that the expected rate of return on R & D investment has declined from 11.4 percent in 1960 to 3.3 percent in 1974. Because the deteriorating rate of return is not likely to attract sufficient future investment in pharmaceutical R & D, Schwartzman advocates that public policy be shaped to encourage profit-motivated R & D.[41] Thomas Stauffer has asserted that the pharmaceutical industry's "phantom rates of return" obscure a deteriorating profitability picture in this industry.[42]

CONCLUSION

The preceding two selections suggest how the structure-conduct-performance framework can be applied to industry analysis. But industries are so diverse that the analytical framework can be only a rough guide. Some characteristics may be very important in one industry and insignificant in others. Government plays a major role in the health care sector both as buyer of services and as regulator. There often is considerable disagreement over whether, in a given situation, government is a solution to a problem or the cause of it. The disagreement ranges over both positive and normative economic questions. Many of the positive economic questions can be analyzed using the concept of market power.

Does a government regulation counter the effect of a structural condition that creates market power and associated undesirable conduct and performance? Or does the regulation operate so as to create or enhance the economic power of some market participants?

The answers to these questions may not provide a complete solution but they are an important component in policy analysis and evaluation. Readers can imagine readily a wide range of policy implications from such evaluations.

NOTE

1. Economists, as well as political scientists, lawyers, and others, have been interested in what one writer has called "the political economy of health care," which concerns the actions of parties to obtain legislation favorable to their positions in the health field. An extensive study of this can be found in Paul J. Feldstein, *Health Associations and the Demand for Legislation* (Lexington, Mass.: Ballinger Publishing Co., 1977).

SUGGESTED READINGS

Baily, Martin N. "Research and Development Costs and Returns: The U.S. Pharmaceutical Industry." *The Journal of Political Economy* 80, no. 1 (January–February 1972): 70–85.

Bays, Carson W. "Case-mix Differences between Non-Profit and For-Profit Hospitals." *Inquiry* 14, no. 1 (March 1977): 17–21.

Comanor, William S. "Research and Technical Change in the Pharmaceutical Industry." *The Review of Economics and Statistics*, May 1965, pp. 182–190.

Peltzman, Sam. *Regulation of Pharmaceutical Innovation: The 1962 Amendments*. Washington, D.C.: American Enterprise Institute, 1974.

Ruchlin, H. S.; Pointer, D. D.; and Cannedy, L. L. "A Comparison of For-Profit Investor-Owned Chain and Non-Profit Hospitals." *Inquiry* 10, no. 4 (December 1973): 13–23.

Rucker, T. Donald. "Economic Problems in Drug Distribution." *Inquiry* 9, no. 3 (September 1972): 43–50.

Schwartzman, David. *Innovation in the Pharmaceutical Industry*. Baltimore: The Johns Hopkins University Press, 1976.

Wardell, William M., and Lasagna, Louis. *Regulation and Drug Development*. Washington, D.C.: American Enterprise Institute, 1975.

REFERENCES FOR WHITE EXCERPT

1. In 1974, 87% of all nonfederal general hospitals in the United States were nonprofit institutions and these hospitals accounted for 95% of all hospital assets. Only 13% of all nonfederal general hospitals were forprofit institutions and they controlled only 5% of all hospital assets.

2. See Davis, K. "Economic Theories of Behavior in Nonprofit Private Hospitals," *Economic and Business Bulletin* (Winter 1972); Harris, J. "The Internal Organization of Hospitals: Some Economic Implications," *Bell Journal of Economics*, 8:2 (Autumn 1977); Newhouse, J. "Toward a Theory of Nonprofit Institutions: An Economic Model of a Hospital," *American Economic Review* (March 1970); Pauly, M. and Redisch, M. "The Not-For-Profit Hospital as a Physicians' Cooperative," *American Economic Review* (March 1973).

3. If a forprofit hospital is the only hospital in town, social and political constraints may well force it to behave like a nonprofit hospital.
4. For example, the Hill-Burton program was recently eliminated, while third-party payers have recently begun to at least partly reimburse forprofit hospitals, as well as nonprofit hospitals, for capital costs.
5. See Bays, C. "Relative Costs and Efficiency in Private Short-Term General Hospitals," unpublished Ph.D. thesis, Department of Economics, University of Michigan, 1975; Rafferty, J. and Schweitzer, S. "Comparison of Forprofit and Nonprofit Hospitals: A Re-evaluation," *Inquiry* (December 1974); Ruchlin, H., Pointer, D. and Cannedy, L. "A Comparison of Forprofit Investor-Owned Chain and Nonprofit Hospitals, *Inquiry* (December 1973); Steinwald, B. and Neuhauser, D. "The Role of the Proprietary Hospital," *Law and Contemporary Problems* (Autumn 1970).
6. For reviews of the marginal cost-pricing literature, see Dreze, J. "Some Postwar Contributions of French Economists," *American Economic Review* (June 1964, Part 2); Farrel, M. "In Defense of Public Utility Price Theory," in Turvey, R. (ed.) *Public Enterprise* (New York: Penguin Books, 1968); Joskow, P. L. "Contributions to the Theory of Marginal Cost Pricing," *The Bell Journal of Economics* (Spring 1976).
7. Feldstein, M. "The High Cost of Hospitals and What to Do About It." *The Public Interest* (Summer 1977).
8. If the motives of nonprofit hospitals vary from hospital to hospital, it is possible that some nonprofit hospitals may engage in the same kind of practices attributed to forprofit hospitals. For example, private nonprofit hospitals in large urban areas are often accused of "dumping" a large share of their nonpaying patients on public nonprofit institutions, especially in cases where these patients are not interesting for research purposes.
9. For a general discussion of this type of behavior, see Joseph, H. "On Interdepartment Pricing of Not-For-Profit Hospitals," *Quarterly Review on Economics and Business* (Spring 1976).
10. Hellinger, F. "Hospital Charges and Medicare Reimbursement," *Inquiry* (December 1975).
11. Direct evidence of quality competition is difficult to obtain. But some studies do suggest that holding case mix fixed, forprofit hospitals tend to use more capital intensive methods of treating patients than nonprofit hospitals. See Bays, op. cit.; Schweitzer, S. and Rafferty, J. "Variations in Hospital Product: A Comparative Analysis of Proprietary and Voluntary Hospitals," *Inquiry* (June 1976).
12. Posner, R. "Taxation by Regulation," *The Bell Journal of Economics* (Spring 1971).
13. Rafferty and Schweitzer, op. cit.
14. Georgette, J. "Staffing by Patient Classification," *Nursing Clinics of North America* (June 1970); Pardee, G. "Classifying Patients to Predict Staff Requirements," *American Journal of Nursing* (March 1968). Also see Aydelotte, M. *Nurse Staffing Methodology: A Review and Critique of Selected Literature,* Division of Nursing, U.S. Public Health Service, DHEW No. (NI) 73-433 (January 1973).
15. Joskow, op. cit.
16. Feldstein, M. "The Welfare Loss of Excess Health Insurance," *Journal of Political Economy* (March/April 1973).
17. Typically, hospital occupancy rates tend to decline on weekends, at least in part because of the preferences of hospital staffs and physicians.

18. Long, M. and Feldstein, P. "Economics of Hospital Systems: Peak Loads and Regional Coordination," *American Economic Review* (May 1967); Ro, K. "Incremental Pricing Would Increase Efficiency in Hospitals," *Inquiry* (March 1969).
19. Dreze, op. cit.
20. Titmuss, R. *The Gift Relationship: From Human Blood to Social Policy* (New York: Harper and Row, 1972).
21. Titmuss, R. ibid, also suggests that markets may provide incentives for supplying low-quality blood. This conclusion is questioned by Sapolsky, J. and Finklestein, S. "Blood Policy Revisited: A New Look at the 'Gift Relationship,' " *The Public Interest* (Winter 1977). However, this is a separate issue from whether or not there are externalities from the gift relationship itself.
22. Pauly, M. "Hospital Capital Investment: The Role of Demand, Profits and Physicians," *The Journal of Human Resources* (Winter 1974).
23. Rafferty, J. "Patterns of Hospital Use: An Analysis of Short-Run Variations," *Journal of Political Economy* (January/February 1971).
24. Steinwald and Neuhauser, op. cit.
25. Schweitzer and Rafferty, op. cit.
26. Of course, nonprofit hospitals may not invest in an optimal fashion either, in which case some general kind of system of planning may be desirable. In this event, there will be no special reason for excluding forprofit hospitals as long as they are willing to produce the kinds of services that planners think are needed.

REFERENCES FOR FIRST MEASDAY EXCERPT

8. Shepherd has estimated an average four-firm concentration ratio of 90 for the pharmaceutical industry, adjusted for noncompeting submarkets. See W. G. Shepherd, *Market Power and Economic Welfare* (New York: Random House, Inc., 1970), Appendix Tables 8 and 9.
9. U.S. Tariff Commission, *Synthetic Organic Chemicals, 1972* (Washington, D.C.: U.S. Government Printing Office, 1974).

REFERENCES FOR FIRST SCHNEE AND CAGLARCAN EXCERPT

14. Douglas Cocks, "Product Innovation and the Dynamic Elements of Competition in the Ethical Pharmaceutical Industry," *Drug Development and Marketing*, ed. Robert B. Helms (Washington, D.C.: American Enterprise Institute for Public Policy Research, 1975), pp. 240–244.
16. Gordon R. Conrad, "Trends in Market Shares for Ethical Pharmaceutical Products," in U.S., Senate, Committee on Small Business, *Hearings on Competitive Problems in the Drug Industry*, Part 5, 90th Cong., 1st and 2nd Sess., 1968, pp. 1788–1805.
17. A. T. Kearney, "Study of Economics of Entry and Exit in the Pharmaceutical Industry" (prepared for the Pharmaceutical Manfacturers Association, April 30, 1974).
18. Lester G. Telser, William Best, John Egan, Harlow N. Higgin Gotham, "The Theory of Supply with Applications to the Ethical Pharmaceutical Industry," *The Journal of Law and Economics* (October, 1975), p. 477.

REFERENCES FOR SECOND MEASDAY EXCERPT

4. Although it has always been unethical for a pharmacist to substitute a different drug for the one prescribed, the protection of individual brands of the same drug is of recent origin. As late as 1953, only 4 states had laws prohibiting brand substitution. The National Pharmaceutical Council, representing the major companies, managed to secure such laws or pharmacy regulations in all 50 states and the District of Columbia by 1965. The tide may have turned in 1974. Laws permitting limited substitution were enacted in Florida and Michigan and narrowly missed passage in at least 10 other states. [This trend has continued since 1974.]
5. U.S. Congress, Senate, Select Committee on Small Business, *Hearings on Competitive Problems in the Drug Industry* (90th Cong., 1st sess., pt. 2, 1967), p. 676.
6. Task Force on Prescription Drugs, "The Drug Prescribers," *Background Papers* (Washington, D.C.: U.S. Government Printing Office, 1968), p. 46.

REFERENCES FOR THIRD MEASDAY EXCERPT

18. U.S. Congress, Senate, Subcommittee on Antitrust and Monopoly, *Administered Prices—Drugs*, Rept. no. 448, 87th Cong., 1st sess., 1961, p. 157.
19. A slightly more modest estimate, $4500 per physician, was provided to the Task Force on Prescription Drugs by Dr. James Goddard, former FDA commissioner. See Task Force on Prescription Durgs, "The Drug Makers and the Drug Distributors," op. cit., p. 28.

REFERENCE FOR FOURTH MEASDAY EXCERPT

30. The companies include Abbott Laboratories; American Home Products; Eli Lilly; Merck & Co.; Chas. Pfizer; Richardson-Merrell; Smith, Kline & French Laboratories; Sterling Drug; Upjohn Co.; and Warner Lambert Pharmaceutical Co. Two other firms in the FTC series for 1958–1968, Rexall (drug manufacturing business sold) and Parke, Davis (merged with Warner Lambert), were replaced by Schering Corp. and G. D. Searle from 1969–1975.

REFERENCES FOR SECOND SCHNEE AND CAGLARCAN EXCERPT

32. See, for example, Harry Bloch, "True Profitability Measures for Pharmaceutical Investment," *Regulation, Economics and Pharmaceutical Innovation*, ed. Joseph D. Cooper (Washington, D.C.: The American University, 1976), pp. 147–156; Robert Ayanian, "Investment in Intangibles and Rates of Return in the Drug Industry," *Drug Development and Marketing*, ed. Robert B. Helms (Washington, D.C.: American Enterprise Institute for Public Policy Research, 1975), pp. 81–96; and Kenneth W. Clarkson, *Intangible Capital and Rates of Return* (Washington, D.C.: American Enterprise Institute for Public Policy Research, 1977).
33. Baxter and Company, "Comparative Rates of Return for Pharmaceutical and Other Firms: A Conceptual and Empirical Analysis" (Washington, D.C.: Baxter and Company, September, 1974).

34. Ezra Solomon, "Alternative Rate of Return Concepts and Their Implications for Utility Regulation," *Bell Journal of Economics and Management* (Spring, 1970), pp. 71–80.
35. J. J. Friedman and Associates, "R & D Intensity in the Pharmaceutical Industry" (Washington, D.C., September, 1973).
36. Gordon R. Conrad and Irving H. Plotkin, "Risk/Return: U.S. Industry Pattern," *Harvard Business Review* (March-April, 1968), pp. 90–99.
37. I. N. Fisher and G. R. Hall, "Risk and Corporate Rates of Return," *Proceedings of the Econometric Society* (December 30, 1973).
38. Alexander Barges and Brian R. Hickey, "Drug Industry Profits," *Financial Analysts Journal* (May-June, 1968), p. 80.
39. Rodney F. Smith, "Ethical Drug Industry Return on Investment" (unpublished Ph.D. dissertation, University of Massachusetts, 1974).
40. Harold A. Clymer, "The Economics of Drug Innovation," *The Development and Control of New Drug Products*, eds. M. Pernarowski and M. Darrach (Vancouver: University of British Columbia, 1972), pp. 121–124.
41. David Schwartzman, *The Expected Return from Pharmaceutical Research* (Washington, D.C.: American Enterprise Institute for Public Policy Research, 1975), pp. 23–42.
42. Thomas R. Stauffer, "Discovery Risk, Profitability Performance and Survival Risk in a Pharmaceutical Firm," *Regulation, Economics and Pharmaceutical Innovation*, ed. Joseph Cooper (Washington, D.C.: The American University, 1976), pp. 93–124.

SOURCES AND PERMISSIONS

a. Reprinted from "Regulating Competition in a Nonprofit Industry: The Problem of Forprofit Hospitals" by William D. White, *Inquiry*, Vol. 16, No. 1 (Spring 1979), pp. 50–61, by permission of the Blue Cross Association. © 1979 by the Blue Cross Association. All rights reserved.

b. Reprinted from "The Pharmaceutical Industry" by Walter Measday, in Walter Adams, ed., *The Structure of American Industry*, 5th ed., pp. 257–262, 269–271, 275–277, by permission of Macmillan Publishing Co., Inc., © 1977.

c. Reprinted from "Economic Structure and Performance of the Ethical Pharmaceutical Industry" by Jerome Schnee and Erol Caglarcan, in Colton Lindsay, ed., *The Pharmaceutical Industry*, pp. 22–23, 37–39, John Wiley & Sons, Inc., by permission of Erol Caglarcan, © 1978.

d. Reprinted from "Pharmaceutical Marketing" by Gilbert Harrell, in Colton Lindsay, ed., *The Pharmaceutical Industry*, pp. 84–85, John Wiley & Sons, Inc., by permission of Erol Caglarcan, © 1978.

Chapter 10

Technological Change

Changes in *technology* have been considerable in health care during this century. New drugs, hospital facilities and equipment, and methods of treatment have revolutionized the practice of medicine. Diseases formerly considered incurable now are susceptible to treatment, while diagnosis and treatment of other conditions are performed in ways undreamed of only a few years ago. Technological advance has not been without its critics, of course. Some have pointed to the depersonalization that seems to accompany highly specialized and technologically sophisticated medical care. Others have questioned whether certain innovations have an effect on health large enough to justify their cost. *Technological change* often is singled out as one reason for the rising cost of health care, and hospitals have been criticized for overinvestment in innovative but expensive equipment.

Economic and social aspects of medical technology represent a very active area of current research. There is extensive recent literature on the subject.[1] The authors necessarily have been quite selective in deciding what topics to cover here and which specific works to include. The selections all make use of the basic economic concepts or research methodology introduced in earlier chapters. This is not to deny, of course, that other approaches yield important insights. The reader undoubtedly will be familiar with some of these approaches and may have had experience with specific cases. It is hoped that the material that follows provides a general context in which to consider future issues and make decisions involving technological change. In addition, it gives a view of one analytical framework used to analyze and evaluate government policy in this area.

A standard treatment of technological change in economic theory views such change as affecting the production function—the relationship between inputs and outputs. This approach is outlined in the next section. The focus then turns to the health care sector specifically and the effects of technological change on costs. Following that, biomedical research is analyzed as an investment, that is, an expenditure now from which returns are expected in the future. A case study reviews the returns on poliomyelitis research that uses cost-benefit analysis, a technique more fully developed in Chapter 11. The next section deals with economic analysis of *diffusion,* the process by which the use of an innovation spreads through a population of users. Finally, the chapter discusses the effects of government policy on technological change.

THE PRODUCTION FUNCTION AND TECHNOLOGICAL CHANGE

The production function is a relationship between quantities of inputs used and the amount of output that can be produced with those inputs. At any given time technology will determine the production function, i.e., the terms on which inputs can yield output. It is important to note that there are always alternative input combinations for producing any output level, and the production function refers to the whole list of alternatives, not just the one chosen. The isoquant diagram is a representation of the production function that emphasizes this point. In Figure 10-1, the isoquant labeled Q_o shows the different capital and labor combinations that produce output level Q_o. For example, at point X the output is being produced by using much capital and a relatively small amount of labor, while point Y shows production of the same output level using much labor and little capital. To take a medical care example, point Y might represent staffing an intensive care unit for ten patients with ten nurses, each equipped with only simple instruments, while point X might represent running the same ten-patient unit using only three nurses and electronic monitoring equipment.

In this context a *technological change* is represented by a downward shift of the isoquant. That is, after the change it is possible to produce output Q_o by using fewer of both inputs. This is shown by the isoquant Q_o', where, for example, the point X' might represent production with new monitoring equipment requiring only two nurses to care for the ten patients. This is an example of a labor-saving technological change. In the medical services industry, technological change sometimes is labor saving but it may have other effects on labor inputs. For instance, the effect of a new device for monitoring patients may be to introduce new capital equipment; but rather than replace labor, the innovation may require a different kind of worker, such as electronics technicians in place of doctors and nurses.

Figure 10-1 Isoquants

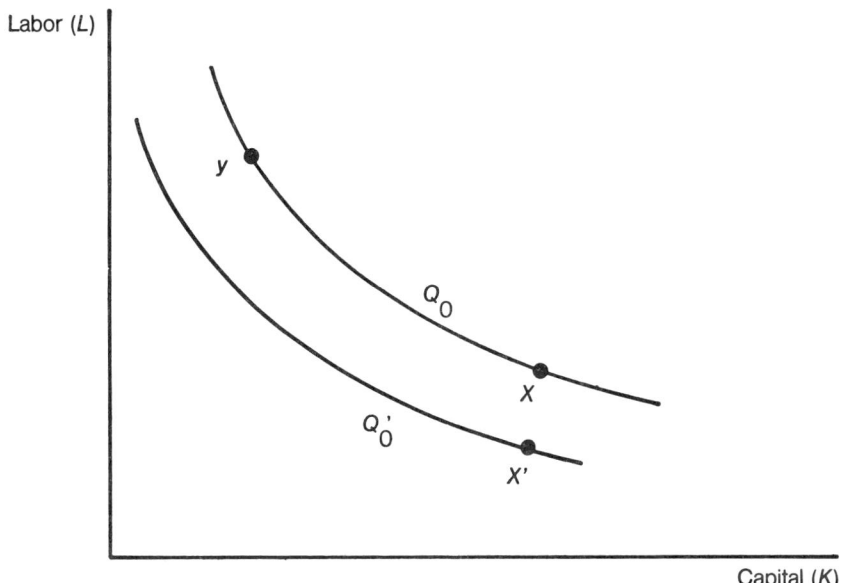

Economists distinguish between a change in technique and technological change. A change in technique means any alteration in the production method used. This can occur in the absence of technological change. If input prices change, the firm will substitute the input whose cost has fallen in relative terms for the one that now is higher. A move along a fixed isoquant thus represents a change in technique that does not require any technological development. The latter requires a shift in the isoquant, i.e., a whole new "menu" of techniques from which the firm can choose. Technological change in medical care often is associated with new equipment but it need not be. New forms of organization, surgical procedures, drugs, or methods of patient management also are types of technological change.

EFFECTS OF TECHNOLOGICAL CHANGE ON COSTS

In the industrial sector the production function approach works best in dealing with process innovation—a change that makes it possible to produce the same output at a lower cost. However, few advances in health care technology fall into that category. More typically they result in production of a different product at somewhat higher cost.

In the next section Martin Feldstein discusses this problem in the context of a model that relates changing technology to hospital costs. His analysis highlights the different effects of a modification in technique and a true technological advance, i.e., an increase in scientific knowledge. He shows that the former can be caused by a demand shift and can result in a cost increase, particularly if the demand increase is related to greater insurance coverage. In addition, even increased scientific knowledge that is potentially cost reducing can have the opposite effect under certain conditions. Feldstein's analytical framework is summarized as follows:

CHANGING TECHNOLOGY[a]

Despite the very rapid change in hospital technology, I know of no previous analysis of the forces that direct this technical change or of its impact on the average cost of care. Rather than attempting a detailed description, this chapter offers a conceptual framework that should be useful for understanding this process and for subsequently developing a more thorough quantitative analysis.

It is important to distinguish between changes of technology due to scientific progress and changes from one technique to another already known technique. Technical change without scientific progress occurs for two different reasons. Traditional economic analysis emphasizes the change that occurs in response to a shift in the relative prices of inputs. Because hospital wage rates have risen much faster than the prices of their other inputs, hospitals have economized on labor by using more disposable items, by automating laboratory and clinical procedures, and in general by other forms of substituting equipment and supplies for personnel. The effect of this substitution has been to prevent costs from rising as fast as they otherwise would have. The importance of this factor as a determinant of the rate of hospital cost inflation in the past and as an influence on future cost increases is a potentially rich but currently unexplored subject for research.[2] The general theory of this type of input substitution is well understood, but because there is insufficient information to examine this process in hospitals, this type of technical change will not be discussed here.

The second reason for technical change without scientific progress is a change in the demand for hospital care. This type of technical change generally yields a new product and not just a different way of producing the old product.[3]

4.1 A Diagrammatic Representation of Technology and Choice

Although actual changes in product and in production technique are often the result of both new scientific knowledge and a changing demand, the logical distinction between changes with and without new scientific knowledge is important for understanding the process of change and its effects on cost. This discussion of technical change can be clarified by using a diagram to represent the two components in the analysis: (1) the relation between cost per patient day (CPPD) and the benefits of hospital care as perceived by patients and (2) the preferences of patients that determine their choice between more expensive hospital care and other forms of consumption.

Figure 10-2 represents the benefit-cost possibility curve, the relation that prevails at a given time, with the particular current state of scientific knowledge, between average cost per patient

Figure 10-2 The Relation of Benefits to Costs

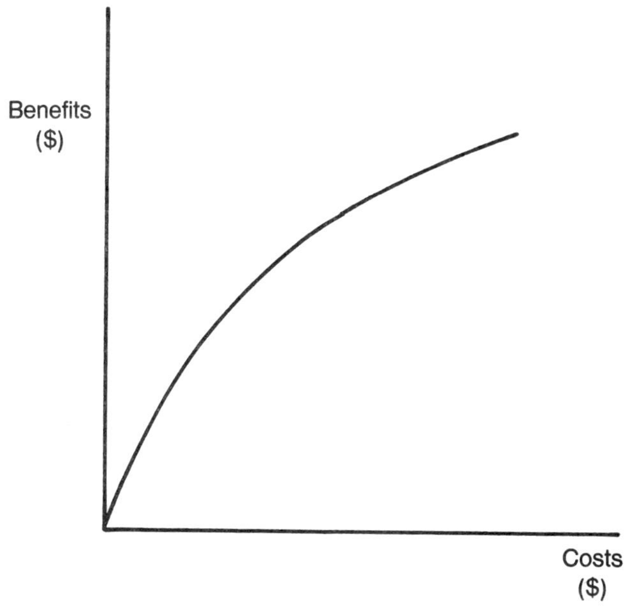

day and the benefit of hospital care as perceived by patients.[4] The term "benefit" should be considered quite broadly to include not only the expected degree of success of medical care but also the patient's comfort while in hospital and the reduction in uncertainty that is provided by more expensive diagnostic procedures. There is no natural physical unit in which the benefits can be measured. It is useful therefore to consider a dollar measure: the maximum amount that an average individual would be willing to pay for the expected medical gains, comfort, and reduced uncertainty.[5] The shape of the benefit-cost curve implies that an increase in cost per patient day raises the level of benefits, but less than proportionately.[6]

What determines the point on the benefit-cost curve where a hospital will choose to operate? That is, what determines the technology that actually prevails? The question is a difficult one, and no definitive answer can be given. In a community in which a single hospital serves the entire population, the chosen technology will reflect the preferences of the patients, the medical staff, and the hospital administration in an indeterminate way. However, when patients can choose among several different hospitals, it is likely that their preferences will dominate in determining the technology.[7] The philanthropic nature of hospitals suggests that this may be approximately true even where hospitals do have some monopoly power. The current analysis will assume that patients' preferences do determine the benefit-cost point that prevails.[8]

"Indifference curve analysis," a diagrammatic method widely used in the economic theory of consumer behavior, can be adapted to represent preferences in the current context. Figure 10-3 shows three indifference lines, labeled I_0, I_1, and I_2.[9] For simplicity we ignore insurance at this point and assume that cost per patient day is the price that the patients pay. . . . Indifference line I_1 represents one set of benefit-cost combinations, among which the "representative" patient is indifferent; he has no preference between the relatively low-cost hospital care (point A) and a higher cost hospital care if the benefits are sufficiently higher (such as point B).[10] By construction, at every point on I_1, the patient values the benefits at $20 more than the price he would have to pay.[11] Points on indifference curve I_2 represent benefit-cost combinations that are preferred to those on indifference curve I_1; point C is more costly than point A but offers much greater benefits. At every point on I_2, the patient values the benefits at

Figure 10-3 Indifference Lines

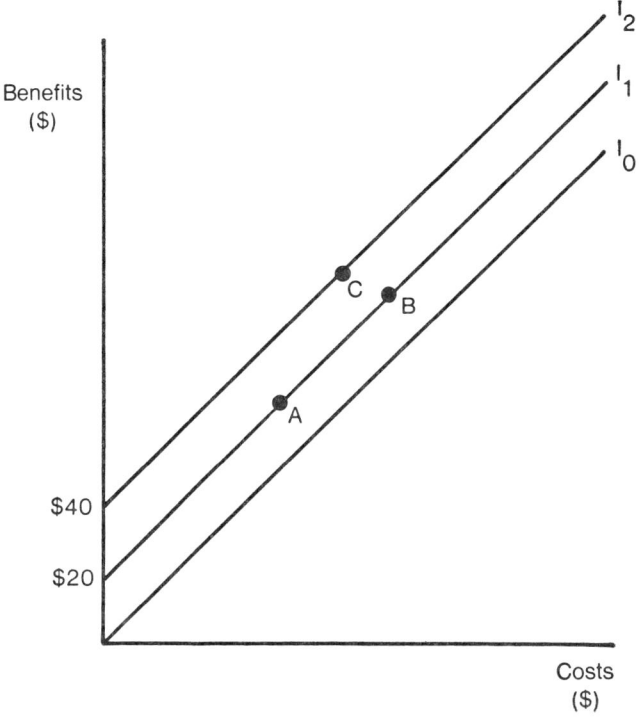

$40 more than their price. Similarly, points on I_0 are less desirable than those on I_1 and I_2; more specifically, these are points at which the charge represents the maximum amount that the patient would be willing to pay for the corresponding benefits. Although only three indifference lines are drawn for illustration, every possible benefit-cost point lies on some indifference line.

Figure 10-4 combines Figures 10-2 and 10-3. Since the only technically feasible benefit-cost combinations lie on or below the benefit-cost possibility curve, it is clear that point E is the benefit-cost combination that the patient prefers. All of the other points on and below the benefit-cost curve lie on lower (i.e., less preferred) indifference lines, and points on higher indifference lines such as I_2 cannot be attained. The technology marked by point E, with the cost per patient day approximately $40, would therefore occur if patients' preferences prevailed.[12]

Figure 10-4 The Preferred Cost Point

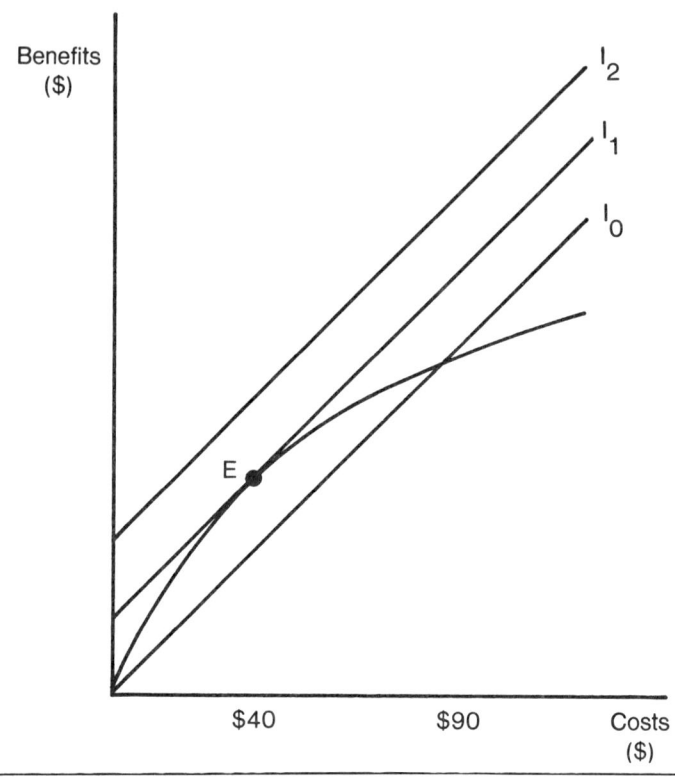

Using this framework, Feldstein is able to analyze the effects of increases in income and insurance coverage, both of which lead to a shift upward in the benefit-costs curve. Scientific progress implies a new "product" at any level of cost per patient day for which the patient is willing to pay more. This also shifts the benefit-cost curve upward. The knowledge that the curve shifts up is not sufficient to explain what happens to the equilibrium point, however. This depends on the slope of the curve as it shifts upward. Feldstein concludes:

> The current discussion is offered as preliminary framework to encourage more sophisticated analysis and to stress several key aspects of the relation between technical progress and health costs that have been generally ignored or incorrectly assessed: (1) the rise in cost per patient day is not evidence that there has been no technical progress or productivity gain; (2) changing demand can alter technology without any scientific progress; (3) technical

progress can increase as well as lower costs; and (4) the current approach to medical research may be biased toward producing information that causes technical progress to increase cost.

Theoretical analysis alone cannot provide actual estimates of the magnitude of technological impacts on health care costs. The task of making such estimates remains a substantial research challenge. There is no consensus on appropriate estimating methodology, and the literature consists largely of case studies of specific technologies. After reviewing the literature that does pertain to costs, Warner concludes:

CAPITAL-EMBODIED MEDICAL COSTS[b]

The literature sheds little light on the quantitative cost importance of capital-embodied technology; neither does it answer the question of whether the tendency to overinvest in and overuse sophisticated services is qualitatively distinct from a similar general tendency in the provision and consumption of medical care. However, an assimilation of the numerous case studies (tempered by an awareness of selection bias) can be combined with the analysis of more general studies to draw some tentative conclusions:

• The high costs associated with capital-embodied technology result principally from the ancillary personnel and supplies required to use the capital equipment. These variable costs, which may include specialized labor (nurses or technicians), run from 1 to 3 or more times capital costs.

• Adoption and use of capital-embodied technology is probably a significant though not primary cause of hospital cost inflation. A methodology was suggested as to how one might estimate both the current cost of such technology and its contribution to inflation. For high-cost equipment, as a guesstimate I place the latter at less than 25 percent of the annual hospital inflation rate. The former would appear to be smaller still.

• The failure of the literature to deal directly and thoroughly with capital-embodied technology reflects the difficulty of defining medical production functions in a uniquely meaningful way. The same problem arises in considering medical technology more generically. In part, this difficulty suggests an arbitrary element in defining and distinguishing these terms.

• The true social cost of a capital-embodied technology, or of any medical care, cannot be evaluated in an output vacuum. That is, lacking knowledge of the benefits derived from a technology, one cannot determine whether the technology's costs are purely inflationary or whether they represent a "good buy," producing a benefit of at least comparable magnitude. Still, theory suggests the existence of strong incentives in the existing medical care system for overutilization of technology; case studies seem to confirm significant and widespread instances of this.

• There are reasons to anticipate continuation of a "technology boom." Given the multiyear lag between research and technology application, the generous funding of R&D a decade ago and the recent emphasis on technology development augur numerous capital-intensive innovations during the next several years. Part of the "technology boom" of recent years undoubtedly [is] owed to the growth in private and public insurance coverage. For example, Russell (1977) documented sharp increases in ICU's and diagnostic radioisotope facilities in small hospitals with the advent of Medicare and Medicaid; electroencephalographs rose rapidly in larger hospitals. It can be argued that "the historical pressures for hospital inflation have been greatly reduced in the mid-1970's. . . . [F]uture increases in demand for hospital services similar to those experienced before are unlikely to occur" (McMahon and Drake, 1976, p. 136). With 90 percent of all direct hospital costs covered by insurance, it is probably correct that the economic pressure for increasing the quantity of services will be small. However, this will not necessarily alter the growing demand for higher *quality* of services, with its attendant implications for the use of sophisticated technology.

Table 10-1 National Expenditures for Health Research and Development by Source of Funds (Amounts in Millions of Dollars)

Source of Funds	1960		1970		1978	
	Amount	Percent	Amount	Percent	Amount	Percent
Federal Government	$448	48.8	$1,667	59.0	$3,789	61.5
State Government	78	8.5	150	5.3	306	5.0
Industry	253	27.6	798	28.1	1,775	28.8
Nonprofit Organizations	139	15.1	215	7.6	291	4.7
Total	918		2,827		6,161	

Source: Adapted from U.S. Department of Health, Education and Welfare, *Health—United States, 1979* (Washington, D.C.: U.S. Government Printing Office, 1980), p. 201.

The general concern is expressed by Gaus and Cooper (1976, p. 11): "Given our tremendous technology-induced costs, it is apparent that in the U.S. today we have neither the capacity to determine how much of what technology is appropriate nor the mechanism to control adoption." In the extreme, the fear is that the state of the art in technology is the binding constraint on medical costs. Unless we learn how to assess the cost-effectiveness of technologies and then how to implement effective controls on adoption and use, we can anticipate that technology will continue to contribute to rapid inflation in the cost of medical care.

INVESTMENT IN BIOMEDICAL RESEARCH

The national investment in health-related research and development for the United States in fiscal 1978 totaled $6.2 billion (Table 10-1). As would be expected, the total expenditure includes a number of quite different activities. There are three general types of activities that usually precede technological innovation in health care: basic research, applied research and development, and clinical testing.[2]

Basic research in biological science lays the groundwork for much technological innovation. Frequently such research is done without clear medical application in mind, and occasionally an advance results serendipitously from lines of inquiry far removed from the health care area that finally benefits. Basic research in physics and chemistry also can lead to medical advances both directly, as in the case of the discovery of x-rays, and indirectly through the development of equipment or techniques useful for doing biological research.

Applied research and development attempts to bring the results of basic research to bear on particular problems. "While basic research in biology seeks to understand vital processes, applied research seeks their manipulation or control."[3] Examples of applied research in nonbiological fields that contribute to medical technology include the development of biomaterials by chemical engineers and of medical electronic instruments.

Clinical testing involves the use of new technologies in human subjects. It ranges from the first use on human beings to large-scale clinical trials.

> The nature of first human use varies with the technology being tested. To test many noninvasive procedures or equipment, the investigator may use himself or coworkers as subjects; little risk may be involved. In other cases, only small samples of blood or

tissue may be required, and these can be obtained from a number of sources including blood banks and hospitals. For invasive or particularly risky procedures, however, careful medical supervision and considerable planning are required. Furthermore, in such cases, first human use raises problems of informed consent by the subject; the individual must be aware that he is participating in an experiment and must agree to become a subject. Clinical testing frequently reveals problems that were not—and perhaps could not have been—anticipated from prior work on animals. In some cases, considerable further research is required; at other times, minor improvements prove to be sufficient. Therefore, continued development of new technology frequently continues apace with further clinical testing.[4]

The innovation process is complex, involving many decision makers and considerable uncertainty. Viewed from an overall economic perspective, however, medical research and development is simply an investment, a use of resources now that, it is hoped, will yield benefits later. In the case of most industrial innovation, the costs and returns are private. The outlays and risks are borne and benefits received by the firm that undertakes the R & D project. Under these circumstances, market competition and the profit incentive provide a guide to the allocation of resources; a particular investment will be undertaken if its expected *rate of return* is greater than that from alternative investments (thus the total investment in R & D will reflect the returns to research and development in relation to other uses of resources).

Actually, even in industrial R & D the market does not provide perfect guidance. There inevitably are some costs and benefits that are not private, that is, that accrue to members of society other than the firm undertaking the investment. In biomedical research this problem is particularly pronounced. Because expenditures are financed by taxes and because the benefits are diffused widely and unpredictably among members of society, private benefits are unidentifiable and the market mechanism gives little direction to investment. (There are, of course, some notable exceptions such as research on drugs and medical equipment by private firms.)

The fact that the resource allocation is decided upon in the absence of profit motivation and market incentives makes the economic problem no less important. Resources have alternative uses, so society should invest in medical R & D only to the extent that returns on this investment are favorable in relation to other possibilities. This rule is easy to state but quite difficult to apply because of the problem of quantifying and estimating the magnitudes of costs and benefits. Nevertheless, some work has been done along these lines. The following excerpt from a well-known article by Burton Weisbrod is an example of an attempt to define and estimate the economic costs and benefits of investment in medical research. Its important concepts and techniques justify its inclusion here despite the out-of-date information on polio cases. (The methodology of cost-benefit analysis is presented more fully in Chapter 11.)

RESEARCH COSTS[c]

The nature of medical research is such that identifying an expenditure with a particular disease is frequently not easy. Expenditures on "basic" research—not directed at any disease—may contribute nonetheless to the development of an operational method for preventing some specific disease. And research aimed at a particular disease may produce results that are useful in dealing with some other disease. As a result, it is often not clear precisely what should be included in an estimate of the cost of research "on" a particular disease—for example, the research leading to the polio vaccines.

The conceptual problem is matched by the empirical problem of obtaining data. In Table 10-2, column (2) shows the time series of amounts awarded for polio research, on the basis of information obtained by the Science Information Exchange (SIE). The data represent awards, not actual expenditures, and then only those research awards (grants and contracts) registered with the SIE by national granting agencies. The SIE series begins with 1946, and I have arbitrarily extended it back to 1930 in the interest of tolerable completeness. Because of the incompleteness of the SIE expenditure data and because of the necessarily arbitrary nature of the extrapolation, two alternative assumptions about the accuracy of the data are utilized in the calculations described below.

The research data in column (2) are in current dollars. In order to take account of price level changes, and in the absence of a truly satisfactory basis for doing so, I used the Consumer Price Index to adjust the expenditure estimates to the 1957 level of prices. The results appear in column (3).

Benefits per Case Prevented

In principle, "benefits" include *all* favorable effects in whatever forms are deemed relevant. As measured here, however, benefits from prevention of polio are only the sum of: (1) the market value

Table 10-2 Estimated Awards for Poliomyelitis Research, 1930–56 (Thousands of Dollars)

Year (1)	Current Dollars (2)	Price Adjusted (1957 = 100) (3)
1930	...	100
1931	...	200
1932	...	300
1933	...	300
1934	...	300
1935	...	300
1936	...	300
1937	...	300
1938	...	300
1939	...	300
1940	...	300
1941	...	100
1942	...	100
1943	...	100
1944	...	100
1945	...	100
1946	242	356
1947	492	631
1948	746	891
1949	1,513	1,823
1950	1,729	2,064
1951	2,609	2,883
1952	2,744	2,967
1953	2,022	2,170
1954	1,920	2,051
1955	2,176	2,332
1956	1,962	2,072

Source: Col. (2), Science Information Exchange; col. (3), for 1946–56, adjustments of data in col. (2) by CPI (1957 = 100); for 1930–45, author's estimates.

of production lost because of premature *mortality* due to polio; (2) the market value of production lost as a result of *morbidity*—illness and disability—caused by polio; and (3) the costs of resources devoted to *treatment* and *rehabilitation* of polio victims. The basic methodology by which each of these three components was estimated is described in detail in my *Economics of Public Health* (Weisbrod 1961, esp. chaps. 7 and 8; hereinafter cited as *EPH*) and will only be summarized briefly here. The present paper extends this earlier work, which dealt only with the benefit side, to an analysis in which the costs incurred to discover the effective vaccines and the costs of vaccinating people—applying the new knowledge—also are considered.

Mortality losses for people of specified ages had been estimated previously (in *EPH*) as the present value of expected future earnings,[2] utilizing 1951 earnings data and U.S. life tables for 1949–51.[3] For women, the market earnings data were supplemented by estimates of the value of household services (*EPH*, appendix 2). From these gross-loss figures were subtracted my estimates of the marginal consumption expenditures attributable to an incremental person in a household—the point being that mortality involves the loss of a consumer as well as a producer.[4] The resulting values of net future earnings were weighted by the actual reported number of deaths attributable to polio among males and females, by age, to obtain the estimated "premature mortality" loss per death from polio (*EPH*, table 6).

Morbidity losses—those resulting from the temporary loss of a producer—were derived from the same age-specific and sex-specific earnings-productivity data used for the mortality-loss estimates, it being assumed that an average of one-fourth of a year of work time was lost per case because of temporary or permanent disability (*EPH*, table 9 and accompanying discussion). For the permanently and totally disabled, the entire remaining working lifetime was lost, but the overwhelming majority of cases produced little or no loss of work time—in part because the effects were very short-term and occurred among children.

Treatment losses are the third form of social cost of polio that had previously been estimated. Prevention of a disease makes treatment costs unnecessary, thereby liberating resources for alternative uses.[5] The range of treatment costs for polio victims has been great, running into many thousands of dollars when respiratory equipment was utilized, but for the large proportion of cases, which have been nonparalytic, these costs have been far smaller. Earlier, I estimated the mean at around $550 per case as of 1950 (*EPH*, p. 80).

These three forms of losses were summed to give an estimated mean loss per case of $1,150—the estimate of the expected benefit per case prevented (*EPH*, p. 90). It is possible that a successful prevention program could bring about a significant change in the labor supply (and, hence, in the marginal productivity of labor) or in the demand for treatment; and in this case the $1,150 figure would be invalid. In the case of polio, however, the disease was not so widespread that substantial effects on factor supply or demand were likely to result from a successful prevention program.

Thus, it was assumed that for each case of polio prevented, a benefit of at least $1,150 resulted—"at least," because, as noted above, benefits in such important forms as reduced pain and suffering have not been considered. This estimated benefit per case prevented is derived from data for various years between 1949 and 1954, but because the data were largely from around 1950, the $1,150 figure was assumed to apply to that year. This figure has been adjusted to prices in 1957—the year of research "success," when the Sabin oral vaccine first became widely available—by the arbitrary use of the CPI, thereby producing a figure of $1,350 in 1957 prices. In some of the calculations described below, a productivity-growth adjustment was also made; more about this later.

Number of Cases Prevented

We turn next to determination of the number of polio cases prevented. This requires estimation of the number of cases expected for each year following 1957, with and without the research success.

Expected Cases—No Research Success

During the period 1920–56 the trend in reported cases of polio was upward, although there was substantial year-to-year variation (Department of Health, Education, and Welfare 1962, p. 17). Some of the "increase" was the result, simply, of improved reporting, and so the incidence rates for the later years should be given heavier weight in a forecast. The procedure actually used, therefore, was to calculate the mean rate for the ten years ending with 1956. This gave an average of some twenty-one new cases annually per 100,000 persons in the population. For the U.S. population in 1957—168 million—this produced an estimate of 36,000 new cases for each year after 1957, holding constant the size and age distribution of the population in that year.[6] Since the U.S. population is actually growing, and for reasons quite independent of the incidence of polio, the absolute number of polio cases would be expected to rise in the absence of a successful research program. The assumption of population constancy is relaxed, later, to assess the sensitivity of the rate of return to this assumption.

Expected Cases—Successful Research Program

Granted that in the absence of the research, 36,000 new cases of polio could be expected each year, it is necessary next to estimate the degree of success of the research. Here an important— if simple—point must be reiterated: knowledge without application is valueless. And since application of new knowledge is rarely costless, we can expect application of new knowledge to be less than complete and immediate. Polio vaccine illustrates this generalization. There are costs of producing and delivering vaccine, and there are implicit costs—in the form of time—for the individual taking it. Thus, we can expect the vaccine to be utilized by less than the entire vulnerable population under fifty, and, consequently, the number of new cases of polio may well not fall to zero.[7] In any event, we must take these application costs into account when we turn to the net benefits of the polio research effort . . . .

The number of new cases expected in a given year after the successful research is a function of the amount of resources devoted to vaccinating people over the previous forty to fifty years or so. The larger the expenditures on application of knowledge— that is, the more people vaccinated—the smaller the number of expected new cases.

In the procedure utilized in this paper, the number of cases expected after 1957 was assumed to equal zero, but alternative assumptions were employed regarding the number of persons who had to be vaccinated—and, hence, the total cost of vaccination— in order to produce this result. Alternative assumptions also were made regarding the cost per person vaccinated. Thus, . . . the number of cases prevented was assumed to equal 36,000, the number of cases expected in the absence of a successful research-vaccination program.

Application (Vaccination) Costs

Turning to the vaccination costs, V, it was assumed that to eliminate polio would have required (1) vaccinating the entire 1957 population under fifty,[8] (2) vaccinating all or, alternatively, none of the subsequent newborn children, assumed constant at the 1957 level of 4.25 million, and (3) incurring a vaccination cost per person of either $0.66 or $3.00 of direct cost plus an opportunity cost of time. The $0.66 figure assumes three "shots" (actually impregnated sugar cubes) at a cost of $0.22 each. This is an estimate of how low the cost might be if mass vaccination techniques were used.[9] It includes the purchase price of the drug, advertising costs, and my estimate of the implicit cost of the time donated by physicians, dentists, pharmacists, and others (utilizing 1959 income data for these occupations, from the 1960 census). The total cost, so computed, was simply divided by the number of persons vaccinated to obtain the average cost estimate of $0.22 per shot, or $0.66 per person receiving the series of three. The $1.00 per shot alternative cost is a rough estimate of the charge made by private physicians (in 1957 prices).

Obtaining a vaccination also requires some of the time of the persons being vaccinated. In my calculations, the average opportunity cost of time per shot received was judged to be around $1.00 for adults and $0.50 for children. These figures are guesstimates. I assumed that about a half hour, including travel time, was required for each of the three shots at an opportunity cost of $2.00 per hour per adult. The lower figure for children (under eighteen) was based on the assumption that, typically, a mother would take more than one child at a time, so that even if the mother herself were not also obtaining a vaccination, the opportunity cost to her of the time required would be well under the $1.00 per hour figure; in addition, in many instances, the vaccination would coincide with a physician visit for some other purpose, thus making the marginal time required rather modest.

Weisbrod then performs several rate-of-return calculations to determine how good an economic investment polio research was. The detailed methodology of his analysis is beyond the scope of this book but is roughly similar to the cost-benefit procedures discussed in Chapter 11. He concludes as follows:

Summary and Conclusion

The resources devoted to polio research in the United States have produced vaccines that are both safe and effective in preventing polio. The analysis in this paper shows that, except under the most extreme assumptions, this research is raising output and reducing treatment expenditures in amounts producing a rate of return on the research and application costs of at least 5 percent, or more probably 11–12 percent.

Because of the narrowness of the operational measure of benefits used in this paper, including its abstraction from the pain and anguish accompanying disease, there is little doubt that the real value of the medically successful polio research—and the price that buyers would pay for the vaccinations—is greater than what is estimated in this paper. The "value" of reduced illness and increased longevity is, one might guess, greater than simply the effects on earnings. In addition, even the more strictly financial benefits are probably understated, in part because of the disregard for the benefits occurring outside the United States.

Empirical findings as to the rate of return on polio research cannot be generalized to other medical research. The approach presented here, however, may have wider applicability.

In the case of some medical research programs, it may be possible to identify the disease or diseases that will be affected if and when the research is fruitful; the closer the research is to the "applied" end of the applied-basic spectrum, the greater the likelihood that such an identification can be made. When it can—when the output of medical research is expected to take the form of a reduction in the incidence, prevalence, or severity of one or more particular diseases—the variables . . . above constitute a checklist of items about which information should be sought by persons responsible for resource-allocation decisions: What is the expected cost of the research program in each period? If the research is "successful," what "benefits" will result in each future period (and with what probabilities) per case of the disease(s) prevented or made less severe? How many cases will be affected in each future period? What application costs, in each future period, will be required in order to realize these benefits from the medical research?

Recognition of the relationship between research and application points up some interesting facets of the "public good" problem and its connection with the question of allocative efficiency in the private sector. Knowledge resulting from (medical or other) research—for example, knowledge about means for preventing polio—has the characteristic of a public or collective-consumption good: its use by one person does not limit its availability to others. Thus, because of the familiar "free rider" problem, the production of medical research (knowledge) in the private market appears likely to be suboptimal. However, since the application of knowledge in some cases, such as polio, involves vaccinations or other procedures that are provided *individually,* exclusion of nonpayers is easily practiced. As a result, when investment in research and investment in the application of the resulting knowledge are considered jointly, the conclusion is that the private market may produce an optimal level of research.

This result, though possible, is by no means necessary. A priori, it is not clear to a private firm that if its research is successful the new knowledge will be such that it can be embodied in a salable commodity such as a vaccination. Even if it can, there is no assurance (except for patent laws) that competitors can be precluded from entering into the production of vaccines. Moreover, to the extent that any research is undertaken privately, we can expect it to emphasize exploration of techniques that lend themselves to low-cost exclusion of consumers—even if other techniques would be more efficient socially. The forms as well as the total "quantity" of research can be nonoptimal.

Another factor influencing the optimality of the private market provision of medical research and application is present when contagious diseases such as polio are involved. Since external benefits accompany the individual internal benefits of vaccination, the decentralized private market is likely to produce nonoptimal numbers of vaccinations; and since the expected profitability of research depends on the expected sales of vaccine, consumer decisions in the market for vaccinations will affect the profitability of research. On the one hand, the occurrence of external benefits tends to cause suboptimal purchase of vaccinations by consumers who disregard the benefits that their vaccinations bestow on others. On the other hand, if consumers also fail to adjust their decisions to the fact that they receive benefits from others who are being vaccinated, a superoptimal level of vaccination may result from individualistic behavior in the private market. The net effect on the vaccination market and, thus, on the research market seems unclear.

This paper has reported on a case study of costs and (certain) benefits of one medical research effort, polio. From the case study, however, we have also come to see how a benefit-cost analysis of medical research requires recognizing the interrelatedness of the research with procedures for applying the fruit of the research. Finally, we have seen that where collective-consumption goods, such as research knowledge, require the use of individual-consumption goods for their application, but where these individual goods produce real external economies, it may not be clear that the private market can be expected to behave inefficiently or, if it does, in which direction the deviation from optimality occurs.

DIFFUSION

The impact of a technological innovation on the economy comes not simply from its introduction by the first user but rather from its adoption by many users. The process by which an innovation spreads from introduction to widespread use is called *diffusion*. The speed and extent of diffusion are important determinants of the total economic consequences of a technological innovation.

The diffusion process is essentially a learning operation. Potential users of the innovation must become aware of its existence, knowledgeable about its properties, and convinced of its usefulness to them before they will try it. Often the innovation itself changes during the diffusion process. If it is a new product, the manufacturer may make modifications and improvements in response to suggestions from early users. A process innovation may be changed or adapted slightly by users to their own requirements. As the diffusion process progresses, the innovation becomes more standardized and the costs of producing and using it typically fall as more experience is gained.

A widely used model of the diffusion process is based on the assumption that the probability that a nonuser will adopt the innovation in a given time period is related to the number of potential users already employing it. (This is similar to models used by epidemiologists to explain the spread of disease.) Under this assumption the diffusion path is represented by an S-shaped curve like that shown in Figure 10-5. Empirical studies have shown that a curve like this provides a good fit to data on a variety of industrial innovations.

Louise Russell analyzed the diffusion process for five hospital technologies that spread widely in the period 1950-1974. Her goals were to determine whether the S-shaped diffusion curve noted in other industries also was found in the hospital industry, to compare the speed of diffusion of hospital technologies with those in other industries, and to observe the effect of Medicare and Medicaid on the diffusion rate. The technologies studied were postoperative recovery room, intensive care unit, respiratory therapy, diagnostic radioisotopes, and electroencephalography. Her meth-

Figure 10-5 Example of a Diffusion Path

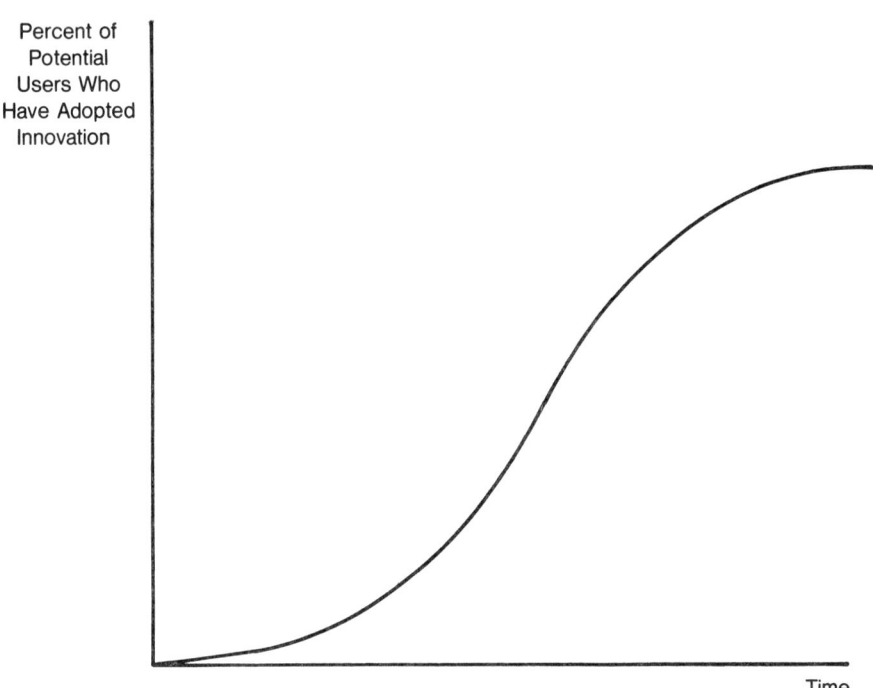

odology involved regression analysis of data from the American Hospital Association Survey of Hospital Facilities. Russell found that the S-shaped curve fit the data well: the diffusion path in the hospital industry was roughly the same as that observed in many other industries. In addition, she found that the speed of diffusion for the hospital technologies was approximately the same as that observed for many industrial innovations. One particularly interesting conclusion was that when Medicare and Medicaid were introduced in the mid-1960s, they served to increase the rate of diffusion for technologies that had not already fully diffused by that time.[5]

An empirical study by John Rapoport examined one technological innovation (radioisotopes) to identify the determinants of the diffusion rate. Using hypotheses suggested by theoretical models of hospital behavior, the study attempted to explain differences in diffusion rates among states as well as among individual hospitals in how long it took them to adopt radioisotopes. The following excerpt presents the general framework of the study and the state cross-section analysis:

CASE STUDY OF RADIOISOTOPES IN U.S. HOSPITALS[d]

Most work by economists on the diffusion of technological innovation has dealt with profit-motivated organizations or individuals. Diffusion of technological innovations among nonprofit firms also raises important resource allocation and policy questions, particularly in the hospital industry where the increasing use of expensive technologically sophisticated equipment often is cited as one reason for the rapid rise in the cost of hospital care. Nuclear medicine, the use of radioactive isotopes for diagnosis and treatment, was first introduced in U.S. hospitals in the mid-1940s and in the past thirty years has become a widely accepted technique. Like many other technological advances, it requires expensive equipment; so that adoption of the innovation by a hospital is not only significant medically but also an important capital investment decision. Thus, the diffusion of nuclear medicine provides a good case study of hospitals' economic behavior.

Hospital Economic Behavior and Diffusion Process

Recent work on the theory of hospitals' economic behavior suggests some hypotheses about the spread of technological innovations among hospitals. Most economic models of hospitals use a multidimensional objective function. Newhouse uses an objective function with two elements, quantity and quality which is maximized subject to a budget constraint [7]. The inclusion of quality in the objective function is particularly important for the diffusion of technological innovations since concern with quality of care is a primary motivation for hospitals to adopt new technology. Indeed, in view of the difficulty of measuring quality directly, the extent and the sophistication of facilities often is taken, at least by the general public, as a measure of the quality of care.

The equipment and services offered by a hospital play a central role in the "conspicuous production" theory of hospital behavior developed by Lee [5]. In his view hospitals are engaged in a type of oligopolistic rivalry for status which is assumed to depend in part on the extent to which expensive highly specialized equipment is available. It is through status that a hospital can attract physicians to its staff, and physicians are the source of patients and thus revenue for a hospital. As Lee puts it: ". . . a part of the expense incurred for expansion of inputs may be regarded as an implicit payment to physicians—a price paid to attract physicians" [5, p. 50].

In Lee's model a hospital competes for status not with all other hospitals but only with others in the same status group. The research-teaching hospitals are the highest status group and are first to adopt an innovation. After spreading among this group of hospitals, the technology then will travel to lower status groups. The importance of grouping of hospitals for analysis also is stressed by Berry who developed a grouping scheme which depends mainly on the number of facilities a hospital has [2]. His work suggests that as hospitals develop they add facilities in particular patterns; thus, a hospital's past development and present mix of facilities can give some indication of its future development.

The demand by hospitals for equipment is, at least in part, derived from the demand for hospital services; thus, factors which influence demand for services also will influence demand for equipment. Physicians play a key role both in the demand for hospital services and in the hospital decision making process leading to equipment acquisition. The model used by Pauly and Redisch views the hospital medical staff as having de facto control of the hospital and as operating as traditional income maximizers [8, 9]. This model would suggest that, at least for some types of innovations, the expected effect on doctors' incomes of a hospital's adoption would be an important determinant of adoption behavior.

The following general hypotheses about the diffusion of innovations are suggested by the above work and are used in this study.[1] First, a hospital's decision to adopt a technological innovation is determined in part by interhospital rivalry for prestige. There would appear to be two ways a hospital can gain a status advantage through the adoption of a particular innovation: it can acquire it before other hospitals, or it can acquire more expensive and sophisticated equipment than other hospitals. One hypothesis tested later in this work is that hospitals in a competitive environment will acquire an innovation earlier and/or spend more on it than hospitals less subject to competitive pressure. Second, there are identifiable groups within the hospital population; the group to which a hospital belongs determines to a great extent the time at which a hospital adopts an innovation. This study uses two groups, teaching hospitals and nonteaching hospitals, and investigates the relationship between them in the diffusion process. Third, variables which influence demand for hospital services—e.g., income—also will influence demand for equipment since the latter is a derived demand. The role of physicians is important in determining demand for hospital services, and an abundance of physicians will lead to high demand. In addition, because of the unique relationship between doctors and hospitals, an innovation will be acquired sooner or more sophisticated equipment will be obtained when the adoption will increase physicians' incomes. Fourth, where adoption of an innovation requires substantial investment, the availability and source of capital funds can influence the decision.

Finally, for many reasons big hospitals are likely to adopt innovations earlier than small ones. Hospital size is a difficult variable analytically since it relates to many aspects of the diffusion process. Size can, itself, be in the objective function; it is certainly one characteristic considered by a hospital in determining what group it should consider itself in competition with; it also is related to a hospital's case mix and function—thus, the demand for equipment. Statistically, hospital size is correlated with almost every other hospital characteristic of interest; therefore, in the regression analyses, two forms of each equation are estimated: one including hospital size as an independent variable and one omitting it. The first equation allows one to see the effect of other variables when size is held constant. Comparison with the second, where size is omitted, gives an indication of the extent to which size itself is important rather than acting as a proxy for other variables.

Description of Diffusion Process in U.S.

According to the American Hospital Association, in 1972 there were 2371 "short term general and other special" hospitals with a diagnostic radioisotope facility which represented 43.5 percent of hospitals in that category which answered the A.H.A. survey [1].[2] The percentage of hospitals having the facilities was much greater in larger than in smaller size classes. An overview of the diffusion process in the United States is provided in Figure 10-6. In the twenty-year period from 1952 to 1972, the number of hospitals offering nuclear medicine service increased roughly eightfold. The last four years of this period saw a considerable increase in the rate of diffusion with the percentage of hospitals having radioisotopes rising by 11.1 percentage points in the period 1969 to 1972: a greater increase than in any previous four-year period. There are large differences among states in the extent of the adoption of the innovation and in the time pattern of the growth rate.

As expected, teaching hospitals adopted the innovation earlier. The percentage of medical school-affiliated hospitals having radioisotopes was over 90 percent by 1960. For each state the year when all medical school affiliated hospitals first reported a radioisotope facility and the year when 10 percent of the nonaffil-

Figure 10-6 Diffusion Curve for Nuclear Medicine in the United States 1952–1972

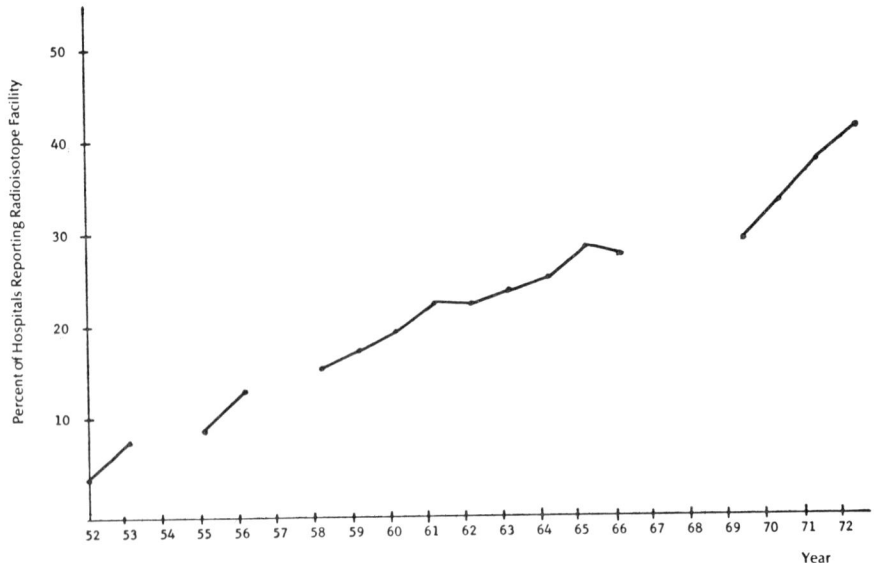

Source: American Hospital Association, *Hospitals* "Guide Issues" [1]. Data for 1954, 1957, 1967 and 1968 not available.

iated hospitals reported having the innovation were determined. This time difference showed how long it took for the innovation to diffuse from one group to the other.[3] The median time difference was three years, but interstate variation was considerable. Speed on intergroup diffusion was associated with hospital size. As a measure of the size of a state's unaffiliated hospitals, I took the percentage of these hospitals larger than 200 beds in 1958, the median year for 10 percent of nonaffiliated hospitals adopting nuclear medicine. The correlation between this size measure and the time difference was -0.61 which was significantly different from zero at the 0.01 level which suggested that where large unaffiliated hospitals were involved the filter-down of the innovation from the higher status group to the lower status group was faster.[4]

Determinants of Diffusion Rate: State Cross Section Analysis

A.H.A. data by states were used for a cross section regression analysis of the determinants of diffusion rates. The most typical diffusion curve seen in earlier studies was an S-shaped pattern, but the data for nuclear medicine did not correspond to this because of the sharp upturn noted in the late 1960s. According to a number of physicians and hospital administrators who were interviewed, there were several large technological improvements in instrumentation and techniques in the late 1960s which made the use of radioisotope imaging a more effective diagnostic tool. Also, the increase in third party coverage due to federal Medicare and Medicaid legislation can have provided economic incentives for hospitals to add radioisotope facilities. What Figure 10-6 represents is an almost completed diffusion cycle and the start of a second one spurred by exogenous economic, technological, and medical factors.

To investigate differences among states in the diffusion process, I plotted diffusion curves for each state. Since data for some years were not available, the percentage of hospitals in each state which reported a radioisotope facility for years at three-year intervals starting in 1952 was calculated.[5] The shape of the diffusion curve in most states was consistent with the national picture; i.e., a curve beginning to level out by 1969 with a sharp upturn in the

1969–1972 period. In the rest of the analysis in this section, the 1969–1972 period is discarded.

A final evaluation of the appropriateness of an S-shaped diffusion curve is made by fitting to the data for each state a logistic function similar to that used by Griliches, Mansfield, and others [4, 6]; that is,

$$P_i(t) = \frac{K_i}{1 + e - (a_i + b_i t)} \qquad (1)$$

where $P_i(t)$ is the proportion of the hospitals in the ith state which have radioisotopes in year t; K_i is the final level of adoption for state i; and a and b are parameters which can be estimated by linear regression. The value of K is set equal to the 1969 value of P, plus 2 percentage points.[6] For eight states the estimated coefficient of t is not significantly different from zero, and these states are dropped from the sample in later analysis.[7] Table 10-3 summarizes the $\bar{R}^2$ values for the remaining states and suggests that the logistic function does provide a fairly good fit to the observed data for what is admittedly a very small sample size. The parameter, b, of the logistic function determines the rate at which the percentage of hospitals adopting the innovation increases between any two levels of adoption measured as percentages of the final level. Since the final levels differ considerably, a measure of the speed of diffusion which is more comparable among states is b, adjusted for differences in K, which I call b^*; i.e., $b^* = bK$.

Why might the speed of diffusion differ among states? If interhospital competition for status and doctors is at work, the number of hospitals in the area would appear to be important.

Table 10-3 Values of $\bar{R}^2$ for the Regression Equation[8]

$$\ln \left(\frac{P}{K - P} \right) = a + bt$$

Value of $\bar{R}^2$	No. of Regressions (States)
.30–.49	2
.50–.69	9
.70–.89	19
.90–.99	12
	42

For example, the only hospital in an isolated rural area would not face severe competition for either doctors or patients since due to travel cost they have no other reasonable choice. (In a longer run sense, the hospital can compete with others in that it can try to attract physicians to the area.) A hospital located in a metropolitan area, on the other hand, will be much more in competition with other hospitals since doctors and patients have several choices. Thus, to the extent that having equipment early helps in the interhospital competition, one would expect hospitals located in urban areas to be quicker to adopt the innovation than those in smaller local areas. In order to become aware of the new technique, convinced of its effectiveness and eventually proficient in its use, potential adopters must maintain a relationship with other doctors already using it. They must see the equipment in operation, must practice using it, and must be able to follow its role in the treatment of specific patients over a fairly long time period. These things are done more easily where the technique is being used in the medical community with which they have day to day contact and where its use is advocated by other physicians whose judgment they respect and with whom they already have established a relationship. For this reason also, the speed of diffusion would be faster in urban areas where such contacts are easier and more frequent. To measure the nature of the typical hospital's local market area using state data is difficult, since a state can contain many different local areas. Two state characteristics were used to try to capture these effects very crudely, though. These were the percent of a state's population which is urban (U) and the area of the state (A) which serves as an indication of the extent to which travel costs can lessen hospital competition and can make activity leading to adoption decisions by physicians more difficult.

Another factor included is the relative availability of physicians which could have two different and opposite effects. More doctors in an area might increase demand for the innovation; however, in areas where doctors are plentiful relative to hospitals' demand for them, the competition for doctors might be less intense than in areas where they are more scarce. To the extent that competition takes place through early equipment acquisition, the rate of adoption would be faster in areas of doctor scarcity. As a measure of the relative abundance of doctors, I used the ratio of doctors in the state to the number of hospital beds (D).

Included as an explanatory variable is the occupancy rate (O) which is included partly as a demand variable but also for two other reasons. First, a high occupancy rate can mean that more internal funds are available to finance new equipment. If this were the case, high occupancy rates would be associated with rapid spread of the innovation. An opposite effect of occupancy rate is suggested by Ginsburg who found that the division of hospitals' investment between expansion of the number of beds and acquisition of sophisticated facilities is related to the occupancy rate. Hospitals with high occupancy rates tend to invest in beds rather than in sophisticated facilities [3]. If this finding is the case, a high occupancy rate would be associated with a slow diffusion rate. Per capita income (I) is included since states with higher income will tend to have higher demand for hospital services and also since hospitals in high income states might have more access to funds from donations. Finally, I include as independent variables the percent of hospitals associated with a medical school (M) and the average hospital size (S).

The above hypotheses can be expressed in the following equation which is estimated by linear regression:

$$b^* = f(S, I, U, A, O, D, M). \qquad (2)$$

The values of the variables all were taken in 1960 or 1961, about the midpoint of the period under consideration. On the basis of the discussion above, S, U, I, and M should appear in the regression with positive coefficients; A should appear with a negative coefficient; and the prediction about the signs of the coefficients of O and D is ambiguous since there are different possible effects of these variables.

The regression estimates are shown in Table 10-4. In equation (2) all the variables, except M, have the expected sign. The coefficients of U, S, and A are significantly different from zero at the 5 percent level. The coefficients of O and D are not statistically significant: a result that could indicate that in each case the two opposite hypothesized effects offset each other. Also, the coefficient of I is not significant. About 80 percent of the variation in the dependent variable is explained by the equation. When hospital size is omitted—equation (2)—the value of $\bar{R}^2$ decreases considerably, and coefficients of other variables change somewhat. This finding indicates that hospital size itself does play an important role. The negative coefficient of M is a surprising and

Table 10-4 Regression Coefficients—Determinants of Diffusion Rates Dependent Variable Is b^* [9]

Independent Variable	(1)	(2)
Constant	−5.49	−21.92*
	(1.0)	(3.0)
Size (S)	.089*	
	(6.2)	
Income (I)	.000028	.0034*
	(.02)	(1.8)
Urban Population (U)	.11*	.16*
	(2.4)	(2.4)
Area (A)	−.019*	−.039*
	(2.1)	(3.1)
Occupancy Rate (O)	−.016	.22*
	(.20)	(2.2)
Doctors (D)	2.73	−.39
	(.64)	(.06)
Medical School Affiliation (M)	−40.46*	−6.43
	(3.2)	(.39)
$\bar{R}^2$	.83	.65
n	42	42

*Significant at 10 percent level.
T-statistics in parentheses.

---

a somewhat puzzling result—suggesting that diffusion is slower in states with a large percentage of teaching hospitals. The coefficient is significant at the 1 percent level. The negative sign appears to be wrong: other evidence has suggested that affiliated hospitals tend to be quick adopters. If that is true, the result must be when there is a relatively large proportion of affiliated hospitals in an area; the rate of adoption among nonaffiliated hospitals is slower than it would be otherwise. This point is considered further below.

To examine further the determinants of diffusion rates, an analysis of the diffusion process based on three subperiods of the twenty-year time span covered by the data was carried out. Because earlier results suggested that medical school-affiliated hospitals and unaffiliated hospitals behaved differently, this analysis was limited to hospitals not affiliated with medical schools. The measure of the rate of diffusion was the difference between the number of hospitals having the facility at the end of the period and at the beginning as a percentage of the number not having it at the beginning. That is, if N_t' was the number of hospitals having a radioisotope facility in year t and if N^t was the total number of hospitals in year t, then the dependent variable for the first period, C_1, was defined

$$C_1 = (N_r^{58} - N_r^{52})/(N^{52} - N_r^{52}) \qquad (3)$$

with C_2 and C_3 being defined similarly for the 1958–1965 and 1965–1972 periods, respectively. This measure represented approximately the percentage of holdouts as of the start of a period who had adopted the innovation by the end of the period.[10]

The set of explanatory variables was similar to that used above with some slight differences due to data availability or differences in the model. The value used for each period was the average of the value in the first and the last year of the time period. Three variables referred to characteristics of the states: the percent of a state's population which was urban (U), per capita income (I), and the doctor/population ratio (D). The percent of hospitals larger than 200 beds (S) was used as an independent variable because of the obvious important role of big hospitals. Since the rate of diffusion in a given time period depended on how much diffusion had taken place before the start of that time period, this rate of diffusion must be taken into account when using a sample of states which can be at different places in their own diffusion processes. I included as an independent variable the percentage of hospitals in the state which had adopted nuclear medicine at the start of the time period (L). Other things being equal, one would expect those states with a relatively high level of adoption at the start of a period to grow slowly during the period.

Two variables were included to capture the effects of different status groups in the hospital population. One was the ratio of medical school affiliated hospitals to unaffiliated hospitals (A). The result of earlier analysis suggested that the presence of many affiliated hospitals in a state tended to retard the spread of nuclear medicine among unaffiliated hospitals. This finding could be true for two reasons. First, in areas with many affiliated hospitals which acquired nuclear medicine early, the nonaffiliated hospitals may have not considered nuclear medicine as appropriate means of competition for their status group and may have turned their attention to other avenues of competition. In areas lacking a large number of affiliated hospitals, the division into status groups may have been less clear; thus, all hospitals saw early acquisition of the technology as a means of competition. Second, there can be simply a demand-side effect; i.e., to the extent that this service was available in teaching hospitals, doctors and patients would seek it there; thus, unaffiliated hospitals would not be faced with a significant demand for it. For both of these reasons, one would expect a high affiliated/unaffiliated ratio to be associated with slow diffusion of the innovation among the unaffiliated hospitals. Finally, the variation of the size distribution of the hospitals can indicate the extent to which they behave as members of noncompeting status groups. If this measure were true, a large variation would be associated with slow diffusion since hospitals feel less compelled to imitate each other in the acquisition of equipment. The measure of the size variation was the coefficient of variation of the bed size distribution (V).

To summarize, the following relationship was tested by linear regression for each of the three time periods,

$$C = f(U,I,D,S,L,A,V) \qquad (4)$$

where the variables were defined above. Coefficients with positive signs for U, I, and S were predicted; while the expected signs for the coefficients of L, A, and V were negative; and either sign for the coefficient of D was possible since there were two opposite effects hypothesized. Regression coefficients are presented in Table 10-5.

The analysis of individual hospital decisions included the effect of additional factors on the diffusion process. Two equations were estimated using observations on 136 hospitals for data. One equation took as the dependent variable the date of first use of radioisotopes, the other took the cost of the original radioisotope facility as the dependent variable. The major results were as follows:

> In summary, the two regression equations indicated the following about hospitals' decisions to adopt radioisotopes. One, hospitals in a competitive environment tended to adopt the innovation earlier. They also tended to acquire more expensive facilities than other hospitals adopting at the same time. Two, those hospitals which adopted early tended to be ones which already were equipped well with specialized facilities; however, hospitals with a wide range of facilities tended to spend less on their initial radioisotope facility. Three, larger hospitals spent more on the initial facility than smaller ones adopting at the same time. Also,

Table 10-5 Regression Results—Determinants of Diffusion Rate among Hospitals Not Affiliated with Medical Schools[11]

	Dependent Variable	Constant	Urban Pop. (U)	Income (I)	Physician Ratio (D)	Hospital Size (S)	Medical School Affiliation (A)	Size Variation (V)	Initial Level of Adoption (L)	$\bar{R}^2$
(1)	C_1	.0309 (.64)	.00125* (1.56)	.000015 (.52)	−.00026 (.81)	.714* (7.19)	−.404* (2.45)	−.047 (1.11)	−.361* (1.75)	.75
(2)	C_1	−.035 (.48)	.0038* (3.5)	.000017 (.40)	−.00040 (.8)		−.32* (1.3)	−.056 (.89)	.24 (.84)	.45
(3)	C_2	−.035 (.53)	.0018* (1.60)	.000047* (1.64)	.000044 (.09)	1.38* (7.70)	−.682* (2.90)	−.104* (1.70)	−1.00* (4.11)	.76
(4)	C_2	−.038 (.37)	.0035* (2.1)	−.000009 (.21)	.000056 (.076)		−.49* (1.3)	−.11 (1.2)	.55* (2.6)	.42
(5)	C_3	.0775 (.41)	.00045 (.20)	.000083* (1.39)	.00188* (1.92)	1.94* (3.50)	−1.69* (4.25)	−.248* (1.59)	−2.018* (3.91)	.51
(6)	C_3	.035 (.16)	.00048 (.19)	.00003 (.46)	.0028* (2.6)		−1.72* (3.8)	−.22* (1.3)	−.37* (1.5)	.38

*Indicates coefficient significant at 10 percent level (one-sided test).
T-statistics in parentheses.

government controlled hospitals tended to spend more than other hospitals. The signs of estimated coefficients were consistent with the following, but coefficients were not statistically significant. Four, hospitals which financed the acquisition with a specific donation tended to be early adopters and to spend less than other hospitals. Five, hospitals in which the physicians using the equipment were paid a straight salary tended to adopt later and to spend less than hospitals where physicians' incomes were tied more closely to use of the new equipment.

Thus, economic analysis has proved useful in understanding diffusion of innovations among hospitals. Diffusion of innovations not requiring capital equipment—for example, drugs, medical procedures, or public health programs—has been less studied by economists. Individuals rather than organizations are the decision makers on them, and because little investment is required, economic motivations are perhaps less important. Some interesting work on diffusion of the use of new drugs among physicians has been done using a sociological approach.[6]

GOVERNMENT POLICY AND TECHNOLOGICAL CHANGE

Government policy can have a significant impact on the rate of diffusion of technological change in health care. Such policy has not always been consistent in the United States. For example, the Regional Medical Programs in the mid-1960s had as one objective the more rapid diffusion of technology. By the early 1970s, however, policy emphasis had shifted and certificate-of-need laws were viewed as a way to limit the diffusion of technology in the interest of cost control. Louise Russell sees a "hierarchy of policy concerns" that may help to identify or classify government policies:

MEDICAL ADVANCES AND THEIR DIFFUSION[e]

Starting at the first, and least controversial, step of the hierarchy, governments may try to promote the adoption of new technologies. In the belief that a particular technology is a good thing, they may try to shorten the natural lags that impede its diffusion. For example, they might help pay for the equipment. They might publish information about its use or about the various models on the market to make it easier for patients, doctors, and hospital administrators to become familiar with it, and, as a consequence, to become comfortable about using it. They might train people to use the technology.

Moving up the hierarchy to step number two, governments may concern themselves with whether new technologies are being used efficiently, in what economists like to call the technical or engineering sense of that word.[1] Without making judgments about the volume of use, they may ask whether that volume is being produced at the lowest possible cost. Are existing facilities used to capacity? Are they large enough to take full advantage of any economies of scale? Are they run by people with enough training, but not too much? Is there "unnecessary" duplication? Considerations of geographic equity and of patient travel times may be brought into the deliberations, and will help determine how much duplication is "necessary" and how much underuse is, in the last analysis, perhaps desirable. Intervention on behalf of greater efficiency is based, of course, on the premise that the unregulated situation is not acceptably efficient and that intervention can improve matters.

These first two steps take as given that the technology is a good thing, that it is beneficial for patients in some fashion and therefore worth having. Implicitly, judgments about benefits are left to the medical profession, individually and collectively, and to patients. Whatever information they absorb is assumed to be correct.

But, in fact, the value of many medical practices has not been proven.[2] The enthusiasms of one era are often discredited in the next. Thus the third step of the hierarchy gets the government into the business of questioning, even testing, the benefits of medical technologies. The simplest way to approach this problem is to make the previously implicit process explicit, and to ask, Does the medical profession, or its most prestigious representatives in the appropriate field, think that the technology is beneficial, and for whom? This approach can take the form of expert conferences that try to arrive at guidelines for the individual physician or of review committees that examine the care given individual patients and recommend, or even enforce, changes.

This still assumes, of course, that whatever steps the profession has taken to learn about the benefits of various technologies are sufficient to support the judgments that are made. The government may decide to question this assumption too, and ask, Has the technology been proven beneficial by persuasive scientific evidence, particularly in the form of randomized controlled trials?

In a randomized controlled trial patients are randomly assigned to a group that receives the new treatment or to a group that receives alternative treatments or a placebo. Objective criteria for success or failure are established at the outset and the trial is designed, if possible, to keep the patients and doctors from knowing which groups are receiving the new treatment, which the alternatives. The point of this last safeguard is to avoid the possibility that the outcome will be influenced by doctors' and patients' beliefs about which alternative is best.

When the government establishes by either expert opinion or controlled trial that a technology is *not* beneficial, it may try to devise means to prevent its use. This is perhaps easiest to do if the technology requires a piece of capital equipment whose purchase can be forbidden. A variation on this approach is to ask which of several more or less equally beneficial alternatives is cheapest and to try to encourage the use of that alternative and the abandonment of the others.

Step number four in the hierarchy brings the government to the crux of the cost problem and into a storm of controversy. At this step, the government explicitly accepts the possibility that it may not be unquestionably desirable to provide every kind of care that has some benefit, however small or costly. The question shifts from, Is it beneficial? to, Is it beneficial *enough?* Are the benefits of the technology enough to justify the costs? The government need not adopt the position that the cutoff point should be the same as that which would be observed in an ordinary market in which the patient paid the full cost of care out of his own pocket. But in moving into this area, it leaves behind the philosophy that everything that is needed, in the sense that it can reasonably be expected to confer some benefit on the patient, will be provided, and accepts the philosophy that some things are so costly in comparison to their benefits that a society faced with limited resources may decide that those resources could be put to better use elsewhere.

Many different government policies influence diffusion. Some are specifically intended to have this effect. Others influence technological change as an objective secondary to their major purpose. Finally, there are policies whose effect on technological change is undesired and perhaps unforeseen by policy makers. The remainder of this section reviews the effects of two government policies on technological change: certificate-of-need laws and federal regulation of new drug development and marketing. Both policies are controversial and are subjects of continuing research. Readers may disagree with the viewpoints expressed but the selections do give a good overview of the issues. Jack Needleman and Lawrence S. Lewin present an analysis of state certificate-of-need laws:

CERTIFICATE OF NEED[f]

Certificate of need is a program of public review and approval of the capital expenditures and service changes of health care providers. Review in most states is conducted by both state agencies and local health systems agencies, with local review advisory and state review final. As part of this review process, judgments are made on the need and desirability of proposed expenditures. In reaching these judgments, reviewers can consider a wide range of factors, including the efficacy or usefulness of the proposed project, the appropriate distribution pattern for the service or equipment sought (both geographically and with respect to the preferred provider or setting), the reasonableness of the financing arrangements, cost and proposed charges and financial feasibility, the adequacy of the proposed staffing and physical layout, and the competence of the provider and overall quality of the services to be offered. Because of the scope of review, certificate-of-need programs directly confront states with the full range of issues affecting the introduction of new medical technology.

These programs are widespread. Currently, 33 states have certification programs. Thirty-seven states have contracted with the federal government to do similar reviews under the authority of Section 1122 of the Social Security Act. Only Missouri has neither program.[3] The National Health Planning and Resource Development Act of 1974, P.L. 93-641, virtually mandates all states to enact certificate-of-need programs.

The programs do not cover all medical equipment purchases, but they are extensive. The federal regulations for state programs require hospitals, nursing facilities, health maintenance organizations, kidney treatment centers, and ambulatory surgical facilities to be subject to review. For these providers, all capital expenditures over $150,000, bed changes, and all new services must be reviewed. The services offered and equipment purchased by private practitioners are not included in most laws, but two states have introduced some controls on physicians' purchases, and more are considering this step.

These programs are intended to serve a number of purposes. There is a concern with cost containment, although it is a very specific one. The impetus for these programs has been a belief that there has been unnecessary overinvestment, leading to inefficient use of capital and additional operational expenses, and encouraging inappropriate utilization of facilities and services. The concern is not with absolute levels of costs, nor with the desirability or impact of expanding medical services per se. Most programs have retained a commitment to assuring access to care that is at least as strong as their cost containment goal.

There have been several analyses of the effects of certificate of need on the investments of health care institutions. Hellinger, based on early data, concluded that certificate-of-need legislation had not lowered hospital investment and that hospitals had increased their investment in the period immediately preceding the enactment of the legislation in anticipation of the program.[4]

Salkever and Bice concluded that certificate-of-need programs had constrained the increase in hospital bed supply but did not reduce total hospital investment. Instead, assets per bed had increased faster in certificate-of-need states, suggesting that investment had been redirected into modernization and special equipment. They also found that certificate of need was associated with decreases in patient days but increases in the costs per day. Since these have opposite effects on the overall costs of health care and the relative magnitude could not be determined, the ultimate impact of certificate of need on total costs was not estimated.[5]

In an update of their analyses with data through 1974,[6] the authors found continued support for their earlier conclusions. An analysis was made of the experience of the five states that had certificate-of-need programs prior to 1971, and for these states the programs were found to be associated with control of assets per bed, although at levels the authors judged not statistically significant. (The significance level was 0.07.) Four of these five states, it should be noted, have institutional rate review programs.

In its 1975 study of the impact of the Section 1122 and other programs to control capital expenditures, Lewin and Associates[7] concluded that these programs had not been particularly successful in controlling hospital investment. Forty-six percent of the 20 states and 40 areawide agencies included in the sample had approved hospital beds in excess of their published 5-year need projection. While approved increases in assets per hospital bed

Table 10-6 Approval Rates by State Agencies under Certificate of Need and 1122 Reviews for Equipment and Service Projects in Sample States

	Applications Received	Percent Approved
Equipment		
CAT scanners	91	96.7
Radiological	106	93.4
Renal dialysis	24	100.0
Cardiac catheter	9	100.0
Other equipment	5	100.0
All equipment	235	95.7
Services		
ICU-CCU	14	92.9
Renal dialysis	14	78.6
Other specialty	69	94.2
Emergency medical services	19	89.5
Other outpatient	73	97.3
Rehabilitation	28	100.0
Other ancillary	8	100.0
All services	224	94.6

between 1972 and 1974 were less than the estimated amount of inflation plus economic growth in most surveyed states with these programs, this could not be compared with the growth of assets in states without this form of regulation. Those states that were most successful in controlling per bed assets generally had some form of institutional reimbursement control.

The Lewin study also found that proposals to purchase equipment and add new hospital services are almost always approved. The principal exceptions are X-ray and other scanner equipment, where the still infrequent denials are largely the result of several institutions applying to purchase the same equipment and only one being approved. A table of approval rates is presented in Table 10-6.

In sum, based on evidence drawn from the first years of operation of these programs, there is little evidence that operating independently they have limited the ability of institutional providers to invest in new technology. There is also some evidence that the process, by defining its coverage in terms of types of providers rather than types of services that require regulation, has encouraged the introduction of secondary and tertiary level technology into primary care settings. For example, the Office of

Technology Assessment reported that 15 percent of CAT scanners were in private physician offices or clinics.[8]

Several factors have influenced this current level of performance by these agencies. The programs are relatively new, as are many of the agencies involved. The ideal situation would be one in which the standards for project review, including definitions of need, were established prior to project submission, so that they could be immediately applied. In most agencies, however, planning activities and standards development have lagged. A frequent pattern has been for agencies to approve the first project (sometimes the first several) of a given type and begin developing a standard for a new service or equipment after the first application has been received.

The standards development process itself has a number of weaknesses. There is now available a considerable body of literature with suggested standards that have been developed at both the national and local levels. These materials cannot simply be adopted by a health planning agency. Rather, they are reviewed to address local circumstances and patterns of treatment. These reviews often blend local health politics with technical adjustments.

In addition, the development of standards for new services, particularly standards regarding the appropriate number of service units, can often only be done once there has been experience with the service. Requests for the new technology, however, will often precede the development of information on efficacy or levels of utilization, placing pressure on review agencies to act before standards can be developed. There has been a tendency in the agencies to grant approval when uncertain. (This is not inevitably the case; it is a function of agency orientation.) In Quebec, under the province's hospital insurance program, which includes both certificate of need and reimbursement authority, the province's announced policy is to limit technological diffusion to services of demonstrated efficacy. As part of this effort, the province had limited the introduction of *in vivo* radioisotope facilities to only a few hospitals and required these to develop research protocols to evaluate the efficacy and cost impact of these services.[9])

There also appear to be some areas in which prior standards development is infeasible, or at least very difficult. Some of the most subtle decisions agencies must make involve determining the appropriate level of technical sophistication in existing services. This includes questions such as: Does a 150-bed community hospital need tomographic or radioisotope capacity in its radiology department? Or, is laboratory volume sufficient to justify an automated analysis and, if so, with what capacity? Standards have not been developed because the decisions involve a great many situational factors that limit general answers. Since these issues do not involve large projects, they have received lower priority in the standards development process than bed planning or plans for entire services. Yet, collectively, these decisions have a major impact on the technological level of routine care.

Finally, there is an issue of whether the entire standards development—and indeed certificate-of-need—process is misoriented. Currently, these efforts are directed at assessing the need and appropriateness of services, beds, and equipment on an absolute standard of whether the service is productively and efficiently used. If so, it is approved. The process does not address the basic issue of establishing priorities to allocate limited resources. No certificate-of-need program has incorporated into its planning process judgments of the rate at which resources should be added to the health care system or medical technology diffused. It is therefore not surprising that these programs seem most able to limit investment in states where reimbursement control programs have introduced separate limits on available resources.

It is within this context that the proposal to limit hospital investment incorporated into the administration's cost containment program [later defeated] should be noted. If adopted, this limit would introduce a fundamental change into the certificate-of-need process. Agencies will be forced to assess projects on the basis of relative as well as absolute need. This has occurred on a limited scale in Rhode Island under the reimbursement control program for hospitals, but for other agencies this would be a new experience. Among its other consequences, it is likely to place basic service expansion into competition with new technology.

The potential impact of certificate-of-need programs on the adoption and diffusion of technology is great. This includes the potential to severely limit the total level of investment. Without the introduction of financial pressures into the certificate-of-need environment, however, the relative ease with which new services and equipment have been approved is likely to continue.

Another area in which government policy may have a major effect on innovation is the drug industry. As noted in Chapter 9, an industry's record of innovation is an important aspect of its overall performance. Many students of the drug industry believe that its innovative performance is below its potential and that this results in large part from government regulation. Gerald D. Laubach writes:

FEDERAL REGULATIONS AND PHARMACEUTICAL INNOVATION[g]

The industry's capability for innovation has been enhanced by the accelerating progress in laboratory hardware and research methodologies since World War II. There are many examples of this vast new power: sophisticated instrumentation, automated techniques, and ingenious devices to measure, probe, and identify—with the net result that many research procedures that were once cumbersome and time-consuming are now routine. Important new methods have been devised for the synthesis of extremely complex chemical substances, for the purification and manipulation of minute quantities of chemical and biological materials, and for the quantitative determination of all sorts of physiological parameters in animals and man. The net effect of all this has been vastly to increase the productive capacity of the individual research scientist. The resulting gain in the effective research potential of the industry over the past twenty-five years is difficult to quantify, but it is surely large.

Another basis for the industry's growing technological power is the vast informational infrastructure in the biomedical field as a whole. This is distinct from the more specific research capabilities of the industry, though it undergirds all of them. Included in this infrastructure is an awesome amount of knowledge—drawn from new insights in chemistry, biochemistry, and physiology—about how living things function. Contemporary insight into the chemical mechanism of biological function, for example, has proven invaluable and often suggests important new hypotheses. As Lewis Thomas, president of the Memorial Sloan-Kettering Cancer Center and one of the country's leading "biology watchers," has put it, there is an "endless list of new discoveries [in cell biology] that have the look of relevance to human problems."[2] Dr. Thomas has also stated: "The scientists who do research on the cardiovascular system are entirely confident that they will soon be working close to the center of things, and they no longer regard the mechanisms of heart disease as impenetrable mysteries."[3]

Finally, the pharmaceutical industry continues its historical pattern of investing an extremely high percentage of its revenues in research and development. Domestic R&D expenditures for prescription drugs in 1977 were 11.5 percent of domestic prescription drug sales. In absolute terms, the domestic R&D expenditures of American pharmaceutical firms on prescription drugs for human use have steadily increased from about $216 million in 1961 to an estimated $1.11 billion in 1978. Even if corrected for inflation, the figure more than doubles. Estimated 1978 expenditures in constant dollars were 235 percent of what they were in 1961.

Sharply contrasting with the excellent possibilities for pharmaceutical innovation, however, is the industry's actual output. The number of fundamentally new pharmaceutical products (so-called new chemical entities) introduced in the United States each year by the industry as a whole has declined from an average of fifty-two two decades ago to sixteen in 1977 and twenty-three in 1978.[4] Even more telling, a recent study indicates that it now takes an average of almost nine years from the time that drug evaluation is begun in human beings to the time when that drug is approved for marketing.[5] A little over a decade and a half ago, this process required about two years.

If spending and innovative potential have both increased and if the need for new drugs remains undiminished, why has actual output been declining? The answer is found in the current environment for therapeutic innovation and specifically in the character of federal drug regulation.

The regulatory environment Laubach refers to stems mainly from amendments to the Food and Drug Act adopted in 1962. These laws, in the interest of promoting safety and efficacy of new drugs, provided for detailed federal regulation of the innovation process. In particular, the Investigational New Drug (IND) regulation required drug companies to increase considerably the time and money spent on clinical research in the drug development process. The government also must review a New Drug Application (NDA) before commercial marketing can begin and this also lengthens the time before the drug is made available. Critics of regulation point to the "drug lag," the long delay that exists between the time a product becomes available in other countries and the time it is approved for use in the United States.

Of course, a balance must be struck. Few would argue that drug safety and efficacy are not desirable policy goals. They are not costless, however. The cost appears in terms of innovations delayed or foregone. Laubach is among many—though certainly not all—analysts who conclude that the cost is far too high under current regulatory policy. He summarizes the economic aspects of that point of view as follows:

ECONOMIC CONSIDERATIONS

The American regulatory system not only prolongs the time necessary for drug development, but it also seriously affects the economics of the pharmaceutical industry. As in the case of the drug lag, considerable documentation is available to demonstrate this point. Economists have conducted cost-benefit analyses showing the net loss to consumers caused by regulation. They have also shown that regulations are a disincentive to pharmaceutical innovation since they make R&D more costly and diminish the return drug companies receive on R&D investments.[27]

It has been estimated that the FDA reviews an average of 120,000 pages of complex data for each NDA; obviously, such paperwork adds tremendously to research costs. The costs are even higher than one would imagine, for the return on a successful new drug must help defray the expense of R&D on substances eliminated in the development process. In 1962, the R&D cost per new chemical entity marketed was estimated to be about $4 million. Today it is over $50 million.[28]

Regulation also reduces the return possible on new drugs by lessening the effective patent life. The exclusive right to market a new drug lasts for seventeen years from the patent issuance date. To protect an invention, a patent application needs to be filed as promptly as possible after the invention has been made. As the drug development process has been lengthened, there is obviously less time left for the developer to enjoy the fruits of his invention. A recent study by the Center for the Study of Drug Development shows that the effective patent life remaining at the time of approval of a new drug for marketing has declined precipitously, from an average of 13.8 years in 1966 to about 8.9 years in 1977.[29] Thus the present system is inequitable, for the more extensive the testing conducted on a new drug to meet regulatory requirements, the shorter will be the time protection (that is, exclusive marketing rights) remaining. The perversity of such a system is obvious: it tends to penalize companies for developing drugs that require lengthy investigation and testing, even though such drugs may be especially important. One obvious remedy would be to make the patent life of a new drug begin only when it is given marketing approval. This approach would give the pharmaceutical industry the full period of protection intended by law.

Another way in which regulation affects the economics of the drug industry is the federal effort to promote generic drugs. HEW has adopted price controls on Medicare and Medicaid drug reimbursements that are set at the level of the lowest-priced generic products. The Federal Trade Commission (FTC) has drafted a model substitution bill for adoption by the states. The thrust of the bill is to encourage the substitution of generic equivalents by a pharmacist, unless otherwise specified by a doctor. And FDA has actively promoted generic prescribing and dispensing.

The federal government's generic policy is in essence a commodity approach to drugs, presupposing that all drugs of a given chemical structure are fundamentally the same and that only price differentiates them. The objective of this policy is to lower drug costs. The lowering of consumer costs is intrinsically desirable, but it should be noted that price competition among multisource drugs has long been increasing as a result of market forces.

A government policy that makes price the only important distinction between products and manufacturers has some important negative effects. Drugs made by different manufacturers will not necessarily have the same therapeutic effects, and in fact there have been a number of bioequivalence problems in recent years. An example of FDA's own recognition of this problem is a directive issued in March 1979 warning the public to accept only the brand-name drug Lasix, not generic furosemide. The reason was that the generic "equivalent" did not meet accepted pharmaceutical standards of efficacy.[30]

A commodity-drug policy must inevitably lead to severe pressures on manufacturing costs, risky economizing in processing and quality control, and product failures. (Consider the simple potential for product "mix-ups"—for example, a lethal drug like digitalis accidentally mislabeled as a multivitamin.) A troubling and inadequately considered issue in the so-called brand/generic debate is the identity and integrity of the source of the drug. Generic substitution tends to create uncertainty for both consumers and physicians as to which manufacturer's product has actually been dispensed. This problem is compounded by the fact that many generic formulations are made to be indistinguishable in appearance from the original product (so-called look-alike formulations). A policy that would make prescription drugs into pure commodities also ignores the social value of the industry's informational programs since it makes no allowance in pricing for the cost of informing physicians and pharmacists of the existence of drugs, of their proper use, or of new findings about them.

In the long run, the government's generic policy must also have a serious impact on research, a pivotal issue that has received comparatively little attention. Because they lower a manufacturer's financial return, generic drugs do not and cannot provide an economic basis for continued investment in therapeutic progress, for the discovery of new drugs or for the discovery and evaluation of new uses for established drugs. A generic drug policy must ultimately alter the character of competition in the drug industry. Historically, competition in pharmaceuticals (as in other research-intensive, high technology industries, where the ratio of intrinsic value of product to price is high) has been based primarily on innovation. But present regulations would increasingly make price the prime basis of competition, thus lessening the incentive and the capability to innovate. Low cost is the only objective served by the government's promotion of generic drugs. As is the case with almost any social policy, zealous pursuit of a single goal to the exclusion of other important considerations produces a one-sided result of dubious public benefit.

The government's promotion of generic drugs, together with the higher costs of research and declining effective patent life, creates economic pressures on research-based companies: costs are higher and returns lower. As a result, American companies have increasingly shifted drug development activities abroad, where regulation tends to be more supportive, development times shorter, and costs lower. The probable consequence will be a further erosion of American leadership in therapeutic research and a further reduction of new drug discoveries in America. In fact, five of the seven economically most important drugs introduced for general use in the United States between 1970 and 1977 were discovered and largely developed in Europe. And many of the most promising current antibiotic developments are taking place in Japan.

In strictly economic terms, current policies toward drugs and pharmaceutical innovation constitute another remarkable paradox. The overall cost of health care and its containment have become prominent concerns in recent years. At the same time, it is well recognized that effective pharmaceutical products can be a highly cost-effective mode of patient care—as compared, for example, to such alternatives as hospitalization or surgical intervention. As Lewis Thomas has put it, the most extravagant health care costs tend to be associated with "halfway technologies."[31] The iron lung for polio is prototypical, compared to which the cost of definitive preventive or curative technologies (in this case, polio vaccine) are trivial. Regulatory constraints on pharmaceutical innovation thus represent a real, but evidently largely unrecognized, barrier to the ultimate goal of health care cost containment.

CONCLUSION

Technological change is one of the most important and pervasive characteristics of the health care sector today. It also is one of the least understood. Even in the industrial sector where technological innovation has been studied for much longer, economic understanding is far from complete. The application of economic analysis to the study of health care technology poses additional problems that are only beginning to be attacked.

The basic concepts are there. Substitution of capital for labor and of one kind of labor for another are results of innovation that cause significant changes in the production process as well as in the cost and quality of service. Production economics provides a framework for study of this phenomenon. Use of resources for biomedical research is an investment promising large future returns. The rate and direction of such investment is subject to economic choice, and tools of investment analysis can be adapted to better inform these choices. Likewise, the decision by a health care organization to adopt an innovation is a decision that can be better understood with economic models of firm behavior. Thus, the basic building blocks of analysis can be identified, but much work remains to be done.

Understanding of technological change is important for government policy making. Government is involved at every step of the way, from allocating funds for basic research, to licensing technicians and other personnel, to influencing diffusion rates. Policies that in themselves apparently are unrelated to technological change can be made obsolete by new technology. New technology also is a fact of life for the professional health administrator who must plan for the future in a rapidly changing environment. In both government and the private sector, improved economic analysis of technological change can have a big payoff in terms of better decision making.

NOTES

1. For the reader interested in looking further into this subject, the following sources are suitable starting places. Both are collections of diverse material and have good bibliographic references:
   - U.S. Department of Health, Education and Welfare, *Medical Technology: The Culprit Behind Health Care Costs?* Stuart Altman and Robert Blendon, eds. Proceedings of the 1977 Sun Valley Forum on National Health (Washington, D.C.: U.S. Government Printing Office, 1979)
   - Committee on Technology and Health Care, Assembly of Engineering, National Research Council and Institute of Medicine, *Medical Technology and the Health Care System: A Study of the Diffusion of Equipment-Embodied Technology* (Washington, D.C.: National Academy of Sciences, 1979)
2. The next few pages follow closely the material in U.S. Office of Technology Assessment, *Development of Medical Technology* (Washington, D.C.: U.S. Government Printing Office, 1976), pp. 70–85.
3. Ibid., p. 71.
4. Ibid., pp. 72–73.
5. Louise B. Russell, "The Diffusion of Hospital Technologies: Some Econometric Evidence," *Journal of Human Resources* 12, no. 4 (Fall 1977): 482–502.
6. A well-known sociological study is James Coleman, Elihu Katz, and Herbert Menzel, "The Diffusion of an Innovation among Physicians," *Sociometry* (December 1957). An example of work by an economist on drug diffusion is Kenneth E. Warner, "A 'Desperation-Reaction' Model of Medical Diffusion," *Health Services Research* (Winter 1975).

SUGGESTED READINGS

Committee on Technology and Health Care, Assembly of Engineering, National Research Council and Institute of Medicine. *Medical Technology and the Health Care System: A Study of the Diffusion of Equipment-Embodied Technology.* Washington, D.C.: National Academy of Sciences, 1979.

Egdahl, Richard H., and Gertman, Paul M. *Technology and the Quality of Health Care.* Germantown, Md.: Aspen Systems Corporation, 1978.

Gordon, G., and Fisher, G., eds. *The Diffusion of Medical Technology: Policy and Research Planning Perspectives.* Cambridge, Mass.: Ballinger Publishing Co., 1975.

Mansfield, Edwin. *Microeconomics: Theory and Applications,* 2nd ed. New York: W. W. Norton & Co., Inc., 1970.

Mushkin, Selma J. *Biomedical Research: Costs and Benefits.* Cambridge, Mass.: Ballinger Publishing Co., 1979.

Russell, Louise B. *Technology in Hospitals: Medical Advances and Their Diffusion.* Washington, D.C.: The Brookings Institution, 1979.

U.S. Department of Health, Education and Welfare. *Medical Technology: The Culprit Behind Health Care Costs?* Stuart H. Altman and Robert Blendon, eds. Proceedings of the 1977 Sun Valley Forum on National Health. Washington, D.C.: U.S. Government Printing Office, 1979.

REFERENCES FOR FELDSTEIN EXCERPT

2. The key to this analysis is an estimate of the technological possibility of input substitution. If this is represented by an assumed constant elasticity of substitution, a rough estimate of the past importance of substitution can be calculated. From 1955 to 1968, hospital wage rates rose approximately 92%, and other input prices, as measured by the wholesale price index, rose 17%. Moreover, in 1955, 62% of total expenses were for labor input. If there were no possibility of substituting other inputs for labor, and the 1955 technology remained in use until 1968, the input cost per patient day would have risen 64%. With an elasticity of substitution of 1, optimal behavior would have limited the cost increase to 59%. *Actual* changes in the use of labor and nonlabor cannot be used to assess the elasticity of substitution because of the changing nature of the product.
3. An increase of demand can also change technology without changing the product if institutions grow in response to the increased demand and a different technology becomes less expensive at the larger scale.
4. This relationship represents the different possibilities that are in principle open to each hospital with its given diagnostic mix of admissions and with fixed input prices. Cost per patient day can be varied by changing the technology of care through different staffing patterns, equipment, and supplies. Each point on the curve therefore represents a particular technological configuration.
5. The benefit-cost possibility curve is therefore not strictly a technological relation, because the benefit measure reflects the evaluation by the patient of the physical outputs. However, this is not important if we assume that the "representative patient" has fixed tastes, income, and insurance coverage. If any of these change, the benefit-cost possibility curve can be modified accordingly. This is developed below.
6. Although an increase in cost may yield more than a proportionate increase in benefits at very low levels of cost per patient day, only the properties of the benefit-cost relation in the range of current operation are important for the analysis here.
7. Although a patient rarely has *many* hospitals among which to choose, the patients of any given hospital will come from different locations and therefore have different hospitals among which to choose. The hospital is therefore in competition with a larger number of institutions than any single patient's range of choice. This spatial characteristic of the market weakens the potential oligopoly power of hospitals. However, because antitrust regulations do not apply to voluntary and public hospitals, there may be more collusion than would prevail in a profit-seeking industry with the same market structure.
8. The assumption that patients' preferences prevail is not crucial to the analysis. If the preferences of the physicians or hospital administration were assumed to prevail instead, the benefits could be redefined in terms of their preferences instead of the patients'.
9. These indifference curves have an unorthodox shape because: (1) the vertical axis measures a "good" and the horizontal axis measures a "bad" (i.e., reduction in the consumption of other goods and services); and (2) the benefits are measured by willingness to pay (dollars).
10. For analytic simplicity we now ignore the effect of cost per patient day and perceived benefits on the demand for patient days. To incorporate admissions and mean stay,

Technological Change 441

or even just total patient days, into the current analysis, it would be necessary to replace simple geometric presentation with a mathematical formulation.

11. To say that the patient "values" the benefits at $20 more than their price is equivalent to saying that he would be willing to pay up to $20 more than that price for those benefits.
12. At any cost per patient day up to approximately $90, the benefits indicated by the benefit-cost possibility curve exceed the cost. The hospital which is a local monopoly could therefore adopt a more expensive technology than the one most preferred by patients and still be able to sell its services. This analysis ignores the price elasticity of demand for patient days; the actual price at which hospitals could maintain their desired occupancy is less than the $90.

REFERENCES FOR WARNER EXCERPT

Gaus, C. and Cooper, B. 1976. "Technology and Medicare: Alternatives for Change" Presented at Conference on Health Care Technology and Quality of Care, Boston University (Nov. 19–20).

McMahon, J. and Drake, D., 1976, "Inflation and the Hospital" in *Health: A Victim or Cause of Inflation?* pp. 130–48, M. Zubkoff, ed., New York: Prodist.

Russell, L., 1977, How much does Medical Technology Cost? Paper presented at the Annual Health Conference of the New York Academy of Medicine, New York City, April 29.

NOTES FOR WEISBROD EXCERPT

2. Alternative discount rates of 10 and 5 percent were used, but the 10 percent calculations are utilized in the present paper. Except for the fact that the present-value estimates were already available from my earlier work (*EPH*), the undiscounted data would have been entered into the internal-rate-of-return formula . . . . In addition, were it not for the fact that these estimates were already available, more recent data—for example, on earnings and life expectancies—would have been used.
3. *EPH*, tables 2 and 3. The assumption was made that age-specific and sex-specific incidence rates for other diseases are independent of those for polio. Thus, a reduction in the incidence of polio—as would result from a successful prevention program—was assumed to leave unchanged the incidence rates, morbidity, and mortality rates from other diseases.
4. For details of the estimation procedure see *EPH*, esp. pp. 33–34, tables 2, 6, and 12, and appendix 1.
5. It might be noted that a freeing of resources from treatment activities would produce no direct effect on the GNP, since treating the sick is regarded as a final output. Notwithstanding the absence of a change in measured GNP, it would seem clear that such a reallocation of resources—made possible by a successful disease-prevention program—would increase economic welfare.
6. The age distribution is relevant because the incidence of polio is markedly age-specific. The incidence among persons over fifty has been virtually zero.
7. Since the number of cases prevented as well as the costs of prevention vary directly with the expenditures on applying knowledge, there is an economic optimum level of application; this may well involve less than complete vaccination of the population. In

fact, as of 1970, 4.6 percent of all U.S. persons under age twenty are estimated to have had no polio vaccinations and an additional 15.2 percent had less than full protection—that is, less than three doses of either the oral or the injected vaccines (Department of Health, Education, and Welfare 1970, p. 13).

SUGGESTED READINGS FOR WEISBROD EXCERPT

U.S. Department of Health, Education and Welfare. *Trends*. Washington, D.C.: U.S. Government Printing Office, 1962.

Weisbrod, Burton A. *Economics of Public Health*. Philadelphia: University of Pennsylvania Press, 1961; referred to as *EPH*.

NOTES FOR RAPOPORT EXCERPT

1. The model of the diffusion process used here is similar in many respects to that proposed by Russell and Burke [10, pp. 141–74].

2. The "short term general and other special" category excludes federal hospitals, psychiatric hospitals, tuberculosis hospitals, and all long-term hospitals. In 1972 there were 2552 hospitals of all types with radioisotope facilities, so clearly most hospitals with the equipment are "short term general and other special." The A.H.A. does not provide a tabulation for just "short term general hospitals." In this section the A.H.A. tabulations are used; but in later sections of the article where I compiled tabulations from the individual hospital listings, I used just short-term general. The difference in number of hospitals between the two groups is quite small: in most years less than 5 percent.

   The set of hospitals with therapeutic radioisotope facilities is a subset of those with diagnostic facilities, and I choose the more inclusive definition since before 1971 the A.H.A. survey does not make the distinction. When I talk about a hospital offering nuclear medicine, I mean that it indicated to the A.H.A. that it has a radioisotope facility.

3. Of course, this is only one possible measure; percentages other than 100 percent and 10 percent could be used.

4. The sample here excludes the eleven states in which there were no affiliated hospitals in the year in which the percentage of unaffiliated first reached 10 percent.

5. Since data were missing from 1967 and 1968, the series skips from 1964 to 1969.

6. Three regressions were computed for each state. In the first K was set equal to the 1969 value of P, plus 2 percentage points; the second used the 1969 value of P, plus 5 percentage points; and the third set K equal to the 1969 value of P, plus 10 percentage points. For well over half the states, the first regression yielded the highest R^2 value.

7. The states dropped were Alaska, Arizona, Delaware, Hawaii, Mississippi, Nevada, North Dakota, and South Dakota. These states had few hospitals with radioisotopes; and one or two hospitals acquiring or dropping the service made large percentage differences, leading to big departures from an S-shaped curve.

8. P is the percentage of hospitals with nuclear medicine in each year as reported to A.H.A.; K is 1969 value of P, plus 2; t is calendar year.

9. Data sources are hospital data from *Hospitals,* "Guide Issues," appropriate years [1]. Urban population data from *City and County Data Book,* various issues. Income, physician/population rate, and state area come from *Statistical Abstract of the United States,* various issues.
10. An alternative measure also was used. This alternative was simply the difference between the percentage of hospitals reporting a radioisotope facility at the end of the period and the percentage reporting it at the beginning. Regression results using this measure of diffusion rate did not differ in important respects from the ones reported. The reason the measure was only approximate was that I was unable to adjust the data for hospitals that appeared or disappeared, changed to medical school affiliated status, or merged during the period, or failed to return the A.H.A. questionnaire in one of the two years.
11. Data sources are the same as given in footnote 9.

REFERENCES FOR RAPOPORT EXCERPT

[1] American Hospital Association, *Annual Guide to the Health Care Field,* Chicago, American Hospital Association, 1971–73. (Before 1971 the survey data were published annually in the Association's journal, *Hospitals,* in the August "Guide Issue.")

[2] R. Berry, "On Grouping Hospitals for Economic Analysis," *Inquiry,* 10:5–12 (December 1973).

[3] P. Ginsburg, "Resource Allocation in the Hospital Industry: The Role of Capital Financing," *Social Security Bulletin,* 35:20–30 (October 1972).

[4] Z. Griliches, "Hybrid Corn: An Exploration in the Economics of Technological Change," *Econometrica,* 25:501–22 (October 1957).

[5] M. L. Lee, "A Conspicuous Production Theory of Hospital Behavior," *Southern Economic Journal,* 38:48–58 (July 1971).

[6] E. Mansfield, *Industrial Research and Technological Innovation,* New York, W. W. Norton and Company, 1968.

[7] J. Newhouse, "Toward a Theory of Nonprofit Institutions: An Economic Model of a Hospital," *American Economic Review,* 60:64–70 (March 1970).

[8] M. Pauly, "Hospital Capital Investment: The Roles of Demand, Profits, and Physicians," *Journal of Human Resources,* 9:7–20 (Winter 1974).

[9] M. Pauly and M. Redisch, "The Not-for-Profit Hospital as a Physician's Cooperative," *American Economic Review,* 63:87–100 (March 1973).

[10] L. B. Russell and C. S. Burke, *Technological Diffusion in the Hospital Sector,* Chicago, National Planning Association, 1975.

NOTES FOR RUSSELL EXCERPT

1. In this chapter, the words "efficiency" and "efficiently" are used in this sense.
2. A. L. Cochrane, *Effectiveness and Efficiency: Random Reflections on Health Services* (London: Nuffield Provincial Hospitals Trust, 1972); Howard H. Hiatt, "Protecting the Medical Commons: Who is Responsible?" *New England Journal of Medicine,* vol. 293 (July 31, 1975), pp. 235–41; Alan K. Pierce and Herbert A. Saltzman, "Conference on the Scientific Basis of Respiratory Therapy," in *Proceedings of the Conference on the*

Scientific Basis of Respiratory Therapy, pt. 2 of *American Review of Respiratory Disease*, vol. 110 (December 1974), pp. 1–15; Paul D. Stolley, "Assuring the Safety and Efficacy of Therapies," *International Journal of Health Services*, vol. 4 (Winter 1974), pp. 131–45.

REFERENCES FOR NEEDLEMAN AND LEWIN EXCERPT

3. Department of Health, Education, and Welfare. Bureau of Health Planning and Resources Development. "Status of Certificate of Need and Section 1122 Programs in the States (as of June 30, 1977)." n.d.
4. Hellinger, Fred J. "The Effect of Certificate-of-Need Legislation on Hospital Investment." *Inquiry* 13 (June 1976) (2): 187–93.
5. Salkever, David S., and Bice, Thomas W. *Impact of State Certificate of Need Laws on Health Care Costs and Utilization.* Washington, D.C.: National Center for Health Services Research, 1976.
6. Memorandum to Ira Raskin, Bureau of Health Planning and Resources Development, from Thomas Bice and David Salkever, on the Implications of CON Findings, March 30, 1977.
7. Lewin & Associates, Inc. *Evaluation of the Efficiency and Effectiveness of the Section 1122 Review Process.* Springfield, Va.: National Technical Information Service, 1976.
8. U.S. Congress, Office of Technology Assessment. "The Computed Tomography (CT or CAT) Scanner and Its Implications for Health Policy." Cited in Institute of Medicine. *Computed Tomographic Scanning: A Policy Statement*, p. 52. Washington, D.C.: National Academy of Sciences, April 1977.
9. Lewin & Associates, Inc. *Government Controls on the Health Care System: The Canadian Experience.* Springfield, Va.: National Technical Information Service, 1976, p. 430.

REFERENCES FOR LAUBACH EXCERPT

2. Lewis Thomas, "Why Two Cells Fuse," *Newsweek*, August 20, 1979, p. 50.
3. Lewis Thomas, "The Medical Lessons of History," *Wall Street Journal*, July 3, 1978.
4. Pharmaceutical Manufacturers Association, "Factbook," 1976, p. 11.
5. Center for the Study of Drug Development, University of Rochester, "Preliminary Analyses of 1977 U.S. Investigational New Chemical Entity (NCE) Study," mimeographed, p. 2.
27. Sam Peltzman, *Regulation and Pharmaceutical Innovation: The 1962 Amendment* (Washington, D.C.: American Enterprise Institute for Public Policy Research, 1974); David Schwartzman, *The Expected Return from Pharmaceutical Research* (Washington, D.C.: American Enterprise Institute for Public Policy Research, 1975); Harold Clymer, "The Economic and Regulatory Climate," in *Drug Development and Marketing*, ed. Robert R. Helms (Washington, D.C.: American Enterprise Institute for Public Policy Research, 1975), pp. 137–54; David Schwartzman, *Innovation in the Pharmaceutical Industry* (Baltimore: The Johns Hopkins University Press, 1976); Henry Grabowski, *Drug Regulation and Innovation: Empirical Evidence and Policy Options* (Washington, D.C.: American Enterprise Institute for Public Policy Research, 1976); and Henry Grabowski, "The Effects of Substitution Laws on Innovation," *Drug Therapy* 8 (December 1978): 91–100.

28. Ronald W. Hansen, "The Pharmaceutical Development Process: Estimates of Development Costs and Times and the Effects of Proposed Regulatory Changes," in *Issues in Pharmaceutical Economics*, ed. Robert L. Chien (Lexington, Mass.: D.C. Heath and Company, 1979), p. 180.
29. "Statement of William Wardell," p. 15.
30. *F-D-C Reports* 41 (April 2, 1979): 15–17.
31. Thomas, "The Medical Lessons of History."

SOURCES AND PERMISSIONS

a. Reprinted from *The Rising Cost of Hospital Care* by Martin Feldstein, pp. 36–42, 51, by permission of Information Resources Press, © 1971.

b. Reprinted from "The Cost of Capital-Embodied Medical Technology" by Kenneth E. Warner, in Committee on Technology and Health Care, *Medical Technology and the Health Care System: A Story of the Diffusion of Equipment Embodied Technology*, pp. 294–296. National Academy of Sciences, 1979.

c. Reprinted from "Costs and Benefits of Medical Research: A Case Study of Poliomyelitis" by Burton Weisbrod, *Journal of Political Economy* 79, no. 3 (1971): 529–534 and 541–543, by permission of The University of Chicago Press. © The University of Chicago, 1971.

d. Reprinted from "Diffusion of Technological Innovation among Nonprofit Firms: A Case Study of Radioisotopes in U.S. Hospitals," by John Rapoport in *Journal of Economics and Business* 30, no. 2 (Winter 1978), pp. 108–113, 116, by permission of Temple University School of Business Administration, © 1978.

e. Reprinted from *Technology in Hospitals: Medical Advances and Their Diffusion* by Louise B. Russell, pp. 133–135, by permission of The Brookings Institution, © 1979.

f. Reprinted from "The Impact of State Regulation on the Adoption and Diffusion of New Medical Technology" by Jack Needleman and Lawrence S. Lewin, in Committee on Technology and Health Care, *Medical Technology and the Health Care* System: *A Study of the Diffusion of Equipment Embodied Technology,* pp. 247–251, 267–268, National Academy of Sciences, 1979.

g. Reprinted from "Federal Regulations and Pharmaceutical Innovation" by Gerald Laubach in *Regulating Health Care: the Struggle for Control,* Proceedings of the Academy of Political Science, 33, no. 4 (1980), pp. 61–63, 72–75, with permission of the Academy of Political Science.

Chapter 11

Economic Evaluation of Health Programs

The idea of program evaluation will not be new to readers of this book. Administrators, planners, and other health professionals constantly face the need to evaluate continuing or new programs. Some evaluations are highly structured, such as those made by the U.S. General Accounting Office or state funding agencies where the analysis must be performed according to legislative mandate. Others are less formal, giving the analyst flexibility to choose both the basis for evaluation and the methods to be used. Evaluation can be done on a very broad scope in the context of major public policy changes. It also can be used as an input to quite specific program decisions.

Evaluation is a large topic, so this chapter is necessarily selective, concentrating on economic evaluation. The reader already familiar with evaluation techniques used by other disciplines should be particularly alert to factors that distinguish an economic approach. Differences include the variables chosen for study, the kinds of questions asked, and the analytical techniques used.

The plan of this chapter is as follows. The next section presents a simple model of the health care system. It develops a set of variables that might form the basis for program evaluation and indicates which ones are of most concern to economists. The following section deals with the analysis of costs. It includes general discussion, a review of cost concepts and measures, and fairly detailed examples of cost finding (accounting) and the interpretation of results. The next sections consider costs in relation to benefits, concentrating on two related but different evaluative methods that are powerful but frequently misused: *cost-benefit analysis* and *cost-effectiveness analysis*. The final section presents the authors' concluding remarks.

VARIABLES IN HEALTH SERVICE ANALYSIS

There can be many meanings to the term evaluation as used in the health field. Fortunately, its common-sense usage as "appraisal with the aim of reaching judgments" will do for purposes here. The term analysis can be used interchangeably with evaluation in this context. The task of evaluation is to assess how well a health system, or a component of it, is functioning according to some accepted basis of judgment.

The focus of evaluation varies with the needs of administrators, planners, and others. An analysis might be made of a single type of health or medical service, of a group of services constituting a program, or of an entire system of delivering care. The concepts in this chapter are applicable to any of these perspectives. However, the illustrative cases tend to focus on programs; hence, the chapter title.

Those in the health field can, and often do, differ over evaluative criteria, such as:

1. pattern of service use
2. consumer satisfaction
3. provider satisfaction
4. equity of care or equality of access
5. efficiency in the delivery of a specific service or a system of health services
6. quality of care
7. effectiveness in promoting health
8. contribution to delivery system reform

Obviously, the relative importance individuals place on the items in their lists is a subjective matter and, indeed, the conclusion they reach about a program often will turn on the judgmental basis or criterion they selected.

The factors involved in selecting criteria for evaluation can be systematized in several ways. One useful approach adapted from the work of R.C. Bradbury[1] is incorporated in Figure 11-1. This defines the health system in terms of basic components: resources, population, services, and health status effects (or other possible outcomes of care); and linkages between components: availability, financial access, utilization, productivity, costs, and effectiveness. Any of these components and linkages might be included in an evaluation, either alone or in combination. It also is possible, of course, to evaluate selected details or elements of a particular component or linkage.

A number of variables that might be considered in health program evaluation have been identified. It should be apparent that some are more "economic" in nature than others. In Figure 11-1, the linkages among system components all have relevance to economic analyses and can be summarized as follows:

1. **Availability of Health Resources:** This describes existing and/or expected volumes of labor (of all kinds), materials, equipment, buildings, and the like that represent inputs in the production process. Factors affecting these elements of supply can be identified through evaluation.
2. **Financial Access:** This linkage incorporates several enabling factors that help explain health service utilization (or lack thereof) such as income, insurance coverage, and entitlement under government programs such as Medicare or Medicaid. When combined with information on prices, data on financial access are indispensable in evaluating program demand.
3. **Utilization of Health Services:** This identifies the pattern of service use related to the characteristics of users. In some instances it also is important to evaluate the characteristics of nonusers. Utilization, of course, is related closely to the economic concept of demand, although it depends in part upon supply as well.
4. **Productivity of Health Resources:** This refers to service output per unit of resource input measured in physical terms—for example, volume of service provided (or even results achieved) per hour of physician input—with the level of other inputs held constant. Productivity represents one measure of efficiency in service provision.
5. **Cost of Providing Services:** This category of efficiency measure goes beyond physical productivity to cover the monetary value of all resources used in producing a service. Costs can be presented per unit of service and per capita (for users or population at risk). They can be segregated for special disease control programs but usually cannot be isolated readily for specific health problems or diagnoses within a delivery institution, such as a hospital.
6. **Effectiveness of Health Services:** This identifies the health status improvement (or lack of it) and other effects of specific services. Epidemiologic techniques and clinical trials are useful in measuring effectiveness, but so too is economics (for example, in measuring the monetary consequences of improved health).

This list captures the predominant economic factors involved in health services evaluation. But a point raised in Chapter 1 is worth repeating here. Economics has no precisely defined boundaries, so health economists have moved into areas that might be assigned more properly to other

Figure 11-1 Health Delivery System

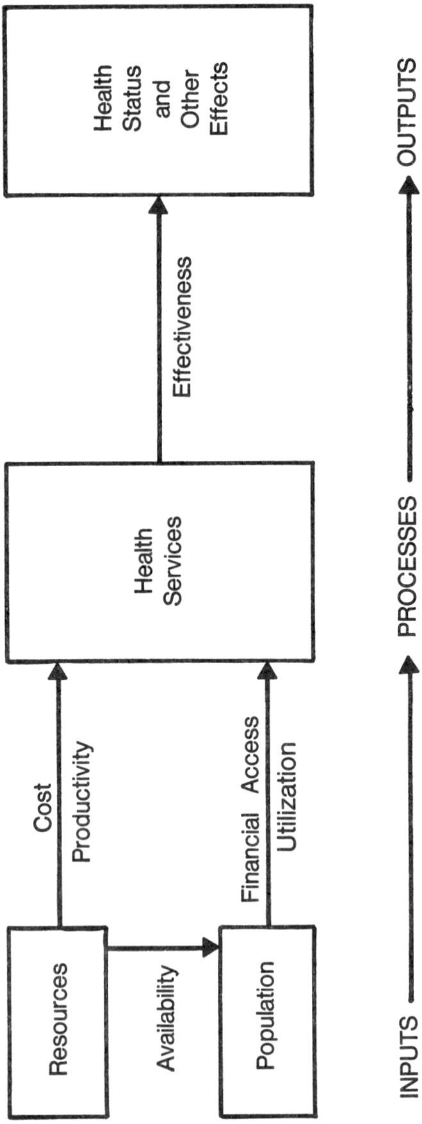

```
Resources ──Availability──▶ Population
   │                              │
   │ Cost                         │ Financial Access
   │ Productivity                 │ Utilization
   ▼                              ▼
         Health Services
              │
              │ Effectiveness
              ▼
      Health Status and Other Effects
```

INPUTS ──▶ PROCESSES ──▶ OUTPUTS

Economic Evaluation of Health Programs 451

disciplines. For example, quality of care clearly falls under the purview of medicine and public health but some economists have incorporated quality measures into their program evaluations.[2] Likewise, equity in the delivery of care is a proper concern of philosophers and political scientists but it, too, has crept into economic evaluations. Such cases of "extended economics" can be justified by arguing that no programmatic implication is truly without economic content, but they are not explored further in this chapter.

ANALYSIS OF COSTS

Cost is of obvious concern to economists. The monetary value of resources used to produce a service was noted in Point 5 above. That notion could be expanded to include more subtle elements, such as the risks incurred by receiving medical care or the threat to societal values implied in some innovative health programs. However, these expansions are far easier to handle in principle than in actual practice, and for the most part are not included in empirical economics. Some additional economic meanings of cost are examined in the selection by Massey et al.:

ECONOMIC COST AND SOME OBSERVATIONS ON ITS MEASUREMENT[b]

First of all, we measure cost in monetary units—dollars, francs, pounds, etc.—only as a convenience. It is closer to the mark to say that what we really want to measure is which ones and how much of our admittedly limited resources are required to implement a given decision. Although most accountants and engineers limit their concept of cost to dollars, some of them perceive that dollars themselves have no intrinsic value, but serve only as a device that permits the aggregation and comparison of many different kinds of resources—tons of cement, man-hours of labor, numbers of skilled engineers, acres of land, and so on. It is economic theory, however, which carries us a step forward when it says economic costs are not X dollars or Y francs nor even Z man-hours. The real cost is to be found in the benefits that could otherwise be obtained by their alternative use. Economic costs are benefits foregone, benefits lost.

When we choose to use some of our limited resources to develop and produce a new public facility, such as a water and power project, then those resources are not available to produce some alternative, perhaps superior, capability. If we undertake programs such as flight to the moon that call our best engineers into research and development for moon flights, then they are not available for other government programs or private production. It is for this reason that economic costs are referred to as opportunity costs. It is in the opportunities or the alternatives foregone that the real meaning of cost is found.

Given this concept of cost, there is reason to doubt the widespread belief that the techniques and methodology of cost measurement are developed and well in hand. Some of the most interesting challenges for cost effectiveness today, and we think, in the foreseeable future, lie in support of system analysis applied to broad public policy problems—such as the distribution of health care, education, or the national system of transportation. Problems of this sort are made up of many complex alternatives and there are a host of opportunities for cost effectiveness analysis to help clarify the issues involved. At the same time, the alternatives to be measured are so broad and far-reaching that they tax existing methods and tools for measurement to the utmost. Let us now return to the subject of cost measurement, with particular emphasis on basic concepts.

Concepts of Cost Measurement

R&D, Initial Investment, and Operating Costs

Resource analysts concerned with cost measurement of large public programs have come to think of these programs as having three distinct cost phases—Research and Development, Initial Investment, and Systems Operations. This summary structure helps to assure comprehensive coverage and time phasing. Development cost includes all outlays incurred to enable us to develop a new capability. Investment costs include those involved in producing the equipment, organizing people initially, and setting up the new system. By system, here, we mean the entire complex of men, facilities, and equipment that is required to implement the new capability. Operating costs are all of the day-by-day expenditures involved in using the new capability or keeping it operationally ready for use over its intended life.

If these three categories are interpreted properly, when combined, they should include all the relevant costs. Note that the appropriate set of categories for a particular analysis will vary, depending on the particular system or decision being analyzed. Thus, for a decision concerning only a change in level of operating an existing system, it may be that only operating costs are involved. However, focusing on the full set of cost categories forces the analyst to consider whether there might not also be some initial investment or even research and development required before this change in level of operations can take place. This three-way categorization also tends to group costs in accordance with the way they behave under alternative conditions.

The basic idea is a simple one. Over the life of a program some costs are one-time or nonrecurring (development and investment); others recur in proportion to the length of time it is in operation and the intensity of its operation. For some analyses, it may be sufficient to combine nonrecurring costs (those incurred up to the point when a program or project becomes operational). This would include development, facilities, equipment, supplies, and perhaps initial training. It certainly includes more than just capital expenditures, as the term "investment" is usually used.

Dollars: The Least Common Denominator?

At the beginning of this discussion we indicated that the real meaning of cost is to be found in the opportunities foregone in deciding to apply resources in one way rather than another. Yet it can be observed, almost universally, that cost measurement operates not in units of real resources but rather in monetary units that we allow to stand, in an abstract way, for the real resources. This practice of measuring an abstraction called value in arbitrary units called dollars is a bit of indirection that greatly increases our ability to manipulate resources in analysis: to summarize, substitute, and calculate in ways that would be impossible with physical measurements of resources.

As a resource, dollars themselves are of little consequence. They are at most printed paper and sometimes less—markings in the books of the Treasury and banking system. Nevertheless, both individually and institutionally, we are willing to accept them as a temporary substitute for the really useful resources of manpower, materials, and facilities. In so doing, we express a collective judgment, a consensus, on the value of the benefits that could otherwise be obtained with the resources. Monetary units are used to represent cost because, and only because, they help us to describe and to evaluate alternatives.

Now it is well not to confuse convenience in cost measurement with good cost measurement. To the extent that dollars help us describe and evaluate alternatives, they are useful. Since we have been asked to comment not only on how cost measurement is done today, but also to make observations on possible limitations and improvements in practice, we would like to examine the use of the dollar proxy a little more closely.

Although the use of money units as a sort of least common denominator is present in the state of the art in cost measurement, it is not necessarily the best of all possible arts. We note especially in costing very large public programs that money costs are sometimes misleading substitutes for real cost. Estimates based on market prices are, after all, marginal prices—valid measures of opportunities foregone for relatively small variations in quantities of resources around the present market equilibrium point.

Massive new public programs may require such large amounts of specific resources that the current market price or marginal cost may constitute a poor basis for assessing the total cost of a program. Conversely, the completion or discontinuation of an unrelated program may release large quantities of a specific resource in the future. This again might render current dollar costs for a specific resource a poor basis for measuring the future cost of even a small program. The good analyst retains a healthy skepticism about even his most fundamental methodology and tools, subjecting their results always to validity checks and tests of reasonableness.

The particular measure of costs chosen depends on the needs of the analyst. The value might be expressed per unit of service (or group of services) of person(s) using, or available to use, the program. Most such measures are averages, which are the easiest values to estimate. Previous chapters noted that the marginal or incremental cost is the appropriate measure to use when decisions are made on the allocation of resources. Unfortunately, because that frequently is difficult to estimate, the marginal concept is honored in intention more often than in practice.

Still another basis for distinguishing among cost measures is time. The appropriate duration for recording costs is a function of the probable time period over which a service or program will operate. Often, expediency restricts the data collection phase of an evaluation to something less than this time period; then, if the study is done at all, the evaluator must be careful to label the limitations of the work. For economists, time applies to costs in another way. The distinction between *short run* and *long run* costs reflects the time required by suppliers to change productive capacity. When resources are fixed—for example, buildings and equipment—the program is said to be operating in the short run. When producers have sufficient time to enter or leave the industry or program, this is referred to as the long run. Because industries and programs differ in the actual time required to change productive capacity, the terms short run and long run do not refer to constant periods of elapsed time. The selections in this chapter, for the most part, are illustrative of short-run analysis.

Uses of Cost Information

Cost data can be of use to many parties—health planners, institutional or program administrators, government policy makers, academic researchers, and others. Not all uses of cost analysis are considered evaluation in the strict sense of the term. Nonetheless, the evaluator has numerous options in the choice of cost analysis to undertake, as indicated in the following selection by the economist Paul Feldstein:

THE USES OF COST ANALYSIS[c]

There are several types of cost analyses, differing in their purposes as well as the type of data needed to conduct them. For both internal (i.e. whether costs are minimized) and external decision-making (i.e. comparisons of the performance between several organizations delivering medical care), the following kinds of cost analyses should be undertaken: the extent of economies of scale for long-run minimization; optimum input mix for minimizing short-run costs.

If data were available to conduct these types of analyses, then we would have the necessary knowledge to do the following:

1. Set up a Cost Control System by diagnosis, by department, by physician and by institutional setting;
2. Be able to forecast future expenses (by provider, diagnostic category, and physician) given changes in the patient or diagnostic mix, changes in prices and wages, etc.;
3. Determine that mix of resources that is least costly for providing treatments and how the optimum mix of resources will change if there are changes in their wages or prices;
4. Determine the scale of operation (for the entire treatment

as well as for the individual settings) that is least costly, i.e. economies of scale. Hence the ability to determine "make or buy" decisions in all phases of the operation;
5. Have the information necessary for setting prices for the care received and also for determining premium levels on a capitation basis;
6. Determine the causes of variations in costs between different plans or organizational forms of delivering medical care;
7. Determine the "profit and loss" at different levels of operations, with different types of patient mix, and how profit and loss would change, given changes in any of the underlying factors affecting costs;
8. Provide part of the necessary information required to conduct cost/benefit analyses of specific programs offered by the plans;
9. Serve as a basis for incentive reimbursement experiments.

The next selection, from a report by James Sorensen and David Phipps, highlights the objectives or needs for costs data on behalf of a mental health center. The points raised are pertinent to most institutions and programs; they are not the only ways of classifying the uses of good cost information. For example, a report of a conference on prepaid group programs, chaired by Sidney Lee, grouped the needs for cost information and analysis into three categories: planning and development, management, and evaluation.[3] Readers may wish to consult the Lee report and apply its categorization to the points contained in the next selection:

OBJECTIVES[d]

Determination of rates for services. The degree of emphasis placed on collections for services varies widely among the many community mental health centers in the United States. At many centers a very intensive effort is made to collect a very high percentage of the expenses incurred for patient services. In other centers there is very little effort expended to make such collections. As the expense of services increases and the availability of general public funds decreases, the need to recover a higher proportion of the expenses from patients and third-party payors becomes increasingly important.

Because of the diversity of services rendered by all centers, frequency of visits or patient contacts, duration and intensity of treatment to various patient group and individual therapy sessions, and the many other variables present, a system for determining patient charges based on averages for most patients (e.g., average cost per patient day) is *unsatisfactory*. Some types of service such as inpatient and partial hospitalization might rely heavily on average cost for the portion of service cost for the usual hospital facilities including room occupancy, meals, laundry, and other housekeeping items, and nursing care because these may be relatively uniform for all patients; on the other hand, the amount of facilities and support services used in outpatient [care] are different and should be accounted for separately. Other expenses such as the direct professional services, pharmacy, x-ray, physical or occupational therapy would probably vary considerably and therefore should *not* be based on averages tied to "patient day" or "patient visit." All special services (including direct professional services) should be accounted for and charged separately. . . .

Negotiation with third-party payors. As the expense of medical care has increased, several third-party payors have made revisions in their contracts to increase the coverage of mental health services and, at the same time, have refused to pay for certain patient charges not covered by their contracts. They have also increased their auditing procedures to determine which charges are being buried in overall or average rates being charged patients, especially those which are not—in their judgment—properly charged. As this trend continues, the individual center will need to have accurate records to prove the validity of charges made to each patient. Direct services offer little problem if adequate records are maintained, but the center must also be able to recover the cost of indirect service as well. This is [w]here a systematic and logical cost-finding methodology becomes imperative if the center expects to recover such charges. The system must be designed to eliminate duplications or omissions and to distribute indirect costs; nonetheless, there are methods that do distribute fairly such costs. If the center is able to accomplish that fair distribution, there should be little argument with third-party payors.

Information for funding agencies and other external groups. So long as a significant portion of a center's total revenues come from public funds—no matter whether from Federal, State or local sources—there will be a need to account to the funding agencies for expenses by whatever break-downs are requested, especially on the cost of various treatment programs. Usually funding agencies are not unreasonable when they ask for valid information about the costs of various treatment programs; the request appears unreasonable often because the center has a poor or undeveloped management information system.

Some mental health program costs have been called into question in recent years because the information furnished to funding agencies has been based on averages. In one agency, for example, as the type of treatment changed from purely custodial care to intensive therapy the expense information furnished led to misleading interpretations; while the daily population had decreased by nearly 80%, the total expense of treatment had more than tripled. The error was in the way the population was related to the type of care and treatment rendered. Treatment modalities vary widely from center to center, as some centers favor the use of high-cost intensive therapy, with a consequent high-turnover in the patient population while others use a longer term approach with lower cost per patient for a given time period and a much lower patient load. Such differences make comparisons of cost per patient a meaningless exercise. Because there is not any unanimity of opinion as to the most effective type of program and when the treatment differs, costs are bound to be unequal if computed on averages. Perhaps from the vantage point of several years' experience and good records both as to costs, on the one hand, and benefits obtained by the population served on the other, some determination is possible as to the most effective treatment modality but unless good records are kept about both elements the answer may never be clearly identified.

Information for managerial analysis. While the need to furnish accurate and meaningful cost information to patients, third party payors, and funding agencies is becoming increasingly important, usually there is minimal opportunity for any of those groups to directly change the expenditure patterns of the center. The specifics of this challenge are usually left to the management of the individual center although some funding sources may think they can and should influence the expenditure patterns of centers. This only highlights the information needs of management.

Rarely is it possible to make good decisions intuitively over an extended period of time. Better decisions should result from better information, but the great opposing forces in gathering information for decision making are accuracy and timeliness. If information is delayed too long in reaching the decision maker, for the sake of greater accuracy, much of its usefulness will have been lost before it reaches the appropriate person. Yet decisions based on inaccurate or misleading information can be extremely harmful. The design of a regular reporting system is important so that information flows smoothly and naturally to the appropriate decision makers in a timely fashion. Even with smooth and timely reports to appropriate personnel, ineffective decisions may still result if the person who receives the information is unable because of his training or lack of time to study the information to act upon the information presented to him. There is a real distinction between information and communication, and, therefore, it is imperative to tailor the information to the user's needs and abilities.

One especially useful managerial application of cost-finding flows from a comparison of the revenue generated by the service with the total cost of operating the service. Management can identify whether or not the service is producing a net income or requiring a subsidy. From this type of analysis, meaningful adjustments to the rate structure may be achieved as well as evaluating the overall financial desirability of the specific service. . . .

A good budgetary system will also fix responsibility and authority for the control of costs and enable the management to assess the effectiveness of the performance of individuals. Each center should have a budget to control expenditures and frequent meaningful comparisons against the budget to ensure performance of the responsible managers and department heads. Cost-finding is useful in rate-setting, negotiation and evaluating the overall financial aspects of a specific service but it is not a substitute for a budgetary control system which provides control over and evaluation of specific individuals responsible for these services.

Cost Finding

Cost finding or accounting is similar for health and other fields and is of use to economists in gathering data to fit their concepts. There are, however, distinctive characteristics of health services and institutions that can complicate the accountant's work. As the foregoing selections indicate, the needs for better data are many and significant. In spite of that, cost finding has not tended to be a strong point of health specialists, especially outside of large institutions such as hospitals.

This is not the place for detailed exposition of cost accounting in general or in health. Yet an evaluator must know how to obtain valid cost data. Not every reader will need to master the details of cost finding (and certainly will not need to become an accountant), but an overview of methodology and some of its possible limitations should be helpful. The general approach is summarized well in the next selection excerpted from the Sorensen and Phipps study of community mental health programs:

Definitions

The term, cost-finding, may be defined as a system of allocating and reallocating costs from a point of data collection into different sets or subsets of costs. Simply stated, cost finding is any method which attempts to charge all relevant costs—both direct and indirect—to *final* producing functions or activities or what accountants have traditionally called "revenue producing functions." (Since accountants trace expenses to the cost centers that produce the final product or services, the term "final producing cost center" has been coined for the Community Mental Health Center (CMHC); viewing the service outputs of the CMHC as "revenue producing" did not seem to describe suitably the intent of a CMHC.) The difficulty in community mental health centers [is] in identifying the appropriate *final* production (or revenue producing) activities. Because of the evolution of type of service concept, one natural way to collect and allocate expenses is by the five basic types of service, i.e., inpatient, outpatient, emergency service, partial hospitalization, and consultation and education. One could choose type of patients such as children, adolescents, adults, and geriatrics as being final (or revenue) producing centers. No matter which of the several possible ways is selected, some rational and systematic method of charging all expenses, both direct and indirect, must be utilized to assign those expenses to the final (or revenue producing) activities. Full cost allocation is appropriate even though some of the defined activities may be subsidized in part or entirely by some level of governmental funding; to know what the total expense was can still meet several needs, even if the final producing cost centers are not "revenue-producing" activities in the usual accounting sense. Individual community mental health centers must establish the method which fits the needs of that center. Because the principle of cost-finding is unaffected by the type of classifications chosen, the original data can be allocated and reallocated to create useful expense categories that reflect the nature of a given center.

The first step in cost finding, then, is to distinguish between "final" and (for want of a better term) "nonfinal" cost or revenue centers. Once this classification has been made, the analyst adds all the direct resource costs in each center for the accounting period in question (usually a month or a year). The final step is to allocate all the costs accumulated by each nonfinal center to the final cost centers. There are several possible allocation methods, including the step-down, double distribution, and simultaneous equations procedures. These methods are well known to accountants and do not require coverage here. In addition, various computational or estimation techniques exist to transform final cost center totals into average or marginal values.

To complete this brief survey of cost finding, some practical considerations and limitations should be noted. For one thing, as fixed resources are permitted to vary, a program's unit costs can change markedly; that is, there can be economies or diseconomies of scale. For another, changes in utilization volume within the same scale of program operations also are likely to modify costs.[4] The mix of cases and persons treated can affect the results, too.

These factors may not concern the accountant whose task it is to conduct the cost finding but they can be of critical importance to the program manager who must assess the validity and generalizability of the results. The problem is difficult because information on the effects of scale, volume, and patient mix frequently is available only for the rather limited range of production represented by current program operations. Beyond this range the manager has little choice but to rely upon informed guesses and assumptions. Fortunately, by using a technique known as *sensitivity analysis*,[5] the analyst can test the degree of impact each assumption will have on the cost finding results. This is described in the context of cost-benefit analysis in a later section.

Interpretation of Cost Results

Assuming that cost finding has been successful, the analyst is ready to interpret the results. Of course, the interpretive plan will have been designed even before the accounting methods are selected and put to use. The specific aims and techniques for interpreting costs depend on the objectives of the evaluation; that is, on the uses to which the results are to be put. Those uses were surveyed previously and need not be repeated here. It is worth recalling that some aims, such as establishing health plan premiums, require per capita costs while for others, costs per unit of service will do.

One final consideration before presenting an actual case study concerns the applicability of experimental conditions to cost analysis. If one program can be compared to another (say through comparison of experimental and control populations served by the two), additional information can be gained on the principal program. In fact, it is difficult to know how to interpret costs in any relative way in the absence of experimental results. Despite the obvious desirability of such comparisons, reasons of time, expense, and cooperation of participants may restrict many evaluations to single programs or services. In those cases, the analyst will need some ingenuity in finding comparative bases for drawing conclusions that reach beyond the program itself.

There is no shortage of studies to illustrate cost finding and interpretation. An excerpt from one is presented in the next selection. It concerns a neighborhood health center in Boston. Each reader might judge the degree to which this study deals successfully with the problems and challenges noted above.

EFFECTS OF MANPOWER UTILIZATION ON COST AND PRODUCTIVITY OF A NEIGHBORHOOD HEALTH CENTER[e]

The data system generated a variety of management and evaluative information. This study primarily considers professional manpower resources, which absorb 48 per cent of the Health Center's annual expenditures; the use of nonprofessional manpower and of complementary nonlabor resources receive less attention. The real manpower input measure used (as distinguished from a monetary measure) is provider time expressed as hours and days worked per month and per year. Utilization of capital items and space was itemized, measured and related directly to individual departments for costing purposes. Departmental and general overhead expenses were allocated to individual departments by several traditional methods. Visits were used as the output measure though other measures might be equally appropriate in different settings.[7,8] Input and output data are tabulated separately for each department, disciplines within departments and even individual providers.

Encounter form and time study data were combined with personnel records and financial information for each department to show who provides what types of services to whom, to tabulate workloads of individual providers per unit of time (month, quarter or year), to look for under- or overstaffing relative to visit volumes and non-patient care activities. The data can be combined for a number of additional uses such as examining cost-effectiveness of manpower mix and resource allocations.

These information outputs were used to accomplish the following objectives:

1. To develop a profile of each department for the purpose of interdepartmental comparisons.
2. To assess manpower utilization with respect to actual and optimal workloads. For example, findings will indicate whether providers in each department can increase visit volumes, under what conditions and whether with or without reduction in non-patient care effort. Workload measures can also be translated into staffing requirements.
3. To examine manpower resource allocations relative to objectives and their respective priorities. For example, is a ten per cent resource allocation to non-patient care effort by medical departments commensurate with the importance assigned (by health center administration and/or by providers) to raising health by preventive and community efforts?
4. To analyze the costs of non-patient care activities and to separate them from the "pure" cost of patient visits. This part of the methodology facilitates computation of the average cost of visits inclusive and exclusive of the cost of community outreach, training, research and self-education.
5. To assess manpower utilization in terms of cost-effectiveness of resource allocations. For example, to the extent that both doctors and nurse practitioners are equally competent in providing certain types of visits, which type of provider produces visits at lowest cost? Furthermore, given differences in cost and practice patterns of different types of providers, what is a rational division of labor within and between departments?

The results section presents illustrative applications of the methodology in each of these areas. [One area is excerpted below.]

● ● ●

Allocation of Departmental Costs between Patient and Non-Patient Care Effort

The methodology presented in this paper enables management to separate the cost of non-patient care activities from the cost of patient visits. Time study data were used to separate patient care from non-patient care activities. Each department's total costs were subdivided based on departmental time distributions. For example, Community Mental Health spent six per cent of total provider time on community outreach, and thus six per cent of the yearly departmental budget was allocated as costs of community outreach. Overhead costs were similarly apportioned between each department's patient visit costs and non-patient care costs.

This allocation method facilitated computation of two sets of average visit costs for each department based on two different departmental cost totals (Table 11-1): the average unadjusted visit cost (column 1) based on total departmental costs divided by yearly visit volumes; and the adjusted or "pure" visit cost (column

Table 11-1 Average Yearly Visit Costs Inclusive and Exclusive of Non-Patient Care Costs and Adjusted Ancillary Costs

Department	Average Unadjusted Visit Costs (1)	Average Adjusted or "Pure" Visit Costs (2)	Differential between 1 and 2 (3)	Non-Patient Care Cost as a Per Cent of Average Unadjusted Visit Cost (Column 1/ Column 3) (4)	Average Adjusted Visit Costs Exclusive of Ancillary Costs (5)
Pediatrics	$19.21	$17.16	$ 2.05	10%	$ 9.54
Internal Medicine	22.55	21.62	.93	4%	13.99
Nursing	20.32	19.42	.90	4%	11.76
Nutrition	11.45	9.16	2.29	20%	9.16
Community Mental Health	32.81	23.06	9.75	30%	23.06
Psychiatry	27.51	21.71	5.80	21%	21.71
Psychology	35.91	24.45	11.46	32%	24.45
Social Services	28.84	23.39	5.45	19%	23.39
Social Work	26.74	24.52	2.22	8%	24.52
Trainees	33.14	21.47	11.67	35%	21.47

Source: Calculations provided by Evaluation Unit for this study.

2), computed by subtracting the costs of non-patient care activities from departmental totals before dividing by yearly visit volumes.

A further variable affecting visit costs is the cost of ancillary services such as radiology, laboratory and nursing support services, which had been prorated between nursing and medical departments according to the share each had of total visits produced by these departments. Another variable, the cost of patient care services delivered in schools and in the community, had likewise been allocated to nursing and medical departments.[15] By identifying and separating these activities, the distributions of visit cost components could be made comparable between departments (Figure 11-2). A second adjustment of visit costs was presented (column 5, Table 11-1), this one exclusive of ancillary service costs.

It can thus be seen that visit costs vary between departments for a variety of reasons. These may include heterogeneity among visits produced by different departments, interdepartmental differences in patient care/non-patient care mix, in visit volumes of providers, in visit lengths, in resource mix utilized and in input prices. For purposes of cost control, it is important to isolate the different reasons for cost variation. By separating the extent to which different departments engage in non-patient care activities and the utilization of ancillary services, departmental costs can be made more comparable.

All departments at the Health Center have multiple objectives and visits represent only one of several outputs. To make interdepartmental visit cost comparisons that are meaningful it is essential to determine and segregate the cost of each output or activity produced by departments. Average unadjusted visit costs (column 1) are derived by allocating all departmental costs as visit costs. By adjusting the figures (column 1) for the cost of non-patient care activities in each department one can compare "pure" visit costs rather than costs of heterogeneous output bundles. Average adjusted or "pure" visit costs (column 2) show notably smaller variation between visit costs of medical and nonmedical departments. However, when the "pure" visit costs of medical and nursing departments are further deflated to eliminate the costs of ancillary services (column 5), cost differences between medical and nonmedical departments widen once more. Other factors that enter into cost variation between departments can be separated out with the above methodology, but are omitted from this discussion.

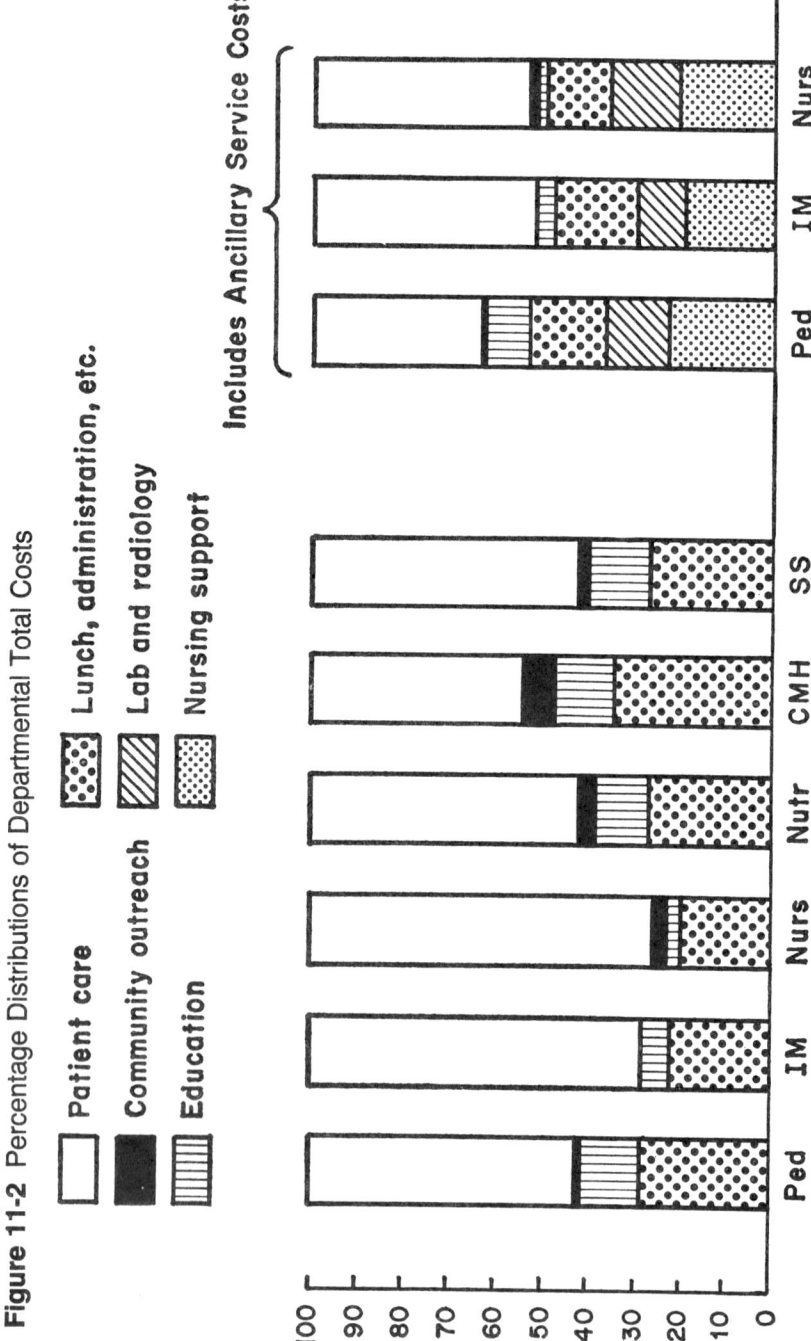

Figure 11-2 Percentage Distributions of Departmental Total Costs

The distinction between unadjusted and "pure" visit costs has particular relevance to methods of financing the Health Center. Most departments are not separately funded for non-patient care activities; inasmuch as patient visits now constitute the primary fee-generating output of the Health Center it may be argued that all costs should be loaded on to visit costs. However, one could equally argue that the training of social workers or sex education in the schools should be financed with education rather than with health care dollars and that patient populations should not be burdened with the cost of non-patient care activities. When these issues are raised and the need to seek alternative sources of financing becomes critical, the cost of non-patient care activities will become an important piece of information.[16]

Department chiefs and Health Center administration can use these cost data to assess whether, given their costs, non-patient care activities should receive greater or lesser emphasis. The figures also enable management to develop patient fees based on "pure" visit costs.[17] Finally, when more is known about end results of patient care, training of health professionals and community preventive effort, cost-effectiveness studies can be conducted to suggest which types of effort yield the largest pay off per dollar.

ANALYSIS OF BENEFITS

When evaluators shift their attention from costs alone to relationships between costs and effects of health care, they are turning to a study of what is, in effect, the production of health. Clearly, health services can have a variety of effects or outcomes. If the results are positive, they can be called benefits. In this discussion, all these terms are used more or less interchangeably. As before, no distinction is made among different types of health services, although their specific effects obviously will vary.

The benefits of care sometimes are presented in the form of "costs" avoided or reduced—for example, a reduction in future medical expenses once a preventive health program has gone into effect. By consensus, positive program consequences have been classified into three categories: *direct, indirect,* and *intangible benefits.* This classification scheme is illustrated in the following selection written a decade ago by Herbert E. Klarman. An eminent health economist in his own right, Klarman here highlights the major issues involved in valuing health benefits under these three headings by summarizing the work of other economists in the field:

APPLICATION OF COST-BENEFIT ANALYSIS TO THE HEALTH SERVICES[f]

Direct Benefits

Direct benefits are that portion of averted costs currently borne which are associated with spending for health services. They represent potential tangible savings in the use of health resources. Certainly in the long run manpower not required to diagnose and treat disease and injury does become available for other uses. It is reasonable to suppose that our economy, like others, has a vast variety of wants in the face of a totality of relatively scarce resources, so that freeing resources for other, desired, objectives represents a contribution to economic welfare.

In the absence of a specific program of services to be evaluated, the measure of direct benefits is usually taken to be total resource costs currently incurred. The appropriateness of this measure as a basis for policy is questionable. . . . Nor is it helpful to take some fraction of the total. In terms of resource use, diminishing marginal productivity is likely to set in as a program expands beyond a certain point. In terms of valuation of benefits, diminishing marginal utility is often a plausible assumption.

While it is usually taken for granted that direct benefits, or the current costs of care that will be averted, can be measured with precision, this is true only when a firm produces a single good or service, such as maternity care in a special hospital. In most instances several goods or services are produced jointly. Under conditions of joint production it is possible to calculate the extra or marginal cost for each product, but not its average unit cost (10, pp. 44–45). When average unit cost figures are presented, they reflect an allocation of overhead and joint costs; and such allocation is necessarily an arbitrary accounting procedure, even where it is systematic and replicable. An alternative procedure, which is no less arbitrary, is to assign to a diagnostic category its proportion of total costs, with the proportion taken from the percentage distribution of patients or services. In the absence of facilities that produce only a single product, it might be helpful to analyze cost data for facilities with varying diagnostic compositions of patient load. However, other factors are also at play, and there is no logical solution to the problem of determining average cost under conditions of joint production of multiple outputs (18, p. 166).

Another complication, which affects the calculation of direct benefits and also of indirect benefits, is the simultaneous presence of two or more diseases in a patient. The presence of disease B when intervention is attempted in disease A serves to raise or lower the costs of intervention and therefore the corresponding benefits (45). The reason that indirect benefits, which represent gains in future earnings, are also affected is that the presence of diseases A and B in a patient may reduce the probability of successful outcome from the treatment of either. The effect is to overstate the benefits expected from reducing the incidence of one or the other disease (51). The magnitude of this effect is not known.

The prevailing tendency is to take direct benefits from a single-year estimate of costs (44). Since survivors will also experience morbidity in the future, some medical care costs are being neglected. Initially this procedure may have been associated with an emphasis on single-year estimates, to the exclusion of present value estimates (50). Once the necessity of present value estimates is recognized, other explanations must be sought for this shortcut. A possible explanation is that survivors will experience only average morbidity in the future; when extra morbidity is absent, there is perhaps no need to deal with morbidity. A more plausible explanation lies in the lack of longitudinal data on the morbidity experience of defined population cohorts.

The fact is that a single-year estimate reflects the prevalence of a disease, not its incidence. It may be that the prevalence figure is sufficiently greater than the incidence figure for chronic conditions, so that it makes ample allowance for future events. Indeed, the prevalence figure in the base year is the same as the sum of the incidence figures for all survivors to this year, if certain factors remain constant, such as the size of population, death rates for the particular diagnostic group, and the incidence rate. When any of these factors follows a rising trend, however, the prevalence figure exceeds the cumulative sum of the past and present incidence figures and falls short of the sum of incidence figures expected in the future.

To the extent that unit costs or prices tend to increase faster in the health services sector than in the economy at large, the value of direct benefits will also increase. In my own work I have incorporated an adjustment for this factor into the discount rate, deriving thereby a *net* discount rate (45, 46). If economic growth were to slow down in this country, the lag in productivity gains of the health services sector behind the economy at large would be reduced, and so would the size of this adjustment.

Transportation expenses for medical care are a resource cost which is disregarded in cost-benefit analysis, although they are allowed as deductions under the individual income tax. When the physician made home calls, his travel expenses were automatically included in health service expenditures. The foremost reason for neglecting them today is, most likely, lack of reliable data. There may be the further, implicit assumption that patients' transportation costs are of a small order of magnitude.

Indirect Benefits

Earnings lost due to premature death or disability, which will be averted, are indirect benefits. Debility as an impairing factor in production has not attained the prominence in empirical studies that Mushkin (41, 51) attached to it from a conceptual standpoint.

Since the publication of Rice's studies (53) it is no longer necessary to estimate loss of earnings on the back of an envelope. Drawing fully on the data resources of the federal government and using unpublished tabulations almost as much as published ones, Rice (43–44) prepared her estimates in systematic fashion. She applied labor force participation rates, employment rates, and mean earnings, inclusive of fringe benefits, to the population cohort in question. For men and women separately, she derived estimates of the present values of lost earnings due to mortality under alternative discount rates and a one-year estimate of lost earnings due to disability or morbidity.

Several elements of the benefit calculation that were still at issue a decade or so ago appear to be more or less settled now, some perhaps prematurely. These can be summarized as follows:

1. Our ordinary concern is with loss in earnings, not income. The latter includes income from property.

2. Consumption by survivors is no longer subtracted from gross earnings in order to arrive at net earnings. Viewed prospectively, everybody is a member of society, including the patient (54).

3. The value of housewives' services is recognized, despite the fact that such services are not traded in the market and are omitted from the GNP. Weisbrod (13, pp. 114–119) developed and applied a complex method for measuring the cost of a substitute housekeeper, but subsequent writers have followed Kuznets (55) in employing a simpler approach, putting the value of the services

of a housewife at the level of earnings of a full-time domestic servant. To employ a single number is the more practical procedure by far. The magnitude of that number is a separate question, however. It is increasingly evident that the value given by the earnings of a domestic servant is not adequate (56). Thus, the accepted value of the housewife's contribution would increase substantially if day care centers for working women were expanded at public cost.

An alternative approach is to value the housewife's contribution at the opportunity cost of her staying out of the labor force (45). Implementation of this approach is impeded by two considerations (57). First, the method is complicated, since values would vary with the individual housewife's educational attainments, type of occupation, amount of job experience, full- or part-time employment status, etc. Second, nonpecuniary factors, which certainly influence the labor force participation rates of women, are difficult to measure and may behave erratically. When total family income permits, the pecuniary opportunity cost of the wife's staying home has been known to be as low as zero or even negative.

4. The employment rate has been typically taken at 96 per cent, or an overall level of 4 per cent unemployment at the level of "full" employment (44). In the 1970s the magnitude of this rate is at issue. Whatever the magnitude, Mushkin's argument is accepted that the health services system should not be charged with failures by the economy to provide jobs to all who seek them (41, 58).

What is often not taken into account is the tendency for persons rehabilitated after serious illness or injury to find fewer job opportunities than persons who have remained healthy and on the job. In my study of syphilis (45), I recognized the loss of earnings due to the "stigma" attached to this and similar diseases. When prevention is feasible, it seems appropriate to assign to it an extra weight or bonus for this reason.

5. Calculations of indirect benefits rest on the implicit assumption that the life expectancies of cohorts of potential survivors are known. Usually standard life tables are employed, separately for men and women. For diseases of low frequency it seems reasonable to disregard any effect on the total death rate occasioned by the deletion of a particular cause of death. For major diseases the problem is important, although simple deletion may be incorrect. As Weisbrod (13, pp. 34–35) recognized more than a decade ago, survivors who have avoided a particular cause of death may have

a higher or lower susceptibility to other, competing causes of death. I compared the effects of simply deleting heart disease as a cause of death on life expectancy and on work-life expectancy. The former was large—11 to 12 years—and the latter was small—less than a year (46). For a disease with heavier impact at the younger ages, the effect on work-life expectancy would be relatively larger, and correspondingly greater attention would have to be paid to the effect of competing causes of death.

Intangible Benefits

Pain, discomfort, and grief are among the costs of illness currently borne, which constitute the intangible benefits of a program of health services that averts them. The benefits accrue partly to the patients and partly to their friends, relatives, and society at large, to the extent that we take pleasure in the happiness of others. That positive external effects in consumption exist is indicated by personal and philanthropic gifts, to the extent that they are not subsidized by the deductibility provisions of the income tax (59). Looming even larger is the averted premature loss of human life. Since none of these effects is traded on the market, none carries a price tag. In attempting to put a value on averting them the question arises: what would one be willing to pay to avoid them?

In my paper on syphilis (45), I estimated willingness to pay for escaping the early and late manifestations of the disease by examining expenditures incurred in connection with other diseases that met certain conditions. After consultation with clinicians I adopted psoriasis as the analogue for early syphilis, and terminal cancer as the analogue for its late stage. The conditions specified were that the expenditures for medical care represented principally a willingness to pay for freedom from the particular disease, since in neither case could direct or indirect tangible benefits, as defined above, be realized. To the extent that payments were made only by the patient (directly or through health insurance), willingness to pay by others was neglected and total willingness to pay was understated.

Neenan (60) has estimated the consumer benefit of a community chest x-ray program for tuberculosis. With the help of some fee data indicating willingness to pay, he obtained very high estimates of value.

Several years have elapsed since intangible benefits were valued. The analogous diseases approach has not been repeated; this suggests that neither the estimates themselves nor the procedures for obtaining them have been found useful. One reason is obvious: the approach is specific, calling for the development of estimates, disease by disease.

A larger body of literature is devoted to the value of human life than to the other types of intangible health benefit. Life insurance holdings are clearly not applicable to bachelors and jury verdicts are inconsistent (13, p. 37). The implications of public policy decisions or governmental spending are difficult to elicit in the absence of information on the alternatives that faced the decision makers (19). Moreover, such valuation may lack stability and consistency (24, pp. 133–134).

Schelling (61) has proposed a different approach. He would measure the value of human life, as distinguished from livelihood, by the amount people are willing to spend to buy a specified reduction in the statistical probability of death. Acton (24, p. 258) applied this approach, and derived an estimate of the value of human life at $28,000. This amount serves as a substitute for the net value of lost earnings and is not an additional sum.

I am not sanguine about the applicability of Acton's numerical estimate to the evaluation of program alternatives. Acton was the first to criticize the defects in his estimate, including the small size of his sample, and its apparent biases. While these defects can be remedied in the future, what troubles me is the likelihood that respondents to this type of question may not grasp its meaning. Do respondents know the actual probabilities of their dying in the coming year? How is a small—e.g. 1 per cent—reduction in statistical probability perceived? How much more is a 10 per cent reduction worth than a 1 per cent reduction? Is it plausible to postulate a strictly linear relationship between increase in risk and willingness to pay to cover it? (54). Moreover, does not the value of a gain depend somewhat on the starting point? (62). If all payments come from the consumer, the distribution of income must exert a sizeable influence; by how much would willingness to pay change if the task of reducing the death rate were viewed as a collective responsibility that is fully financed from public funds?

Titmuss (63) regards the value of human life as priceless and beyond valuation. Yet implicit values are being placed on human life whenever public policy decisions are made on highway design, auto safety, airport landing devices and traffic control measures, mining hazards, factory safeguards, etc. In emphasizing voluntary giving, the sense of community that the gift relationship in blood both reflects and promotes, Titmuss seems to be pointing to a large external benefits component that is neglected when life-time earnings are taken as the proxy for the value of human life. Although the concern for the altruistic motive is salubrious and appropriate, the conclusion does not follow that human life is priceless.

As Mishan (54) observes, a rough measure of a precise concept is superior to a precise measure of an erroneous concept. It is agreed that the notion of the value of human life, apart from livelihood, is sound. A numerical estimate of this value would be useful in comparing the worthwhileness of alternative programs. Comparisons of programs would gain in relevance and aptness if all benefits were counted, including the saving of human life or improvements in life expectancy. This potential gain is much more likely to be realized if all benefits are entered into the model, rather than if some appear only in footnotes.

It should be clear from the foregoing selection that there is no single, unique measure for the benefits of health services, even those restricted to health status. Some analysts have selected a single indicator of indirect benefits—for example, the decrease in time lost from work because of illness (one factor in the earnings reduction category in the Klarman piece). Others have opted for one or another composite index of effects; some of these measures are complicated, indicating that they probably score better in theory than in practice. Another commonly cited list of outcome indicators is attributed to Kerr White. They are his "five D's"—death, disease, disability, discomfort, and discontent.[6] Specified as "D's" averted, they, too, can serve as indicators of program benefits.

Every benefit indicator has its limitations. As a general rule, outcomes are necessary to study but difficult to estimate well.[7] It is always a challenging problem to determine the relationship between specific inputs or sets of inputs and specific outcomes. Solving this "attribution problem" is so difficult that some analysts have fallen back, unhappily, on using inputs to represent outcomes—for example, valuing hospital care in terms of patient days.

No simple answers are offered here. Instead, it is argued that each person conducting or interpreting program evaluations must be aware of the advantages and limitations of the possible measures and should focus on the

Table 11-2 Present Value of the Economic Costs of 119,600 New Cases of Syphilis by Type of Cost and Stage of Discovery and Treatment, United States, 1962 (Dollar Amounts in Millions Except for Cost Per Case)

Type of Cost	Total	P & S Stages*		Early Latent Stage	Late Latent Stage	Late Stage
		Not Reported	Reported			
Medical Care Expenditures	$ 19.5	$ 3.0	$ 5.0	$ 1.8	$ 2.5	$ 7.2
Output Loss Due to Treatment Time or Disability	40.7	1.5	1.9	0.8	1.2	35.3
Reduction in Earnings Due to "Stigma"	51.0	11.9	11.1	7.8	19.3	0.9
Consumer Benefit Loss	6.3	1.0	1.7	0.4	1.2	2.0
Total Cost	$117.5	$17.4	$19.7	$10.8	$24.2	$45.4
Number of Cases (in thousands)	119.6	20.0	33.4	17.0	48.2	1.0
Cost per Case (dollars as shown)	$985	$870	$590	$635	$500	$45,400

Source: [Author's calculations using data from various sources.]
[*"P & S Stages" = Primary & Secondary Stages.]

---

one(s) least likely to distort the purposes of the particular study. Inevitably, simplifying assumptions (carefully labeled) will need to be made.[8]

The valuation of health benefits is difficult but not hopeless. This section closes on a positive note with an excerpt from a well-regarded case of benefit estimation—Klarman's 1965 work on the effects of syphilis control programs.

SYPHILIS CONTROL PROGRAMS[g]

Economic Benefits

Table 11-2 has presented the figures against which the benefits of a specified program can be measured.

Eradication

The present value of the benefits accruing from total eradication would be $117.5 million realized in perpetuity, or $2.95 billion (at a discount rate of 4 percent). Since the disease is communicable, it cannot recur in the absence of an external source of infection. An added benefit is the control and surveillance mechanism, which could presumably be abandoned and its averted cost realized in perpetuity. In 1962, $6 million were spent; discounted at 4 percent, this yields a present value of $150 million.

In sum, the present value of eradicating syphilis, on the above assumptions, would be $3.1 billion. More than 40 percent of this amount, or $1.3 billion, is due to "stigma" (evaluated mostly at 1 or 0.5 percent of earnings subsequent to the discovery of syphilis).

The distribution of total benefits by type is (in percent): medical care expenditures, 15.8; output loss due to treatment time or disability, 32.9; reduction in earnings due to "stigma," 41.3; consumer benefit loss, 5.1; abandonment of control mechanism, 4.9.

Direct costs are one fifth of the total (15.8 + 4.9 = 20.7 percent). Indirect costs, in the conventional sense, are one third but mount to three fourths when the reduction in earnings due to "stigma" is taken into account (32.9 + 41.3 = 74.2 percent).

Reduction and Control

In all fairness, it must be said that in the absence of radical technological innovations or social changes, eradication in the strict sense is not feasible. A surveillance and control mechanism would almost certainly be required to prevent infection by travelers from abroad and is also likely to be required in practice in a free civilian society as new generations grow up, to keep the disease at a tolerable level. It has been officially recommended that the annual expenditures for operating such a mechanism be raised to $10 million.[55] In perpetuity the present value of such an annual expenditure amounts to $250 million; this can be viewed as an increase in cost of $100 million over 1962, or as an equivalent reduction in prospective benefit.

Alternative levels of control. Acceptable control of syphilis can be attained at alternative levels. The level of incidence achieved is in part a function of the amount spent on the surveillance and control mechanism. As the incidence of the disease declines, the reservoir from which infections are drawn is diminished, but tracing additional cases becomes increasingly difficult and costly.

The benefits of reducing incidence by a given amount or proportion could be uniquely determined if the distribution of cases were the same at each incidence level. Thus, if the number of new cases declined by 80,000 and the remaining 40,000 cases were distributed in the same way as the original 120,000 by sex, race, source of treatment, and stage of discovery, the annual benefit (apart from any changes in expenditures for the control mechanism) would be $78.5 million. It is unlikely, however, that the distribution of cases would be the same at each incidence level. Surely one factor would be the route by which a given level is attained.

The distribution of the resulting number of cases by stage of discovery is of obvious importance in calculating the benefits of a control program. On the face of it, a case discovered and treated in the latent stage of syphilis costs considerably less than a case treated in the primary or secondary stage (Table 11-2). Would it, then, not make sense to postpone treatment? The answer is "no," for the heaviest cost attaches to a late case. A person treated in the infectious stages is certain to avoid the late complications. The probability of developing neurosyphilis or syphilitic heart disease increases as the discovery and treatment of the patient is postponed to the latent stage. This is particularly true if the administration of penicillin is circumscribed.

Perhaps it would be appropriate to view the cost of a latent case as consisting of two components: the several types of cost shown for that stage in Table 11-2, and some fraction of the cost of a late case, corresponding to the probability of developing these complications. Unfortunately, in light of the discussion on the incidence of late cases, nothing more definitive on this score can be said.

Communicability. It was disappointing that we were unable to determine the ultimate effect on the incidence of syphilis of an initial reduction (or increase) of given amount, because the chain of communicability was broken. There is some doubt whether an adequate epidemiological theory exists that applies to the conditions of syphilis.[56] And if such a theory does exist, it certainly has not yet been applied. Letting the model operate over a large number of syphilis generations (the full interval of infectiousness) would be necessary before concluding whether a specified change in incidence would ultimately lead to stability at some other level, to fluctuations around that level, to a gradual decline (or rise) toward an asymptote, or to eradication (or explosion to an epidemic).

On the average, a case discovered and treated in the primary stage of syphilis is infectious to sex partners for four and a half weeks; in the secondary stage, twice as long (nine weeks); and in a latent stage, almost three times as long (twelve weeks). To the extent that sexual activity is independent of the stage in which a case is discovered, there is a better chance of reducing the incidence of syphilis by finding infected persons early rather than later.

Conceivably the time element might also be important from another standpoint. If the infectious agent tends to acquire resistance to a drug, then speed in prosecuting a program becomes essential. There is, however, no evidence that the syphilis organism is becoming resistant to penicillin.

"Stigma." However estimated, the "stigma" factor looms very large once it is recognized. Any change in procedures, whether technological or administrative, that would contribute to the elimination or reduction of "stigma" due to having had syphilis, would yield a large economic benefit. An obvious, partial remedy is to strengthen the safeguards surrounding the disclosure of official information concerning persons with a history of syphilis.[57] The value of "stigma" cannot really be measured without a survey of two populations under controlled conditions. Even then a difference in earnings could reflect other factors as well. To repeat, the estimates presented in this paper are illustrative and reflect only the stated assumptions.

Conclusions

1. Estimates are presented of the economic benefits (costs averted) of controlling syphilis. The largest amount would, of course, accrue from complete eradication. Short of that, a continuing surveillance and control mechanism would be required, which might well cost more in the future than it did in 1962. In addition, all the other costs would continue for the thousands of new cases of syphilis incurred each year. The magnitude of these costs would depend not only on the number of cases, but also on the stage in which they are discovered and treated.

2. Among the costs calculated in this paper—in addition to medical care expenditures and output loss due to treatment time

or disability—are reductions in earnings due to "stigma" and loss in consumer benefit. Since the latter two are seldom if ever calculated, they warrant close scrutiny. Cost due to "stigma" is particularly high, constituting almost 44 percent of the economic costs calculated for the 119,600 new cases of syphilis in 1962. The loss in consumer benefit does not reflect a cost in resources; rather, it represents an attempt to measure the value of avoiding a psychic cost.

3. It was unfortunately not possible to calculate realistically the costs associated with the communicability of syphilis. The probable outcome of an initial change in incidence of specified magnitude is a critical question and warrants intensive exploration.

4. The costs calculated in this paper are tantamount to potential benefits—that is, they represent benefits to the extent that they can be averted. No attempt was made to calculate the direct costs of alternative control programs capable of yielding specified benefits. It is virtually impossible to estimate such costs in the absence of an adequate epidemiological theory on the spread of syphilis.

COST-BENEFIT ANALYSIS

The focus turns now from benefits alone to the task of relating them to costs. A fundamental economic question exists for each and every health program: do its benefits justify its costs? That is, should an expenditure of funds (and a concomitant decision to tie up scarce resources) be made?

The general analytic approach to answering that question is termed *cost-benefit* or *benefit-cost* analysis (the two are the same). It is a technique for judging the economic merit of a program by computing and then comparing all of its associated costs and benefits. Details of cost-benefit analysis vary among economists but the general framework is the same. The usual steps in the analysis are:

1. Identify the nature of the relevant costs and benefits.
2. Value the costs and benefits in monetary terms.
3. Calculate the present value of the cost and benefit streams over time.
4. Compare the present values of costs and benefits.
5. Interpret the results as an aid to decision making.

Each of these steps can present conceptual problems and lead to considerable controversy. Steps 1 and 2 were discussed in earlier sections. The last three steps are considered briefly here.

Health programs involve costs and benefits that extend over time. A typical program will have capital and start-up costs when it is initiated and *operating costs* throughout its existence. Benefits often are not realized immediately but come into being during the later years of the program and may even continue after it has ended. Costs and benefits, therefore, take the form of time streams of values. Although the program's effects extend over future time, a decision to undertake it must be made at a prior point in time. The calculation of *present value* involves deriving a single number to represent a whole time stream of numbers. The technique of *discounting* by which this can be accomplished is discussed in detail below. At this stage, it simply is noted that the correct concepts for use in cost-benefit analysis are the present value of costs, C, and the present value of benefits, B.

These factors often are compared by using the benefit-cost ratio, Z. The benefit-cost ratio is simply the present value of benefits divided by the present value of costs, that is

$$Z = \frac{B}{C}$$

Here B and C represent the present value of benefit and cost streams for the entire proposed program. A modification useful in some applications is the marginal benefit-cost ratio where the two elements apply to a proposed expansion of an existing program. Another comparison is made by computing the value of *net benefits*, that is, the present value of benefits minus the present value of costs.

How are benefit-cost comparisons to be interpreted? Consider first the case of a single proposed program. A cost-benefit analysis is done and the benefit-cost ratio is found to be less than one. What does this indicate? Since the present value of costs is greater than the present value of benefits, society values the resources more in their current use than in the proposed new program. It should not be undertaken. Suppose, alternatively, that the benefit-cost ratio turns out to be greater than one, say, 1.6. Does this mean that the program should be initiated? It does have economic merit—the benefits are greater than the costs. Before a decision is made, however, alternative uses of funds should be checked. Suppose another project could be accomplished at the same cost but with a benefit-cost ratio of 2.1. If funds are limited and only one of the two projects could be undertaken, then it should be the latter one.

This suggests another use for the benefit-cost ratio—the evaluation of a list of different proposed projects. Suppose an agency has a certain amount of funds available for investment, with many possible projects.

One approach to allocating the funds is, for each project, (1) to compute the benefit-cost ratio, (2) to rank the projects in descending order according to the value of the benefit-cost ratios, (3) to implement the first project on the list, the second project, and so on until funds run out. With this procedure the agency can provide the maximum possible benefit to society with its limited investment funds.

As useful as the benefit-cost ratio is, it does not tell the whole story. In particular, it gives no indication of the total impact or scale of the program. For this it is necessary to refer to the present value of benefits minus the present value of costs, $B - C$. Suppose each of two projects has a B/C ratio of 1.5. For one project the present value of costs is $10,000 and for the second it is $1,000,000. The net benefit, $B - C$, associated with the first project is $5,000, for the second, $500,000. Clearly, the second project will have a much greater favorable economic impact, a fact that would have been overlooked had only the benefit-cost ratio been evaluated.

The choice of the best criterion for decision making is a basic question but not the only one for practical cost-benefit analysis. Another is the issue of which effects (or benefits) can be attributed to which health service. Still another is whether to measure intangible benefits in monetary terms or in any common unit at all, and what to do when market prices do not appear to represent social values correctly because of monopoly or externalities.

Of all the issues in applied economic evaluation, the calculation of present values represents one of the most controversial. It is a technique with which the reader should become familiar. The following excerpt from the work of Robert Haveman discusses the methodology and its implications for cost-benefit analysis:

THE ECONOMICS OF THE PRIVATE SECTOR[h]

1. The Treatment of Time One of the primary applications of benefit-cost analysis is in evaluating the worth of long-lived public undertakings—investment programs which produce outputs for many years into the future and whose operation entails costs in future years. An example of such a public investment undertaking is the construction of a large dam to control floods.

A significant problem arises in evaluating long-lived public investments because of the different time periods in which benefits and costs are experienced. This problem exists because of a very basic proposition: *A dollar of benefits (or costs) not expected until next year is worth less than a dollar of benefits (or costs) expected today.* That is to say, time matters. The value of something depends on *when* one will gain use of it—a dollar has a specific value only at a specific date. Thus, a dollar placed in a savings account a year ago has become $1.05 today (at 5 percent interest per year) and will become $1.1025 next year. Likewise, a dollar not expected until next year is worth about 95¢ today if the interest rate is 5 percent. A dollar's value is a function of (depends on) time.

In benefit-cost analysis, both inputs and outputs are valued in terms of dollars—a common unit of account—so the benefits and costs can be compared and decisions can be based on the outcome. When time matters, the money unit by which we value inputs and outputs becomes a rubber yardstick. Dollars are no longer equal to dollars. To be accurate, then, we must not only state inputs and outputs in terms of dollars, but we must state them in terms of dollars of the same date.

It has become common practice to measure all future benefits and costs in terms of *today's dollars*. This makes sense because decisions must be made today between alternatives which have no future benefits and costs and alternatives which do. To compare these alternatives, both present and future benefits and costs are stated in terms of their *present value*.

From the effect of time on values, it is clear that if receiving $1 of income is deferred, its *present value* is less than $1. Conversely, if I have $1 today, I can turn it into more than $1 in a future year by loaning it at some rate of interest. For example, if the interest rate is 5 percent, I can turn the dollar I hold today into $1.05 a year from today. However, if I expect to receive $1.05 a year from today, the *present value* of that $1.05 is about $1. A simple formula for this is

$$P(1 + r) = F_1 \qquad (1)$$

in which P is the present value, r is the rate of interest, and F_1 is the amount received one year in the future. For example, if I have $1 today ($P$) and if the interest rate (r) is 10 percent (or .10), the $1 can be turned into $1.10 a year from today:

$$\$1\ (1.10) = \$1.10 \qquad (2)$$

If I keep my $1 invested at 10 percent for 2 years, it turns into $1.21. This is determined by going through the same calculation two times:

$$\$1\ (1.10)\ (1.10) = \$1.21 \qquad (3)$$

While the above formulae are correct for calculating the future value of something owned today, they are awkward for going in the other direction—for calculating the present value of something not expected until the future. The formulae can be easily revised to go from future to present values as follows:

$$P = \frac{F_1}{1 + r} \tag{4}$$

and

$$P = \frac{F_t}{(1 + r)^t} \tag{5}$$

According to the second formula, the *present value (P)* of some amount expected in year t (F_t) is $\frac{F_t}{(1 + r)^t}$ when the interest rate is r percent. This process of calculating present values is called *discounting*.

In symbolic terms, the numerator of the benefit-cost ratio—the *present value of the net benefits*—is

$$\sum \frac{B_t}{(1 + r)^t}$$

in which Σ means "summation over all the years," B_t stands for the benefits expected in the tth year, and $(1 + r)$ is the discounting factor by which values expected in the future are turned into today's values. Similarly, the denominator of the benefit-cost ratio—the *present value of capital and future operation costs*—is

$$K + \sum \frac{O_t}{(1 + r)^t}$$

in which K is the capital or construction costs (assumed to occur in the current year) and O_t are the operation, maintenance, and repair costs expected in the tth year. The full benefit-cost ratio (Z) is stated as

$$Z = \frac{\sum \frac{B_t}{(1 + r)^t}}{K + \sum \frac{O_t}{(1 + r)^t}}$$

or the ratio of the present value of the benefits over the present value of capital plus future operation costs.[18]

We have noted that the procedure used to calculate present values is called *discounting*. From our description of this process, it is clear that the size of the interest rate used in discounting is very important. The effect of the interest rate on benefit-cost calculations was described in a congressional report. The present value of benefits and costs shown there were calculated from formulae like those presented in the previous paragraph. The report stated:

> **The following table [Table 11-3] presents a simple example of the impact of the discounting procedure on the economic evaluation of an investment.**

Table 11-3 The Effect of Discounting on the Evaluation of a Typical Investment, Using Discount Rates of 0, 3, 5, and 10 percent [Dollar Amounts in Thousands]

	Interest rate (in percent)			
	0	3	5	10
Value today [present value] of total benefits	$15,000	$10,448	$8,456	$5,442
Value today [present value] of total costs	7,500	6,741	6,409	5,906
Benefit-cost ratio	2.00	1.55	1.32	0.92
Present value of benefits minus present value of costs	7,500	3,707	2,047	-464

As Haveman points out, the time factor raises a methodological question. The determination of present values through discounting is an accepted practice among cost-benefit analysts, but how is the proper *rate of discount* determined? This is no mere theoretical exercise. A high *discount rate*, other things equal, will tend to lower the present value of future program benefits; a low discount rate, on the other hand, will make these benefits appear higher. The same is true for program costs. Note, however, that if benefits follow costs in time, the effect of discounting will be relatively more pronounced on the benefit stream than on the cost stream. By exploiting this feature, the analyst can significantly affect the final result. The U.S. Army Corps of Engineers, for example, has been accused of manipulating cost-benefit analyses to justify dam construction projects through its use of a low discount rate.

In reviewing the literature on cost-benefit analysis, the reader will be struck by the fact that most studies use what, today, appear to be ridiculously low discount rates. It would be wrong, however, to take this as evidence of conscious manipulation. The interest rate chosen should reflect underlying economic conditions. The high inflation rates that characterized the economy during the latter half of the 1970s make that task more difficult. Clearly, the faster prices are rising the less future values will be worth, so the greater must be the discount rate used in the analysis. In effect, the inflation rate should be added to some "pure" discount rate to obtain the proper rate.

For some purposes and with some data the limitations of cost-benefit analysis can be overwhelming, and the technique should not be used. However, if the problems noted up to this point are kept in mind and the evaluator is thorough in conducting the study, it can be useful for appraising restricted sets of services or programs. An example of one such attempt is provided in the following selection by Kenneth Steiner and Harry Smith on PKU screening. The reader should be forewarned that this particular research effort contains a number of flaws and questionable assumptions. It is included here because it points up well the kind of pitfalls that can hamper the application of cost-benefit analysis in real life situations. A critique is provided at the end of the selection.

COST-BENEFIT ANALYSIS OF A PKU SCREENING PROGRAM[i]

The cost-benefit approach was used successfully to measure the cost-benefit parameters of a phenylketonuria (PKU) screening program for Mississippi and relating the costs to the benefits.

Phenylketonuria is a hereditary condition in which the patient possesses a simple Mendelian autosomal, recessive gene. It is caused by a rare, inborn error of metabolism and usually results in mental retardation. This disease is somewhat unique in the area of mental deficiency as it is readily detected, and when diagnosed early in life, the deficiency can be modified or prevented with dietary treatment. PKU develops because of the patient's inability to metabolize phenylalanine properly. The result is a deficiency in the amount of phenylalanine that is converted to tyrosine, and large amounts of phenylalanine are found in the blood and spinal fluid. There are no physical standards for comparison in the diagnosis of children with suspected PKU at birth. The child will be apparently normal, but at three or four months of age signs of retardation will appear. The first noticeable change will be the infant's loss of interest in his surroundings, followed by a decrease in mental development, which finally ceases at the age of 10 to 14.

Costs of PKU

The costs associated with PKU were categorized into two areas: direct costs and indirect costs. Direct costs were defined as the actual expenditures for medical and other services attributable to the disease, reflecting the use of resources. These include both personal and non-personal costs. Personal service expenditures included the cost of hospital care, professional medical care, and pharmaceutical services, to list the major items. Non-personal service expenditures included medical supplies, drugs, medical research cost, government grants, charges for depreciation of facilities, and any other non-personal cost associated with the disease.[4,5]

Indirect costs were defined as a loss of economic productivity attributable to the disease, resulting from either death or disability. These indirect costs were calculated on the basis of the annual loss of production as measured by the loss of wages for the work years or months attributable to disease. It was presumed that the patients would have been gainfully employed in a full employment period.[6] The median incomes of the population segmented by age and sex were used in this study. Future earnings were discounted at the rate of 4 percent to ascertain their current value.[7]

The total cost per case, direct and indirect, served as the measure of benefits derived from preventing that case. Three types of benefits are identifiable: 1) reduction in the use of health resources; 2) gains in economic output; and 3) satisfaction from better health. Much too little attention has been given to the latter benefit, accounting to some economists.[8,9] But this benefit, the satisfaction or feeling of well-being of the patient, is very difficult to measure, especially in economic terms. Thus this factor is normally treated as a bonus or windfall to society after all the other calculations are made.

There are two basic approaches in the application of the cost-benefit analysis—the retrospective and the prospective approaches. Both approaches were used in this study. The retrospective approach measures the direct and indirect costs of the current population with a disease entity, PKU in this instance. After these calculations are made, an estimate of the costs of screening, detecting, and treating these patients from among the entire population encompassing the life spans of the patient population is calculated.

The other technique, utilizing the prospective approach, calculates the cost of screening, detecting, and treating all of the live-births in a given year. The future savings (cost to society) of preventing the direct medical cost of the people who are successfully detected and treated plus the indirect costs of future economic productivity of these patients are compared to the cost of screening and detection.

Results of the Retrospective Method

Information from the three mental institutions in Mississippi provided the data for computing the direct and indirect costs associated with PKU patients. Demographic characteristics of the patients provided the base line data as shown in Table 11–4. The direct costs for all mentally retarded patients in the three institutions are summarized in Table 11–5.

Since PKU patients were not identified among the retarded patients in the three Mississippi institutions, the direct cost of maintaining PKU patients had to be estimated by the most reliable

Table 11-4 Age and Sex Distribution of Mentally Retarded Patients in Mississippi Mental Institutions in 1967

Age	Male	Female	Total
Under 5	3	0	3
5–9	32	36	68
10–14	83	49	132
15–19	158	74	232
20–24	176	74	250
25–34	260	148	408
35–44	234	175	409
45–54	201	210	411
55–64	148	234	382
65+	84	109	193
Total	1,379	1,109	2,488

Table 11-5 Summary of Direct Costs for Institutionalized Mentally Retarded Patients

	Whitfield	Ellisville	Meridian	Total
Personal services				
Cost/patient/year	$ 1,847	$ 1,241	$ 1,322	$ 1,512[a]
Number of patients[b]	1,094	1,248	146	2,488
Total	$2,020,618	$1,548,768	$193,012	$3,762,398
Non-personal services				
Depreciation	$ 83,510	$ 78,215	$ 13,041	$ 174,766
Imputed interest	113,991	66,951	12,040	192,982
Research grants	—	—	—	73,346
Total	$ 197,501	$ 145,166	$ 25,081	$ 441,094
Total direct cost	$2,218,119	$1,693,934	$218,093	$4,203,492

[a]Rounded average for the three institutions.
[b]The numbers represent the mentally retarded patient population; there were other patients with various mental disorders in these institutions.

means available. First, the personal service costs for all patients in the institutions were calculated on a per patient per year basis. These figures were multipled by the known number of mentally retarded patients in all the three institutions. This gave an overall annual cost of $3,762,398 for personal services for all mentally retarded patients in the three institutions. The total non-personal service cost per year for the three institutions was $367,748. In addition, $73,346 in research grants was awarded to other institutions to study mental retardation during the baseline year. The total annual direct cost was $4,203,492. Based on the reported statistic that 1 percent of all mentally retarded patients are PKU patients,[10] the best estimate of the direct cost per year per PKU patient was 1 percent of $4,203,492 or $42,035. PKU patients have been reported to be institutionalized 30 years on the average;[11] therefore, the estimated total direct cost for PKU patients was $1,261,050.

Indirect costs are measured by the loss of income. It was assumed that once a mentally retarded patient was institutionalized, he remained incapacitated for life and was a complete loss to the work force. The indirect costs for all the institutionalized mental retardates were computed and reported in Tables 11–6 and 11–7.

The total estimated indirect cost for the mentally retarded population was $105,354,512. One percent of this amount, $1,053,545, was allocated to the PKU patient population. The sum of the direct and indirect costs was summarized in Table 11–8.

Table 11-6 Adjusted Present Value of Lifetime Earnings for Males: Amount Discounted at 4 Percent, Adjusted to 1967 Dollars and for Mississippi, by Age

(1) Age	(2) Earnings[a]	(3) Inflator factor[b]	(4) Inflated lifetime earnings[c]	(5) Lifetime earnings deflated[d]	(6) Number of mentally retarded[e]	(7) Adjusted lifetime earnings for mentally retarded[f]
0–4	$ 62,026	1.090	$ 67,608	$34,480	3	$ 103,440
5–9	79,333	1.090	86,473	44,101	32	1,411,232
10–14	96,736	1.090	105,442	53,775	83	4,463,325
15–19	114,613	1.090	124,928	63,713	158	10,066,654
20–24	126,688	1.192	151,012	77,016	176	13,554,816
25–34	125,801	1.141	143,539	73,205	260	19,033,300
35–44	104,629	1.158	121,160	61,792	234	14,459,328
45–54	71,676	1.178	84,434	43,061	201	8,655,261
55–64	37,168	1.143	42,483	21,666	148	3,206,568
65+	6,560	1.155	7,577	3,864	84	324,576
Total						$75,278,500

[a]From: Rice, D. P. *Estimating the Cost of Illness*, Health Economics Series No. 6, Publication #947-6 (Washington, D.C.: GPO, May 1966) Table 24, p. 93.
[b]Ratio of 1966 median income to 1963 median income.
[c]Column 2 times column 3.
[d]Column 4 times ratio of 1967 median income for Mississippi to 1967 median income for U.S.
[e]Obtained from Table 11-4.
[f]Column 5 times column 6.

Source: Column 3 derived from: U.S. Bureau of the Census, *Current Population Reports*, Series P-60, No. 43, "Income of Families and Persons in the United States: 1963" (Washington, D.C.: GPO, September 29, 1964) Table 20, p. 36; and *ibid.*, No. 53, "Income in 1966 of Families and Persons in the United States" (Washington, D.C.: GPO, December 28, 1967) Table 20, p. 38.

The total cost (the sum of direct and indirect costs) to society to care for the 25 PKU patients (1 percent of the 2,488 institutionalized mentally retarded patients) was $2,314,595.

Estimated Detection Cost

This cost was compared to the estimated program cost to have detected this number of PKU patients and maintained them at a self-supporting status in society. This estimated cost was computed retrospectively as follows. The incidence rate of PKU

Table 11-7 Adjusted Present Value of Lifetime Earnings for Females: Amount Discounted at 4 Percent, Adjusted to 1967 Dollars and for Mississippi, by Age

(1) Age	(2) Earnings[a]	(3) Inflator factor[b]	(4) Inflated lifetime earnings[c]	(5) Lifetime earnings deflated[d]	(6) Number of mentally retarded[e]	(7) Adjusted lifetime earnings for mentally retarded[f]
0–4	$36,280	0.964	$34,974	$17,837	0	$ 000,000
5–9	46,289	0.964	44,623	22,758	36	819,288
10–14	56,422	0.964	54,391	27,739	49	1,359,211
15–19	64,936	0.964	62,598	31,925	74	2,362,450
20–24	67,960	1.150	78,154	39,859	74	2,949,566
25–34	65,608	1.110	72,825	37,141	148	5,496,868
35–44	58,801	1.119	65,798	33,557	175	5,872,475
45–54	47,634	1.130	53,826	27,451	210	5,764,710
55–64	33,816	1.116	37,739	19,247	234	4,503,798
65+	12,525	1.361	17,047	8,694	109	947,646
Total						$30,076,012

[a]From: Rice, D. P. *Estimating the Cost of Illness, op. cit.*, Table 24, p. 93.
[b]Ratio of 1966 median income to 1963 median income.
[c]Column 2 times column 3.
[d]Column 4 times ratio of 1967 median income for Mississippi to 1967 median income for U.S.
[e]Obtained from Table 11-4.
[f]Column 5 times column 6.
Source: For Column 3: Same as in Table 11-6.

Table 11-8 Total Costs for Institutionalized PKU Patients in 1967[a]

Direct costs	
30-year extended direct costs	$1,261,050
Indirect costs	
Present value of lifetime earnings lost	1,053,545
Total direct and indirect costs	$2,314,595

[a]Determined by taking 1 percent of the respective costs for mentally retarded patients.

Table 11-9 Retrospective Analysis of Program Costs

Number of screening tests required	660,000[a]
Cost of initial screening	$561,000[b]
Cost of retesting within six weeks	$561,000[b]
Number of confirmation tests required	3,300[c]
Cost of confirmation tests	$ 12,375[d]
Cost of retesting while on special diet	$ 3,937[e]
Cost of special diet for seven years	$127,750[f]
Administrative cost (10% of other costs)	$126,606
Total program cost	$1,392,668

[a] Figure rounded to the nearest 1,000.
[b] Based on mean cost of $.85 per test from a survey of 42 health departments.
[c] Based on national statistic of 0.5 percent cases requiring confirmation test.
[d] Based on mean cost of $3.75 from survey of the health departments.
[e] Based on average cost of $3.75 per test once every two months for 7 years.
[f] Based on national statistics of an average cost of $2.00 per day per patient.

among a white population is 1:15,000,[12] while the incidence rate among the non-white population is 1:100,000.[13] The 1967 ratios of live-births among white and non-white populations in Mississippi were 49 percent and 51 percent, respectively. Based on 46,714 live-births in 1967, 1.76 PKU cases would have been detected if all 46,714 newborns had been tested, or 1 case of PKU could be found in 26,542 newborns. Therefore, testing approximately 660,000 newborns over a period of 14 years would have been required to have detected the 25 institutionalized PKU patients. The cost of screening the newborns and treating this number of patients has been outlined in Table 11-9.

This total, $1,392,668, is the estimated cost to detect and treat the 25 suspected PKU patients in the Mississippi mental institutions. This figure can then be compared to the total cost of institutionalization and earnings lost of $2,314,595. The resulting cost-benefit ratio was calculated to be 1 to 1.66. Stated positively, each dollar spent in the detection and control of the disease would have yielded a net gain of $0.66 above the cost of the detection and control program.

Results of the Prospective Method

The prospective method based on 1967 live-births in Mississippi was thought to yield more valid results than the retrospective method. As previously noted, testing the 46,714 live-births in 1967

Table 11-10 Program Costs for Live-Birth Data

Number of live-births in Mississippi in 1967	46,714
Average cost per screening test	$0.85
Number of confirmation cases	233.6
Number of cases of whites	1.52
Number of cases of nonwhites	.24
(A) Cost of initial screen test	$39,707
(B) Cost of retest at six weeks	$39,707
(C) Cost of confirmation at $3.75 per test	$ 876
(D) Diet cost of 1.76 cases for seven years	$ 8,994
(E) Cost of retest while on diet	$ 278
(F) Administration cost	$ 8,956
Total cost of program	$98,518

would have detected an average of 1.76 PKU cases. The total costs to conduct such a screening program were tabulated in Table 11-10.

It was assumed that the total number of live-births would be tested initially and again within six weeks. Also, it was assumed that an average number of confirmation tests would be made, and a test monitoring the PKU urine level would be performed every two months. A diet cost of $2.00 per patient per day was used in the computations, which is the highest cost reported in the literature.[14] The statistics used in Table 11-10 maximized the cost of the detection and treatment program.

Based on the data used in the retrospective method, the direct cost of institutionalized care was estimated at $1,690 per case per year. If the 1.76 cases had been detected in 1967, it would have cost $89,232 for institutional care for 30 years, the minimum expected length of time of institutionalization, or $210,588 for the 70.8 years of normal life expectancy of a one-year-old child born in 1967. The indirect cost for loss of future earnings, discounted at 4 percent per annum,[7] totaled $45,830. The total direct and indirect costs were $135,062 for 30 years of institutional care and $256,418 for 70.8 years of institutional care. These data yielded cost-benefit ratios of 1 to 1.37 and 1 to 2.60, respectively.

Again, the gain to society using live-birth data and the prospective method was substantial, even if we use the minimum of 30 years of institutionalization. In all of the calculations, costs of the detection and control programs were maximized, while direct and indirect costs (benefits) were minimized.

Conclusion

The conclusion to be drawn from this study is that a PKU screening program is beneficial not only to the person who has the disease but also to society. The retrospective approach yielded a cost-benefit ratio of 1:1.66. Using the more valid prospective approach, the cost-benefit ratio was 1:1.37 when the direct costs were minimized to correspond to the 30 year average time a patient is institutionalized. A ratio of 1 :2.60 resulted when the full life expectancy was used. Neither the time and money spent for a PKU preventive program nor the economic benefits derived from such a program reveal the additional financial burden and amount of personal care required by the families of the undiagnosed patients. In addition, the emotional stress which is inflicted upon the families cannot be measured in economic terms.

• • •

Is PKU screening worthwhile? From a humanistic standpoint it certainly would appear to be, and indeed the procedure has been in widespread use for years. In research published subsequently to Steiner and Smith, the economic benefits of such screening have been reaffirmed.[9] The issue then is not so much the authors' results as how they were obtained. Is the analytical framework appropriate? Are all program benefits and costs identified properly? Are the identified benefits and costs valued correctly?

A point to begin with is the analytical framework. Steiner and Smith use as their decision criterion the benefit-cost (B/C) ratio that shows the return in benefits for each dollar spent in screening costs. While there is nothing inherently wrong in using a ratio criterion, it generally is considered inferior to the net benefit approach. Why? For one thing, the ratio does not indicate the magnitude of returns once costs are accounted for. This can lead to some ambiguity because it is entirely possible to have a high ratio combined with a low net return and vice versa.

Another problem is that the B/C ratio value is highly sensitive to whether program effects are defined as true benefits or as costs averted. For example, Steiner and Smith consider the institutional costs averted by eliminating future PKU retardates to be a primary program benefit; that is, they add it into the numerator of the ratio. But PKU institutionalization could be considered just as logically as a program cost that is reduced through screening. In this case, the averted cost would be subtracted from the denominator rather than added to the numerator. It does make a difference. According to their calculation under the retrospective method

$$\frac{B}{C} = \frac{\$2,314,595}{\$1,392,668} = 1.66$$

But, by shifting the $1.2 million in institutional costs from numerator to denominator, we obtain

$$\frac{B}{C} = \frac{\$1,053,545}{\$\ \ 131,618} = 8.01$$

In so doing, the rate of return is increased nearly five-fold without changing any of the facts in the case. The net benefit approach is superior because it is not susceptible to this type of manipulation or reinterpretation. (In the above example $B - C = \$921,927$ regardless of how institutional costs are treated.)

After the analytical framework has been chosen, the next step in benefit-cost analysis is to identify all relevant program effects. This is a more troublesome task than might first be imagined because any change in a social system may have secondary and tertiary implications that are difficult to foresee. Consider the case at hand. Steiner and Smith correctly identify savings in hospitalization as a positive result of a screening program. But what of those PKU patients who were never institutionalized or who were awaiting hospitalization? Presumably the costs for these individuals also would be averted with a successful screening program. Moreover, the Steiner and Smith assumption that research on PKU would cease once screening begins might be questioned. Is this a realistic assumption? Did research on polio stop with the introduction of the Salk and Sabin vaccines?

It is virtually impossible to conduct cost-benefit analysis without making some assumptions about causes or effects. When such situations arise, the careful researcher will do three things: (1) state explicitly what each assumption is, (2) justify it according to the most reliable information available, and finally (3) give the reader some idea of just how sensitive the final result is to the assumption made. The third factor (referred to in economics literature as sensitivity analysis) is probably the most important. A particular assumption may be dubious and yet make relatively little difference in the benefit-cost ratio or net benefit estimate. For example, the authors of this book question the inclusion of the PKU research grant as a cost averted because of screening, but the amount of the research grant ($73,346) is so small that excluding it would have a minimal effect on the cost-benefit calculations.

It is not possible to be as sanguine about another Steiner and Smith assumption. It is apparent that the value of program benefits (institutional costs averted and additional lifetime earnings generated) is highly sensitive to their estimates of PKU incidence in Mississippi. At one point, they cite a nationally reported statistic that 1 percent of all mentally retarded patients are PKU victims. At another point they rely upon a personal communication to justify a PKU incidence rate of 1:15,000 among a white population. How strong is this evidence? The reader is left in doubt. The figures may be appropriate for Mississippi, but then again they may not (particularly if incidence is highly race-specific). If they are not accurate, a relatively small shift in magnitude (say from 1.0 to 0.5 percent of institutionalized mentally retarded patients) would be enough to produce negative net benefits under the screening program.

Even if it is assumed that the incidence figures are reliable, there are other considerations that might affect the study results significantly. On the benefit side, Steiner and Smith assume that a 1 percent reduction in the census for three state hospitals would result in a proportionate reduction in total direct costs, including those for depreciation and imputed interest on these facilities. Since depreciation and interest are fixed costs, there will be no savings here.[10] More serious is the fact that except in the case of lifetime earnings, they fail to discount future costs and benefits to present values. The 30-year estimate of $1.2 million in institutional costs averted thus is overstated by a wide margin. The same is true to a lesser degree in the case of the seven-year cost of special diets for detected PKU cases.

Additional criticisms of the article could be noted,[11] but the reason for the exercise should be clear at this point. Unless extreme caution is taken in conducting cost-benefit analysis, the effort may go for naught. This case review indicates that a medical intervention probably does produce positive economic returns as well as inestimable benefits in lifelong health to those affected. However, a detractor of public health expenditures, by using the type of critique developed here, might make a convincing case that these benefits are not sufficiently strong to warrant the expenditures involved.

COST-EFFECTIVENESS ANALYSIS

Cost-effectiveness analysis is a technique for judging the relative economic merit of a particular program in comparison with its alternatives. The analyst attempts to find which program or approach among several alternatives provides the largest benefit for a given cost or (equivalently) yields a particular benefit (or set of benefits) at the lowest expenditure. It is different from cost-benefit analysis in that it imposes no requirement to measure costs and benefits in the same units. If a benefit can be scaled in nonmonetary terms—say, in number of years of life saved by a program or some other objective achieved by it—then the alternative ways to obtain a given level of that benefit can be compared on the basis of their monetary costs.

This technique is most modest, but frequently more practical, than cost-benefit analysis under many conditions. However, it is not without its own limitations. An obvious one is that either the benefit or cost variable must be fixed in size in the calculations. Cost-effectiveness analysis does not reveal how big the benefit should be or what programmatic scale (and cost) should be taken as given. Another restriction is that the attribution problem cannot be avoided. The analyst *must* be able to relate services specifically to effects or outcomes. That suggests another challenge: how to deal with the situation in which a program (or a service) yields more than one type of outcome? Unless there is some common denominator for all relevant benefits, they cannot be summed for a complete analysis.

A final theoretical problem with cost-effectiveness analysis should be mentioned. When benefits accrue over a period longer than one year, the question of discounting still remains. Monetary gains received later are worth less than ones received during the present year, as acknowledged in connection with cost-benefit studies. But what about nonmonetary benefits, such as years of life saved? Some would argue that these, too, must be discounted to estimate their present value.[12] Whenever discounting is required, the nagging problem of the appropriate rate will haunt the evaluator. To this and other assumptions made, sensitivity analysis ought to be applied.

Notwithstanding such problems and qualifications, the positive side of cost-effectiveness analysis and its potential superiority over cost-benefit studies should be stressed. To show some of the potentialities of the technique, providing lessons for both administrators and planners, this chapter concludes with a final case study. The setting in Botswana might appear exotic, with questionable applicability to the United States. However, the issues treated are pertinent to this country—for example, in relation to rural health care—and its analytic methods clearly are relevant. The article's selection of effectiveness indicators, especially the "likely effective patient contact," might be noted and compared with others to be found in the literature.[13] The reader should examine this report critically to judge how well the limitations of cost-effectiveness analysis mentioned above are handled and to decide what alternative measures might have been used.

MOBILE HEALTH SERVICES: A STUDY IN COST-EFFECTIVENESS[j]

Critical examination of resource allocation within the health sector is essential for the efficient and effective deployment of services. This is even more crucial in Third World countries owing to their relative poverty. In many developing countries difficulties are experienced in providing health services for the population at even the most minimal level. In such situations different approaches to increasing health care coverage have been attempted and increased mobility of health workers has been an integral part of many of these attempts.[3, 4, 7, 13] In certain instances relatively sophisticated transport systems, including aircraft,[8, 9, 11, 19] have been proposed for such work. The protagonists of aircraft have argued enthusiastically for their more widespread use in health services,[9, 22, 23] while others have been less certain of the place of mobile health services[6, 14, 15, 16] and in particular aircraft.[10]

The present article illustrates how cost-effectiveness techniques were employed in a developing country, Botswana, to make recommendations regarding the use of transport, including aircraft, in the health services in the context of the delivery of care from both fixed and mobile units. The study described herein is based upon actual conditions in Botswana, with regard both to patient profiles and health manpower and services; as such, alternative hypotheses concerning basically different cost-effective strategies for health delivery were not considered, *e.g.*, the use, of Chinese-type village health workers.

Botswana: The Country

Botswana is a large country (220,000 sq. miles) lying at the center of the Southern African Plateau. The population is mainly engaged in subsistence agriculture and especially the raising of cattle. Almost 600,000 people were enumerated at the 1971 census; of these less than a tenth were urban and over half lived in villages of less than 500 people. The per capita income is estimated at £92 (1973–1974). This figure is deceptive in that income distribution is skewed to favor the urban employed; the periurban per capita income is about £55 and the rural per capita income £25. The economy is growing at an annual rate of approximately 12 per cent, due mainly to recent mining developments. It is stated government policy to devote a large proportion of the revenue generated from these undertakings to development in rural areas. Health services (government and mission) have been largely concentrated upon curative hospital based care. In Botswana there are 12 general hospitals (six government and six mission), one long-stay mental hospital, six health centers and 45 clinics. Outpatient and inpatient surveys show that the majority of patients travel less than 10 miles for these services (83 per cent of outpatients and 69 per cent of inpatients). When this information is combined with data on population distribution, differential utilization rates can be produced. These show that people living less than 5 miles from health facilities utilize outpatient services nearly 5 times more often than do people living further than 10 miles away. For hospital inpatients, people living less than 10 miles from a hospital have admission rates almost 10 times higher than those living further than 25 miles away. Hospital services consume almost three-quarters of the government's recurrent health budget. The average government expenditure on health is £3.2 per capita (1974–1975), however for people living less than 5 miles from hospitals government expenditure is £7.5 per capita and for those living further than 25 miles only £0.9 per capita.

In an attempt to redress the present imbalance in the allocation of health service resources the Botswana government is employing mobile units and is considering both their expansion and the establishment of a flying health service to increase the coverage of population with basic health care.

Methods

Visits were made to the African Medical and Research Foundation (AMRF) based in Nairobi, Kenya and the Lesotho Flying Doctor Service in Maseru, Lesotho. Available data on their operations were reviewed.

In Botswana mobile health services were examined in two areas: 1) those delivering primary patient care using land and air transport, and 2) those making supportive visits to permanently staffed basic health facilities. To provide baseline data against which it would be possible to measure the work of the mobile services in terms of cost-efficiency (where the output of service was defined as the number of patient contacts) and cost-effectiveness (where the outcome of service was defined as the number of patient contacts in which the diagnosis and treatment was likely to be efficacious) four permanently staffed rural clinics were examined.

Mobile Services Delivering Primary Care. Two mobile services (one using a lorry and the other a Cessna-185 light aircraft) that delivered primary patient care were studied. They served similar populations in adjacent administrative districts extending about 250 miles into the Kalahari Desert. The distance traveled and number of patients seen on the particular trips examined were representative of normal (other) journeys. The journeys studied took place during February and March, 1975.

Patient Characteristics. Details of all patients seen were recorded by questionnaire. The first part of this questionnaire, containing mainly demographic items, was completed by trained Botswana assistants. The second part, containing details of diagnosis, treatment, and disposal, was completed by the doctor seeing the patient.

Outcomes of Service. Outcomes of service were looked at from two viewpoints: i. The likely developments if the contact had not occurred. Conditions were classified into one of the eight following outcome groups.

1. Probable death
2. Possible death
3. Probable complications of an acute illness or condition
4. Possible complications of an acute illness or condition
5. Complications unlikely, but a possible longer natural history of an acute illness or condition
6. Possible complications of a chronic illness or condition
7. Relief of discomfort in a condition likely to be self-limiting
8. Short-term relief in a chronic or degenerative condition

ii. The likely effectiveness of diagnosis and treatment. Conditions were classified into one of the four following outcome groups.

1. Efficacious treatment was likely at one visit.
2. Efficacious treatment may have required continuing care or access to it.
3. Efficacious treatment required continuing care.
4. Treatment likely to be only palliative, placebo or of dubious efficacy.

The decision as to which diagnoses fell into each of the above classifications was made after discussions leading to consensus decisions with a number of other doctors (Table 11-11). There

Table 11-11 Outcomes of Service

Likely Developments If the Contact Had Not Occurred

---

1. *Probable death* (out of 898 patients seen, none fell into this category). Examples of diagnoses in this group are: meningitis, tetanus, diphtheria, trypanosomiasis.
2. *Possibe death* (out of 898 patients seen none fell into this cateogry). Examples of diagnosis in this group are: severe tuberculosis, severe gastroenteritis, kwashiokor.
3. *Probable complications of an acute illness or condition.* Examples of diagnoses in this group are: measles, pneumonia, gastroenteritis, ear infections, incomplete abortion.
4. *Possible complications of an acute illness or condition.* Examples of diagnoses in this group are: eye infections, lower respiratory infections (other than pneumonia), urinary tract infections, accidents, antenatal patients.
5. *Complications unlikely but a possible longer natural history of an acute illness or condition.* Examples of diagnoses in this group are: tonsilitis, skin infections.
6. *Possible complications of a chronic illness or condition.* Examples of diagnoses in this group are: tuberculosis, pelvic inflammatory disease, syphilis, anaemia, malnutrition, psychiatric illness.
7. *Relief of discomfort in a condition likely to be self-limiting.* Examples of diagnoses in this group are: upper respiratory infections, herpes simplex.
8. *Short-term relief in a chronic or degenerative condition.* Examples of diagnoses in this group are: arthritis, dyspepsia, peptic ulceration.

Likely Effectiveness of Diagnosis and Treatment

---

1. *Efficacious treatment was likely at one visit.* Examples of diagnoses in this group are: gonorrhoea, scabies, extraction of carious teeth, eye infections.
2. *Efficacious treatment may have required continuing care or access to it.* Examples of diagnoses in this group are: respiratory infections, skin infections (excluding scabies), pelvic inflammatory disease, urinary tract infections, ear infections, gastro-enteritis in people aged five years and above, minor trauma.
3. *Efficacious treatment required continuing care.* Examples of diagnoses in this group are: tuberculosis, malnutrition, gastro-enteritis in children aged less than five years, psychiatric disorders, including epilepsy, major trauma, antenatal care, child welfare care, family planning.
4. *Treatment was likely to be only palliative, placebo, or of dubious efficacy.* Examples of diagnoses in this group are: menstrual disorders, vague digestive, and bone, muscular and joint disorders (excluding trauma).

are some problems of validity and repeatability for both classifications. However these concern only a minority of conditions and a small proportion of total contacts.

Costs. Costs (1974) for both mobile services were calculated. These included costs of transport (fixed and variable), salaries, drugs, and equipment. The transport costs for the land mobile service were estimated using data from the Botswana Government Central Transport Organization. They calculated that the cost was £0.26 per mile for the vehicle used. This included running and fixed (capital discounted over three years and annual maintenance) costs. For the air mobile service, actual costs were not available since the service was operated by a mission society. The cost of chartering a similar aircraft (a Cessna-185) was obtained from a local light-aircraft charter company. The actual day-equivalent salaries for the people making the trip were obtained. Drugs used were noted and priced at the government Central Medical Stores. A nominal sum was included for the equipment used on the journeys made by each mobile service.

Fixed Clinics. Four rural clinics located in three of the seven health regions of Botswana were examined. The clinics are reasonably representative of those in rural Botswana. Utilization data for different categories of care (including curative outpatients, antenatal, child welfare, family planning, and home visiting) were obtained for 1974. Actual annual costs for each clinic were calculated; failing this, estimates were obtained from the Ministries of Health and Local Government and Lands. Considerable effort was made to ensure that these estimates were realistic. For capital costs of clinic buildings current (1974–1975) costs for equivalent buildings were used. Annual maintenance costs were calculated at 10 per cent of capital costs for furniture and equipment and 2.5 per cent for buildings. Arbitrary lifetimes were taken of 30 years for buildings, 15 years for furniture and 10 years for equipment. Equivalent annual costs were produced for capital items *e.g.*, buildings, furniture, equipment, vehicles, generators, by using the standard accounting procedure of annuity costing (a 10 per cent annuity rate was employed).

Supportive Visits to Permanently Staffed Clinics. Regional medical officers were accompanied on visits to permanently staffed rural health facilities during which time referral clinics were held. Details of patients seen in these clinics were recorded by questionnaire. Other activities carried out during these visits were noted and the costs of such visits calculated.

Results

Mobile Services Delivering Primary Patient Care. The patients seen on each mobile trip were similar with regard to age, sex, diagnostic grouping, and distance traveled for care. On the air-delivered service 145 patients were seen, and 753 patients were seen on the land service. The great majority of patients (95 per cent) traveled less than five miles to the services.

Outcomes of Service. The services were similar in the proportions of patients seen by each method of classifying outcome. In viewing the outcome of patients' conditions, in terms of the likely development if the contact had not occurred, it appeared that the services might have prevented (at least in the short run) some form of medical complication in over half the patients seen (Table 11–12). However, when outcome is viewed from its likely effectiveness only a minority of patients (7 per cent for females and 20 per cent for males) seen was likely to have been treated efficaciously (Table 11–13). It was considered that almost one-third of the patients seen certainly required continuing care (32 per cent for females and 21 per cent for males). This second method of considering likely outcome is the more important one since it corresponds more closely with the requirements for health service provision.

Costs. Transport costs formed a far higher proportion of total costs in the air-delivered service as compared with the land one, 57 per cent as against 27 per cent (Table 11–14).

Fixed Clinics. When patient outcomes at fixed clinics were viewed by the effectiveness of diagnosis and treatment (outcome classification 2) it was considered that a majority (91 to 94 per cent) of patient contacts were likely to be effective. This was a far higher proportion than for the mobile services. This was due primarily to the continuous availability of care at these clinics in contrast to the periodic nature of the mobile services.

Supportive Visits. As expected, where a referral system is operating, most (77 per cent) of the screened patients seen had either:

1. Complications of their medical conditions
2. Not responded to conventional treatment
3. A relatively uncommon condition
4. An atypical presentation

Table 11-12 Mobile Services Compared According to Likely Outcome If No Contact Had Been Made

	Air Service			Land Service			Totals	
	Observed		Expected	Observed		Expected		
Likely Outcome	No.	%		No.	%		No.	%
Probable death	0	(0)	0	0	(0)	0	0	(0)
Possible death	0	(0)	0	0	(0)	0	0	(0)
Probable complications of an acute illness or condition	28	(19)	22	106	(14)	112	134	(15)
Possible complications of an acute illness or condition	35	(24)	44	237	(31)	228	272	(30)
Complications unlikely but a possible longer natural history of an acute illness or condition	20	(14)	14	66	(9)	72	86	(10)
Possible complications of a chronic illness or condition	16	(11)	13	63	(8)	66	79	(9)
Relief of discomfort in a condition likely to be self-limiting	4	(3)	6	33	(4)	31	37	(4)
Short-term relief in a chronic or degenerative condition	42	(29)	47	248	(33)	243	290	(32)
Totals	145	(100)		753	(99)*		898	(100)

*Does not add to 100 due to rounding.
Note: $\chi^3 = 9.483$ on five degrees of freedom; $0.1 > p > 0.05$.

5. Or, required more sophisticated investigations and/or treatment than the permanent staff of the clinic were able to provide

The importance of these regular supportive visits extends beyond the seeing of referred patients. The other activities carried out during these visits appear in many cases to be far more important. Organizational and administrative arrangements are dis-

Table 11-13 Mobile Services and Likely Effectiveness of Diagnosis and Treatment

Likely Effectiveness of Diagnosis and Treatment	Air Service						Land Service					
	Female		Male		Total		Female		Male		Total	
	No.	%	No.	%	No.	%	No.	%	No.	%	No.	%
Efficacious treatment was likely at one visit	6	(7)	13	(22)	19	(13)	34	(7)	47	(19)	81	(11)
Efficacious treatment may have required continuing care or access to it	36	(41)	20	(34)	56	(39)	161	(32)	99	(40)	260	(35)
Efficacious treatment required continuing care	23	(26)	10	(17)	33	(23)	163	(32)	55	(22)	218	(29)
Treatment likely to be only palliative, placebo or of dubious efficacy	22	(25)	15	(26)	37	(26)	145	(29)	49	(20)	194	(26)
Totals	87	(99)*	58	(99)*	145	(101)*	503	(100)	250	(101)*	753	(101)*

*Does not add to 100 due to rounding.

Table 11-14 Costs, Costs per Patient Contact and Cost per Likely Effective Patient Contact, for Mobile Services (in £)

Cost Factors	Costs	
	Air Service	Land Service
Transport	116.45*	127.39†
Equipment	4.14‡	5.52§
Drugs‖	37.04	215.21
Salaries¶	44.48	127.51
Total**	202.11	475.63
Number of patients seen	145	753
Cost per patient contact	1.39	0.63
Number of patients seen where diagnosis and treatment likely to be efficacious at one visit	19	81
Cost per likely effective patient contact	10.64	5.87

*Inclusive cost, local charter rate for a Cessna-185 aircraft of £0.27 per land mile.
†Inclusive cost, the Botswana Government Central Transport Organization estimate of £0.26 per mile for vehicle used, a five-ton Bedford lorry.
‡Includes a canopy, drug containers, etc.
§Includes a small generator, drug containers, etc.
‖Drugs used noted and priced at government Central Medical Store's prices.
¶Mid-point salaries of personnel making trips for days involved.
**No central administrative costs included.

cussed as are details of individual patient management and community health issues. However, quantification of the effectiveness of such activities is difficult. While it would have been preferable to study the effectiveness of different visiting patterns on the provision of care at randomly selected and control clinics, this was not possible in the time available. Nonetheless, the organization of clinics, the morale of the staff and the rapport with the visitor appeared far higher when visiting was regular and reasonably frequent (about every two weeks).

Cost-Efficiency and Cost-Effectiveness of the Mobile Services Compared with the Stationary Clinics. The average cost-per-patient-contact was similar for the fixed clinics* and the land-delivered service, but for the air-delivered service the comparable figure was more than double. In comparison with the fixed clinics the average cost per effective patient contact was almost 8 times

Table 11-15 Comparison of Cost per Patient Contact and Cost per Likely Effective Patient Contact for Fixed Clinics and Mobile Clinics (in £)

	Costs		
	Fixed	Mobile Clinics	
Cost Factors	Clinic	Air	Land
Per patient contact	0.68	1.39	0.63
Per likely effective patient contact	0.75	10.64	5.87

greater for the land service and just over 14 times greater for the air service (Table 11-15).

The average cost per referred patient (Table 11-16) seen during the supportive visits to permanent clinics was less than half the average cost per effective patient contact for the land-delivered mobile service and less than a quarter of that for the air-delivered service. It must be stressed that the justification of supportive visits extends far beyond the seeing of referred patients. The visits are important in emphasizing preventive and community care, in

Table 11-16 Cost per Referred Patient Seen at Permanently Staffed Fixed Clinics

Cost Factors	Costs (in £)
Referral clinics	4
Number of patients seen	78
Transport*	79.29
Regional medical officer's salary†	64.44
Total	143.73
Visit cost per referred patient	1.84
Cost per referred patient including clinic "overhead" costs‡	2.52

*Central Transport Organization's estimates of £0.13 per mile for a Land-Rover and £0.18 for a Ford F.250 four-wheel drive vehicle. Visits to two clinics were made in Land-Rovers and to two others in Ford F.250s.

†Regional medical officer's day salary £16.10. Although the whole of this cost is applied to seeing referred patients, it is obvious that other important duties are also performed.

‡Clinic "overhead" costs taken as £0.68, the mean cost per patient contact of the four fixed clinics examined (see Table 11–15).

lessening the isolation of rural clinics, and in continuing the education of the staff at these units.

The Health-Planning Implications of These Findings

The comparison of alternative primary care delivery systems by their cost-effectiveness shows that static facilities are to be greatly preferred to mobile services.† The most efficient use of transport in association with primary care is to convey skilled but scarce health personnel to peripheral and often isolated permanently staffed facilities. In Botswana many of these rural units are at present visited both infrequently (some only every 6 to 12 weeks) and irregularly. Several possible transport strategies to provide more adequate support to all rural clinics were examined and costed. These models included the consideration of different mixes of transport types *i.e.*, land vehicles (both two- and four-wheel drive) and light aircraft. The constraints within which the proposed system should function were identified as:

1. The relatively small number of doctors (especially those who wished or were able to leave their hospitals).
2. The large distances between clinics and the poorly developed road system.
3. Every clinic should be visited fortnightly, and a visit should last about four hours.
4. Expenditure of approximately £0.25 per capita (1974–1975) for all government health sector transport. (This figure is an average of actual expenditure over the previous six years at 1974–1975 prices.)

Given the above constraints the cheapest option was to use land vehicles to visit those clinics located relatively close to regional health headquarters and light aircraft to visit only the most distant facilities. Two simple criteria‡ for deciding which clinics should be visited by aircraft were evolved. Those clinics that are located by virtue of distance or difficult terrain at such traveling time from regional health headquarters by road that: 1) more than a day is required for the visit to one clinic; and 2) a total stay of more than four nights from the base is involved in any one trip (it is agreed amongst people making such trips that stays of four nights away from their base in one stretch, or in one 14 day period is an upper acceptable limit on a regular basis).

Discussion

Mobile health units have been employed by the health services of many developing countries in an attempt to increase population coverage. They have initially appeared to be attractive. Two of the many reasons being that, 1) they are able to make contact with relatively large numbers of individuals and therefore appear to be a way of spreading care more widely, and 2) they depend to a great extent upon central organization and minimally upon the active participation of visited communities.

However, when the effectiveness of the medical care offered is examined more critically and compared with that available from permanently staffed facilities the fallacy of the initial (above) attraction is apparent. As Bodenheimer[3] has stated, mobile health services have as their main disadvantage that of being periodic in nature. The present attempt in Botswana to quantify the impact of this periodic delivery of care in relation to its effectiveness suggests that, by contrast, fixed facilities are far more cost-effective. In addition there is a greater possibility of active community participation in relation to a fixed clinic, especially if this unit is adequately supported by the central health organization. It is in this supportive area that mobility is likely to be most efficient, especially given the austere constraints of trained manpower and finance encountered in developing countries (together with other additional barriers to rural development).

The use of all mechanical transport (*i.e.*, that powered by petrol or diesel fuel) must be viewed critically.[21] It is important to establish the medical (service) needs for mobility before setting out to meet them. In certain countries mobile health services have been envisaged "as the spearhead of development"[9] preparing communities for the eventual provision of more permanent services. Unfortunately in most developing countries resources are so constrained that such an approach to the delivery of services is not possible. Frequently the proposed interim development preempts or unnecessarily delays the eventual achievement of the more desirable end-point, *i.e.*, static clinics.

In addition to the use of transport connected with primary health care, mobility in health services has been used in several other roles. These include:

1. Specialist clinical rounds on a scheduled basis[23]

2. Scheduled visits not necessarily involving direct patient care, *e.g.*, the delivery of medical and general supplies, administration[22]
3. Vertical health programs, *e.g.*, communicable disease control,[12] maternal and child health,[14, 18] and family planning
4. Emergency/ambulance evacuation of patients[1, 2, 4]

A case can be made for transporting specialists regularly from central hospitals to more isolated district ones, in an attempt to extend and improve available health care. A decision regarding the most appropriate form of transport to be used can be made by the use of criteria similar to those developed for supportive visits to primary care facilities. Visits concerned with the delivery of supplies are usually carried out more efficiently when combined with supportive visits. Vertical health programs are more effective when incorporated into basic health care programs.[17] Often the most dramatic and appealing use of transport is in the capacity of ambulance evacuation. The main disadvantage of this use is high cost per journey. For example, in 1973 the average recurrent cost per ambulance flight by the Nairobi-based AMRF was just over £100,[1] and for the Australian Royal Flying Doctor it was approximately £250.[2] However, the disparity in per capita health expenditure for these two countries is very large. Kenya is spending about £1.30[20] per capita, while Australia is spending almost £60.[5]

It is important that the use of all mechanical transport, and in particular aircraft, be restricted only to those activities which, given the disease patterns and population age structure, are likely to have the highest cost-benefit ratio. In the context of the majority of Third World countries this will rule out the use of aircraft for emergency services and virtually restrict its use to a supportive relationship to fixed units that could not otherwise be as efficiently reached by land vehicles. Consequently there is an absolute need to integrate the aircraft into the ongoing health delivery system. It is virtually inevitable that, unless the use of aircraft is tightly scheduled, they will be called upon when emergencies do arise and be diverted from more effective activities. Anyway, when aircraft are available many so-called emergencies turn out not to be "red" emergencies. The case for the availability of aircraft for ambulance purposes, on the basis that emergencies simply must be met, cannot be justified in terms of rational health planning within the "needs" and resources of most developing countries. To provide such services would be an instance of resource allocation based upon emotion and could be accomplished only at great cost to the potential health care of the whole community.

CONCLUSION

It is worth emphasizing, in conclusion, that this chapter has presented a selective view of the evaluation of health care. Coverage was limited to economic appraisals of care—and to certain economic factors at that. Costs, benefits, and the relationship between them were stressed. Necessarily in a book like this other evaluative elements, such as quality of care, were omitted or played down. Ample literature is available for extending studies to those matters.

Good data on costs are essential to administrators, planners, and other health field specialists of all kinds. Economic evaluation of costs can supplement the techniques of cost analysis commonly used in basic management, planning, and program development. The main point here is to understand such basic economic concepts as opportunity cost, and to know how they can be properly transformed into useful measures of costs. The specific measures employed in a given situation will depend on the needs of the user and the availability of sound data.

Simple cost accounting concepts should be understood by most, and perhaps all, health specialists. This does not mean that everyone need be skilled in accounting per se. Accountants certainly will see much more to costs than others must master. If this chapter has demonstrated new ways to estimate cost values and use them to evaluate programs, it will have done its job.

Measuring the benefits of health services represents a very difficult part of evaluation. Yet, what is the ultimate point of program assessment if it is not to judge how well the activity has contributed to the better health of its clients? Measures of improvement need not be confined to physical status but may extend to effects on attitudes and practices, among other indicators. Economists have their own preferred measures of program benefits (or positive effects), some of which are applied readily in practice while others are relevant primarily on a theoretical level.

The fundamental economic notion of relating inputs to outputs suggests the logic behind comparisons of program costs to benefits. One noteworthy expression of this relationship is cost-benefit analysis. At its most basic level, this tool provides a method for making the essential judgment: Does a program pay? Are its benefits at least equal to its costs, properly measured? In actual applications, such as the choice among competing programs, cost-benefit analysis presents numerous conceptual and technical difficulties. It is hoped that this chapter has shown the requisites of good cost-benefit analysis and some of the pitfalls in less adequate ones.

The other common technique that economists use in appraising health programs is cost-effectiveness analysis. It, too, presents potential difficulties but is often safer and more useful for practical policy making, especially when deciding which of several ways to reach a common objective is the best in economic terms.

The reader is not expected to emerge from this book with a blueprint for conducting either type of analysis. If the authors have provided an appreciation of some accomplishments as well as limitations of economic evaluation, we will have met our goal.

NOTES

1. R.C. Bradbury, "Policymaking and the Planning Process," *American Journal of Health Planning* 1 (April 1977): 40. An earlier approach aimed at economists can be found in M.S. Feldstein, "An Aggregate Planning Model of the Health Care Sector," *Medical Care* 5 (November-December 1967): 369–381.

2. See discussion in Chapter 6, *Quality of Medical Care Assessment Using Outcome Measures*, U.S. Department of Health, Education and Welfare, Health Resources Administration, National Center for Health Services Research, DHEW Publication No. (HRA) 77-3176, 1977.

3. Sidney Lee, "Discussion on Cost Analyses and Data Needed for a Better Appreciation of Choices in the Provision of Medical Care," in Paul M. Densen et al., eds., *University Medical Care Programs: Evaluation,* U.S. Department of Health, Education and Welfare, Health Services and Mental Health Administration, DHEW Publication No. (HSM) 72-3010 (Washington, D.C.: U.S. Government Printing Office, December 1971), pp. 125–131.

4. An example of a check on the utilization factor using a useful ratio computation can be found in Robert L. Robertson, Bernardo Barona, and Ricardo Pabón, "Hospital Cost Accounting and Analysis: The Case of Candelaria," *Journal of Community Health* 3, no. 1 (Fall 1977): 74–75.

5. A good summary of sensitivity analyses of various types in cost-benefit studies is provided in Peter G. Sassone and William A. Shaffer, *Cost-Benefit Analysis: A Handbook* (New York: Academic Press, 1978), Chapter 8.

6. Kerr White, "Evaluation of Medical Education and Health Care" in Willoughby Lathem and Anne Newburg, eds., *Community Medicine* (New York: Appleton-Century-Crofts, Inc., 1970), p. 246.

7. The advantages and limitations of outcomes measures are especially well summarized in U.S. Department of Health, Education and Welfare, National Center for Health Services Research, *Needed Research in the Assessment and Monitoring of the Quality of Care,* by Avedis Donabedian, DHEW Publication No. (PHS) 78-3219 (Washington, D.C.: U.S. Government Printing Office, July 1978), pp. 5–7.

8. Two sources to read on assumptions required are: Herbert E. Klarman, "Syphilis Control Programs" in Robert Dorfman, ed., *Measuring Benefits of Government Pro-*

grams (Washington: Brookings Institution, 1965), esp. pp. 369–374; Robert L. Robertson, "Issues in Measuring the Economic Effects of Personal Health Services," *Medical Care* 5 (November–December 1967): 362–368.

9. Robert Scheffler and Lynn Paringer, "A Review of the Economic Evidence on Prevention," *Medical Care* 18, no. 5 (May 1980): 480–481.
10. Interest, depreciation, and other fixed costs might be averted in the long run when it comes time to replace existing facilities with institutions of smaller size reflecting the reduced census. To account properly for such savings it would be necessary to calculate the remaining life of existing facilities and to deduct fixed costs averted only for the years following the anticipated replacement dates.
11. Some of these additional concerns are suggested by the following questions: Is the discount rate of 4 percent too low? Should the earnings figures be weighted to reflect the racial composition of Mississippi's population? Is the economic value of preventing retardation among females really less than half that for men? Is it realistic to project 30 years of institutional costs without considering the effect of inflation? Is it appropriate to use a dietary cost of $2 per meal in 1967, given that the reference source was from 1961? Why was a seven-year dietary program used in the prospective method? (Do dietary needs cease after seven years?) Do the dietary costs reflect the entire food cost or just the additional costs over and above those of normal meals? Are there no start-up costs associated with introducing a screening program, such as training and education, that should be included as program costs?
12. For a provocative article on this issue, see Carolyn A. Watts, Morgan Jackson, and James P. LoGerfo, "Cost Effectiveness Analysis: Some Problems of Implementation," *Medical Care* 17, no. 4 (April 1979): 430–434.
13. For those preferring studies closer to home, two of the many possibilities are cited here. For a relatively theoretical piece using a "quality adjusted life years" indicator and illustrative data, see Richard Zeckhauser and Donald Shepard, "Where Now for Saving Lives?," *Law and Contemporary Problems* 40 (Autumn 1976): 5–45. A more empirical article is Peter G. Goldschmidt, "A Cost-Effectiveness Model for Evaluating Health Care Programs: Applications to Drug Abuse Treatment," *Inquiry* 13, no. 3 (March 1976): 29–47. It employs an indicator of the impact of drug abuse treatments called "effectiveness measure units" that scales successful contacts in terms of months of drug-free life after treatment.

SUGGESTED READINGS

Barlow, Robin. "The Economic Effects of Malaria Eradication." *The American Economic Review* 57 (May 1967): 130-148.

Bogen, Leslie I. "Cost-Benefit Analysis: Caveat Emptor" (Editorial). *American Journal of Public Health* 69 (December 1979): 1210-1211.

Bradbury, R.C. "Policymaking and the Planning Process." *American Journal of Health Planning* 1 (April 1977): 37-43.

Cochrane, A. L. *Effectiveness and Efficiency: Random Reflections on Health Services.* London: Nuffield, Provincial Hospitals Trust, 1972.

Cooper, Barbara, and Dorothy P. Rice. "The Economic Cost of Illness Revisited." *Social Security Bulletin* 39 (February 1976): 21-36.

Donabedian, Avedis. *Needed Research in the Assessment and Monitoring of the Quality of Medical Care.* Hyattsville, Md.: U.S. Department of Health, Education and Welfare, Public

Health Service, National Center for Health Services Research, DHEW Publication No. (PHS) 78-3219, July 1978.

Goldschmidt, Peter G. "A Cost-Effectiveness Model for Evaluating Health Care Programs: Application to Drug Abuse Treatment." *Inquiry* 13 (March 1976): 29-47.

Goldsmith, Seth B. "A Re-evaluation of Health Status Indicators." *Health Services Reports* 88 (December 1973): 937-941.

———. "The Status of Health Status Indicators." *Health Services Reports* 87 (March 1972): 212-220.

Heller, Peter S. "Issues in the Costing of Public Sector Outputs: The Public Services of Malaysia." Washington: World Bank, Staff Working Paper No. 207, June 1975.

Lee, Sidney S. (Chairman). "Discussion on Cost Analysis and Data Needed for a Better Appreciation of Choices in the Provision of Medical Care." In *University Medical Care Programs: Evaluation*, edited by Paul M. Densen, et al. Rockville, Md: U.S. Department of Health, Education and Welfare, Health Services and Mental Health Administration, National Center for Health Services Research and Development, DHEW Publication No. (HSM) 72-3010, December 1971: 125-131.

Lewis, Charles E. "The State of the Art of Quality Assessment—1973." *Medical Care* 12 (October 1974): 799-806.

McCaffree, Kenneth M. "The Cost of Mental Health Care Under Changing Treatment Methods." *American Journal of Public Health* 56 (July 1966): 1013-1025.

McKean, Roland N. *Public Spending*. New York: McGraw-Hill Book Company, 1968: Chaps. 3 and 8.

Mushkin, Selma J. "Health as an Investment." *Journal of Political Economy* 70 (October 1962), Part 2 (supplement): 129-157.

Rice, Dorothy P. *Estimating the Cost of Illness*. Washington, D.C.: U.S. Department of Health, Education and Welfare, Public Health Service, Publication No. 947-6, May 1966.

Rice, Dorothy P., and Cooper, Barbara S. "The Economic Value of Human Life." *American Journal of Public Health* 57 (November 1967): 1954-1966.

Robertson, Robert L. "Issues in Measuring the Economic Effects of Personal Health Services." *Medical Care* 5 (November-December 1967): 362-368.

Robertson, Robert L. et al. "Costs and Financing Policies at a Neighborhood Health Center." *Inquiry* 10 (September 1973): 36-48.

Robertson, Robert L. et al. "Costs of Mental Health Services in a Colombian Hospital." *American Journal of Public Health* 67 (October 1977): 972-974.

Sassone, Peter G., and Schaffer, William A. *Cost-Benefit Analysis: A Handbook*. New York: Academic Press, 1978.

Schelling, T.C. "The Life You Save May Be Your Own." In *Problems in Public Expenditure Analysis*, edited by Samuel B. Chase. Washington, D.C.: The Brookings Institution, 1968: 127-162.

Sorkin, Alan L. *Health Economics in Developing Countries*. Lexington, Mass.: Lexington Books, D.C. Heath and Company, 1976: esp. 33-35, 43-57, 93-95, 126-130, 136.

U.S. Department of Health, Education and Welfare, Health Resources Administration, National Center for Health Services Research. *Quality of Medical Care Assessment Using Outcome Measures*. Hyattsville, Md: NCHSR, DHEW Publication No. (HRA) 77-3176, August 1977.

Watts, Carolyn A.; Jackson, Morgan; and Logerfo, James P. "Cost-Effectiveness Analysis: Some Problems of Implementation." *Medical Care* 17 (April 1979): 430-434.

Weisbrod, Burton A. *Economics of Public Health*. Philadelphia: University of Pennsylvania Press, 1961.

White, Kerr L. "Evaluation of Medical Education and Health Care." In *Community Medicine*, edited by Willoughby Latham and Ann Newbury. New York: Appleton-Century-Crofts, Inc., 1970: 241-262.

Zeckhauser, Richard, and Shepard, Donald. "Where Now for Saving Lives?" *Law and Contemporary Problems* 40 (Autumn 1976): 5-45.

REFERENCES FOR BUTTER ET AL., EXCERPT

7. Reder, M. W., Some problems in the Measurement of Productivity in the Medical Care Industry, in Fuchs, V. R. (Editor), *Production and Productivity in the Service Industries*, New York, National Bureau of Economic Research, 1969.
8. Kovner, J. W., Measurement of Outpatient Office Visit Services, *Health Services Research*, 4, 112-127, Summer, 1969.
15. More specifically, 32 per cent of total nursing time spent both at the Health Center and in the community represents patient care time, but could not be attributed to visit-specific activities. The cost of this share of nursing time was divided equally between nursing and medical visits because the activities in question are more closely related to patient care than to non-patient care functions.
16. This issue will be discussed in more detail in a forthcoming paper by Robert L. Robertson, Gordon T. Moore and Irene Butter. [See Robertson et al., *Inquiry*, in the Suggested Readings at the end of this chapter.]
17. See the forthcoming paper by Robertson, Moore and Butter.

REFERENCES FOR FIRST KLARMAN EXCERPT

10. McKean, R. N. *Efficiency in Government Through Systems Analysis*. John Wiley & Sons, Inc., New York, 1958.
13. Weisbrod, B. A. *Economics of Public Health*. University of Pennsylvania Press, Philadelphia, 1961.
18. Klarman, H. E. *The Economics of Health*. Columbia University Press, New York, 1965.
19. Freeman, A. M. Project design and evaluation with multiple objectives. In *Public Expenditures and Policy Analysis*, edited by R. H. Haveman and J. Margolis, pp. 347–363. Markham Publishing Company, Chicago, 1970.
24. Acton, J. P. Evaluation of a Life-Saving Program: The Case of Heart Attacks. Doctoral Dissertation, Harvard University, Cambridge, 1970.
41. Mushkin, S. J., and Collings, F. d'A. Economic costs of disease and injury. *Public Health Rep.* 74(9): 795–809, 1959.
43. Rice, D. P. *Economic Costs of Cardiovascular Diseases and Cancer*. Health Economics Series No. 5. U.S. Government Printing Office, Washington, D.C., 1965.
44. Rice, D. P. *Estimating the Cost of Illness*. Health Economics Series No. 6. U.S. Government Printing Office, Washington, D.C., 1966.
45. Klarman, H. E. Syphilis control programs. In *Measuring Benefits of Government Investments*, edited by R. Dorfman, pp. 367–410. The Brookings Institution, Washington, D.C., 1965.

46. Klarman, H. E. Socioeconomic impact of heart disease. In *The Heart and Circulation,* Vol. 2, pp. 693–707. Federation of American Societies for Experimental Biology, Washington, D.C., 1965.
50. Klarman, H. E. Conference on the economics of medical research. In Report of the President's Commission on Heart Disease, Cancer, and Stroke, Vol. 2, pp. 631–644. U.S. Government Printing Office, Washington, D.C., 1965.
51. Mushkin, S. J. Health as an investment. *Journal of Political Economy* 70(5): 129–157, 1962.
53. Rice, D. P., and Cooper, B. S. The economic value of human life. *Am. J. Pub. Health* 57(11): 1954–1966, 1967.
54. Mishan, E. J. Evaluation of life and limb. *Journal of Political Economy* 79(4): 687–705, 1971.
55. Kuznets, S. *National Income and Its Composition, 1919–1938,* pp. 22–23. National Bureau of Economic Research, New York, 1947.
56. Walker, K. E., and Gauger, W. H. The Dollar Value of Household Work. New York State College of Human Ecology, Cornell University, Ithaca, New York, 1973 (processed).
57. Sirageldin, I. A-H. *Non-Market Components of National Income.* Institute for Social Research, University of Michigan, Ann Arbor, 1969.
58. Gelman, A. C. *Multiphasic Health Testing Systems: Reviews and Annotations.* U.S. Government Printing Office, Washington, D.C., 1971.
59. Vickrey, W. S. One economist's view of philanthropy. In *Philanthropy and Public Policy,* edited by F. G. Dickinson, pp. 31–56. National Bureau of Economic Research, New York, 1962.
60. Neenan, W. B. *Normative Evaluation of a Public Health Program.* Institute of Public Administration, University of Michigan, Ann Arbor, 1967.
61. Schelling, T. C. The life you save may be your own. In *Problems in Public Expenditure Analysis,* edited by S. B. Chase, pp. 127–162. The Brookings Institution, Washington, D.C., 1968.
62. Thurow, L. *Investment in Human Capital,* p. 134. Wadsworth Publishing Company, Inc., Belmont, California, 1970.
63. Titmuss, R. M. *The Gift Relationship,* p. 198. Pantheon Books, New York, 1971.

REFERENCES FOR SECOND KLARMAN EXCERPT

55. Baumgartner and Task Force, *The Eradication of Syphilis,* pp. 8, 19.
56. Helen Abbey, "An Examination of the Reed-Frost Theory of Epidemics" and J. de Oliveira Coste Maia, "Some Mathematical Developments on the Epidemic Theory Formulated by Reed and Frost," *Human Biology,* Vol. 24 (September 1952), pp. 201–33 and 167–200, respectively; see pp. 202 and 168 for assumptions.
57. Cockburn, *The Evolution and Eradication of Infectious Diseases,* p. 171.

REFERENCE FOR HAVEMAN EXCERPT

18. These present value formulae, it should be noted, are very close to formula 5 in the previous paragraph. The main difference is that the formulae in the benefit-cost ratio have a summation sign (Σ) in them. . . .

REFERENCES FOR STEINER AND SMITH EXCERPT

4. Rice, D. P. "Estimating the Cost of Illness," *American Journal of Public Health* 57:424–440 (1967).
5. Rice, D. P. *Estimating the Cost of Illness,* Health Economics Series No. 6, PHS Publication #947-6 (Washington, D.C.: GPO, May 1966) p. 3.
6. Fein, R. *Economics of Mental Health,* (New York: Basic Books, 1958).
7. Rice, *Estimating the Cost of Illness, op. cit.,* Parts II & III, Appendix B.
8. Marshall, A. W. "Cost-Benefit Analysis in Health." Paper presented in Monterey, California, November 10, 1965, and reproduced by the Rand Corporation.
9. Klarman, H. E. *The Economics of Health* (New York: Columbia University Press, 1965).
10. Hsia, D. Y. Y. "Recent Developments in Inborn Errors of Metabolism," *American Journal of Public Health* 50 :1653–1661 (1960).
11. Cunningham, G. C. "Two Years of PKU Testing in California," *California Medicine* 111:11–16 (1969).
12. Hormuth, R. P., specialist in services for mentally retarded children, Children's Bureau, Department of Health, Education and Welfare, personal communication.
13. Katz, H. P. and Menkes, J. H. "Phenylketonuria Occurring in an American Negro," *Journal of Pediatrics* 65 :71–74 (1964).
14. Centerwall, W. R.; Centerwall, S. A.; Acosta, P. B.; and Chinnock, R. F. "Phenylketonuria. I. Dietary Management of Infants and Young Children," *Journal of Pediatrics* 59:93–101 (1961).

NOTES FOR WALKER AND GISH EXCERPT

* This is the case in Botswana and is due in part to the relatively low utilization rates at fixed facilities.

† Which is not to claim that the mere addition of facilities can be automatically equated with better health for the largest possible number of especially poor rural inhabitants.

‡ Although it was not possible to develop scientific criteria, based upon wide discussion and field criteria, it was felt that the criteria actually selected would be able to meet any reasonable test of suitability.

REFERENCES FOR WALKER AND GISH EXCERPT

1. African Medical and Research Foundation: Annual Report for 1973. Nairobi, Kenya, 1974.
2. Australian Information Service: The Flying Doctor. Canberra, Australia, 1974.
3. Bodenheimer, T. S.: Mobile units: A solution to the rural health problem? Med. Care 7:144, 1969.
4. Bolton, J. M.: Medical services to the Aborigines in West Malaysia. Br. Med. J. 2:818, 1968.
5. Cochrane, A. L.: World health problems. Can. J. Public Health 66:280, 1975.

6. Cox, P. S. V.: The value of mobile medicine. East Afr. Med. J. 46:548, 1969.
7. Denny, K. M.: A Review of Alternative Approaches to Health Care in Developing Countries: Mobile Health Teams. Cambridge, Mass., Management Sciences for Health, 1974.
8. Duncan, J.: The Flying Doctor Service of Africa. World Med. J. 13:102, 1966.
9. Flying Doctor Development Service Limited: Flying Doctor Services and Rural Development: Report of a Seminar held at Birmingham University, 1969. Birmingham 31, England, Flying Doctor Development Service, 1969.
10. Great Britain, Parliament. Hansard's Parliamentary Debates (Commons), 972:309, 1974.
11. Jackman, E.: Flying Doctor Services in Zambia. In Medical Geography Techniques and Field Studies, N. D. McGlashan, Ed. London, Methuen, 1972.
12. Jogan, B., and Rogers, I.: Mobile leprosy control in the Luapula Province of Zambia. Lepr. Rev. 44:120, 1973.
13. King, M. (Ed.): Medical Care in Developing Countries, sec. 2:10. Nairobi, Oxford University Press, 1966.
14. Korte, R., and Patel, P. M.: Operational aspects of mobile and stationary young child clinics in Lushoto, Tanzania J. Trop. Pediatr. 20:90, 1974.
15. Long, E. C.: Health problems of Central America. Trop. Doct. 2:89, 1972.
16. Paddock, W., and Paddock, E.: Mobile Health Clinics Become a Shell Game, Ch. 4. In *We Don't Know How*, an Independent Audit of What They Call Success in Foreign Assistance. Ames, Iowa State University Press, 1973.
17. Soper, F. L.: The Relation of the Mass Campaigns for the Prevention of a Specific Disease to the General Health Services. WHO/PHA/Mass Campaigns/5, 1969.
18. Van der Mei, J., and Belcher, D. W.: Comparing under-five programmes in a hospital-based clinic and in satellite mobile clinics. Trop. Geogr. Med. 26:449, 1974.
19. Vuturo, A. F., and Jensen, R. T.: Considerations for planning and implementing a flying health service: Experiences in the Ryuku Islands. Milit. Med. 136:736, 1971.
20. WHO Regional Office for Africa. The Place of Hospitals in Public Health Services and Their Role in African Communities: Report on a Seminar 1974. AFR/PHA/132, p. 47, 1974.
21. WHO/UNICEF. Joint Study on Alternative Approaches to Meeting Basic Health Needs of Populations in Developing Countries. JC/UNICEF-WHO/75.2, p. 17, 1974.
22. Wood, A. M.: Communication with Rural Areas by Radio, Light Aircraft and Mobile Land Units. J. R. Coll. Surg. Edinb. 16:202, 1971.
23. Wood, A. M.: The Use of Modern Forms of Transport in Community Medicine. In Health and Disease in Africa: East African Medical Research Council Conference, Nairobi, 1970, G. C. Gould, Ed., Kampala, East African Literature Bureau, 1970.

SOURCES AND PERMISSIONS

a. Adapted from "Policymaking and the Planning Process," by R.C. Bradbury, *American Journal of Health Planning* 1 (April 1977), p. 40, by permission of American Health Planning Association, © 1977.
b. Reprinted from H.G. Massey et al., "Cost Measurement: Tools and Methodology for Cost Effectiveness Analysis" by H.G. Massey et al., P-4762, pp. 5-7, 13-14, by permission of The Rand Corporation, © 1972.

c. Reprinted from "Cost Analyses and Data Needed for a Better Appreciation of Choices in the Provision of Medical Care" by Paul Feldstein, in Paul M. Densen, et al., eds., *University Medical Care Programs: Evaluation*, pp. 119-120, U.S. Department of Health, Education and Welfare, Health Services and Mental Health Administration, National Center for Health Services Research and Development, DHEW Publication No. (HSM) 72-3010, December 1971.

d. Reprinted from *Cost-Finding and Rate-Setting for Community Mental Health Centers* by James Sorensen and David Phipps, with others, pp. 2-2–2-7, 2-1–2-2, U.S. Department of Health, Education and Welfare, National Institute of Mental Health, DHEW Publication No. (HSM) 72-9138, 1972.

e. Reprinted from "Effects of Manpower Utilization on Cost and Productivity of a Neighborhood Health Center" by Irene Butter et al., *Milbank Memorial Fund Quarterly* 50 (October 1972), Part I, pp. 426-427, 439-444, by permission of Milbank Memorial Fund Quarterly, © 1972.

f. Reprinted from "Application of Cost-Benefit Analysis to the Health Services and the Special Case of Technologic Innovation" by Herbert E. Klarman, *International Journal of Health Services* 4 (May 1974), pp. 331-335, by permission of author and Baywood Publishing Co., © 1974.

g. Reprinted from "Syphilis Control Programs" by Herbert E. Klarman, in Robert Dorfman, ed., *Measuring the Benefits of Government Investments*, pp. 404-410, by permission of The Brookings Institution, © 1965.

h. Reprinted from *The Economics of the Public Sector*, 2nd ed., by Robert H. Haveman, pp. 161-163, by permission of John Wiley & Sons, Inc., © 1976.

i. Reprinted, with permission of the Blue Cross Association, from "Application of Cost-Benefit Analysis to a PKU Screening Program" by Kenneth Steiner and Harry Smith, *Inquiry* 10, no. 4 (December 1973), pp. 35-40. Copyright © 1973 by the Blue Cross Association. All rights reserved.

j. Reprinted from "Mobile Health Services: A Study in Cost-Effectiveness" by Godfrey Walker and Oscar Gish, *Medical Care* 15 (April 1977), pp. 267-276, by permission of J.B. Lippincott, Co., © 1977.

Glossary

Allocative Efficiency: Using inputs and producing outputs in the proper combinations to satisfy society's wants. (See also: **Economic Efficiency, Efficiency, Technical Efficiency**)

Assignment: In health insurance and government health programs, the process whereby a provider accepts from the payer an agreed-upon fee for each service delivered. If assigned, no additional charges may be billed to the patient other than allowed by deductible, coinsurance, or copayment provisions imposed by the payer.

Average Cost: The cost per unit for producing a certain number of units of a product; that is, total cost divided by number of units produced. (Contrast with: **Marginal Cost**)

Average Per Diem (APD): A method of cost apportionment for hospital reimbursement whereby total allowable costs are allocated among third-party payers according to the percentage of total patient days accounted for by each payer. (Contrast with: **Ratio of Charges-to-Charges Applied to Costs**)

Average Revenue: The per unit revenue derived from selling a certain number of units of a product; that is, total revenue divided by number of units produced. (Contrast with: **Marginal Revenue**)

Balance Billing: A reimbursement technique whereby providers receive a portion of their fees from a third-party payer and must bill patients for the balance due.

Benefit-Cost Analysis: Equivalent to cost-benefit analysis. (See also: **Cost-Benefit Analysis, Cost-Effectiveness Analysis**)

Bilateral Market Power: The existence of market power on both the demand and supply sides of the market. The extreme case is bilateral monopoly where a single buyer faces a single seller. The existence of bilateral market power complicates and may even preclude the establishment of an equilibrium price in the market. (See also: **Market Power**)

Budget Line: A line on a graph that depicts the collection of points representing combinations of the quantities of two products that can be purchased with a given amount of income at current product prices.

Capital: Productive resources of physical types, the purchase of which constitutes investment; sometimes used loosely to refer to funds involved in business. (See also: **Capital Costs, Human Capital, Investment**)

Capital Costs: Equivalent to investment costs. (See also: **Capital, Development Costs, Investment Costs, Operating Cost**)

Capitation: A method of reimbursement whereby the provider collects, in advance, a set fee that entitles the patient to any quantity of covered services deemed necessary by the provider over a specified period of time, usually a month. (See also: **Panel**)

Carrier: A third-party payer for the Medicare Supplementary Medical Insurance program. (See also: **Third-Party Payer**)

Ceteris Paribus: Holding constant all factors other than the single variable in question for an analysis.

Coinsurance: A type of cost sharing by consumers under third party payment by which a consumer must pay a particular percentage of the total bill. (See also: **Copayment, Deductible**)

Comparative Statics: The study of the relationship between two static equilibrium points (for example, two equilibrium prices), one before and the other after a particular change is introduced into the system, holding all other influences constant. (See also: **Equilibrium Price**)

Concentration Ratio: The percentage of total industry sales (or assets or employment) accounted for by the largest 4, 8, or 20 firms.

Conduct: Behavior of firms in an industry toward one another as well as toward suppliers, employees, and customers. (See also: **Firm, Industry**)

Constant Dollars: Monetary values after the effects of inflation have been removed; that is, current dollars, deflated. (See also: **Current Dollars, Deflation**)

Consumption: The expenditure for, and use of, products that yield utility directly, and thus are valued for their own sake. (See also: **Utility**; Contrast with: **Investment**)

Copayment: A type of cost sharing by consumers under third party payment by which a consumer must pay a particular portion of the bill for specific services (for example, office visits or prescriptions). (See also: **Coinsurance, Deductible**)

Correlation: The quantitative association (relationship) between two variables, or the statistical study of that association. (See also: **Correlation Coefficient (Simple), Multiple Correlation Coefficient**)

Correlation Coefficient (Simple): A numerical value indicating the degree of association (relationship) between two variables as determined by statistical analysis. (See also: **Correlation, Multiple Correlation Coefficient**)

Cost-Benefit Analysis: An analytic technique for judging the economic merit of a product or program by comparing its costs and benefits. (See also: **Benefit-Cost Analysis, Cost-Effectiveness Analysis**)

Cost-Effectiveness Analysis: An analytic technique for judging the relative economic merit of one product or program in comparison with its alternatives. (See also: **Benefit-Cost Analysis, Cost-Benefit Analysis**)

Cost Function: The relationship between costs and corresponding quantities produced (or sold) of a product for a firm, with variables such as resource price held constant.

Cross-Elasticity of Demand: The responsiveness (in percentage terms) of quantity demanded of one product to the change (in percentage terms) in the price of another product, with other variables held constant). (See also: **Elasticity of Demand**)

Cross Section: A type of statistical analysis using data that apply to variables for several different units for a single period of time. (See also: **Longitudinal Analysis, Time Series**)

Cross-Subsidization: In health insurance and reimbursement, an instance where one class of patient or service is priced below cost and losses are made up from revenue received from another class of patient or service.

Glossary 521

Current Dollars: Monetary values at the current level of prices, as recorded or observed. (See also: **Constant Dollars, Deflation**)

Customary Charge: Synonymous with usual fee or prevailing fee. (See also: **Prevailing Fee, UCR Reimbursement, Usual Fee**)

Dead Weight Loss: An economic loss to society as a whole, as opposed to a loss by one person offset by a gain to another. A health services example: the value of time lost in waiting in a queue. (See also: **Queue**)

Deductible: A type of cost sharing by consumers under third-party payment by which a consumer must pay a particular initial amount of the bill before any third-party coverage begins. (See also: **Coinsurance, Copayment**)

Deflator (Deflating, Deflation): As applied to index numbers: the process of removing the effects of inflation from a measure of expenditure change over time. The result is an expenditure measure in constant dollars. (See also: **Constant Dollars, Current Dollars**)

Demand: The quantity of a product that one or a group of consumers is willing to purchase at a given price during a particular period of time. (See also: **Demand Curve, Demand Function, Derived Demand, Law of Downward-Sloping Demand**)

Demand Curve: The graph of a demand function relating price and quantity demanded. (See also: **Demand, Demand Function, Law of Downward-Sloping Demand**)

Demand Function: The relationship between quantity demanded and factors determining it, such as prices, income, and tastes. Often used to refer simply to the relationship between a good's price and quantity demanded, assuming other variables are held constant. (See also: **Demand, Demand Curve, Law of Downward-Sloping Demand**)

Derived Demand: Demand for a factor of production or an intermediate good. The demand depends on or is derived from consumer demand for the final output. (See also: **Demand, Factor of Production, Intermediate Good**)

Development Costs: The outlay of funds for all nonrecurrent (one-time) resources used to develop a new product or service for market. (See also: **Capital Costs, Investment Costs, Operating Costs**)

Diffusion: The process by which the use of an innovation spreads through a population of users. (See also: **Technological Change**)

Diminishing Marginal Utility: The fact that for most persons successive quantities purchased and used of a product will yield decreasing increments of utility (satisfaction). (See also: **Marginal Utility, Utility, Utility Function**)

Direct Benefits: In the case of health services: medical costs averted (and resources saved) by a reduced need to use and pay for health services due to the provision of past and present services. (See also: **Indirect Benefits**)

Discounting: The process of computing the present value of some benefit or cost to be received in the future by application of a rate of discount to the future value. (See also: **Discount Rate, Present Value, Rate of Discount**)

Discount Rate: The annual rate at which one or a group of persons would reduce the value of a future benefit or cost in order to compute its present value. Also called Rate of Discount. (See also: **Discounting, Interest Rate, Present Value, Rate of Discount, Rate of Return**)

Diseconomies of Scale: The situation in production when a firm's average cost of producing a product rises as its scale increases; in such a case there are said to be decreasing returns to scale. (See also: **Average Cost, Returns to Scale, Scale**; Contrast with: **Economies of Scale, Scale Economies**)

Dummy Variable: A variable defined for statistical purposes to represent a characteristic that has only a "yes-no" type of measure rather than quantitative values.

Economic Efficiency: The achieving of a particular level of output at a minimum cost for the inputs (resources) used. (See also: **Allocative Efficiency, Efficiency, Technical Efficiency**)

Economies of Scale: The situation in production when a firm's average cost of producing a product falls as its scale increases; in such a case there are said to be increasing returns to scale. Also called Scale Economies. (See also: **Average Cost, Returns to Scale, Scale**; Contrast with: **Diseconomies of Scale**)

Effective: As applied to a medical regimen: "Capable of achieving efficacious therapies to all persons who could or should benefit from them." (Source: White in *Community Medicine*.) (See also: **Efficacious, Efficient**)

Efficacious: As applied to a medical regimen: More useful and beneficial, on the basis of objective evidence, "for the purposes for which it is advocated." (Source: White in *Community Medicine*.) (See also: **Effective, Efficient**)

Efficiency: Using available resources in the way that will yield the maximum possible benefits (output). (See also: **Allocative Efficiency, Economic Efficiency, Efficient, Technical Efficiency**)

Efficient: As applied to a medical regimen: Prudent use of resources "in achieving the effective delivery of efficacious regimens." (Source: White in *Community Medicine*.) (See also: **Effective, Efficacious, Efficiency**)

Elastic Demand: A demand function for which the percentage change in quantity demanded exceeds the corresponding percentage change in price (or income). (See also: **Elasticity of Demand, Income-Elasticity of Demand, Price-Elasticity of Demand**; Contrast with: **Inelastic Demand**)

Elasticity of Demand: The responsiveness (in percentage terms) of quantity demanded of a product to changes in some variables such as price, income, age, etc. (See also: **Cross-Elasticity of Demand, Elastic Demand, Income-Elasticity of Demand, Inelastic Demand, Price-Elasticity of Demand**)

Endogenous Variable: A variable whose value is determined within the system under study, that is, is influenced by the system. (Contrast with: **Exogenous Variable**)

Equilibrium Price: The price at which the total quantity demanded of a product is equal to the total quantity supplied in a market; graphically, the price at which the demand curve and supply curve intersect (cross). (See also: **Demand Curve, Market, Supply Curve**)

Equity: The fairness of a situation; for example, equal benefits or opportunity to obtain them for all consumers and potential consumers in an economic system.

Excess Demand: The situation in a market in which the quantity demanded exceeds the quantity supplied at the prevailing price. (See also: **Shortage**; Contrast with: **Excess Supply, Surplus**)

Excess Supply: The situation in a market in which the quantity supplied exceeds the quantity demanded at the prevailing price. (See also: **Surplus**; Contrast with: **Excess Demand, Shortage**)

Exogenous Variable: A variable whose value is determined outside of the system under study, that is, is not influenced by the system. (Contrast with: **Endogenous Variable**)

Expansion Path: Points of economically efficient factor use for different levels of output; graphically, the line composed of points where isocosts and isoquants are tangent. (See also: **Isocost, Isoquant**)

Externalities: Economic effects of production or consumption that are felt by parties beyond the immediate producer or consumer of a product; they can be positive effects (benefits) or negative effects (costs). (See also: **Social Benefit, Social Cost**)

Factor of Production: An input to a productive process; it can take the form of labor, machinery, or other resources. (See also: **Productive Resources, Resource**)

Fee-for-Service: A common method of reimbursement where the rate bases are specific services delivered and rates are derived from professional fees. (See also: **Rate Base, Rate Determination**)

Firm: One decision-making unit concerned with production, or one seller of a particular product. (See also: **Industry, Market, Oligopoly**)

Fiscal Agent: A third-party payer for state Medicaid programs. (See also: **Third-Party Payer**)

Gross National Product: The total monetary value of the final output of an economy during a period of time such as a year; under certain definitions, it is equivalent to total national income for that period. (See also: **Income**)

Human Capital: Labor or its characteristics in terms of future productive capacity; for example, the educational characteristics of one or more persons. (See also: **Capital**)

Hypothesis Test: A test (as in statistics) of a general proposition, based on available evidence. (See also: **Significance Test**)

Income: The flow of products, or entitlement to products through monetary receipts, over a given period of time for one person or a group of people. (See also: **Gross National Product, Income Distribution**; Contrast with: **Wealth**)

Income Distribution: The division (often measured in percentage terms) of the income of a group of persons among those persons. (See also: **Income**)

Income-Elasticity of Demand: The responsiveness (in percentage terms) of quantity demanded of a product to the change (in percentage terms) in income of its buyers, with other variables held constant. (See also: **Elastic Demand, Elasticity of Demand, Inelastic Demand**)

Index Number: An expression of the percentage change in the values of a particular variable (or set of them) in relation to its value in a base period, holding other variables constant. (See also: **Laspeyres Index, Paasche Index**)

Indifference Curve: A graph that contains a curve depicting the collection of points representing combinations of quantities of two products, all of which points have the consumer equally satisfied. (See also: **Marginal Rate of Substitution, Utility, Utility Function**)

Indirect Benefits: In health services: Values of positive effects of past and present health services in the form of improved production, longer life, reduced disability, lessened pain, and the like; essentially, all the benefits except direct ones. (See also: **Direct Benefits**)

Industry: The group of providers (firms) producing or selling a particular product within a particular area; the scope of the area will depend on the product. (See also: **Firm, Market, Oligopoly, Performance**)

Inelastic Demand: A demand curve for which the percentage change in quantity demanded is less than the corresponding percentage change in price (or income). (See also: **Elasticity of Demand, Income-Elasticity of Demand, Price-Elasticity of Demand**; Contrast with: **Elastic Demand**)

Interest Rate: The annual rate of charge imposed on the use of resources or funds. (See also: **Discount Rate, Rate of Discount, Rate of Return**)

Intermediary: A third-party payer for the Medicare Hospital Insurance Program. (See also: **Third-Party Payer**)

Intermediate Good: A product that is created for subsequent use in producing a final product; an intermediate result between inputs and final output.

Investment: The expenditure for, and use of, products that provide a flow of other outputs over time; the latter are the outputs valued for their utility by consumers. (See also: **Capital, Utility;** Contrast with: **Consumption**)

Investment Costs: The value of all resources used, or outlays of funds, "involved in producing the equipment, organizing people initially, and setting up the new system;" all are one-time (nonrecurrent) outlays. (Source: Massey et al., *Cost Measurement*.) (See also: **Capital Costs, Development Costs, Operating Costs**)

Isocost: A line composed of points showing alternative input combinations that can be purchased for a given total cost. (See also: **Isoquant**)

Isoquant: A line composed of points showing alternative input combinations, all of which yield the same output level. (See also: **Isocost, Marginal Technical Rate of Substituting**)

Laspeyres Index: A type of index number in which the change in the value of price is computed for the collection of quantities purchased during the base period. (See also: **Index Number, Weights;** Contrast with: **Paasche Index**)

Law of Downward-Sloping Demand: The fact that for most products there is an inverse relationship between price and quantity demanded, hence, downward-sloping demand curves. (See also: **Demand, Demand Curve, Demand Function**)

Least Squares Method: A technique for computing regression estimates. (See also: **Multiple Regression, Regression, Simple Regression**)

Level of Significance: The degree of probability that a particular result of a statistical test could have occurred due simply to chance. (See also: **Significance Test**)

Longitudinal Analysis: Equivalent to time series analysis. (See also: **Cross Section, Time Series**)

Long Run: A time period for production that is long enough for the number of firms to change and for each firm's inputs (resources) to change in quantity so that no inputs necessarily are fixed in quantity; during such a period, a firm's scale can change. (See also: **Scale;** Contrast with: **Short Run**)

Macroeconomics: The study of economic questions at the level of the entire economy or large aggregates in it, such as all consumer expenditure. (Contrast with: **Microeconomics**)

Marginal Analysis: The type of economic analysis that involves the balancing of marginal revenue or marginal benefit and marginal cost to reach decisions. (See also: **Marginal Benefit, Marginal Cost, Marginal Revenue**)

Marginal Benefit: The additional benefit derived by producing and using one more unit of a product. (See also: **Marginal Analysis**)

Marginal Cost: The additional cost of producing one more unit of a product. (See also: **Marginal Analysis;** Contrast with: **Average Cost**)

Marginal Productivity: The measure of the increase in output resulting from the addition of one more unit of input (resource), with all the other inputs held constant. (See also: **Productivity**)

Marginal Rate of Substitution: The rate at which a consumer is willing to trade one product for another and remain equally satisfied. (See also: **Indifference Curve;** Contrast with: **Marginal Technical Rate of Substitution**)

Marginal Revenue: The additional revenue derived from selling one more unit of a product. (See also: **Marginal Analysis;** Contrast with: **Average Revenue**)

Marginal Technical Rate of Substitution: The terms on which two inputs can be substituted, one for the other, in producing a given output level; graphically, the slope of an isoquant. (See also: **Isoquant;** Contrast with: **Marginal Rate of Substitution**)

Marginal Utility: The additional satisfaction to a person from consuming one more unit of a product. (See also: **Diminishing Marginal Utility, Utility, Utility Function**)

Market: The group of buyers and sellers interacting to trade a particular product (in a particular area). (See also: **Industry, Market Power, Market Structure**)

Market Power: The situation in which one or a small number of market participants acting jointly can affect the price of the product. (See also: **Bilateral Market Power, Market, Shadow Pricing**)

Market Structure: Characteristics of a market, including (especially) the size distribution of firms in the industry, ease of entry into the industry, and the number and size distribution of buyers in the industry. (See also: **Firm, Industry, Market**)

Microeconomics: The study of economic questions at the level of small units: the individual, the firm, and the industry. (Contrast with: **Macroeconomics**)

Monopoly: A firm with total market power; that is, an industry with only one firm. (See also: **Firm, Industry, Market Power, Price Setter;** Contrast with: **Oligopoly**)

Moral Hazard: In insurance literature: the loss-producing propensity of the insured; in economics literature: price-elasticity in the demand for services covered by insurance.

Multiple Correlation Coefficient: A numerical value indicating the degree of association (relationship) between a dependent variable and a set of two or more independent ones; the square of this value (R^2) tells the percentage of variation in the dependent variable that is "explained" by all the independent variables together. (See also: **Correlation, Correlation Coefficient [Simple]**)

Multiple Regression: Regression analysis in a case involving one dependent and more than one independent variable. (See also: **Least Squares Method, Regression, Regression Coefficient, Simple Regression**)

Net Benefits: In the case of health services: The present value of benefits minus the present value of costs. (See also: **Present Value**)

Normative Economics: The study of what ought to happen, as determined by application of values rather than facts. (Contrast with: **Positive Economics**)

Oligopoly: An industry with a few large rival firms who recognize their interdependence. (See also: **Firm, Industry;** Contrast with: **Monopoly, Price Setter**)

Operating Costs: The value of all resources used, or outlays of funds, "involved in using the new capability or keeping it operationally ready for use over its intended life;" all are recurrent outlays. (Source: Massey et al., *Cost Measurement.*) (See also: **Capital Costs, Development Costs, Investment Costs**)

Opportunity Cost: The true cost of a product, which is the value of the best alternative output (product) whose production is forgone when the necessary resources are used to produce the first product instead.

Paasche Index: A type of index number in which the change in the value of price is computed for the collection of quantities purchased during the period to which the number applies. (See also: **Index Number, Weights;** Contrast with: **Laspeyres Index**)

Panel: The group of patients eligible to receive services under a capitation form of reimbursement. (See also: **Capitation**)

Payer: (See: Third-Party Payer)

Perfect Competition: The situation in a market with many well-informed buyers and sellers who are able to move freely for purposes of making transactions. (See also: **Price Taker, Shadow Pricing**)

Performance: The overall effect of an industry on society in terms (for example) of efficiency, technological progressiveness, and product quality. (See also: **Industry**)

Population: In statistics, the full group on which information and conclusions are desired and from which a sample might be drawn. (See also: **Sample, Significance Test**)

Positive Economics: The study of what happens, or is expected to happen, and why; it involves the examination of facts but not values. (Contrast with: **Normative Economics**)

Present Value: The value as if received today of some benefit or cost to be received or incurred in the future; it is equal to the "discounted" value of the future benefit or cost. (See also: **Discounting, Discount Rate, Net Benefits, Rate of Discount**)

Prevailing Fee: A term used by Medicare carriers to indicate a percentile limit on usual fees charged by practitioners for a given service. Under Medicare, prevailing fees are set at the 75th percentile of usual charges. Payers using UCR terminology define prevailing fees as customary charges. (See also: **Customary Charge, Reasonable Fee, UCR Reimbursement, Usual Fee**)

Price Discrimination: Charging different prices for the same good or service where the differences in price are not related to the cost of production or distribution.

Price Elasticity of Demand: The responsiveness (in percentage terms) of quantity demanded of a product to the change (in percentage terms) in its price, with other varibles held constant. (See also: **Elastic Demand, Elasticity of Demand, Inelastic Demand**)

Price Setter: A firm in a monopolistic, oligopolistic, or noncompetitive market that is sufficiently large to establish or at least influence the market prices for outputs sold. (See also: **Monopoly, Oligopoly;** Contrast with: **Price Taker**)

Price Taker: A firm in a competitive industry where output prices are established by market forces, not the individual actions of the firm in question. (See also: **Perfect Competition;** Contrast with: **Price Setter**)

Production Function: A specification of the terms by which inputs can be transformed into a particular output.

Productive Resource: Equivalent to a factor of production. (See also: **Factor of Production, Resource**)

Productivity: The output per unit of input of a particular resource with all other resources taken as given (held constant). (See also: **Marginal Productivity**)

Public Good: A product (for example, national defense) having the following characteristics: a person who refuses to pay for it cannot be excluded from consuming it; all persons consume the same amount, with one's consumption not reducing another's.

Queue: A waiting line (as in the case of consumers waiting to receive medical services). (See also: **Dead Weight Loss**)

Rate Base: In reimbursement methodology, the item or service covered by the third-party payer; three common classes of rate bases are services, patients, and time. (See also: **Fee-for-Service, Rate Determination**)

Rate Determination: In reimbursement, the method of assigning dollar values to rate bases. (See also: **Fee-for-Service, Rate Base**)

Rate of Discount: Equivalent to the discount rate. (See also: **Discounting, Discount Rate, Interest Rate, Present Value, Rate of Return**)

Rate of Return: The annual rate of gain, or accrual of benefits, produced in return for the use of resources or funds. (See also: **Discount Rate, Interest Rate, Rate of Discount**)

Ratio of Charges-to-Charges Applied to Costs (RCCAC): A method of cost apportionment for hospital reimbursement whereby total allowable costs are allocated among third-party payers according to the percentage of dollar charges accounted for by each payer. (Contrast with: **Average Per Diem**)

Reasonable Fee: Under UCR reimbursement methodology, the lowest of the actual charge, the usual fee, or the percentile maximum on usual fees designated at the prevailing fee. (See also: **Prevailing Fee, UCR Reimbursement, Usual Fee**)

Regression: The statistical technique for fitting a line to a scatter of points that relate two or more variables for purposes of testing whether a relationship exists among those variables. (See also: **Least Squares Method, Multiple Regression, Regression Coefficient, Simple Regression**)

Regression Coefficient: A value derived from regression analysis that shows the specific numerical effect of an independent variable on the dependent variable; in the case of multiple regression analysis, this applies with all other independent variables held constant. (See also: **Multiple Regression, Regression, Simple Regression**)

Relative Value Schedule (RVS): In health insurance, a ranking of medical procedures using RVS units; reimbursement is determined by multiplying the number of RVS units by a dollar conversion factor. (See also: **Relative Value Unit**)

Relative Value Unit: In health insurance, a measure of the value of a specific medical procedure relative to all other procedures; medical procedures are assigned various numbers of units, depending on the time and skill required to perform them. (See also: **Relative Value Schedule**)

Resource: Equivalent to a factor of production. (See also: **Factor of Production, Productive Resource**)

Returns to Scale: The measure of the relationship between the firm's average cost and scale of operation. (See also: **Average Cost, Diseconomies of Scale, Economies of Scale, Scale, Scale Economies**)

Risk: A known probability that a particular event or outcome will occur (or not occur). (See also: **Risk Aversion, Uncertainty**)

Risk Aversion: Behavior that demonstrates a preference for certainty rather than risk; more technically, the choice of a certain outcome over a probabilistic one with an equal or greater expected value. (See also: **Risk**)

Sample: A selected component of a larger group. (See also: **Population, Significance Test, t-Test**)

Scale: The size of a producing unit; technically, an increase in scale means an increase of all factor inputs by the same proportion. (See also: **Diseconomies of Scale, Economies of Scale, Long Run, Returns to Scale, Scale Economies, Short Run**)

Scale Economies: Equivalent to economies of scale. (See also: **Economies of Scale, Returns to Scale, Scale**; Contrast with: **Diseconomies of Scale**)

Scarcity: The insufficiency of supply of productive resources needed to provide all the products (goods and services) that people want; it is a fact of economic life in every society.

Sensitivity Analysis: "A systematic testing of the key assumptions to see how uncertainty in these values affects" the final result. (Source: Massey et al., *Cost Measurement*.)

Shadow Pricing: "The process of adjusting faulty market observations" in order to yield real economic values of inputs and outputs for analytic and decision-making purposes; for example, adjusting labor input costs for aggregate unemployment and adjusting product prices for market power or lack of competition. (Source: Haveman, *The Economics of the Public Sector*, 2nd ed.) (See also: **Market Power, Perfect Competition**)

Shortage: Equivalent to excess demand. (See also: **Excess Demand**; Contrast with: **Excess Supply, Surplus**)

Short Run: A time period for production that is short enough for certain inputs (resources) of a firm to remain fixed in quantity (and cost) while other types of inputs might vary in quantity; during such a period, the firm's scale is unchanged. (See also: **Scale**; Contrast with: **Long Run**)

Significance Test: A statistical hypothesis test of some proposition about a population based on evidence from a sample. (See also: **Hypothesis Test, Level of Significance, Population, Sample, Statistically Significant, t-Test**)

Simple Regression: Regression analysis in a case involving one dependent and only one independent variable. (See also: **Least Squares Method, Multiple Regression, Regression, Regression Coefficient**)

Social Benefit: The sum of (a) private benefit to a consumer of a product (the usual type of benefit) and (b) external benefit—that is, the benefit received by others who are not the direct consumers (as in the case of a vaccination). (See also: **Externalities, Social Cost**)

Social Cost: The sum of (a) private cost to a producer of a product (the usual type of cost) and (b) external cost—that is, the cost borne by nonproducers (as in the case of pollution). (See also: **Externalities, Social Benefit**)

Standard Error: A measure of how close the computed regression coefficient is likely to be the true (population) value.

Statistically Significant: A particular result of a statistical test that is very unlikely to have occurred because of chance. (See also: **Significance Test**)

Stochastic Variable: A variable whose value is random or probabilistic.

Supply: The quantity of a product that one seller or a group of sellers is willing to sell at a given price during a particular period of time. (See also: **Supply Curve, Supply Function**)

Supply Curve: The graph of a supply function relating price and quantity supplied. (See also: **Supply, Supply Function**)

Supply Function: The relationship between price of a product and quantity supplied for one seller or a group of sellers, with other variables (such as cost) held constant. (See also: **Supply, Supply Curve**)

Surplus: Equivalent to excess supply. (See also: **Excess Supply**; Contrast with: **Excess Demand, Shortage**)

Target Income Hypothesis: A theory that states that as annual income rises, a worker reaches a point where the potential for further income will be traded off for more leisure time, so higher rates of pay will lead to less rather than more work's being performed.

Technical Change: Equivalent to technological change. (See also: **Technological Change, Technology**)

Technical Efficiency: Obtaining the maximum possible output from the use of a given combination of inputs (resources). (See also: **Allocative Efficiency, Economic Efficiency, Efficiency**)

Technological Change: "The advance of technology, . . . often taking the form of new methods of producing existing products and new techniques of organization, marketing, and management." (Source: Mansfield, *Microeconomics*, p. 465.) (See also: **Technical Change, Technology**)

Technology: "Society's pool of knowledge regarding the industrial and agricultural arts." (Source: Mansfield, *Microeconomics*, p. 465.) (See also: **Technical Change, Technological Change**)

Third-Party Payer: In health insurance and government health programs, the organization charged with administrative and claims payment functions. The term originated from the triumvirate of patient, provider, and insurer, with the last-named designated as the third party. (See also: **Carrier, Fiscal Agent, Intermediary, Payer**)

Time Series: A type of statistical analysis using data that apply to variables for a single observation unit for several time periods; sometimes called longitudinal analysis. (See also: **Cross Section, Longitudinal Analysis**)

Transfers: Payments not made in return for goods or services or for use of resources; for example, a public assistance payment.

t-Test: A common type of statistical significance test permitting a conclusion based on the probability of occurrence of the event found from sampling; contains a t-statistic. (See also: **Sample, Significance Test**)

UCR Reimbursement: A common method of fee-for-service payment of physicians and other health care practitioners based on Usual, Customary, and Reasonable fees. (See also: **Customary Fee, Prevailing Fee, Reasonable Fee, Usual Fee**)

Uncertainty: The existence of insufficient information to know (or predict) the probability that a particular event or outcome will occur. (See also: **Risk**)

Usual Fee: Term used by health insurance companies to indicate the median fee charged by a practitioner for a given service over a period of a year or more. Under Medicare terminology, the usual fee is defined as the customary charge. (See also: **Prevailing Fee, UCR Reimbursement**)

Utility: The satisfaction derived by a consumer from purchasing and using a product. (See also: **Diminishing Marginal Utility, Indifference Curve, Investment, Marginal Utility, Utility Function**)

Utility Function: A relationship between the quantities of goods consumed by an individual and the satisfaction (utility) derived from the consumption; graphically, the utility function can be represented by a family of indifference curves. (See also: **Diminishing Marginal Utility, Indifference Curve, Marginal Utility, Utility**)

Wealth: The assets, in monetary and/or physical terms, held at a particular point in time by one person or a group of people. (Contrast with: **Income**)

Weights: In index numbers, values applied to a variable to adjust it in order to reflect its relative importance in the index. (See also: **Laspeyres Index, Paasche Index**)

Index

A

Abbott Laboratories, 373, 382
Ability to pay, 2
AC. *See* Average cost
Access to care, 1, 309, 429, 448
Acton, J., 120, 473
Acute medical care, 7
Adjustment lags, 367-369
Administrators, 241
Admission costs, 52
Adoption, 414, 421, 422
Advertising
  costs of, 408
  of drugs, 376, 378, 379
  of health care services, 32, 270, 351
African Medical and Research
  Foundation (AMRF), 498, 509
Age elasticity of demand, 120
Age and utilization, 120
Aggregate measures of hospital
  costs, 52-58
AHA. *See* American Hospital
  Association
Alchian, Armen, 246

Allocation
  efficiency of, 26, 519
  and prices, 23-26
AMA. *See* American Medical
  Association
American Home Products, 382
American Hospital Association
  (AHA), 52, 85, 89, 90, 210, 221,
  222, 412, 415, 417
  Annual Survey of, 84
American Medical Association
  (AMA), 263, 269
AMRF. *See* African Medical and
  Research Foundation
Annual Survey, AHA, 84
Anticipation effects on insurance,
  116
Antitrust laws, 352
APD. *See* Average per diem
Appointment calendars, 175, 176
Appropriate rate of wage increase,
  86
AR. *See* Average revenue
Army Corps of Engineers, 484
Assembly of facts, 36

Assignment, 75, 304, 311
  defined, 519
Attribution problem, 474
Auditing procedures, 457
Australian Royal Flying Doctor, 509
Availability of health resources, 449
Available income, 99
Average case, 52
Average cost (AC), 166, 208
  defined, 519
  and marginal costs, 218
Average cost (AC) curves, 166, 201
Average cost-pricing, 356, 360-364, 369
Average fee, 75
Average patient day, 52
Average per diem (APD) reimbursement, 324, 325, 326
  defined, 519
Average price, 76-78, 79
  customary price ratio to, 77
Average revenue (AR), 168
  defined, 519
Averted costs, 476, 478, 493

B

Bad debts, 304
Bailey, Richard M., 261, 266
Balance billing, 304
  defined, 519
Baltimore City Health Department, 377
Barges, Alexander, 384, 385
Beds
  availability of, 271
  ratio of to plant assets, 236-237
Behavior
  observations of, 37
  risk, 117
  risk-averse, 118
Benefit-cost analysis. *See* Cost-benefit analysis
Benefits, 478, 479, 493
  See also Cost-benefit analysis
  analysis of, 467-479

cost of, 493
defined, 396, 467
direct, 467, 468-470, 521
external, 410, 474
fringe, 470
future, 495
indirect, 467, 470-472, 523
intangible, 467, 472-475
internal, 410
limitations on insurance, 116
marginal, 524
net, 480, 493, 495, 525
nonmonetary, 496
social, 528
Berki, Sylvester, 193, 198, 204
Berry, Ralph E., Jr., 219, 414
Bice, Thomas W., 429
Bilateral market power, 298, 519
Billed charges, 303, 322
Biomedical research, 401-411
Black market price, 75
BLS. *See* Bureau of Labor Statistics
Blue Cross of Greater Philadelphia, 211
Blue Cross of Northeastern Pennsylvania, 336
Blue Cross plans, 292, 293, 294, 305, 322, 325
Blue Cross of Western Pennsylvania, 210
Boan, J. A., 265
Bodenheimer, T. S., 508
Boundaries of health, 7-8
Bradbury, R. C., 448
Brand loyalties to drugs, 379
Breakeven constraints, 224, 231
Budget line, 107, 109, 111
  defined, 519
Budgets, departmental, 334-335, 338, 464
Bulk sales, 299
Bureau of the Census, 372
Bureau of Labor Statistics (BLS), 52, 62, 63, 64, 65, 67, 68, 71, 72, 73, 74, 75, 76, 81, 86
Buyers' market power, 29

C

Caglarcan, Erol, 373, 383
California Department of Health, 281
Capacity, 426
 constraints of, 224
 productive, 433
Capital, 392, 438
 See also Investment; Utility
 defined, 519
 human, 523
 utilization of, 462
Capital costs, 399, 483, 501
 See also Investment costs
 defined, 519
Capital-embodied medical costs, 399-401
Capital expenses, 89, 453
Capital funds, 415
Capital input per day of hospital care, 236
Capitation, 164, 308, 335, 338
 defined, 520
Carter, Jimmy, 344
Case mix, 338
Cases treated, 338
Cash flow maximization, 221, 226-227, 229, 236, 240
Cash flow rates, 233
CAT scanners, 431
Census Bureau, 372
Center for Health Administration Studies (CHAS), 122, 126
Center for the Study of Drug Development, 435
Certainties, 39
Certificate-of-need legislation, 14, 354, 368, 425, 427, 428-433
CES. *See* Consumer Expenditure Survey
Ceteris paribus, 7, 19, 23, 24, 119, 209
 defined, 520
Charity and prices, 173-174
CHAS. *See* Center for Health Administration Studies
Chassin, M. R., 271, 283
Chiswick, Barry, 35
Chiswick, Stephen, 35
Choices, 100, 162, 163
 economic, 2
 personal, 2, 5-6
 social, 5-6
 and technology, 395-399
Civilian Health and Medical Program of the Uniformed Services (CHAMPUS), 294
Claims payment agents, 292
Clinical testing, 402
Clymer, Harold A., 385
CMHC. *See* Community Mental Health Center
Cobb-Douglas form, 208
Coefficients of elasticity, 112, 122
Coefficients of utilization index, 215
Coinsurance, 17, 115, 122, 131, 133, 134, 137
 See also Copayments; Deductibles
 defined, 520
 and demand, 129
 effects of, 130-138
Collection costs, 304
Collection ratio, 304
Collective-consumption goods, 411
Colorado Blue Cross, 335
Commerce Clearing House, 324
Commerce Department, 87, 89
Commercial insurance companies, 292, 293
Commodity-drug policy, 436
Community Mental Health Center (CMHC), 460
Comparative Financial and Statistical Information, 210
Comparative statics, 165
 See also Equilibrium price
 defined, 520
Competition, 13, 15, 162, 299, 349, 353-370, 358, 359, 369, 370, 410, 415, 437
 for HMOs, 259

among hospitals, 14
perfect, 27, 32, 349, 351, 526
among pharmaceutical companies, 371-380
pressures of, 222
price, 351, 358, 436
pure. *See* perfect
quality, 358
theory of, 297
Competitive markets, 25, 27
defined, 13
Complementary goods, 114
Composite output measure, 206
Concentration ratios
defined, 520
in pharmaceutical industry, 371, 373
Condition of entry, 350
Conduct, 350
defined, 520
Connecticut Hospital Association, 335
Conrad, Gordon R., 384, 385
Conrad-Plotkin model, 384
"Conspicuous production," 413
Constant dollars, 75, 520
Constraints, 152
breakeven, 224, 231
capacity, 224
economic, 163, 259
income, 106-107, 111
institutional, 163, 195, 259, 268
legal, 163, 259
price, 106-107, 111
professional, 195
social, 195
technological, 163
time, 165
Consumer behavior, 396
Consumer Expenditure Survey (CES), 64, 73-74
Consumer income, 19
Consumer Price Index (CPI), 52, 403
Consumer services, 9-10
Consumption, 520
Consumption economics, 4

Consumption externality, 30
Consumption goods, 99
Continuing consumer expenditure survey, 73-74
Continuing point-of-purchase survey, 74
Controlled experiment, 37
Controlled fee, 75
Cooper, B., 401
Copayments, 115, 116, 520
See also Coinsurance; Deductibles
Corporate practice of medicine, 268, 270
Correlation, 42, 520
Correlation coefficient, 44, 47
Cost accounting, 510
Cost-based reimbursement, 323, 325, 326
Cost-benefit analysis, 410, 435, 447, 456, 461, 468-479, 486, 496, 510, 511, 519
defined, 519, 520
Cost-benefit curve, 396, 397, 398
Cost-benefit ratio, 480, 481, 491, 493, 494
Cost containment, 272, 277, 309, 429, 432, 437, 459, 465
Cost Control System, 455
Cost-effectiveness, 452, 463, 467, 498, 505, 507, 511
analysis of, 447, 495-510
defined, 520
Cost-efficiency, 498, 505
Cost finding, 459-461
defined, 460
interpretation of results of, 461-462
methodology of, 457
Cost functions, 163, 189, 196
defined, 520
estimation of, 204
of hospitals, 200-219
Cost-of-living adjustments, 315
Cost-of-living index. *See* Consumer Price Index (CPI)
Cost per admission, 52

Cost per capita, 52
Cost per case, 75
Cost per effective patient contact, 505, 506
Cost per patient contact, 505
Cost per patient day (CPPD), 52, 207, 395, 396, 457, 458
Cost per referred patient, 506
Cost per service, 75
Cost per visit, 465, 467
Cost-plus pricing hypothesis, 229
Cost-price ratio, 437
Cost-pricing, 222
Cost-related reimbursement, 323
Costs, 303, 449
  See also Expenses
  admission, 52
  advertising, 408
  allocation of, 461
  analysis of, 451-467
  apportionment of, 324
  average, 166, 208, 218, 519
  averted, 476, 478, 493
  benefit, 493
  capital, 399, 483, 501, 519
  capital-embodied medical, 399-401
  categories of, 453
  collection, 304
  control of. *See* Cost containment
  in CPI, 74-76
  defined, 451
  departmental, 463-467
  development, 521
  direct, 460, 461, 476, 479, 486, 487, 492
  direct resource, 461
  drug, 436
  estimated, 489-491
  expected treatment, 361
  external, 203
  final, 460
  fixed, 166, 303, 495, 501
  future, 495
  health care, 1, 15
  hospital, 51, 52-58, 53, 54, 212-215
  and hospital size, 201
  indirect, 460, 476, 486, 487, 488, 492
  institutional, 493
  investment, 452, 524
  labor, 303
  long run, 454
  maintenance, 501
  manufacturing, 436
  marginal, 20, 166, 168, 177, 206, 218, 228, 524
  measurement of, 452-455
  medical supply, 303
  nonfinal, 460
  nonrecurring, 453
  office supply, 303
  operating, 226, 429, 452-453, 453, 459, 480, 483, 525
  opportunity, 2, 5, 6, 7, 25, 29, 175, 176, 200, 303, 451, 452, 471, 510, 525
  overhead, 261, 263, 324, 462, 464
  private, 29, 30, 115
  production, 20, 115, 163, 169, 177
  real, 451
  recovery of, 221-222, 258
  research, 403-411, 435, 486
  resource, 468, 470
  and revenues, 21
  risk, 304
  service, 457, 488, 501
  short run, 454
  social, 29, 30, 115, 399, 405, 528
  and technological change, 393-401
  and technology, 431
  time, 134-137, 174-177, 408
  total, 52, 208
  transportation, 203, 266, 419, 470, 502
  vaccination, 407-408
  variable, 166, 399, 501
Cost-volume-revenue relationship, 327, 328, 329
Cost weights of market basket items, 66, 67, 70
CPI. *See* Consumer Price Index

CPPD. *See* Cost per patient day
CPR. *See* Customary and prevailing charge
"Cream skimming," 354, 361
Cross-elasticity of demand, 113, 114, 263
　See also Elasticity of demand
　defined, 520
Cross section, 51, 122, 136, 207
　See also Longitudinal analysis; Time series regression
　defined, 520
Cross-subsidization, 323, 325, 326
　defined, 520
Consumer Price Index (CPI), 54, 56, 58, 59, 61-76, 79, 81, 87, 88, 89, 406
　for all urban consumers, 71-72
　calculation of, 66-67
　and costs, 74-76
　formula for, 69-70
　future revisions of, 73-76
　history of, 63-64
　limitations of, 68-69
　revision of 1978, 70-71
　shortcomings of, 75, 81
　uses of, 63
Curley, 383
Current dollars
　See also Constant dollars; Deflation
　defined, 521
Customary charge, 75, 76-83
　See also Prevailing fee; Usual, customary and reasonable reimbursement; Usual fee
　average price ratio to, 77
　defined, 521
Customary and prevailing charges (CPR), 305, 307, 311, 312, 321

D

Data availability, 84
Davis, Karen, 220, 258

Dead weight loss, 175
　See also Queues
　defined, 521
Death rates, 471
Deductibles, 17, 115, 116, 127, 128
　See also Coinsurance; Copayments
　defined, 521
Deferred spending, 332
Deflation
　See also Constant dollars; Current dollars
　defined, 521
Degrees of freedom, 47
Delivery
　by foundations, 278-283
　organization of, 111
　system of, 128
Delta Dental plans, 292, 293
Demand, 16-20, 165, 169, 185, 294, 355, 356, 367, 369, 395, 398, 414, 415, 419, 420, 423, 449
　See also Supply and demand
　age elasticity of, 120
　analysis of. *See* Demand analysis
　characteristics of, 111-121
　and coinsurance, 129
　cross-elasticity of, 113, 114, 263
　defined, 95, 521
　derived, 19, 521
　for drugs, 377
　elasticity of. *See* Demand elasticity
　empirical studies of, 121-123
　equation for, 125
　estimation of, 138
　excess, 22, 522
　for health insurance, 117-119
　and HMOs, 259
　for hospital services, 223
　and income changes, 107
　income-elasticity of, 121
　increase in, 166
　inelasticity of. *See* Demand inelasticity
　and insurance, 114-117

Index 537

for physician services, 131-134, 136
and price changes, 107, 109
price elasticity of, 526
and revenue, 168
shift in, 19, 297, 394
theory of, 98-101
and utilization, 98
as value-free concept, 98
for voluntary hospitals, 193
Demand analysis, 4
applications of, 119-121
Demand creation, 105, 106
Demand curve, 16, 17, 99, 109, 111, 124, 168, 294, 296
defined, 521
derivation of, 107-110
and elasticity, 18
shifts in, 18
Demand elasticity, 17, 18, 111-114, 116, 119, 120, 136, 222, 522
defined, 522
and insurance, 298
Demand function, 108
defined, 521
Demand inelasticity, 17, 113, 116, 294
in pharmaceutical industry, 375, 377
Demsetz, Harold, 246
Densen, P. M., 276, 277
Departmental budgets, 334-335, 338, 464
Departmental costs, 463-467
Depreciation, 226, 324
Derived demand, 19
defined, 521
Development costs, 521
Diversity of markups, 222
Diagnosis-related groups (DRGs), 219, 344
Diffusion, 392, 411-413, 415-425, 431, 432
See also Technological change
defined, 521
Diffusion curve, 416

Diffusion cycle, 417
Diffusion path, 412
Diminishing marginal utility, 100, 101
defined, 521
Direct benefits, 467, 468-470
See also Indirect benefits
defined, 521
Direct costs, 460, 476, 479, 486, 487, 492
Direct resource costs, 461
Disability, 405
Disaggregated production function, 198
Disaggregation, 72
Discounting, 480, 483, 484, 492, 496, 501
See also Present value
defined, 521
Discount rates, 469, 470
defined, 521, 527
Discounts on insurance payments, 322
Diseconomies of scale, 201, 264
See also Economies of scale
defined, 521
Distribution, 2, 6-7, 126
double, 461
geographic, 315-318, 426
of physicians, 315
of specialties, 315-318
Diversity of markups, 222
Division of labor, 201
Doctors. *See* Physicians
Donabedian, A., 272, 274
Double distribution, 461
Dowling, William, 198, 199, 200, 326, 343, 344
Downward-sloping demand law, 17
defined, 524
Drake, D., 400
Dreze, J., 364
DRG. *See* Diagnosis-related groups
Drug industry. *See* Pharmaceutical industry
"Drug lag," 434

Dual billing system, 242
Dummy variable, 51
  defined, 522

E

Economic analysis objections, 4
Economic behavior, 3
Economic choices, 2
Economic conditions, 23
Economic constraints, 163, 259
Economic efficiency, 26, 259
  defined, 522
  of HMOs, 260-262
Economic indexes, 59
Economic methodology, 36-39
Economic model of price
  determination, 13
Economic output, 4
Economics, 99
Economics, defined, 2
Economics of Public Health (EPH),
  404, 405
Economic Stabilization Program
  (ESP), 54, 56, 58, 82, 83, 336
Economic statistics, 36
Economic theory of the firm, 291
  and HMOs, 258
Economic theory of groups, 262-264
Economies of scale, 201-204, 260,
  264, 266, 350, 355, 426, 455
  See also Diseconomies of scale
  defined, 522
Effectiveness, 449
  defined, 522
Efficaciousness, defined, 522
Efficiency, 26-27, 338, 351, 366, 368
  allocative, 26, 519
  defined, 522
  economic, 26, 259, 260-262, 522
  of group practices, 269
  of prospective rate setting, 332-333
  and quality, 183-185
  and size of medical practices, 265,
    266
  of solo practices, 269
  technical, 26, 177
Egan, Douglas M., 265
Elasticity coefficient, 113, 122, 136
Elasticity of demand, 17, 18,
  111-114, 116, 119, 120, 136, 222,
  520
  See also Cross-elasticity of
    demand; Inelasticity of demand
  defined, 522
  and insurance, 298
Empirical research, 204, 210,
  228-229, 265, 268
  on demand, 121-123
Employment rate, 471
Endogenous variable, 522
Engineering approach to production
  function, 195
Enrolled population, 257
Entry barriers, 350, 351
Environmental health services, 7
Environmental pollution, 29
EPAPD. *See* Expenses per adjusted
  patient day
EPC. *See* Expenses per capita
*EPH. See Economics of Public
  Health*
EPPD. *See* Expenses per patient day
Equilibrium, 175
  market, 21-23
  monopoly, 28
Equilibrium prices, 21, 22, 25
  See also Comparative statics
  defined, 522
Equity, 6-7, 26-27, 175, 426, 448, 451
  defined, 522
ESP. *See* Economic Stabilization
  Program
Estimation
  of cost functions, 204
  of detection cost, 489-491
  of marginal costs, 206
  of production function, 196-200
Ethical drugs, 371
Ethics, 176
Excess demand, 22
  defined, 522

Index 539

Excess supply, 22
  defined, 522
Exclusions under insurance, 115
Exogenous variable, 522
Expansion path, 182
  defined, 522
Expected loss, 118
Expected treatment costs, 361
Expenditures. *See* Expenses
Expenses
  See also Costs
  capital, 453
  depreciation, 226, 324
  and insurance, 79-83
  nonlabor, 90
  operating, 226, 429
  out-of-pocket, 226, 356
  overhead, 462
  patterns of, 458
  payroll, 90
  of physician services, 134
Expenses per adjusted patient day (EPAPD), 52, 54, 56
Expenses per capita (EPC), 52, 54, 58
Expenses per patient day (EPPD), 52, 54, 56, 58, 85
"Extended economics," 451
External benefits, 410, 474
External cost, 203
Externalities, 29-31, 364-367
  See also Social benefits; Social costs
  defined, 29, 523
Extrapolation of past trends, 138

F

Facilities utilization, 138-155
Factor, defined, 15
Factor inputs, 234-236
Factor prices, 27
Factor of production, 15
  defined, 523

FDA. *See* Federal Drug Administration
Federal Drug Administration (FDA), 435, 436
Federal Employee Health Program, 272
Federal Employees Health Benefits Plan (FEHBP), 294
Federal Reserve Board, 61
Federal Trade Commission (FTC), 14, 352, 436
Fee-for-service (FFS) payment, 105, 164, 258, 268, 300, 303, 307, 308
  defined, 523
FEHBP. *See* Federal Employees Health Benefits Plan
Fein, Rashi, 261
Feldstein, Martin S., 77, 79, 85, 87, 89, 196, 198, 199, 200, 219, 225, 356, 362, 394, 398
Feldstein, Paul J., 51, 83, 218, 364, 455
FFS. *See* Fee-for-service payment
Final cost, 460
Final good, 19
Final goods market, 15
Final producing cost center, 460
Financial access, 449
Firm
  defined, 161, 523
  objectives of, 162
  size of, 162, 350
  theory of, 258, 291
First-come-first-serve, 176
Fiscal agents, 291, 523
Fisher-Hall model, 384
Fisher, I. N., 384
"Five D's," 474
Fixed costs, 166, 303, 495, 501
Fixed fees, 75, 304, 306, 307
Fixed input proportions, 177
Fixed variable fee systems, 306
Food and Drug Act, 434
Forecast financial statements, 138-155
Forecasting, 51, 83-91, 138

For-profit hospitals
  capital input per day of care in, 236
  investments in, 367, 368-369
  labor input per day of care in, 236
  vs. nonprofit hospitals, 228, 240
  quantity of services of, 231-234
  regulation of, 352-370
Foundations. *See* Medical care foundations
Four-firm concentration ratio, 371
Frech, H. E. "Ted," 263
Free rider, 264, 410
Freezing of usual charges, 306
Friedman, J. J., 383
Fringe benefits, 470
FTC. *See* Federal Trade Commission
Fuchs, Victor, 8, 76, 81, 173
Fuel price indexing, 89
Full insurance coverage, 116
Fully employed economy, 2
Funding agencies, 457-458
Future costs, 495
Future savings, 487

G

Gaus, C. R., 273, 401
General Accounting Office, 447
Generic products, 436
Genetic factors in health, 8
Geographical definition of market, 16
Geographic distribution, 315-318, 426
Georgette, J., 361
Geographers, 1
GHP. *See* Group Health Plan
Gift relationship, 365, 366
Ginsburg, Paul, 263, 420
GNP. *See* Gross National Product
Government health programs, 291, 292, 293
Government licensing, 28, 165, 350

Government policy, 5, 352
  and technological change, 425-438
Government regulation, 163
  of for-profit hospitals, 352-370
  of pharmaceutical innovation, 433-438
Grants, 403
Griliches, Z., 418
Gross National Product (GNP), 5, 470
  defined, 523
Gross National Product (GNP) Deflator, 61
Gross revenue, 303
Group Health Plan (GHP) of Palo Alto, Calif., 129, 131, 137
Group insurance policies, 299
Group practices, 263
  efficiency of, 269
  vs. solo practices, 264, 269
Growth maximization, 228, 233

H

"Halfway technologies," 438
Hall, G. R., 384
Harrell, Gilbert D., 380
Haveman, Robert, 481, 484
Health
  boundaries of, 7-8
  definition of, 7
  genetic factors in, 8
  and lifestyle, 8
  measurement of, 4
  status of. *See* Health status (HS)
Health Care Financing Administration, 306, 309
Health economics, defined, 4
Health, Education and Welfare (HEW), 436
Health insurance, 77, 106, 355, 356, 394, 398, 400, 431, 472
  See also Third party payers
  demand for, 117-119
  demand under, 114-117

and expenditures, 79-83
growth of, 79, 80
impact of, 296
and price discrimination, 173
supply and demand under, 295
universal, 126, 127, 128
Health Insurance Plan (HIP), New
    York, 273, 276, 277
Health maintenance organizations
    (HMO), 271-278, 293, 308
  appraisal of performances of,
    259-264
  characteristics of, 257-258
  concept of, 257-259
  and medical outcome
    effectiveness, 283-284
  objectives of, 278
  quality of care by, 277
  types of, 258
  and utilization, 270-271
Health status (HS), 101, 103
  defined, 100
  production of, 102-106
  utility function for, 111
Health systems agencies (HSA), 428
Hellinger, Fred J., 358, 429
HEW. See Health, Education and
    Welfare
Hickey, Brian R., 384, 385
Hierarchy of policy concerns, 425
HIP. See Health Insurance Plan,
    New York
HMO. See Health maintenance
    organizations
Hoffmann-LaRoche Pharmaceutical
    Company, 372
Holahan, John, 271
Hospital behavior, 413
  theories of, 220-241
Hospital costs
  aggregate measures of, 52-58
  forecasting of, 51
  increases in, 54, 212-215
  measures of, 53
  trends in, 55
Hospital expenditure rates, 83-91

Hospital nonlabor input price index,
    87
Hospital output measurement, 52
Hospital prices measurement, 81
Hospital resources, 193
  allocation of, 203
Hospitals
  behavior of. See Hospital behavior
  cost functions of, 200-219
  costs in. See Hospital costs
  hotel services of, 9, 335
  objectives of, 163, 220
  optimal size of, 202
  pricing in, 221
  production functions of, 193-200
  size of, 247
  types of, 190
Hospitals, 210
Hospital services, demand for, 223
Hospital wages, 84
"Hotel" services of hospitals, 9, 335
HS. See Health status
HSA. See Health systems agencies
Hsiao, W. C., 321
Human capital, 523
Hypothesis building, 38
Hypothesis formulation, 36
Hypothesis test, 38, 40
  defined, 523

I

Imperfect information, 32
Incentives, 309, 310, 318, 326, 327,
    330-332, 338
Income
  available, 99
  consumer, 19
  defined, 523
  loss of, 488
  net, 229-231, 242
  per capita, 420, 422, 497
  predetermined goals for, 171
  redistribution of, 27
  rise in, 19

target, 171-173, 182
  and utilization, 120
Income changes and demand, 107
Income constraints, 106-107, 111
Income distributions, 2, 26, 27, 351, 352
  defined, 523
Income-elasticity of demand, 121
Income tax, 472
IND. *See* Investigational New Drug
Indemnity plans, 304
Independent health plans, 292
Independent (individual) practice association (IPA), 258, 308
Indexes, 58-61
Index of Industrial Production, 61
Indexing of prevailing fees, 306
Index number, 59
  defined, 523
Indifference curve, 100, 101, 107, 108, 396
  defined, 523
Indifference lines, 397
Indifference map, 101
Indirect benefits, 467, 470-472
  See also Direct benefits
  defined, 523
Indirect costs, 460, 476, 486, 487, 488, 492
Individual-consumption goods, 411
Individual practice association (IPA), 258, 308
Individual purchasing decisions, 95
Industrial organization
  defined, 349
  economics of, 4
Industry, 438
  defined, 523
Inelasticity of demand, 17, 113, 116, 294, 523
  See also Elasticity of demand
  in pharmaceutical industry, 375, 377
Inflation, 310-312
Information, 104, 351
  availability of, 32

Ingbar, M. L., 219, 221
Innovation, 391, 411, 414, 415, 418, 422, 425, 432, 434, 437, 438
  in pharmaceuticals, 433-438
  process of, 402
  technological, 352
Inputs, 163
  analysis of, 391, 462, 510
  substitution of, 394
Institute of Medicine, 97
Institutional constraints, 163, 195, 259, 268
Institutional costs, 493
Institutional rate review programs, 429
Institutional reimbursement, 322-326
Insurance
  See Health, Life, Major medical, Malpractice insurance
Insurance companies, 291
Intangible benefits, 467, 472-475
Intellectual experiments, 37
Interest rates, 523
Intergroup diffusion, 417
Intermediary, 291
  See also Third party payer
  defined, 523
Intermediate good, 15, 19
  defined, 524
Internal benefits, 410
Internal rate structure, 221
InterStudy, 97
Investigational New Drug (IND), 434
Investment, 452-453
  See also Capital; Capital costs; Utility
  analysis of, 438
  in biomedical research, 401-411
  decisions on, 163
  defined, 524
  in for-profit hospitals, 367, 368-369
  lags in, 369
  needs for, 221, 222, 229

Investment costs, 452
  defined, 524
Investment goods, 99
IPA. *See* Independent (individual) practice association
Isocost, 181
  defined, 524
Isoquant, 393
  defined, 524
Isoquant curve, 178
Isoquant diagram, 392

J

Johnston, John, 204, 208

K

Kaiser Plans, 137, 266, 272, 273
Kaiz, Edward M., 222
Kefauver, Sen., 375, 379
Kessel, Reuben A., 267
Keynes, John Maynard, 185
Klarman, Herbert E., 77, 223, 270, 273, 467, 474, 475
Kovner, Joel, 266
Kramer, Marcia, 76, 81, 173
Kuznets, S., 470

L

Labor, 15, 84, 392, 394, 438, 449, 451, 463, 470, 471, 497, 508
  productivity of, 86. *See also* Productivity
  shortages of, 1
  substitution of, 177-183, 184
  utilization of, 463
Labor costs, 303
Labor Department, 61
Labor economics, 4
Labor function, 178
Labor input per day of care, 236
Laspeyres Index, 60, 61
  defined, 524
Laubach, Gerald D., 433, 434

Lave, Judith, 204, 210, 219
Lave, Lester, 204, 210, 219
Law of diminishing marginal utility, 100, 101
Law of downward sloping demand, 17
  defined, 524
Least-cost techniques, 356, 369
Least squares, 43
  defined, 524
Lee, M. L., 413, 414
Lee, Sidney, 456
Legal constraints, 163, 259
Legal monopoly, 28
Leisure time, 171
Lengths of stay, 338
Lesotho Flying Doctor Service, 498
Level of significance, 524
Lewin and Associates, 429
Lewin, Lawrence S., 428, 430
Licensing, 28, 165, 350
Life expectancy, 474, 492
Life insurance, 473
Life insurance examinations, 8
Life styles, 8
Linear programming, 198, 199, 200
Linear regression, 43, 423
Linked competitive markets, 27
Loan, Frank, 314
Local markets, 419
Logistic function, 418
Longitudinal analysis, 122, 136
  See also Cross section; time series
  defined, 524
Long, Millard F., 222, 364
Long run, 201, 454
  defined, 524
Long-run average cost curves, 201
Loss
  of earnings, 470, 473
  expected, 118
  of income, 488
  probabilities of, 119
  of production, 486
Low income persons, 1
Luft, H. W., 272

M

Macroeconomics, 4
  defined, 524
Maintenance costs, 501
Major medical insurance, 127
"Make or buy" decisions, 456
Market structure, 350
Maldistribution of physicians, 315
Malpractice insurance, 89
Management information system, 458
Managerial analysis, 458-459
Manpower. *See* Labor
Mansfield, Edwin, 418
Manufacturing costs, 436
Marginal analysis, 2, 3, 20
  defined, 524
Marginal benefits, 524
Marginal costs (MC), 20, 166, 168, 177, 228
  and average costs, 218
  curve, 166
  defined, 524
  estimated, 206
  of production, 115
Marginal private benefits, 115
Marginal productivity, 103, 180, 468
  defined, 524
Marginal rate of substitution (MRS), 101, 102, 178
  defined, 524
Marginal revenue (MR), 20, 168, 228
  defined, 524
Marginal social cost, 115
Marginal technical rate of substitution (MTRS), 178, 180
  defined, 525
Marginal utility, 3, 100, 101, 175, 468
  defined, 525
  diminishing, 521
Market, 15-16
  defined, 15, 525
  equilibrium of, 21-23
  failure of, 27-32
  mechanism of, 402
  model of, 15
  structure of, 525
Market analysis, 16
Market basket, 64-65, 66, 67, 73
Market power, 28-29
  bilateral, 298, 519
  defined, 525
  problems in, 350
Markups, 221
  diversity of, 222
Marshfield Clinic, 274, 275
Massey, H. G., 451
Maximum liability limits, 115, 116
MC. *See* Marginal cost
McMahon, J., 400
Measday, Walter, 371, 375, 378, 381
Measurement
  of hospital costs, 53
  of hospital output, 52
  necessity of, 36-39
  of quality, 206
Medicaid, 27, 291, 292, 294, 304, 305, 309-310, 312, 315, 316, 317, 321, 356, 400, 411, 412, 417, 436, 449
  physicians' participation in, 312-315
Medical care, 7
Medical care foundations, 258, 259, 273, 277, 278, 280, 281, 308
Medical Economics, 266
Medical ethics, 176
"Medically necessary," 324
Medical staff role, 241
Medical supply costs, 303
Medical technology. *See* Technology
Medicare, 291, 292, 294, 305, 306, 307, 309-310, 311, 312, 315, 316, 317, 321, 356, 400, 411, 412, 417, 436, 449
  physicians' participation in, 312-315
Medicare and Medicaid Guide, 324
Memorial Sloan-Kettering Cancer Center, 433

Merck Pharmaceutical Company, 372, 382
Michigan Blue Cross, 334
Michigan Board of Pharmacy, 376
Microeconomics, 4
  defined, 525
Millmaster Onyx, 373
Mishan, E. J., 474
Monetay units, 453, 454
Monopoly, 267, 297, 350, 351, 355, 396
  defined, 525
  equilibrium of, 28
  legal, 28
  pure, 28
  theoretical, 349
Moral hazard, 114, 311
  defined, 525
Morbidity, 404, 405, 469
Mortality, 10, 404, 405, 470
Mosquito control, 32
MR. *See* Marginal revenue
MRS. *See* Marginal rate of substitution
MTRS. *See* Marginal technical rate of substitution
Multipart pricing, 364
Multiple correlation coefficient, 525
Multiple regression, 46-51, 59, 121, 130, 210
  defined, 525
Multispecialty groups, 164
Multivariate analysis, 121, 130-138
Mushkin, Selma J., 470, 471
Mutual insurance companies, 292, 293

N

National defense, 32
National economic index, 312
National Guidelines for Health Planning, 95-98
National Health Planning and Resource Development Act, 428
National Opinion Research Center (NORC), 122, 126
Natural logarithms of variables, 51
NDA. *See* New Drug Application
Need for investment, 221, 222, 229
Needleman, Jack, 428
Neenan, W. B., 472
Negotiated rate, 75
Nelson, Sen., 381
Nerlove, Marc, 205
Net benefits, 480, 493, 495
  See also Present value
  defined, 525
Net discount rate, 469
Net future earnings, 405
Net income, 242
  of nonprofit hospitals, 229-231
Net price, 79
Net revenue, 303
New Drug Application (NDA), 434, 435
Newhauser, D., 367
Newhouse, Joseph, 129, 136, 137, 138, 224, 260, 265, 413
Nonaffiliated hospitals, 417, 421
Nonassignment, 304
Noneconometric approach to demand forecasting, 138
Nonexcludability in consumption, 31
Nonfinal cost, 460
Noninvasive diagnostic technologies, 6, 401
Nonlabor expenses per patient day, 90
Nonlabor price index, 89
Nonmonetary benefits, 496
Nonprice rationing devices, 128
Nonprofit firms, 21, 202
Nonprofit hospitals, 228
  behavior of, 220-241
  capital input per day of care in, 236
  vs. for-profit hospitals, 228, 240
  labor input per day of care in, 236
  motives of, 353

net incomes of, 229-231
as physicians' cooperative, 241-248
profitability of, 229
profits of, 228, 229, 331
quantity of services of, 231-234
theory of, 245-247
Nonprofit insurance carriers, 292, 293
Nonprofit private corporations, 164
Nonprofit status of voluntary hospitals, 220
Nonrecurring costs, 453
NORC. *See* National Opinion Research Center
Normative economics, 3, 4
  defined, 525
Not-for-profit. *See* Nonprofit
Nurse practitioners, 184

O

Objective function, 189, 220, 413
Objectives
  of firms, 162
  of HMOs, 278
  of hospitals, 163, 220
  of PGPs, 258
Observations of behavior, 37
Occupancy rates, 233, 420
Office supply costs, 303
Office of Technology Assessment, 430-431
Office waiting time, 175, 176
Oligopoly, 349, 350
  defined, 525
Olson, Mancur, Jr., 262
Operating costs, 226, 429, 452-453, 459, 480, 483
  defined, 525
Operations research, 196
Opportunity costs, 2, 5, 6, 7, 25, 29, 175, 176, 200, 303, 451, 452, 471, 510
  defined, 525
Optimal size of hospitals, 202

Organized medicine, 28, 29, 268
Outpatient clinics, 263
Out-of-pocket expenses, 226, 356
Out-of-pocket price, 75, 114, 294
Outputs
  analysis of, 391, 462, 510
  definition of, 163
  maximization of, 221, 222-224
  and quality maximization, 221
Overbooking, 175
Over-the-counter drugs. *See* Proprietary drugs
Overhead costs, 261, 263, 324, 462, 464

P

Paasche Index, 60, 61, 525
Palo Alto Medical Clinic, 137
Panel, defined, 525
Pardee, G., 361
Paringer, L., 314
Patents, 28, 350, 410, 435, 437
Patient cost sharing, 115, 136
Patient day, 52
Patient load, 458
Patient mix, 461
"Patient related," 324
Patients' time values, 175, 176
Pauly, Mark, 119, 241, 245, 264, 367, 414
Payroll expenses, 84, 90
Payroll expenses per patient day (PEPPD), 84
Peak-load pricing, 364
Peer review, 271
Penick Pharmaceutical Company, 373
PEPPD. *See* Payroll expenses per patient day
Per capita income, 420, 422, 497
Per case rates, 335-336, 341
Perceived medical production function, 111
Percentile adjustments, 306

Per diem rates, 335-336, 341
Perfect competition, 27, 32, 349, 351
    defined, 526
Performance
    defined, 526
    evaluation of, 351, 352
Personal choices, 2, 5-6
Personal habits, 8
Personal values, 3, 5, 7, 99, 100
Personnel per one hundred census (PP100C), 84, 85
Personnel shortages. *See* Labor
Pertschuk, Michael, 14, 15
Per visit revenue, 168
Pfizer Pharmaceutical Company, 372
Pfouts, Ralph, 205
PGP. *See* Prepaid group practice
Pharmaceutical industry, 370-380
    innovation in, 433-438
    marketing in, 380-385
Pharmaceutical Manufacturers Association (PMA), 371, 381
Phelps, Charles, 122, 123, 125, 129, 136, 137, 138
Phipps, David, 456, 460
Physician office visits, 99, 123-129, 127
    demand for, 136
Physician Productivity and the Demand for Health Manpower, 182
Physicians
    as de facto controllers of hospitals, 241-248
    demand creation by, 105, 106
    demand for services of, 131-134
    distribution of, 315
    expenditures for services of, 134
    incentives for, 318
    independence of, 14
    licensing of, 28
    maldistribution of, 315
    motivation of, 21
    participation of in Medicare, Medicaid, 312-315
    productivity of, 182, 260, 261
    profit-maximizing, 177
    as purchasing agent for drugs, 376
    quality of, 266
    ratio of to population, 422
    reimbursement of. *See* Reimbursement
    scarcity of, 419
    validation role of, 8
Physicians' cooperatives, 241-248
Physicians' Desk Reference, 378
Plant assets ratio to beds, 236-237
Plotkin, Irving H., 384, 385
PMA. *See* Pharmaceutical Manufacturers Association
Point-of-Purchase Survey, 73, 74
Political scientists, 1
Pollution, 29
Population, 39
    defined, 526
Positive economics, 3, 4, 5
    defined, 526
PP100C. *See* Personnel per one hundred census
Predetermined income goals, 171
Predictions, 36, 39
    See also Forecasting
Present values, 470, 495
Preferred cost point, 398
Premiums for HMOs, 257
Prepaid group practice (PGP), 258, 259, 268, 270, 271, 278, 280, 284
    economic efficiency of, 260
    hospital utilization for, 275
    objectives of, 258
Prescription drugs. *See* Ethical drugs
Present value, 469, 476, 479, 480, 481, 482, 483
    See also Discounting; Net benefits
    defined, 526
Prevailing fees, 75, 305
    defined, 526
    indexing of, 306
Preventive care, 7, 99
Price changes, 19, 114

and demand, 107, 109
Price competition, 351, 358, 436
Price constraints, 106-107, 111
Price discrimination, 173, 174, 176,
  351, 356, 357-360, 364, 369, 370
  defined, 526
Price elasticity of demand, 111
  defined, 526
Price-fixing agreements, 351
Price received fees, 75
Prices, 16, 20, 23, 168, 292, 393, 394,
  396, 449, 455, 465, 469, 472
  and allocation, 23-26
  average, 76-78, 79
  average operating costs as, 222
  black market, 75
  changes in. *See also* Price changes
  and charity, 173-174
  constant dollar, 75
  cost-per-case, 75
  cost-per-service, 75
  customary, 76-83, 79
  data collection on, 65
  definitions of, 75
  determination of, 13
  equilibrium of, 21, 22, 25, 522
  factor, 27
  hospital, 81, 221
  increases in, 22, 166
  multipart, 364
  net, 79
  out-of-pocket, 75
  peak-load, 364
  in pharmaceutical industry, 375
  policy on, 350
  and profits, 166-171,n172
  regional difference in, 90
  regulation of, 359
  and resource scarcity, 25
  setting of, 456
  shadow, 75, 527
  and target incomes, 171-173
Price setters, 291
  defined, 526
Price takers, 291
  defined, 526

Primary care, 430, 499
Primary factor of production, 15, 19
Private benefits, 30, 31, 115
Private cost, 29, 115
Private cost curves, 30
Private insurance companies, 292
Private sector economics, 481-495
Probabilities, 39
  of loss, 119
  of successful treatment, 225
Problems of health industry, 1
Producer Price Index, 87
Production, 2, 404, 433, 438, 470
  capacity for, 455
  of health status, 102-106
  loss of, 486
  primary factor of, 15, 19
Production costs, 20, 163, 119, 177
Production function, 102, 103, 111,
  163, 189, 193-200, 258, 391
  defined, 526
  disaggregated, 198
  estimated, 196-200
  and technological change, 392-393
  of treatment, 198
Productive resources
  defined, 526
  scarcity of, 2
Productivity, 86, 177-183, 340, 398,
  449, 469, 486
  defined, 526
  marginal, 103, 180, 468, 524
  of physicians, 182, 260, 261
  studies of, 265
Product safety, 351
Professional associations, 28, 29
Professional constraints, 195
Professional Standard Review
  Organizations (PSRO), 281
Profitability, 20
Profit and loss, 456
Profit making orientation, 164, 166
Profit maximization, 162, 175, 182,
  220, 221, 224, 225, 227-228, 229,
  233, 241, 244, 353
  by physicians, 177

Profits, 303, 351, 352
  of nonprofit hospitals, 228, 229, 231
  of pharmaceutical industry, 381, 383-385
  and prices, 166-171, 172
Proprietary drugs, 371
Prospective analysis, 486, 487, 491-492
Prospective rate setting, 326-333
  and hospital operation, 337-343
PSRO. *See* Professional Standard Review Organizations
Psychologists, 1
Public good, 31-32
  defined, 526
Pure competition. *See* Perfect competition
Pure monopoly, 28

Q

Quality, 200, 309, 310, 338, 366, 413, 448, 451
  changes in, 68, 83
  and CPI, 68
  definitions of, 224, 225, 247, 248
  and efficiency, 183-185
  and externalities, 364-367
  and HMOs, 259, 277
  of innovations, 352
  measurement of, 206
  of physicians, 266
  variations in, 203
  willingness to pay for, 185
Quality competition, 358
Quality maximization, 221, 224-225, 234, 240
Quality-quantity maximization, 240
Quantity of innovations, 352
Quantity maximization, 224
Quantity-quality maximization, 225
Quantity of services
  of for-profit hospitals, 231-234
  of nonprofit hospitals, 231-234

Queues, 174-177, 367
  defined, 526

R

Rafferty, J., 359, 367, 368
Rand Health Insurance, 273
Rapoport, John, 412
Rate base, 301, 304
  defined, 526
Rate charged per service, 304
Rate determination, 300, 302
  See also Prices, determination of
  defined, 526
Rate of discount. *See* Discount rate
Rates of return, 402, 408
Rate structure, 459
Ratio of charges-to-charges applied to costs (RCCAC), 324, 325, 326
  defined, 526
Rationing mechanisms, 23, 173, 176, 177
  by need, 367
  nonprice, 128
RCCAC. *See* Ratio of charges-to-charges applied to costs
R&D. *See* Research and development
Real cost, 451
Reasonable cost, 323
Reasonable fees, 305
  defined, 527
Recovery of costs, 221-222, 258
Reder, Melvin W., 223, 225, 226
Redisch, Michael, 241, 245, 414
Redistribution of income, 27
Regional differences in prices, 90
Regional Medical Programs, 425
Regression analysis, 41-45, 121, 131, 415, 420
  defined, 527
  and forecasting, 51
  multiple, 46-51, 59, 121, 130, 210, 525
  simple, 41-45, 528
  time-series, 51, 122, 202, 207, 529

Regression coefficient, 43, 46, 423
  defined, 527
Rehabilitation, 99, 404
Reimbursement
  and inflation, 310-312
  institutional, 322-326
  methodology of, 299-302
  for professional services, 303-309
Reinhardt, Uwe, 104, 105, 182, 266
Relative value schedule (RVS), 307
  defined, 527
Relative value unit, 307
  defined, 527
Research cost, 403-411, 435, 486
Research and development (R&D), 400, 402, 434, 435, 452-453
  in pharmaceuticals, 383, 384, 385
Resources
  allocation of, 402, 409, 413,n463, 498, 510
  cost of, 468, 470
  defined, 527
  of hospitals, 193
  productive, 526
  scarcity of, 5, 25
  transfer of, 24
Retrospective analysis, 486, 487-489
Retrospective cost-based reimbursement, 325, 326
Retrospective demand studies, 121
Returns to scale, 201
  defined, 527
Revenue, 226
  average, 168, 519
  and cost, 21
  and demand, 168
  gross, 303
  marginal, 20, 168, 228, 524
  net, 303
  per visit, 168
  total, 168
Revenue producing functions, 460
Revenue-sharing, 261
Reynolds, Lloyd, 36
Rice, Dorothy P., 470
Richardson-Merrell, 382

"Right" to health care, 14, 27
Risk
  aversion to, 118, 527
  behavior toward, 117
  costs of, 304
  defined, 527
  in pharmaceutical industry, 382, 384
  vs. uncertainty, 102
Risk-neutral attitudes, 118
Roemer, M. I., 272, 273
Ro, K., 364
Rural hospitals, 209
Russell, Louise, 400, 411, 412, 425
RVS. *See* Relative value schedules

S

Sabin vaccine, 406, 494
Salkever, David S., 429
Salk vaccine, 494
Sample, 39-41
  defined, 527
  size of, 47
  time-series, 51
Samuelson, Paul, 99
San Joaquin Foundation for Medical Care, 280, 281, 282
Satisfaction. *See* Utility
Scale, defined, 527
Scale economies. *See* Economies of scale
Scarcity
  See also Shortage
  defined, 527
  of physicians, 419
  of productive resources, 2
  of resources, 2, 5, 25
Schelling, T. C., 473
Schering Pharmaceutical Company, 382
Schieber, G. J., 317
Schnee, Jerome, 373, 383
Schwartzman, David, 385
Schweitzer, F., 359, 368

Science Information Exchange
  (SIE), 403
Scitovsky, Anne, 129, 131, 137
Seasonal Factor Method, 67
Seasonally adjusted indexes, 67-68
Seattle Prepaid Health Care Project,
  278
Self-insurance plans, 293
Self-regulation, 15
Sensitivity analysis, 461, 494, 496
  defined, 527
Service cost, 457, 488
Shadow pricing, 75
  defined, 527
Shepherd, W. G., 267
Shiskin, Julius, 71
Shonick, W., 272, 273
Shortage, 22, 23
  See also Scarcity
  defined, 528
  of personnel, 1
Short run, defined, 528
Short run cost, 208, 454
SIE. *See* Science Information
  Exchange
Significance, 47
Significance level, defined, 524
Significance test, 39-41
  defined, 528
Simple regression, 41-45
  defined, 528
Simultaneous equations, 461
Site-specific HMOs, 258
Size
  and costs, 201, 202
  of firms, 162, 350
  of hospitals, 201, 202, 247
  of medical practices, 266
  of pharmaceutical companies, 371
Skill mix index, 85
Sliding fee, 75
Sloan, Frank, 313, 344
Smith, Harry, 485, 493, 494, 495
Smith, Rodney F., 385
SMSA. *See* Standard Metropolitan
  Statistical Areas

Snyder, Nelda M., 129, 131, 137
Social benefits, 30, 31
  See also Externalities; Social cost
  defined, 528
Social choices, 5-6
Social constraints, 195
Social cost, 29, 115, 399, 405
  See also Externalities; Social
    benefits
  defined, 528
Social cost curve, 30
Social Security Act, 312, 428
Social Security Bulletin, 129
Social values, 7
Sociologists, 1
Sole proprietorships, 164
Solomon, Ezra, 383
Solo practices, 164-185, 263
  efficiency of, 269
  vs. group practices, 264, 269
  tax advantages of, 268
Sorensen, James, 456, 460
Sorkin, Alan L., 201
Specialization, 184, 201
  distribution of, 315-318
Specialized facilities, 236-240
Squared correlation coefficient, 47
S-shaped curves, 411, 412, 417, 418
Standard error, defined, 528
Standard Metropolitan Statistical
  Areas (SMSA), 71, 72
Standards development, 431, 432
Stason, W. B., 321
State laws against corporate practice
  of medicine, 268
Statistical formula for CPI, 66
Statistical inference, 38
Statistical significance, 39-41, 47
  defined, 528
Statistics, 36
  and production function, 195
  sampling in, 39-41, 47, 51, 527
*Statistics and Econometrics: A
  Problem-Solving Text*, 35
Status groups, 414, 417, 422, 423
Stauffer, Thomas R., 385

Steiner, Kenneth, 485, 493, 494, 495
Steinwald, Bruce, 344, 367
Step-down, 461
Stigma, 471, 476, 478, 479
Structural characteristics of health
  industry, 190-193
Structure-conduct-performance
  approach, 350-352, 385
Subspecialties of economics, 4
Substitutability, 18, 114
  degree of, 178
  input, 394
  labor, 184
  technical, 195
Supply, 20-21, 295, 449
  See also Supply and demand
  defined, 528
  excess, 22, 522
  price inelasticity of, 295, 296
  and third party payment, 294
Supply curve, 20, 296
  defined, 528
  shifts in, 21
Supply and demand, 13, 349
  See also Demand; Supply and
    insurance, 295
Supply function, 20
Supply incentive, 20
Surgical procedures, 319, 321
Surplus, 22, 23
  defined, 528
  of personnel, 1
Survey research, 37
Survivor model of medical practices,
  264-270
Symtomatic treatment, 99
System analysis, 452
Systems operations, 452

T

Target income, 171-173, 182
  defined, 528
Tariff Commission, 372
Tastes, 19
Taxes, 472

for small groups, 268
Taylor, Lester D., 219, 221
Teaching hospitals, 209
Technical efficiency, 26, 177
  defined, 528
Technical production function, 196
Technical substitutability, 195
Technological change
  See also Diffusion
  and costs, 393-401
  defined, 528
  and government policy, 425-438
  and production function, 392-393
Technological constraints, 163
Technological diffusion, 431, 432
Technological innovation, 352
Technological progressiveness, 351
Technology, 6, 103, 111, 352
  and choices, 395-399
  cost impact of, 431
  defined, 529
  "halfway," 438
"Technology boom," 400
Technology matrix, 199
Theoretical monopoly, 349
Theorizing, 38
Theory of the firm, 258, 291
Therapeutic classes of drugs, 372
Third party payers, 193, 291, 292,
  293, 456, 457
  See also Health insurance;
    Intermediary
  defined, 529
  economic models of, 294-299
  growth of, 78
Thomas, Lewis, 433, 438
Time-based payment schemes, 308
Time constraints, 165
Time cost, 134-137, 174-177, 408
Time cost elasticity of demand, 120
Time-and-motion studies, 178
Time series cost function, 209
Time series regression, 51, 122, 202,
  207
  See also Cross section;
    Longitudinal analysis

defined, 529
Time values of patients, 175, 176
Timing of payment, 292
Titmuss, R., 365, 473, 474
Today's dollar, 482
Total budget method, 333-334, 338, 341
Total cost, 52, 208
Total expenses per patient day, 85, 90
Total revenues, 168
Transfers, 27
  defined, 529
Transportation costs, 203, 266, 419, 470, 502
Transportation time, 426
Travel. *See* Transportation
Treatment, 404
Treatment losses, 405
Treatment modalities, 458
Trial-and-error approach to fee adjustment, 173
T-statistic, 46, 47, 50
T-test, 40
  defined, 529

U

UCR. *See* Usual, customary and reasonable fees
Unaffiliated hospitals, 422, 423
Uncertainty
  defined, 529
  vs. risk, 102
Universal insurance, 126, 127, 128
University of Chicago, 122
Urban hospitals, 209
U.S. City Average Index, 62
Usual, customary and reasonable (UCR) fees, 75, 305, 306, 307, 309
  See also Customary fees
  defined, 529
Usual fees, defined, 529
Utility, 3, 99, 108
  See also Capital; Investment
  defined, 529

diminishing marginal, 521
marginal, 100, 101, 175, 468, 521, 525
Utility function, 99-102, 101, 111
  defined, 529
Utility maximization, 221, 225-226, 240, 247, 248
Utilization, 1, 138-155, 311, 429, 431, 449, 498
  and age, 120
  and demand, 98
  and HMOs, 259, 270-271
  and income, 120
  necessary vs. unnecessary, 98
Utilization coefficient, 215-217
Utilization differentials, 98

V

Vaccination costs, 407-408
Validation services, 8-10
Value of human life, 473, 474
Values, 3, 5, 7, 99, 100
Variable costs, 166, 399, 501
Verification, 38
Vertical health programs, 509
Voluntary hospitals
  demand for, 193
  growth in, 190, 192
  nonprofit status of, 220

W

Wages, 84, 307, 455, 486
  increases in, 86
  rates of, 394
Waiting rooms, 175, 176
Walters, Alan, 204, 208
Warner, Kenneth E., 399
Washington's State Hospital Commission, 334
Wealth, defined, 529
Weights, 66, 67, 70
  See also Laspeyres Index; Paasche Index
  defined, 529

Weisbrod, Burton, 221, 403, 404, 408, 470, 471
White, Kerr, 474
White, William D., 352
Wholesale Price Index (WPI), 87, 88
Willingness to pay, 472

Work-life expectancy, 472
WPI. *See* Wholesale Price Index

Y

Yale-New Haven Hospital, 138, 155
Yett, Donald E., 265

About the Authors

John Rapoport is Professor of Economics and Chairman of the Economics Department at Mount Holyoke College. He holds an A.B. from Dartmouth College and a Ph.D. in Economics from the University of Pennsylvania (1970). His areas of specialization, in addition to health economics, include industrial organization and the economics of technological change. He has published works in those areas and has served as consultant to various organizations.

Robert L. Robertson is Professor of Economics at Mount Holyoke College. He holds a B.S. from Cornell University and a Ph.D. from the University of Wisconsin. His articles have been published in a variety of journals; other work has appeared in book chapters and research contract reports. Dr. Robertson is a coauthor of two manuals for evaluating health services, one published in the United States, the other in Colombia. His consulting on health care has extended through the United States, Canada, and Latin America.

Bruce C. Stuart is Associate Professor of Health Planning and Administration at The Pennsylvania State University. He received a B.A. from Whitman College in 1965 and graduate degrees in economics from Washington State University in 1968 (M.A.) and 1970 (Ph.D.). Dr. Stuart taught at the University of Massachusetts at Amherst, where he was chairman of the Health Administration Program from 1974 to 1978. He also has worked in state government and directed the Health Research Division of the Michigan Department of Social Services from 1971 to 1974. He is the author of numerous monographs and articles on health financing and economics.

RA
410
.R36